The Theory and Practice
of
Counselling Psychology

To Hughie and Lesley Toner
und für Karlheinz Pilny

The Theory and Practice of Counselling Psychology

Richard Nelson-Jones

CASSELL

Cassell Educational Limited
Villiers House
41-47 Strand
London
WC2N 5JE

First published by Holt, Rinehart and Winston Ltd
Reprinted 1988, 1989, 1990, 1991 (twice), 1992, 1993, 1994

British Library Cataloguing in Publication Data

Nelson-Jones, Richard
  The theory and practice of counselling psychology.
  1. Psychology
  2. Counselling
  I. Title
  150′.2436   BF131

ISBN 0 304 31500 1

Text set in 10/12 pt Linotron Times
Printed in Great Britain by
Redwood Books, Trowbridge, Wiltshire

Preface

The aim of this book is to provide a basic survey of the field of counselling psychology for students, trainers and practitioners in English-speaking parts of the world. Furthermore, I hope this book will help to establish counselling psychology as a recognized area of psychology in Britain as well as clarify and confirm its role in other English-speaking countries. The main focus of counselling psychology is on the needs of people who are less disturbed rather than very seriously disturbed. Indeed, such people may be functioning reasonably well, yet still below their potential. Thus the book includes material on ways of helping people with everyday concerns such as personal relations, work, leisure and studying, to mention but a few.

Readers of the book may be trainers, trainees and students in educational institutions. At present, counselling psychology is taught mainly at the postgraduate level, either on a large number of counsellor training courses or as a part of many other professional courses, such as those in occupational, educational and clinical psychology. I hope, however, that this book will encourage the teaching of counselling psychology to undergraduates as well as be helpful for initial and in-service teacher training. Furthermore, this book is intended to support the training of voluntary counsellors in several areas, including: marital, family, educational, youth, pastoral care, health-related, disablement, pregnancy/abortion, homosexual/bisexual, bereavement, suicide prevention, women's, and cross-cultural counselling. Needless to say, additional training specific to these various ideas is likely to be desirable.

Training tends to be a continuous process. The practitioner of counselling psychology frequently feels and sometimes expresses a need for further education to keep up with developments in a rapidly growing field. Possibly some parts of this book may expand the knowledge and stimulate the thinking of such persons. Additionally, both professional and lay readers may find this book useful for self-help, since counselling psychology is central to our own lives as well as to the lives of our clients.

The book has a number of distinctive features which I hope will appeal to those teaching, learning and practising counselling psychology. I have started by explaining what counselling psychology is and by introducing the theory and practice parts of the book. The theory part gives a basic, but selective, survey of the humanistic, psychoanalytic and behavioural models. These have been chosen since they are the main models underlying counselling practice. Additionally, material on occupational choice and development theory is provided. The practice part draws mainly on humanistic and behavioural theories and attempts to offer the reader some specific guidelines on how to perform various aspects of the counselling psychologist's role. I have tried to relate both theory and practice to the reader as a person. By this I mean that, in the theory part, I have concluded each chapter with self-referent exercises through which readers may assess the relevance of the material to their own lives. Furthermore, in the practice part, I have included a number of practical exercises and questions which readers are encouraged to work through and hence improve their knowledge and skills. These practical exercises and questions are focused on *professional development* rather than on *self-understanding*. Indeed, the main thrust of the book is on the practice of counselling psychology.

In presenting the material I have striven for clarity and conciseness. Sub-headings have been used throughout to highlight the structure of material. I have tended to use the terms 'counselling psychology' and 'counselling', and 'counselling psychologist' and 'counsellor', interchangeably. In regard to the gender of personal pronouns, usually I have used plural pronouns and thus circumvented the issue. Where this is not the case, female and male personal pronouns have been used in the odd and even numbered chapters respectively. The genders of personal pronouns used in quotations have not been altered.

I wish to acknowledge a debt of gratitude to all those writers and researchers whose work I have mentioned. I hope that readers will be diligent in following up my references to primary sources and regard this textbook as a first, rather than a final, step in approaching the material.

I wish also to thank the many people who offered comments on drafts of various parts of the manuscript. They are, in alphabetical order: Chris Barker, Martin Cole, Peter Coxhead, Martin Davies, Peter Daws, Wendy Dryden, Caroline Haddon, Douglas Hamblin, Ruth Holdsworth, Douglas Hooper, John Marzillier, C. H. 'Pat' Patterson, Michael Reddy, Donald Super, Keith Taylor, Brian Thorne and Keith Wyld. Their comments have improved the standard of the book, and its shortcomings are mine and not theirs. Nigel Springett was a good and congenial research assistant in helping identify and collect reference material, while Wendy Bayliss provided invaluable and patient support at the typewriter. Last, I wish to thank my editorial team at Holt-Saunders both for having faith in the book and also for helping me improve its quality. In alphabetical order, they are: David Inglis, Helen Mackay, Tom Perlmutter (now in Canada) and David Roberts.

A further thought is that the writing of this book was alternated with and made much easier by many trips to the golf course. No longer being able to use the effort of its writing as an excuse, now I may have to face the grim reality about why my handicap is rather high!

I hope you find your time with the book a rewarding experience. I shall be glad to receive suggestions for its improvement as well as information on overseas developments in counselling psychology.

Kenilworth and the University of Aston   *Richard Nelson-Jones*
 in Birmingham   May 1981

Contents

1 – Introduction: What is Counselling Psychology?

SUMMARY: *Counselling may be viewed in different ways: first, as a helping relationship characterized by certain 'core' counsellor-offered conditions; second, as a set of activities and methods; and third, as an area of special focus for the delivery of counselling services; namely, catering to the needs of the less disturbed. Counselling is a psychological process and no really valid distinctions can be drawn between the activities of counselling and psychotherapy. 'Counselling psychology', which incorporates psychological education and consultancy, is a broader term than 'counselling'. Attempts to define counselling psychology are described and a further definition is offered.*

Counselling psychology also may be defined in terms of its theory and practice. The concept of a theory is discussed. A theory, if it is to be stated adequately, needs to cover four areas: basic assumptions, acquisition, perpetuation, and change or modification of behaviour. The contents of the theory part of the book are reviewed. Counselling psychology theories fall into three main groups: humanistic, psychoanalytic and behavioural. Additionally, occupational choice and development theory is represented, though it tends to be more derivative than original.

Counselling psychology practitioners may be viewed as decision-makers. The decisions they have to make fall into three categories: role, treatment and responding decisions. A treatment decision-making model of counsellor interventions in relation to client needs is presented and discussed. This model provides a rationale for the selection of material in the practice part of the book, with the contents of each chapter being described briefly. Counselling psychology is a developing field and the importance of experiential as well as academic learning is stressed.

USES OF THE TERM 'COUNSELLING'

The term 'counselling' is used in a number of ways. For instance, counselling may be viewed as a special kind of *helping relationship*, or as a set of *activities* and methods, or as defining an *area* in which services are provided. We will discuss each of those uses prior to a discussion of the term 'counselling psychology'.

Counselling as a Helping Relationship

One way of defining counselling involves stipulating some central qualities offered by counsellors in their interviewing relationships with clients which most counsellors would regard as necessary, and some, such as Rogers[1] and Patterson,[2] as both necessary and sufficient for client changes to occur. Suffice it for now to say that these counsellor-offered qualities, sometimes called the 'core conditions', are empathic understanding, respect for the client's potential to lead his or her own life and congruence or genuineness. They are viewed as representing not only the counsellor's *skills*, such as reflection of feeling and content, but also the counsellor's fundamental *attitude* to clients or capacity for altruistic care and concern.[3] The term 'active listening' is another way of expressing this basic counselling relationship.[4] Those who view counselling predominantly as a relationship tend to be adherents of the theory and practice of client-centred or person-centred counselling.

Counselling as a Set of Activities

There are numerous counsellors who would support the position that, while the counsellor-client relationship is important, it is not necessarily sufficient for client changes to occur. Thus counselling may be viewed as a set of activities and methods, including an empathic relationship, which counsellors use when working with their clients. These activities and methods may represent theoretical viewpoints, such as the rational-emotive, psychoanalytic or behavioural, other than the person-centred viewpoint.

Counselling, however, is a psychological process whether it is viewed as a helping relationship, characterized by the core conditions, or a set of activities and methods derived from differing theoretical positions. Reasons for the fundamental association between psychology and counselling include the following. First, the *objectives* of counselling are of a psychological nature, for example helping clients explore, understand and alter their self-conceptions and behaviour so that they may cope with life more effectively. Second, the underlying *theories* from which counselling objectives are derived are psychological. The great majority of leading counselling theorists have been psychologists: Rogers is a prime example. Third, the *process* of counselling is psychological. It is a continuing interaction between two or more persons engaging in various kinds of behaviour. A number of attempts have been made to identify and describe the behaviours of the effective counsellor. These invariably involve psychological concepts such as empathy, respect and congruence for the client-centred counsellor and reinforcement and modelling for the behavioural counsellor. Furthermore, tests and measures evaluating psychological constructs such as interest and aptitude may form part of the counselling process. Additionally, client behaviours during the counselling process may be described in psychological terms, such as self-exploration and transference. Fourth, psychological *research* contributes both to creating counselling theories and to evaluating counselling processes and outcomes.[5]

Counselling and Psychotherapy

Attempts to differentiate between counselling and psychotherapy are never wholly successful. For instance, Tyler observes: 'The aim of therapy is generally considered to be personality *change* of some sort. Let us use counselling to refer to a helping process, the aim of which is not to change the person but to enable him to utilise the resources he now has for coping with life'.[6] However, ability to mobilize coping resources might be considered as personality change, hence invalidating Tyler's distinction. There is a series of other possible distinctions between counselling and psychotherapy which, while suggesting differing emphases, are arguable and scarcely define discrete activities. For instance, counselling is client-centred rather than therapist-centred, emphasizes the relationship rather than specific techniques, is based on humanistic rather than psychoanalytic or behavioural theory, and takes place in non-medical as contrasted with medical settings.

Both counselling and what are better termed the 'psychological therapies' are based ideally on 'informed and planful application of techniques derived from established psychological principles'.[7] Both make use of a variety of theoretical models and 'stress the need to value the client as a person, to listen sympathetically and to hear what is communicated, and to foster the capacity for self-help and self-responsibility'.[8] Indeed, some psychologists, such as Truax and Carkhuff,[9] use the terms 'counselling' and 'psychotherapy' interchangeably, and Patterson[10] concludes that there are no essential differences upon which agreement can be found.

Counselling as a Special Area for Providing Services

It seems probable that no really valid distinction can be made between counselling and the psychological therapies in terms of the activities involved in the counselling or therapeutic process. Rather the distinction between counselling and the psychological therapies, where it exists, rests more on differing client populations and settings. In general, counselling focuses on less disturbed clients in non-medical settings, whereas the psychological therapies focus on moderately to severely disturbed clients, including those diagnosed as psychotic, in in-patient and out-patient medical settings. An additional distinction may be that different client populations have differences as well as similarities in their presenting problems. For instance, counsellors may be more concerned with occupational-choice problems and difficulties in studying than are their psychological therapy counterparts. A study by Manning and Cates[11] further illustrates this point and provides an insight into specialization within American psychology in areas relevant to counselling. Based on a factor analysis of the responses of 2900 psychologists, specialities loading on the 'clinical practice' factor were projective techniques, psychopathology, psychotherapy and individual assessment. Specialities loading on the 'school-clinical' factor were behaviour problems, pupil assessment, exceptional children, therapeutic processes and reading problems. Those loading on the 'psychotherapy' factor were family therapy, group therapy and psychotherapy. Specialities loading on the 'general counselling' factor were vocational problems, assessment, educational problems, personal adjustment, student personnel, counselling theory, therapy and rehabilitation.

DEFINING COUNSELLING PSYCHOLOGY

While agreeing that counselling can legitimately be viewed as a helping relationship, as a set of activities, and as defining a special area for providing services, the term 'counselling psychology' implies something rather more than all of these, either individually or collectively.

Psychological Education and Consultancy

Although counselling is a major intervention focused on the needs of the less disturbed, recently in America there has been a growing emphasis on psychological education, reflecting an attempt by psychologists to engage more in developmental and preventive, as contrasted with remedial, work. Ivey observes that counselling and psychotherapy are but one aspect of a broad helping role which he calls the psychoeducator model. Ivey uses psychoeducation to indicate both an overall model involving counselling, training and consultation and also the training and counsultation parts of that overall model. Training elements might involve listening skills, parent effectiveness training and life planning workshops, while consultation could have an institution or a community as its focus.[12] Likewise, in Britain, Hopson and Hough[13] have argued for developing the curriculum area of personal and social education in secondary schools and further education. Additionally, preparatory training in effective parenting might be considered another facet of psychological education in the schools, though psychological education is best viewed within the framework of life-long education. Psychological education and counselling have much in common, in that they both involve the central counselling skills of listening, understanding and being sensitive to the developmental status, needs and feelings of pupils or clients. Psychological education, however, has more of a preventive emphasis than counselling, tends less to make the assumption of disturbance, and can be applied to fairly large groups in non-psychological settings such as classrooms. Another aspect of psychological education in recent years has been a particular emphasis on consultancy work for changing the systems, such as schools and industrial organizations, which have been instrumental in contributing to counselling problems.

Counselling Psychology

The term 'counselling psychology' is in common usage in America, Australia and Canada. There have been a number of previous attempts to define counselling psychology, though none emanating from Britain. In 1952, the Committee on Counselor Training of the American Psychological Association's (APA) then Division of Counseling and Guidance stated that the professional goal of the counselling psychologist was to foster the psychological development of the individual, which includes all people on the adjustment continuum and not just those suffering from more severe psychological disturbances.[14] In 1956, a Committee on Definition of the APA's Division of Counseling Psychology (formerly Division of Counseling and Guidance) observed that the counselling psychologist was a psychologist who used varying combinations of exploratory experiences, psychometric techniques, and psychotherapeutic interviewing to assist people to grow and develop.[15] This committee added it was their conviction that counselling psychology was still evolving as a speciality area. A more recent definition of counselling psychology is that of Ivey:

> Counseling psychology may be defined as the most broadly-based applied psychological speciality. Its practitioners may be working in community settings, schools, hospitals or industry. They may be conducting psychotherapy or counseling, involved in education or program development, or managing community change activities.[16]

Counselling psychology is distinguished, albeit with much overlap, from fields like psychiatry and clinical and educational psychology by its emphasis on well-being and self-actualizing rather than on sickness and maladjustment. Super, while acknowledging his over-simplification, states that the essential difference between clinical and counselling psychology is that clinical psychologists tend to look for what is wrong and how to treat it, while counselling psychologists tend to look for what is right and how to use it.[17] However, professionals in these other applied fields all, to some degree, use counselling relationships and activities as part of their work.

To conclude this section, here is a reply to the question 'What is counselling psychology?'. Counselling psychology is an applied area of psychology which has the objective of helping people to live more effective and fulfilled lives. Its clientele tend to be not very seriously disturbed people in non-medical settings. Its concerns are those of the whole person in all areas of human psychological functioning, such as feeling and thinking, personal, marital and sexual relations, and work and recreational activity. Its methods include counselling relationships and activities, psychological education and consultancy, and self-help. People using the methods of counselling psychology include professional psychologists, paid and voluntary counsellors, and social workers. The settings for provision of counselling psychology services include education, medicine, industry and numerous community and voluntary agencies. Counselling psychology is distinguished from psychiatry, clinical psychology and educational psychology mainly by its emphasis on well-being and self-actualizing rather than on sickness, severe disturbance and maladjustment.

THEORY IN COUNSELLING PSYCHOLOGY

Counselling psychology also may be defined in terms of its theory and practice. Thus another way of approaching the question 'What is counselling psychology?' is to look at some of the decisions made regarding what to include in this basic textbook on the subject. We review such decisions first in relation to theory and then in relation to practice.

What is a Theory?

In the first part of this book we look at some of the theoretical foundations which underlie the practice of counselling psychology. Hall and Lindzey state that a theory is an unsubstantiated hypothesis or a speculation concerning reality which is not yet definitely known to be so and that when the theory is confirmed it becomes fact.[18] Perhaps more simply, a theory may be viewed as an intellectual model designed to explain and predict phenomena, in this case human behaviour. Whether or not a theory is a good one depends on the extent to which it achieves this aim. Furthermore, accurate explanation and prediction of human behaviour lay a sound foundation for models of practice or of interventions focused on altering behaviour. Kurt Lewin reputedly stated that nothing is so practical as a good theory.

There are a number of dimensions against which theories of human behaviour may be viewed. For instance, some theories are fairly comprehensive, in that they attempt to explain and predict large segments of behaviour. Others are more circumscribed, in that they focus on smaller segments of behaviour, such as aspects of our thinking or communicating. Another dimension of theories of human behaviour is the extent to which they focus on pathology, suffering and maladjustment as contrasted with effective human functioning. Yet another dimension is the extent to which theories are concerned with the whole human life cycle rather than with portions of it, such as childhood development. Two other important aspects are the extent to which theories lay the basis for effective practical interventions and the extent to which they stimulate the generation of testable research hypotheses.

Theoretical Models

Allport has suggested that the psychological theories which underlie counselling practice fall into three main groups. In an article published in 1962, he observed that however excellent the natural eyesight of counsellors may be, they always look at their clients through professional spectacles, with three lenses being worthy of special scrutiny.[19] These were: (a) man seen as a reactive being, as in behaviourism; (b) man seen as a reactive being in depth, as in psychoanalysis; and (c) man seen as a being-in-process-of-becoming, in which he mentioned trends, including holism, personalitistics and existential psychology, which might be grouped as humanistic psychology. Some 20 years later, the behavioural, psychoanalytic and humanistic theoretical lenses which Allport identified still seem to be the main ones underlying the practice of counselling psychology, although the humanistic and behavioural models appear to have the greater number of adherents among counsellors.

The theory part of this book aims to provide a basic coverage of each of the three main counselling models as well as an overview of occupational choice and development theory. Within each of the three main theoretical models there are different emphases, thus necessitating decisions about inclusion and exclusion of specific counselling theories. The first main theoretical model, the humanistic, is presented in Chapters 2, 3 and 4, with a distinction being made between humanistic-perceptual and humanistic-rational theories. The client-centred or person-centred approach is a humanistic-perceptual approach which emphasizes the role of oversocialization in hindering people's capacity to perceive themselves and their environment accurately. The humanistic-rational approaches, while acknowledging the importance of over-socialization, also emphasize the contribution of undersocialization, in the form of faulty thinking and poor coping strategies, to causing people to sustain self-defeating patterns of behaviour. Humanistic-rational theory is represented by a discussion of the rational-emotive, reality therapy, and transactional analysis theoretical view-points.

The second major theoretical model, the psychoanalytic, is presented in Chapter 5, which gives a fairly detailed, but by no means exhaustive, account of Freud's thinking. Freud has been chosen as the sole representative of the psychoanalytic writers because his work was seminal in providing a stimulus for other writers and comprehensive in conception, and also because many later psychologists could learn from his writing style and ability to present ideas clearly. A further reason for choosing only Freud is that the main orientation of this book is humanistic and behavioural approaches to counselling psychology.

Chapters 6 and 7 provide an introduction to the work of six leading behavioural theorists. These theorists all emphasize the importance of discovering the principles of learning through appropriate animal and human experimentation. Behavioural theory is cumulative, in that later theorists build on the work of earlier ones. Furthermore, there are a number of different behavioural viewpoints. The six theorists, whose work is presented selectively, are Pavlov, Watson, Skinner, Wolpe, Eysenck and Bandura. They represent both a historical and a theoretical range within the behavioural position.

Occupational or vocational psychology is an important area of counselling psychology. Although occupational choice and development theories tend to be more derivative than original, they are included here as Chapters 8 and 9 for a number of reasons. First, they illustrate the relevance of basic theory to a specific applied area. Second, occupational psychology, despite its importance to many clients, tends to receive insufficient emphasis on many counselling courses. This may be reinforced by the tendency of some counselling textbooks to ignore or very briefly present the area. Third, many trainees seem to need help in seeing the relevance of occupational psychology to their work as counsellors. Chapter 8 focuses mainly on the developmental viewpoints of Ginzberg and Super and on the behavioural viewpoint of Krumboltz and his colleagues. Chapter 9 covers the 'modern differentialist' position of Holland, and also the structural or sociological viewpoint, mainly as represented by Roberts.

The chapter concludes with a section on occupational choice and development theory as it relates to leisure.

Counselling theories need to have four main elements if they are to be stated adequately. These elements are: (1) a statement of the basic assumptions underlying the theory; (b) an explanation of the acquisition of functional and dysfunctional behaviour; (c) an explanation of the perpetuation or maintenance of functional and dysfunctional behaviour; and (d) practical ways of changing or modifying behaviour. A further important element of a theory is what it states about counselling goals and the way in which people might best lead their lives. Consequently, each of the theories presented in Chapters 2 to 5 is in a standardized format with sections on a vignette of the theorist's life, basic assumptions, acquisition, perpetuation, change and goals. The change sections tend to be relatively brief, not least because the second part of the book is devoted to the practice of counselling psychology. At the end of each chapter, including Chapters 6 to 9, there are self-referent exercises the object of which is to help readers to understand the contents of the chapter through exploration of its relevance to their own lives. Chapters 6 to 9, the two behavioural and two occupational theory chapters, have not been written in a standardized format. This is partly because the subject matter does not lend itself so easily to this approach and partly because each of these chapters covers the work of at least three theorists.

Some of the chapters in the theory part of the book are closely related to chapters in the practice part. For instance, Chapters 2 and 11 taken together form an introductory section on the theory and practice of person-centred counselling. Similarly, Chapters 6, 7 and 12 form an introduction to behavioural counselling, and Chapters 8, 9, 17 and 18 an introduction to occupational counselling. In these instances it is possible to read the theory either independent of the chapter or chapters on practice or in conjunction with them.

With the possible exception of occupational choice and development theory, the theories presented in Part One have been developed primarily with the needs of the more disturbed sections of the population in mind. Although the distinction is somewhat artificial, they are theories which focus more on *remediation* of deficiencies than on *enhancement* for reasonably functioning people. While each of the theories is relevant to the needs of the less disturbed, there is a need in counselling psychology for the development of further theories with greater emphasis on the dimensions of higher-level human functioning. Kagan, making a similar point, states: 'We need a different *level* of theory and a different *type* of theory'.[20]

PRACTICE IN COUNSELLING PSYCHOLOGY

The Counsellor as a Decision-maker

Throughout this book we take the view that the counsellor is a decision-maker. Decisions in counselling practice fall into three categories: *role*, *responding* and *treatment* decisions. Role decisions are those pertaining to how counsellors distribute their time between various activities, such as individual counselling, group counselling, and psychological education. All counsellors continually make responding decisions as a result of individual and series of client statements. For instance, person-centred counsellors are always making decisions about the formulation and communication of empathic responses. Counsellors who adopt an eclectic stance (perhaps, if adequately thought through, better termed an integrative stance) also have to make treatment decisions about *what* method or methods to adopt with *which* client or clients and *when*. Similarly, clients will be making decisions about what they are prepared to disclose, the areas they wish to work on and the treatment methods they find congenial. Hence counselling may be viewed as an interactional process involving a series of decisions, of varying degrees of interrelatedness, on the part of both counsellor and client.

Another way of viewing counsellor-client interaction is to view each party engaged in a continuing process of making and testing hypotheses. These hypotheses may concern each other, themselves, the counselling relationship and any specific treatment approaches which may be used. Depending on the way the hypotheses are evaluated, further hypotheses will be formulated in a continuing interplay between two persons in a particular environmental context. However, whether the counselling participants are viewed as decision-makers or as hypothesis-makers, their interaction is seldom, if ever, a purely rational process, since such meetings are 'complicated by the disjunctive force of the anxiety experienced by both participants'.[21]

The decisions that counsellors make and their perceptions of their clients' needs are influenced heavily by their theoretical positions. Figure 1.1 presents a treatment-decision model of counsellor methods in relation to client needs drawn mostly from

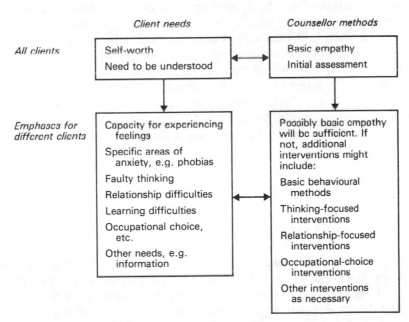

Figure 1.1 A treatment decision-making model of counsellor methods in relation to client needs

humanistic and behavioural practice. The model suggests that, to a large extent, all clients have common needs from counselling, for example having their worth as human beings validated and respected and feeling that their concerns are understood by their counsellors. Resulting from these needs, certain counsellor methods, such as a relationship involving empathic understanding and an adequate initial assessment, are necessary for all clients. However, while for all clients these counsellor methods are *necessary*, for most clients they are *insufficient* to maximize counselling outcomes. Different clients may need, as a result of their initial and subsequent assessments, additional counsellor interventions beyond empathic understanding. For instance, a basic behavioural method like systematic desensitization may be the best treatment method for a circumscribed phobic area, whereas other interventions may be more appropriate for thinking, relationship, learning and occupational-choice problems and decisions. Thus, as well as offering a fundamental relationship, counsellors need to possess a range of psychological knowledge and skills to help as many of their clients as much as possible. The decision-making model depicted in Figure 1.1 relates mainly to the decisions of counsellors offering a fairly comprehensive service and has less relevance to the decisions of specialist counsellors, such as those focusing on career choice or on sexual concerns.

Knowledge and Skills Required for Practice

The treatment-decision model in Figure 1.1 provides the rationale for the selection of the material for the chapters in Part 2 of this book, each of which serves to elaborate the model. Chapter 10, which focuses on counselling goals and on stages in the process of counselling, is intended as a bridging chapter between the theoretical and practical parts of the book. Chapter 11 develops the idea of a fundamental counselling relationship characterized by the skills and attitudes of basic empathy. Such empathy is a necessary ingredient of virtually all successful counselling relationships, though it is often insufficient on its own. Much of the chapter is in the form of a training manual, comprising a series of exercises with accompanying text, designed to teach basic empathy. Chapter 12 describes a number of basic behavioural counselling methods, including relaxation, systematic desensitization, behaviour rehearsal and reinforcement methods. The chapter concludes with practical exercises for learning each basic behavioural counselling method.

Chapter 13, on the initial interview and psychiatric considerations, is basically a chapter on assessment in counselling. A five-stage model of the initial interview is presented and discussed. Such interviews have four main objectives: to establish a working alliance with the client; to form a working model of the client; to formulate working goals; and to decide on working methods. Counsellors undertaking assessment interviews need to be sensitive to psychiatric considerations, and in Chapter 13 the following are described: indications of severe disturbance, possible psychosomatic symptoms, and the major psychiatric drugs. A growing area in counselling psychology is a focus on helping clients to think more effectively. Chapter 14 reviews client areas of thinking difficulty and then suggests numerous counsellor interventions focused on altering ineffective thinking.

Chapter 15 is on personal, marital and sexual relationship concerns. Basically relationships involve effective sending and receiving of appropriate verbal, vocal and bodily communications. The chapter covers such areas as effective listening, appropriate self-disclosure, conflict resolution and approaches to sexual dysfunction. Also, approaches to clients with concerns about homosexual and bisexual orientation are discussed. Much counselling is conducted in educational settings where many pupils and students present with learning-competence concerns. Chapter 16 reviews approaches to concerns such as effective use of study time, procrastination, examination anxiety, mathematics anxiety, and public-speaking anxiety.

Chapters 17 and 18 cover occupational counselling and careers education. Chapter 17 focuses on testing and occupational information, both emphases helping to distinguish occupational from other kinds of counselling. Chapter 18 reviews developmental, behavioural and differentialist approaches to careers and to leisure counselling. The chapter also discusses careers education, which involves educating people, particularly in the schools, to make career decisions wisely. Methods for helping pupils to attain specific careers education objectives are described. Also, the role of computers in careers counselling and education is discussed.

Chapters 19 and 20 focus on group approaches to counselling psychology. Chapter 19, on group counselling, includes a rationale for counsellors working with groups of clients, preparatory considerations in establishing counselling groups, and considerations relating to the counsellor's role in the group process. Some approaches to counselling which either exclusively or heavily emphasize group work are reviewed briefly, namely psychodrama, gestalt therapy, integrity groups and conjoint family therapy. Chapter 20 discusses definitions of psychological education. Numerous examples of psychological education are described, such as: personal and social education in the schools and in higher education; women's programmes; public education about homosexual and bisexual orientation; and education for effective parenting. Also, counsellor skills relating to psychological education are identified and discussed.

In conclusion, we reiterate that counselling psychology is a broader field than counselling. This book attempts a fairly comprehensive coverage of the present position of this still developing field. Readers are encouraged to go to original or primary sources to follow up areas of interest in more detail and, where possible, to keep abreast of the theoretical and research literature in the area. Lastly, counsellors, both in training and later in practice, learn by *doing*. A textbook such as this cannot adequately be understood unless it is supplemented by suitable opportunities for experiential education.

NOTES

1. Rogers, C. R. (1957) The necessary and sufficient conditions of therapeutic personality change. *Journal of Consulting Psychology*, **21**, 95–104.
2. Patterson, C. H. (1974) *Relationship Counseling and Psychotherapy*. New York: Harper and Row.

3. Rogers, C. R. (1975) Empathic: an unappreciated way of being. *The Counseling Psychologist*, **5**, 2, 2–10.
4. Gordon, T. (1970) *Parent Effectiveness Training*. New York: Wyden.
5. Nelson-Jones, R. (1980) Do counselling and psychology make counselling psychology? *Counselling News*, **32**, 32–35.
6. Tyler, L. (1961) *The Work of the Counsellor* (2nd edition) p. 12. New York: Appleton-Century-Crofts.
7. Meltzoff, J. & Kornreich, M. (1970) *Research in Psychotherapy* p. 6. New York: Atherton.
8. Division of Clinical Psychology (1979). *Report on the Working Party on the Psychological Therapies* p. 6. Leicester: British Psychological Society.
9. Truax, C. R. & Carkhuff, R. R. (1967) *Toward Effective Counseling and Psychotherapy*. Chicago: Aldine.
10. Patterson, C. H. (1974) *Relationship Counseling and Psychotherapy* pp. 12–13. New York: Harper and Row.
11. Manning, T. T. & Cates, J. (1977) Specialisation within psychology. *American Psychologist*, **27**, 462–467.
12. Ivey, A. E. (1976) Counseling psychology, the psychoeducator model and the future. *The Counseling Psychologist*, **6**, 3, 72–75.
13. Hopson, B. & Hough, P. (1976) The need for personal and social education in secondary schools and further education. *British Journal of Guidance and Counselling*, **11**, 16–27.
14. Committee on Counselor Training, Division of Counseling and Guidance (1952). Recommended standards for training counseling psychologists at the doctorate level. *American Psychologist*, **7**, 175–181.
15. Committee on Definition, Division of Counseling Psychology (1956) Counseling psychology as a specialty. *American Psychologist*, **11**, 282–285.
16. Ivey, A. E. (1979) Counseling psychology – the most broadly-based applied psychology specialty. *The Counseling Psychologist*, **8**, 3, 3–6. Full reference pp. 3–6.
17. Super, D. E. (1977) The identity crisis of counseling psychologists. *The Counseling Psychologist*, **7**, 2, 13–15.
18. Hall, C. S. & Lindzey, G. (1970) *Theories of Personality* p. 10. New York: John Wiley.
19. Allport, G. W. (1962) Psychological models for guidance. *Harvard Educational Review*, **32**, 373. Full reference pp. 373–381.
20. Kagan, N. (1977) Presidential address: Division 17, August 1977. *The Counseling Psychologist*, **7**, 2, 7. Full reference pp. 4–7.
21. O. A. Will's introduction to Sullivan, H. S. (1954) *The Psychiatric Interview* p. XI. New York: W. W. Norton.

Part One: Theory

2–Humanistic Theory: Person-centred

SUMMARY: *Person-centred or client-centred theory emphasizes the importance of people's subjective self-concept, which consists of the ways in which they perceive and define themselves. Through a group enterprise, Rogers has been particularly influential in developing the theory. The actualizing tendency inherent in the organism to maintain and enhance itself is man's single motivating drive. Very early on in life humans start developing a self-concept. Many of the self-conceptions which form the self-concept are likely to be based on the organism's own valuing process. However, other self-conceptions reflect internalized conditions of worth or the values of others treated as if they were based on the organism's own valuing process. Thus a conflict arises between the actualizing tendency and the self-concept, which is a subsystem of the actualizing tendency, in that conditions of worth impede accurate perception of both inner and outer experiences.*

Subception is the mechanism by which the organism discriminates experience at variance with the self-concept and, depending on the degree of threat inherent in the experience, the organism may defend its self-concept by denying the experience or distorting its perception. People are psychologically well to the extent that their self-concepts allow them to perceive all their significant sensory and visceral experiences. Unconditional positive regard from others expressed through empathic understanding is important both in developing adequate self-concepts and in dissolving conditions of worth. Rogers' and Maslow's goals for counselling and living are reviewed, and six key characteristics of the self-concepts of fully functioning or self-actualizing persons are identified, namely, realistic perception, rationality, personal responsibility, self-regard, capacity for good personal relations, and ethical living.

INTRODUCTION

The humanistic model, while acknowledging that people are influenced by their childhood and also by their current learning experiences, posits that they can play a part in fashioning their own lives to the extent that they are psychologically well. Probably the most influential exponent of the humanist position in counselling psychology is Carl Rogers, founder of the client-centred approach to counselling and psychotherapy, more recently called the person-centred approach. This chapter on person-centred theory is drawn mainly from Rogers' writings. Rogers, however, has been influenced by psychologists such as Combs, Snygg and Maslow, and the work of these psychologists is included where it appears to add to or clarify the Rogerian contribution to the person-centred position. This appears to be in line with Rogers' own statement that the development of the position is basically a group enterprise.[1]

Carl Rogers

Carl Ransom Rogers (1902–   ) was born in Illinois, America, the fourth of six children. He lived his childhood in a close-knit family in which hard work and a highly conservative, almost fundamentalist Protestant Christianity were almost equally revered.[2] When Rogers was twelve his parents bought a farm and this became the family home. He shared little of his private thoughts and feelings with his parents because he knew these would have been judged and found wanting. Until he went to college he was a loner who read incessantly and who adopted his parents' attitude toward the outside world, summed up in the statement: 'Other persons behave in dubious ways which we do not approve in our family'.[3] Such dubious ways included playing cards, going to the cinema, smoking, dancing, drinking and engaging in other even less mentionable activities. He was socially incompetent in other than superficial contacts and, while at high school, had only one date with a girl. He relates that his fantasies during this period were bizarre and would probably have been classified as schizoid by a psychological diagnostician.[4]

Rogers entered the University of Wisconsin to study agriculture, but later changed to history, feeling that this would be a better preparation for his emerging professional goal of becoming a minister. His first real experience of fellowship was in a group there who met in a YMCA class. When he was 20, Rogers went to China for an international World Student Christian Federation Conference and, for the first time, emancipated himself from the religious thinking of his parents, a fundamental step towards becoming an independent person. Also, at about this time Rogers fell in love, and, on completing college, married. This marriage was to last until his wife Helen's death in 1979.

In 1924 Rogers went to Union Theological Seminary, but after two years moved to Teachers College, Columbia University, where he was exposed to the instrumentalist philosophy of John Dewey, the highly statistical and Thorndikean behavioural approaches of Teachers College, and the Freudian orientation of the Institute for Child Guidance where he had an internship. Along with his formal learning, he was starting to understand relationships with others better, and was beginning to realize that, in close relationships, the elements that 'cannot' be shared are those that are the most important and rewarding to share.[5] Rogers received his MA from Columbia University in 1928 and then spent twelve years in a community child guidance clinic in Rochester, New York. In 1931, he received his PhD from Columbia University and in 1939 published his first book, entitled *The Clinical Treatment of the Problem Child*.[6] During this period Rogers felt that he was becoming more competent as a therapist, not least because his experience with clients was providing him with valuable learning and insights which contributed to a shift from diagnosis to listening. Furthermore, such a relationship approach met his own needs, since, stemming from his early loneliness, the therapeutic interview was a socially approved way of getting really close to people without the pains and longer time-span of the friendship process outside therapy.[7]

In 1940, Rogers accepted a position as a professor of psychology at Ohio State University and two years later published *Counselling and Psychotherapy*,[8] the contents of which were derived primarily from his work as a therapist rather than as an academic psychologist. From 1945 to 1957 he was professor of psychology and executive secretary of the university counselling centre at the University of Chicago, where non-directive, or client-centred therapy, as it came to be called, was further developed and researched. In 1957 Rogers was appointed professor of psychology and psychiatry at the University of Wisconsin, where he examined the impact of the client-centred approach to hospitalized schizophrenics. From 1962–1963 he was a fellow at the Center for Advanced Study in the Behavioral Sciences at Stanford University. In 1964 he went to the Western Behavioral Sciences Institute at La Jolla, California, as a resident fellow. Then, in 1968, with some colleagues, he formed the Center for Studies of the Person at La Jolla, where he is still a resident fellow. During the latter part of his career Rogers has developed a great interest in the application of client-centred ideas to group work and to community change.

Although the years since 1940 have been very successful for Rogers and his ideas, they have also contained professional and personal struggles. Two struggles of professional significance have been those with psychiatry and with behaviouristic psychology.[9] Rogers has fought to gain greater recognition for the contribution of psychologists, as contrasted with psychiatrists, so that they can be allowed to practise psychotherapy and to have administrative responsibility over 'mental health' work. Also, he has constantly been highlighting the philosophical and practical issues involved in a humanistic or person-centred as against a behaviouristic view of human beings. On a more personal level, Rogers has continued struggling to become a more real, open and growing person. Furthermore, he has had to handle personal crises, such as the long illness and subsequent death of his wife.

Throughout most of his professional career Rogers has been not just a counselling theorist and practitioner, but an *author* with a deep commitment to clear and cogent communication. In fact, he sees the theme of his life 'as having been built around the desire for clarity of communication, with all its ramifying results'.[10] As well as those already mentioned, his books include *Client-centred Therapy*,[11] *On becoming a Person*,[12] *The Therapeutic Relationship and its Impact: A Study of Psychotherapy with Schizophrenics*,[13] *Freedom to Learn*,[14] *Encounter Groups*,[15] *Becoming Partners:*

Marriage and its Alternatives,[16] *Carl Rogers on Personal Power*,[17] and *A Way of Being*.[18] A chronological bibliography of Rogers' books and articles published in the period 1930–1980 is printed at the end of *A Way of Being*.

In all probability, Rogers, like a number of other leading theorists, has been influenced heavily by his own early emotional deprivations to design a counselling approach to overcome their effects and hence to meet his own companionship and growth needs. Other influences have included his interview experiences with clients and the theoretical, practical and research work of his colleagues. He also claims that serendipity or 'the faculty of making fortunate and unexpected discoveries by accident' has been important.[19] Rogers enjoys gardening and finding the right conditions for plants to grow. As with plants, so with people. While regarding the following saying from Lâo-Tsze as an oversimplification, Rogers considers that it sums up many of his deeper beliefs about human growth.[20]

> If I keep from meddling with people, they take care of themselves,
> If I keep from commanding people, they behave themselves,
> If I keep from preaching at people, they improve themselves,
> If I keep from imposing on people, they become themselves.

BASIC CONCEPTS

In 1951 Rogers presented his theory of personality and behaviour as the final chapter of *Client-centred Therapy* and, eight years later, in an edited publication entitled *Psychology: A Study of Science*[21] he presented an updated version of his theory, which he still regards as the fullest statement of his theoretical position. He observes that this and any theory should be a stimulus for further creative thinking rather than a dogma of truth.

Perceptual or Subjective Frame of Reference

Combs and Snygg state that, broadly speaking, behaviour may be observed from either the point of view of an outsider or the point of view of the behaver himself.[22] It is sometimes stated that the former is viewing behaviour from the external frame of reference while the latter is viewing behaviour from the internal, subjective or perceptual frame of reference. Rogers writes of his fundamental belief in the subjective, observing that 'Man lives essentially in his own personal and subjective world, and even his most objective functioning, in science, mathematics, and the like, is the result of subjective purpose and subjective choice'.[23] It is this emphasis on the subjective, perceptual view of clients which has led to the term 'client-centred'. The perceptions of the client are viewed as his version of reality.

In a later paper,[24] Rogers stresses again that the only reality a person can possibly know is the word which that individual perceives and experiences at this moment. The notion that there is a 'real world', the definition of which can be agreed upon by everyone, is a luxury that the human race cannot afford, since it leads to false beliefs, like faith in technology, which have brought our species to the brink of annihilation. His alternative hypothesis is that there are as many realities as there are people. Furthermore, people are increasingly 'inwardly and organismically rejecting the view of one single, culture-approved reality'.[25]

Actualizing Tendency

The actualizing tendency is the single basic motivating drive. It is an active process representing the inherent tendency of the organism to develop its capacities in the direction of maintaining, enhancing and reproducing itself. The actualizing tendency is operative at all times in all organisms and is the distinguishing feature of whether a given organism is alive or dead. Rogers observes, from his experiences with individual and group counselling and from his attempts to provide students in classes with 'freedom to learn', that 'the most impressive fact about the individual human being seems to be the directional tendency toward wholeness, toward actualisation of potentialities'.[26] Thus the cornerstone of both his therapeutic and his political thinking is that people move towards self-regulation and their own enhancement and away from control by external forces.

The actualizing tendency is viewed as basically positive and assumes that man 'has the capacity to guide, regulate, and control himself, providing only that certain definable conditions exist'.[27] The person-centred approach posits a unitary diagnosis that all psychological difficulties are caused by blockages to this actualizing tendency and, consequently, the task of counselling is to release further this fundamentally good motivating drive. Maslow reiterates this assessment of man's basic nature when he writes that the human being does seem to have instinct remnants and that clinical and other evidence suggests that those weak instinctoid tendencies are good, desirable and worth saving.[28]

Often, however, individuals appear to have two motivational systems, their organismic actualizing tendency and their conscious self. As the self-concept develops, the actualizing tendency is expressed in the actualizing of the self-concept, which may or may not be synonymous with the actualizing of the organism. Maslow writes of the basic conflict in humans between defensive forces and growth trends and observes that the actualizing tendency may involve both deficiency and growth motivations.[29] However, given a certain emotional environment, growth motivations will become increasingly strong.

Experience

Rogers uses the term 'sensory and visceral experience' in a psychological rather than a physiological sense. Perhaps another way of stating sensory and visceral experience is the undergoing of facts and events, which are potentially available to conscious awareness, by the organism's sensory and visceral equipment. The individual may not be aware of much of his experience. For instance, when sitting, you may not be aware of the sensation on your buttocks until your attention is drawn to it. However, this experience is potentially available to conscious awareness. The total range of experience at any given moment may be called the 'experiential', 'perceptual' or 'phenomenal' field. Rogers stresses that physiological events such as neuron discharges or changes in blood sugar are not included in his psychological definition of experience.[30]

Perception and Awareness

Perception and awareness are virtually synonymous in person-centred theory. When an experience is perceived, this means that it is in conscious awareness, however dimly, though it need not be expressed in verbal symbols. Another way of stating this is that 'perceiving' is 'becoming aware of stimuli or experiences'. Rogers views all perception and awareness as transactional in nature, being a construction from past experience and a hypothesis or prediction of the future.[31] Perception or awareness may or may not correspond with experience or 'reality'. When an experience is symbolized accurately in awareness, this means that the hypothesis implicit in the awareness will be borne out if tested by acting on it. Many experiences may not be symbolized accurately in awareness because of defensive denials and distortions. Other experiences, such as buttocks sitting on a chair, may not be perceived, since they may be unimportant to the actualizing tendency.

Awareness, or conscious attention, is one of the latest evolutionary developments of the human species. One way in which Rogers regards it is as 'a tiny peak of awareness, of symbolizing capacity, topping a vast pyramid of non-conscious organismic functioning'.[32] Figure 2.1 attempts to illustrate this. When a person is functioning

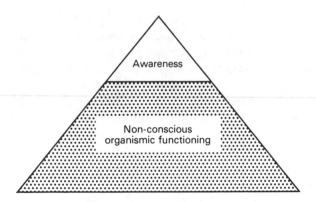

Figure 2.1 Pyramidal view of awareness and non-conscious organismic functioning.

well, awareness is a reflection of part of the flow of the organism at that moment. However, all too often people are not functioning well, and organismically they are moving in one direction while their aware or conscious lives are struggling in another.

ACQUISITION: DEVELOPMENT OF SELF-CONCEPT

Person-centred theory may become clearer to the reader if a distinction between self and self-concept is maintained. The self may be viewed as the real, underlying, organismic self expressed in popular sayings such as 'To thine own self be true' and 'To be that self which one truly is'. The self-concept is a person's perception of himself, which does not always correspond with his own experiencing or organismic self. Thus, ideally the actualizing tendency refers to self-actualizing where aspects of self and of self-concept are synonymous or congruent. However, where self and self-concept are incongruent, the desire to actualize the self-concept may work at cross purposes with the deeper need to actualize the organismic self. The above distinction is always implicit, if not always explicit, in Rogers' writings.

Organismic Valuing Process

The concept of an organismic valuing process is central to the idea of a real or true and unique self. A person's organismic valuing process relates to the continuous weighing of experience and the placing of values on that experience in terms of its ability to satisfy the actualizing tendency. For instance, the behaviour of an infant indicates that he prefers those experiences, such as curiosity and security, which maintain and enhance his organism and rejects those, such as pain and hunger, which do not.[33] This weighing of experience is an organismic rather than a conscious symbolic process. The source of the valuing process or values placed on the various experiences seems to be clear in the infant who reacts to his own sensory and visceral evidence. As people grow older, their valuing process is effective in helping them to achieve self-enhancement to the degree that they are able to be aware of and perceive the experiencing which is going on within themselves.

Early Development of Self-concept

The self-concept is the self as perceived, or what a person refers to as 'I' or 'me'. Initially, the self-concept may be made up largely of self-experiences, events in the phenomenal field discriminated by the individual as 'I', 'me', or 'self', even though in a pre-verbal way. For instance, an infant who discovers his toes may incorporate the fact that he has toes into his self-concept. Also, the infant who is hungry may incorporate into his self-concept the fact that he negatively values hunger. As the young person interacts with the environment, more and more of his experience may become symbolized in awareness as self-experience. Not least through interaction with significant others who treat him as a separate self, he develops a self-concept which includes both his perceptions about himself and the varying positive and negative values attached to these self perceptions.

Conditions of Worth

A need for positive regard from others is a learned need developed in early infancy. Positive regard means here the perception of experiencing oneself as making a positive difference in the experiential field of another. It is likely that on many occasions the young person's behaviour and experiencing of his behaviour will coincide with positive regard from others and hence meet his need for positive regard. For instance, smiling at parents may reflect a pleasurable experience as well as generating positive regard.

However, on other occasions, the young person may feel that his experiencing conflicts with his need for positive regard from significant others. Rogers gives the example of the child who experiences satisfaction at hitting his baby brother, but who experiences the words and actions of his parents as saying 'You are bad, the behaviour is bad, and you are not loved or lovable when you behave this way'. An outcome of this may be that the child does not acknowledge the pleasurable values of hitting his baby brother emanating from his own experience, but comes to place a negative value on the experience because of the attitudes held by his parents and his need for positive regard. Thus, instead of an accurate symbolization of the experience, such as 'While I experience the behaviour as satisfying, my parents experience it as unsatisfying', may come a distorted symbolization, such as 'I perceive this behaviour as unsatisfying'.[34] Such values, which are based on others' evaluations rather than on the individual's own organismic valuing process, are called conditions of worth.[35] All too often 'individuals are culturally conditioned, rewarded, reinforced, for behaviors that are in fact pervasions of the natural directions of the unitary actualizing tendency',[36] so creating conditions of worth.

The concept of conditions of worth is important because it means that the individual develops a second valuing process. The first is the organismic valuing process which truly reflects the actualizing tendency. The second is a conditions of worth process, based on the internalization or 'introjection' of others' evaluations, which does not truly reflect the individual's actualizing tendency and which serves to impede it. The individual, however, has a false awareness in regard to this second valuing process, since he feels that decisions based on it are in fact based on his organismic valuing process. Thus experiences may be sought or avoided to meet false rather than real needs.

Effect of Conditions of Worth on Self-concept

Individuals differ in the degree to which they internalize conditions of worth, depending on the emotional quality of their environment and the extent of their need for positive regard. For some, their self-concepts will develop so as to allow much of their experience to be accurately perceived. However, even the most fortunate are likely to internalize some conditions of worth, and the less fortunate are fated to internalize many.

Some common examples of conditions of worth are: 'Achievement is very important and I am less of a person if I do not achieve', 'Making money is very important and, if I do not make much money, then I am a failure', and 'Sexual fantasies and behaviours are mostly bad and I should not like myself for having them'. Thus conditions of worth entail not only internalized evaluations of how individuals should be, but also internalized evaluations about how they should feel about themselves if they perceive that they are not the way they should be. Rogers believes that it is common for most individuals to have their values largely introjected, held as fixed concepts and rarely examined or tested.[37] Thus, not only are they estranged from their experiencing, but their level of self-regard is lowered and they are unable to prize themselves fully. Furthermore, by internalizing conditions of worth, they have internalized a process by which they come to be the agents of lowering their own level of self-regard or, more colloquially, of 'self-oppression'.

PERPETUATION: ROLE OF SELF-CONCEPT IN SUSTAINING MALADJUSTMENT

For the counsellor working with clients the question is not so much how clients become the way they are, as what is causing them currently to perpetuate behaviour which does not meet their real needs. The concept of perpetuation, or of how maladjusted behaviour and perceptions are sustained, often in the face of conflicting evidence, is critical to a full understanding of person-centred theory and practice. Person-centred theory may be viewed as a theory of human information processing or of the processing of experiences into perceptions. This is a process in which, especially for those who are disturbed, conditions of worth play a large part.

Processing of Experience

Rogers observes that when experiences occur in the life of an individual there are four possible outcomes.[38] First, like the sensation of sitting, they may be ignored. Second, they may be accurately perceived and organized into some relationship with the self-concept either because they meet a need of the self or because they are consistent with the self-concept and thus reinforce it. Third, their perception may be distorted in such a way as to resolve the conflict between self-concept and experiencing. For instance, a student with a low academic self-concept may receive some positive feedback about an essay and perceive 'The teacher did not read it properly', or 'The teacher must have low standards'. Fourth, they may be denied or not perceived at all. For example, a woman may have had her self-concept deeply influenced by a strict moral upbringing and thus be unable to perceive her cravings for sexual satisfaction.

Figure 2.2 represents the processing of experience by low-functioning and high-functioning persons. It has been mentioned that individuals have two valuing processes, their own organismic valuing process and an internalized process based on conditions of worth. The low-functioning person is out of touch with his own valuing process for large areas of his experiencing. In these areas his self-concept is based on

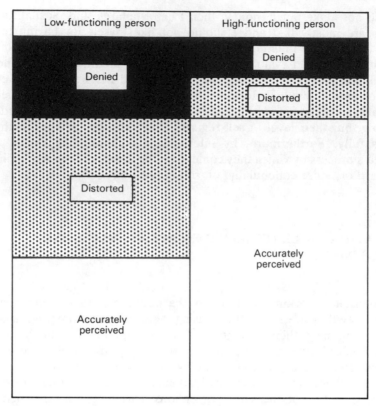

Figure 2.2 Diagrammatic representation of processing of experience by low-functioning and high-functioning people.

conditions of worth which cause him to distort and deny much of his experiencing. On the other hand, the high-functioning person has fewer conditions of worth and thus is able to perceive most of his experiences accurately.

People may be viewed as being in the process of actualizing their self-concepts. The self-concept of the high-functioning person allows him to perceive most significant sensory and visceral experiences and thus self-concept actualizing is almost the same as self-actualizing or actualizing the organismic self. The low-functioning person, however, is engaged in a process of self-concept actualizing which allows relatively little self-actualizing based on the organism's own valuing process. An outcome of this is that the high-functioning person is able to interact with others and his environment on the basis of largely realistic information, whereas the low-functioning person does not have that capacity to any great extent.

Incongruence between Self-concept and Experience

When experiences are accurately symbolized and included in the self-concept, there is a state of congruence between self-concept and experience or, stated another way, between the self-concept and the organismic self. When, however, experience is denied and distorted, there exists a state of incongruence between self-concept and experience. This state of incongruence may exist where experiences are positive as well as where they are negative. Counselling clients tend to have low self-concepts and frequently deny and distort positive feedback from outside as well as inhibit positive feelings from within.

Subception, Defence and Anxiety

Rogers uses the concept of subception or pre-perception to explain the mechanism by which sensory and visceral experiences relevant to the actualizing tendency may be denied or inaccurately perceived.[39] He quotes McCleary and Lazarus' finding that 'Even when a subject is unable to report a visual discrimination he is still able to make a stimulus discrimination at some level below that required for conscious recognition'.[40] Subception involves a filtering of experience in such a way that experiences contradictory and threatening to the self-concept may be excluded or altered. Thus the organism may discriminate the meaning of an experience without using the higher nerve centres involved in conscious awareness or perception. The process of subception is the mechanism of defence of the self-concept in response to threats to its current structure or set of self-conceptions. Anxiety is a state of uneasiness or tension which is the response of the organism to the 'subception' that a discrepancy or incongruence between self-concept and experience may enter perception or awareness, thus forcing a change in the currently prevailing self-concept. The term 'intensionality' is used to describe characteristics of the individual who is in a defensive state. Intensional reactions include seeing experience in absolute and rigid terms, overgeneralization, confusing facts and evaluation, and relying on abstractions rather than on reality testing.[41]

Breakdown and Disorganization

This brief section relates to serious disturbance. The self-concept of a very low-functioning person blocks his accurate perception of large areas of his significant sensory and visceral experience. If, however, a situation develops in which a significant experience occurs suddenly, or very obviously, in an area of high incongruence, the process of defence may be unable to operate successfully. Thus, not only may anxiety be experienced to the extent to which the self-concept is threatened, but, with the process of defence being unsuccessful, the experience may be accurately symbolized in awareness. The individual is brought face-to-face with more of his denied experiences than he can handle, with an ensuing state of disorganization and the possibility of a psychotic breakdown. Rogers mentions that he has known psychotic breakdowns to occur when the individual has sought 'therapy' from many different sources simultaneously and also when a client has been prematurely faced with material revealed under the influence of sodium pentathol.[42] Once acute psychotic behaviours have been exhibited, the defensive processes may work to protect the individual against the pain and anxiety generated by the perception of the incongruence.

Importance of Self-concept

A person's self-concept, especially certain self-perceptions which are viewed as central, has been demonstrated to be fundamental to understanding how psychological maladjustment is perpetuated. The self-concept is so important to people because it is the constellation of their perceptions about themselves and, as such, the means by which they interact with life in such a way as to meet their needs.[43] An effective self-concept allows people to perceive their experience realistically, whether it originates within their organism or in their environment; in other words, it lets them be open to their experience.

An ineffective self-concept may be maintained tenaciously for a number of reasons. First, as with the effective self-concept, the ineffective self-concept is perceived as the means of need gratification and the source of personal adequacy. Second, the ineffective self-concept contains within it many conditions of worth which may have been functional at one stage of the person's life, but which have outgrown any usefulness they once possessed. Nevertheless, because they originate from the individual's need for positive regard, they may be deeply embedded in the structure of the self-concept as a kind of 'emotional baggage'. Third, the more deeply embedded such conditions of worth have become the more tenaciously they are maintained, since to alter them would involve the anxiety of perceiving the incongruence between these self-perceptions and experiencing. Fourth, the conditions of worth have the effect of lowering the sense of worth of the individual and thus make it less likely that he will have the confidence to acknowledge and face his incongruence. There is a threshold area for both high-functioning and low-functioning people in which they may be able to assimilate incongruent perceptions into their self-concepts. This threshold area appears to be narrower and more tightly defined for low-functioning people.

DIMENSIONS OF SELF-CONCEPT

Since the idea of self-concept, sometimes expressed as 'self-structure', 'perceived self', 'phenomenal self', or just 'self', is so fundamental to person-centred theory, we will briefly review some of its dimensions.

Content Areas

The self-concept is a unique complex of many different self-conceptions which constitute an individual's way of describing and distinguishing himself. Table 2.1

shows some of the content areas of self-conception, though individuals vary in the importance they attach to these various areas and also in the kinds of self-conceptions they have in the areas. For instance, the shape of his nose may be felt as important by one person while another may be scarcely aware of it. The self-concept may be described in self-referent statements such as 'I am a good carpenter', 'I like ice-cream' and 'Meeting new people makes me nervous'.

Characteristics

Table 2.1 also lists nine characteristics of a person's self-concept.

Table 2.1 *Some content areas and characteristics of a person's self-concept*

Some content areas	Some characteristics
Bodily	Structure or process
Social	Contents
Sexual	Central-peripheral
Feelings and emotions	Congruence-incongruence
Tastes and preferences	Conditions of worth
Intellectual	Subception and defence
Occupational	Intensionality-extensionality
Philosophy and values	Level of self-regard
	Real-ideal

Structure or process

The self-concept may be viewed as a structure made up of different self-conceptions related to each other in various ways. Also, the self-concept is the means or process by which we interact with the environment and by which experience is denied, distorted or accurately perceived.

Contents

The contents of the self-concept include all the different self-conceptions in any of the content areas.

Central – peripheral

Combs and Snygg distinguish between the phenomenal self, the organization or pattern of all those aspects which the individual refers to as 'I' or 'me', and the self-concept, those perceptions about self which are most vital to the individual himself and which may be regarded as his very essence.[44] For all people, some self-conceptions are much more central than others, and everyone has his unique way of ordering self-conceptions as central or peripheral, even though this is often more implicit than explicit.

Congruence–incongruence

Many self-conceptions may match the reality of a person's experiencing, in which case there is congruence between self-conception and experience. Other self-conceptions may be different in varying degrees from the reality of a person's experiencing, in which case a state of incongruence exists.

Conditions of worth

Incongruence implies that a self-conception is based on a condition of worth rather than on the organism's own valuing process. For example, an incongruent self-conception for a particular individual may be 'I want to be a doctor', whereas a congruent self-conception for that individual may be 'I want to be an artist'. Being a doctor may be based on values internalized from parents, whereas being an artist represents the organism's own valuing process.

Subception and defence

This is an area of self-concept as a process. Experiences may be denied or distorted by the process of subception. This defends existing self-conceptions by preventing the person from perceiving incongruence and hence possibly changing both self-conceptions and behaviour.

Intensionality–extensionality

Intensionality describes characteristics of a self-concept in a defensive state, for example rigidity and absence of adequate reality testing. Extensionality describes characteristics of a mature self-concept, such as seeing experience in limited, differentiated terms and testing inferences and abstractions against reality.[45]

Level of self-regard

Another way of expressing 'level of self-regard' is 'the degree to which individuals prize themselves'. Rogers states that when the individual's self-concept is such that no self-experience can be discriminated as more or less worthy of positive regard than any other, then he is experiencing unconditional positive self-regard.[46] 'Level of self-acceptance' is a further way of stating 'level of self-regard'.

Real–ideal

Whereas real self-conceptions represent my perceptions of how I am, ideal self-conceptions represent my conceptions of how I would most like to be. Both real and ideal self-conceptions form parts of an individual's self-concept complex.

CHANGE: CONDITIONS FOR FACILITATING DEVELOPMENT AND REINTEGRATION

The client-centred or person-centred view is that the conditions for the development of adequate self-concepts and those for the reintegration of inadequate self-concepts are essentially the same. Both contain the characteristics of good and loving interpersonal relationships. Implicit in this is the notion that significant experiences for the development of adequate and, regrettably, also of inadequate self-concepts are not restricted to childhood and adolescence.

Family Life

The adequacy of the self-concepts of parents affects the ways in which they relate to their children. Gordon has emphasized that the level of self-acceptance or self-regard of parents may be related to their degree of acceptance of the behaviour of their children, though this is not something which is static.[47] Figure 2.3 is a diagrammatic representation, albeit oversimplified, of the possible effects of parents on their children. Rogers observes that parents are able to feel unconditional positive regard for a child only to the extent that they experience unconditional self-regard. Furthermore, the greater the degree of unconditional positive regard that parents experience toward the child, the fewer the conditions of worth in the child and the higher the level of its psychological adjustment. Put simply, high functioning parents create the conditions for the development of high-functioning children.[48] By 'unconditional positive regard' Rogers means prizing a child even though the parent may not value equally all of his behaviours. In 1970 Gordon published his book, *Parent Effectiveness Training*, based on Rogerian principles, which attempts to teach parents how to listen to and talk with their children, thus helping the attitude of prizing to be communicated to children.[49]

Reintegration in Counselling

Chapter 11 develops the concepts of the person-centred practice of counselling in some detail, but for now it is sufficient to state that a decrease in the defensive processes of the self-concept involves a decrease in conditions of worth and an increase in unconditional self-regard. To facilitate this reintegrative process, the

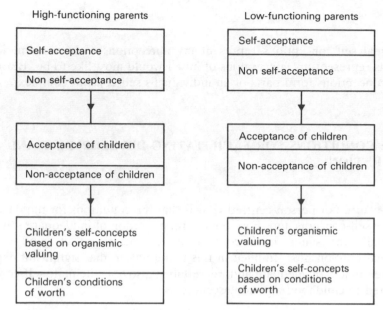

Figure 2.3   Degree of self-acceptance of parents in relation to their acceptance of their children and to the extent of conditions of worth in their children's self-concepts.

counsellor must communicate a basic attitude of unconditional positive regard for the client by means of empathic understanding. Empathic understanding involves the healing help of the 'gentle and sensitive companionship of an empathic stance' in which the personal meanings and nuances of the client are understood and communicated back with accuracy by the counsellor.[50] When the client perceives such a quality in the counselling relationship the process of dissolving conditions of worth is under way.

Groups, Marriage, Education and Politics

The person-centred position sees contributions to the development of adequate self-concepts not only being made in family life and in counselling, but also as being potentially available in many other human situations. In part this reflects an interest in working with adults as well as with children. It also acknowledges that most people are less self-actualizing than is desirable because they are cluttered up with conditions of worth. Thus Rogers appears increasingly to have turned his attentions to the problems of the less disturbed.

Encounter groups may help people to alter their self-concepts 'as they explore their feelings in an accepting climate and receive tough and tender feedback from people who care'.[51] Relationships between partners, whether marital or otherwise, can also have growth-inducing properties in which conditions of worth dissolve and level of self-regard increases. Rogers gives a moving case of Joe's steady and healing concern for and trust in Irene's potential, despite her self-conception that 'no one can love all of me. The core of me is dark and unlovable'.[52]

Rogers has also turned his attention to the under-realized potential of educational institutions for creating emotional climates for the development of healthy self-concepts.[53] He particularly favours significant experiential learning which is self-initiated and reflects the concerns of the student rather than those of the teacher or administrator. Furthermore, he has focused on the politics of interpersonal and intergroup relationships and sees his faith in the actualizing tendency as indicating a more democratic sharing of power and control.[54]

GOALS FOR COUNSELLING AND FOR LIVING

Person-centred goals are the same for clients, for counsellors and for everyone. Statements of such goals include those by Rogers,[55, 56, 57, 58] Maslow[59, 60] and Combs and Snygg.[61] Rogers also made a later statement on the qualities of the person of tomorrow who can live in a vastly changed world.[62] He considers that a 'paradigm shift' is taking place from old to new ways of conceptualizing the person. Table 2.2

Table 2.2   *Rogers' and Maslow's goals for counselling and for living*

Rogers	*Maslow*	*Rogers*
Overall goal The fully functioning (mature) person	*Overall goal* The self-actualizing (psychologically healthy) person	*Overall goal* The person of tomorrow
Qualities Open to experience and able to perceive realistically	*Qualities* Superior perception of reality	*Qualities* Openness to the world, both inner and outer
Rational and not defensive	Increased acceptance of self, of others and of nature	Desire for authenticity
Engaged in existential process of living	Increased spontaneity, simplicity and naturalness	Scepticism regarding science and technology
Trusts in organismic valuing process	Increase in problem-centring	Desire for wholeness as a human being
Construes experience in extensional manner	Increased detachment and desire for privacy	The wish for intimacy
Accepts responsibility for being different from others	Increased autonomy and resistance to enculturation	Process persons
Accepts responsibility for own behaviour	Greater freshness of appreciation	Caring for others
Relates creatively to the environment	More frequent peak experiences	Attitude of closeness towards nature
Accepts others as unique individuals	Increased identification with human species	Anti-institutional
Prizes himself	Deeper, more profound inter-personal relations	Trust of the authority within
Prizes others	More democratic character structure	Material things unimportant
Relates openly and freely on the basis of immediate experiencing	Greatly increased creativeness	A yearning for the spiritual
Communicates rich self-awareness when desired	Superior ability to discriminate ethical values	

illustrates Rogers' and Maslow's goals for counselling and for living as well as Rogers' conceptualization of the person of tomorrow. Although Rogers writes about the fully functioning person and the person of tomorrow, Maslow about self-actualizing, and Combs and Snygg about adequate persons, there are a number of common themes in their descriptions.

Realistic Perception

A self-concept which allows all significant sensory and visceral experiences to be perceived is the basis for effective functioning. Rogers frequently uses the term 'openness to experience' to describe the capacity for realistic perception and observes that 'There is no need for the mechanism of "subception" whereby the organism is forewarned of experiences threatening to the self'.[63] Realistic perception makes for more efficient behaviour in that people have a wider perceptual field and are able to behave more often from choice than from necessity.[64] Realistic perception may also increase the possibility of spontaneity and creativity, since people are less bound by the strait jacket of conditions of worth. In other words, realistic perception enables people to engage in an existential process of living where they are alive, able to handle change, and alert to the range of their choices for creating their lives.

Rationality

A feature of realistic perception is that it allows for rationality. When people are in touch with their actualizing tendency their behaviour is likely to be rational in terms of maintaining and enhancing their organism. Maslow observes that the neurotic is not emotionally sick; he is cognitively *wrong*.[65] Similarly Rogers states 'The tragedy for most of us is that defenses keep us from being aware of this rationality, so that consciously we are moving in one direction, while organismically, we are moving in another'.[66] A characteristic of this rationality is what was earlier described as extensionality rather than intensionality.

Personal Responsibility

The term 'personal responsibility' refers to people's taking responsibility *for* their self-actualizing and not just feeling responsible *to* others.[67] This covers Rogers' ideas of individuals' trust in their organismic valuing process, trust of the authority within, acceptance of responsibility for their own behaviour, and also acceptance of responsibility for being different from others. It also incorporates Maslow's idea of increased autonomy and resistance to enculturation. Personally responsible people, within the existential parameters of death and destiny, are capable of taking control of their lives and of self-actualizing. The person-centred philosophy in many aspects is one of self-control, self-help and personal power, hopefully within the context of caring relationships. Acknowledgement of personal responsibility is a central part of the self-concept of an effective person.

Self-regard

Another important part of the self-concepts of an effective person is self-regard. One way of expressing this is that the individual possesses a high degree of unconditional self-regard, or self-acceptance. It is a self-regard based on a person's organismic valuing process rather than on the praise and needs of others. People with a high degree of unconditional self-regard will prize themselves, even though they may not prize all their behaviours and attributes. Combs and Snygg observe that it is not only the number, but the importance of the positive self-conceptions that defines the adequate personality.[68] Perhaps self-acceptance is a more fundamental way of stating the desired quality, since positive self-conceptions or evaluations may reflect conditions of worth which impede realistic perception.

Capacity for Good Personal Relations

Self-acceptance means that a person is less likely to be defensive and hence more likely to accept others. Good personal relations incorporate Rogers' notions of accepting others as unique individuals, prizing others, relating openly and freely to them on the basis of immediate experiencing, and having the capacity, when appropriate, to communicate a rich self-awareness. Such personal relations also incorporate Maslow's notions of increased acceptance of others, deeper more profound interpersonal relations, and a more democratic character structure. These relations are characterized by mutual concern for both persons' self-actualizing. They are also characterized by good listening and authenticity, involving appropriate self-disclosure. Rogers considers congruence, genuineness, or 'realness' to be probably the most important element in the ordinary interactions of life, while empathy has the highest priority where the other person is anxious and vulnerable.[69]

Ethical Living

Person-centred theory is based on a view of the person as at core a trustworthy organism.[70] This shows itself in the social relations of self-actualizing people in at least two ways. First, they are capable of a wide identification with other human beings, so they are likely to seek others' self-actualizing along with their own. Consequently, they are careful not to infringe on the rights of others while pursuing their own ends. Second, they appear to be able to distinguish sharply between ends and means and between good and evil. Maslow has described such people, atheists included, as religious people or people who walk in the path of God.[71] Qualities which are likely to contribute to such people's ethical living are: trust in internal rather than in external authority; an indifference to material things, such as money and status symbols; an attitude of closeness to and reverence for nature; and a yearning and seeking for spiritual values that are greater than the individual.

Other attributes of effective persons, such as desire for privacy and more frequent mystic or peak experiences, are mentioned in the person-centred literature, but will not be described further here. The central attributes of fully functioning or self-actualizing people are the six we have identified: realistic perception, rationality, personal responsibility, self-regard, capacity for good personal relations, and ethical living. All these attributes are both the ends and the means of the actualizing tendency and all involve effective self-conceptions. Self-actualizing people possess actualizing self-concepts!

SELF-REFERENT EXERCISES

It may help you to understand this chapter better if, either with paper and pencil or in your head, you think about and answer the following questions.

1.   Review the concept of the actualizing tendency in relation to yourself.

2.   How would you describe your self-concept? For instance, what self-referent sentences would describe your view of yourself in each of the content areas listed in Table 2.1?

3.   Which of the above self-conceptions are central to your view of yourself?

4.   Are you aware of any of your conditions of worth and, if so, what are they? (Remember that your conditions of worth may be both positive and negative, indicating either how you should or how you should not be.)

5.   Examine a past or current relationship which you feel has helped or is helping you to attain a more adequate self-concept. What characteristics of the other person in this relationship do you consider were or are helpful?

6.   Examine a past or current relationship which you feel has hindered you from attaining a more adequate self-concept. What characteristics of the other person in this relationship do you consider were or are harmful?

7.   Assess yourself on each of the following attributes of fully functioning or self-actualizing people: realistic perception, rationality, personal responsibility, self-regard, capacity for good personal relations, and ethical living.

NOTES

1.   Rogers, C. R. (1959) A theory of therapy, personality, and interpersonal relationships, as developed in the client-centred framework. In S. Koch (Ed.), *Psychology: A study of Science* (Study 1, Volume 3) p. 194. New York: McGraw-Hill. Full reference pp. 184–256.

2. *Ibid.* pp. 185–188. Rogers' introduction to this chapter is a personal statement of his early development as a psychological theorist.
3. Rogers, C. R. (1980) *A Way of Being* p. 28. Boston: Houghton Mifflin.
4. *Ibid.* p. 30.
5. *Ibid.* p. 33.
6. Rogers, C. R. (1939) *The Clinical Treatment of the Problem Child.* Boston: Houghton Mifflin.
7. Rogers, C. R. (1980) *A Way of Being* p. 34. Boston: Houghton Mifflin.
8. Rogers, C. R. (1942) *Counseling and Psychotherapy.* Boston: Houghton Mifflin.
9. Rogers, C. R. (1980) *A Way of Being* pp. 53–59. Boston: Houghton Mifflin.
10. *Ibid.* p. 66.
11. Rogers, C. R. (1951) *Client-centered Therapy.* Boston: Houghton Mifflin.
12. Rogers, C. R. (1961) *On Becoming a Person.* Boston: Houghton Mifflin.
13. Rogers, C. R., Gendlin, E. T., Kiesler, D. J. & Truax, C. (1967) *The Therapeutic Relationship and its Impact: A Study of Psychotherapy with Schizophrenics.* University of Wisconsin Press.
14. Rogers, C. R. (1969) *Freedom to Learn.* Columbus, Ohio: Charles E. Merrill.
15. Rogers, C. R. (1970) *Encounter Groups.* London: Penguin.
16. Rogers, C. R. (1973) *Becoming Partners: Marriage and its Alternatives.* London: Constable.
17. Rogers, C. R. (1977) *Carl Rogers on Personal Power.* London: Constable.
18. Rogers, C. R. (1980) *A Way of Being.* Boston: Houghton Mifflin.
19. *Ibid.* p. 64.
20. *Ibid.* p. 42. Rogers cites as his source of the Lâo-Tsze saying Friedman, M. (1972) *Touchstones of Reality.* New York: E. P. Dutton.
21. Rogers, C. R. (1959) A theory of therapy, personality, and interpersonal relationships, as developed in the client-centred framework. In S. Koch (Ed.), *Psychology: A Study of Science* pp. 184–286. New York: McGraw-Hill.
22. Combs, A. W. & Snygg, D. (1959) *Individual Behavior* (Rev. ed.) pp. 16–36. New York: Harper and Row.
23. Rogers, C. R. (1959) A theory of therapy, personality, and interpersonal relationships, as developed in the client-centred framework. In S. Koch (Ed.), *Psychology: A Study of Science* p. 191. New York: McGraw-Hill.
24. Rogers, C. R. (1980) *A Way of Being* pp. 96–108. Boston: Houghton Mifflin.
25. *Ibid.* p. 106.
26. Rogers, C. R. (1977) *Carl Rogers on Personal Power* p. 240. London: Constable.
27. Rogers, C. R. (1959) A theory of therapy, personality, and interpersonal relationships as developed in the client-centred framework. In S. Koch (Ed.), *Psychology: A Study of Science* p. 221. New York: McGraw-Hill.
28. Maslow, A. H. (1970) *Motivation and Personality* (2nd ed.) pp. 117–129. New York: Harper and Row.
29. Maslow, A. H. (1962) *Toward a Psychology of Being* pp. 19–41, and pp. 42–56. Princeton, New Jersey: Van Nostrand.
30. Rogers, C. R. (1959) A theory of therapy, personality, and interpersonal relationships as developed in the client-centred framework. In S. Koch (Ed.), *Psychology: A Study of Science* pp. 197–198. New York: McGraw-Hill.
31. *Ibid.* pp. 198–200.
32. Rogers, C. R. (1977) *Carl Rogers on Personal Power* p. 244. London: Constable.
33. Rogers, C. R. (1967) Toward a modern approach to values: the valuing process in the mature person. In C. R. Rogers & B. Stevens, *Person to Person: The Problem of Being Human* pp. 13–28. London: Souvenir Press. First published in slightly altered form in 1964 in the *Journal of Abnormal and Social Psychology*, **68**, 160–167.
34. Rogers, C. R. (1951) *Client-centred Therapy* pp. 498–503. Boston: Houghton Mifflin.
35. Rogers, C. R. (1959) A theory of therapy, personality, and interpersonal relationships as developed in the client-centred framework. In S. Koch (Ed.), *Psychology: A Study of Science* pp. 209–210. New York: McGraw-Hill.

36. Rogers, C. R. (1977) *Carl Rogers on Personal Power* p. 247. London: Constable.
37. Rogers, C. R. (1967) Toward a modern approach to values: the valuing process in the mature person. In C. R. Rogers & B. Stevens, *Person to Person: The Problem of Being Human* p. 20. London: Souvenir Press.
38. Rogers, C. R. (1951) *Client-centred Therapy* pp. 503–507. Boston: Houghton Mifflin.
39. *Ibid*. pp. 506–507.
40. McCleary, R. A. & Lazarus, R. S. (1949) Autonomic discrimination without awareness. *Journal of Personality*, **18**, 171–179.
41. Rogers, C. R. (1959) A theory of therapy, personality, and interpersonal relationships as developed in the client-centred framework. In S. Koch (Ed.), *Psychology: A Study of Science* p. 205. New York: McGraw-Hill.
42. *Ibid*. pp. 229–230.
43. Combs, A. W. & Snygg, D. (1959) *Individual Behavior* pp. 37–58. New York: Harper and Row.
44. *Ibid*. pp. 126–132.
45. Rogers, C. R. (1959) A theory of therapy, personality, and interpersonal relationships as developed in the client-centred framework. In S. Koch (Ed.), *Psychology: A Study of Science* pp. 205–207. New York: McGraw-Hill.
46. *Ibid*. pp. 207–209.
47. Gordon, T. (1970) *Parent Effectiveness Training* pp. 29–61. New York: Wyden.
48. Rogers, C. R. (1959) A theory of therapy, personality, and interpersonal relationships as developed in the client-centred framework. In S. Koch (Ed.), *Psychology: A Study of Science* p. 241. New York: McGraw-Hill.
49. Gordon, T. (1970) *Parent Effectiveness Training*. New York: Wyden.
50. Rogers, C. R. (1975) Empathic: an unappreciated way of being. *The Counseling Psychologist*, **5**, 2, 2–10. Reproduced in Rogers, C. R. (1980) *A Way of Being* pp. 137–163. Boston: Houghton Mifflin.
51. Rogers, C. R. (1970) *Encounter Groups* p. 70. London: Penguin.
52. Rogers, C. R. (1973) *Becoming Partners: Marriage and its Alternatives* pp. 87–108. London: Constable.
53. Rogers, C. R. (1969) *Freedom to Learn*. Columbus, Ohio: Charles E. Merrill.
54. Rogers, C. R. (1977) *Carl Rogers on Personal Power*. London: Constable.
55. Rogers, C. R. (1961) *On Becoming a Person* pp. 163–182. Boston: Houghton Mifflin.
56. *Ibid*. pp. 183–196.
57. Walker, A. M., Rablen, R. A. & Rogers, C. R. (1960) Development of a scale to measure process changes in psychotherapy. *Journal of Clinical Psychology*, **16**, 79–85.
58. Rogers, C. R. (1959) A theory of therapy, personality, and interpersonal relationships as developed in the client-centred framework. In S. Koch (Ed.), *Psychology: A Study of Science* pp. 205–207. New York: McGraw-Hill.
59. Maslow, A. H. (1962) *Toward a Psychology of Being* pp. 23–24. Princeton, New Jersey: Van Nostrand.
60. Maslow, A. H. (1970) *Motivation and Personality* (2nd ed.) pp. 149–160. New York: Harper and Row.
61. Combs, A. W. & Snygg, D. (1959) *Individual Behavior* pp. 237–264. New York: Harper and Row.
62. Rogers, C. R. (1980) *A Way of Being* pp. 339–356. Boston: Houghton Mifflin.
63. Rogers, C. R. (1959) A theory of therapy, personality, and interpersonal relations as developed in the client-centred framework. In S. Koch (Ed.), *Psychology: A Study of Science* p. 206. New York: McGraw-Hill.
64. Combs, A. W. & Snygg, D. (1959) *Individual Behavior* pp. 250–252. New York: Harper and Row.
65. Maslow, A. H. (1970) *Motivation and Personality* (2nd ed.) p. 153. New York: Harper and Row.
66. Rogers, C. R. (1961) *On Becoming a Person* p. 195. Boston: Houghton Mifflin.
67. Nelson-Jones, R. (1979) Goals for counselling and psychotherapy: responsibility as an

integrating concept. *British Journal of Guidance and Counselling*, **7**, 154. Full reference pp. 153–168.

68. Combs, A. W. & Snygg, D. (1959) *Individual Behavior* pp. 240–242. New York: Harper and Row.
69. Rogers, C. R. (1975) Empathic: an unappreciated way of being. *The Counseling Psychologist*, **5,** 2, 9. Reproduced in Rogers, C. R. (1980) *A Way of Being* pp. 137–163. Boston: Houghton Mifflin.
70. Rogers, C. R. (1977) *Carl Rogers on Personal Power* p. 7. London: Constable.
71. Maslow, A. H. (1970) *Motivation and Personality* (2nd ed.) p. 169. New York: Harper and Row.

3 – Humanistic Theory: Reality and Rational-emotive

SUMMARY: *Reality therapy emphasizes the importance of acknowledging reality as the basis for responsible behaviour. Acting responsibly enables people to fulfil needs for love and worth and thus attain a success identity. The opposite of a success identity is a failure identity. Failure identities are caused by denying or ignoring reality, irresponsible behaviour and the loneliness and pain caused by lack of involvement in worthwhile relationships and activity. The Western world is now an identity society, with the emphasis on role and personal fulfilment, rather than a survival society, with the emphasis on attainment of economic goals. The identity society, however, has numerous casualties. Parents and schools must get involved with children, teach them how to behave responsibly and meet their needs for love and worth. Seven principles are described for counselling people with failure identities.*

Rational-emotive therapy (RET) emphasizes how people create and sustain their emotional disturbance through irrational thinking and self-talk. People have an innate tendency to irrationality as well as to rationality. While the culture, parents and the media foster irrationality, this is sustained by the individual's continually reindoctrinating herself. RET posits an ABC framework, with A the activating event, B the belief or beliefs about the activating event, and C the consequence. Where beliefs are irrational they obscure the reality of the activating event and thus the consequences can be highly inappropriate. Ellis lists twelve major irrational ideas or beliefs relating to how we, others and the environment should be. Characteristics of irrational beliefs include demandingness, overgeneralization, self-rating, awfulizing, attribution errors, anti-empiricism, and repetition. Changing irrational beliefs involves D, detecting and disputing the beliefs, to produce E, a new effect or consequence. The practice of RET involves cognitive, emotional and behavioural approaches. RET aims to minimize clients' self-defeating outlooks which cause anxiety and hostility and also to help them to acquire a more realistic and tolerant philosophy of life.

The distinction between humanistic-perceptual theory, as represented by person-centred, and humanistic-rational theory, as represented by reality and rational-emotive, is one of degree rather than of kind. Both theoretical positions acknowledge that the way in which people perceive their world affects the extent to which they are rational. A major difference, however, is that while humanistic-perceptual theory emphasizes oversocialization, in the form of conditions of worth blocking capacity for experiencing and realistic perception, humanistic-rational theory emphasizes under-socialization, in the form of faulty thinking and irresponsible behaviour sustaining people's inability to meet their needs. This chapter describes the theory underlying two approaches, reality therapy and rational-emotive therapy, which heavily emphasize people's responsibility for perpetuating their own disturbances and lack of fulfilment. We start with reality therapy and then discuss rational-emotive therapy. Although the major focus here is on theory, the practice of each approach is also discussed very briefly.

REALITY THERAPY

Introduction

William Glasser, a California-based psychiatrist, is the originator of reality therapy. Clients have failed to learn the behaviours necessary for them to meet their psychological needs and, consequently, the task of the reality therapist is to educate them to become more responsible and realistic and hence more successful at attaining their goals. Glasser and Zunin write: 'The crux of the theory is personal responsibility for one's own behaviour, which is equated with mental health'.[1] The principles of reality therapy are relevant to people trying to attain success identities in their everyday lives as well as to those with serious behavioural and emotional problems.

William Glasser

William Glasser (1925–   ) grew up in Cleveland, Ohio, where he studied chemical engineering at Case Institute of Technology. At 19 he is reported as suffering from acute shyness, though this did not prevent him from marrying during his college years.[2] For three years he studied for a PhD in clinical psychology at Western Reserve University, but then decided to become a psychiatrist. In 1953 Glasser obtained his MD from Western Reserve and, in 1957, finished his psychiatric residency at the University of California at Los Angeles.

After an attempt at private practice which was hampered by a shortage of referrals, Glasser accepted a position with the California Youth Authority as head psychiatrist at the Ventura School for Girls, where he started experimenting with the techniques and principles of reality therapy. He published his first book *Mental Health or Mental Illness?*[3] in 1961 and four years later published his influential *Reality Therapy*.[4] In 1966

Glasser began consulting in the California school system, spending much time in elementary schools in the deprived Watts area of Los Angeles. In 1969, as a result of this experience, he published *Schools Without Failure*.[5] In the same year he stopped working at Ventura and opened the Institute for Reality Therapy in Brentwood, a suburb of Los Angeles. Also, that year he created the Educator Training Center to research and develop programmes for the prevention of school failure. In 1972 Glasser published *The Identity Society*[6] and since then his interests have been focused mainly on institutional change. However, he still maintains a major interest in the prevention of crime and drug abuse.

Basic Concepts

Identity

Reality therapy asserts that all humans, regardless of culture, have a single basic need. This is the need for 'an identity: the need to feel that we are somehow separate and distinct from every other living being on the face of this earth . . .'[7] Glasser considers that around the year 1950 there was a shift in the Western world from a survival society, in which people were oriented towards *goals* such as a secure profession, to an identity society, in which people were oriented towards *roles* and trying to gain a successful identity. Many of the older generation, once secure, have started to be concerned about personal fulfilment. Many of the younger generation, however, having known economic security all their lives, are more concerned with attaining a successful identity than with survival. The need for a successful identity is viewed as a health or growth force. Thus it might be said that reality therapy sees humans' underlying nature as pro-social. However, people may have failure as well as success identities.

Involvement

Glasser sees the 10 000 years up to approximately 1950 as the survival society. However, this was preceded by 3.5 million years of a primitive survival society, in which the need for intelligent co-operation became part of people's nervous system, and then by half a million years of a primitive identity society, in which the need for intelligent co-operation evolved into the need for involvement or the need for people to be with their fellow humans. Glasser writes: 'To succeed in the post-1950 identity society, we must base our knowledge of man not upon the learned behavior of 10 000 years – antagonism and hostility – but upon the innate behavior of four million years – cooperation and friendly competition'.[8] The need for involvement is built into the human nervous system, which uses pain to encourage people to get involved with each other.

Love and worth

Security was the key to success in the survival society, but love and worth are the bases for a successful identity in the new identity society. In his earlier book, *Reality Therapy,* Glasser emphasizes that there are two basic needs: the need to love and be loved, and the need to feel that we are worth while to ourselves and to others.[9] The need to love and be loved means involvement with people for whom one cares and respects. To feel worth while people must perform a task which increases their self-worth and often helps others to do the same. Being worth while entails maintaining a satisfactory standard of behaviour and, where people do not act to improve their conduct when it falls below their standards, they will feel pain as acute as the pain they feel when they fail to love or to be loved. The outcomes of failing to meet the sub-goals for a successful identity of love and worth are loneliness, pain and a failure identity. Glasser sees the identity society as fraught with loneliness and failure, since many have not learned how to attain love and worth.

Responsibility

Responsibility is defined as 'the ability to fulfil one's needs, and to do so in a way that does not deprive others of the ability to fulfil their needs'.[10] Inability to meet the needs of love and worth is described as irresponsibility. Thus, responsible behaviour is the means of obtaining love and worth, which together make a success identity. On the other hand, irresponsible behaviour causes loneliness and pain, which together make a failure identity.

   Although some mental disturbances are caused by biochemical disorders or brain damage, most are best described as irresponsibility. The concept of mental illness and its accompanying classificatory system, such as 'schizophrenic' and 'neurotic', is a scientific fantasy. Glasser believes that in most instances the symptoms are chosen not so much because of a person's past but rather because they are lonely and failing now. He considers that no symptom is chosen without reason and that people with a failure identity focus on a symptom companion to reduce the pain of loneliness. The patient must assume the responsibility of learning successful involvement with others which involves facing loneliness and failure and admitting that her symptom is her own choice.[11] When needs are successfully fulfilled by means of responsible behaviour, then all symptoms disappear.

Reality

Glasser acknowledges that the psychiatric patient's or the delinquent's behaviours have meaning and validity to them. Nevertheless, he considers that their lack of success in meeting their needs has a common characteristic in that they deny the reality of the world around them. This denial may be partial or total, as in the case of a chronic backward patient in a state hospital. The aim of reality therapy, however, is not only to help people to face reality but also to enable them to meet their needs within its framework.

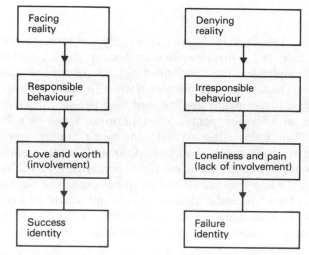

Figure 3.1   The four-link chain implicit in Glasser's reality therapy.

Figure 3.1 draws together the various strands underlying Glasser's reality therapy. The facing or denying of reality is critical to the steps in attaining a success or failure identity. Figure 3.1, however, is a simplified diagram, since it does not show the middle ground, into which most fall, where we only partially face reality. The unpalatable truth is that all of us sometimes behave irresponsibly, not only the mental patient or the delinquent.

Acquisition: Formation of Identity and Development of Responsibility

Sources of identity

Glasser and Zunin list the sources which enable people to clarify and understand who they are.[12] First, we tend to associate with and psychologically incorporate into ourselves people whom we love and admire. Similarly, we reject people we dislike. Second, we gain identity by reflecting on the causes and concerns on which we spend our time and energies. Third, our behaviour in crises may give us further information about ourselves. Fourth, we learn from the feedback, reflections and mirroring of our identity that we receive from others. Fifth, our beliefs, values and philosophy contribute to our identity, as does the sixth source, our socio-economic status relative to others. Last, our physical image and structure help us to define our identity.

Around the age of four or five the individual may start forming a failure identity, depending on how she or he develops 'the social skills, verbal skills, intellect, and thinking ability which enable him to begin defining himself in terms of being a successful or unsuccessful person'.[13] Prior to this age most children regard themselves as successful. However, once they start identifying themselves as successful or unsuccessful they tend to associate with others of similar identities and the success and failure groups become progressively more polarized.

Parental involvement

Glasser views the teaching of responsibility as the most important task of all higher animals. He observes that humans are not driven by instinct to care for and teach responsibility to their children, but have developed the intellectual capacity to be able to teach responsibility well.[14] The need for children to have love, support and warm human involvement is emphasized. However, within the context of this involvement parents must teach responsibility to their children.

Preferably early, since it is easier to acquire responsibility without having to undo previous faulty learning, parents can teach responsibility by behaving in various ways to their children. First, they can set a good example or model responsibility and commitment to each other. Second, they can help their children to meet their needs through the appropriate use of discipline rather than through punishment. Children need to feel that their parents actively care enough to show them responsible ways to behave. Discipline gives the child the power to change any restriction by changing her behaviour. It is saying to a child: 'Look, we don't want to put a lot of restrictive rules on you. If you do something wrong and foul up, well everybody does that sometimes. So let's figure out a way to do it right. Sit down for an hour and figure something out, and then we'll talk about it'.[15] Parents, however, may have to suffer the intense anger of a child and yet persist in firmly holding her to a responsible course of action.

Other elements of parental involvement in teaching children responsibility include spending time talking with, listening to and discussing matters with them, getting them to formulate and express their thoughts and wants clearly, encouraging them in independent social involvement with other children, and discussing their own and family plans. Glasser perceives the family as a place where children can be helped to understand how to meet their needs within the reality of living within our society. He views excessive viewing of television as the greatest obstacle to a child's socialization between the ages of two and five, since it does not fulfil the nervous system's need for involvement and deprives the child of social play.[16]

School involvement

Although parental involvement is very important, it is vital that schools be involved in helping children towards success rather than failure identities. Many children who go to school have already started having failure identities, while others will have to struggle to maintain their success identities while at school. Glasser feels that many children fail at school because teachers deny that the child's humanity and needs for love and worth are primary. Consequently, instead of developing a warm, personal involvement with children and then helping them towards responsibility with a relevant curriculum which encourages them to think through issues, teachers focus on rewarding children for attaining goals which may have little relevance for them. The critical school years, not just for socio-economically disadvantaged pupils, are between the ages of five and ten. Children who have experienced much failure in school by the age of ten will have had their confidence and motivation destroyed and will be acquiring failure identities. Again, it is preferable to have children initially acquiring success identities in relation to schooling than to place them in positions of needing corrective educational experiences which may be unavailable.

Glasser strongly believes that elementary schools can help children become more responsible if they: (a) focus on thinking and problem-solving rather than on memorizing; (b) ensure that what children learn in school is relevant to their world and vice versa; (c) teach children to make decisions and to plan; (d) give prime importance to the communication skills of reading, writing and speaking; (e) predominantly use heterogeneous classes, with the possible exception of teaching reading, in which children are grouped only by age; (f) understand where children need help and do more work rather than labelling some as failures, or leading them to believe they are failures through the use of a grading system; and (g) introduce classroom meetings in which the teacher leads the whole class in a non-judgemental discussion about what is relevant and important to them.[17]

The concept of personal responsibility underlies Glasser's thinking on schools. He does not believe in a deterministic position which states that young people are precluded from success because they are the products of adverse home and socio-economic circumstances. This is for two main reasons: first, because it removes personal responsibility for failure, and second, because the position does not acknowledge that success is potentially available to all young people.[18]

Perpetuating a Failure Identity

Glasser stresses that the identity society has numerous casualties who, unable to gain a successful identity, suffer the pain of a failure identity. He considers that at present there are insufficient social pathways to success and that consequently there are two societies: 'the failure society, those who identify themselves as failures and are motivated by pain to reduce the pain in ways that do not lead to involvement; and the success society, those who identify themselves as successes and are motivated by pleasure to become more involved'.[19]

We have already seen that failure identities may be both caused and perpetuated by inadequate involvement on the part of parents and the school system. However, many individuals try to reduce and thus sustain their pain by engaging in behaviours which only further separate them from genuine involvement with others. These ways include social withdrawal, alcoholism, drug abuse, promiscuous sex and delinquen-cy. In fact, Glasser considers that 'all symptoms, psychological or psychosomatic, and all hostile, aggressive, irrational behaviour are products of loneliness and personal failure'.[20] Such persons may not believe that loving and worthwhile involvements are open to them. This in itself is a denial of reality and one which has profound implications of motivation for change. Furthermore, such people may need to learn the behaviours and skills which will help them out of their self-involvement. In a sense, the mentally disturbed or irresponsible person 'has changed the real world into his own fantasy to make him feel more comfortable'.[21] This denial of reality blocks responsible behaviour and perpetuates a failure identity. Since failures tend to associate with other failures, this further sustains, if not deepens, the sense of failure.

Changing a Failure Identity

Glasser views therapy as a special kind of teaching or training which attempts to help the client to gain, in a relatively short time, the realism and responsible behaviour which should have been achieved during normal growing up.[22] The goal of reality therapy is a successful identity based on being able to meet the needs of love and worth through realism and responsible behaviour.

Glasser describes four qualities necessary to be a successful reality therapist.[23] He considers the more these qualities are present, the more effective the therapist will be as a change agent. First, the therapist needs to be very responsible and able to meet her needs within the context of reality. Second, the therapist needs the strength and integrity to be able to stand up to patients or clients requesting collusion in their irresponsibility. Third, the therapist must accept and understand people who are isolated and in pain through failure to meet their needs. Fourth, the therapist must have the capacity to become emotionally involved with irresponsible patients or clients and to be affected by their suffering.

Reality therapy consists of a series of principles which are meant to be applied flexibly depending on the needs of the client. Since these principles will not be described as a separate therapy in the practice part of this book, they are listed briefly here. The Glasser and Zunin article[24] lists eight principles, whereas Glasser in *The Identity Society*[25] lists seven, which are described below.

Involvement

The therapist needs to be warm and friendly in order to break through the sense of failure and self-involvement of the client. The involvement, acceptance, caring and willingness to discuss personal experiences on the part of the therapist is the bridge by which clients develop the confidence to make lasting involvements of their own. Being involved also means being honest about the limits of the involvement, such as length of appointments and attitude to contact between appointments. Reality therapy focuses on warm, involving conversations on a wide range of topics. It discourages long discussions about the client's problems, since this is seen as increasing irresponsible self-involvement.

Focus on current behaviour

Reality therapy focuses on changing behaviour rather than thinking or feeling. Clients are encouraged to become very aware of their current behaviour. The emphasis is on what they are doing rather than on why they are doing it. They are helped to understand that their current behaviour is their own choice. Furthermore, they are helped to understand their assets.

Evaluating behaviour

The reality therapist encourages clients to make value judgements about whether or not their behaviour is the best choice. The concept of alternatives is stressed, since often people with emotional problems see few, if any, alternatives to their current unsatisfactory behaviour. The question which is continuously explicit or implicit is 'How is this behaviour helping you to meet your needs?'.

Planning responsible behaviour

The reality therapist assists clients in understanding, clarifying and defining their immediate and long-term life goals. Plans should be feasible in terms of the client's abilities and motivation. They should not attempt too much too soon, since a failing person may need small successes to build up confidence for more difficult tasks.

Commitment

The reality therapist assists the client in making a commitment, verbal or written, to carrying out a reasonable plan. This commitment is viewed as very important, since the key to feelings of self-worth is the ability to make and follow through plans.

No excuses

The reality therapist assumes that a commitment to a reasonable plan can always be fulfilled. Consequently, no excuses are accepted and clients are asked whether they are going to fulfil their commitment or not. In instances where a plan does turn out to be unreasonable, therapist and client work together to make a better one.

No punishment

When a client succeeds, praise is given. Punishment, however, is viewed as weakening the involvement with the client and also as reinforcing a failure identity. Any kind of negative statement by a therapist is punishment. The negative consequences stemming from not carrying out plans are viewed as being quite different from punishment.

Although the above section on changing a failure identity has focused on an individual therapeutic or counselling relationship, group reality therapy is also regularly used. Furthermore, these principles can be applied in institutions such as schools, prisons and industrial organizations. They are also relevant to family life, parent education and, last but not least, to effective self-help.

Goals for Counselling and for Living

The overall goal for counselling and for living is a successful identity. Attaining a successful identity has the following ingredients: first, neither denying nor ignoring the reality of the world in which we live; second, accepting personal responsibility for our behaviour; third, behaving responsibly, including formulating and carrying out reasonable plans; fourth, loving and being involved with and committed to others as well as being loved in return; fifth, engaging in activities which are worth while to ourselves and probably to others; sixth, living up to a reasonable standard of ethical behaviour. People with successful identities are succeeding in their search for personal fulfilment in the evolving identity society.

RATIONAL-EMOTIVE THERAPY

Introduction

Whereas Glasser's reality therapy sees failure to face reality in terms of irresponsibility, Ellis's rational-emotive therapy (RET) sees such failure more in terms of irrationality. Undoubtedly the irresponsible person is irrational and vice versa, but there is a difference in emphasis. Ellis considers that emotionally disturbed individuals act in irrational and illogical ways. He views earlier statements of his central hypothesis as coming both from the Stoic philosopher, Epictetus, who wrote 'Men are disturbed not by things, but by the views which they take of them', and from Shakespeare, who states in *Hamlet*: 'There's nothing either good or bad but thinking makes it so'.[26]

Albert Ellis

Albert Ellis (1913–) was born in Pittsburgh, Pennsylvania, and grew up in New York City. His childhood was difficult and his parents divorced when he was twelve. In 1934, despite an early ambition to become the Great American Novelist, he received a bachelor's degree in business administration from the City University of New York. Early occupations included a business matching trousers to still usable jackets and being personnel manager of a gift and novelty firm. Ellis devoted much of his spare time to writing fiction, but with time and publishing difficulties turned to writing exclusively non-fiction, especially concerned with the 'sex-family revolution'.
Discovering that he liked counselling as well as writing, in 1942 Ellis entered the clinical psychology programme at Columbia University, obtaining a master's degree in 1943 and a doctorate in 1947. Ellis started private practice in family and sex counselling soon after obtaining his MA. After his doctorate, Ellis's ambition was to become an outstanding psychoanalyst and so he completed a training analysis with an analyst from the Karen Horney group and began to practise psychoanalysis under his

teacher's direction. In the late 1940s Ellis was the senior clinical psychologist at Greystone Park State Hospital in New Jersey and was also an instructor at Rutgers University and New York University. He became chief psychologist at the New Jersey Diagnostic Center and then at the New Jersey Department of Institutions and Agencies. However, the bulk of Ellis's professional life has been spent in private practice.

Ellis increasingly doubted the efficacy of psychoanalysis and started using some of the active-directive methods he employed in family and sex counselling. Before undergoing analysis, Ellis had worked through many of his own problems by reading and practising the philosophies of Epictetus, Marcus Aurelius, Spinoza and Bertrand Russell, and so he started teaching clients the philosophic principles that had helped him.[27] Ellis first started using RET in 1955 and gave his first paper on it at the American Psychological Association's annual meeting in Chicago on 31 August, 1956.[28] In 1959 The Institute for Rational Living, Inc., a non-profit-making scientific and educational organization, was founded to teach the principles of rational living. In 1968 the Institute for Advanced Study in Rational Psychotherapy was founded as a training organization chartered by the Regents of the University of the State of New York. In 1978 the latter institute changed its name to the Institute for Rational-Emotive Therapy. These two institutes have their headquarters in New York City and branches in several cities in the United States and in other countries, all carrying on activities to disseminate the rational-emotive approach.[29] Ellis has published well over 30 books and 300 articles on RET, sex and marriage.[30]

Basic Concepts

Rationality

Ellis considers that virtually all humans have two goals: first, to stay alive, and second, to feel relatively happy and free of pain.[31] RET sees these basic goals as choices or preferences rather than needs or necessities. Rationality consists of thinking in ways which contribute to the attainment of the chosen goals of survival and happiness, whereas irrationality consists of thinking in ways which block or interfere with their attainment. It consists of striking a sensible balance between short-range and long-range hedonism, or between the pleasures of the here-and-now and the longer-range pleasures gained through present discipline.[32] Thus rationality may be defined as the use of reason in pursuit of chosen short-range and long-range hedonism.

Reason and emotion

In an early paper on 'Rational psychotherapy' Ellis proposed three hypotheses which are fundamental to understanding RET.[33] First, thinking and emoting are closely related. Second, thinking and emoting are so closely related that they usually accompany each other, act in a circular cause-and-effect relationship, and in certain (though hardly all) respects are essentially the same thing, so that one's thinking becomes one's emotion and emoting becomes one's thought. Third, both thinking and emoting tend to take the form of self-talk or internalized sentences and, for all practical purposes, the sentences that people keep saying to themselves are or become their thoughts and emotions. Thus people's internal self-statements are capable of both generating and modifying their emotions.

Appropriate and inappropriate emotions

RET is not a therapy of no emotions; rather it emphasizes appropriate emotions. Inappropriate emotions are those which interfere with achieving a sensible balance between short-range and long-range hedonism. For instance, it may be appropriate for people in an alien and difficult world to be fearful, cautious or vigilant so that they may take any necessary steps for realistic protection. Anxiety, however, is seen as an inappropriate emotion, since it is based on irrational thinking or insane beliefs and, in fact, may interfere with or block realistic behaviour. Similarly, hostility may have a sane and an insane part. The sane part of hostility involves acknowledging discomfort or annoyance as a basis for action designed to overcome or minimize the irritation. The insane part of hostility may involve blaming others and the world in such a way as to block effective action and possibly generate even more unhappiness for oneself and further hostility from others. Thus emotions are appropriate when they are accompanied by rational or sane beliefs which are functional in that they do not block the possibility of effective action and attainment of hedonistic goals.[34]

The above discussion has focused on negative emotions, such as anxiety and hostility, but pleasurable and enjoyable emotions can also be very appropriate. In fact, a sensible balance between achieving short-range and long-range hedonistic goals, by definition, involves a balance between achieving short-range and long-range appropriate pleasurable emotions.

Biological tendencies

RET sees people as having strong innate as well as acquired tendencies to be both rational and irrational. By 'innate' Ellis means that the organism has a natural easy predisposition to behave in certain ways and has a difficult time modifying or eliminating such behaviour. Ellis believes that all the major human irrationalities exist in virtually all humans regardless of culture and educational level. Human fallibility has an inherent source. The facts that people seem so easily conditioned into dysfunctional thinking and behaviour and that it is so hard to modify are both viewed as evidence for an innate tendency to irrationality.[35] On the one hand humans have a great potential to be rational and pleasure-producing, but on the other they also possess a huge potential to be destructive of self and others, illogical and continually to repeat the same mistakes. People's failure to accept reality almost always causes them to manifest the characteristics of emotional disturbance.

Acquisition: Development of Irrationality

Ellis's emphasis is much more on how people sustain their irrationality than on how they develop it. He considers that psychology has focused on how people originally become illogical and that this by no means indicates how people maintain or perpetuate their illogical behaviour, or what they should do to change it.[36] Consequently, Ellis's treatment of the development of irrationality is cursory.

Given that human beings are born with a distinct proneness to irrationality, this tendency is frequently exacerbated by their environment, especially early in life, when people are most vulnerable to outside influences. Ellis sees humans as basically highly suggestible, but acknowledges the existence of innate individual differences.[37] Irrational ideas, which once might have been appropriate in view of the helpless state of the child, are acquired for a number of reasons. First, the young child is unable to think clearly, in particular insisting on immediate rather than on future gratification and being unable accurately to distinguish real from imagined fears. Second, the child is dependent on the planning and thinking of others. Third, parents and members of the family group themselves have irrational tendencies, prejudices and superstitions which they inculcate into the child. Fourth, this process is exacerbated by the indoctrinations of the mass media.[38]

The process of development of irrationality does not end with indoctrination. Ellis believes that humans largely create their own emotional disturbances through not developing and exercising their capacity for rational choice. Instead, they re-indoctrinate themselves with the original prejudices and superstitions which they acquired during childhood.[39] Furthermore, they often tend to resist giving up these ideas partly because of their innate tendency to irrationality.

Perpetuation: Sustaining Irrationality

Ellis's major theoretical contribution has been his analysis of how, helped by their innate tendencies, people sustain or perpetuate their irrationality and hence their self-defeating emotions and behaviour.

ABC framework

RET operates within an ABC framework. The outline of this framework will be explained briefly before a more detailed example is given. Within the *ABC* framework:

A is the activating event, consisting of the existence of a fact, or event, or the behaviour or attitude of another person.
B consists of the beliefs or self-verbalizations of the individual about *A*.
C is the consequence or reaction of the individual, be it happiness or emotional disturbance, which erroneously may be presumed to follow directly from *A*.

Ellis considers that humans, for good or for ill, largely control their own emotional destinies. This is through the innate, acquired and continuously re-indoctrinated beliefs they hold or, in *ABC* terms, what happens at *B*. Thus the emotional and behavioural consequences of the various activating events in our lives are controlled by our belief systems. Furthermore, though we have powerful tendencies in the opposite direction, we are capable of learning to control and modify our beliefs and hence our consequences.

Figure 3.2 consists of an example based on an RET rational self help form.[40] In this

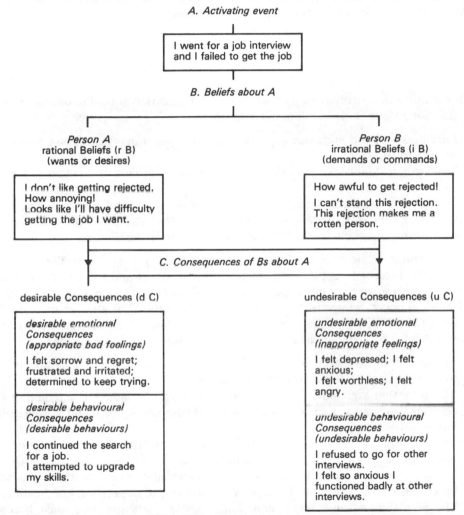

Figure 3.2 An example within Ellis's *ABC* framework. Adapted with permission from Ellis, Albert. *Rational Self Help Form*. New York: Institute for Rational Living, Inc., 1976. Copyright.

example the activating event *A* consists of going for a job interview and failing to get the job. Though it is likely that people might have a mixture of rational and irrational beliefs triggered by this event, for the purposes of the example Person *A* and Person *B* will have exclusively rational and irrational beliefs respectively. Person *A*'s rational beliefs represent wants or desires, whereas Person *B*'s irrational beliefs represent commands or demands, often called 'demandingness' in RET. Person *A*, possessing rational beliefs or taking a rational view of her failure to get a job, feels appropriate emotions such as sorrow and regret, but is still able to behave rationally either by deciding to continue searching for a job or by attempting to upgrade skills. Person *B*, however, places irrational demands on herself which lead to dysfunctional emotions, such as anxiety and depression. Furthermore, Person *B*, through subverbalizing or thinking irrational beliefs, is unable to act in ways which on a rational, hedonistic calculation would lead to greater happiness and less pain.

Irrational beliefs

Ellis considers that virtually every disturbed feeling is closely linked to one or more of the following three basic irrational beliefs:

1. 'I *must* do well and must win approval for all my performances, or else I rate as a rotten person.'
2. 'You *must* act kindly and considerately and justly toward me or else you amount to a louse.'
3. 'The conditions under which I live *must* remain good and easy, so that I get practically everything I want without too much effort and discomfort, or else the world turns damnable, and life hardly seems worth living?'[41]

In his writings, Ellis has amplified the above three points about the demands emotionally disturbed people make on themselves, others and the world by stating that there are a number of more specific irrational beliefs. In an early work Ellis listed 11 irrational beliefs which cause and sustain disturbance,[42] but another more recent list gives 12 such beliefs. Ellis uses the words 'belief' and 'idea' interchangeably, and below is his list of 12 major irrational ideas, in no set order of importance:

1. The idea that you must – yes, must – have sincere love and approval almost all the time from all the people you find significant.
2. The idea that you must prove yourself thoroughly competent, adequate, and achieving; or that you must at least have real competence or talent at something important.
3. The idea that life proves awful, terrible, horrible, or catastrophic when things do not go the way you would like them to.
4. The idea that emotional misery comes from external pressures and that you have little ability to control your feelings or rid yourself of depression and hostility.
5. The idea that if something seems dangerous or fearsome, you must become terribly occupied with and upset about it.
6. The idea that you will find it easier to avoid facing many of life's difficulties and self-responsibilities than to undertake some rewarding forms of self-discipline.
7. The idea that your past remains all-important and that, because something once strongly influenced your life, it has to keep determining your feelings and behaviour today.

8. The idea that people and things should turn out better than they do; and that you have to view it as awful and horrible if you do not quickly find good solutions to life's hassles.
9. The idea that you can achieve happiness by inertia and inaction or by passively and uncommittedly 'enjoying yourself'.
10. The idea that you must have a high degree of order or certainty to feel comfortable; or that you need some supernatural power on which to rely.
11. The idea that you can give yourself a global rating as a human and that your general worth and self-acceptance depend on the goodness of your performances and the degree that people approve of you.
12. The idea that people who harm you or commit misdeeds rate as generally bad, wicked or villainous individuals and that you should severely blame, damn and punish them for their sins.[43]

Characteristics of irrational beliefs

In addition to listing irrational beliefs, some of their more common characteristics should be mentioned. These include the following.

Demandingness. RET makes a distinction between desires, preferences and wishes on the one hand, and demands on the other. Emotional disturbance occurs when an individual 'commands, insists and dictates' that her wishes or preferences must be satisfied.[44] These demands may be in relation to self, others, or the environment. Implicitly or explicitly they almost invariably contain words like 'must' or 'should'. Ellis views 'shoulds' and 'musts' as absolutistic thinking or magical demands which create and sustain disturbance. He also uses the term 'musturbating' to describe these irrational demands.[45] Other words illustrating this characteristic are 'perfectionism', 'grandiosity' and 'intolerance'.[46]

Overgeneralization. Ellis views RET as a form of semantic therapy which strives after greater precision in thought and speech. He has been heavily influenced by Korzybski, who has focused on overgeneralization as a characteristic of fallible humans.[47] One kind of overgeneralization is to take a single observation such as 'I failed at that test' and then expand it into the generalization 'I will always fail; I have no ability to succeed at it'.

Self-rating. A further kind of overgeneralization consists of self-rating. Ellis acknowledges that people can have fortunate and unfortunate traits, but stresses the importance of people learning to accept themselves unconditionally. In other words, while it may be functional in terms of living and enjoying life to rate given characteristics, it is dysfunctional and irrational then to evaluate personal worth. Three negative effects of self-rating are that it wastes time and energy, it tends to be inconsistent, and it often becomes demandingly perfectionist and hence causes serious interference with performance. The favoured philosophic solution to the problem of personal worth is to be truly self-accepting rather than self-evaluating.[48]

Awfulizing. Awfulizing is allied to demandingness. If I, someone, or something is not the way that I demand that they should or must be, then this is awful, terrible, or horrible.[49] It may also be viewed as catastrophic. Awfulizing leads to heightened emotionality which interferes with the capacity for rational problem-solving. As with all the characteristics of irrational beliefs, awfulizing hinders the individual from perceiving accurately the activating event and hence changing or solving the noxious happenings at point *A*.

Attribution errors. Here attribution means attributing causes and motives to our own and others' behaviour and to external events and internal physical states. Misattributions, such as falsely blaming oneself or others, frequently contribute to emotional disturbance.[50] Many irrational beliefs involve misattributions.

Anti-empiricism. Anti-empiricism means that an irrational belief cannot be empirically validated or disproven. Ellis sees RET as relying on induction from empirical evidence and on logical deduction from fact-based hypotheses.[51] Irrational beliefs are incapable of logico-empirical validation.

Repetition. Irrational beliefs tend, once acquired, to occur again and again. Ellis continually stresses that people have a strong tendency to reindoctrinate themselves with their self-defeating ideas.

Changing to Rational Beliefs

A further discussion relevant to Ellis's ideas about counselling practice will be provided in the later chapter on counselling approaches focused on thinking. Here we simply mention a few central ideas in RET treatment.

First, RET focuses heavily on changing irrational beliefs or the iBs in its *ABC* framework. Thus the major objective of RET is to substitute rational and functional beliefs for irrational and dysfunctional beliefs.

Second, while the *ABC* framework is sufficient for RET theory it needs expansion into an *ABCDE* framework to take into account counselling practice. *D* stands for disputing or debating irrational beliefs. For instance, in the example in Figure 3.2 of the person who goes for a job interview and fails to get the job, disputing iBs would involve a rational examination of the following questions: 'Why is it awful to get rejected for a job?', 'Why can't I stand this rejection?' and 'How does this rejection make me a rotten person?'. *E* stands for the effects of successfully disputing or debating irrational beliefs. These effects are of three kinds: cognitive, similar to rational beliefs; emotional, consisting of appropriate feelings; and behavioural, consisting of desirable behaviours. An example of a cognitive effect is: 'I can stand rejection, though I'll never like it'. An emotional effect might be 'I feel concerned but not anxious', while a behavioural effect might be 'I am sending out more letters applying for jobs'.[52,53]

Third, RET focuses on changing irrational beliefs into rational beliefs in three main ways: cognitive, emotive and behavioural. The cognitive emphasis involves an active-didactic approach to helping the individual detect and dispute his demanding-ness. The key to detection of irrational beliefs is *cherchez les* 'shoulds', *cherchez les* 'musts', or look for the shoulds and look for the musts.[54] Emotional-evocative therapy may include role-playing situations involving irrational beliefs, modelling to show the client how to think and behave differently, and exhortation. Behavioural methods include homework, using imaginative techniques and self-reinforcement.[55]

Fourth, RET may be conducted on an individual, group, or combination of individual and group counselling basis. Furthermore, it frequently uses additional aids, such as homework sheets, directed reading and cassette recordings of interviews.

GOALS FOR COUNSELLING AND FOR LIVING

Ellis writes that the methods of RET combine to attain one major goal: 'the minimization of the client's central self-defeating outlook and his acquiring a more realistic, tolerant philosophy of life'.[56] Elsewhere he writes: 'The concrete constructive goals of psychotherapy are derivatives of the two primary goals: the minimization of the client's anxiety and hostility'.[57] The route to the minimization of self-defeating thinking and negative emotions is the adoption of a rational philosophy of life entailing a logical approach to the problems of living.

Ellis considers that virtually all psychotherapies are hedonistic in that they encourage the individual to minimize needless pain and to maximize pleasure, including love and creative work.[58] Deriving from the minimization of negative thinking and feeling are a number of positive goals, which he acknowledges as overlapping considerably with the goals of as diverse a group as Freud, Skinner, Maslow and Rogers. These goals are: (a) self-interest; (b) self-direction; (c) tolerance; (d) acceptance of uncertainty; (e) flexibility; (f) scientific thinking; (g) commitment; (h) risk-taking; and (i) self-acceptance.[59]

SELF-REFERENT EXERCISES

It may help you to understand this chapter better if, either with paper and pencil or in your head, you think about and answer the following questions.

Reality Therapy

1.   Do you consider that Glasser's distinction between a survival society and an identity society is a valid one? On these dimensions, how do you assess the society in which you live?

2.   Do you consider that you possess a success identity, a failure identity, or a mixture of the two? Identify specific success and failure elements.

3.   Assess the extent to which you have satisfactory involvements with other people. Identify ways in which you act irresponsibly in meeting your need for love and make a plan or plans for behaving more responsibly.

4.   Assess the extent to which you are performing tasks which enhance your sense of self-worth. Identify ways in which you act irresponsibly in meeting your need for worth and make a plan or plans for behaving more responsibly.

Rational-emotive Therapy

5.   Identify areas in which you are demanding and perfectionist in relation to yourself.

6.   Identify areas in which you are demanding and perfectionist in relation to others.

7.   Place at least one of your areas of irrational beliefs into an *ABC* framework as depicted in Figure 3.2.

8.   Assess the extent to which your thinking contains the following characteristics:

(a) overgeneralizing;
(b) self-rating;
(c) awfulizing;
(d) attribution errors.

NOTES

Reality Therapy

1. Glasser, W. & Zunin, L. M. (1973) Reality therapy. In R. Corsini (Ed.), *Current Psychotherapies* p. 287. Itasca, Illinois: Peacock. Chapter reference pp. 287–315.
2. Berges, M. (1976) A realistic approach. In A. Bassin, T. E. Bratter & R. L. Rachin (Eds), *The Reality Therapy Reader* p. 7. New York: Harper and Row.
3. Glasser, W. (1961) *Mental Health or Mental Illness?* New York: Harper and Row.
4. Glasser, W. (1965) *Reality Therapy*. New York: Harper and Row.
5. Glassser, W. (1969) *Schools without Failure*. New York: Harper and Row.
6. Glasser, W. (1975) *The Identity Society* (Rev. ed.). New York: Harper and Row.

7. Glasser, W. & Zunin, L. M. (1973) Reality therapy. In R. Corsini (Ed.), *Current Psychotherapies* p. 292. Itasca, Illinois: Peacock.
8. Glasser, W. (1975) *The Identity Society* p. 235. New York: Harper and Row.
9. Glasser, W. (1965) *Reality Therapy* p. 9. New York: Harper and Row.
10. *Ibid.* p. 13.
11. Glasser, W. (1975) *The Identity Society* pp. 26–71. New York: Harper and Row.
12. Glasser, W. & Zunin, L. M. (1973) Reality therapy. In R. Corsini (Ed.), *Current Psychotherapies* p. 295. Itasca, Illinois: Peacock.
13. *Ibid.* pp. 294–295.
14. Glasser, W. (1965) *The Reality Therapy* p. 16. New York: Harper and Row.
15. Berges, M. (1976) A realistic approach. In A. Bassin, T. E. Bratter & R. L. Rachin (Eds), *The Reality Therapy Reader* p. 8. New York: Harper and Row.
16. Glasser, W. (1975) *The Identity Society* pp. 103–128. New York: Harper and Row.
17. Glasser, W. (1969) *Schools without Failure.* New York: Harper and Row.
18. Glasser, W. & Zunin, L. M. (1973) Reality therapy. In R. Corsini (Ed.), *Current Psychotherapies* p. 291. Itasca, Illinois: Peacock.
19. Glasser, W. (1975) *The Identity Society* p. 38. New York: Harper and Row.
20. *Ibid.* p. 71.
21. Glasser, W. & Zunin, L. M. (1973) Reality therapy. In R. Corsini (Ed.), *Current Psychotherapies* p. 296. Itasca, Illinois: Peacock.
22. Glasser, W. (1965) *Reality Therapy* p. 30. New York: Harper and Row.
23. *Ibid.* pp. 22–24.
24. Glasser, W. & Zunin, L. M. (1973) Reality therapy. In R. Corsini (Ed.), *Current Psychotherapies* pp. 298–304. Itasca, Illinois: Peacock.
25. Glasser, W. (1975) *The Identity Society* pp. 77–102. New York: Harper and Row.

Rational-emotive Therapy

26. Ellis, A. (1962) *Reason and Emotion in Psychotherapy* p. 54. New York: Lyle Stuart.
27. Gregg, G. (1973) A sketch of Albert Ellis. *Psychology Today*, p. 61. Accompanying this sketch is an article by Ellis entitled 'The no cop-out therapy', pp. 56–62.
28. Ellis, A. (1977) The basic clinical theory of rational emotive therapy. In A. Ellis & R. Grieger (Eds), *Handbook of Rational-emotive Therapy* p. 3. New York: Springer Publishing Co.
29. Ellis, A. (1973) Rational-emotive therapy. In R. Corsini (Ed.), *Current Psychotherapies* p. 169. Itasca, Illinois: Peacock. Chapter reference pp. 167–206.
30. Gregg, G. (1973) A sketch of Albert Ellis. *Psychology Today*, p. 61.
31. Ellis, A. & Harper, R. A. (1977) *A New Guide to Rational Living* p. 201. Hollywood. Wilshire Book Co.
32. Ellis, A. (1973) *Humanistic Psychotherapy: The Rational-emotive Approach* pp. 12–13. New York: Julian Press.
33. Ellis, A. (1958) Rational psychotherapy. *The Journal of General Psychology*, **59**, p. 36. Full reference pp. 35–49.
34. Ellis, A. (1973) *Humanistic Psychotherapy. The Rational-emotive Approach* pp. 147–162. New York: Julian Press.
35. Ellis, A. (1977) The basic clinical theory of rational-emotive therapy. In A. Ellis & R. Grieger (Eds), *Handbook of Rational-emotive Therapy* pp. 14–20. New York: Springer Publishing Co.
36. Ellis, A. (1962) *Reason and Emotion in Psychotherapy* pp. 56–57. New York: Lyle Stuart.
37. Ellis, A. (1977) Personality hypotheses of RET and other modes of cognitive-behaviour therapy. *The Counseling Psychologist* **7**, 1, 7. Full reference pp. 2–42.
38. Ellis, A. & Harper, R. A. (1961) *A Guide to Rational Living* p. 184. Englewood Cliffs, N.J.: Prentice-Hall.

39. Ellis, A. (1973) Rational-emotive therapy. In R. Corsini (Ed.), *Current Psychotherapies* p. 168. Itasca, Illinois: Peacock.
40. Ellis, A. (1976) Rational self help form. New York: Institute for Rational Living.
41. Ellis, A. (1977) The basic clinical theory of rational-emotive therapy. In A. Ellis & R. Grieger (Eds), *Handbook of Rational-emotive Therapy* p. 11. New York: Springer Publishing Co.
42. Ellis, A. (1962) *Reason and Emotion in Psychotherapy* pp. 60–88. New York: Lyle Stuart.
43. Ellis, A. (1977) Irrational ideas (handout). New York: Institute for Rational Living.
44. Ellis, A. (1973) Rational-emotive therapy. In R. Corsini (Ed.), *Current Psychotherapies* pp. 181–182. Itasca, Illinois: Peacock.
45. Ellis, A. (1977) The basic clinical theory of rational-emotive therapy. In A. Ellis & R. Grieger (Eds), *Handbook of Rational-emotive Therapy* p. 10. New York: Springer Publishing Co.
46. Ellis, A. (1973) Rational-emotive therapy. In R. Corsini (Ed.), *Current Psychotherapies* p. 182. Itasca, Illinois: Peacock.
47. Korzybski, A. (1933) *Science and Sanity*. Lancaster, Pa: Lancaster Press. Paperback edition: San Francisco: Institute for General Semantics, 1973.
48. Ellis, A. (1973) *Humanistic Psychotherapy. The Rational-emotive Approach* pp. 17–29. New York: Julian Press.
49. Ellis, A. (1977) The basic clinical theory of rational-emotive therapy. In A. Ellis & R. Grieger (Eds), *Handbook of Rational-emotive Therapy* p. 10. New York: Springer Publishing Co.
50. Ellis, A. (1977) Personality hypotheses of RET and other modes of cognitive-behaviour therapy. *The Counseling Psychologist*, **7**, 1, 9.
51. Ellis, A. (1973) *Humanistic Psychotherapy. The Rational-emotive Approach* p. 12. New York: Julian Press.
52. Ellis, A. (1976) Rational self-help form. New York: Institute for Rational Living.
53. Ellis, A. (1977) The basic clinical theory of rational-emotive therapy. In A. Ellis & R. Grieger (Eds), *Handbook of Rational-emotive Therapy* pp. 8–32. New York: Springer Publishing.
54. *Ibid.* p. 8.
55. Ellis, A. (1973) Rational-emotive therapy. In R. Corsini (Ed.), *Current Psychotherapies* p. 8. Itasca, Illinois: Peacock.
56. *Ibid.* p. 184.
57. Ellis, A. (1973) *Humanistic Psychotherapy. The Rational-emotive Approach* p. 161. New York: Julian Press.
58. *Ibid.* pp. 12–13.
59. *Ibid.* pp. 159–161.

4 – Humanistic Theory: Transactional Analysis

SUMMARY: *Transactional analysis was originated by Eric Berne and comprises a theory of personality, a theory of social interaction, and an analytic tool for psychotherapy. Humans start from a fundamentally OK life position, which early experiences often cause them to lose. Ego states are patterns of feeling, thinking and behaviour. Each person has three ego states: Parent, Adult and Child, which represent parental and cultural influences, reality-oriented data processing, and childlike wishes and impulses, respectively. Further analysis of ego states tends to focus on elaborating the Parent and Child. At any time the ego state which is most cathected with psychic energy will have executive power. People are motivated principally by stimulus, recognition, and structure hungers. Six ways of structuring social time are: withdrawal, rituals, activities, pastimes, games and intimacy. Transactions involve the exchange of strokes, or units of recognition, between the ego states of those involved in a social interaction. Transactions between ego states can be complementary, crossed or ulterior.*

Scripts are preconscious life plans by which people structure their time and have their destinies determined. They are based on early decisions when the young person moves into one of the Not-OK life positions and relinquishes some autonomy in order to acquiesce with parental injunctions. The script matrix is a way of conceptualizing directives given from the ego states of parents to those of their child. Four ways in which parents hamper the ego-state development of their children are through injunctions, attributions, discounts and lying. Games, which involve ulterior transactions and a payoff, are developed on the basis of a script decision and justify a life position. Ways in which maladaptive behaviour is perpetuated include: script payoffs, game payoffs, the illusion of autonomy involving ego-state contamination, ego-state exclusion and inadequate information. The subdivisions of transactional analysis are structural analysis of ego states, transactional analysis, game analysis and script analysis. Action-oriented exercises are also used sometimes. The goals of transactional analysis include autonomy through the development of an integrated Adult. Three features of autonomous people are awareness, spontaneity and intimacy.

INTRODUCTION

Transactional analysis is a further humanistic approach which emphasizes the development of rationality in clients as well as the use of reasoning as a counselling method. Eric Berne, the originator of transactional analysis, stated that the criterion distinguishing his approach from other approaches is that it is based on the personality theory of Child, Parent and Adult ego states. The dividing line between what is and what is not transactional analysis rests on whether or not human behaviour is explained in terms of such ego states.[1] (Throughout this chapter Parent, Adult and Child start with a capital letter when describing ego states.)

Although Berne was strongly influenced by Freud, the theory and practice of transactional analysis are very different from those of psychoanalysis. Berne sees an element of his approach, called script analysis, as being 'para-Freudian' rather than anti-Freudian,[2] and conceivably the same might be said for the whole of transactional analysis. He also differs from other humanistic theorists and from Freud in his greater emphasis on social psychology, or the analysis of social, as well as intrapsychic, transactions.

Eric Berne

Eric Berne (1910–1970) was born Eric Lennard Bernstein in Montreal, Canada, and grew up in a poor Jewish section of the city. His father appears to have been a dedicated general practitioner who often took Berne on his rounds. His mother was a professional writer and editor who, after her husband died in 1921, supported Berne and his sister by her writing. James considers that Berne's inner boy was traumatized by his father's death.[3] Certainly his father appears to have had a strong influence on Berne, whose goal was always to cure patients. This influence is reflected in the Latin dedication in Berne's seminal book *Transactional Analysis in Psychotherapy*, a translation of which is 'In Memory of My Father David, Doctor of Medicine, Master of Surgery, and Doctor to the Poor'.[4] Berne's having a journalist mother appears to have been a strong influence on his writing about curing patients.

Berne studied English, psychology and pre-medicine at McGill University in Montreal and received his BA in 1931. In 1935 he obtained his MD and Master of Surgery degree from the same institution. Berne then went to the United States, where he became an American citizen. After an internship at Englewood Hospital in New Jersey, he next became a psychiatric resident at Yale University School of Medicine. Reacting to the anti-Semitism of this period, he changed his name to Berne and began a private psychiatric practice in Norwalk, Connecticut. He also contracted the first of three marriages, each of which ended in divorce. Berne became Clinical Assistant at Mt Zion Hospital in New York and, in 1941, began training at the New York Psychoanalytic Institute, being analysed by Paul Federn, a former colleague of Freud.[5]

In 1943 Berne entered the Army Medical Corps as a psychiatrist and it was during the war period that he started working with groups.[6] On his discharge in 1946 he moved to Carmel, California, and finished *The Mind in Action*, since revised and now published as *A Layman's Guide to Psychiatry and Psychoanalysis*.[7] He also resumed his psychoanalytic education at the San Francisco Psychoanalytic Institute and underwent a training analysis with Erik Erikson. In 1950 he took a position at Mt Zion Hospital, San Francisco, and restarted private practice. For the remainder of his life he worked both in San Francisco and in Carmel, 125 miles away.

From his days in the army, Berne developed a research interest in intuition and developed the concept of ego image, which is a therapist's intuitive image of a person which in some ways describes his ego. Ego images are largely based on observation and listening to what patients say about themselves.[8] During the period 1954 to 1958 Berne developed his ideas on: the diagnosis of ego states or structural analysis; the analysis of individual transactions; the analysis of a series of transactions with covert as well as overt content, otherwise known as game analysis; and the longitudinal view of a patient's whole life from which it was possible to extrapolate and predict his future, now called script analysis.[9] Berne's first transactional analysis group started in September 1954[10] and his ideas were developed further in a series of regular seminars in Carmel which, in 1958, were succeeded by the San Francisco Social Psychiatry Seminars, now called the Eric Berne Seminars.[11]

Berne was moving away from orthodox psychoanalysis and, in 1956, his application for membership of the Psychoanalytic Institute of San Francisco was rejected for the third time. Of this event he comments: '. . . after fifteen years the psychoanalytic movement and the writer officially parted company (on the most friendly terms) . . .'[12] When, some years later, the Psychoanalytic Institute offered him membership, he declined with thanks. Berne had increasingly felt that the effective therapist had to be more active than was allowed in orthodox psychoanalysis and had to practise transactionally rather than from the head of a couch. At the November 1957 Western Regional Meeting of the American Group Psychotherapy Association in Los Angeles he presented a paper entitled 'Transactional analysis: a new and effective method of group therapy', which was published in 1958.[13] During three successive summers he broadened his experience by going to the South Pacific to study socialization and mental illness in various island cultures. By 1961 he had visited mental hospitals in about 30 different countries in Europe, Asia, Africa and the islands of the Atlantic and Pacific to test his ideas in various racial and cultural settings.[14]

Berne's most systematic book *Transactional Analysis in Psychotherapy*[15] was published in 1961. In 1963 he published a discussion of the application of transactional analysis to groups in *The Structure and Dynamics of Organizations and Groups*.[16] In 1964 his ideas on analysing psychological games were publicly presented in *Games People Play*,[17] though these ideas had appeared three years earlier in a private edition of the book. The principles of transactional analysis for psychotherapists are explained in his 1966 book *Principles of Group Treatment*,[18] and his ideas on script analysis are developed in *What Do You Say After You Say Hello?*,[19] published posthumously in 1972. Berne also wrote *The Happy Valley*[20] for children and *Sex in Human Loving*[21] for non-professionals as well as for professionals. The *Transactional Analysis Bulletin* started in 1962 with Berne as editor. In 1964 the International Transactional Analysis Association (ITAA) was formed, and it remains a main training and accreditation body for transactional analysis,[22] though now the European

Association for Transactional Analysis also performs training and accreditation functions.

During the 1960s, along with his writing and private practice, Berne held a number of appointments. These included Consultant in Psychiatry to the Surgeon General, US Army; Attending Psychiatrist to the Veterans Administration Mental Hygiene Clinic; Lecturer in Group Therapy, Langley-Porter Neuropsychiatric Clinic; Visiting Lecturer in Group Therapy, Stanford Psychiatric Clinic; and Adjunct Psychiatrist, Mt Zion Hospital, San Francisco.[23] Early in 1970 Berne and his third wife were divorced, and he died of a heart attack on 15 July of that year. Berne's work has been continued by a number of his colleagues who attended the San Francisco seminars, including Claude Steiner, who has focused on developing script analysis.[24, 25]

It is interesting to speculate on Berne's own life script. The son of a doctor and a writer, he spent his life curing and writing about curing people. Some idea of his professional ideals may be gleaned from the introduction to his *Principles of Group Treatment*, which is written for those who wish to become 'real doctors' as contrasted with the 'non-real' or 'unreal' variety. A 'real doctor': (a) has the overriding consideration throughout his practice of curing his patients; (b) plans his treatment so that at each phase he knows what he is doing and why he is doing it; (c) clearly distinguishes research and experimentation from good medical or surgical care, the former always being subsidiary to the latter; and (d) takes complete responsibility for the welfare of his patients.[26] The development of transactional analysis represents Berne's own commitment to being a 'real doctor'.

BASIC CONCEPTS

Berne saw transactional analysis both as a theory of personality and social interaction and as a method of psychotherapy.[27] Some of his assumptions and basic concepts are presented below.

The Fundamental OK Position

Berne had a positive view of human nature which is stated in the transactional-analytic position 'I am OK; you are OK'. Another way he expressed this is by his statement 'Every human being is born a prince or a princess; early experiences convince some that they are frogs, and the rest of the pathological development follows from this'.[28]

Related to the basic assumption of human OKness are two further assumptions. First, Berne regarded practically every human being as possessing the complete neurological apparatus for adequate reality-oriented or Adult functioning. The only exceptions were those with the most severe type of organic brain injuries. Thus the therapeutic task is that of how to strengthen this already existing apparatus so that it may take its normal place in the patient's psychic organization.[29] Second, Berne believed that people have a built-in drive to both mental and physical health. The transactional analyst's job is to help nature by removing obstructions to patients' emotional and mental development, so letting them grow in their own directions.[30]

Ego States

Central to transactional analysis is the notion of ego states. One definition of an ego state is that it represents a consistent pattern of feeling and experience directly related to a corresponding consistent pattern of behaviour.[31] Elsewhere, Berne has written:

> An ego state may be described phenomenologically as a coherent system of feelings related to a given subject, and operationally as a set of coherent behaviour patterns; or pragmatically as a system of feelings which motivates a related set of behaviour patterns.[32]

Though not always emphasized by Berne, ego states involve thinking as well as feeling and behaviour.

Each human being exhibits three kinds of ego states, and at any given moment any individual in a social grouping will predominantly exhibit one or another of these states. The three ego states, depicted in Figure 4.1, are described as follows.

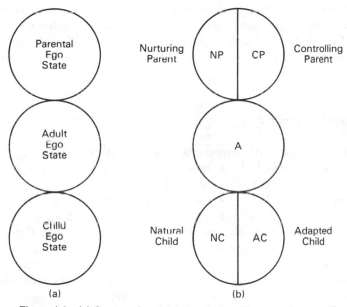

Figure 4.1   (a) Structural and (b) descriptive diagrams of personality.

1. A *Parental* or exteropsychic *ego state* is a set of feelings, thoughts, attitudes, and behaviours which resemble those of parental figures. It is both an accumulation of data and a way of relating to people. The Parental ego state may be seen in one of two forms. The *controlling* or prejudicial Parent is manifested as a set of seemingly arbitrary and rigid rules, usually prohibitive, which may either agree or disagree with the rules of a person's culture. The *nurturing* Parent is manifested as

sympathy and care for another individual or for oneself. Thus the Parent can be over-controlling and inhibiting or supportive and growth-enhancing. The Parent ego state may also influence a person's Adult or Child ego states. The function of the Parent is to conserve energy and to diminish anxiety by making certain decisions 'automatic'.

2. An *Adult* or neopsychic *ego state* autonomously and objectively appraises reality and makes judgements. Berne likens the neopsyche to a partially self-programming probability computer and stresses that the criterion of its adequacy is the use made of data available to a given individual.[33] Characteristics by which an Adult ego state may be recognized include organization, adaptability and intelligence.

3. A *Child* or archaeopsychic *ego state* is a set of feelings, thoughts, attitudes and behaviour patterns which are archaic relics of an individual's childhood. Berne considers that we all carry within ourselves a little boy or girl who feels, thinks, acts and responds just as we did when we were children of a certain age. The Child ego state is exhibited in two major forms. The *adapted* Child is manifested by feelings and behaviour which inferentially are under parental influence, such as sulking, compliance, withdrawal and inhibition. The *natural* Child is manifested by spontaneous expression such as self-indulgence, creativity and rebelliousness. Berne considered the natural Child to be the most valuable part of the personality. The proper function of a 'healthy' Child is to motivate the Adult so as to obtain the greatest amount of gratification for itself. This it does by letting the Adult know what it wants and by consulting the Parent about its appropriateness.

Structural Analysis of Ego States

Structural analysis consists of diagnosing and separating one feeling-thinking-and-behaviour pattern or ego state from another. Further analysis of ego states does not provide new ego states, but rather subdivisions of the existing ones. Such analysis tends to be called second-order structural analysis and can get very detailed. In particular, it focuses on further analysis of the Parent and Child.

In Figure 4.2 the Parent is divided into two components, one derived from the father and one derived from the mother. Children incorporate the whole of each parent into their Parent ego state, including the ways in which their parents exhibited thinking and feeling when expressing values. Consequently, second-order structural analysis includes the Parent, Adult and Child ego states of both parents.

Within the Child ego state, Parent, Adult and Child ego states, which were already there when the child made its basic decision concerning its life script, can be observed. Berne sometimes called the parent in the Child the 'electrode',[35] and Steiner describes it as the 'Pig Parent'.[36] Berne called the parent in the Child the electrode because when it 'pushes the button', the person automatically does something negative. Examples of such negative behaviour, the origins of whose injunctions are unclear, include excessive alcohol consumption, reckless gambling, and getting sexually turned off if coming on too strong.[37]

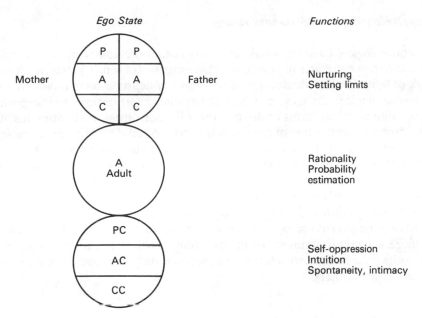

Figure 4.2 Second order structural diagram of personality.[34]

Berne saw the adult in the Child (AC) as a keen and perceptive student of human nature, which he called the Professor.[38] Steiner calls AC the Little Professor and observes that it is the ego state which Berne himself used in his studies on intuition, when he would guess the occupations of people using his own intuition.[39] The adult in the Child is the source both of intuitive and creative thinking and of delusion, since it may not always be right. The child in the Child ego state (CC) is the source of innate wants and feelings.[40] Spontaneity is a central characteristic of the child in the Child, but sometimes this spontaneity can be self-destructive.

Psychic Energy and Cathexis

Transactional analysis is a dynamic theory of personality in that it uses the concepts of psychic energy and of cathexis or distribution of energy. At a given moment the ego state which is most strongly cathected will have executive power. Berne writes of the 'flow of cathexis' which represents shifts in ego states. He considers that the most convenient way of acknowledging the differentiation of ego states is to view each state as having a boundary which separates it from other ego states. Ego states are viewed as semi-permeable under most conditions. Shifts in ego state depend on three factors: (a) the forces acting on each state; (b) the permeability of the boundaries between ego states; and (c) the cathectic capacity of each ego state. Berne observes that it is the quantitative balance between these three factors which determines the clinical condition of the patient and thus indicates the therapeutic procedures.[41]

Stimulus, Recognition and Structure Hunger

The psychobiological basis of social psychiatry is that the ability of human beings to maintain coherent ego states depends on a changing flow of sensory stimuli. Berne cites the work of Spitz,[42] which demonstrates that sensory deprivation in infants results not only in psychological changes, but also in organic deterioration. Berne posits that there are three principal forms of drive, hunger or motivation. First, stimulus hunger, with the most favoured forms of stimuli being those offered by physical intimacy. The dangers of over-stimulation as well as those of under-stimulation are acknowledged. Second, there is recognition hunger, which may be viewed as a partial transformation of infantile stimulus hunger. Berne uses the term 'stroking' to denote any act implying recognition of another's presence. There are numerous rituals, such as saying 'Hello!', which imply recognition and give gratification. Biologically, even negative recognition has an advantage over no recognition at all. Put colloquially, 'Folks need strokes!'[43] Third, there is structure hunger, or the everyday problem of how to structure one's waking hours.[44] Such time structuring is concerned only with social time or the time people spend with others.

Time Structuring

Berne observes that if two or more people are in a room together they have six possible kinds of social behaviour or time structuring from which to choose.[45] These are discussed below.

Withdrawal

Here two people do not overtly communicate with one another, for example if they are on a tube train or are withdrawn schizophrenics. In withdrawal, people remain wrapped up in their own thoughts.

Rituals

Rituals are stylized signs of mutual recognition dictated by tradition and social custom. At the simplest level, two people saying 'Good morning' would be engaging in a ritual.

Activities

Activities, more commonly called work, are not just concerned with dealing with the material means of survival. They also have a social significance in that they offer a framework for various kinds of recognition and satisfactions. Berne considered that work transactions were typically Adult-to-Adult, oriented mainly towards external reality.

Pastimes

Pastimes are semi-ritualistic, topical conversations which last longer than rituals but are still mainly socially programmed. Pastimes might include 'Isn't Everything Awful' and 'Motor Cars'. The focus of pastimes tends to be external to the participants rather than directly self-referent.

Games

Games, in contrast to pastimes, are sequences of transactions which are based more on individual than on social programming. A psychological game is a set of covert or ulterior as well as overt transactions which lead to a predictable outcome or payoff. Frequently these payoffs involve negative feelings or 'rackets' such as anger and depression. Collecting racket feelings is known as collecting 'trading stamps', which may some day be cashed in for behaviours such as a good cry or going out and buying some new clothes. More drastically, 'trading stamps' may be cashed in for divorce or attempted suicide. Each game has a motto by which it can be recognized, for example 'Why Don't You? – Yes But' and 'If It Weren't For You'.

Intimacy

Berne defines bilateral intimacy as 'a candid, game-free relationship, with mutual free giving and receiving and without exploitation'.[46] Intimacy represents individual and instinctual programming in which social programming and ulterior motivations are largely, if not totally, suspended. Intimacy is the most satisfying solution to stimulus, recognition, and structure hunger, but unfortunately it is not very common for people to live as 'princes' and 'princesses'. Berne's idea of intimacy includes, but is not restricted to, sexual intimacy.

Types of Transactions

In transactional analysis a stroke or unit of recognition is viewed as the fundamental unit of social interaction. An exchange of strokes constitutes a transaction. Thus rituals, activities, pastimes, games and intimacy may all be viewed as involving transactions. During transactions, at any given time each person is likely to have one of their three ego states predominantly energized or cathected. Thus transactions take place between ego states and, at its simplest level, transactional analysis involves diagnosing the ego states involved in a stimulus and response exchange. In other words, the transactional stimulus may come from the Parent, Adult or Child of one person and the transactional response from the Parent, Adult or Child of the other person.

There are three main types of transactions: complementary, crossed and ulterior.

Complementary transactions

Complementary transactions are ones in which the directions of the stimulus-response transactions are consistent, such as discussing the ills of the world (Parent–Parent), talking about work (Adult–Adult), or having fun together (Child–Child). Another way of stating this is that complementary transactions are ones in which people receive a response from the ego state that they have addressed. An example of a complementary transaction is given in Figure 4.3. There are nine possible types of

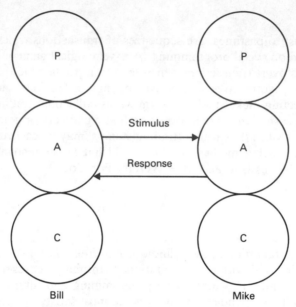

Figure 4.3   A complementary transaction. Stimulus: 'Pass me the salt.' Response: 'Here it is.'

complementary transactions (PP, PA, PC, AP, AA, AC, CP, CA, CC). Berne's first rule of communication is that communication will proceed smoothly as long as transactions are complementary.[47] In the example in Figure 4.3 Mike responds (a) from the ego state addressed by Bill and (b) to the ego state from which Bill addressed him.

Crossed transactions

In a crossed transaction the transactional response (a) comes from an ego state different from the one addressed, and/or (b) may go to an ego state which did not send the original stimulus. Berne's second or converse rule of communication is that communication is broken off when a crossed transaction occurs. In fact, communication may continue after crossed transactions, but on another subject. Figure 4.4 is an example of a crossed transaction. There are 72 possible types of crossed transactions, but only a few occur frequently.

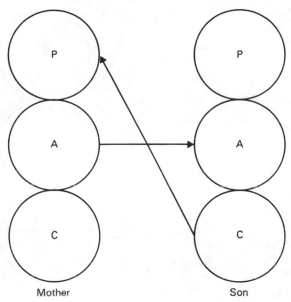

Figure 4.4   A crossed transaction. Stimulus: 'Would you please help with the washing-up?' Response: 'Why do you always keep asking me?'

Ulterior transactions

An ulterior communication is where, under the guise of an overt and socially more acceptable communication, an individual engages in an underlying and socially more risky communication. Another way of viewing this is that in much human interaction there is an underlying psychological as well as an overt social agenda. Psychological games, by definition, involve ulterior transactions.

Ulterior transactions may occur in everyday situations such as when a salesman says to a customer, 'Perhaps you shouldn't buy that beautiful and expensive fur coat', when his psychological message is 'Come on, I want you to buy it'. Another everyday situation in which ulterior transactions may occur is in potential sexual situations. Figure 4.5 is an illustration of such an ulterior transaction. Transactional analysts lay great stress on open and direct communication, including intimacy, and thus do not encourage time structuring that involves ulterior transactions.

ACQUISITION: DEVELOPMENT OF PERSONALITY

The Script

Berne regards a script as a preconscious life plan by which people structure their time. Scripts determine their destinies, including their approach to relationships and to

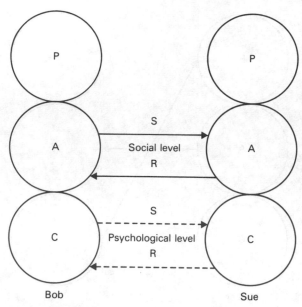

Figure 4.5 An ulterior transaction.
Social level – Bob: 'That was a great film. How about coming back to my place for a drink?'
Sue: 'Yes, I'd like that.'
Psychological level – Bob: 'Let's have some fun together.'
Sue: 'I'm available.'

tasks. He considers that they are usually based on childlike illusions which may persist throughout a whole lifetime.[48] People's scripts are the product of parental programming plus the decisions they made in response to parental programming, and lead them to have an illusion of personal autonomy when in fact they are carrying out, often unthinkingly, the directives of their scripts. At times, however, some people may question their scripts and this may cause identity crises which may or may not be resolved satisfactorily by removal of some of the blockages to genuine autonomy and a well-functioning Adult. Berne's view of human life, as contrasted with human nature, is pessimistic, as he tends to see humans as driven by script directives which lead to ways of time structuring seriously detrimental to the attainment of autonomy and creative activity.

The Script Matrix

The script matrix is a diagram used to help understand the development of people's scripts.[49] It is helpful to an understanding of the transmission of scripts if the matrix depicts a second-order structural breakdown of the Child. Figure 4.6 depicts such a script matrix for a hypothetical person, Mary. The diagram aims to show how script directives are transmitted to her. Although, during her upbringing, it is desirable for Mary to experience much of the nurturing Parent ego state of her parents and also their reasoning Adult and spontaneous Child, she may also be experiencing negative

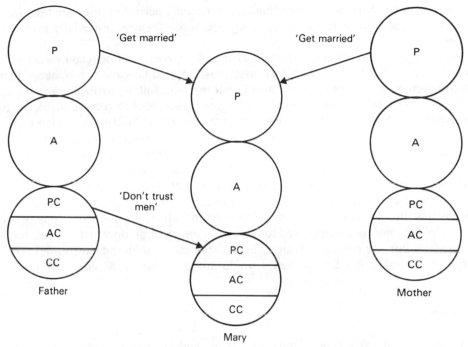

Figure 4.6 Script matrix showing transmission of script directives.

directives from the parent in the Child ego state of one or both of her parents. As depicted in Figure 4.6, the directives to Mary may be contradictory.

Although a chapter in Berne's 1961 book *Transactional Analysis in Psychotherapy* is devoted to analysis of scripts, he acknowledges the valuable work of Steiner in devising the script matrix and in helping to develop script theory. Berne proposed that it was the parent of the opposite sex who usually tells the child what to do and the parent of the same sex who usually demonstrates how to do it. Steiner added that it was the Child in the parent who gives the restrictive directives or injunctions and the Adult in the parent who gives the child the pattern or programme of behaviour.[50]

Injunctions, Attributions, Discounts and Lying

Although directives from parents can be nurturing and conducive to the child's emotional development, they can also be restrictive, reflecting the fears and insecurities of the Child in the parent.

Injunctions tend to be expressed as 'Don'ts', 'Oughts' and 'Shoulds'. They can be relatively mild or highly restrictive. Steiner gives the following as injunctions by which people learn to block intimacy: (a) do not give strokes if you have them to give; (b) do not ask for strokes when you need them; (c) do not accept strokes if you want them; (d) do not reject strokes when you do not want them; and (e) do not give yourself strokes. He considers that the above injunctions are the basis of depression.[51] Other injunctions may stop people from thinking, especially perhaps if they are female. Still others may interfere with the capacity to experience feelings, especially perhaps for males.

However, Steiner believes that children are also strongly influenced by *attributions*, or being told what they are and what they must do, and how they are feeling. Family reinforcement schedules tend to reward children who follow attributions and punish children who disobey injunctions.[52] Children are also liable to receive *discounts* from their parents. Steiner regards a discount as a crossed transaction in which a person says something from an Adult ego state to another person's Adult and the other person responds from his or her Parent or Child.[53] For instance, children's inquisitiveness may be discounted by parental rebuffs. More generally, a discount in TA is the minimization of some aspect of oneself, another person, or a situation.

Children's awareness can also be undermined either by their parents' overtly *lying* to them or by the more covert lying involved in half-truths and omissions of truth. Thus children may not be exposed to important information on which to base realistic perception. Steiner considers lying to be the rule rather than the exception in human affairs,[54] though many TA advocates would not go so far as to agree with this.

Decisions

On the basis of early transactions related to feeding, toilet training, weaning and family relationships, the young person starts developing a view of the world. Where a child is given unconditional protection he is less likely to develop a restrictive script. When, however, parents make their nurturing conditional on their child's submission to their injunctions and attributions, the child may make a conscious decision to adhere to parental wishes even though this means the sacrifice of autonomy. These decisions tend to be made in the pre-school years and are as realistic as the capacity of the adult in the Child or Little Professor at the time of the decision.[55] As a result of this decision, however, the child tends to take a different and more negative position and also develops a script. Berne acknowledged, however, that some scripts could be winner's scripts.

Life Positions

The fundamental assumption of transactional analysis is that of human OKness as expressed in the statement or life position 'I'm OK – You're OK'. By making a decision the child moves out of this position where he is likely to develop the full use of his various ego states. Instead, he adopts one of three other life positions, namely: 'I'm Not OK – You're OK'; 'I'm OK – You're Not OK'; and 'I'm Not OK – You're Not OK'. Each of these three 'Not OK' positions reflects and sustains impaired ego state development. Also, 'Not OK' positions militate against the development of intimacy and are the bases on which individuals play out their games.[56] Just as stimulus, recognition and structure hunger can be viewed as motivators, it is also possible to view the need to justify a basic life position as a motivator. Perhaps, though, it is more accurate to consider position hunger as a refinement of the other motivators, indicating how their fulfilment is to be attained.

Berne gives an example of a decision leading to a life position in the case of Rita.[57] Rita, when little, used to run to greet her father when he came home from work. As time went on her father's behaviour became erratic because of his drinking and he would push Rita away. One day her father had a particularly bad row with her mother. Rita, who was 6 years, 2 months and 23 days, was bewildered and frightened and at 5 p.m. that afternoon she made a decision that she would never again love a man. In order to maintain her decision, Rita took a position regarding her father that, even when amiable and sober, he was fundamentally bad. Over time she generalized her position to most other men, the Not-OKness of whom she epitomized in the slogan 'All men are beasts'. Her position also became the basis of a game in which her seductive behaviour provoked 'decent' men to make advances, which she then rejected. Berne observes that Rita's seductive manoeuvres were an attempt to establish an intimate relationship which she was unable to carry through.

Development of Games

During children's upbringing they are taught the rituals, activities and pastimes appropriate to their situations in life. They also learn games through significant experiences in their family life from their earliest months. Berne gives as an example of how a game might be learned the case of three-year-old Mike who, when his seven-year-old brother was allowed to leave the dinner table and lie down because of a stomach-ache, said 'I have a stomach-ache too', as though he wanted the same consideration.[58] Mike's parents, however, did not co-operate and thus may have saved him from the game of pleading illness (social transaction) in order to gain some privilege for himself (ulterior or psychological transaction). Berne considered that games are imitative in nature, and also that they are deliberately initiated by the neopsychic adult or Little Professor in the Child, frequently between the ages of two and eight.[59] As illustrated by Rita, games are often formulated to help justify a life position.

The Counterscript

In the development of a script, the person is given not only script injunctions and attributions from their parents' parent in the Child, but also counterscript messages from their parents' nurturing Parent. Berne uses the word 'prescription' for counter-script messages and observes that prescriptions are usually transmitted from grandparents.[60] Examples of prescriptions are 'Be a good boy (or girl)!' and 'Work hard'. Script injunctions and counterscript prescriptions are often contradictory, and life may involve an alternation between compliance first to one and then to the other. The counterscript may lead to a period of time in which an unhappy life plan gives way to a happier period. However, in the end the script injunctions always prevail, though again the possibility of winner's scripts should be acknowledged. Steiner indicates that an alcoholic's nurturing Parent may give the counterscript 'Be sober' while the parent in the Child is giving the injunction 'Don't think! Drink'.[61] In Figure 4.6 Mary's parents' nurturing Parent counterscript prescription was 'Get married' while her father's parent in the Child injunction was 'Don't trust men'. Frequently injunctions are transmitted non-verbally by approval or disapproval of certain kinds of behaviour, and this may make them harder to acknowledge than when they are transmitted more openly.

PERPETUATION OF MALADAPTIVE BEHAVIOUR

In the preceding section the ways in which people acquire scripts and games were described. The question to be answered in this section is why people persist in acting out scripts and playing games rather than enjoying autonomy and intimacy, or, in other words, why people stay frogs when it might seem more rewarding to revert to being a prince or princess. Part of the answer is that both scripts and games have their rewards or payoffs.

Script Payoffs

Berne defines the script payoff as the ultimate destiny or final display that marks the end of a life plan.[62] He considers that there are four main payoffs in clinical practice: be a loner, be a bum, go crazy or drop dead.[63] While these ultimate destinies are one way of viewing the concept of script payoff, another way is to look at it in terms of current as contrasted with ultimate rewards. Steiner observes that when a person enters his counterscript phase, despite a superficial sense of well-being, he experiences a deep visceral discomfort. However, the individual experiences visceral comfort when reverting to script behaviour. This is because adherence to script injunctions represents acquiescence to parental wishes, albeit the parental parent in the Child, and thus is associated with the well-being and comfort of parental protection. Steiner notes that an alcoholic, even in the pain of a hangover, is receiving approval for acquiescing to the parental Child's injunction 'Don't think! Drink'.[64] Steiner is perhaps more pessimistic about scripts than many other TA counsellors.

Game Payoffs

Games too have their payoffs, which are related to the life positions adopted in their players' scripts. For instance, the payoff in Rita's script was manipulating men to boorish behaviour which confirmed her position that men are Not-OK. Berne observes that, beyond their social function of time structuring, games are urgently needed by some for the maintenance of their health. Their life positions are so precariously maintained that to interfere with or deprive them of the payoffs from their games may cause disturbance, or even psychosis. Thus game analysis must be approached cautiously.[65]

An example of a game with a payoff is 'If It Weren't for You'. A person can complain endlessly that if it were not for a husband, wife, child, boss or some other person, they could engage in an activity from which at present they feel restricted. Sometimes, however, these other people are being used to defend the person against the realization that, if it were not for them, he or she might be unable to perform a difficult or anxiety-evoking task. Also, if the task were performed, it would no longer be possible to cause the other person discomfort by saying 'If It Weren't For You'. This game validates the life-position that others are Not OK.

The Illusion of Autonomy

Berne considered that only the strongest can live without illusions and that one of the illusions which is hardest to relinquish is that of autonomy or self-determination.[66] An autonomous person knows what is practical and Adult, what he accepts that comes from others, and what he does that is determined by early impulses. The illusion of autonomy is where a person does not acknowledge feelings and behaviours which come from his Child and Parent ego states, but instead believes that they come from the Adult ego state. Berne makes a distinction between delusions and illusions, both of which are contaminations of the Adult ego state and, as such, prevent it from accurately processing information. Delusions are the prejudices and directives from parents which a person treats as though they were his own ideas. Illusions are those wishful ideas, impulses and early tastes coming from the Child which are accepted as Adult and rational. The significance of the illusion of autonomy is that an individual, being unaware of the delusions and illusions which are causing 'frog-like' behaviour, lacks the necessary insight and motivation for change. Thus destructive ways of time structuring are sustained rather than ameliorated. What is needed is a re-alignment and strengthening of the Adult ego-boundary to allow accurate processing of all relevant information.

Exclusion

With a truly autonomous person the ego-boundaries are strong, yet appropriately permeable to allow psychic energy to move between Parent, Adult and Child ego states. The illusion of autonomy indicates a structure where ego-boundaries are insufficiently well defined and the Adult ego state is being contaminated by the Parent and/or Child ego states. Exclusion, on the other hand, occurs in situations where psychic energy becomes exclusively cathected in a constant Parent, a constant Adult, or a constant Child.[67] Thus one ego-state is strongly cathected while the other two are decommissioned. Berne considered that the excluding Parent is to be found in 'compensated' schizophrenics, where exclusion is the principal defence against confused Child or archaeopsychic activity. He gives us an example of an excluding Adult, Dr Quint, who had a sincere commitment to data processing as a way of life, yet possessed no healthy Child or Parent characteristics. Narcissistic impulsive personalities exhibit the excluding Child, where both rational and nurturing and limit-setting ego states are avoided. The excluding Parent, Adult or Child may defend itself by, for instance, the use of intellectualization, as in the case of the excluding Adult.

Inadequate Information

The last point to be made regarding the perpetuation of maladaptive behaviour is that the effectiveness of the Adult is dependent on the adequacy of the information available to it. Furthermore, it may need to develop some skills of effective Adult functioning, including the ability to collect and adequately assess relevant information. James and Jongeward state that the computer phrase 'Garbage in, garbage out' applies to the Adult or, for that matter, to any other ego state.[68]

CHANGING MALADAPTIVE BEHAVIOUR

Transactional analysis is an umbrella term for four different, but interrelated, approaches to treatment. These approaches, which are briefly discussed below, are structural analysis, transactional analysis, game analysis and script analysis. Berne saw a progression from structural analysis, through transactional and game analysis, to script analysis, though he realized that the script analysis state was not always attained.[69] Frequently, if not always, transactional analysis involves the use of contracts or agreements on the part of both clients and therapists regarding their roles in achieving clearly stated objectives.

Structural Analysis

As mentioned earlier, structural analysis consists of diagnosing and separating one feeling-thinking-and-behaviour pattern or ego state from another. Structural analysis helps clients or patients to identify and become aware of both the existence and the contents of their ego states. Its aim is to free the individual to have appropriate access to all his ego states without debilitating exclusions and contaminations. A related aim is to help the Adult to remain in control of the personality in stressful situations. Ego states may be viewed not only in terms of their content, but also in terms of the degree to which they are cathected both before and after treatment. Dusay has devised a diagram called the egogram which graphs the extent to which each of a person's ego states are cathected.[70] He also posits that the amount of psychic energy within a person is constant and that if energy is taken away from one ego state more will be available for other ego states. Thus, as treatment progresses, the parent in the Child ego state may be less strongly cathected, while the Adult and natural Child ego states may attain stronger cathexes.

Transactional Analysis

Berne saw the aim of transactional analysis as social control or the ability of the Adult to decide when to release the Parent or Child and when to resume the executive.[71] If a person does not have social control, others can consciously or unconsciously activate that person's Parent or Child ego states in ways which may not be helpful. Transactional analysis proper, as Berne called it, is the analysis of single transactions by means of transactional diagrams.[72] Clients are helped to understand the ego state transactions involved in situations and relationships in which they are experiencing difficulty as a means towards greater competence at handling them.

Game Analysis

Game analysis is another way of attaining social control. Just as an understanding of structural analysis is a prerequisite of transactional analysis, so an understanding of analysis of single transactions is a prerequisite of understanding the more complex series of transactions called games. In game analysis the client is encouraged to learn more satisfying ways of structuring time and acquiring strokes. The methods of game analysis include helping a client to see what game he is playing, what the moves are, what the racket or bad feeling payoffs are, and how the games justify a life position. It is also important to help the client to express constructively the natural Child need or feeling which he has been discounting.[73]

Script Analysis

The script analyst must take care not to behave in ways which promote a client's script. The purpose of script analysis is to get the client out of his script and thus to behave autonomously. The therapist needs to listen carefully to and observe his client's verbal and non-verbal behaviour for script signs or signals. Additionally, script analysis may involve the use of a script checklist to help both analyst and client to know the client's script.[74] Script analysis aims to help clients to abandon their early decisions, *previously* made in different circumstances and with an incomplete neo-psychic or Adult apparatus, by *now* making and enacting redecisions for change.

A script antithesis is a therapeutic intervention which directly contradicts a parental injunction and thus brings temporary or permanent release from a script.[75] Berne considered that the final common pathway of a patient's behaviour is the preconscious dialogue between Parent, Adult and Child, or voices in the head, which can easily be brought into consciousness. Redecision can be helped by getting into the client's head another voice, that of the therapist. This process involves the three 'Ps' of script antithesis: potency, permission and protection. Potency is defined by whether the therapist's voice in the client's head has been powerful enough to prevail over the voices or injunctions of the client's parents in the Child. Permissions can be positive or negative. Positive permissions or licences involve the therapist's saying 'Let him do it!', whereas with negative permissions or releases the therapist is saying 'Stop pushing him into it!'. When a client follows a script antithesis and goes against a parental injunction, his Child may get very anxious. Protection means that during the period of change the client or patient can call upon the therapist to exercise his potency again in time of need.

Further Methods

Gestalt and psychodrama methods may be used in conjunction with transactional analysis. For instance, the Gestalt 'empty chair' technique, by which the client moves from one chair to another playing parts of himself, may be used to elicit voices in the head. Also, psychodramatists may supply trained assistants who play some roles while the client plays the other. James and Jongeward's *Born to Win* offers an example of transactional analysis theory highlighted by Gestalt exercises.[76] Also, some clients may be referred to dance classes or sensory-awareness groups as an adjunct to transactional analysis. The permission class is a teacher-run group which follows the prescription of the transactional analyst, especially where bodily contact for clients seems desirable. For instance, a transactional analyst may feel that a client needs to give and receive hugging and sends him to a prescription class to do exercises focused on hugging.[77]

GOALS FOR COUNSELLING AND FOR LIVING

Achieving autonomy or the integrated Adult are two ways of stating the goals of transactional analysis. In a sense autonomy is a more colloquial term for the integrated Adult.

Autonomy

Autonomy refers to the capacity for 'non-script' behaviour which is reversible, 'with no particular time schedule, developed later in life, and not under parental influence'.[78] Autonomous behaviour is the opposite of script behaviour. It involves the overthrow of and then persistent struggle against sinking back into: (a) the weight of a whole tribal or family historical tradition; (b) the influence of the individual's parental, social and cultural backgrounds; and (c) seeking ulterior payoffs from games. Furthermore, autonomy consists of the active development of personal and social control so that significant behaviour becomes a matter of free choice. Berne summarizes the process of the attainment of autonomy as 'obtaining a friendly divorce from one's parents (and from other Parental influences) so that they may be agreeably visited on occasion, but are no longer dominant'.[79]

The attainment of autonomy involves the person's regaining three basic capacities of the fundamental OK position: awareness, spontaneity and intimacy.[80]

Awareness

Awareness means the capacity to see and hear directly and not in the way in which one was brought up. It means living in the here-and-now, open to the sensations coming from the environment in the way a painter, poet or musician might be.

Spontaneity

Spontaneity means the capacity to feel directly and to express feeling directly and not in the way in which one was brought up. The spontaneous person can choose feelings, be they Parent, Adult or Child feelings.

Intimacy

Intimacy means the capacity to relate to another person or persons in an aware, spontaneous, loving and game-free way. Berne regarded intimacy as essentially a function of the natural, uncorrupted Child.

The Integrated Adult

With the integrated Adult, certain child-like and parent-like qualities get integrated into the Adult ego state in a manner different from contamination. The integrated Adult can have both child-like qualities, such as charm and openness of nature, and ethical qualities, such as courage, sincerity, loyalty and reliability, which Berne observed as meeting a world-wide ethos.[81] Thus the integrated Adult or neopsychic ego state ideally should exhibit three kinds of elements or tendencies: first, archaeo-psychic elements like personal attractiveness and responsiveness; second, neopsychic elements like objective data-processing; and third, exteropsychic elements like personal responsibility.

SELF-REFERENT EXERCISES

It may help you to understand this chapter better if, either with paper and pencil or in your head, you think about and answer the following questions.

1.   Do a first-order PAC structural analysis on yourself (Figure 4.1(a)) indicating thoughts, feelings and behaviours belonging to your:

    (a) Parent ego state;
    (b) Adult ego state;
    (c) Child ego state.

2.   Assume that you have 100 units of energy to divide among your nurturing Parent, controlling Parent, Adult, natural Child, and adapted Child ego states. In terms of the way you usually feel and behave, distribute the 100 units of energy among the five areas.

3.   Into which of the four life positions would you place yourself: 'I'm OK – You're OK'; 'I'm Not OK – You're OK'; 'I'm OK – You're Not OK'; and 'I'm Not OK – You're Not OK'? Give reasons for your choice.

4.   Draw a script matrix for yourself as in Figure 4.6 and indicate some of the main script injunctions and counterscript prescriptions you received from your parents.

5.   Identify any early decisions you made which are no longer appropriate. Formulate appropriate statements of redecision which will allow you to change the ways in which you are currently scripted to feel and behave.

6.   Take a relationship with a significant other in your life (parent, spouse, child, colleague, etc.) and analyse one or more of the transactions in it in terms of the Parent, Adult and Child ego state, or states, cathected in each person.

7.   Try to identify some of the games you play, including the moves involved and their negative feeling payoff or your racket. Suggest an easily remembered name for each of your games.

8.   Assess yourself on each of the following goals of transactional analysis:

   (a)   autonomy;
   (b)   awareness;
   (c)   spontaneity;
   (d)   intimacy;
   (e)   the integrated Adult ego state.

NOTES

1.   Berne, E., Steiner, C. M. & Dusay, J. M. (1973) Transactional analysis. In R. R. M. Jurjevich (Ed.), *Direct Psychotherapy* (Volume 1) Coral Gables, Florida: University of Miami Press. p. 373. Full reference pp. 370–393.
2.   Berne, E. (1972) *What Do You Say After You Say Hello?* p. 400. London: Corgi Books.
3.   James, M. and Contributors (1977) *Techniques in Transactional Analysis: For Psychotherapists and Counsellors.* p. 21. Massachusetts: Addison-Wesley.
4.   Berne, E. (1961) *Transactional Analysis in Psychotherapy.* New York: Grove Press. The Latin version of the dedication is: *In Memoriam Patris Mei David Medicinae Doctor et Chirurgiae Magister atque Pauperibus Medicus.*

5. Gregg, G. (1973) Eric Berne: a drive to simplify and make it. *Psychology Today*, April, 50–51.
6. Berne, E. (1966) *Principles of Group Treatment*. Foreword. New York: Oxford University Press.
7. Berne, E. (1968) *A Layman's Guide to Psychiatry and Psychoanalysis*. Harmondsworth: Penguin Books. First published in 1947 as *The Mind in Action*.
8. Steiner, C. M. (1974) *Scripts People Live* pp. 12–15. New York: Bantam Books.
9. Berne, E., Steiner, C. M. & Dusay, J. M. (1973) Transactional analysis. In R. R. M. Jurjevich (Ed.), *Direct Psychotherapy* (Volume 1) pp. 371–373. Coral Gables, Florida: University of Miami Press.
10. Dusay, J. M. (1971) Eric Berne's studies of intuition 1949–1962. *Transactional Analysis Journal*, **1**, 39. Full reference pp. 34–44.
11. Holland, G. A. (1973) Transactional analysis. In R. Corsini (Ed.), *Current Psychotherapies* p. 357. Itasca, Illinois: Peacock. Full reference pp. 353–399.
12. Berne, E. (1961) *Transactional Analysis in Psychotherapy*, Preface, p. 13. New York: Grove Press.
13. Berne, E. (1958) Transactional analysis: a new and effective method of group therapy. *American Journal of Psychotherapy*, **12**, 735–743.
14. Berne, E. (1961) *Transactional Analysis in Psychotherapy*, Preface, p. 11. New York: Grove Press.
15. *Ibid.*
16. Berne, E. (1963) *The Structure and Dynamics of Organizations and Groups*. Philadelphia: J. B. Lippincott Co.
17. Berne, E. (1964) *Games People Play*. New York: Grove Press.
18. Berne, E. (1966) *Principles of Group Treatment*. New York: Oxford University Press.
19. Berne, E. (1972) *What Do You Say After You Say Hello?* London: Corgi Books.
20. Berne, E. (1968) *The Happy Valley*. New York: Grove Press.
21. Berne, E. (1970) *Sex in Human Loving*. Harmondsworth: Penguin Books.
22. James, M. and Contributors (1977) *Techniques in Transactional Analysis: For Psychotherapists and Counselors* pp. 23–28. Reading, Massachusetts: Addison-Wesley.
23. Holland, G. A. (1973) Transactional analysis. In R. Corsini (Ed.), *Current Psychotherapies* p. 357. Itasca, Illinois: Peacock.
24. Steiner, C. M. (1971) *Games Alcoholics Play*. New York: Grove Press.
25. Steiner, C. M. (1974) *Scripts People Live*. New York: Bantam Books.
26. Berne, E. (1966) *Principles of Group Treatment*, Introduction. New York: Oxford University Press.
27. Berne, E. (1972) *What Do You Say After You Say Hello?* p. 20. London: Corgi Books.
28. Berne, E. (1966) *Principles of Group Treatment* pp. 289–290. New York: Oxford University Press.
29. *Ibid.* p. 221.
30. *Ibid.* p. 63.
31. Berne, E. (1972) *What Do You Say After You Say Hello?* p. 443. London: Corgi Books.
32. Berne, E. (1961) *Transactional Analysis in Psychotherapy* p. 17. New York: Grove Press.
33. *Ibid.* pp. 68–80. Also Berne, E. (1964) *Games People Play* pp. 23–28. New York: Grove Press; and Berne, E. (1972) *What Do You Say After You Say Hello?* pp. 409–413. London: Corgi Books.
34. Steiner, C. M. (1974) *Scripts People Live* pp. 51–58. New York: Bantam Books. Also Berne, E. (1972) *What Do You Say After You Say Hello?* pp. 11–13, 116. London: Corgi Books.
35. Berne, E. (1972) *What Do You Say After You Say Hello?* pp. 115–117. London: Corgi Books.
36. Steiner, C. M. (1974) *Scripts People Live* p. 53. New York: Bantam Books.
37. Berne, E. (1972) *What Do You Say After You Say Hello?* p. 116. London: Corgi Books.
38. Berne, E. (1961) *Transactional Analysis in Psychotherapy* p. 207. New York: Grove Press; and Steiner, C. M. (1974) *Scripts People Live* p. 104. New York: Bantam Books.

39. Steiner, C. M. (1974) *Scripts People Live* p. 53. New York: Bantam Books.
40. Woollams, S., Brown, M. & Huige, K. (1974) *Transactional Analysis in Brief* pp. 4–6. Michigan: Huron Valley Institute. A more recent TA book is: Woollams, S. & Brown, M. (1979) *The Total Handbook of Transactional Analysis*. Englewood Cliffs: Prentice-Hall.
41. Berne, E. (1961) *Transactional Analysis in Psychotherapy* pp. 37–43. New York: Grove Press.
42. Spitz, R. (1945) Hospitalism, genesis of psychiatric conditions in early childhood. *Psychoanalytic Study of the Child*, **1**, 53–74.
43. English, F. (1973) TA's Disney world. *Psychology Today*, April, 47. Full reference pp. 45–50 and p. 98.
44. Berne, E. (1961) *Transactional Analysis in Psychotherapy* pp. 83–85. New York: Grove Press. Also Berne, E. (1964) *Games People Play* pp. 13–16. New York: Grove Press.
45. Berne, E. (1972) *What Do You Say After You Say Hello?* pp. 22–26. London: Corgi Books.
46. *Ibid.* p. 25.
47. Berne, E. (1964) *Games People Play* pp. 29–34. New York: Grove Press.
48. Berne, E. (1972) *What Do You Say After You Say Hello?* pp. 25–26. London: Corgi Books.
49. Steiner, C. M. (1974) *Scripts People Live* p. 67. New York: Bantam Books.
50. Berne, E.(1972) *What Do You Say After You Say Hello?* pp. 279–298. London: Corgi Books.
51. Steiner, C. M. (1974) *Scripts People Live* pp. 137–138. New York: Bantam Books.
52. *Ibid.* pp. 71–75.
53. *Ibid.* p. 144.
54. *Ibid.* pp. 155–160.
55. *Ibid.* pp. 82–89.
56. Berne, E. (1972) *What Do You Say After You Say Hello?* pp. 84–96. London: Corgi Books.
57. Berne, E. (1966) *Principles of Group Treatment* pp. 264–267. New York: Oxford University Press.
58. Berne, E. (1964) *Games People Play* pp. 58–60. New York: Grove Press.
59. *Ibid.* p. 60.
60. Berne, E. (1972) *What Do You Say After You Say Hello?* pp. 118–120. London: Corgi Books.
61. Steiner, C. M. (1974) *Scripts People Live* pp. 104–109. New York: Bantam Books.
62. Berne, E. (1972) *What Do You Say After You Say Hello?* p. 446. London: Corgi Books.
63. *Ibid.* pp. 110–113.
64. Steiner, C. M. (1974) *Scripts People Live* pp. 104–109. New York: Bantam Books.
65. Berne, E.(1964) *Games People Play* pp. 61–62. New York: Grove Press.
66. Berne, E. (1972) *What Do You Say After You Say Hello?* pp. 147–156. London: Corgi Books.
67. Berne, E. (1961) *Transactional Analysis in Psychotherapy* pp. 44–47. New York: Grove Press.
68. James, M. & Jongeward, D. (1971) *Born to Win* p. 241. Reading, Massachusetts: Addison-Wesley.
69. Berne, E. (1961) *Transactional Analysis in Psychotherapy* pp. 90–91. New York: Grove Press.
70. Dusay, J. M. (1972) Egograms and the 'constancy hypothesis'. *Transactional Analysis Journal*, **2**, 3, 27–41.
71. Berne, E. (1961) *Transactional Analysis in Psychotherapy* p. 90. New York: Grove Press.
72. Berne, E. (1972) *What Do You Say After You Say Hello?* p. 447. London: Corgi Books.
73. Woollams, S., Brown, M. & Huige, K. (1974) *Transactional Analysis in Brief* pp. 26–31. Michigan: Huron Valley Institute.
74. Berne, E. (1972) *What Do You Say After You Say Hello?* pp. 417–439. London: Corgi Books.

75. *Ibid.* pp. 349–378.
76. James, M. & Jongeward, D. (1971) *Born to Win.* Reading, Massachusetts: Addison-Wesley.
77. Berne, E. (1972) *What Do You Say After You Say Hello?* pp. 371–372. London: Corgi Books.
78. *Ibid.* p. 418.
79. Berne, E. (1964) *Games People Play* p. 183. New York: Grove Press.
80. *Ibid.* pp. 178–181.
81. Berne, E. (1961) *Transactional Analysis in Psychotherapy* pp. 194–195. New York: Grove Press.

5 – Psychoanalytic Theory

SUMMARY: *Psychoanalytic theory groups human instincts into two broad categories, the erotic or life instincts and the death or destructive instincts. The energy of the life instincts is termed 'libido'. To a large extent people are motivated by the pleasure principle. Mental life takes place on conscious, preconscious and unconscious levels. The mental apparatus consists of three agencies: the id, which is constantly striving for instinctual satisfaction; the super-ego, which represents parental and moral influence; and the ego, which aims to meet the instinctual demands of the id on the basis of the reality principle. The ego has three task-masters – the external world, the id and the super-ego – and each may cause it anxiety. Psychical energy is distributed among the three mental agencies, which may be in harmony or in conflict with each other.*

People are sexual from infancy, though they tend to be subject to amnesia about this. Humans are constitutionally bisexual and infantile sexuality contains great tendencies to perversion. Sexual development takes place in two phases: a pre-genital phase up to the end of the fifth year and a genital phase starting at menarche and puberty. The period in between is the latency period. There are some differences in sexual development between the sexes, including development during the Oedipus situation. While the child's ego is relatively weak, it develops defensive mechanisms to ward off the strong sexual impulses emanating from the id. Thus much of its early sexual life becomes repressed or is not allowed access to consciousness. Excessive repression may lead to the development of neurosis. Since the ego is weakened by having to maintain the repression, it does not have access to the repressed material, and the repressed impulses become transformed into neurotic symptoms. The aim of psychoanalysis is to strengthen the client's ego by lifting childhood repressions, filling in gaps in memory and allowing acts of judgement to be made through the ego's present strength rather than its previous weakness. Concepts of psychoanalytic treatment like free association, transference and interpretation are discussed briefly.

INTRODUCTION

The previous three chapters have focused on humanistic theory, which emphasizes people's capacity to bring much of their behaviour under conscious control. The present chapter deals with a second main model of human behaviour underlying counselling psychology – the psychoanalytic model, which sees people as being more under the sway of their instincts. Around the turn of the century Freud started writing about psychoanalysis. His theory is considered worthy of inclusion in this book for a number of reasons. First, psychoanalytic theory provides a tremendously fruitful source of concepts concerning personality. For instance, Freud's instinct theory throws light on the biological basis of human functioning, while his ideas on defensive mechanisms provide a valuable insight into the ways in which people sustain self-defeating behaviour. Second, psychoanalytic theory possesses a unique historical interest not only in terms of its being an early major psychological theory, but also because of its influence on other theorists. The humanistic psychologists have been affected in varying degrees by Freud. For example, the points of contact with transactional analysis include the tripartite structure of personality and the import-ance of early experience. Also, Rogers' concept of levels of awareness resembles Freud's idea of levels of consciousness. Others influenced by Freud include Jung, Adler, Horney, Sullivan and Fromm, the last four of whom are often termed the 'neo-Freudians'. Third, psychoanalytic concepts regarding practice, such as free association, interpretation, transference and resistance, merit the attention of all counsellors. Fourth, some counselling psychologists are of an analytic orientation, as are, it seems, a greater proportion of psychiatrists. Some analysts use 'pure' Freudian theory; others accept some of his ideas while modifying others. Communication with such people is likely to be facilitated by an understanding of their theoretical framework.

Sigmund Freud

Sigmund Freud (1856–1939) was born at Freiberg, a small town in what is now Czechoslovakia. He was the eldest son of his father's second wife, who subsequently bore five daughters and two other sons. Jones writes of Freud's mother's pride in and love for her first-born and also mentions that between the ages of two and two and a half Freud's libido had been aroused towards his mother on seeing her naked.[1] Freud writes: 'My parents were Jews, and I have remained a Jew myself'.[2] His father, Jakob, was a wool merchant who, when Freud was four, moved his family to Vienna. Freud's early years in Vienna were hard and, throughout his upbringing, his family appears to have been short of money.

When he was nine Freud went to high school (Sperl Gymnasium), where he was at the top of his class for seven years, enjoyed special privileges, and was required to pass few examinations. Freud was a hard worker who enjoyed reading and studying. On leaving school with distinction at 17 he faced the choice of a career, which for a Viennese Jew had to be in industry, business, law or medicine. He recalls not feeling any particular predilection for medicine, since his interests were directed more towards human concerns than natural objects. Freud writes '. . . and it was hearing Goethe's beautiful essay on Nature read aloud by Professor Carl Brühl just before I left school that decided me to become a medical student'.[3]

In 1873 Freud enrolled at the University of Vienna to study medicine, though when he was there his academic interests were more wide-ranging. In 1876 he began the first of his researches, a study of the gonadic structure of eels. Soon afterwards he entered Ernst Brücke's physiological laboratory, where he worked, with short interruptions, from 1876 to 1882. During this period Freud focused chiefly on work connected with the histology of nerve cells. He found 'rest and satisfaction' in Brücke's laboratory as well as scientists 'whom I could respect and take as my models'.[4] He thought especially highly of Brücke himself. Freud recalls being decidedly negligent in pursuing his medical studies. Nevertheless, in 1881 he passed his final examinations to become a Doctor of Medicine with the grade of 'excellent'.

In 1882 Freud left Brücke's laboratory, where the year before he had been appointed a demonstrator. For financial reasons, probably influenced by his having fallen in love, Freud decided to earn his living as a physician. He entered the General Hospital of Vienna, where he gained experience in various departments and became an active researcher in the Institute of Cerebral Anatomy. During this period 'with an eye to material considerations, I began to study nervous diseases'.[5] Because of inadequate opportunities for learning this subject, Freud was forced to be his own teacher. He published a number of clinical observations on organic diseases of the nervous systems and, in 1885, was appointed lecturer in neuropathology. Around this period Freud both took and conducted research into the use of cocaine. Jones observes: 'For many years he suffered from periodic depressions and fatigue or apathy, neurotic symptoms which later took the form of anxiety attacks before being dispelled by his own analysis'.[6] Cocaine apparently calmed the agitation and eased the depression. Jones also mentions that all his life Freud was subject to severe bouts of migraine which were refractory to any treatment.[7]

On the award of a travelling fellowship Freud went to Paris where, from October 1885 to February 1886, he studied at the Sâlpetrière (hospital for nervous diseases) under Charcot. He was very impressed with Charcot's investigations into hysteria, confirming the genuineness of hysterical phenomena, including hysterical paralyses and contractures by hypnotic suggestion. In 1886 he returned to Vienna to marry Martha Bernays and to set up a private practice as a specialist in nervous diseases. His 'therapeutic arsenal contained only two weapons, electrotherapy and hypnotism. . .'.[8] He soon dropped electrotherapy and increasingly realized the limitations of hypnotic suggestion. During the period 1886 to 1891 he did little scientific work, though in 1891 he jointly published the first of his studies on the cerebral paralyses of children.

In the early 1880s Freud had developed a close friendship with Joseph Breuer, a prominent Viennese physician, who told him how, between 1880 and 1882, he had successfully treated a young girl with hysterical symptoms. His method was to hypnotize her deeply and then encourage her to express in words her reminiscences of earlier emotional situations which were oppressing her. In the late 1880s Freud began repeating Breuer's technique with his own patients, being aware 'of the possibility that there could be powerful mental processes which nevertheless remained hidden from the consciousness of man'.[9] In 1893 Freud and Breuer wrote a preliminary paper on the cathartic method and, in 1895, published their book *Studies on Hysteria*.[10]

During the 1890s the transition from catharsis to psychoanalysis proper took place. Jones writes: 'there is ample evidence that for ten years or so – roughly comprising the nineties – he suffered from a very considerable psychoneurosis . . . yet it was just in the years when the neurosis was at its height, 1897–1900, that Freud did his most original work'.[11] Although he showed no conversion symptoms, he had extreme alterations of mood between elation and self-confidence, and depression and inhibition. In the latter moods Freud could neither write nor concentrate, apart from his professional work. Additionally, he had occasional attacks of dread of dying and also anxiety about travelling by rail.

During the period 1887 to 1900 Freud had an intense friendship with Fleiss, a nose and throat specialist two years younger than himself. Fleiss saw sexual problems as central to his own work and encouraged Freud and gave him permission to develop his theories. Jones notes Freud's dependency on Fleiss's good opinion and calls him Freud's 'sole public' during this period. Jones rated Fleiss as intellectually much inferior to Freud.[12]

Against this background, Freud started developing his ideas on the sexual bases of neuroses, abandoned hypnotism yet retained his practice of requiring the patient to lie on a sofa while he sat behind, and, during 1897 to 1899, wrote his major work, *The Interpretation of Dreams*.[13] In the summer of 1897 Freud undertook a psychoanalysis of his own unconscious, and this self-analysis generated material for the book. Freud discovered his childhood passion for his mother and jealousy for his father, which he considered a pervasive human characteristic; he termed it the Oedipus complex. It took eight years to sell the first edition of 600 copies of *The Interpretation of Dreams*. Jones observes of Freud's self-analysis: 'The end of all that labor and suffering was the last and final phase in the evolution of Freud's personality. There emerged the serene and benign Freud, henceforth free to pursue his work in imperturbable composure'.[14] Fromm's biography is less kind, suggesting that Freud continued to exhibit some insecurity and egotism in areas of both his professional and his personal life.[15] In 1905 Freud published what is perhaps his other major work, *Three Contributions to the Theory of Sex*, which traces the development of sexuality from its earliest childhood beginnings.[16]

In his autobiographical study Freud observed that, after the preliminary cathartic period, the history of psychoanalysis falls into two phases. From 1895–96 until 1906 or 1907 he worked in isolation, but thereafter the contributions of his pupils and collaborators increasingly grew in importance.[17] The historical development of Freud's ideas will be left at this stage. Suffice it to say that for the remainder of his life he published numerous books and articles not only on psychoanalysis as a method of treating the disturbed, but also on the relevance of his theories to everyday life. In 1910, at a congress held at Nuremberg, the analysts formed themselves into an International Psychoanalytical Association divided into a number of local societies, but under a common president. By 1935 the number of the Association's supporters had increased considerably.[18] The growth of psychoanalysis, however, was not smooth, and it aroused considerable antipathy.

Freud was in the habit of smoking an average of 20 cigars a day and, in 1923, learned that he had cancer of the jaw. He lived the last 16 years of his life in pain which was often extreme, and a total of 33 operations were performed on his jaw. In 1938 Nazism caused Freud to leave Austria with his family and settle in his admired England, which he had first visited when he was 19. He died in London a year later. The following is Freud's summary of his life's work:

> Looking back, then, over the patchwork of my life's labours, I can say that I have made many beginnings and thrown out many suggestions. Something will come of them in future, though I cannot myself tell whether it will be much or little. I can, however, express a hope that I have opened up a pathway for an important advance in our knowledge.[19]

Elsewhere, Freud had observed that he was by temperament a conquistador or adventurer, with the accompanying traits of curiosity, boldness and tenacity.[20] A modern term for Freud might be an 'ideas person'.

BASIC CONCEPTS

Although many of Freud's basic concepts are to be found in *The Interpretation of Dreams*, he was developing and refining his ideas continuously. Thus the same concept may appear in different sources, only some of which will be mentioned here. In general, this chapter represents Freud's later presentation of his theory.

The Pleasure Principle

Originally presented as the unpleasure principle,[21] the pleasure principle follows from the constancy hypothesis that 'the mental apparatus endeavours to keep the quantity of excitation in it as low as possible or at least to keep it constant'.[22] Thus everything which increases the quantity of excitation will be felt as unpleasurable and anything which diminishes it will be experienced as pleasurable. Freud qualified the idea of the dominance of the pleasure principle by observing that, although in the mind there exists a strong tendency towards the pleasure principle, there are also other forces opposing it, with the final outcome not always fulfilling the tendency towards pleasure.

The Instincts

Instincts represent somatic or biological demands upon the mind. While acknowledging the possibility of distinguishing many instincts, Freud assumed that these could be grouped into two basic instincts, *Eros* and the *destructive instinct*. The erotic instincts 'seek to combine more and more living substance into even greater unities', while the death instincts 'oppose this effort and lead what is living back to an inorganic state'.[23] Eros includes the instincts of self-preservation, the preservation of the species, ego-love and object-love, and its energy is called *libido*. Throughout life the basic instincts may either work together (for instance the sexual act is also an act of aggression) or oppose each other.

Freud saw instincts as historically acquired and conservative, writing: 'It seems, then, that an instinct is an urge inherent in life to restore an earlier state of things'.[24] Given the assumption that living things appeared later than inanimate ones and arose out of them, the death instinct may be viewed as a compulsion to repeat this earlier inorganic state. Consequently, the aim of all life is death. Eros, however, does not follow the same formula. Freud considered that sexual instincts were the single exception among the instincts in seeking to restore an earlier state of things.[25, 26]

Freud viewed the inclination to aggression as an original instinctual disposition in humans. He quoted Plautus: '*Homo homini lupus*',[27] a translation of which is 'Man is a wolf to man'. The aggressive instinct is the derivative and main representative of the death instinct. The evolution of civilization represents the struggle between the life and death instincts in the human species. The fateful question that Freud posed at the end of *Civilization and its Discontents* was whether Eros would assert itself, 'But who can foresee with what success and what results?'.[27]

The Unconscious and Consciousness

Heavily influenced by his study of dreams, Freud made a distinction between the unconscious and consciousness. He observed: 'The interpretation of dreams is the royal road to a knowledge of the unconscious activities of the mind'.[28] From the very beginning, he stated that there were two kinds of unconscious. First, there is the *unconscious* (Ucs), or unconscious proper, which is material that is inadmissible to consciousness through repression. In other words, with the unconscious the censorship on material coming into awareness is very strong indeed. The object of psychoanalysis is to help make some of this material accessible to awareness, though during the process strong resistances may be aroused, not least because of the forbidden sexual connotations of much of what is being repressed.

The second kind of unconscious is the *preconscious* (Pcs), which consists of everything that can easily exchange the unconscious state for the conscious one. Thus the preconscious is latent and capable of becoming conscious, while the unconscious is repressed and is unlikely to become conscious without great difficulty. Material may remain in the preconscious, though usually it finds its way into consciousness without any need for psychoanalytic intervention. The preconscious may be viewed as a screen between the unconscious and consciousness, with, as in the case of dreams, modifications being made in unconscious material through censorship.

Consciousness (Cs or Pcpt Cs) has the function of a sense organ for the perception of psychical qualities. Unlike the two kinds of unconscious, consciousness has no memory and a state of consciousness is usually very transitory. Material becomes conscious, or flows into the consciousness sense-organ, from two directions: the external world and inner excitations. Furthermore, the function of speech enables internal events such as sequences of ideas and intellectual processes to become conscious.[29, 30, 31]

The Structure of the Mental Apparatus

Freud structured the mental apparatus into three systems or agencies: the id, the ego and the super-ego. Psychological well-being depends on whether these three systems are interrelating effectively. Figure 5.1 is Freud's own sketch of the structural relations of the mental apparatus, though he acknowledges that the space occupied by the unconscious id ought to have been much greater.[32]

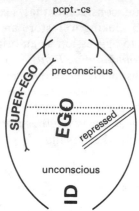

Figure 5.1   Structural relations of the mental apparatus. Acknowledgement is made to Sigmund Freud Copyright Ltd, The Institute of Psycho-Analysis and the Hogarth Press Ltd for permission to reprint this diagram from *New Introductory Lectures on Psycho-Analysis* in Volume XXII of the Standard Edition of *The Complete Psychological Works of Sigmund Freud*, translated and edited by James Strachey, and to W.W. Norton & Company, Inc. Copyright (c) 1965, 1964 by James Strachey.

The *id* or 'it' is the oldest of these systems and contains everything that is inherited and fixed in the constitution. The instincts, which originate in the somatic organization, find their mental expression in the id. The id, filled with energy from the instincts, strives to bring about the satisfaction of instinctual needs on the basis of the pleasure principle. Thus the activity of the id is directed towards securing the free discharge of quantities of excitation. The psychical processes of the id are known as primary processes because they are present in the mental apparatus from the first.[33] Furthermore, no alteration in the id's mental processes is produced by the passage of time. Freud viewed the id as 'a chaos, a cauldron full of seething emotions', which 'knows no judgements of values: no good and evil, no morality'.[34] The id consists of wishful impulses. It is not governed by logic, and this applies especially to the law of contradiction, since it contains contrary impulses side by side. In short, the id is the individual's primary subjective reality at the unconscious level.

The *ego* or 'I' is first and foremost a bodily ego ultimately derived from bodily sensations, in particular those coming from its surface. The ego is a portion of the id which has undergone a special development or modification through the influence of the external world. The ego acts as an intermediary between the id and the external world and ideally represents reason and common sense, whereas the id contains instinctual passions and would destroy itself without the intervention of the ego. The ego strives to bring the reality principle to bear upon the id in substitution for the pleasure principle. The processes of the ego, which include perception, problem-solving and repression, are later developments or secondary processes, in contrast to the original or primary processes of the id. Nevertheless, the ego seeks pleasure and the avoidance of unpleasure, differing from the id only in the means of attaining common ends. A foreseen increase in unpleasure is met by a signal of anxiety. As Figure 5.1 shows, the perceptual-conscious system is the outer layer of the ego, which also includes much preconscious and unconscious material.

The ego is in control of voluntary movement, but interposes thought between experiencing a need and acting on it. The ego deals with external events through perception, memory, avoiding excessive stimuli, adapting to moderate stimuli, and engaging in activities designed to modify the external world to its advantage. Regarding internal events in relation to the id, the ego attempts to control instinctual demands by deciding the timing and manner of their gratification or by suppressing their excitations. Freud makes the analogy of the id being the horse, while the ego is the rider. He observes that often, however, the ego is weak in relation to the id and so is in the habit of transforming the id's will into action as if it were its own.[35,36,37]

The third agency is the *super-ego*, which is a residue formed within the ego in which parental influence is prolonged. Parental influence may be defined broadly as including cultural, racial and family influences. As the person grows up, the nature of the 'parental' influence may vary, partly because parents may behave differently. Also, teachers, admired figures in public life and many others may contribute to the development of an individual's super-ego, which normally departs more and more from original parental influences.

The function of the super-ego, which engages in self-observation, is to contain the demands of the id through moral influence on the ego. Originally the child engages in instinctual renunciation through fear of loss of love or through fear of aggression from an *external* or parental authority. Subsequently a secondary situation develops in which the external restraint is internalized and thus instinctual renunciation comes about through fear of an *internal* authority, or super-ego.

A characteristic of the super-ego is the ego-ideal, based on the admiration which the child felt for the perfection it saw in its parents and which it strives to emulate. In fact the terms 'super-ego' and 'ego-ideal' are virtually synonymous. The ego-ideal consists of both precepts – 'You ought to be like this' – and prohibitions – 'You ought not to be like that'. These precepts and prohibitions are based in part on the identifications and repressions resulting from the resolution of the Oedipus complex. They represent the individual's conscience, transgressions of which are likely to result in a sense of inferiority and guilt and also possibly in a need for punishment. Freud observed: 'The super-ego is the representative for us of every moral restriction, the advocate of a striving towards perfection – it is, in short, as much as we have been able to grasp psychologically of what is described as the higher side of human life'.[38]

In addition to the demands of the instincts and of the external world, the ego has to take into account the demands of the super-ego. Individuals vary in the severity of their super-egos, which may be benign or punitively harsh and restricting. Conflicts can arise between ego and super-ego, with large portions of both agencies remaining unconscious.[39, 40, 41, 42]

Anxiety

Freud defined anxiety as a specific state of unpleasure accompanied by motor discharge along definite pathways.[43] He saw anxiety as the universal reaction to the situation of danger and the ego as the sole seat of anxiety. In later life, a source of anxiety which is involuntary occurs whenever a dangerous situation arises. Another source is anxiety generated by the ego when danger is merely threatened and the ego feels weak in relation to it. Hence there are three kinds of anxiety, one for each of the ego's three 'taskmasters': (a) *realistic* anxiety regarding the dangers of the external world; (b) *moral* anxiety regarding conflict with the super-ego; and (c) *neurotic* anxiety regarding conflict with the strength of the id's instinctual impulses. Thus anxiety is either a reaction to actual danger or a signal involving the perception of impending danger.[44,45]

Psychical Energy, Cathexis and Anti-cathexis

Psychoanalysis is often referred to as having a dynamic view of psychology. What this means is that the concept of psychical or mental energy and its distribution among the id, ego and super-ego is central to psychoanalysis. The id is the source of this somatically based psychical energy, being filled with energy reaching it from the instincts. Sexual excitation is an example of instinctual psychical energy. As the ego and the super-ego are formed they also become charged with energy.

The words 'cathexis' and to 'cathect' describe the idea of psychical energy being drawn to mental agencies and processes, somewhat analogous to an electric charge.[46] Cathexes are the charges of instinctual energy seeking discharge, whereas anti-cathexes are charges of energy which block and inhibit such discharge. The id has only primary-process instinctual cathexes seeking discharge. However, the ego and the super-ego have both urging cathexes and restraining anti-cathexes.[47,48] Throughout life the ego is the avenue by which libidinal cathexes are transferred to objects and into which they may also be withdrawn again. Two characteristics of libidinal cathexes are mobility, the ease with which they pass from one object to another, and, in contrast, fixation, or being bound to particular objects.

Bisexuality

Freud observed that it was a long-known anatomical fact that in every normally formed male or female there are traces of the apparatus of the other sex, though in atrophied form. Anatomically there may have been an original predisposition to bisexuality, which in the course of the development of the human species has largely been altered to monosexuality.[49]

Psychologically Freud considered that the sexual impulse is probably entirely independent of its object and therefore not originated by chemical attraction. Another way of stating this is that there is only one libido and it cannot be assigned a sex. Therefore the direction of both heterosexual and homosexual object selection requires further explanation. By studying covert sexual excitations, psychoanalytic research discovered that all men were capable of homosexual object selection and actually accomplish this in the unconscious. Furthermore, homosexual libidinous feelings 'play no small role as factors in normal psychic life' and an even greater role as 'causative factors of disease'. Freud considered that the same free attachment to male and female objects as observed in childhood and primitive and prehistoric states forms the basis on which both normal and homosexual or inverted sexual development takes place. A degree of homosexuality is congenital in everyone, with the final determination of sexual behaviour being the result of the intensity of constitutional predisposition as well as of life experiences and restrictions in one or the other direction. Both the woman and the man develop out of a child with a bisexual disposition.[50]

DEVELOPMENT OF PERSONALITY

Infantile Sexuality and Amnesia

Freud distinguished between the sexual impulse, the sexual object, and the sexual aim. The sexual impulse is the sexual aspect of libido, the sexual object is the person in whom sexual attraction is lodged, and the sexual aim refers to the action, such as touch or intercourse, towards which the sexual impulse strives. Freud further made a sharp distinction between 'sexual' and 'genital', considering that sexual life consists of gaining pleasure from erotogenic zones of the body and that this is not necessarily in the service of reproduction. Additionally, sexual life includes affectionate and friendly impulses often called 'love'. In a sense, all adult sexual behaviour whose goal is not reproduction, a heterosexual object and intercourse may be considered perverse. Adult sexual behaviour does not suddenly emerge at puberty but has developed out of prior sexual dispositions and experiences.

Sexual life starts soon after birth. Infantile sexuality, in the absence of genital maturation and of ego and super-ego development, lacks a central co-ordinating focus. Instead the component sexual instincts seek their own pleasure. Infantile sexuality is fundamentally auto-erotic in that the infant finds its pleasure in the object of its own body. Freud considered that the infantile sexual disposition contained great tendencies to perversion and that normal sexual behaviour develops partly in response to organic changes and partly as a result of psychic inhibitions and repressions.

The years of childhood are when the individual is most impressionable. Nevertheless, people are largely unaware of the beginnings of their sexual life and tend to view their childhood as if it were a prehistoric time. However, infantile and childhood sexual experiences leave deep traces in the individual's psychical life, acting as significant determinants for future development. Freud used the term 'infantile amnesia' to refer to the phenomenon by which a veil is drawn over early sexual experiences.[51, 52]

Sexual Development

The onset of sexual life is diphasic. The first or pre-genital phase of sexual development is a steady process which reaches a climax towards the end of a child's fifth year. After this there is a lull or period of latency. The second or genital phase starts with the re-emergence of the sexual impulse at menarche or puberty. The pre-genital and genital phases of sexual organization are distinguished by whether or not the genital zones have assumed a dominating role.

The pre-genital phase itself consists of three separate phases of sexual organization through which individuals normally pass smoothly, though fixations or arrested development may occur at each phase. Both sexes seem to pass through the early stages of sexual development in the same manner. The first organ to be an erotogenic zone is the mouth, and hence sexual development starts with the *oral* phase. The infant's act of sucking goes beyond that needed for the taking of nourishment to what may be viewed as the seeking of sexual organ-pleasure independent of nourishment. The oral phase can be further subdivided. The first sub-stage is where there is a focus only on oral incorporation, whereas the second sub-stage is 'oral-sadistic', with the emergence of biting activity. These two sub-stages of the oral phase are the first manifestation of the phenomenon of ambivalence.

The second organ to become an erotogenic zone is the anus, and normal sexual development proceeds from the oral to the *sadistic-anal* phase. The active aspect of this phase is the impulse for mastery (sadism), with the strengthening of the musculature of the body and control of sphincter functions. The erotogenic mucous membrane of the anus also manifests itself as an organ with a passive sexual aim. Character traits associated with this phase are orderliness, parsimoniousness and obstinacy, which together define the so-called 'anal character'.

The third organ to become an erotogenic zone is the genital apparatus. The period of sexual development in which the male sexual organ (the phallus) and the female clitoris become important is known as the *phallic* phase, which starts in about the child's third year. Here pleasure is obtained from masturbation. During the phallic phase the sexuality of early childhood reaches its greatest intensity and it is during this phase that male and female sexual development become differentiated.

The *Oedipus* phase is part of the phallic phase for both sexes. Put simply, at an early age the little boy develops an object-cathexis for his mother and identifies with his father. During the phallic phase the body's libidinal object-cathexis of his mother intensifies and he wishes to get rid of his father and to take his father's place with his mother. The threat of castration causes the boy to abandon and repress his incestuous wishes. The resolution of the boy's Oedipus complex involves renouncing his object-cathexis of his mother, which may lead to an identification with his mother or, more normally, to an intensification of his identification with his father, consolidating the masculinity in his character. The Oedipus situation is often more complex because of the child's bisexual disposition. Thus, instead of affection for his mother and ambivalence towards his father, he may have a mixture of affection for and ambivalence towards each parent. Freud observes that 'in both sexes the relative strength of the masculine and feminine sexual dispositions is what determines whether the outcome of the Oedipus situation shall be an identification with the father or with the mother'.[53] Perhaps it is more accurate to consider the outcome as a predominant rather than an exclusive identification with one or the other parent. He further asserts that, especially with neurotics, a bisexual Oedipus complex should be assumed.

As with the boy, the girl's mother is the first object of her love. During the phallic phase the clitoris is her predominant erotogenic zone. Freud considered that during the girl's development to femininity she should change both her predominant erotogenic zone (to the vagina) and also the sex of her love object. The powerful attachment of the girl to her mother is ended when the girl, discovering the inferiority of her clitoris and the fact that she does not have a penis, holds her mother responsible. Penis envy or the wish for a penis is a very important feminine trait. The wish for a penis-baby from the father replaces the wish for a penis, and it is at this stage that the girl has entered her Oedipus situation, desiring the father and wishing to be rid of the mother. Again the situation may be complicated by her bisexual disposition. Girls remain in their Oedipus situation for an indeterminate length of time and resolve it late and often incompletely. Whereas the boy is encouraged to surmount the Oedipus complex through fear of castration, the girl has no such motivation. As time goes by the female Oedipus complex weakens, partly as a result of inevitable disappointments from her father.

The period from around the beginning of the child's sixth year, probably later for girls, to menarche and puberty constitutes the sexual latency period. Latency may be total or partial and, during this period, sexual inhibitions develop. One of the mechanisms by which sexual energy is diverted is called sublimation or the displacement of libido to new aims and cultural pursuits. Furthermore, as the individual develops, libidinous impulses may call forth contrary anti-cathexes or reactions (reaction formations) such as disgust, shame and morality.

The *genital* phase, which starts at menarche or puberty, involves the subordination of all sources of sexual feeling to the primacy of the genital zones. Earlier libidinal cathexes may be retained, included in sexual activity or preliminary or auxiliary acts, or in some way repressed or diverted. Puberty brings a greater increase of libido in boys, but in girls there is an increase in repression, especially regarding clitoral sexuality. Also at menarche and puberty, along with the overcoming of incestuous object-choices, comes the breaking away from parental authority. Given a reasonably adequate prior sexual development, the individual is now ready to engage in a heterosexual genital relationship.[54, 55, 56, 57]

Identification

Identification is an important concept for understanding ego and super-ego development. Identification may be viewed in three ways: first, as the original form of emotional tie with an object; second, as a regressive substitute for a libidinal object-tie by means of introjection of the object with the ego, so that the ego assumes the characteristics of the object (e.g. a female patient imitating her father's cough); and third, as a feeling generated by the perception of a common quality with another person who is not libidinally cathected.[58] The development of the super-ego may be seen in terms of identification with the parental agency, by which the young person, wishing to be like them, moulds her ego after the fashion of those taken as her models. Identification is part of the normal process of development. However, the ego may be restricted, as well as enhanced, depending on the nature of the identification.

Defensive Mechanisms

During the child's early years its ego is relatively feeble, yet it has to deal with strong instinctual sexual impulses. At this stage anxiety may be generated by loss of an object or loss of love, which may persist into later life. Later sources of anxiety include fear of castration during the phallic phase, and fear of the super-ego during and after the latency period.

In order to cope with the sources of anxiety the ego utilizes defensive mechanisms. Freud doubted that the ego could do without them during normal development. In many instances, however, the ego pays a high price for the use of the mechanisms, since they restrict its functioning, also using in their anti-cathexes psychical energy which might better be expended elsewhere. Defensive mechanisms are infantilisms which operate unconsciously and may impede realistic behaviour long after they have outlived their usefulness. An individual does not make use of all the possible mechanisms of defence, but selects some, which become fixated in her ego.[59] The establishment of defensive mechanisms is largely a feature of the child's struggle against its sexuality during the first five years of life.

When the ego observes that an emerging instinctual demand may place it in danger, the defensive ways in which it strives to contain the instinctual cathexis include the following.

Repression

The process of repression is of two kinds. First, material which is in the preconscious and hence admissible to consciousness is pushed back into the unconscious. Second, unconscious material may be forbidden by censorship to enter the preconscious and hence has to remain unconscious. For example, either kind of repression might apply to an individual's latent sexually perverted impulses. Repression is the central underlying defensive mechanism of the ego, the basis of all other defences.

Sublimation

Sublimation involves displacing instinctual sexual impulses into socially more acceptable channels. For instance, a painter may be expressing her sexuality in displaced form in her art. Sublimation is not necessarily pathological.

Reaction-formation

In reaction-formation the ego acknowledges impulses contrary to the ones by which it is threatened. For instance, sexual impulses may be warded off by excessive shame, disgust and loathing of sexuality.

Denial

With denial, the ego wards off some claim from the external world, which it experiences as painful, by denying the perceptions that would involve acknowledging the reality of the situation. For example, a person may deny feedback from others about her aggressiveness.

Fixation

Where people get highly anxious about moving on to the next phase of their sexual development, they may lag behind or become fixated in varying degrees to an earlier stage in terms of satisfaction of their instincts. For instance, a child may cling dependently to its mother's love rather than make new object-cathexes.

Regression

Another danger in sexual development is that, under threat, an individual will return to an earlier phase at which she may previously have been fixated. In fact, regressions may be of two kinds: a return to the incestuous objects first cathected by the libido and a return of the sexual organization as a whole to an earlier phase.

Projection

With projection, the ego deals with the threat of an unacceptable instinctual impulse by externalizing it. Thus an individual, instead of acknowledging the extent of her own libidinal and aggressive impulses, may become very aware of such characteristics in others and actually attribute them incorrectly.[60, 61, 62, 63]

Normal Development

To summarize, the Freudian view of the normal development of personality may be seen in terms of three interrelated strands. One strand involves the individual's libidinal development, which starts with a mixture of constitutional and infantile predispositions which mature into genital sexuality in successive but overlapping phases, interrupted by the latency period. The second strand involves the development of both the ego, as it gains in ability to mediate between instinctual demands and the reality of the external world, and the super-ego, based on identifications with parental influences. The third strand is the establishment of favoured defensive mechanisms on the part of the ego to ward off the anxiety caused by the strength and persistence of the id's libidinal impulses. Thus normal development may be viewed as passing through successive stages of sexual maturation without major fixations and regressions, developing an ego which copes reasonably effectively with the external world, developing a super-ego based on identifications which are constructive and not punitively moralistic, and evolving defensive mechanisms which drain off some of the energy of the id without serious restriction of ego functioning. Normal development is a dynamic process entailing a continuing distribution and redistribution of psychical energy among id, ego and super-ego, the three systems of the mental apparatus.

Development of Neurosis

Freud saw biological, phylogenetic and psychological factors as each contributing to neurosis. The biological factor is that the human animal is born relatively unfinished and thus has to undergo a protracted period of helplessness and dependence. This helplessness creates the initial situation of danger regarding fear of object loss, which in turn creates the human's need to be loved, which it never renounces.

The phylogenetic factor is inferred from the interruption in human sexual development of the latency period, whereas the sexual maturation of related animals proceeds uninterrupted. Freud believed that something momentous must have taken place in the history of the human species to bring about this situation and that its pathogenic importance is that most of the instinctual demands of infantile sexuality are treated as dangers to be guarded against by the ego. Furthermore, there is the danger that the sexual impulses of puberty will follow their infantile prototypes into repression.

The psychological factor involves three elements which together make for a pathogenic neurotic conflict. The first element is that of frustration of libidinal impulses or the damming up of the sexual instinct by the ego. Repressions are especially likely to take place in infancy and early childhood, when the ego is underdeveloped and feeble in relation to the strength of the sexual impulses. Freud observed: 'We recognize the essential precondition of neuroses in this lagging of ego development behind libidinal development'.[64] The process of repression takes place under the influence of anxiety, in that the ego anticipates that satisfaction of the emerging sexual cathexis will lead to danger. In fact the ego allows an initial reproduction of the feared unpleasure. This feeling of anxiety brings the unpleasure-pleasure mechanism into operation and so causes the ego to repress the dangerous instinctual impulse. By the act of repression, however, the ego has renounced a portion of its organization and the repressed instinctual impulse remains inaccessible to its influence.

The second psychological element is that the frustrated sexual impulses may not disappear, instead getting transformed into neurotic symptoms. Freud saw symptoms such as hysterical or conversion symptoms as the substitute satisfactions for the frustrated sexual instincts. Repression, however, does not always result in symptom formation. For instance, in a successful dissolution of the Oedipus complex the repressed sexual impulses may be destroyed, with their libido being put permanently to other uses.

The third psychological element is that, while the repressions may be effective during early childhood and the latency period, they may turn out to be inadequate with the re-awakening and intensification of the sexual instincts at menarche and puberty. When this occurs the individual may experience an intense neurotic conflict with all its suffering. Without assistance in undoing its repressions, the ego will have little or no influence over the transformed instincts of the repressed id. Furthermore, the conflict is often heightened through an alliance of the id and super-ego against the ego.

Freud gives as an example of normal and neurotic development the story of the caretaker's and the landlord's little daughters. When young, the two girls played games which took on a sexual character, including exciting each other's genitals. These experiences awakened sexual impulses which afterwards found expression in masturbation. The caretaker's daughter, unscarred by her early sexual activity, which she regarded as natural and harmless, took a lover and became a mother. While still a child the landlord's daughter, as a result of education, got the idea that she had done something wrong. She turned into an intelligent and high-minded girl who renounced her sexuality and whose subsequent neurosis precluded her from marrying. While consciously unaware of her sexual impulses, unconsciously these impulses were still attached to her experiences with the caretaker's daughter. Freud observes that, owing to the higher moral and intellectual development of her ego, she came into conflict with the demands of her sexuality.[65, 66, 67, 68, 69]

PERPETUATION OF NEUROSIS

Freud considered that neuroses are acquired only during early childhood, up to the age of six, even though the symptoms of the neurotic conflict may not appear until much later. He acknowledged the truth of the common assertion that 'the child is psychologically father of the man . . .'.[70] The neurotic person, despite her suffering, is unable to heal her disordered ego and thus her misery is perpetuated. The reason for this is that, by definition, the significant repressions made by her weak childhood ego are unconscious. Thus her ego pays the price of its defensive operations by not having conscious access to the material through which the neurotic conflict might be resolved. Her ego is weakened by its repressions and her personality functioning is impaired by psychical energy being utilized in harmful defensive anti-cathexes. Also, as long as the repressions continue, so do the conditions for the formation of neurotic symptoms through the rechannelling of frustrated libidinous impulses.

In a broader sense, perpetuation of neurosis results from the unsatisfactory way in which society tries to regulate sexual matters. Freud considered that what is described as morality, or the group super-ego, requires a bigger sacrifice of libidinal impulses than is necessary or desirable. He found it impossible to side with conventional sexual morality and considered that anyone with real self-knowledge would be protected against the dangers of morality, while possibly adopting a life-style different from the conventions of their society.[71]

PSYCHOANALYTIC THERAPY

Objectives and Limitations

A definition of a neurotic is someone who is incapable of enjoyment and efficiency. To be capable of enjoyment the neurotic needs to be able to deploy her libido onto real objects instead of transforming it into symptoms. To live efficiently the ego needs to have the energy of the libido at its disposal rather than wasting energy in warding off libidinous impulses through repression. Furthermore, the individual's super-ego needs to be such as to allow her libidinal expression and the efficient use of her ego. Thus the objectives of psychoanalysis are threefold: (a) the freeing of impulse; (b) the strengthening of reality-based ego functioning, including widening its perceptions so that it appropriates more of the id; and (c) the alteration of the contents of the super-ego so that it represents human rather than punitive moral standards.

Psychoanalysis is a process of re-educating the ego. Repressions were instituted when the client's ego was weak, but now not only has her ego grown stronger, but it possesses an ally in the analyst. Methods by which the analyst helps the weakened ego to lift its repressions, gain insight and make realistic decisions are discussed below. The pathogenic conflicts of neurotics are different from normal mental conflicts because of the ego's weakness relative to the other mental agencies.

Freud considered psychoanalytic treatment effective for a number of nervous diseases, such as hysteria, anxiety states and obsessional neurosis. Since the alliance between the analyst and the client's ego is a mutual one, the client's ego needs to have retained a minimum degree of coherence or reality orientation. This is not to be expected with psychotics, with whom, therefore, psychoanalysis is contra-indicated.[72, 73]

Free Association

The fundamental rule or contract between analyst and client is that of free association. The client must tell the analyst everything that occurs to her, even if it is disagreeable and even if it seems meaningless. As far as possible, the client is encouraged to put her self-criticism out of action and tell the analyst all her thoughts, feelings, ideas, memories and their associations. The object of free association is to help lift repressions by making unconscious material conscious.

Resistance

Free association, however, is not really free, in that the client is associating within the context of the analytic situation. Thus everything that occurs to her has some reference to that situation and she is likely to resist reproducing the repressed material. At its simplest level, resistance involves intentionally not adhering to the fundamental rule. Even if this level of resistance is overcome, resistance will find less obvious means of expression. The client's ego is fearful of potential unpleasure caused by exploring material that it has repressed in the unconscious. The ego protects itself from the repressed id by means of anti-cathexes. The more threatening the repressed material is, the more tenaciously the ego clings to its anti-cathexes and the more remote are the client's associations from the unconscious material that the analyst seeks.

Freud described all the forces that oppose the work of recovery as the client's resistances. One resistance is the repression resistance described above. A second resistance is the transference resistance, which will be mentioned shortly. A third is the client's resistance to foregoing the gain from her illness. A fourth resistance is that of the id, which may resist a change in the direction of its satisfaction and need to 'work through' to a new mode of satisfaction. The fifth kind of resistance, emanating from the super-ego, is the unconscious sense of guilt or need for punishment which resists any success through analysis. Freud considered this the most powerful factor and the one analysts most dreaded. The struggle to overcome resistances is the main work of psychoanalysis and this part of analytic treatment cannot easily be hurried. Forces helping the analyst to overcome resistances are the client's need for recovery, any intellectual interest she may have in the analytic process and, most important, her positive transference with the analyst.[74, 75, 76]

Interpretation

Interpretation is the means by which material that is repressed and unconscious is transformed into preconscious material and consciousness. Furthermore, the analyst employs interpretation not only to understand the impulses of the id, but also to help the client to gain insight into the defensive mechanisms and resistances that her ego uses both to cope with the repressed material and to thwart the analytic endeavour. Part of the work of interpretation consists of filling in memory gaps. The analyst interprets the impulses that have become subject to repression and the objects to which they have become attached with the aim of helping the client to replace these repressions by acts of judgement appropriate to her present-day rather than to her childhood situation. The analyst works with the client's ego, encouraging it to overcome resistances and to take control of her hitherto repressed libidinal energy. Unconscious impulses are exposed to criticism by being traced back to their origin.

The material for interpretation is obtained from a number of sources. These include the client's free associations, her parapraxes or slips of the tongue, her dreams, and her transference relationship with the analyst. Freud considered appropriate timing of the interpretations very important, since if they were attempted at the wrong time they would meet with resistance. Therefore the client needs to be very close to the moment of insight before an interpretation is made.[77, 78] The later stages of psychoanalysis involve a working through by repeated interpretation, and this is often the most difficult and frequently an incomplete part of therapy.

Interpretation of Dreams

An important – sometimes the most important – part of the psychoanalytic technique is the interpretation of dreams. During sleep the ego reduces its repression and thus unconscious material becomes conscious in the shape of dreams. Freud saw dreams as wish-fulfilments, being the disguised fulfilment of repressed wishes. However, even in sleep the ego still retains some censorship over repressed material and the latent dream thoughts are distorted so as to make the manifest dream content less threatening. Dreams, in fact, are compromises between repressed id impulses and the defensive operation of the ego. The interpretation of a dream involves understanding the latent dream thoughts which are disguised by the process of dream work. Elements of dream work involve condensing the latent dream thoughts into a much smaller dream content, displacing the psychical intensity between elements, and using symbolism.[79, 80]

Transference

From early in his career Freud attached great importance to his relationship with the client. He discovered that the client perceives the analyst as the reincarnation of an important figure from her childhood and transfers onto him moderate to intense feelings and emotions appropriate to this earlier model. Freud speaks of transference-love and observes that this love is ambivalent, being a mixture of affection with a reverse side of hostility, exclusiveness and jealousy. In the transference the client reproduces, rather than just remembers, mental attitudes and defensive reactions connected with her neurosis.

The transference may start by being positive, which helps the analyst, since the client works to please him. However, almost invariably it becomes negative and hostile, thus turning into a resistance. The transference represents a development of the original neurosis into a transference neurosis in relation to the analyst. Handling this transference is a critical skill of the analyst, who must point out the prototype of these feelings in her childhood. The revival of the pathogenic conflict gives the analyst access to much repressed material, insight into which helps to strengthen the client's ego.[81,82]

GOALS FOR COUNSELLING AND FOR LIVING

On the one hand the goals of analysis and of living may be viewed in terms of absence of negative qualities. Such negative qualities include neurotic symptoms and suffering, debilitating repressions, a weak ego and a punitive super-ego. On the other hand, the goals may be viewed as the presence of positive qualities, albeit the inverse of the negative qualities. Such positive qualities are sometimes expressed as efficiency and enjoyment or the ability to work and to love. Sometimes terms like 'a strong ego' or 'ego-strength' are used. Ego-strength means that the ego is effective in channelling and finding satisfaction for the libidinous impulses of the id at the same time as adhering to realistic moral standards. Thus a workable integration is achieved between the individual's ego, id and super-ego which, while not without its conflicts, defensive mechanisms and repressions, nevertheless allows her to meet her significant instinctual needs on the basis of reality.

SELF-REFERENT EXERCISES

It may help you to understand this chapter better if, either with paper and pencil or in your head, you think about and answer the following questions.

1.   List as many of your instincts as you are able. Do you consider that Freud's idea about the destructive instincts applies to you?

2.   Can you think of material or events in your life which might be seen as evidence for unconcious mental processes? If so, provide examples (e.g. dreams).

3.   Think back over your own sexual development. Are you aware of having been sexual as an infant, having passed through pre-genital, latency, and genital phases of sexual development, and having experienced an Oedipus situation? If you are unaware of such experiences, do you think it might be because you are repressing them?

4.   What are some of the significant influences which contributed to the formation of your super-ego? With what moral guidelines, if any, do you consider that your super-ego restricts you from the realistic pursuit of pleasure?

5.   Assess the adequacy with which your ego deals with each of its three taskmasters: (a) your instinctual impulses; (b) the external world; and (c) your super-ego. Do you suffer from neurotic and/or reality and/or moral anxiety?

6.   Are you aware that your ego uses defensive mechanisms to ward off anxiety? If so, what are they? Do you consider that your use of defensive mechanisms is normal or neurotic?

NOTES

1. Jones, E. (1963) *The Life and Work of Sigmund Freud* pp. 6–7. Edited and abridged in one volume by Lionel Trilling and Steven Marcus. New York: Anchor Books. Also available in a Penguin edition.
2. Freud, S. (1935) *An Autobiographical Study* p. 12. London: Hogarth Press.
3. *Ibid.* p. 14.
4. *Ibid.* p. 15.
5. *Ibid.* p. 18.
6. Jones, E. (1963) *The Life and Work of Sigmund Freud* pp. 54–55. New York: Anchor Books.
7. *Ibid.* p. 110.
8. Freud, S. (1935) *An Autobiographical Study* p. 26. London: Hogarth Press.
9. *Ibid.* p. 29.
10. Freud, S. & Breuer, J. (1956) *Studies on Hysteria*. London: Hogarth Press. Original edition 1895.
11. Jones, E. (1963) *The Life and Work of Sigmund Freud* p. 194. New York: Anchor Books.
12. *Ibid.* pp. 182–203.
13. Freud, S. (1976) *The Interpretation of Dreams*. Harmondsworth, Middlesex: Penguin Books. Original edition 1900. The 1976 volume is part of The Pelican Freud Library, which contains many of his works.
14. Jones, E. (1963) *The Life and Work of Sigmund Freud* p. 205. New York: Anchor Books.
15. Fromm, E. (1959) *Sigmund Freud's Mission*. London: George Allen and Unwin.
16. Freud, S. (1962) *Three Contributions to the Theory of Sex*. New York: E. P. Dutton. Original edition 1905.
17. Freud, S. (1935) *An Autobiographical Study* p. 101. London: Hogarth Press.
18. *Ibid.* pp. 135–136.
19. *Ibid.* pp. 129–130.
20. Jones, E. (1953) *The Life and Work of Sigmund Freud*, Trilling's introduction, p. XI. New York: Anchor Books.
21. Freud, S. (1976) *The Interpretation of Dreams* pp. 729–730, 759–764. Harmondsworth, Middlesex: Penguin Books.
22. Freud, S. (1961) *Beyond the Pleasure Principle* p. 3. London: Hogarth Press, Original Edition 1920.
23. Freud, S. (1973) *New Introductory Lectures on Psychoanalysis* p. 140. Harmondsworth, Middlesex: Penguin Books. Original edition 1933 (1932).
24. Freud, S. (1961) *Beyond the Pleasure Principle* p. 30. London: Hogarth Press.
25. *Ibid* pp. 28–37.
26. Freud, S. (1949) *An Outline of Psychoanalysis* pp. 19–32. New York: W. W. Norton. Originally published posthumously in 1940. Written just before Freud's death, this is an excellent introduction to psychoanalysis.
27. Freud, S. (1962) *Civilization and its Discontents* p. 92. New York: W. W. Norton. Original edition 1930.
28. Freud, S. (1976) *The Interpretation of Dreams* p. 769. Harmondsworth, Middlesex: Penguin Books.
29. *Ibid.* pp. 680–700.

30. Freud, S. (1949) *An Outline of Psychoanalysis* pp. 33–45. New York: W. W. Norton.
31. Freud, S. (1962) *The Ego and the Id* pp. 3–8. London: Hogarth Press. Original edition 1923.
32. Freud, S. (1973) *New Introductory Lectures on Psychoanalysis* p. 111. Harmondsworth, Middlesex: Penguin Books.
33. Freud, S. (1976) *The Interpretation of Dreams* pp. 719–720, 745–769. Harmondsworth, Middlesex: Penguin Books.
34. Freud, S. (1973) *New Introductory Lectures on Psychoanalysis* pp. 106–107. Harmondsworth, Middlesex: Penguin Books.
35. Freud, S. (1962) *Ego and the Id* pp. 9–17. London: Hogarth Press.
36. Freud, S. (1973) *New Introductory Lectures on Psychoanalysis* pp. 107–111. Harmondsworth, Middlesex: Penguin Books. Lecture 31, entitled 'Dissection of the psychical personality', deals with all three mental agencies (pp. 88–112).
37. Freud, S. (1949) *An Outline of Psychoanalysis* pp. 13–18. New York: W. W. Norton.
38. Freud, S. (1973) *New Introductory Lectures on Psychoanalysis* p. 98. Harmondsworth, Middlesex: Penguin Books.
39. Freud, S. (1962) *Civilization and its Discontents* pp. 70–80. New York: W. W. Norton.
40. Freud, S. (1949) *An Outline of Psychoanalysis* pp 17–18. New York: W. W. Norton.
41. Freud, S. (1962) *The Ego and the Id* pp. 18–29. London: Hogarth Press.
42. Freud, S. (1973) *New Introductory Lectures on Psychoanalysis* pp. 88–112. Harmondsworth, Middlesex: Penguin Books.
43. Freud, S. (1936) *The Problem of Anxiety* p. 70. New York: W. W. Norton. Originally published in 1926 under the title *Inhibitions, Symptoms and Anxiety*.
44. *Ibid.* pp. 69–84, 108–109.
45. Freud, S. (1973) *New Introductory Lectures on Psychoanalysis* pp. 110–127. Harmondsworth, Middlesex: Penguin Books. Lecture 32 is entitled 'Anxiety and instinctual life', pp. 113–144.
46. Freud, S. (1949) *An Outline of Psychoanalysis* pp. 19–24. New York: W. W. Norton. (Especially James Strachey's footnote on p. 23.)
47. Freud, S. (1973) *New Introductory Lectures on Psychoanalysis* pp. 106–109, 121–124. Harmondsworth, Middlesex: Penguin Books.
48. Hall, C. S. (1954) *A Primer of Freudian Psychology* pp. 36–54. New York: Mentor Books. This book is highly recommended as a secondary source.
49. Freud, S. (1962) *Three Contributions to the Theory of Sex* p. 7. New York: E. P. Dutton.
50. *Ibid.* pp. 1–34, in particular the long note on pp. 10–11. This discussion is focused on male homosexuality. Mention of female homosexuality is made in Freud's lecture on 'Femininity', No. 33 in Freud, S. (1973) *New Introductory Lectures on Psychoanalysis* pp. 145–169. Harmondsworth, Middlesex: Penguin Books.
51. *Ibid.* pp. 35–65.
52. Freud, S. (1973) *Introductory Lectures on Psychoanalysis* pp. 362–382. Harmondsworth, Middlesex: Penguin Books. Lecture 21 is entitled 'The development of the libido and sexual organizations'.
53. Freud, S. (1962) *The Ego and the Id* p. 23. London: Hogarth Press.
54. Freud, S. (1962) *Three Contributions to the Theory of Sex* pp. 35–98. New York: E. P. Dutton.
55. Freud, S. (1962) *Ego and the Id* pp. 18–29. London: Hogarth Press.
56. Freud, S. (1962) *An Outline of Psychoanalysis* pp. 25–32. New York: W. W. Norton.
57. Freud, S. (1973) *New Introductory Lecture on Psychoanalysis* pp. 145–169. Harmondsworth, Middlesex: Penguin Books.
58. Freud, S. (1959) *Group Psychology and the Analysis of the Ego* pp. 37–42. London: Hogarth Press. The book was originally published in 1921.
59. Freud, S. (1950) Analysis terminable and interminable. In S. Freud, *Collected Papers*, Vol. V pp. 316–357. London: Hogarth Press. Originally published in 1937.
60. Freud, S. (1973) *Introductory Lectures on Psychoanalysis* pp. 327–343. Harmondsworth, Middlesex: Penguin Books. Lecture 19, on 'Resistance and repression'.

61. Freud, S. (1962) *Three Contributions to the Theory of Sex* pp. 38–41. New York: E. P. Dutton.
62. Freud, S. (1949) *An Outline of Psychoanalysis* pp. 118–119. New York: W. W. Norton.
63. Hall, C. S. (1954) *A Primer of Freudian Psychology* pp. 85–97. New York: Mentor Books.
64. Freud, S. (1949) *An Outline of Psychoanalysis* p. 113. New York: W. W. Norton.
65. Freud, S. (1973) *Introductory Lectures on Psychoanalysis* pp. 383–403. Harmondsworth, Middlesex: Penguin Books. Lecture 22 entitled 'Some thoughts on development and regression-aetiology'. This includes the example of the landlord's and caretaker's daughters.
66. Freud, S. (1973) *New Introductory Lectures on Psychoanalysis* pp. 113–144. Harmondsworth, Middlesex: Penguin Books.
67. Freud, S. (1936) *The Problem of Anxiety* pp. 93–101. New York: W. W. Norton.
68. Freud, S. (1962) *Three Contributions to the Theory of Sex* pp. 26–30. New York: E. P. Dutton.
69. Freud, S. (1949) *An Outline of Psychoanalysis* pp. 103–119. New York: W. W. Norton.
70. *Ibid*. pp. 83–87.
71. Freud, S. (1973) *Introductory Lectures on Psychoanalysis* pp. 485–486. Harmondsworth, Middlesex: Penguin Books.
72. *Ibid*. pp. 489–490.
73. Freud, S. (1949) *An Outline of Psychoanalysis* pp. 63–64. New York: W. W. Norton.
74. *Ibid*. pp. 72–79.
75. Freud, S. (1964) *The Question of Lay Analysis*. pp. 61–62. New York: Anchor Books. Originally published in 1926.
76. Freud, S. (1936) *The Problem of Anxiety* pp. 102–107. New York: W. W. Norton.
77. Freud, S. (1973) *Introductory Lectures on Psychoanalysis* pp. 501–517. Harmondsworth, Middlesex: Penguin Books. Lecture 28 on 'Analytic therapy'.
78. Freud, S. (1949) *An Outline of Psychoanalysis* pp. 70–79. New York: W. W. Norton.
79. Freud, S. (1976) *The Interpretation of Dreams*. Harmondsworth, Middlesex: Penguin Books.
80. Freud, S. (1973) *New Introductory Lectures on Psychoanalysis* pp. 35–59. Harmondsworth, Middlesex: Penguin Books. Lecture 29 entitled 'Revision of the theory of dreams'.
81. Freud, S. (1973) *Introductory Lectures on Psychoanalysis* pp. 482–500. Harmondsworth, Middlesex: Penguin Books. Lecture 27 on 'Transference'.
82. Freud, S. (1949) *An Outline of Psychoanalysis* pp. 65–70. New York: W. W. Norton.

6 – Behavioural Theory: Pavlov, Watson and Skinner

SUMMARY: *Behavioural theory may be viewed both as an overall theory and as an experimentally based attempt to describe the laws or principles by which human behaviour is learned and maintained. Pavlov conducted extensive researches into the functioning of the cerebral hemispheres of dogs. He discovered the conditioned reflex, otherwise known as classical or respondent conditioning. For example, by pairing a conditioned stimulus (metronome) with an unconditioned stimulus (food), a dog comes to acquire a salivary response in the presence of the conditioned stimulus alone.*

Watson viewed behaviourist psychology, termed 'behaviourism', as an objective experimental branch of natural science focused on the behaviour of human beings. He distinguished between unlearned and learned responses. Most stimuli to which humans respond are learned. Three main habit systems are formed by conditioning: (a) visceral or emotional; (b) manual; and (c) laryngeal or verbal. Some experiments on an 11-month-old boy called Albert illustrate the conditioning of an emotional fear response to a white rat, its transfer to other furry animals, and its persistence. A further experiment on another child unconditioned his fear of furry animals. The cure for personality problems is unconditioning and conditioning.

Skinner views behaviour as being shaped and maintained by its consequences. While acknowledging the importance of classical conditioning, he goes beyond this to focus on the action of the environment after *the response has been made. Operant conditioning emphasizes that behaviour operates on the environment to generate consequences. Reinforcers are events which strengthen the probability of a response. Contingencies of reinforcement, which describe the interaction between the organism and its environment, are: (a) the occasion on which a response occurs; (b) the response itself; and (c) the reinforcing consequences. Other concepts reviewed here are: positive and negative reinforcement, primary and conditioned reinforcers, schedules of reinforcement, maintenance and extinction of behaviour, shaping and successive approximation, stimulus discrimination and control, and stimulus generalization. Skinner's ideas on the self, self-control, psychotherapy and environmental design are also described.*

INTRODUCTION

So far we have explored the humanistic and psychoanalytic models which underlie counselling psychology. The next two chapters focus on the third main model, the behavioural model. Behaviour therapy, or behavioural counselling, views itself as being firmly rooted in experimentally derived principles of learning. However, behavioural theory is an overall theory as well as an experimentally based attempt to describe the specific laws or principles of human behaviour. As an overall theory the distinctive emphasis is on the overwhelming role of environmental contingencies in influencing the acquisition and perpetuation of behaviour. In its most radical form the behavioural model sees human actions as derived solely from two sources: biological deprivations, such as hunger and sexual tension, and the individual's learning history. There is no place for concepts such as mind and free will. However, a distinction increasingly emerging in behavioural counselling and therapy is that between approaches based solely on stimulus-response connections and those which also take into account cognitive mediating variables. The latter emphasis appears less deterministic than the former. The practice of modern behavioural counselling is covered later, especially in Chapter 12 and also, to a certain extent, in Chapters 14 and 15.

As a set of experimentally derived principles of learning, the behavioural model offers a greater degree of specificity in analysing observable, as contrasted with intrapsychic, human behaviour than that offered by either the humanistic or the psychoanalytic models. Much of the research on which the behavioural model is based has been performed on animals such as dogs, cats and pigeons. Consequently, this raises the issue of the generalizability of a model derived largely from non-human animals in laboratory settings to humans in naturalistic settings. Nevertheless, the point remains that, at the molecular level or level of observations of specific behaviours, behavioural psychologists have made a distinctive contribution to the development of a theoretical framework for counselling psychology.

Defining learning involves indicating both what the term includes and what it excludes. Hilgard and Bower provisionally offer the following definition:

> Learning is the process by which an activity originates or is changed through reacting to an encountered situation, provided that the characteristics of the change in activity cannot be explained on the basis of native response tendencies, maturation, or temporary states of the organism (e.g. fatigue, drugs, etc.).[1]

Learning is a process which involves the acquisition of and, in varying degrees, the retention of behaviours. Although it may be helped or hindered by factors such as maturation and fatigue, it refers to those elements in the acquisition and retention of behaviours which are not attributable to these factors.

The structure of these two chapters differs from that of the preceding ones. Each aims to introduce the reader to some key behavioural concepts through discussing selectively the ideas and experimental work of three leading theorists. This chapter focuses on Pavlov, Watson and Skinner, while the next chapter focuses on Wolpe, Eysenck and Bandura. The theorists are presented in roughly historical order, though their working lives may overlap.

PAVLOV'S CLASSICAL CONDITIONING

Ivan Petrovich Pavlov (1849–1936) was a Russian physiologist who, in the course of his investigations into the activities of the digestive glands, started to record all the external stimuli falling on his experimental dogs at the time their reflex reactions, such as the secretion of saliva, were manifested. Pavlov did not begin his investigations into the functioning of the cerebral hemispheres of dogs until he was 50, but spent the remainder of his life on this research, eventually with a large staff.[2] Although he is best known for the discovery of the conditioned reflex, his researches were far more extensive.

Pavlov considered that both instincts and reflexes were alike in being the inevitable responses of the organism to internal and external stimuli. 'Reflex' was the preferred term since it had been used from the beginning with a scientific connotation. The whole nervous activity of animals is based on inborn reflexes, which may be either excitatory or inhibitory. Such reflexes 'are regular causal connections between certain definite external stimuli acting on the organism and its necessary reflex reaction'.[3] The inborn reflexes alone are inadequate to ensure the continued existence of the organism, and the more specialized interaction between the animal and the environment is provided through the medium of the cerebral hemispheres. The 'most general function of the hemispheres is that of reacting to signals presented by innumerable stimuli of interchangeable signification'.[4]

In his book *Conditioned Reflexes*, subtitled 'An investigation of the physiological activity of the cerebral cortex', Pavlov describes the precautions taken to build a laboratory so as to eliminate, as far as possible, any stimuli outside his control. In order to register the intensity of the salivary reflex, all the dogs used in his experiments were subjected to a minor operation which consisted of transferring the opening of the salivary duct from the mucous membrane of the mouth to the outside skin.[5] In the experimental laboratory a dog would be harnessed to a stand in one section of a double chamber, while the experimenter was in the other section.

In the following experiment a conditioned reflex was obtained by pairing or linking up the action of a new stimulus with an unconditioned reflex. An experimental dog was introduced to a routine in which stimulation by a metronome was linked with feeding. If the dog was then placed in the experimental condition its salivary glands remained inactive as long as no special stimulus was introduced. However, when it was allowed to hear the sounds of a beating metronome, salivary secretion began after nine seconds, and in the course of 45 seconds 11 drops were secreted. Furthermore, in this experiment the dog turned in the direction from which it had customarily received food and began to lick its lips vigorously.

In another experiment food was shown to the animal. After five seconds salivary secretion began, and in the course of 15 seconds six drops were collected. In yet another experiment food was introduced into the dog's mouth and secretion began in one to two seconds.

Food in the dog's mouth, as contrasted with the sight of food or the association of food with the beating of a metronome, produces an inborn reflex. This reflex is brought about by the physical and chemical properties of the food acting upon the mucous membrane of the mouth and tongue. However, even salivation at the sight of food is a learned reflex, as is salivation at the beating of the metronome. Both the sight of food and the beating of the metronome are signals, and the reaction to them involves signalization through the activity of the cerebral hemispheres. Thus inborn reflexes do not involve learning or signalization, while conditioned reflexes are learned and do involve signalization. The definition of reflexes as causal connections between definite external stimuli and their necessary reflex reactions still holds true when signalization is involved. The difference is that the reflex reaction to signals depends on more variables than those entailed in unconditioned reflexes.[6]

In a further experiment on the same dog, contrary to the usual routine, stimulation by the metronome was not followed by feeding. The stimulus of the metronome was repeated for periods of 30 seconds at intervals of two minutes. Pavlov gives details indicating a lengthening of the latency period prior to secretion and a diminution of drops of saliva over successive trials. He writes that the phenomenon of the weakening of a reflex to a conditioned stimulus which is repeated a number of times without reinforcement might appropriately be termed 'extinction of conditioned reflexes'. Indeed, if the above experiment had been continued, the conditioned reflex would have disappeared entirely.[7]

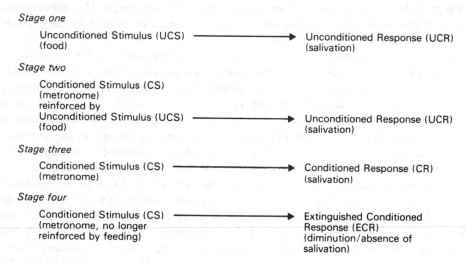

Figure 6.1 Diagrammatic representation of Pavlov's experiments on the conditioning and extinction of a dog's salivary response to the beating of a metronome.

Figure 6.1 diagrammatically depicts metronome experiments, with the term 're-sponse' substituted for 'reflex'. Food in the mouth is an unconditioned stimulus (UCS), which automatically elicits the inborn response of salivation (UCR). Through repeated reinforcement consisting of stimulation by the metronome followed by feeding, the metronome becomes a conditioned stimulus (CS), thus becoming a signal for food and eliciting the conditioned response of salivation (CR). However, if the metronome (CS) is no longer reinforced by feeding, then the conditioned response (CR) undergoes extinction and diminishes, or even disappears (ECR).

The learning of a conditioned response in the above manner has come to be termed classical or respondent conditioning. Pavlov and his colleagues explored many other areas, such as conditioned inhibition and the generalization of stimuli, but these researches will not be described here. Suffice it for now to say that Pavlov's experimental work constitutes a lasting and fundamental influence in the behavioural approach to counselling psychology.

WATSON'S CONDITIONED BEHAVIOURISM

John Broadus Watson (1878–1958), sometimes viewed as the founder of behaviourism, led an unusual life. He was born in Greenville, South Carolina, to an energetic and religious mother and a philandering father, who left home when Watson was 13 years old. Watson was educated at Furman University in Greenville and at the University of Chicago, where his doctoral thesis was on animal education. Watson married when he was 25. At 30, he became professor of psychology at Johns Hopkins University in Baltimore and at the age of 36 he was elected president of the American Psychological Association. During the 1910s Watson moved his emphasis from animal to human observation and experimentation, and from 1913 he worked hard at establishing behaviourism as a method of psychology.

In his personal life Watson had a decided tendency to respond to female stimuli, a characteristic with which his wife was prepared to live while the relationships were not really serious. However, in 1919 Watson, who was then 41, met an overwhelming stimulus in the person of a 19-year-old graduate student called Rosalie Raynor. In 1920 Watson was forced to submit his resignation from Johns Hopkins University on the grounds of adultery with a student, and no other university would offer him a place. Divorced in late 1920, Watson married Rosalie in January 1921 and lived happily with her until her tragic death from illness in 1936. After leaving university life Watson became a highly successful advertising man with J. Walter Thompson's and later with Esty's. Watson did some research on children with Mary Cover Jones in the 1920s and also some popular psychological writing. His two children by his second marriage, Billy and Jimmy, were brought up by behavioural methods, including an absence of overt shows of parental affection so that they would not become dependent. Billy, who became a psychiatrist interested in Freudian ideas, committed suicide a few years after Watson's death in 1958, while Jimmy underwent psychoanalysis.[8] Watson's books include *Animal Education*,[9] *Behavior*,[10] *Psychology from the Standpoint of a Behaviorist*,[11] *Behaviorism*[12] and *The Psychological Care of the Infant and Child*.[13] A bibliography of Watson's work can be found at the end of David Cohen's biography, *J. B. Watson, the Founder of Behaviourism*.[14]

Behaviourism

To the behaviourist 'the subject matter of human psychology is *the behaviour of the human being'.*[15] Furthermore, the behaviourist views psychology as a purely objective experimental branch of natural science, with its theoretical goal being the prediction and control of behaviour. In his 1913 paper 'Psychology as the behaviorist views it', Watson observed that he had devoted nearly 12 years to experimentation on animals and that it was natural that he should drift to a theoretical position in harmony with his experimental work.[16] What is observable is the real field of psychology and what can be observed is what the organism does or says, i.e. its behaviour.

Watson considered that there were two points of view dominant in the American psychological thinking of his time: introspective or subjective psychology, which he termed the old psychology, and the new and objective psychology of behaviourism. Concepts such as consciousness and introspection, the subject matter of the old psychology, were magic.[17] Psychology, being an objective and experimental branch of the natural sciences, needs such concepts as little as do the sciences of chemistry and physics. As the behaviour of animals can be investigated without referring to consciousness, so can the behaviour of man. In fact 'the behaviour of man and the behaviour of animals must be considered on the same plane; as being equally essential to a general understanding of behaviour'.[18]

Stimulus, Response and Conditioning

Both man and animal adjust themselves to their environments by means of hereditary and habit equipments. Through the process of evolution humans have developed sense organs, such as the eye, skin and viscera, which are most sensitive to differing kinds of stimuli. A stimulus, or thing that evokes a reaction, may come from objects in the external environment. Also, humans are affected constantly by stimuli in their internal environment arising from tissue changes in their bodies. By means of conditioning there is an ever-increasing range of stimuli to which people respond.

Stimuli evoke responses which usually involve the organism moving or altering in such a way that the stimulus no longer arouses reaction. One classification of responses is that between overt and implicit. Another general classification is between learned and unlearned responses. Unlearned responses include all the things people do from earliest infancy, such as perspiration and breathing, prior to the processes of conditioning and habit formation which produce learned responses.

The Watsonian behaviourist sees all psychological problems and their solutions as being schematized in *stimulus* (or the more complex *situation*) and *response* terms, often abbreviated to S-R terms. In the ideal behaviourist world, given the response the stimuli can be predicted and given the stimuli the response can be predicted. Figure 6.2 illustrates this view of psychological problems.

Stimuli may be unconditioned in that from birth they call forth definite responses, such as the responses of turning the eyes away from or closing the eyes to light. On the other hand, most stimuli to which humans respond are conditioned or learned, for example all the printed words to which humans respond. Similarly, responses may be unconditioned, as in the above light example, but very frequently they are conditioned, as in the case of a two-year-old child who has learned to substitute screaming for laughter at the sight of a dog.[20] Watson observed that the whole body of man is

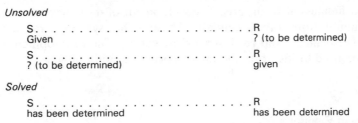

Figure 6.2 Watson's schematization of unsolved and solved psychological problems.[19]

built around the keynote 'rapid-, and when needed, complicated reactions to simple and complex stimuli'.[21]

Hereditary Equipment

Watson viewed humans as animals born with certain types of structure, subject to individual variations, which force them to respond to stimuli in certain ways. For instance, at birth the human responds with breathing, heart beat, sneezing, etc. These kinds of reactions are the human's unlearned behaviour. Some unlearned behaviours, such as suckling and unlearned grasping, are short lived. Others, such as blinking, menstruation and ejaculation, begin later in life and last much longer. Unlearned behaviours form a relatively simple list of human responses, each of which, including our respiration and circulation, becomes conditioned shortly after birth. The concept of instinct is redundant in psychology, since observation of children indicates that everything which people tend to call 'instinct' is largely the result of training or conditioning and, as such, is part of the human's learned behaviour.

Watson developed the idea of the activity stream, a 'ceaseless stream of activity beginning when the egg is fertilised and becoming more complex as age increases'.[22] Each human action system starts with an unlearned beginning and is then made more complex by conditioning. For instance, vocal responses constitute unlearned behaviour while talking represents a conditioned action system.[23]

Determinism and Habit Formation

The Watsonian behaviourist is a strict determinist positing: 'the child or adult has to do what he does do. The only way he can be made to act differently is first to untrain him and then to retrain him'.[24] Watson considered that, given total control over a dozen healthy infants from birth, he could take any one at random and train him to become any type of specialist he might select, including doctor, lawyer, artist, beggar-man and thief.[25] Inheritance of capacity, talent, temperament, mental constitution and characteristics does not really exist, since these things depend on training.

Habit formation probably starts in embryonic life and is very rapid after birth.

Though very helpless at birth, greater development of three habit systems differenti-ates the human from other animals. These habit systems are: (a) visceral or emotional; (b) manual; and (c) laryngeal or verbal. The development of emotional habits will be used to illustrate the importance of conditioning.

Conditioning of Emotions

Watson states that there are three types of unlearned beginnings of emotional reactions, or unlearned emotional responses, to stimuli. These responses are fear, rage and love. These emotional reactions might be viewed as unconditioned reflexes or responses. For instance, a loud sound is a fundamental stimulus for eliciting the fear response.

Watson and Raynor did a series of experiments on an 11-month-old boy called Albert.[26, 27] The first experiment involved the establishment of a conditioned emotional response of fear to a white rat. This was achieved by linking on some trials the loud sound of the striking of a bar with Albert's touching the white rat. When later the white rat was presented alone, Albert exhibited fear responses of crying, falling over and crawling away. A second experiment showed that there was a transfer of the conditioned fear response, though less strong, from the white rat to other furry animals (rabbit, dog) and objects (fur coat, cotton wool) when five days later they were presented to him. The above tests were carried out on a table covered with a mattress in a small, well lit room. A further experiment indicated, after 31 days, the persistence in a less intense form of both the conditioned fear response to the rat and the transferred fear responses to the fur coat and the rabbit. Watson and Raynor concluded that it was probable that many of the phobias in psychopathology are conditioned emotional reactions of either the direct or the transferred type. Emotion-al disturbances can be retraced to conditioned and transferred responses set up in infancy and childhood to all three of the fundamental human emotions.

Watson and Raynor did not remove Albert's conditioned emotional responses prior to his discharge from hospital, to be adopted by a family that lived outside Baltimore. However, Mary Cover Jones, an associate of Watson's, conducted an experiment in which Peter, a boy of about three years, was unconditioned or reconditioned of his 'home grown' fears of a rabbit, a white rat and related stimuli.[28, 29] The experimenters were given permission to give Peter his lunch of crackers and a glass of milk. Just as he began to eat his lunch, the rabbit was displayed in a cage of wire mesh just far enough away not to disturb his eating. Gradually the rabbit was brought closer and closer and finally Peter would eat with one hand and play with the rabbit with the other. There was a transfer of unconditioning of fear responses to other furry objects, with degrees of success varying from total to greatly improved.

Watson contended that human emotional life is the result of the wear and tear of environmental forces. Through experiments such as those described above, it was beginning to be understood how emotional reactions could be conditioned and unconditioned. Watson was excited and cautiously optimistic about the place of his natural science approach in the treatment of the emotionally disturbed.[30]

Thinking and Memory

Watson argued that 'thinking' referred to all subvocal word behaviour. In other words, thinking is the same as talking to oneself. Furthermore, language development represents the conditioning of verbal responses on unlearned vocal sounds. Sometimes the subvocal use of words has become an automatic habit. On other occasions, for example in reacting to a new situation, human thinking is similar to the trial-and-error behaviour of a rat in a maze. When subjects are asked to think aloud it is easy to see how they worked out their problem by word behaviour. New verbal creations, such as a poem, are arrived at by manipulating words and shifting them about until a new pattern is arrived at. There is no such thing as personal meaning in the behaviourist's theory.

Memory is viewed as the retention of verbal habits. If people meet a stimulus again after a period of time they do the habitual thing they learned to do when the stimulus was first present. For instance, a person who meets a friend after an absence will say the old words and exhibit the old visceral reactions.[31]

Personality and Diagnosis

Watson defined personality as 'the sum of activities that can be discovered by actual observation of behaviour over a long enough time to give reliable information. In other words, personality is the end product of our habit systems'.[32] Thus personality is defined in terms of behaviours or habits which may be observed objectively and which may give rise to accurate predictions of future behaviour. The method of studying personality is to take a cross-section of the habit systems in the activity stream at a given time, say at the age of 24. Among the activities there are dominant habit systems in each of the three broad clusters of habit systems, i.e. visceral, manual and laryngeal. An example of a dominant habit system in the laryngeal field is that of a great talker, whereas shyness may be a dominant habit system in the visceral field. Watson considered most judgements of personality to be superficial, made without a real study of the individual and often causing people serious injury as a result. He suggested five ways of obtaining a more accurate estimate of personality, namely by studying the individual's (a) education chart, (b) achievement chart, (c) spare time and recreation record, (d) emotional make-up under the practical situations of daily living and (e) by using psychological tests.

There is no need to introduce the concept of mind into the so-called mental diseases. Diagnosis should involve an analysis of behaviour as suggested above. Personality problems are behaviour disturbances and habit conflicts which need to be cured by unconditioning and conditioning.[33]

Ethics

The behaviourist is not interested in morals or ethics except as a scientist. Watson considered that to guide human behaviour on experimentally sound lines was beyond existing knowledge, since far too little was known about the human body and its needs.[34] However, behaviourism is the foundation of all future experimental ethics. He possessed a vision of behaviouristic freedom unshackled by those customs and conventions which needlessly and harshly restrict the individual because they are not based on a sound understanding of the principles of behaviour. The behaviourist would like to develop a world of people 'so that their speech and their bodily behavior could equally well be exhibited freely everywhere without running afoul of group standards'.[35]

SKINNER'S OPERANT BEHAVIOURISM

Burrhus Frederick Skinner (1904–　　) was born in Susquehanna, Pennsylvania, and held early academic appointments at the Universities of Minnesota and Indiana. In 1948 he became professor of psychology at Harvard, where he had previously obtained his MA and PhD. He spent the remainder of his academic career there. His books include: *The Behavior of Organisms*;[36] *Walden Two*, a novel about a behavioural utopia;[37] *Science and Human Behavior*;[38] *Verbal Behavior*;[39] *Schedules of Reinforcement*, co-written with C. B. Ferster;[40] co-authorship with J. G. Holland of a programmed textbook, *The Analysis of Behavior*;[41] *Contingencies of Reinforcement*;[42] *Beyond Freedom and Dignity*;[43] and *Particulars of My Life*.[44]

Like Watson, Skinner was dedicated to a science of behaviour which deals with facts and searches for lawful relations among the events in nature. Pavlov's and Watson's experiments involved classical or respondent conditioning in which the organism was passive while being conditioned. In 1913, the noted experimental psychologist Thorndike propounded his Law of Effect that: 'When a modifiable connection between a situation and a response is made and is accompanied or followed by a satisfying state of affairs, that connection's strength is increased: when made and accompanied by an annoying state of affairs its strength is decreased'.[45] The Law of Effect went beyond the conditioning of reflexive responses to emphasize that the satisfying or annoying after-effects of connections influence them. Skinner's distinctive contribution to psychology has been to elaborate the importance of the after-effects or consequences of behaviour. His fundamental principle is that 'Behavior is shaped and maintained by its consequences'.[46] He has been assiduous in conducting experiments which map out the details of this principle. He considers that he has gone beyond stimulus and response to take into account the action of the environment upon the organism *after* the response has been made. We now review some of Skinner's basic concepts derived from experimental research with pigeons and rats, prior to discussing some implications for human behaviour.

Basic Concepts

Operant behaviour

Skinner observes that a response which has occurred cannot be predicted or controlled, but all that can be predicted is the probability of a similar response occurring in the future. The unit of a predictive science of behaviour is an operant. The term 'operant' emphasizes the fact that behaviour *operates* on the environment to generate consequences. Thus the consequences define the properties with respect to which responses are viewed as similar. Skinner uses the term 'operant' both as an adjective, as in operant behaviour, and as a noun, which indicates the behaviour defined by a given consequence. He acknowledges that Pavlov called all events which strengthened behaviour in his dogs 'reinforcement' and the resulting changes in their voluntary and involuntary behaviour 'conditioning'. However, the critical difference is that in Pavlov's work the reinforcer is paired with the *stimulus*, whereas in operant behaviour it is contingent upon a *response*. Classical and operant conditioning are the only two possible kinds of conditioning.[47]

Contingencies of reinforcement

Skinner stresses the role of the environment in shaping and maintaining behaviour. Behaviour both operates on the environment to produce consequences and also is controlled or contingent upon the consequences produced by that environment. Any adequate description of the interaction between an organism and its environment must specify three elements: (a) the occasion on which a response occurs; (b) the response itself; and (c) the reinforcing consequences. The interrelationship of these three elements constitutes the contingencies of reinforcement. For example, in an experiment with pigeons, any stimuli deriving from the experimental space, such as sound or light, and from the operanda of the experiment, such as a translucent disc on the wall which may be pecked, and from any special stimulating devices prior to the response, are the 'occasion' of the response. The response itself might be pecking the disc and the reinforcing consequence might be food provided at a time when the pigeon is hungry.[48]

Positive and negative reinforcement

The probability of a response is increased after both positive and negative reinforcement. Positive reinforcements consist of presenting something, such as food, water or sexual contact, in a situation. Negative reinforcements consist of removing something, such as a bright light or an electric shock, from the situation. Thus the difference between positive and negative reinforcement hinges on whether it is the presence or absence of a given reinforcer which increases the probability of a response. The withdrawal of a positive reinforcer has the same effect as the presentation of a negative reinforcer.[49] Skinner did not consider punishment, by definition, to be a negative reinforcer since it does not necessarily permanently reduce a tendency to respond in a certain way and, also, it may have harmful side-effects.[50]

Primary and conditioned reinforcers

Skinner considers that all reinforcers eventually derive their power from evolutionary selection and that it is part of 'human nature' to be reinforced in particular ways by particular things. For instance, both the positive reinforcer of food and the negative reinforcer of escape from a dangerous situation have obvious survival value.[51] Only a small part of behaviour is immediately reinforced by food, water, sexual contact or other reinforcers of evident biological significance. Such reinforcers are the primary or unconditioned ones. Most behaviour is emitted in response to reinforcers which have become associated with or conditioned to primary reinforcers. For instance, if each time food is given to a hungry pigeon a light is turned on, the light eventually becomes a conditioned reinforcer. The light may then be used to condition an operant in the same way as food. A conditioned reinforcer is generalized when it is paired with more than one primary reinforcer. The importance of this is that a generalized conditioned reinforcer, such as money, is useful because it is not attached to just one state of deprivation, such as hunger, but to many. Therefore, under this kind of reinforcement, a response is more likely to occur. Other generalized conditioned reinforcers are attention, approval and affection.[52]

Schedules of reinforcement

Ferster and Skinner observe that many significant features of the shaping and maintenance of behaviour can be explained only by reference to the properties of schedules of reinforcement, and also that intermittent reinforcement can be a very important source of reinforcement in its own right and not just the poor relation of inevitable or continuous reinforcement.[53]

Non-intermittent schedules of reinforcement. These are:
1. Continuous reinforcement, where every response emitted is reinforced.
2. Extinction, where no responses are reinforced.

Intermittent schedules of reinforcement. These include:
1. Fixed interval, in which the first response occurring after a given period of time (for example, five minutes) is reinforced, with another period beginning immediately after the reinforcement.
2. Fixed ratio, in which every *n*th response is reinforced. (The word 'ratio' refers to the ratio between responses and reinforcements.)
3. Variable interval, in which reinforcements are scheduled according to a random series of intervals having a given mean and lying between arbitrary values.
4. Variable ratio, in which reinforcements are scheduled according to a random series of ratios having a given mean and lying between arbitrary values.
5. Multiple, in which one schedule of reinforcement is in force in the presence of one stimulus and a different schedule in the presence of another stimulus. For instance, there is a fixed interval when the key in the pigeon's experimental box is red, and a variable interval when the key is green.

6.   Differential reinforcement of rate of response, in which a response is reinforced only if it follows the preceding response after a specified interval of time (e.g. three minutes) or before the end of a given interval (e.g. half a second).[54, 55, 56]

Maintenance and extinction

Skinner does not consider the term 'learning' to be equivalent to 'operant conditioning'. Learning emphasizes acquisition of behaviour, whereas operant conditioning focuses on both acquisition and maintenance of behaviour. Thus behaviour continues to have consequences, and if these consequences or reinforcements are not forthcoming then extinction occurs. For instance, when a pigeon's behaviour, such as the lifting of its head, which has been reinforced by the consequence of food, no longer continues to receive this reinforcement, the head lifting tends to occur with a reduced frequency. Similarly, when people engage in behaviour which no longer has rewarding consequences, they find themselves less inclined to behave that way. Schedules of reinforcement are relevant to extinction. For example, the resistance to extinction generated by intermittent reinforcement may be much greater than that under continuous reinforcement. The task of a science of behaviour is to account for the probability of a response in terms of its history of reinforcement and extinction. Skinner uses the term 'operant strength' to indicate the probability of a given response and observes that with humans the condition of low operant strength resulting from extinction often requires treatment. For instance, psychotherapy might sometimes be viewed as a system of reinforcement designed to reinstate extinguished behaviour.[57]

Shaping and successive approximation

Behaviour may be shaped by reinforcing successive approximations to the desired response. Skinner gives the example of teaching a pigeon to bowl by swiping, with a sharp sideward movement of its beak, a wooden ball down a miniature alley towards a set of toy pins. When he and his colleagues waited for the complete response, which was to be reinforced by food, nothing happened. Then they decided to reinforce any response which had the slightest resemblance to a swipe and, afterwards, to select responses which more closely approximated the final form. This was a highly successful procedure and within minutes the pigeon was striking the ball as if it had been a champion squash player. In another experiment, by reinforcing successive approximations, a rat was conditioned to pull a string to get a marble from a rack, pick up the marble with its forepaws, carry it across the cage to a vertical tube rising two inches above the floor, lift the marble, and drop it into the tube.[58]

Stimulus discrimination and control

Operant behaviour is emitted through important connections with the environment. For instance, in a pigeon experiment, neck-stretching is reinforced when a signal light is on and allowed to extinguish when a signal light is off. The contingencies of reinforcement are that a stimulus (the light) is the occasion, the response is stretching the neck, and the reinforcement is food. The process through which the response is eventually more likely to occur when the light is on is called discrimination. Another way of viewing discrimination is to say that a response has come under the control of a discriminative stimulus or, more briefly, under stimulus control. Once an operant discrimination has been conditioned, the probability of the response occurring may be increased or decreased by presenting or removing the discriminative stimulus. An example of the effect of stimulus control on humans is the increased probability of purchasing behaviour through the effective display of merchandise in a shop.[59]

Stimulus generalization

When the reinforcing effect of one stimulus spreads to other stimuli, the effect is that of generalization or induction. For instance, if a response to a round, red spot one square inch in area is reinforced, a yellow spot of the same size and shape may also be reinforcing through the common properties of size and shape. However, by reinforcing only responses to the red spot with the above dimensions, and by extinguishing the response to the yellow spot, the red spot may be given exclusive discriminative control. An example of stimulus generalization in everyday life is reacting to people in a similar way because they resemble someone we know.[60]

Some Implications for Human Behaviour

The self

Skinner regards a self as a repertoire of behaviours appropriate to a given set of reinforcement contingencies. The traditional view of the causation of behaviour regards man as an autonomous agent responsible for his own life. The scientific view is that a person is a member of a species shaped by evolutionary contingencies of survival whose behaviour is under the control of the environment in which he lives. Although Skinner acknowledges the nomad on horseback in Outer Mongolia and the astronaut in outer space as being different people, he considers that if they had been exchanged at birth they would have taken each other's place[61] (though this might be interfered with by genetic factors which set limits on learning). The ways in which people perceive and know are determined by environmental contingencies. Also, consciousness or awareness is a social product shaped by the environment. Furthermore, the complex activity called thinking is explicable in terms of contingencies of reinforcement. Thus the self is a repertoire of behaviours acquired through an environmental history of reinforcement and maintained or extinguished through current contingencies of reinforcement.[62, 63]

Self-control

A functional analysis of behaviour implies discovering the independent variables which, once they are controlled, in turn control behaviour. In self-control, people manipulate events in their environments to control their behaviour. Self-control involves two interrelated responses. First, there is the controlling response which acts on the environment to alter the probability of the second or the controlled response. For instance, an adult may engage in the controlling response of walking away so that he is able to control his response of anger. Similarly, removal of discriminative stimuli, such as food, may help to avoid over-eating. On the other hand, presence of certain discriminative stimuli may make desirable behaviours more probable. For instance, a certain desk may act as a stimulus to study behaviour and a knot in a handkerchief may reinforce acting at a later date.[64] Even problems in the private world inside the skin are amenable to self-control through problem-solving behaviour which, as usual, has been built into the environment.[65]

Psychotherapy

Some of the emotional and motivational manifestations of what is called mental disease may be extreme consequences of variables used in controlling the normal organism. In other words, much of the behaviour involved in mental disease is learned and therefore the role of psychotherapy is to change behaviour by manipulating the client's contingencies of reinforcement. Psychotherapy may be viewed as a form of control, the aim of which is frequently to correct the undesirable effects of excessive or inconsistent control exercised by other agencies to restrict the individual's selfish, primarily reinforced behaviour. These other agencies of control include parents and educational and religious institutions. Skinner considers that the use of punishment as a measure of control is responsible for many of the avoidance or escape responses and emotional by-products characteristic of mental disease.

Diagnosis in psychotherapy consists of a functional analysis to discover variables which can be used to alter unwanted behaviour. If the therapist is able adequately to identify and control these intervening variables, this leads directly to the control of dependent variables. One intervening variable in psychotherapy is the therapist's ability to be a controlling agent or potent reinforcer. Despite the client's aversive condition, which should make promise of relief reinforcing, usually the therapist's initial power is slight. However, as time goes by the therapist may become an important source of reinforcement, with approval being especially effective.

The main tool of the therapist is to be a non-punishing audience or to respond in ways which are incompatible with punishment. This may have two effects. First, behaviour which has hitherto been repressed may begin to appear in the repertoire of the client. Second, some of the effects of punishment may become extinguished. For instance, a client who feels less wrong or sinful may be less likely to emit the kinds of operant behaviour which provide escape from these self-generated stimuli. Skinner writes: 'It is clear that psychology and psychodynamics overlap, these two fields being distinguished not in terms of subject matter or the causal factors to which appeal is made, but only in technique . . .'.[66]

Not all unwanted behaviours, however, are caused by excessive use of punishment. Therefore further techniques are needed, depending on the outcomes of the functional analysis. For example, in instances where ethical and parental control have been inadequate, therapy may consist of supplying additional controlling contingencies. With the total lack of control of the psychotic it is difficult to discover effective controlling contingencies.

At other times the therapist may need to construct new controlling contingencies either by strengthening responses already in the individual's repertoire or by building additional responses. Furthermore, the therapist may have to teach a client techniques of self-control, especially if the client is still likely to be subject to continued excessive or inconsistent control. Skinner acknowledges that the use of active techniques to add, strengthen and possibly to teach self-control for specific responses may be the second stage in a therapeutic process, only to be engaged in after the therapist has established himself as a non-punishing audience. Furthermore, it may be important for the therapist to help a client to change his behaviour in such a way that he may find a solution for himself, since sometimes telling a client what is wrong does nothing to alter the relevant intervening variables. In such an instance the client's behaviour in respect of his problem is a relevant intervening variable.

In psychotherapy there is always the possibility that the therapist will misuse the power to control. One form of countercontrol to prevent this abuse is the ethical standards of the psychotherapeutic profession. Nevertheless, there is still mistrust of the possibility of therapeutic control and therefore some theories of psychotherapy deny that, in the final analysis, behaviour can be controlled and that psychotherapy is one of the controlling agencies.[67, 68]

Environmental design

Psychotherapy is a form of control designed to correct the problems caused by other controlling agencies. Usually it is based on the assumption, common in our culture, of autonomous man who wishes both to be free from aversive features of the environment and also to receive credit for ethical behaviour. People find it difficult to accept the fact that all control is exercised by the environment. A technology of behaviour which will help humans to design better environments is available. Although such environments will exercise control over behaviour, their task is to release people for more reinforcing activities, consequently also reducing the need for corrective psychotherapy. The basic premise for the design of a culture is that behaviour can be changed by changing the conditions of which it is a function. Humans are the products of both biological and cultural evolutions. Though man is controlled by a culture, it is largely of his own making. The task of evolving a more effective culture may be seen as a gigantic exercise in self-control.[69] Skinner affirms his belief in operant behaviourism by concluding *Beyond Freedom and Dignity* with the following statement: 'A scientific view of man offers exciting possibilities. We have not yet seen what man can make of man'.[70]

SELF-REFERENT EXERCISES

It may help you to understand this chapter better if, either with paper and pencil or in your head, you think about and answer the following questions:

1. Are you aware of any of your reactions, emotional or otherwise, which have been classically conditioned? If so, please describe them.

2. List at least six stimulus-response connections in your life (e.g. traffic light stimuli and car-driving responses).

3. Describe the contingencies of reinforcement in a situation in which you either have been or are being operantly conditioned. Specify: (a) the occasion; (b) the response; and (c) the reinforcer(s).

4. Give examples in your own life of the following concepts:
    (a)   a positive and negative reinforcer;
    (b)   a primary, a conditioned and a generalized reinforcer;
    (c)   an intermittent schedule of reinforcement;
    (d)   self-control of a behaviour through manipulating its consequences;
    (e)   shaping a behaviour through successive approximation;
    (f)   extinction of a behaviour;
    (g)   stimulus discrimination;
    (h)   stimulus generalization.

5. Do you consider that your life is totally determined by the evolutionary history of the human species and by your environment? Give reasons for your position on this issue.

NOTES

1. Hilgard, E. R. & Bower, G. H. (1966) *Theories of Learning* (3rd ed.) p. 2. New York: Appleton-Century-Crofts.
2. *Ibid*. p. 48.
3. Pavlov, I. P. (1927) *Conditioned Reflexes* (Anrep translation) p. 16. Oxford: Oxford University Press.
4. *Ibid*. p. 16.
5. *Ibid*. pp. 17–22.
6. *Ibid*. pp. 22–24. The description of the three experiments forms part of Lecture 2, pp. 16–32, which is reproduced in Pavlov, I. P. (1955) *Selected Works*. pp. 188–205. Moscow: Foreign Languages Publishing House.
7. *Ibid*. pp. 48–49. Description of extinction experiment.
8. Cohen, D. (1979) *J. B. Watson, The Founder of Behaviourism*. London: Routledge and Kegan Paul.
9. Watson, J. B. (1903) *Animal Education*. Chicago: University of Chicago Press

10. Watson, J. B. (1914) *Behavior*. New York: Holt.
11. Watson, J. B. (1919) *Psychology from the Standpoint of a Behaviorist*. Philadelphia. Lippincott. 2nd ed. 1924; 3rd ed. 1929.
12. Watson, J. B. (1931) *Behaviorism*. London: Kegan Paul, Trench and Traubner.
13. Watson, J. B. (1928) *The Psychological Care of the Infant and Child*. New York: W. W. Norton.
14. Cohen, D. (1979) *J. B. Watson, The Founder of Behaviourism* pp. 290–293. London: Routledge and Kegan Paul.
15. Watson, J. B. (1931) *Behaviorism* p. 2. London: Kegan Paul, Trench and Traubner.
16. Watson, J. B. (1913) Psychology as the behaviorist views it. *Psychological Review*, **20**, 175. Full reference pp. 158–177.
17. Watson, J. B. (1931) *Behaviorism* pp. 1–5, London: Kegan Paul, Trench and Traubner.
18. Watson, J. B. (1913) Psychology as the behaviorist views it. *Psychological Review*, **20**, 176.
19. Watson, J. B. (1931) *Behaviorism* pp. 22–23. London: Kegan Paul, Trench and Traubner.
20. *Ibid*. pp. 11–47.
21. *Ibid*. p. 91.
22. *Ibid*. p. 139.
23. *Ibid*. pp. 93–129.
24. *Ibid*. p. 183.
25. *Ibid*. p. 104.
26. Watson, J. B. & Raynor, R. R. (1920) Conditioned emotional reactions. *Journal of Experimental Psychology*, **3**, 1–14.
27. Watson, J. B. (1931) *Behaviorism* pp. 158–164. London: Kegan Paul, Trench and Traubner.
28. Jones, M. C. (1924) A laboratory study of fear: the case of Peter. *Pedagogical Seminary*, **31**, 308–315.
29. Watson, J. B. (1931) *Behaviorism* pp. 172–176. London: Kegan Paul, Trench and Traubner.
30. *Ibid*. pp. 141–195.
31. *Ibid*. pp. 224–251.
32. *Ibid*. p. 274.
33. *Ibid*. pp. 269–304.
34. *Ibid*. p. 47.
35. *Ibid*. p. 303.
36. Skinner, B. F. (1938) *The Behaviour of Organisms*. New York: Appleton-Century-Crofts.
37. Skinner, B. F. (1948) *Walden Two*. New York: Macmillan.
38. Skinner, B. F. (1953) *Science and Human Behavior*. New York: Macmillan.
39. Skinner, B. F. (1957) *Verbal Behavior*. New York: Appleton-Century-Crofts.
40. Ferster, C. B. & Skinner, B. F. (1957) *Schedules of Reinforcement*. New York: Appleton-Century-Crofts.
41. Holland, J. G. & Skinner, B. F. (1961) *The Analysis of Behavior*. New York: McGraw-Hill.
42. Skinner, B. F. (1969) *Contingencies of Reinforcement*. New York: Appleton-Century-Crofts.
43. Skinner, B. F. (1971) *Beyond Freedom and Dignity*. Harmondsworth, Middlesex: Penguin Books.
44. Skinner, B. F. (1976) *Particulars of My Life*. London: Jonathan Cape.
45. Thorndike, E. L. (1932) *The Fundamentals of Learning* p. 176. New York: Teachers College Bureau of Publications.
46. Skinner, B. F. (1971) *Beyond Freedom and Dignity* p. 23. Harmondsworth, Middlesex: Penguin Books.
47. Skinner, B. F. (1953) *Science and Human Behavior* pp. 59–90. New York: Macmillan.
48. Skinner, B. F. (1969) *Contingencies of Reinforcement* pp. 3–28. New York: Appleton-Century-Crofts.

49. Skinner, B. F. (1953) *Science and Human Behavior* p. 73. New York: Macmillan.
50. *Ibid.* pp. 182–193.
51. Skinner, B. F. (1971) *Beyond Freedom and Dignity* p. 104. Harmondsworth, Middlesex: Penguin Books.
52. Skinner, B. F. (1953) *Science and Human Behavior* pp. 76–84. New York: Macmillan.
53. Ferster, C. B. & Skinner, B. F. (1957) *Schedules of Reinforcement* p. 3. New York: Appleton-Century-Crofts.
54. *Ibid.* whole book, especially pp. 5–7.
55. Skinner, B. F. (1969) *Contingencies of Reinforcement* pp. 24–25. New York: Appleton-Century-Crofts.
56. Skinner, B. F. (1953) *Science and Human Behavior* pp. 91–106. New York: Macmillan.
57. *Ibid.* pp. 69–72, and p. 98.
58. Skinner, B. F. (1958) Reinforcement today. *The American Psychologist*, **13**, 94–99. Reprinted in Skinner, B. F. (1961) *Cumulative Record*. New York: Appleton-Century-Crofts.
59. Skinner, B. F. (1953) *Science and Human Behavior* pp. 107–128. New York: Macmillan.
60. *Ibid.* pp 129–140.
61. Skinner, B. F. (1971) *Beyond Freedom and Dignity* pp. 180–181. Harmondsworth, Middlesex: Penguin Books.
62. *Ibid.* pp. 180–210.
63. Skinner, B. F. (1953) *Science and Human Behavior* pp. 283–294. New York: Macmillan.
64. *Ibid.* pp. 227–241.
65. Skinner, B. F. (1971) *Beyond Freedom and Dignity* p. 190. Harmondsworth, Middlesex: Penguin Books.
66. Skinner, B. F. (1961) *Cumulative Record* p. 200. New York: Appleton-Century-Crofts.
67. *Ibid.* pp. 194–202.
68. Skinner, B. F. (1953) *Science and Human Behavior* pp. 359–383. New York: Macmillan.
69. Skinner, B. F. (1971) *Beyond Freedom and Dignity*. Harmondsworth, Middlesex: Penguin Books.
70. *Ibid.* p. 210.

7 – Behavioural Theory: Wolpe, Eysenck and Bandura

SUMMARY: *Wolpe offers a reciprocal inhibition explanation for some conditioned inhibition. Reciprocal inhibition involves eliciting one response in order to bring about a decrease in the strength of a simultaneous response. Wolpe induced neurotic fear responses in experimental cats and then used his reciprocal inhibition principle to decondition them to the point where they could eat in an experimental cage where previously they had received electric shocks. A number of responses incompatible with anxiety may be used in conjunction with counselling. These include relaxation, assertive and sexual responses.*

Eysenck considers that a theory of neurosis has to explain not only the failure of extinction, but the enhancement of neurotic conditioned responses that remain unreinforced. His incubation theory posits that certain conditioned responses have drive properties which, when the conditioned stimulus only is presented, produce a conditioned response of fear/anxiety identical to the unconditioned response. Such a CR provides positive reinforcement for the CS-only presentation, thus causing it to evoke more fear or enhance/incubate the CR. Incubation allows the CR to exceed the strength of the UCR. Conditions which favour incubation are discussed.

Bandura's social learning theory views humans as determinants of environments as well as environments as determinants of human behaviour. Cognitive mediating processes are central to the interpretation of stimuli, to motivation and to self-regulation. Behaviour is acquired through the response consequences of first-hand experience and, in particular, through observational learning or modelling. Modelling involves attentional, retention, motor reproduction and motivational processes. Expectancy is an important antecedent determinant of behaviour and perceived self-efficacy, or knowing that one can successfully execute a behaviour required to produce certain outcomes, is the critical expectancy in analysing avoidance behaviour. Three kinds of reinforcement are external, vicarious and self-regulated. Self-regulated reinforcement involves the administration of rewards contingent upon the attainment of subjective self-evaluative standards. The distinctive counselling technique emanating from social learning theory is participant modelling, which is described briefly.

Behavioural theory started being formulated around the turn of the century. The last chapter focused on Pavlov and Watson, two of the 'founding fathers' of the behavioural approach, and on Skinner, whose work has been published since the 1930s. There were, of course, many other important early contributors to behavioural theory, such as Edward Thorndike and Clark Hull.[1] The period since the late 1950s has seen further contributions to both the theoretical and applied development of the behavioural approach. Wolpe, Eysenck and Bandura are three of the leading more recent behaviourist writers. Their work, some of which is discussed in this chapter, illustrates the continuing search for greater refinement of the principles of behaviour.

WOLPE'S RECIPROCAL INHIBITION

Joseph Wolpe (1915–) was a lecturer in the department of psychiatry at the University of Witwatersrand, Johannesburg, South Africa. In the late 1940s, as a result of laboratory experiments with cats as subjects, he developed a method based on reciprocal inhibition for de-conditioning neurotic fear responses. Wolpe then applied his experimental findings in his clinical work, with great success. In 1958 both the experimental work and its clinical and counselling derivatives were published in *Psychotherapy by Reciprocal Inhibition*.[2] This book created a great stir and acted as a major impetus to the burgeoning development since the early 1960s of behavioural approaches to clinical and counselling concerns. Wolpe emigrated to the United States, where he became professor of psychiatry at Temple University in Pennsylvania. His other books include *The Practice of Behaviour Therapy*[3] and *Theme and Variations: A Behaviour Therapy Casebook*.[4] At present he is editor of the *Journal of Behaviour Therapy and Experimental Psychiatry*. Wolpe acknowledges his debt to other learning theorists, especially Pavlov and Hull, in developing his approach to the learning and unlearning of neurotic behaviour. This approach is summarized in his statement: 'fundamental psychotherapeutic effects follow reciprocal inhibition of neurotic responses'.[5]

Theory

Extinction: conditioned, reactive and reciprocal inhibitions

This first paragraph is fairly technical and some readers may wish to omit it. Wolpe, in a discussion of the extinctive or unlearning processes, observed that a partial recovery of the response, known as spontaneous recovery, takes place if the stimulus is not applied for some time. The partial nature of spontaneous recovery indicates that two elements are involved in the inhibition of a response during extinction: reactive inhibition, which describes an inhibitory state dissipating with time, and negative conditioning, which leads to a permanent decrease in response probability. The Miller-Mowrer explanation of the extinctive process posits that every time an organism makes a response to a stimulus, there follows a fatigue effect which has an inhibitory effect on a closely following repeat of the same response. Stimuli present at the time are in closest contiguity with the drive reduction associated with cessation of the activity and, in some measure, become conditioned to an inhibition of a response to which previously they were positively joined. The result of this is that, at the next presentation of these stimuli, the strength of the response decreases, even after a time interval long enough to eliminate all reactive inhibition effects. However, when the response is a reinforced one, the positive effects override the development of conditioned inhibition. In other words, in this explanation of conditioned inhibition, the inhibition is built up during extinction through traces of the conditioned stimuli being simultaneous with reactive inhibition of the conditioned response.

Wolpe offered a further explanation of conditioned inhibition. He noted that old habits are often eliminated by allowing new habits to develop in the same situation. The term *reciprocal inhibition* encompasses 'all situations in which the elicitation of one response appears to bring about a decrement in the strength of evocation of a simultaneous response'.[6] He hypothesized that if an incompatible response were to inhibit the conditioned response and lead to significant drive reduction, then a significant degree of conditioned inhibition of the original response would be developed.[7] Eventually, his work led to his framing the following general reciprocal inhibition principle:

> If a response antagonistic to anxiety can be made to occur in the presence of anxiety-evoking stimuli so that it is accompanied by a complete or partial suppression of the anxiety responses, the bond between these stimuli and the anxiety responses will be weakened.[8]

Neurotic behaviour

Wolpe defined neurotic behaviour as 'any persistent habit of unadaptive behaviour acquired by learning in a physiologically normal organism'.[9] Neurotic behaviour almost invariably involves anxiety, which is the autonomic response pattern that is characteristically a part of the organism's response to noxious stimulation. To Wolpe, 'anxiety' and 'fear' are terms that can be used interchangeably. The criterion for the severity of a neurosis is generally the level of unadaptive anxiety. Anxiety impairs the functioning of the organism in many ways, including impairments of mental co-ordination, mental activity and sexual performance. Human neuroses, like animal neuroses, are learned in situations which evoke high anxiety.

Experimentation

The learning and unlearning of neurosis in cats

The subjects were 12 domestic cats between the ages of six months and three years. Lasting neurotic effects were induced in all the cats by the administration of several electric shocks in a small experimental cage. Six of the cats were subject to a procedure by which, after control observations, the cat was given five to ten grid shocks preceded by a 'hoot' lasting two to three seconds. The other six cats were subject to a different procedure in which they were first conditioned to perform food-approach responses to a buzzer. This response was strongly reinforced over eight to 16 experimental sessions. The next stage of the procedure involved sounding the buzzer and shocking the cat when it made its food-approach response until it ceased to do so. The mean number of shocks required was four.

The immediate responses of the cats to the shocks included combinations of the following: rushing hither and thither, clawing at the cage, getting up on hind legs, crouching, trembling, howling, pilo-erection and rapid respiration. Persistent responses displayed by all animals were: (a) resistance to being put into the experimental cage; (b) signs of anxiety when inside the cage; and (c) refusal to eat meat pellets anywhere in the cage even after one, two or three days' starvation. The above symptoms were invariably intensified by presentation of the original auditory stimuli. Furthermore, all cats showed some of these symptoms outside the experimental cage.

The learned neurotic reactions of six of the cats were associated with inhibition of feeding. This suggested to Wolpe that under different conditions feeding might inhibit the neurotic reactions. The neurotic anxiety reactions were subsequently removed, or unlearned, in all cats by getting them to eat in the presence of successively larger doses of anxiety-evoking stimuli. The cats were subject to a number of procedures. One procedure was to place the cat in the experimental cage and move pellets of meat towards its mouth on the flat end of a four-inch rod held in the experimenter's hand, in the hope that the human hand would act as a stimulus to overcome the inhibition to eating. After some persistence, four out of the nine cats undergoing this procedure were induced to eat. However, only one of the three cats whose food-approach responses had been shocked was induced to eat in this way. The three cats not subject to the human-hand procedure were induced to eat by Masserman's 'forced solution' procedure. This involved repetitions of a procedure, in the experimental cage, of gradually pushing a hungry, neurotic cat by means of a movable barrier towards an open food box containing appetizing food.

The five cats which remained unaffected by the human-hand method were eventually induced to eat in the experimental cage by a procedure which involved a 'hierarchy' of anxiety-evoking rooms ranging from the most anxiety-evoking, the experimental room or Room A, to the least anxiety-evoking, which turned out to be the passage outside Room D. The five cats initially ate at different points in the hierarchy, but by a method of gradual ascent all cats were eventually induced to eat in Room A and then in the experimental cage. By similar methods the cats' neurotic responses to the conditioned auditory stimuli were inhibited.

Wolpe explained the success of his experiments by stating that, when stimuli to incompatible responses are present simultaneously, the occurrence of the response that is dominant in the circumstances involves the reciprocal inhibition of the other. Thus, as the number of feedings increased, the anxiety responses gradually became weaker, so that to stimuli to which there was initially an anxiety response there was ultimately a feeding response with inhibition of anxiety.[10,11]

Application

Reciprocal inhibition in psychotherapy

In overcoming the neurotic reactions of clients or patients, Wolpe considers it vital to determine which stimuli actually or potentially evoke them currently. Suffice it for now to say that Wolpe's method involves deciding which of a number of incompatible responses can most appropriately be used to obtain reciprocal inhibition of neurotic anxiety responses. Wolpe lists eight incompatible responses at the disposal of the counsellor or therapist, through which deliberate intervention for change may be made. These are:

1. assertive responses;
2. sexual responses;
3. relaxation responses;
4. respiratory responses;
5. 'anxiety-relief' responses;
6. competitively conditioned motor responses;
7. 'pleasant' responses in the life situation (with drug enhancement):
8. (a)   interview-induced emotional responses;
   (b)   abreaction.[12]

Relaxation, as part of systematic desensitization, is probably the main incompatible response used in behavioural counselling and therapy. Here progressively anxiety-evoking scenes on a hierarchy are presented by the therapist to the imagination of a relaxed client, the idea being that the relaxation response progressively reciprocally inhibits the anxiety response to a particular situation, such as fear of examinations. Systematic desensitization is discussed in much more detail in Chapter 12. Assertive responses and sexual responses are also commonly used as incompatible responses, the former for interpersonal anxieties and the latter for sexual anxieties.[13,14] There is a long-standing debate about the mediating processes of the behavioural changes brought about by systematic desensitization. Whatever the outcome of this debate, Wolpe has been a pioneering figure in the development of the behavioural approach to counselling psychology.

EYSENCK'S INCUBATION THEORY OF NEUROSIS

Hans J. Eysenck (1916–   ) left his native Germany in 1934 and, after a period of study in France, settled and continued his education in England. After the 1939–45 war he became a senior research psychologist at the Maudsley Hospital in London, soon founding and becoming director of the psychology department in the hospital's Institute of Psychiatry. In 1955 he was appointed professor of psychology at the University of London. Eysenck has been a prolific writer and his many books include: *The Structure of Human Personality*;[15] *Behaviour Therapy and the Neuroses*;[16] with S.

Rachman, *The Causes and Cures of Neurosis*;[17] *The Biological Basis of Personality*;[18] and *You and Neurosis*.[19] For many years Eysenck edited the journal *Behaviour Research and Therapy*. He has influenced extensively the development of the theory and practice of the behavioural approach to counselling psychology. As early as 1965 Wolpe wrote: 'The now popular term *behavior therapy* . . . owes its wide promulgation and acceptance to Eysenck'.[20]

Other Theories of Neurosis

Eysenck observed that neurotic behaviour, a distinctive feature of which is that behaviour followed by negative consequences is not eliminated, neither follows Skinner's law of reinforcement nor can be explained adequately in Skinnerian terms. He considered that Watson's view of neurosis as classically conditioned emotional responses was not elaborated in any detail. For instance, Watson never adequately explained the lack of extinction of neurotic responses. A further gap in Watson's work is that no explanation was offered for the phenomenon that, in many neuroses, not only does extinction fail to take place, but also there is an incremental enhancement effect, so the unreinforced conditioned stimulus (CS) may produce increases in anxiety (CR) with each presentation of the CS. This enhancement of the unreinforced CR, even more than the failure of extinction, is the central paradox of the neurotic reaction.[21,22]

Innate and Acquired Sources of Neurosis

Eysenck acknowledged four sources of neurotic fear/anxiety responses. First, they may be innate, for example when the degree of fear is strong on first encountering the stimulus object. Second, they may be attributed to 'preparedness', when the fear is weak but the conditioning easy at the first encounter of the stimulus. Preparedness means that certain fears are highly 'prepared' to be learned by humans. Both innate fears and those to which the concept of preparedness applies reflect the evolutionary development of the species. Third, fears may be learned through modelling (imitation). Fourth, and the most important source of the learning of fear responses, is classical or Pavlovian conditioning. The main unconditioned stimulus (UCS) generating fear responses is neither pain nor the three stimuli suggested by Watson (loud noises, loss of support, and physical constraint), but frustration or 'frustrative non-reward', which can have physiological and behavioural consequences identical to those of pain. Eysenck's biological theory of personality states that introverts condition more readily than extroverts, thus being more likely to acquire neurotic fear responses.

Extinction and Incubation

Eysenck tentatively proposed his incubation theory of neurosis, hoping to encourage the collection of relevant clinical and research data. He realized it went considerably beyond ascertained fact and was extrapolated heavily from animal experimentation. While a CS-only presentation always provokes a decrease in CR strength, it may also provoke an increase. Thus there are two possible consequences of CS-only presentation. The first is *extinction* of the CR, and the other is enhancement of the CR or *incubation* of the anxiety/fear responses. Extinction occurs if the decreasing exceed the increasing tendencies, while incubation takes place if the increasing exceed the decreasing tendencies.[23] There are two classes of CR: those which have drive properties and those which do not, the former leading to enhancement and the latter leading to extinction. A CR leading to extinction, when the CS alone is presented, is a dog's salivation, since the salivation does not produce the hunger drive. However, giving rats a shock after a CS-only presentation does produce a CS-induced drive, or enhancement, and rats will learn new activities and practise established ones.

Eysenck argues that fear/anxiety is a response which possesses drive properties and hence not only resists extinction, but is enhanced by presentation of the CS. By definition, the initial position is that the UCS produces fear/anxiety, while the CS does not. Pairing the UCS with the CS leads to a situation in which, after conditioning, the presentation of the CS alone produces a CR of fear/anxiety which is identical to the UCR. It is the drive properties of the CR which make it functionally equivalent to the UCR, so providing reinforcement for the CS-only presentation. Thus where the CR, for example fear/anxiety, has drive properties, presentation of CS-only stimuli produces incubation (enhancement) of the CR. A positive feedback cycle is established in which the fear/anxiety associated with the CS-only presentation is itself a painful event, and the stimuli associated with the CS, by classical conditioning, come to evoke more fear.[24] This process is responsible for not only the continuation but also the growth of neurotic responses.

Incubation has the effect of allowing the CR to exceed the strength of the UCR. Furthermore, it may account for the slow growth of neurotic responses over a period of time, with a few exposures to CS only. There is much evidence that the duration of the CS-only presentation is a critical factor, with short rather than long presentations favouring incubation of fear/anxiety responses. There is less evidence that a strong as opposed to a weak UCS presentation does so. Eysenck observed that stable extroverts extinguish more readily than other extroversion-neuroticism groupings, while neurotic introverts show most evidence of incubation.[25]

Eysenck considered that his revision of the law of extinction made possible the acceptance of a conditioning model of neurosis. His theory demonstrates the interaction between theory and research in the search for a fuller understanding of the laws of behaviour. His incubation theory of neurosis is built on previous theory and research, and requires further experimental work which may, in turn, lead to a modification of the theory. His work demonstrates that behavioural theory is still developing and should not prematurely be regarded as dogma, an attitude which conflicts with the behaviourist's scientific emphasis.

BANDURA'S SOCIAL LEARNING THEORY

Albert Bandura (1925–), who has been chosen to represent the cognitive-behavioural theorists, is a professor of psychology at Stanford University in California. He has written numerous journal articles based mainly on his experimental work. His books include: *Social Learning and Personality Development*, with Richard Walters;[26] *Principles of Behavior Modification*;[27] *Aggression: A Social Learning Analysis*;[28] and *Social Learning Theory*.[29] Bandura felt that traditional ways of studying human behaviour had been too circumscribed and mechanistic. His response was to evolve a theoretical viewpoint called social learning theory, which is described below.

Basic Concepts

Reciprocal determinism

Three possible paradigms for conceptualizing human behaviour are environmental, personal and reciprocal determinism. In the environmental determinism paradigm, which is the Skinnerian position, behaviour (B) is the consequence (F) of environmental contingencies (E), otherwise expressed as $[B = F(E)]$. In the personal determinism paradigm, which is the humanistic position, the environment (E) is determined (F) by behaviour (B), otherwise expressed as $[E = F(B)]$. The social learning paradigm views human behaviour (B) in terms of a continuous reciprocal interaction between cognitive behavioural (P) and environmental (E) determinants. This reciprocal determinism position may be depicted as:

Although environmental control has been minutely researched, personal control tends to have been neglected. Nevertheless, the fact remains that environments have causes as well as conseqences. Environmental determinists, such as Skinner, are inconsistent when they assert that people are controlled by external events and, at the same time, advocate that they apply a technology of behaviour to obtain intentional control over their environments. Furthermore, psychological perspectives on determinism influence behaviour. For instance, personal determinists may be more likely to develop self-directed personalities. In the final analysis, however, human behaviour is the result of reciprocal interaction of external events and personal determinants such as genetic endowment, acquired competencies, reflective thought and self-initiative.[30,31] In short, Bandura has brought personal determinism into behavioural theory.

Mediating cognitive processes

Cognitive events are, among others, imagery, representation of experience in symbolic form and thought processes. External events affect behaviour through mediating cognitive processes. Also, cognitive processes are highly relevant to motivation and self-regulation. Thus cognition has a causal influence on behaviour. Furthermore, any theory that denies that thoughts can regulate actions cannot adequately explain complex human behaviour.[32]

Whereas early classical and even operant conditioning may be viewed as an S → R or stimulus → response model, Bandura's is much more an S → O → R or stimulus → organism's mediating cognitive processes → response model. However, even this three-link chain does not do justice to his notion of the interaction of personal and environmental determinisms.

Human nature

Except for elementary reflexes, people are not equipped with inborn repertoires of behaviour and hence must learn them. Biological factors, however, set limits to the learning process. For instance, genes and hormones affect physical development which, in turn, influences behavioural potentialities. Additionally, as in the case of speech, there is a rudimentary natural endowment on which new responses may be formed on the basis of learning. Often, experiential and physiological influences are not easily separable and thus it may be more fruitful to analyse the determinants of behaviour rather than to try to categorize proportions of behaviour as learned or innate.[33] Bandura writes of human nature 'as a vast potentiality that can be fashioned by direct and vicarious experience into a variety of forms within biological limits'.[34] Furthermore, not only do environments fashion humans, but humans fashion environments.

Acquisition of Behaviour

Response consequences

One way in which new behaviour is learned is by direct experience. This involves experiencing the positive and negative consequences of actions. However, the process of learning does not stop here, since people notice the effects of their responses. Thus reinforcement does not automatically strengthen a tendency to respond, but does so by altering informational and motivational cognitive variables. In other words, contrary to the mechanistic view, consequences determine behaviour largely through intervening thoughts. The term 'reinforcement' is misleading, since it has connotations of automatic responding and of 'strengthening' responses, like driving a car, which may not be able to be further strengthened. Regulation of behaviour is a concept preferable to reinforcement.[35]

Modelling

It is unnecessary for people to learn all their behaviour from the consequences of their own responses. Most learning takes place on a vicarious basis through observation of other people's behaviour and its consequences for them. Observational learning or modelling may be used both for the acquisition of new responses and for the inhibiting or disinhibiting of existing responses.[36, 37]

There are conflicting theories about the necessary and sufficient conditions for the acquisition of new responses on an observational basis. For instance, the Skinnerian analysis of modelling rests on the three-component paradigm $S^d \rightarrow R \rightarrow S^r$, where S^d denotes the modelled stimulus, R represents an overt matching response, and S^r designates the reinforcing stimulus. Bandura criticizes this scheme for failing to account for learning which takes place: (a) where observers do not perform the modelled responses in the same setting as demonstrated; (b) where neither the model nor the observer may be reinforced; and (c) when the responses may be performed much later. There is an important distinction between acquisition and performance, in that modelled behaviour may be acquired but not performed and, hence, not reinforced. Bandura's view is that observational learning occurs through symbolic processes during exposure to modelled activities and this in itself is sufficient to produce learning. However, his research suggests that modelling plus enactment of the modelled behaviour may be a more potent form of learning to overcome fears than modelling alone.[38]

In the social learning analysis of modelling there are four component processes:

1. *Attentional processes.* If people are to learn from modelling it is important that they pay attention to and accurately perceive the modelled behaviour. One set of attentional variables concerns characteristics of the modelling stimuli, such as availability, distinctiveness, personal attractiveness, and the functional value of the modelled behaviour. Another set of attentional variables revolves around observer characteristics, such as sensory capacities, arousal level, perceptual habits, and past reinforcements.
2. *Retention processes.* To be effective modelling must be remembered. This involves either imaginal storing of information or, more frequently, coding of modelled events into readily usable verbal symbols. Further aids to retention include either imaginal rehearsal of the modelled behaviour or actually carrying it out.
3. *Motor reproduction processes.* At some stage, symbolic representations of modelled behaviour will probably need to be translated into effective action. Variables influencing reproduction of the behaviour include the observer's physical capacities, whether their response repertoire already includes the necessary component responses, and the ability to make corrective adjustments when trying out the new behaviour.
4. *Motivational processes.* The distinction between learning and performance is highlighted by the fact that people are not motivated to enact everything they learn. The observer is more likely to adopt the modelled behaviour, if it: (a) brings external rewards; (b) is internally positively valued; and (c) has been

observed to bring rewards to the model. Anticipation of reinforcement is one of the factors affecting which aspects of modelled behaviour are observed or ignored.[39]

Bandura considers modelling, leading to observational learning through symbolic processes, to be the principal mode of transmitting new modes of behaviour; also, that the range of modelled influences has increased with advances in communications technology.[40] Diffusion of ideas does not necessarily mean that they will be adopted. Furthermore, through reciprocal determinism people can influence the models to which they are exposed.

Regulating Behaviour

Antecedent determinants and self-efficacy

Social learning theory heavily emphasizes the role of expectancy or anticipation as an antecedent determinant of behaviour. The $S \rightarrow R$ model, in which people automatically respond to stimuli, is erroneous, since it fails to take into account the fact that humans interpret stimuli. Reactions to given stimuli are not the automatic results of conditioning but are largely self-activated on the basis of learned expectations. Expectations may be learned either through first-hand experience or observationally. Environmental cues, such as distinctive features of places, persons or things, provide the person with information on which to base expectations of the probable consequences of different courses of action.

Self-efficacy is a central concept for understanding and analysing changes in fearful or avoidant behaviour.[41,42] Bandura distinguishes between an efficacy expectation, 'the conviction that one can successfully execute the behaviour required to produce the outcomes', and an outcome expectation, 'a person's estimate that a given behaviour will lead to certain outcomes'.[43] The distinction is made because it is possible for people to know that a given behaviour will produce a certain outcome, but still be unsure about whether they can perform the behaviour successfully.

Another way of viewing self-efficacy is as an expectation of personal mastery. Granted the necessary skills and adequate incentives, such an expectation is likely to influence both whether a task will be initiated and also the strength and persistence of coping behaviour. Three dimensions on which efficacy expectations vary are magnitude, generality and strength. Mastery expectations may differ in relation to the magnitude of the tasks to be performed. Some efficacy expectations may relate to a specific treatment, whereas others will generalize beyond specific situations. Furthermore, some mastery expectations will be strong and lead individuals to persevere despite difficulties, whereas other expectations may be weak. A meaningful expectancy analysis requires a detailed assessment of each of the dimensions of magnitude, generality and strength.

Expectations of personal efficacy are based on the five major sources of information described below. Any method of treatment may work with one or more of these sources.

Performance accomplishments. Personal experiences of success provide the most fundamental source of efficacy expectations. Success raises efficacy expectations, whereas repeated failure lowers them. Two treatment strategies which focus on performance improvements are participant modelling and participant desensitization, in both of which the client is inducted into successful performance of feared tasks.

Vicarious experience. Efficacy expectations may be altered by observing others and noting the consequences of behaviour for them. Efficacy expectations induced by modelling are unlikely to be as strong as those induced by successful task performance. Modelled behaviour for which the successful consequences are clear is likely to lead to stronger efficacy expectations than where the consequences are non-existent or ambiguous.

Verbal persuasion. Verbal persuasion, such as suggestion and exhortation, may also influence self-efficacy. However, persuasion may only raise expectations without providing a base on which competency may be established and, hence, is likely to be a weak source of efficacy expectations.

Emotional arousal. When people are tense and anxious, their physiological state or level of emotional arousal is likely to influence their efficacy expectations. High arousal usually debilitates performance and thus lowered expectations of efficacy are, in part, based on lowered performance. The converse is that an appropriate level of arousal is likely to facilitate rather than debilitate performance.

Situational circumstances. Even within an area of anxiety, such as public speaking, some situations will present more of a threat to a person's expectations of efficacy than others. For instance, size of audience and familiarity with and difficulty of subject matter are situational variables which might affect public-speaking self-efficacy.

Consequent determinants and self-regulation

The distinction between antecedent and consequent determinants of behaviour is somewhat artificial, since consequences affect behaviour largely through the expectations they create. Nevertheless, human behaviour is still very much regulated by its consequences. Two kinds of regulatory consequences are external reinforcement and vicarious external reinforcement. Since they have symbolic and self-reactive capacities, humans are also capable of internally administering their own consequences or of self-regulation. In self-regulation, sometimes called self-reinforcement, 'individuals regulate their behaviour by making self-reward conditional upon matching self-prescribed standards of performance'.[44]

Self-regulated reinforcement influences motivation in two main ways. First, the self-evaluative standards that people adopt specify the requirements for positive self-reinforcement. Second, the same self-evaluative standards provide negative feedback where performance is insufficient, and this also may provide an incentive.

Three component processes in self-regulated reinforcement are the evaluation of the performance, the judgemental process and the self-response.[45]

1. *Evaluation of performance.* There are a number of evaluative dimensions on which behaviour may be measured. For instance, writing may be measured in terms of quantity, quality and originality. Social behaviour may be measured on such dimensions as authenticity or deviancy. Needless to say, these 'objective' evaluative dimensions vary according to the nature of the activity.

2. *Judgemental process.* Self-evaluations tend to go beyond 'objective' measures and become translated or interpreted into subjective self-appraisals. The same performance may represent success to one person and failure to another. These personal standards are acquired partly through differential reinforcement by others, e.g. parents, and partly through modelling. The process of self-evaluation tends to involve comparisons with reference points. An important source of reference is self-comparison, where the measure of adequacy may be based on past performance. Social comparison, where people assess their success in relation to others, for example in regard to their incomes, is another source of personal standards. A further element in the judgemental process is whether or not the individual values the behaviour highly or not. Last, people are more likely to generate consequences for themselves when they hold themselves responsible for their performance than when they attribute their behaviour to external factors.

3. *Self-response.* The outcome of the judgemental process applied to measures of performance might be viewed in terms of self-produced consequences. In valued activities, favourable self-evaluations activate rewarding self-responses, whereas unfavourable self-evaluations generate negative consequences. Thus personal satisfaction and dissatisfaction are determined not only by the actual level of performance but by the standards used to judge level of performance. Dysfunctional self-evaluative systems tend to be those in which the individual has extremely harsh standards, thus giving rise to depression and feelings of worthlessness.

The ability of humans intentionally to influence their behaviour through self-produced consequences gives them a capacity for self-direction, albeit within the confines of reciprocal determinism. People have considerable potential to regulate their own feelings, thoughts and actions. There are two stages in the self-regulatory process in which incentives operate. First, there is the need to create the necessary self-reward contingencies to provide motivation for engaging in the activity. Second, there is the actual process of self-reward for attaining the required performance. Furthermore, self-evaluative influences operate only if activated and are sensitive to situational cues. For instance, a high level of aggressiveness may be perceived as appropriate in certain military situations and inappropriate in civilian life.

A number of factors maintain systems of self-regulation. Threat of negative sanctions for not adhering to the desired self-regulation may sustain the necessary behaviour. Personal benefits from self-regulated behaviour may include the absence of aversive outcomes, such as being overweight, and the presence of positive outcomes, such as mastering a desired skill. Additionally, people tend to regulate their own behaviour by choosing reference groups who share similar self-reinforcement standards. Also, modelling may lend support to self-regulatory behaviour through observation of others successfully regulating their behaviour through contingent self-reinforcement.

CHANGING BEHAVIOUR

Participant Modelling

Perhaps Bandura's most distinctive contribution to changing behaviour in counselling and clinical settings has been the approach termed participant modelling.[46,47] Participant modelling goes beyond vicarious modelling by attempting to ensure that the client engages in successful performance of the feared task. The required behaviour is approached by a hierarchy of progressively more difficult tasks. For each task the counsellor first models the behaviour and then subjects are instructed to perform it. If difficulties arise, the counsellor introduces performance aids to ensure success. One such aid is joint performance with the counsellor. As treatment progresses the supplementary aids are withdrawn until clients' feelings of self-efficacy in relation to the task are such that they can cope on their own.

Concluding Comments

Eysenck observes that, whereas his view of behaviourism is basically a physiological one, Bandura's cognitive view of behaviourism is based on a body–mind dichotomy which he has failed to justify. Eysenck views failure expectations as epiphenomena to the fundamental physiological processes described in his induction theory of neurosis.[48] Wolpe observes that emotional reconditioning processes involving anxiety reduction take place during participant modelling. He states that elimination of anxiety responses is the primary therapeutic requirement and that increases in self-efficacy expectations logically *follow*, and hence are secondary to, fear diminution.[49] These criticisms have been presented to illustrate that there are differences as well as similarities in the views of the more recent behavioural theorists. Also, it may be inferred that, in the scientific search for the principles underlying behaviour, much theorizing and laboratory and clinical experimentation remain to be done.

GOALS FOR COUNSELLING AND FOR LIVING

Krumboltz has observed that behavioural goals for counselling: (a) should be capable of being stated differently for each client; (b) should be compatible with, though not necessarily identical to, the values of the counsellor; and (c) are such that the degree to which they are attained should be externally observable. He further suggests that there are three types of goals, albeit sometimes interrelated, which meet his criteria and fall within the scope of the counsellor's responsibilities. These are: altering maladaptive behaviour, e.g. increasing socially assertive responses; learning the decision-making process, e.g. making a list of possible courses of action; and preventing problems, e.g. implementing a system of helping young men and women to select compatible marriage partners.[50] The goals of counselling are not always scientifically derived, since behaviourists recognize that there are many influences on the client's choice of goals and on the counsellor's choice of methods.

At the risk of introducing a level of generality which behavioural counsellors, with their emphasis on specific goals for individual clients, might find uncongenial, there follows an attempt to derive a series of goals for counselling and for living from the writings of the six behavioural theorists discussed in this and the preceding chapter. Such goals include:

1.   absence of deficits in behavioural repertoires;
2.   absence of weaknesses in behavioural repertoires;
3.   absence of debilitating anxiety reactions;
4.   capacity to relax;
5.   ability to assert oneself;
6.   adequacy at sexual functioning;
7.   capacity for self-control by shaping environmental consequences;
8.   capacity for self-control by cognitive self-regulation;
9.   adequacy as a behavioural model.

The above goals are for individuals. Of the behavioural theorists, Skinner in particular has focused on the need for groups to design environments in which humans can behave in more reinforcing ways. Thus, further behavioural goals might focus on groups and include the capacity for group self-control, both by shaping environmental consequences and also by cognitive self-regulation.

SELF-REFERENT EXERCISES

It may help you to understand this chapter better if, either with pencil and paper or in your head, you think about and answer the following questions.

1.   Can you give any examples from your own life of engaging in an incompatible activity in order to inhibit the anxiety you were experiencing in conjunction with another activity? If so, please describe them.

2.   Can you think of any of your 'neurotic' behaviours which not only have failed to extinguish but have actually been enhanced with the passage of time? If so, please describe them.

3.   Indicate any significant activity that you have learned by observing modelled behaviour. Describe the processes by which observational learning became an effective way of acquiring the desired behaviour.

4.   Discuss the concept of perceived self-efficacy in relation to one or more areas of your behaviour. Do you consider it a central mediating variable in whether or not you behave effectively?

5.   Give examples in which your current self-evaluative standards are:
(a) helping you to regulate your behaviour effectively and obtain positive self-reinforcement;
(b) hindering you from effectively regulating your behaviour and thus causing self-disparagement.

NOTES

1. Hilgard, E. R. & Bower, G. H. (1966) *Theories of Learning* (3rd ed.). New York: Appleton-Century-Crofts. For a review of the work of some important contributors to behavioural theory.
2. Wolpe, J. (1958) *Psychotherapy by Reciprocal Inhibition.* Stanford: Stanford University Press.
3. Wolpe, J. (1973) *The Practice of Behaviour Therapy* (2nd ed.). Oxford: Pergamon Press.
4. Wolpe, J. (1976) *Theme and Variations: A Behaviour Therapy Casebook.* Oxford: Pergamon Press.
5. Wolpe, J. (1958) *Psychotherapy by Reciprocal Inhibition* p. IX (Introduction). Stanford: Stanford University Press.
6. *Ibid.* p. 29.
7. *Ibid.* pp. 17–31.
8. *Ibid.* p. 71.
9. *Ibid.* p. 32.
10. *Ibid.* pp. 37–75.
11. Wolpe, J. (1976) *Theme and Variations. A Behaviour Therapy Casebook* pp. 31–80. Oxford. Pergamon Press. This is about one of the cats used in the experiments described in this chapter.
12. Wolpe, J. (1958) *Psychotherapy by Reciprocal Inhibition* p. 113. Stanford: Stanford University Press.
13. *Ibid.* pp. 105–220. For a discussion of practical applications of reciprocal inhibition.
14. Wolpe, J. (1973) *The Practice of Behaviour Therapy* pp. 80–179. Oxford: Pergamon Press. For a discussion of assertive training, systematic desensitization and treatment of inhibited sexual responses.
15. Eysenck, H. J. (1970) *The Structure of Human Personality* (3rd ed.). London: Methuen.
16. Eysenck, H. J. (1960) *Behaviour Therapy and The Neuroses.* Oxford: Pergamon Press.
17. Eysenck, H. J. & Rachman, S. (1965) *The Causes and Cures of Neurosis.* London: Routledge and Kegan Paul.
18. Eysenck, H. J. (1967) *The Biological Basis of Personality.* Springhill: C. C. Thomas.
19. Eysenck, H. J. (1977) *You and Neurosis.* Glasgow: Fontana/Collins.
20. Wolpe, J. (1965) *The Practice of Behaviour Therapy* p. vii. Oxford: Pergamon Press.
21. Eysenck, H. J. (1976) The learning theory model of neurosis – a new approach.

Behaviour Research and Therapy, **14**, 251–267. The major statement of the incubation theory of neurosis.

22. Eysenck, H. J. (1977) *You and Neurosis* p. 61–106. Glasgow: Fontana/Collins. A further statement of the incubation theory.

23. Eysenck, H. J. (1968) A theory of the incubation of anxiety/fear responses. *Behaviour Research and Therapy*, **6**, 309–321.

24. *Ibid*. pp. 312–316.

25. Eysenck, H. J. (1976) The learning theory model of neurosis – a new approach. *Behaviour Research and Therapy*, **14**, 260.

26. Bandura, A. & Walters, R. (1963) *Social Learning and Personality Development*. New York: Holt, Rinehart and Winston.

27. Bandura, A. (1969) *Principles of Behavior Modification*. New York: Holt, Rinehart and Winston.

28. Bandura, A. (1973) *Aggression: A Social Learning Analysis*. Englewood Cliffs, NJ: Prentice-Hall.

29. Bandura, A. (1977) *Social Learning Theory*. Englewood Cliffs, NJ; Prentice-Hall.

30. *Ibid*. pp. 9–13.

31. *Ibid*. pp. 194–213.

32. *Ibid*. pp. 160–191.

33. *Ibid*. pp. 16–17.

34. *Ibid*. p. 13.

35. *Ibid*. pp. 17–22.

36. *Ibid*. pp. 22–55. For a discussion of the role of modelling in originating behaviour.

37. Bandura, A. (1969) *Principles of Behavior Modification* pp. 118–216. New York: Holt, Rinehart and Winston. Chapter 3 is a lengthy exposition on modelling entitled 'Modelling and vicarious processes'.

38. Bandura, A., Adams, N. E. & Beyer, J. (1977) Cognitive processes mediating behavioural change. *Journal of Personality and Social Psychology*, **35**, 3, 125–139.

39. Bandura, A. (1977) *Social Learning Theory* pp. 22–29. Englewood Cliffs, NJ: Prentice-Hall.

40. *Ibid*. pp. 54–55.

41. Bandura, A. (1977) Self-efficacy: toward a unifying theory of behavioural change. *Psychological Review*, **84**, 2, 191–215.

42. Bandura, A. (1977) *Social Learning Theory* pp. 78–85. Englewood Cliffs, NJ: Prentice-Hall.

43. Bandura, A. (1977) Self-efficacy: toward a unifying theory of behavioural change. *Psychological Review*, **84**, 2, 193.

44. Bandura, A. (1976) Self-reinforcement: theoretical and methodological considerations. *Behaviourism*, **4**, 2, 135. Full reference pp. 135–155.

45. Bandura, A. (1977) *Social Learning Theory* pp. 128–158. Englewood Cliffs, NJ: Prentice-Hall. For a discussion on self-regulation.

46. Bandura, A., Jeffery, R. W. & Wright, C. L. (1974) Efficacy of participant modelling as a function of response induction aids. *Journal of Abnormal Psychology*, **83**, 56–64.

47. Bandura, A., Adams, N. E. & Beyer, J. (1977) Cognitive processes mediating behavioural change. *Journal of Personality and Social Psychology*, **35**, 3, 125–139.

48. Eysenck, H. J. (1978) Expectations as causal elements in behavioural change. *Advances in Behaviour Research and Therapy*, **1**, 171–175.

49. Wolpe, J. (1978) Self-efficacy theory and psychotherapeutic change: a square peg for a round hole. *Advances in Behaviour Research and Therapy*, **1**, 231–236.

50. Krumboltz, J. D. (1966) Behavioral goals for counselling. *Journal of Counseling Psychology*, **13**, 153–159.

8 – Occupational Choice and Development Theory: Developmental and Behavioural

SUMMARY: *Occupational choice and development considerations are pertinent to both work and leisure. Perhaps the four main theoretical viewpoints relating to careers are the developmental, behavioural, differentialist and structural viewpoints. The two main developmental theorists are Ginzberg, with his periods of occupational choice, and Super, with his stage theory of vocational self-concept development and implementation. Originally Ginzberg hypothesized that occupational choice was a process, largely irreversible, with compromise being an aspect of every choice. The process, involving periods of fantasy, tentative and realistic choice, was largely completed by the mid-20s. Ginzberg later revised his position to take into account the ideas that occupational choice could be a life-long process, not necessarily irreversible, and that people optimized the fit between themselves and the world of work.*

Super uses the notion of self-concept as an integrating focus. The five stages of vocational self-concept development are growth, exploration, establishment, maintenance and decline. Career development involves the formation and implementation of vocational self-concepts. It is a compromise process affected by biological heritage, personal and social determinants, opportunity to play various roles, and feedback. Vocational maturity refers to the manner in which people cope with the tasks appropriate to their life stage. Possible dimensions of vocational maturity for adolescents are autonomy, planfulness, exploration, career decision-making, knowledge and realism.

Krumboltz et al offer a behavioural approach to career development based on social learning theory. The development of career preferences and decision-making skills involves a complex interaction of four sources of influence: genetic endowment and special abilities, environmental conditions, learning experiences, and task-approach skills. Learning experiences may be instrumental, with behaviour being shaped by its consequences, or associative, e.g. learning by observing modelled behaviour. Instrumental and associative learning experiences can be positive or negative in helping people to develop adequate career preferences and realistic decision-making skills. Goodstein's analysis of the effects of anxiety on career decision-making is also reviewed briefly.

The term 'occupational choice and development theory' is used here in preference to 'vocational theory' or 'careers theory'. This is because the concept of occupations, or how people fill their time, encompasses both work and leisure activities. The term 'vocational' not only requires a further term, avocational, to describe leisure, but also has religious connotations of a divine call which may be inappropriate. Similarly, the term 'careers' requires a further term to describe non-career activities.

The scope of counselling psychology as applied to people's occupational life encompasses three main areas: (a) occupational choice and career development in the world of work; (b) occupational adjustment; and (c) the choice and development of leisure occupations. The next two chapters focus mainly on the first, but part of Chapter 9 is devoted to the third of these areas, which is becoming increasingly important as the impact of cybernetic advances makes itself felt. Needless to say, other roles, such as spouse, parent and citizen, might be regarded as occupations.

CHOICE AND DEVELOPMENT RELATING TO WORK

Crites suggests that there are five major approaches to career counselling: trait and factor, client-centred, psychodynamic, developmental and behavioural.[1] Daws writes of the differentialist, or talent-matching, and the developmental approaches to vocational guidance, but acknowledges the structural approach, that occupational choice is 'to be explained only in terms of a history of significant antecedent socially structured experiences' as a third approach to understanding work choice processes.[2] Holland and Gottfredson mention the developmental and the differentialist views as the two main traditions for understanding careers.[3] Although writers differ and each counselling theory may provide its own theoretical model for understanding the career choice process, in the next two chapters the approaches are grouped into four main theoretical viewpoints: developmental, behavioural, differentialist and structural. Historically the differentialist preceded the developmental and behavioural viewpoints. However, in line with the predominant orientations of the practice part of this book, we review the developmental and behavioural positions first.

DEVELOPMENTAL VIEWPOINT

The developmental viewpoint emphasizes the processes and stages of occupational choice and adjustment within the individual's life-span. The theoretical viewpoints tend to overlap, with, for instance, developmental and differentialist considerations influencing each other, since, on the one hand, individual differences in part reflect different developmental influences and, on the other hand, developmental theory needs to be sensitive to individual variations. Perhaps the main contributors to the developmental position have been Eli Ginzberg and Donald Super, to whose work we now turn. Anne Roe, who has written about the effects of different kinds of parenting on people's orientation towards other people and hence on their choice of career, might be considered to be another developmental theorist.[4,5]

Ginzberg's Occupational Choice Theory

Eli Ginzberg (1911–   ) has been professor of economics and Director of the Conservation of Human Resources Project at Columbia University. He was also chairman of the American National Manpower Advisory Committee. For much of his career he has been interested in empirical studies into borderline areas involving psychology and economics. Dissatisfied with the existing state of occupational choice theory, Ginzberg and his colleagues, Axelrad, Herma and Ginsburg, conducted research with a view to formulating a theory of occupational choice. In 1951 their findings and deliberations were published in *Occupational Choice: An Approach to a General Theory*.[6] In 1972 Ginzberg offered a restatement of the theory in light of further evidence.[7]

The original book was based largely on a sample of white American males, either Protestant or Catholic, of Anglo-Saxon background, and from fairly affluent families. There were eight interviews of different individuals at each of eight stages in the educational process: sixth grade in elementary school; eighth, tenth and twelfth grades in high school; the freshman and senior years in college; first-year graduate students and advanced graduate students. Additional interviews were conducted with 17 boys from a deprived economic environment and ten girls from Barnard College. Needless to say, the sources of data influence the findings.

Ginzberg and his colleagues viewed their original theory as a 'tentative formulation'. Although this early theory was based on a developmental approach, he considers that his reformulated theory represents more of a sociopsychological approach. The three basic elements in the 1951 statement of the theory of occupational choice are: (a) that it is a *process*; (b) the process is largely *irreversible*; and (c) *compromise* is an essential aspect of every choice.[8] Each of the major elements in the 1951 formulation is reviewed here along with its 1972 revision.

Process

The original theory stated that the process of occupational decision-making could be analysed in terms of three periods – fantasy, tentative and realistic – each of which may be differentiated by the way the individual 'translates' his impulses and needs into an occupational choice. These three stages may be seen in Table 8.1. During the period of *fantasy* choices the child thinks of an occupation in terms of the wish to be an adult, and choices are arbitrary and made without reference to reality.

The period of *tentative* choices is divided into the interest, capacity, value, and transition stages. Pubescent boys and girls first approach their occupational choice in terms of current likes and interests. During the capacity stage children take their capacity or suitability for an occupation into consideration much more. At around 15

Table 8.1 *Ginzberg's periods of occupational choice and Super's stages of voca-tional self-concept development*

Ginzberg's periods of occupational choice	Super's stages of vocational self-concept development
1. Fantasy choices (ages 6–11)	1. Growth stage (birth–14)
2. Tentative choices (ages 11–17)	Fantasy (4–10)
Interest stage (11–12)	Interest (11–12)
Capacity stage (13–14)	Capacity (13–14)
Value stage (15–16)	2. Exploration stage (ages 15–24)
Transition stage (17)	Tentative (15–17)
3. Realistic choices (age 17–mid 20s)	Transition (18–21)
Exploration	Trial, little commitment (22–24)
Crystallization	3. Establishment stage (ages 25–44)
Specification	Trial, commitment and
4. Lifelong choice process	stabilization (25–30)
	Advancement (31–44)
	4. Maintenance stage (ages 45–64)
	5. Decline stage (age 65 onwards)
	Deceleration (65–70)
	Retirement (71 onwards)

or 16 years of age young people enter the value stage, where they become aware for the first time of a range of occupational-choice factors connected with their goals and values. In the transition stage, or around the time young Americans move from high school to college, individuals start shifting their focus from predominantly subjective factors, such as interests, capacities and values, to the reality considerations of work, such as working conditions, length of preparation and financial rewards.

The period of *realistic* choices is divided into the exploration, crystallization, and specification stages. During the exploration stage the college freshman tries to acquire the information and experience that will help him to make an occupational choice. Sources of occupationally related data include exploring various subjects of study and talks with teachers and careers advisers. Crystallization is the culmination of the preceding choice processes. At this stage the individual has made an assessment of many relevant subjective and external factors and has become committed to a vocational objective, even though the details may remain unclear. The specification stage, which involves specialization and planning within the area of choice, is the time when such details are clarified. For instance, during the crystallization stage a person may decide to become a physicist, then during the specification stage will decide which branch of physics and whether to work in academic life, government or industry.

Ginzberg and his colleagues acknowledged that there would be variability within the occupational-choice process. For example, entry to both the tentative and realistic choice periods may differ by as much as two years. Furthermore, some individuals pursue a chosen occupation, such as doctor or engineer, from an early age, whereas the more typical pattern involves a narrowing down from an initially broad range of options to a specific choice. Some individuals present a major deviation in the occupational-choice process through their inability to crystallize a choice. There is some evidence that such deviations reflect basic emotional difficulties.[9]

In Ginzberg's 1972 restatement he no longer considered the process of occupational decision-making to be limited to a decade, but believed it could be a life-long process as long as people expect to make decisions about work and career. For instance, even some professional people may move into related and sometimes even different types of work. Furthermore, the career patterns of women often involve career development and decisions marked by movements between home and work. Three principal factors which contribute to a 'lifelong dynamizing of the choice process' are: (a) the feedback going on between a person's original career choice and the satisfactions and opportunities of their actual work experience; (b) the degrees of freedom that emerge through changing family circumstances, such as when children grow up; and (c) the pressures arising out of a job that force a person to look for new employment or accept early retirement.[10]

Irreversibility

The original theory stated that the process of occupational choice was largely irreversible. The essential resource that becomes committed during this process is time. Time pressures come from two sources. First, in our culture people are expected to perform various developmental tasks, such as occupational adjustment, within various time parameters, and getting behind may involve difficulties in obtaining financial support as well as being out of step with peers. Second, if mistakes have been made, it may take additional time to get the necessary education and training for new occupational choices. The greater the amount of time invested in the previous decision, the more likely this is to be the case. Psychological barriers can also influence people not to change earlier decisions, since this may involve admitting mistakes and failure, which may be threatening to self-esteem. Also, a change of occupational choice involves the capacity to admit that certain values may not be so important as previously thought.[11]

Ginzberg's 1972 restatement modifies, if not reverses, the notion of irreversibility in that, while earlier decisions have a shaping influence on people's later careers, so do the continuing changes that they undergo in work and in life. For instance, if a young worker succeeds in obtaining employment with a large company with an internal training and promotion scheme, earlier occupational decisions may become relatively unimportant in determining eventual occupation.[12]

Compromise

The original formulation asserted the inevitability of compromise in crystallizing an occupational choice. During the tentative period the individual strives to establish a compromise between interests, capacities and values. This might be seen as a compromise between subjective factors. Another kind of compromise is that between subjective factors, such as interest, and educational requirements for different occupations. For example, a prospective medical student may not have much time to pursue an interest in English literature. In the final analysis, occupational choice represents a compromise between subjective factors and the world of work by which the individual hopes to gain maximum work satisfaction.[13]

In his 1972 restatement Ginzberg prefers the dynamic term '*optimization*' to the static term 'compromise'. People are in a continuing search to find the best occupational fit between their changing desires and circumstances. Each time they consider altering their work and career, they go through a process of analysing the costs and gains and of trying to optimize the gains.[14]

Ginzberg's reformulated theory is that 'occupational choice is a lifelong process of decison-making in which the individual seeks to find the optimal fit between his career preparation and goals and the realities of the world of work'.[15] He still considers individuals as the prime movers in the decision-making process, especially if they are prepared to take advantage of available options for shaping their lives and careers. However, individuals face many past and present constraints on occupational choice, especially if they grow up in adverse circumstances. Such circumstances include coming from a low-income family, limitations of parental education and values, schools which entrap young people in, rather than liberate them from, low-income environments, and guidance in the educational system that does not reflect the lessened discrimination in work settings against women and minority groups.[16]

Super's Self-concept Theory of Vocational Development

Like Ginzberg, Donald E. Super (1910–   ) has spent the major part of his professional life at Columbia University in New York City, where he became professor of psychology and also head of the psychology division at Teachers College. Super, in fact, is further connected to Ginzberg in that he conducted a review of the American literature on occupational choice for Ginzberg et al's 1951 book.[17] Super also has links with Britain, having been a student at Oxford University and having held a three-year, post-retirement senior research fellowship with the National Institute for Careers Education and Counselling, based in Cambridge.

Until the early 1950s American vocational guidance had been heavily dominated by the talent-matching or differentialist approach espoused by the pioneer of the vocational guidance movement, Frank Parsons, whose position was that vocational choice consists of three phases: (a) knowledge of self; (b) knowledge of the world of work; and (c) a true assessment of the relations between these two groups of facts.[18] What appeared to Super to be a mechanical matching of men and occupations, often involving the General Aptitude Test Battery of the US Employment Service and Strong's Vocational Interest Blank, was incompatible with the growing developmental and clinical emphasis in psychology. His work represents an attempt to bridge the gap between vocational psychology and personality theory by conceptualizing occupational choice as the formulation and implementation of a self-concept.[19] In Super's important work, *The Psychology of Careers*,[20] he uses the notion of self-concept as an integrating focus for vocational choice and development throughout the whole of the individual's life-span. Furthermore, the role of the occupational counselling psychologist is viewed as helping the client to develop, clarify and implement a satisfactory and realistically based vocational self-concept.

Elements of vocational self-concept theory

Super sees three elements in the process by which self-concept affects vocational development, namely, the processes of formation, translation and implementation of the self-concept. From infancy people start developing a concept of themselves, and this process goes on throughout life. Exploration is one way in which people engage in the *formation* of self-concepts. For instance, an adolescent may try to write poetry or do some metal-work. Self-differentiation, a process in which people note differences from others in the way they react and approach tasks, also contributes to self-concept formation. Identification with people within the family or with those who visit the home is another way. Role playing, either in imagination or in overt behaviour, gives people the opportunity to explore self-concepts, as indeed do reality-testing experiences, which either strengthen or modify self-concepts. *Translation* of self-concepts into occupational terms may come about through such processes as identification with an adult in a favoured occupational role, experience in roles in which people may find themselves, and awareness of possession of talents and capacities that lend themselves to particular occupations. The *implementation* of a self-concept may come about as professional training, such as that required for engineering or teaching, is entered, or it may take place as individuals enter their first jobs. Futhermore, the development of a career may be viewed as a continuing process of self-concept implementation.[21]

Stages of vocational self-concept development

Super based his stages of vocational self-concept development, depicted in Table 8.1, on the psychological life stages defined by Buehler as a result of her analysis of life histories.[22] The processes of exploration, establishment, maintenance and decline involve all aspects of living and are pertinent to both females and males, with the age limits to be considered as approximations. Self-concept development takes place as follows.[23,24]

Growth. During the growth stage (age 0–14) the child's vocational self-concept begins to be formed by the processes, such as identification, described in the previous section. Although fantasy needs are important early in this stage, interests and capacities come to play an increasingly prominent role.

Exploration. The exploration stage (age 15–24) lasts from adolescence into early adulthood. During this stage individuals explore themselves, other people's occupational roles, and the occupational world. Sources of occupational self-concept data are contacts with others, activities, experiences, and role-playing in the home, school and in part-time work. At first occupational choices are likely to be tentative and tried out in fantasy, discussion with others and role experimentation. In the transitional phase reality considerations become more important as the young person takes the first steps in implementing a vocational self-concept. A period of trial implementation of the self-concept in a chosen occupation then follows.

Establishment. During the *establishment* stage (age 25–44) there may be problems of trial and floundering as the young adult attempts to gain a secure vocational self-concept. In some instances there will be shifting of jobs, which may either lead to the person's finding his life's work or be the precursor of a series of jobs. Especially in the professions, there may be little trial and floundering. With the vocational self-concept becoming firmer, an effort is made to advance and establish a secure place in the world of work.

Maintenance. By the maintenance stage (age 45–64) the individual is likely to be well established and the task may be less that of breaking new ground than that of successfully preserving an existing self-concept. However, challenges may arise, for example from new developments in a field, which may entail mastery of additional competencies. In general, the maintenance stage is likely to be one of fruition and self-fulfilment. However, for those who have not achieved stabilization in a suitable occupation, the maintenance period is likely to be one of frustration. Wise people start adjusting their self-concepts and planning for retirement during this stage.

Decline. The decline stage (age 65 on) is characterized by a slowing down of physical and mental processes and by decreasing energy. Here the task is that of adjusting to a new self by changing a self-concept, with related work habits, which has remained relatively stable for a generation. In the deceleration phase the individual may take on a lighter load and in other ways alter work patterns to suit declining capacities. Part-time jobs and hobbies may replace full-time occupation. Although there are great variations in the age of retirement and in complete stopping of work, this is handled constructively by some while others find it a period of difficulty and disappointment.

Life-span, life-space career self-concept development

In a later paper[25] Super broadens his view of self-concept development to take into account the variety of roles that people play in their life-space at any one of the life-stages in their life-span. Super identifies nine major roles (child, student, 'leisurite', citizen, worker, spouse, homemaker, parent, and pensioner) and four principal theatres in which the roles are played (home, community, school and workplace). He defines a career as the combination and sequence of roles played by a person during his lifetime. Career self-concept development takes into account the combinations, interactions and varying roles played by people during each life-stage. The combination of roles at any given time constitutes a person's life-style. The importance of the varying roles is operationally defined by the amount of *time* and *emotion* invested in them. But time and emotional investment in specific roles may fluctuate at different stages of the life-cycle. Within a person's overall life-cycle there are numerous decision points concerned with adding, dropping or modifying roles. Often decisions about roles are interrelated, for example possible decisions about obtaining work and getting married.

Determinants of career self-concept development

Super acknowledges that the decision points of a life career take place within a variety of interacting economic, social and psychological determinants.[26] These determinants affect role preferences, choices, entry, changes and performance. Economic and general determinants include business cycles, technological change and war. Social determinants include socioeconomic status, education, citizenship, race, religion and gender. Psychological and personal determinants include biological heritage, intelligence, special aptitudes, interests and needs.

A theory of vocational self-concept development

In an early paper,[27] Super criticized Ginzberg's theory of occupational choice as insufficiently describing the compromise process. He offered a summary statement of a comprehensive theory of vocational self-concept based on ten propositions. It should be noted that this statement refers mainly to self-concept development in work. The ten propositions are described briefly here.

1. Individual difference in aptitudes, interests and values are significant for vocational development.
2. Multipotentiality, or the fact that individuals have the potential for self-realizing in a number of different occupations, is a well-established fact.
3. Occupational ability patterns, the characteristic patterning of abilities and interests required for different occupations, are highly relevant to job satisfaction and success.
4. Vocational preferences and competencies change with time and experience, thus making the formation, translation and implementation of a vocational self-concept a continuous process.
5. This continuous process may be depicted in a series of life stages of vocational self-concept development.
6. Career patterns, the level, frequency, duration and stability of jobs, have personal, socioeconomic and chance determinants.
7. Development of vocational self-concepts through the life stages can be guided by the provision of adequate opportunities for the maturation of abilities and interests, including counselling and reality testing.
8. Vocational development involves the continuous development and implementation of a self-concept and, as such, is a compromise process in which the evolving self-concept is a product of biological heritage, personal and social determinants, opportunity to play various roles, and feedback about the results of role playing.
9. Role playing, whether in fantasy, discussion or overt behaviour involving actual try-outs, is central to the compromise process.
10. Work not only involves doing a job but also involves a way of life and, furthermore, is relevant to personal as well as vocational adjustment, both of which are most likely to result when people's vocational self-concepts and life-styles are congruent with their aptitudes, interests and values

Vocational maturity

Vocational development is viewed as one aspect of individual development in the same manner as social, emotional and intellectual development. Super observes: 'The concept of vocational development leads logically to that of vocational maturity'.[28] He views vocational development as a continuum and vocational maturity as the degree of development attained on this continuum. Following Ginzberg et al, he identifies five dimensions of vocational maturity – the degrees to which individuals: (a) are oriented to making vocational choices; (b) have adequate information about jobs and are capable of carrying out plans; (c) are increasingly consistent in their vocational preferences; (d) show increasing crystallization of abilities and traits to provide a basis for consistent action; and (e) demonstrate an increasing wisdom in their vocational preferences.[29] Thus vocational maturity refers to the readiness and manner in which people cope with the developmental tasks of their life stages.

For some years Super and his colleagues have been working on a satisfactory measure of vocational maturity for adolescents. Super et al's *Career Development Inventory*[30] has attained a number of versions. Resulting from his work in Britain in the late 1970s, Table 8.2 indicates some of Super's more recent thinking on the dimensions of vocational maturity. The concept of vocational maturity arising out of Super's and Ginzberg's work has generated much research interest. Further measures of vocational maturity include Westbrook's *Cognitive Vocational Maturity Test*,[32,33] Crites' *Career Maturity Inventory*[34,35] and Daws' *Keele Occupational Crystallisation Self-Appraisal Form*.[36]

Concluding Comments

The occupational choice and development stages of both Ginzberg and Super have been formulated in an American context, and it would be interesting to find out the extent to which occupational choice and development processes are similar in Britain. Therefore it is welcome that a start has been made in Britain on developing indices of vocational maturity or, in other words, of effective occupational decision-making.

It is interesting to speculate on the extent to which vocational maturity reflects emotional maturity. Super's notion of vocational choice being a process involving the formation and implementation of occupational self-concepts still leaves unanswered the central developmental concern of whether the individual's occupational self-concept is based on conditions of worth or on other people's values rather than the individual's own. In other words, the process of occupational choice involves not just an external compromise between the individual and the world of work, but also some form of internal compromise between the individual's own needs and residues of parental and cultural influences. The notion of autonomy in Super's recent work goes some, but not all, of the way towards evaluating the extent to which people are open to their *own* experience and, also, do not have their decision-making processes distorted by anxiety and unexamined internalizations of other people's values. Such considerations may be critical as a counselling psychologist helps an adolescent with occupational choice, or works with an older person handling a mid-career crisis.

Table 8.2 *Vocational maturity: career development attitudes, knowledge and skills suggested for Britain*[31]

Dimension	Description
Autonomy (a) Attitude (b) Behaviour	Shows appropriate balance, at each life stage, of dependence and independence in decision-making, locus of control, acceptance of responsibility for decisions, and taking consequences.
Planfulness (a) Attitude: looks ahead (b) Behaviour: plans and acts	Recognizes impending developmental tasks and changing opportunities. Takes short-term, medium-term and long-term planning needs into account; identifies steps to take and seeks ways of implementation; recognizes contingencies and sees alternatives.
Exploration (a) Attitude, with cognitive component (b) Behaviour	Is willing to use appropriate resources (people, materials, activities) for the exploration of educational and occupational opportunities and for self-understanding. Uses school and community resources to learn about them and self with good results.
Career decision-making Cognitive, with strong attitudinal component	Knows decision-making principles and can apply them to career decisions at various stages of a career. Considers alternatives, seeks information about the various determinants and the weight to give them; knows satisfactions sought and probable attainability; understands and can assess different styles of decision-making.
Knowledge Cognitive (a) World of work (b) Knowledge of preferred occupational field	Knows about a variety of occupations and something of the mores of the world of work, including needed education and training, entry requirements and methods, duties, supply and demand, working conditions, and advancement and retirement. Knows the important facts about the occupational field that appeals most.
Realism (Late maturing) (a) Attitude (b) Cognitive	Recognizes that self and situational knowledge may be limited and seeks to improve these; knows something of own capacities and personality and relates these to educational and occupational opportunities; has stable but flexible goals and is consistent in efforts to attain them; identifies new objectives as new situations require.

Acknowledgement of permission to reproduce the material in Table 8.2 is made to the Career Development Research Seminar, NICEC, a working paper by J. M. Kidd, E. G. Knasel, D. E. Super and R. Ward.

Implicit in the developmental viewpoint is a focus on life planning and self-directed development. The role of educational institutions and of counsellors is that of facilitating the processes involved in the various stages of occupational choice and development. Thus the developmental emphasis lends support to careers education as well as to counselling interventions. Furthermore, educational and counselling interventions may be appropriate during each of the life stages and should not be restricted to the initial period of occupational preference, choice and entry. For instance, some people might benefit from education and counselling concerning their impending or actual retirement.

BEHAVIOURAL VIEWPOINT

The behavioural viewpoint, or perhaps more correctly behavioural viewpoints, involves the transfer to the area of occupational choice and development of many of the concepts presented earlier from behavioural theory, such as reinforcement and modelling. It has a distinctly developmental emphasis in as much as contingencies of reinforcement etc. can influence individuals at any point before, during or after their working lives. Also, it acknowledges both differentialist and structuralist considerations. However, compared with the differentialist and developmental viewpoints, it is a relative newcomer to occupational psychology, with almost all the behavioural theorizing and experimentation relating to careers being conducted since the early 1960s. Perhaps the leading proponent of the behavioural approach to careers work has been Krumboltz, and it is his social learning theory of career selection which is presented here. This is followed by a short report of another behavioural theoretical position.

Krumboltz's Social Learning Theory

John Krumboltz (1928–   ) has been a professor in the school of education at Stanford University in California, where Bandura is a professor of psychology. Krumboltz's social learning theory of career selection in part reflects Bandura's influence. For many years Krumboltz and his colleagues have been conducting a series of experiments on the processes of career selection, with particular emphasis on career decision-making processes such as the reinforcement and modelling of information-seeking and exploratory behaviour.[37,38,39] Krumboltz et al offer an attempt at a social learning explanation of both the acquisition of educational preferences and skills and also the decision-making processes involved in the selection of courses, occupations and fields of work.[40]

Influencers of career decision-making

People's career decisions are influenced by the interactions of genetic factors, environmental conditions, learning experiences and performance skills. Table 8.3 depicts what Krumboltz et al perceive to be the four influencers of career decision-making. At every decision-making point there are a number of decision options and,

Table 8.3 *Krumboltz et al's four influencers of career decision-making*[41]

Genetic endowment and special abilities	Environmental conditions and events	Learning experiences	Task approach skills
Race Sex Physical characteristics Physical handicaps Examples of predispositions interacting with environment intelligence musical ability artistic ability muscular co-ordination	Number and nature of job opportunities Number and nature of training opportunities Social policies and procedures for selecting trainees and workers Rate of return for various occupations Labour laws and union rules Physical events such as earthquakes, droughts, floods, hurricanes Availability of and demand for natural resources Technological developments Changes in social organization Family training experience and resources Education system Neighbourhood and community influences	Instrumental learning experiences acting on environment to produce consequences Associative learning experiences responding to external stimuli, e.g. classical conditioning, modelling	Problem-related skills Performance to standards and values Work habits Perceptual and cognitive processes, e.g. attending, encoding Mental sets Emotional responses

once made, decisions increase or decrease the options available for future decisions. *Genetic endowment* and *special abilities* may set limits on an individual's educational and occupational preferences, skills and entry. Sometimes, as in the case of musical ability, career possibilities are opened up by the favourable interaction of genetic potential and environmental circumstances. *Environmental conditions and events* may be outside the influence of individuals, though at other times individuals may influence their environments. In general, individuals can have little impact on macro-environmental conditions such as technological developments, but more influence on micro-environmental conditions such as the hiring behaviour of a prospective employer.

People's past and current *learning experiences* influence their educational and occupational choice and development. One major learning category is that of *instrumental* learning experiences, which reflect Skinner's reinforcement ideas. People's occupational behaviours are shaped by successive reinforcement experiences, which both provide consequences for past behaviours and influence probabilities of future behaviours. The other major category is that of *associative* learning experiences where, in the first instance, the individual's response pattern to external stimuli is reactive rather than enactive. This category of experience covers observational learning, in which the individual observes the behaviours of real or fictitious models. Furthermore, it includes contiguous associations in which a previously neutral situation may be paired with some emotionally positive or negative reaction, for example by hearing remarks like 'All lawyers are crooked'. Pavlovian classical conditioning is also included here, as in the case of a man who does not want to become a physician because as a boy he became nauseous at the sight of blood.

Resulting from interactions between the three previously mentioned influencers, individuals bring to each new task or problem a set of *task-approach skills*. Krumboltz et al define task-approach skills as 'cognitive and performance abilities and emotional predispositions for coping with the environment, interpreting it in relation to self-observation generalisations, and making covert or overt predictions about future events'.[42] Table 8.3 lists some broad categories of task-approach skills. More specific task-approach skills relating to career decision-making include value clarifying, problem defining, alternative generating, information seeking, evaluating consequences of alternatives, eliminating and selecting alternatives, and planning.[43]

Self-observation generalizations

Krumboltz et al introduce cognitive mediating variables into their theory of career selection by means of self-observation generalizations. A self-observation generalization is defined as 'an overt or a covert self-statement evaluating one's own actual or vicarious performance in relation to learned standards'.[44] Individuals observe their performance in relation both to others' performances and to their own past performance. Self-observation generalizations may be explicit, such as 'Last time I went for a job interview I got on well and I know I can do well again', or vague, such as in a feeling of discomfort or anxiety before an interview. Self-observation generalizations are not necessarily accurate, since originally they may have been based on inaccurate feedback from significant others and can be maintained wrongly by people continuing to reinforce these inaccurate self-observations. Career interests and preferences are self-observation generalizations derived from prior learning experiences. Interests, as such, do not cause occupational selection, since they in turn are caused by prior learning experiences. Thus career interests and preferences are not static but can be influenced by future learning experiences.

Learning experiences and career preference

Although learning experiences produce preferences, actual entry into training or work is not a simple function of preferences but is influenced by many of the complex environmental factors mentioned earlier, such as availability of employment opportunities. In fact, environmental, economic, social and cultural events impinge upon learning experiences. For instance, a drop in the birthrate may reduce the demand for teachers, which may in turn make approach behaviours regarding teaching less positively reinforced. Occupational selection is a life-long process involving the sequential cumulative effects of numerous learning experiences, their interaction with environmental circumstances, and the individual's reactions and self-observation generalizations to these factors. Krumboltz et al give the example of Barbara, a white female with no physical handicaps who, given one set of learning experiences and environmental circumstances, when aged 30 works as a waitress. However, Barbara, given a different set of learning experiences and environmental circumstances, at the same age works as a general practitioner in a poor rural area.[45]

Educational and occupational preferences are viewed as evaluative self-observation generalizations acquired mainly through positive and negative learning influences. Table 8.4 gives illustrative examples of instrumental and associative learning experiences which are conducive or detrimental to developing self-observation generalizations which constitute preferences for various courses, occupations or fields of work. A more concrete example of positive instrumental learning experiences influencing career selection would be that of boys who are consistently positively reinforced for their science performance being more likely to indicate an interest in a science career than those not so reinforced. An example of negative associative learning through the vicarious reinforcement of models might be that of students acquiring reservations about expressing a career preference for teaching because some of their teacher-trained friends are unable to find teaching jobs.

Learning experiences and career decision-making skills

Career decision-making skills are viewed as a subset of task-approach skills. Like career preferences, career decision-making skills are acquired mainly through learning experiences. Table 8.5 gives illustrative examples of learning experiences helpful or harmful to developing effective career decision-making skills. For instance, pupils and students who are given a course in decision-making skills and whose efforts on the course are positively reinforced may be more likely to apply those skills to future

Table 8.4 *Illustrative positive and negative instrumental and associative learning experiences influencing career preferences*[46]

Mode of learning	Learning experiences influencing preferences	
	Positive	Negative
Instrumental	Being positively reinforced for engaging in activities associated with the successful performance of a course, occupation, field of work.	Being punished and/or not being reinforced for engaging in activities associated with the successful performance of a course, occupation, field of work.
Associative	Observing a valued model being reinforced for engaging in activities associated with the successful performance of a course, occupation, field of work.	Observing a model receiving punishment and/or little or no reinforcement for engaging in activities associated with the successful performance of a course, occupation, field of work.
Associative	Being exposed to positive words and images associated with a course, occupation, field of work.	Being exposed to negative words and images associated with a course, occupation, field of work.
Instrumental and associative	Being consistently positively reinforced by a valued person who models and/or advocates engaging in a course, occupation, field of work.	

Table 8.5 *Hypothesized positive and negative instrumental and associative learning experiences influencing career decision-making skills*[47]

Mode of learning	Learning experiences influencing career decision-making skills	
	Positive	Negative
Instrumental	Being positively reinforced for cognitive and performance skills and emotional responses necessary for career planning, self-observing, goal setting and information seeking.	Being negatively reinforced for cognitive and performance skills and emotional responses necessary for career planning, self-observing, goal setting and information seeking.
Associative	Observing real or vicarious models engaged in effective career decision-making strategies.	Observing real or vicarious models receiving punishment and little or no reinforcement for attempting to engage in career decision-making activities.
Availability of learning experience	Having access to people and other resources with the necessary career decision-making information.	Having little or no access to people and other resources with the necessary career decision-making information.

problems than are pupils and students whose decision-making efforts are constantly overruled and punished. Similarly, pupils and students who observe models engaging in effective decision-making strategies may be more likely to engage in similar behaviour than are those not observing the models. Furthermore, pupils and students who have ready access to careers information and simulated vocational problem-solving material may be more likely to develop career decision-making skills than are those who do not. Within the limits of practical research designs, instrumental and associative learning experiences lend themselves to being formulated into testable hypotheses to be proved or disproved. As indicated earlier, Krumboltz and his colleagues are assiduous researchers.

Implications for counselling

The processes of career selection are complex, since they represent the interaction of many influences over a long period of time. The role of the careers counsellor is to help clients to obtain a set of decision-making skills by which career preference, training and entry decisions can be made as rationally as possible. Furthermore, counsellors should help clients both to set up appropriate career-exploration learning experiences and to evaluate the personal consequences of these experiences.

Another Behavioural Viewpoint

Anxiety-focused

Goodstein raises the issue of anxiety in behavioural approaches to career problems.[48,49] Anxiety is defined as 'a learned or acquired emotional reaction to an originally neutral stimulus'.[50] Goodstein observes that there are two general reasons for maladaptive career choice behaviour, both involving anxiety. First, clients may have had inadequate opportunity to acquire adequate information for formulating and implementing vocational plans, the consequence of which may be anxiety stemming from failure to make such plans. Here anxiety seemingly plays a small role in the aetiology of the problem, and is mainly the cause of clients' not availing themselves of other non-counselling resources for vocational problem-solving.

Second, clients' failure to engage in adaptive and adequate career-choosing responses may not be the result of lack of opportunity, but rather inability to collect information or use opportunities because of the interfering effects of anxiety. For some people, making a vocational decision may arouse intense anxiety. Goodstein observes that it could mean becoming independent of parents or defying them, or becoming committed to an academic or work endeavour for which the client does not feel ready. One way to contain the anxiety may be to avoid making the vocational decision, which is difficult, since there are strong social pressures on adolescents and young adults to make such decisions.

The behavioural counsellor must decide in each instance the degree to which vocational indecision represents *consequent* anxiety, through lack of opportunity to acquire adequate vocational information, and the degree to which it represents *interfering* anxiety, which has prevented the client from acquiring or using the skills relevant to decision-making. In the former instance the counselling approach is more likely to be focused on the acquisition of information. However, in the latter the counselling approach may need to start by identifying the cues that arouse the anxiety so that it may be eliminated or reduced; then, if necessary, engaging in skills acquisition and development.[51]

Concluding Comment

The developmental and behavioural viewpoints on occupational choice and development seem to converge in a number of areas. For example, Krumboltz et al's ideas of
acquisition of self-observation generalizations that affect career selection bear affinity
to the developmental ideas about the formation and implementation of vocational
self-concepts. Also, the developmental descriptions of dimensions of vocational
maturity go some way to being behavioural descriptions of career decision-making
skills. One of the reasons for the similarity between the developmental and behavioural viewpoints described here is that Krumboltz et al's social learning theory of
career selection is a cognitive-behavioural rather than a radical behavioural position
based on a straightforward S–R paradigm.

SELF-REFERENT EXERCISES

It may help you to understand this chapter better if, either with pencil and paper or in
your head, you think about and answer the following questions:

1.   Give examples of your occupational choices in relation to the following
        periods of Ginzberg's theory:

        (a) fantasy choices;
        (b) tentative choices;
        (c) realistic choices.

2.   If possible, within the framework of Super's developmental stages identify
        critical factors in the formation and implementation of your vocational
        self-concept. Please be as specific as possible.

3.   Assess your levels of vocational maturity on the following dimensions (see
        Table 8.2 for fuller descriptions):

        (a) autonomy;
        (b) planfulness;
        (c) exploration;
        (d) career decision-making;
        (e) knowledge;
        (f) realism.

4.   Regarding the development of your own *career preferences*, give at least
        one example of each of the following:

        (a) a positive instrumental learning experience;

(b)   a negative instrumental learning experience;
(c)   a positive associative learning experience;
(d)   a negative associative learning experience.

5.   Regarding the development of your own *career decision-making skills*, give
          at least one example of each of the following:

(a)   a positive instrumental learning experience;
(b)   a negative instrumental learning experience;
(c)   a positive associative learning experience;
(d)   a negative associative learning experience.

NOTES

1.   Crites, J. O. (1974) Career counselling: a review of major approaches. *The Counseling Psychologist*, **4**, 3, 3–23.
2.   Daws, P. P. (1978) The changing purpose of vocational guidance. In Scottish Council for Research in Education. *School and After: A European Symposium* pp. 115 126. Windsor: NFER.
3.   Holland, J. L. & Gottfredson, G. D. (1976) Using a typology of persons and environments to explain careers: some extensions and clarifications. *The Counseling Psychologist*, **6**, 3, 20–29.
4.   Roe, A. (1956) *Psychology of Occupations*. New York: Wiley.
5.   Roe, A. (1957) Early determinants of vocational choice. *Journal of Counseling Psychology*, **4**, 212–217.
6.   Ginzberg, E., Ginsburg, S. W., Axelrad, S. & Herma, J. L. (1951) *Occupational Choice: An Approach to a General Theory*. New York: Columbia University Press.
7.   Ginzberg, E. (1972) Toward a theory of occupational choice: a restatement. *Vocational Guidance Quarterly*, March, 169–176.
8.   Ginzberg, E., Ginsburg, S. W., Axelrad, S. & Herma, J. L. (1951) *Occupational Choice: An Approach to a General Theory* p. 186. New York: Columbia University Press.
9.   *Ibid.* pp. 59–130, 185–198.
10. Ginzberg, E. (1972) Toward a theory of occupational choice: a restatement. *Vocational Guidance Quarterly*, March, 169–170.
11. Ginzberg, E., Ginsburg, S. W., Axelrad, S. & Herma, J. L. (1951) *Occupational Choice: An Approach to a General Theory* pp. 193–196. New York: Columbia University Press.
12. Ginzberg, E. (1972) Toward a theory of occupational choice: a restatement. *Vocational Guidance Quarterly*, March, 171.
13. Ginzberg, E., Ginsburg, S. W., Axelrad, S. & Herma, J. L. (1951) *Occupational Choice: An Approach to a General Theory* pp. 196–198. New York: Columbia University Press.
14. Ginzberg, E. (1972) Toward a theory of occupational choice: a restatement. *Vocational Guidance Quarterly*, March, 171–172.
15. *Ibid.* p. 172.
16. *Ibid.* pp. 173–175.
17. Ginzberg, E., Ginsburg, S. W., Axelrad, S. & Herma, J. L. (1951) *Occupational Choice: An Approach to a General Theory* p. 16. New York: Columbia University Press.
18. Parsons, F. (1909) *Choosing A Vocation*. Boston: Houghton Mifflin.
19. Super, D. E. (1963) *Career Development: Self-concept Theory* pp. 1–16. New York: College Entrance Examination Board. Reprinted in Zytowski, D. G. (ed.) (1968)

Vocational Behavior: Readings in Theory and Research pp. 194–207. New York: Holt, Rinehart and Winston.

20. Super, D. E. (1957) *The Psychology of Careers.* New York: Harper and Row.
21. Super, D. E. (1968) Career development: self-concept theory. In D. G. Zytowski (ed.), *Vocational Behavior: Readings in Theory and Research* pp. 203–205. New York: Holt, Rinehart and Winston.
22. Buehler, C. (1933) *Der Menschliche Lebenslauf als Psychologisches Problem.* Leipzig: Hirzel.
23. Super, D. E. (1957) *The Psychology of Careers* pp. 69–161. New York: Harper and Row.
24. Super, D. E. & Jordaan, J. P. (1973) Career development theory. *British Journal of Guidance and Counselling,* **1,** 3–4. Full reference pp. 3–16.
25. Super, D. E. (1980) A life-span, life-space approach to career development. *Journal of Vocational Behavior,* **16,** 282–298.
26. Super, D. E. & Bohn, M. J. (1970) *Occupational Psychology* pp. 145–146. London: Tavistock Publications.
27. Super, D. E. (1953) A theory of vocational development. *American Psychologist,* **8,** 4, 185–190. Reprinted in Hopson, B. & Hayes, J. (1968) *The Theory and Practice of Vocational Guidance* pp. 13–23. Oxford: Pergamon Press.
28. Super, D. E. (1957) *The Psychology of Careers* p. 185. New York: Harper and Row.
29. *Ibid.* pp. 187–189.
30. Super, D. E., Thompson, A. S., Lindeman, R. H., Jordaan, J. P. & Myers, R. A. (1981) *Career Development Inventory.* Palo Alto: Consulting Psychologists Press. The *Users' Manual* is written by Thompson and Lindeman, with the collaboration of the others, same date.
31. Table 8.2 is from a handout sent to the author by Professor Super on 17 July 1979. It comes from a working paper by J. M. Kidd, E. G. Knasel, D. E. Super and R. Ward, Career Development Research Seminar, NICEC, Cambridge.
32. Westbrook, B. W. (1970) *Cognitive Vocational Maturity Test.* Raleigh, NC: North Carolina State University.
33. Westbrook, B. W. (1974) Content analysis of six career development tests. *Measurement and Evaluation in Guidance,* **7,** 172–180.
34. Crites, J. O. (1973) *Career Maturity Inventory.* Monterey: California Test Bureau/McGraw-Hill.
35. Crites, J. O. (1974) Problems in the measurement of vocational maturity. *Journal of Vocational Behavior,* **4,** 25–31.
36. Daws, P. P. (1975) The Keele occupational crystallisation self-appraisal form. *British Journal of Guidance and Counselling,* **3,** 114–116.
37. Krumboltz, J. D. & Thoresen, C. E. (1964) The effect of behavioral counseling in group and individual settings on information seeking behavior. *Journal of Counseling Psychology,* **11,** 324–333.
38. Jones, G. B. & Krumboltz, J. D. (1970) Stimulating vocational exploration through film-mediated problems. *Journal of Counseling Psychology,* **17,** 107–114.
39. Krumboltz, J. D. & Baker, R. D. (1973) Behavioral counseling for vocational decisions. In H. Borow (ed.), *Career Guidance for a New Age* p. 235. Boston: Houghton Mifflin.
40. Krumboltz, J. D., Mitchell, A. M. & Jones, G. B. (1976) A social learning theory of career selection. *The Counseling Psychologist,* **6,** 1, 71–81.
41. *Ibid.* pp. 71–73.
42. *Ibid.* p. 74.
43. Krumboltz, J. D. & Baker, R. D. (1973) Behavioral counseling for vocational decisions. In H. Borow (ed.), *Career Guidance for a New Age* p. 240. Boston: Houghton Mifflin.
44. Krumboltz, J. D., Mitchell, A. M. & Jones, G. B. (1976) A social learning theory of career selection. *The Counseling Psychologist,* **6,** 1, 74.
45. *Ibid.* pp. 75–76.
46. *Ibid.* pp. 76–79. Table 8.4 has been made up from material contained in these pages.
47. *Ibid.* pp. 79–80. Table 8.5 has been made up from material contained in these pages.

48. Goodstein, L. D. (1965) Behavior theoretical views of counseling. In B. Stefflre (ed.), *Theories of Counseling* pp. 140–192. New York: McGraw-Hill.
49. Goodstein, L. D. (1972) Behavioral views of counseling. In B. Stefflre and W. H. Grant (eds), *Theories of Counseling* (2nd ed.) pp. 243–286. New York: McGraw-Hill.
50. Goodstein, L. D. (1965) Behavior theoretical views of counseling. In B. Stefflre (ed.), *Theories of Counseling* p. 160. New York: McGraw-Hill.
51. Goodstein, L. D. (1972) Behavioral views of counseling. In B. Stefflre and W. H. Grant (eds), *Theories of Counseling* (2nd ed.) pp. 260–263. New York: McGraw-Hill.

9 – Occupational Choice and Development Theory: Differentialist, Structural and Leisure

SUMMARY: *The differentialist viewpoint stresses the matching of people and jobs. A 'modern differentialist' approach to occupational choice and development is that of Holland. He suggests that most people can be categorized by their resemblance to one of six personality types: realistic, investigative, artistic, social, enterprising and conventional. People may also be categorized by their personality pattern or sub-types, which vary on the dimensions of differentiation and consistency. Six kinds of environmental models correspond to the six personality types. Environmental models may also be assessed according to their patterns. People's occupational behaviour is determined by the degree of congruence between their personality type and environmental model.*

The structural viewpoint emphasizes the differences between people's occupational choice and development arising from their different positions in the social structure. Blau et al's economic, sociological and psychological conceptual schema illustrates that structural considerations influence both job choosers and selectors. Roberts argues that occupational choices in Britain are heavily circumscribed, since different groups of school leavers have differential access to the various opportunities, depending on socio-economic, educational, family and neighbourhood influences. Career preferences are the outcomes of anticipatory socialization rather than of free choice. Because choices are socially determined, the impact of careers education and guidance is likely to be marginal. Daws suggests a flexible structural model in which careers education programmes counteract harmful socialization. Furthermore, there is evidence of a growth in occupational mobility and educational opportunity in Britain, indicating rather more mutable opportunity structures than previously. Finally, brief mention of decision theory is made, with a distinction between decision-making processes and styles.

Counselling for leisure is likely to become increasingly important. A developmental viewpoint stresses the formation and implementation of a healthy leisure self-concept. A differentialist position attempts to identify the predominant patterns of leisure activity as a basis for matching people with specific activities. This chapter concludes by suggesting some goals for counselling and for living relating to both work and leisure.

In the preceding chapter we reviewed the developmental and behavioural models of occupational choice and development relating to work. In this chapter the differentialist and structural models are presented, with brief mention of decision theory also being made. Additionally, there is a section on occupational choice and development relating to leisure, an increasingly important topic in the Western world.

DIFFERENTIALIST VIEWPOINT

The differentialist viewpoint may be seen as involving job analysis and person analysis and trying to achieve the optimum match between the two sets of characteristics derived from these analyses. Super observes that matching theories 'have tended to assume that individuals make only one choice of, are once selected for, or are consistently conveyed or impelled by personal or situational characteristics toward, an occupation which is in some way (even if not in others) appropriate to their personal or social characteristics'.[1] The psychological approach to matching has tended to focus, singly or in various combinations, on aptitudes, interests and personality. Furthermore, as described in Chapter 17, psychometric measures have been devised for these characteristics.

There are many writers who might be classified as differentialists, including Frank Parsons and E. G. Williamson of America and Alec Rodger of Britain. This section, however, focuses on the 'modern differentialist' theoretical model of John Holland, who observes that the goal of vocational guidance, matching people and jobs, has remained the same over the years, with the only major shift being to see the process of vocational decision-making in the context of a person's development.[2] Both developmental and behavioural writers acknowledge the importance of individual differences in career development, though neither approach offers a theoretical model matching people to occupations.

Holland's Theory of Vocational Choices and of Careers

John L. Holland (1919–   ) has been a vocational counsellor in educational, military and psychiatric settings. In 1959, when he first published his theory of vocational choices, he was working as a researcher for the American National Merit Scholarship Corporation. Holland then moved to Johns Hopkins University (where he has been a professor), developed his theory and conducted much research into its efficacy. Holland acknowledges that the stimulus for his matching theory came in part from Murray's ideas of personal 'needs', which represent significant determinants of behaviour within the person, and of environmental 'press', which have the power to affect the well-being of the person either beneficially or adversely.[3]

The first formulation of Holland's theory of vocational choices was published in 1959 as a journal article.[4] Second and third formulations of the theory were published in book form in 1966 and 1973 respectively.[5,6] In 1976 he published a further article, with some extensions and clarifications of the theory.[7] Here he described his typology as a 'modern differentialist view'. Over the years Holland has broadened his theory into a theory of careers which deals with vocational problems throughout a person's life, including work choices, changes, satisfaction and performance.

Basic assumptions

Holland considers that this theory has four basic assumptions:

1. Most persons can be categorized by their resemblance to one of six *personality types:* realistic, investigative, artistic, social, enterprising and conventional.
2. There are six kinds of *environmental models* corresponding to the six personality types.
3. People search for the kinds of environments which will let them exercise the skills, abilities, attitudes and values of their personality type.
4. People's behaviour is determined by the interaction between their personality type and the characteristics of their environment.[8]

By elaborating these four basic assumptions into a theory, Holland aimed both to explain vocational behaviour and to develop practical ideas for helping people with their vocational problems.

Development of personality types

Table 9.1 lists some of the main characteristics in which personality types are similar to each other and different from other personality types. The clustering of similarities for the various characteristics of each personality type represents common outcomes of the interaction between heredity and the environmental influences experienced in growing up in north American culture. Thus, for instance, people may develop into realistic personality types with similar self-concepts, values, occupational preferences, etc.

The processes through which people grow to resemble one type or another are

Table 9.1   *Characteristics and order of development of characteristics for Holland's personality types*[9]

Characteristics of personality types	Order of development of characteristics
Self-concepts	(Heredity)
Perception of the environment	↓
Values	Activities
Achievement and performance	↓
Differential reaction to environmental rewards, stress, etc.	Interests
	↓
Preference for occupation and occupational role	Competencies
Coping style	↓
Personal traits	Disposition

reinforcement and modelling. Parents, schools, neighbourhoods and friends offer environments which both provide opportunities for and reinforce certain behaviours more than others. For instance, each parental type may provide environmental opportunities and deficits which positively reinforce or extinguish the behaviour of their children. Realistic parents are likely to provide reinforcement for realistic activities, investigative parents for investigative activities, and so on. Furthermore, depending on their personality types, the significant others in the growing child's environment are likely to engage in or model some behaviours more than others. Additionally, cultural, socio-economic and sex-role socialization factors lead to the development of different types, through differential encouragement of activities, interests and competencies.[10]

The second column of Table 9.1 indicates that, in developing the characteristics of personality types, the order is from environments influencing the development of activities to dispositions. For instance, preferred activities and aversions develop out of the interaction of the child's heredity, her early activity and her environmental circumstances. These preferences may later become well defined interests which, in turn, lead to the development of specialized competencies as well as the lack of development of other potential competencies. The differentiation of interests and competencies creates a characteristic disposition or personality type distinguished by similarities on the characteristics of personality types, such as self-concept, listed in the first column of Table 9.1.

Descriptions and assessment of personality types

Holland's formulation of personality types has three main sources. First, his experience as a vocational counsellor and clinician. Second, his interpretation of the interest and personality literature over a period of years, especially factor analytic studies, confirmed his observation that 'several broad factors account for most human interests, traits and behaviours'.[11] Third, his construction of the *Vocational Preference Inventory* from interest materials led to six scales which correspond to his present personality types.[12] He claims he was later impressed and reassured by Guilford's comprehensive factor analysis of human interests deriving six major factors which are very similar to his personality types. Guilford's factors are: mechanical, scientific, social welfare, clerical, business and aesthetic.[13]

The special heredity and experiences of people lead to the outcomes of the characteristics of Holland's six personality types. Table 9.2 indicates some illustrative characteristics for each type. In his 1966 formulation Holland provided conceptual definitions, which resemble the kinds of environmental demands that are congenial to them, of each personality type.[14] In short, the types prefer occupations or situations in which they can engage in favoured activities and avoid uncongenial ones. Also, they prefer occupations in which they can use their special problem-solving competencies.

Personality types may be assessed by qualitative and quantitative methods. Qualitatively, a classification may be made by comparing people's educational and vocational interests or their employment with occupations assumed to be typical of each personality type. Quantitative methods include the *Vocational Preference*

Table 9.2   *Personality types and related environmental models in Holland's theory of careers*[15, 16]

Title of personality type and of related environmental model	Personality types		Environmental models	
	Illustrative characteristics	Dominant demands and opportunities	Typical settings and occupations
Realistic	Practical, masculine, materialistic, stable, conforming, frank, genuine, asocial, persistent, uninsightful.	Explicit, ordered, systematic, manipulation of objects, tools, of machines, and animals.	Settings: filling station, farm, construction project. Occupations: aircraft mechanic, civil engineer, electrician, filling station attendant.
Investigative	Intellectual, analytical, rational, curious, critical, methodical, precise, independent, reserved, introverted.	Observation and symbolic, systematic, creative investigation of physical, biological, or cultural phenomena.	Settings: research laboratory, library. Occupations: biologist, mathematician, astronomer, anthropologist, research analyst.
Artistic	Imaginative, intuitive, impulsive, emotional, feminine, original, non-conforming, complicated, introspective, independent.	Ambiguous, free, unsystematized activities and competencies to create art forms or products.	Settings: play rehearsal, dance studio, study. Occupations: writer, artist, architect, actor, drama teacher.
Social	Sociable, responsible, helpful, friendly, idealistic, persuasive, co-operative, feminine, insightful, kind.	Manipulation of others to inform, train, develop, cure or enlighten.	Settings: schools, colleges, mental hospitals, churches. Occupations: social worker, personnel director, clergyman, college professor, rehabilitation counsellor.
Enterprising	Energetic, domineering, acquisitive, adventurous, ambitious, self-confident, impulsive, exhibitionistic, optimistic, sociable.	Manipulation of others to obtain organizational or self-interest goals.	Settings: car lot, estate agent's office, retail outlets. Occupations: automobile dealer, banker, manager/administrator.
Conventional	Conforming, orderly, obedient, persistent, practical, conscientious, inhibited, inflexible, self-controlled, unimaginative.	Explicit, ordered, systematic manipulation of data, such as keeping records, organizing written and numerical data, operating data-processing machines.	Settings: bank, accounting firm, post office, file room, business office. Occupations: teller, book-keeper, key punch operator, typist, mail clerk.

John Holland, MAKING VOCATIONAL CHOICES: A Theory of Careers © 1973, pp. 11–36. Adapted by permission of Prentice-Hall, Inc., Englewood Cliffs, New Jersey, USA.

Inventory, the *Self-directed Search* and the *Strong Vocational Interest Blank*, now the *Strong–Campbell Interest Inventory*. For instance, scores on the realistic, intellectual, social, conventional, enterprising and artistic scales of the *Vocational Preference Inventory* are one way of typing a person.[17,18] Another way is to use the subscales of Holland's *Self-directed Search*. For example, the realistic activity, competency, self-rating and occupation subscales of the *Self-directed Search* correspond to the realistic type, etc.[19,20] The *Strong Vocational Interest Blank*[21] has been used in two ways. Six Strong scales have been selected to represent each of the personality types. Also, Campbell and Holland have created six scales from Strong items to approximate the six scales of the *Vocational Preference Inventory*, thus providing a further way of measuring personality type.[22]

Holland views people's personality *patterns* as their profile of resemblances to personality *types*. He acknowledges that a simple, six-category scheme of personality types is unrealistic and observes that, by allowing a simple ordering of people's resemblance to each of the six types, this provides the possibility of 720 different personality patterns.[23] In fact, Holland seems to type people in descending order of their three highest scale scores. For instance, based on *Vocational Preference Inventory* scores, person A may be social-investigative-artistic, while person B may be investigative-realistic-enterprising. Holland's *Occupations Finder* lists appropriate occupations based on a three-subtype personality pattern code, such as REI.[24]

The concepts of *differentiation* and *consistency* may be applied to personality types and patterns. For instance, people may range from being strongly defined or differentiated in terms of one personality type to being poorly defined or undifferentiated. Furthermore, some personality patterns are considered to be more consistent than others. In Figure 9.1, the shorter the distance between types, the greater their similarity or psychological resemblance. Taking their two highest *Vocational Preference Inventory* scale scores, the hexagon in Figure 9.1 may be used to define people's profile pattern as being consistent or inconsistent. Proximity on the hexagon, for

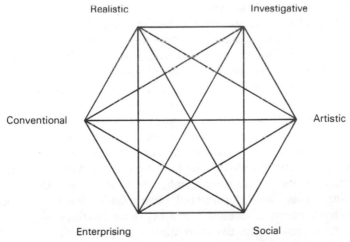

Figure 9.1 Holland's hexagonal model for defining the relationships among personality types, environmental models and their interactions.[25]

example with a realistic-investigative pattern, indicates consistency, while lack of proximity, for example with a conventional-artistic pattern, indicates inconsistency.

A number of hypotheses about occupational and other kinds of behaviour may be made from the personality type formulations. For example, it is hypothesized that people's personality types and patterns determine the direction of their vocational choices, and also, that differentiation and consistency of personality pattern contribute to effective vocational functioning. Furthermore, it is hypothesized that people's personality patterns determine their choice of leisure activities and also their degree of social responsiveness to others.[26]

Descriptions and assessment of environmental models

In addition to Murray's ideas of environmental 'press', Holland derived his ideas on the need to assess environments from Linton's notion that the major force of an environment is transmitted through other people.[27] Holland defines an environmental model as 'the situation or atmosphere created by the people who dominate a given environment' and observes that 'it is possible to classify people and environments in the same terms and thus to predict the outcomes of pairing people and environments'.[28] Thus an office full of realistic types, such as engineers, would be expected to have a different atmosphere from an office of social types, such as rehabilitation counsellors. Environments, however, are rarely homogeneous, and thus it is important to be specific. For instance, colleges and universities may provide different environments depending on the departments in which students or staff work.

Table 9.2 illustrates the dominant demands and opportunities of the six environmental models. It also lists some typical settings and occupations. The demands of the environmental models are such that they reinforce the characteristics of the personality types which correspond to them. Thus investigative types seek out investigative environments, which in turn reinforce the self-concepts, behaviours, attitudes and values characteristic of investigative types.

Astin and Holland have developed the *Environmental Assessment Technique* as a way of measuring environmental models.[29] Again the principle is that the psychological force of an environment is transmitted by the people in it. Thus, by assessing the occupations and training or vocational preferences of a population in terms of personality types, it is possible to obtain a profile or *pattern* for an environment. Holland gives an example in which a population in a business environment is composed of the following percentages of types: realistic, 10 per cent; investigative, 4 per cent; social, 6 per cent; conventional, 64 per cent; enterprising, 14 per cent; and artistic, 2 per cent. The environmental pattern of this business might be represented as CERSIA, which in particular would emphasize conventional characteristics.[30]

Like personality patterns, environmental patterns may vary on *differentiation* and *consistency* dimensions. A differentiated environment, such as a predominantly conventional environment, is likely to reinforce a well defined group of behaviours, whereas the guidelines in an undifferentiated environment will be much more ambiguous. The consistency of the psychological force of an environment may be assessed by using the hexagon model given earlier (Figure 9.1). Again, the shorter the distance between the two predominant groupings of personality types in an environ-ment, the greater the psychological similarity of the environment and vice versa.

A number of hypotheses about people's vocational and educational behaviour and personal effectiveness may be made from the environmental model formulations. For instance, it is hypothesized that each model environment, including educational environments, attracts its own personality type and also reinforces its own characteris-tic achievement; also, that differentiation and consistency of environments each promote vocational satisfaction. Furthermore, each model environment reinforces a characteristic group of social behaviours.

Personality type and environmental model interactions

Holland and Gottfredson observe that the quality of a person's vocational coping is a function of the interaction between personality type and environmental model and the consistency and differentiation of each.[31] The interaction between personality type and environmental model can be assessed by the degree of matching or *congruence*.[32] Congruence may be viewed as a continuum ranging from exact matching of people and environments to people's being in totally dissimilar environments from their personality types. An example of matching is an enterprising type in an enterprising environment. From the hexagon (Figure 9.1) it may be seen that an example of a personality type in an adjacent environment is a realistic type in an investigative or a conventional environment. Examples of a high degree of incongruence would be enterprising types in investigative environments and social types in realistic environ-ments. People in environments which are congruent are provided with the oppor-tunity to engage in congenial activities, have their self-image reinforced, and avoid activities they dislike. Conversely, people in incongruent environments may be faced with activities they dislike, lack of opportunity to engage in congenial activities, and colleagues who do not reinforce their self-image. An obvious example of incon-gruence is an artistic type in a conventional environment, which requires structured activities and routine competencies, whereas the artistic environmental model is ambiguous, unsystematized and values creativity and self-expression.

The dimensions of *consistency* and *differentiation* are also relevant to interactions between people and environments. Consistent environments provide consistent demands and opportunities which are likely to be highly satisfactory to individuals whose personality patterns are similarly consistent. The interaction of consistent people with consistent environments is likely to result in more predictable outcomes than where either or both are inconsistent. Furthermore, the congruence of differentiated people in differentiated environments, or of well defined people in similar well defined environments, may make for vocational satisfaction. The interaction of undifferentiated people in undifferentiated environments is likely to be much less predictable, since neither has a clearly identified focus.

The interaction of person and environment has implications for stability and change of both vocational choice and employment behaviour. For instance, the direction of people's vocational choice is likely to be stable if they are in congruent environments, whereas incongruent interactions are more likely to lead to change in vocational choice.

Holland considers vocational achievement and satisfaction to be enhanced by congruent work environments. Where there are incongruent interactions, people may attempt to resolve the incongruence either by altering their behaviour within or by reshaping their current environment, or by moving to a different environment.[33] Furthermore, people who are in reasonably congruent environments may change jobs to achieve greater congruence. People with consistent and differentiated personality patterns are likely to find it easier to make vocational choice and change decisions than those whose vocational identity is more ambiguous. Since the majority of people seem to be successful in finding congruent work, people tend to be sustained in their personality types, with change of personality type being exceptional.[34]

Implications for practice

Holland and Gottfredson consider that the typology suggests a new vocational assistance orientation, which they tentatively call the 'Exploratory View'. This view accepts clients' definitions of their problems and helps them to explore themselves and the world of work by providing materials, such as self-administered and self-scored inventories and vocational information, that they can use with little aid. Here counselling is seen as a back-up resource for the client's self-directed search, to be used only if personal initiative and easily available search materials are insufficient.[35] Holland notes that his typology provides a framework for organizing occupational information as well as for assessing clients.[36] The practical implications of his typology are further elaborated in Chapter 18.

Concluding comments

Holland's theory of careers has a number of strengths. He presents it very clearly His focus on personality types rather than on interests leads to a fuller analysis of the characteristics of people than that provided by interest measures. While interest measures describe one dimension of a person, the concept of personality type goes beyond this to include illustrative characteristics, coping styles, and preferred demands and opportunities. Similarly, his focus on environmental models goes further in describing the psychological impact of a job environment than that provided by traditional job descriptions. The outcome of his personality type–model environment typology may be that counselling clients engage in a less superficial exploration of their occupational self-concepts and of the world of work than might otherwise be the case. The typology also lends itself to the formulation of vocational assessment devices and provides a classification scheme for occupational information, as indicated by Holland's *Occupations Finder*.[37] Furthermore, the typology both has some research support and lends itself to generating testable research hypotheses about vocational choice and behaviour.

One criticism of the personality type formulations is that they insufficiently take into account the level of development or maturity of the person. People may be describing their personality types in terms of their current levels of development rather than their potential levels. Thus, there is a risk that they may prematurely label themselves as certain personality types in ways that may curtail rather than foster deeper exploration of their personalities and their vocational self-concepts. Another criticism of Holland's work is that, for some people, it needs to be supplemented by further training in making and implementing vocational decisions. Thoresen and Ewart comment that average occupational interest profiles, while they provide useful points of reference, 'offer no guide to how one might develop the mastery of self and environment needed to make and implement career-related decisions'.[38]

Holland acknowledges some weaknesses of his typology. He considers that the hypotheses about vocational environments need much more research exploration. Also, although the hypotheses about person-environment interactions are promising, they still need more testing, as do the formulations about personality type development. Additionally, he acknowledges that many important personal and environmental contingencies lie outside the scope of the typology.[39] The latter, of course, might need to be taken into account in counselling specific clients.

As time goes by, Holland's typology may need updating as different developmental experiences affect personality types and also as different influences, such as technological change, affect environmental models. Holland observes that his typology has implications for leisure activities. It would be good to see the leisure aspect of the typology developed, as well as its implications for friendship and marital interactions. Crowley provides some tentative evidence that Holland's work has relevance in Britain, though his own *Work Environment Schedule* fails to identify clearly the enterprising and investigative environmental models.[40] A rigorously developed personality type–environmental model typology for Britain seems highly desirable. The writer's hypothesis is that such a typology would differ little from Holland's.

STRUCTURAL VIEWPOINT

The structural viewpoint is a sociological approach which emphasizes the differences between people's occupational choice and development arising from their different positions in the social structure. Law observes that differentialist theories may use either a psychological vocabularly, for example in Holland's typology, or a sociological vocabulary.[41] The structural viewpoint, which predominantly uses a sociological vocabulary, is outlined here rather than developed in depth. The viewpoint has implications for counselling practice which are controversial, and there is a continuing debate in British counselling circles, for example between Roberts and Daws, about the degree and immutability of sociological determinism.[42,43,44,45,46]

Blau et al's Overall Conceptual Schema

Blau and his colleagues were an interdisciplinary team who devised a conceptual framework which attempted to illustrate the economic, sociological and psychological aspects of the process of occupational choice.[47] They observed that not only the process of *choice* but also the process of *selection* must be taken into account in explaining why people end up in different occupations. The social structure affects both choice and selection by influencing the personality development of the choosers and by providing the socioeconomic framework for selection.

Occupational choice involves a series of decisions about employment in which individuals compromise their preferences with the realities of being able to enter a given occupation. Occupational selection involves a series of decisions by selectors in which they compromise their preferences in the light of the quantity and quality of available candidates. Occupational *entry* must be seen in terms of the interaction between individual choosers and selecting agencies, both of whom are influenced by a number of long-term, medium-term and short-term determinants.

Figure 9.2 sets out many of the historical, social, economic, technological and psychological variables influencing occupational choice, selection and development. For instance, the immediate determinants on the part of choosers include the extent and adequacy of their occupational information, their qualifications, their social characteristics, and the way they value differing rewards. The immediate determinants for selectors include the demand for new members in the occupation existing at the time, the functional or technical qualifications needed for optimum performance of the job, the non-functional or subjective requirements of the job (e.g. good looks), and the kinds of monetary and other rewards offered by the employment conditions. A final point is that for both choosers and selectors the consequences of past decisions become determinants of future ones.

Opportunity Structure as Determinants of Occupational Entry

Blau et al's conceptual schema is an interdisciplinary approach to understanding the processes of occupational choice and selection. A more exclusively sociological viewpoint is that provided by Roberts, who posits that *opportunity structure* rather than *occupational choice* is the key concept in understanding both the transition from school to employment and the patterns of career development in Britain. Developmental theorists overestimate the degree of effective choice that people have when they interpret careers in terms of fulfilment of ambitions. Instead, the degree of occupational choice that people have is structured by a number of interlocking factors including a stratified occupational system, different levels of educational attainment, and the types of homes from which they come.

Roberts sees the relative desirability of different occupations as providing a hierarchical structure of occupations. Different groups of school leavers have highly differential access to these various opportunities. He observes that key variables in predicting the type of job a school leaver will obtain are 'his educational qualifications and to a lesser extent the occupational status of his parents, together with the local job opportunity structure'.[48] Social class differences in Britain pervade educational opportunity and attainment and, hence, socioeconomic opportunity. Furthermore, once a person is in a career, job movement may be predicted less by aspirations and

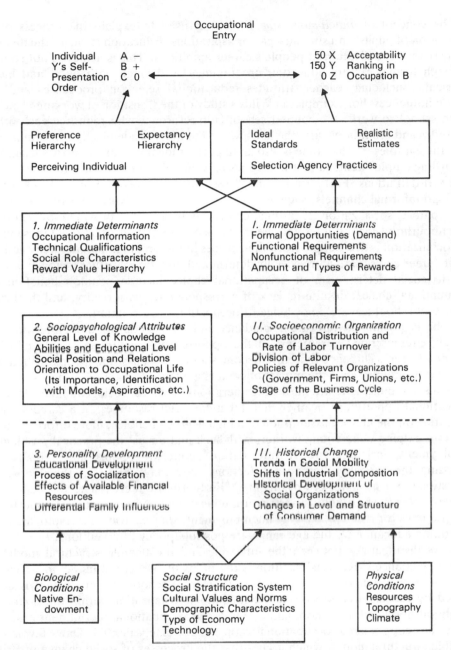

Occupational
Entry

Individual	A −		50 X	Acceptability
Y's Self-	B +		150 Y	Ranking in
Presentation	C 0		0 Z	Occupation B
Order				

Preference Expectancy	Ideal Realistic
Hierarchy Hierarchy	Standards Estimates
Perceiving Individual	Selection Agency Practices

1. Immediate Determinants	*I. Immediate Determinants*
Occupational Information	Formal Opportunities (Demand)
Technical Qualifications	Functional Requirements
Social Role Characteristics	Nonfunctional Requirements
Reward Value Hierarchy	Amount and Types of Rewards

2. Sociopsychological Attributes	*II. Socioeconomic Organization*
General Level of Knowledge	Occupational Distribution and
Abilities and Educational Level	Rate of Labor Turnover
Social Position and Relations	Division of Labor
Orientation to Occupational Life	Policies of Relevant Organizations
(Its Importance, Identification	(Government, Firms, Unions, etc.)
with Models, Aspirations, etc.)	Stage of the Business Cycle

3. Personality Development	*III. Historical Change*
Educational Development	Trends in Social Mobility
Process of Socialization	Shifts in Industrial Composition
Effects of Available Financial	Historical Development of
Resources	Social Organizations
Differential Family Influences	Changes in Level and Structure
	of Consumer Demand

Biological	*Social Structure*	*Physical*
Conditions	Social Stratification System	*Conditions*
Native En-	Cultural Values and Norms	Resources
dowment	Demographic Characteristics	Topography
	Type of Economy	Climate
	Technology	

Figure 9.2 Blau et al's schema of the process of occupational choice and selection. Reprinted with permission from the *Industrial and Labor Relations Review*, Vol. 9, No. 4 (July 1956), p. 534. c 1956 by Cornell University. All rights reserved.

preferences than by the jobs people currently hold and the connections between these and future jobs. Thus opportunity structures restrict choices not only at the point of work entry, but also during working life.

The concept of *anticipatory socialization* is used to explain the process of the formation of pupils' and students' career aspirations. Education is one of the means of anticipatory socialization of people's career ambitions. This is achieved not so much through formal careers education programmes as through both overt and hidden curricula, including teacher attitudes, educational selection procedures and peer group influences. For example, in Willis's study of the transition of working-class boys from school to work, the counter-school culture group, who reinforce each other's attitudes and aspirations, are 'the lads', while the more academically conforming boys are 'the ear 'oles'.[49] The home is also an important means of anticipatory socialization regarding employment, in that it supplies role-models and transmits attitudes, values and self-definitions. Furthermore, much recruitment to occupations still takes place through informal channels, such as personal contacts involving relatives. Additional anticipatory socialization regarding employment may be provided by churches, neighbourhood communities and the media. The cumulative effect of all these means of socialization is that people learn their places in the occupational hierarchy and thus their career choices are more socially determined than free. Further factors contributing to social determinism of occupational choice include people's belief in free occupational choice, despite its lack of correspondence with reality, and the limited nature of school leavers' knowledge of occupational information.

Roberts' position is that careers guidance and careers education operate within the closely circumscribed parameters of the opportunity structures available to school leavers. Careers guidance therefore becomes a matter of assisting people within their existing structures. Thus the impact of careers guidance is marginal, since work entry depends so much on structural considerations such as socioeconomic class and educational opportunity. Rather than focus financial resources on a careers service operating on the illusory assumption of a high degree of choice, more effort should be put into helping some young workers with such matters as: the practical problems of employment, including precise information about job opportunities; realistically assessing the probably limited satisfactions they may expect in their jobs; and adjusting to the demands of working life.[50] Furthermore, there is a need for a focus on *careers policies* which help to restructure educational and occupational opportunity. Programmes for reducing teenage unemployment, sharing available employment and extending education up the age range are possible policy interventions.[51]

Daws distinguishes between the inflexible and the flexible structural models of careers guidance.[52] Roberts' position is the inflexible structural model in which, for the majority of school leavers, the transition from school to employment is determined by conservative processes of anticipatory socialization within the home, the neighbourhood and the school and by restrictive occupational recruitment practices. Thus the scope for real occupational choice is extremely limited. Daws favours the flexible structural model, which argues that the processes of social change in Britain are widening the range of occupations available to the majority of school leavers and that careers guidance and education can significantly help people to take advantage of these extensions of social opportunity. Furthermore, careers programmes also have socialization functions which help young people to explore their overall life-style and not merely their educational and occupational choices, force them to think about the socialization processes to which they have been subjected, and help them to transcend socially imposed barriers to a full awareness of choice and opportunity. Thus money spent on careers programmes based on developmental assumptions, such as an emphasis on choice, may be well rather than ill spent and such programmes may be a catalyst of desirable social change.[53]

Daws considers that Roberts insufficiently acknowledges the extent of social mobility, and hence the degree of mutability of opportunity structures, in Britain. Halsey provides some evidence that opportunity structures are slowly but steadily becoming less rigid.[54] For example, in 1911 the richest 5 per cent of the nation owned 86 per cent of its private capital, whereas by 1970 they owned 55 per cent. Regarding university entry, Table 9.3, which is based on a sample of 10 000 men in England and

Table 9.3 *Percentage of British males who reached university, by date of birth and occupation of fathers*[55]

| Date of birth | Professional, administrative and managerial | Occupation of father | | Semi-skilled or unskilled manual | Total |
		Inspectoral, supervisory and non-manual	Skilled manual		
1910–29	12.3	2.81	1.37	0.64	2.63
1930–49	22.73	7.73	4.14	1.92	6.88

Wales in 1972, suggests that inequality declined for those born in the 1930–49 period relative to that for those born in the 1910–29 period. Nevertheless, for the later born group, upper-middle-class children had a three times better than average chance of entry, whereas the lower working class had less than half the average chance. There has also been a move to less rigid opportunity structures in the schools, as shown by less streaming in primary and secondary education and by fewer than 20 per cent of today's children being subjected to selective educational procedures at 11-plus.[56] Additionally, there is more opportunity for 'second chance' entry to further and higher education at a later age, through open-access policies of recruitment in colleges of education and through the establishment of the television- and radio-based Open University. Regarding occupational mobility, recent data indicate a significant increase in the volume of *absolute* intergenerational change in class membership as measured by socioeconomic criteria.[57] Daws observes that this 'is attributable to an increase in the volume of middle-class labour-market demand, a process which has been evident since the nineteenth century'.[58] However, he adds that there is no evidence of a change in *relative* occupational mobility or, in other words, in mobility which cannot be attributed to a structural change in the labour market.

Apart from socioeconomic classification, there are a number of social characteristics which may, singly or in different combinations, be pertinent to occupational opportunity. These include gender, religion, race, age, physical handicap and size of community. Gender is very important indeed. Taking medical education as an example, in Britain in 1968 the proportion of medical students who were women was about 24 per cent; in Canada in 1968–69 women comprised about 14 per cent of medical students; in the United States in 1967–68 just over 10 per cent of the entering class were women; while in Russia in 1963 60 per cent of medical students were women.[59] The attribution of female and male stereotypes to various occupations is a major way in which both choosers and selectors restrict opportunity. Size of community may affect not only choice of occupation, but also the area of focus within an occupation. For instance, in the late 1960s over twice as many first-year Canadian medical students who came from communities of under 1000 people stated a preference for general practice, rather than a clinical speciality or other fields of medicine, than did students coming from communities of 100 000 or more.[60] In an area such as Northern Ireland, whether a person ascribes to the Protestant or the Catholic religion may still have significant consequences for their occupational opportunities. Also, in virtually every part of the world, racial and cultural minorities consider, usually with some reason, that they are being discriminated against in obtaining suitable employment.

Concluding Comments

The structural position, as it tends to get stated in Britain, is mainly in terms of opportunity structures being limited by social class and educational opportunity. Other barriers to occupational opportunity seem insufficiently emphasized, especially sex-role stereotyping in regard to both female and male self-definitions and to the attribution of desirable characteristics for occupations. Furthermore, assumptions about the desirability of being higher up the occupational hierarchy are not necessarily valid. People can work congenially or uncongenially in either high-level or low-level occupations. Thus not only the *level* of work, but also the *type* of work, including social psychological considerations, is important.

The psychological and sociological perspectives on occupational development are not mutually exclusive. Ideally, school leavers should be helped to know themselves and the world of work in such a way that they can transcend unrealistic socialization, whether it is in relation to their social class origins, their gender or other people's ideas about what constitutes a hierarchy of desirable occupations. Restructuring of opportunities, for example by employment legislation affecting women and minorities, can be important, especially if translated effectively into the attitudes and behaviours of choosers and selectors. Nevertheless, careers counselling and education still have an important role to play. Rather than do away with such programmes, a more desirable result of criticism would be to improve their quality, not least by sharpening careers counsellors' and educators' awareness of and ability to handle the interplay of psychological and sociological variables in their clients' lives.

DECISION THEORY

To complete our discussion of choice and development theory relating to work, brief mention is made of decision theory. Needless to say, the developmental, behavioural, differentialist and structural viewpoints all contain explicit and implicit statements about the way career decisions are made. Though the distinction is somewhat artificial, the counselling literature specifically focused on decision-making can be classified according to whether it emphasizes *process* or *style*. Tiedeman attempts to describe the *process* of decision-making within the framework of vocational development.[61,62] The process of *each* decision can be divided into two periods, a period of anticipation and a period of implementation and adjustment. The period of anticipation can be divided into four stages: exploration, crystallization, choice and specification. The period of implementation and adjustment is characterized by three stages: induction, in which the primary mode of reaction is responsive; transition, in which the primary mode of reaction becomes assertive; and maintenance. A conception of self evolves and is expressed through a series of vocational decisions, each potentially consisting of the seven distinct phases above and each also capable of being considered in a wider context of past and future decisions. Additionally, behavioural writers have focused specifically on the process of decision-making, and in the practice part of this book we discuss Krumboltz and Baker's views on the skills of effective decison-making[63] and Thoresen and Ewart's use of behavioural self-control to help clients to become better architects of their occupational lives.[64]

Arroyba defines decision-making *style* as 'a way of approaching, responding to, and acting in a decision-making situation; that is the overall manner in which a decision is made. It is a label which is applied to the making of a specific decision, rather than to the decision-maker'.[65] In the early 1970s, Gelatt and his colleagues listed eight such styles: impulsive, fatalistic, compliant, delaying, agonizing, planning, intuitive/inner harmony, and paralysis.[66] Using Gelatt et al's work as a guideline, Arroyba identified six styles which, using cluster analysis, fell into three groupings: (a) compliant; (b) no thought, emotional, intuitive; and (c) logical and hesitant.[67] Passivity-activity is the major dimension underlying her decision-making styles: for instance, the 'compliant' style features a high degree of passivity, whereas the 'logical' and 'hesitant' styles involve extensive and active personal consideration and effort. Arroyba's work suggests that the same person may adopt different styles depending on her perception of situations, thus indicating that the concept of style might be more useful as a way of classifying behaviours rather than people.

Ultimately there is considerable overlap between the processes and style of effective decision-making. For example, Arroyba's 'logical' style and Gelatt et al's 'planning' style are those of effective, objective and rational decision-making. Where the concept of style appears to have some distinctive usefulness for counselling practice is in identifying ineffective decision-making behaviours depending on clients' subjective perceptions of particular situations.

CHOICE AND DEVELOPMENT RELATING TO LEISURE

There appears to be a growing concern with leisure choice and development in counselling psychology. Sometimes leisure activities are described as avocational or non-occupational to make a distinction between them and work. Dimensions of a definition of leisure may include time, freedom of choice, and function.[68] For instance, on the temporal dimension, leisure might be perceived as either non-work time or time remaining after basic needs, such as sleep, work and family obligations, have been met. On the freedom dimension, leisure might be taken as the freedom to occupy a period of time in any way that is desired. On the function dimension, possible views of leisure include a means towards self-realizing or personal meaning and fulfilment, a therapeutic activity for disturbed people, diversion, recreation and refreshment, compensation for unrewarding work, and avoidance behaviour.

There are a number of reasons relating to time, freedom of choice, and function why leisure is an appropriate concern for counselling psychologists. Time available for leisure activities forms at least a part of everyone's life and is the major part for some, such as the retired and the unemployed. Furthermore, leisure time is likely to increase with the shortening of the working week. The choosing of leisure outlets is relevant to satisfactory identity formation and self-realizing. Also, the need for assistance with choice may become greater with the increasing number of possible leisure activities. Some remedial and growth functions of leisure have already been mentioned above.

Overs observes that, because of their generic counselling skills, including an understanding of motivation, coping strategies and adjustment problems, counselling psychologists are *potentially* well qualified to conduct avocational counselling at a sophisticated level. However, in order to realize this potential many will need to change their attitude to value leisure participation more highly. Also, information about avocational activities must be learned and skills in handling clients with avocational concerns have to be acquired.[69]

Concern with leisure is still recent in counselling psychology. Consequently, there has been little theoretical and applied work on leisure choice and development relative to that concerning the world of work. It seems possible to extrapolate theoretical insights relevant to leisure choice and development from developmental, behavioural, differentialist and structural writings concerning work-choice processes. However, there is within the developmental and differentialist viewpoints some writing focused specifically on leisure. Additionally, there is a sociological literature on leisure which is not reviewed here.

Developmental Viewpoint

In a later paper, Super mentioned 'leisurite' as one of the nine roles in his life-span, life-space approach to career development.[70] Indeed, it is possible to view the development of leisure occupations in terms of a continuous process of forming and implementing self-concepts throughout the life-stages. Super, however, has never developed his ideas on leisure self-concepts in any detail. Nevertheless, almost all of the ten propositions of this theory of vocational development[71] appear relevant, with little alteration, to avocational development. This even suggests the possibility of an overall theory of occupational choice and development incorporting both vocational and avocational elements.

McDowell considers that the concepts of leisure life-space and leisure self-concept are central to a theory of leisure choice and development.[72] A client's leisure self-concept consists of perceptions built upon and from personal needs, beliefs, attitudes and values. Three elements of the leisure self-concept are: (a) the self as seen by the self; (b) the self as perceived by others; and (c) the self as one would like to be. The leisure self as seen by the self consists of a person's current attitudes to and involvement in leisure. Unhealthy leisure modes consist of viewing leisure in terms of such phrases as 'I ought' and 'I should' and 'I don't have the time'. People who form and implement leisure self-concepts which allow them to do what they want to do are in a healthy leisure mode. Sometimes people collude in letting others keep a false perception of their leisure selves by not openly acknowledging their real leisure interests. A more healthy leisure mode is for people to be open about their real leisure self-concepts and interests. One of the main objects of leisure counselling is to help clients to bridge the gap between their real and their ideal leisure self-concepts. Often an element of this is helping them to become better at planning their leisure involvement. McDowell's approach to leisure choice and development appears to be an extension of humanistic-perceptual theory into this area.

Differentialist Viewpoint

Holland's model of vocational choice is oriented mainly to the world of work. An attempt at a differentialist theory of leisure choice is that of McKechnie, who suggests that psychological analysis of individual differences in leisure activity should: (a) identify the predominant types or patterns of leisure activity; and (b) explore the personality and demographic correlates of participation in these patterns.[73] He devised a list of 121 leisure activities which have high participation rates in the United States, called the *Leisure Activities Blank*. This instrument asks subjects to rate their past participation and future participation intentions for each of the activities. He administered the LAB to just under 300 subjects stratified on age (for people over 20) and sex, and living in a relatively affluent area of California.[74] Factor analyses of LAB-past and LAB-future data were performed separately. Six factors best accounted for the LAB-past data, while eight factors best accounted for the LAB-future data. Table 9.4 shows the eight LAB-future factors. Additionally,

Table 9.4. *Leisure Activities Blank: future factors and illustrative activities*[75]

Factor	Illustrative activities
Adventure	Bicycling, horseback riding, sailing, canoeing
Mechanics	Auto repair, electronics, metalwork, woodwork
Crafts	Designing clothes, jewellery making, sewing, weaving
Easy living	Social dancing, nightclubs, social drinking
Intellectual	Attending concerts, going to plays, bridge
Ego recognition	Acting, modern dance, judo, squash
Slow living	Dining out, gardening, reading magazines
Clean living	Baseball, basketball, child-related activities

adjectives are given to describe high and low scorers on each factor. For instance, high scorers on the 'adventure' factor are often described as 'adventurous', 'alert' and 'ambitious', whereas low scorers are 'absent-minded', 'awkward' and 'conservative'. McKechnie considers that leisure counselling must employ multivariate techniques of appraisal which can reliably and validly predict initial and long-term adjustment of clients to leisure situations.

Concluding Comments

The area of effective use of leisure is important to people's psychological well-being. Leisure activities are likely to be somewhat culture-related, depending on such variables as historical customs (e.g. cricket rather than baseball) and climate. Thus it is unwise to rely on theory and instruments developed in other countries. It is hoped that progress will be made in the coming years in developing a British literature and indigenous instruments in the area of leisure choice and development, as well as in similar developments in other English-speaking countries.

GOALS FOR COUNSELLING AND FOR LIVING

Some goals for counselling and for living may be extrapolated from the various viewpoints on occupational choice and development. Ginzberg stresses the importance of the optimization of the fit between people's changing desires and circumstances and the world of work. Super emphasizes vocational maturity and suggests six component dimensions: autonomy, planfulness, exploration, career decision-making, knowledge and realism. Vocationally mature people are more likely to gain both occupational and personal fulfilment through the successful implementation of a self-concept which is realistic in terms of their own capacities and the nature of the world of work. The behavioural viewpoint emphasizes the learning of effective career decision-making skills, including the capacity to set up exploratory career learning experiences, and Goodstein mentions the need to unlearn maladaptive anxiety reactions affecting occupational choice.

Holland believes that vocational satisfaction, stability and effective performance are more likely to occur if there is congruence between people's personality types and patterns and the environments in which they find themselves. Furthermore, both consistency and differentiation of their personality patterns may contribute to the ease with which choices are made and to vocational satisfaction. The structural position emphasizes careers policies to change social structures, such as the educational system, as ways of correcting imbalances in occupational opportunity. However, as Roberts observes, life chances tend to be arranged in zero-sum equations, with it being impossible for everyone to climb to the summit of the occupational structure.[76] The flexible structural position also focuses on helping people to overcome the adverse effects of their socialization and take advantage of the increasing range of opportunities arising from social change.

Developmental goals for leisure are being able to formulate and implement a healthy leisure self-concept. This involves freedom from the constrictions of unrealistic 'oughts' and 'shoulds'. Differentialist goals involve the matching of people with the predominant types or patterns of leisure activity so that suitable leisure occupations may be identified.

SELF-REFERENT EXERCISES

It may help you to understand this chapter better if, either with paper and pencil or in your head, you think about and answer the following questions:

1.   Which of Holland's six personality types best describes you? Please give reasons.

2.   Assess the degree to which your personality pattern resembles each of Holland's six personality types. What are the three leading dimensions of your personality pattern? To what degree is your personality pattern:

   (a) differentiated;
   (b) consistent?

3.   What is the predominant environmental model of your current main work or study environment? What are the other two main environmental models represented in this environment?

4.   Assess the degree of congruence between your personality pattern and your current main work or study environment. What implications does this have for your:

   (a) vocational stability;
   (b) vocational satisfaction;
   (c) level of performance?

5.   During your life, what structural considerations have been important in determining or influencing your educational and occupational choices and development? Describe the structural considerations in relation to the specific areas in which they have influenced you.

6.   Do you consider the distinction between decision-making process and style to be valid? Give reasons for your answer.

7.   As best as you are able, analyse for one or more situations:

   (a) your decision-making processes;
   (b) your decision-making style or styles.

8.   Do you consider that you have a healthy or unhealthy leisure mode? Give reasons.

9.   Describe your leisure profile in terms of the dimensions of McKechnie's *Leisure Activities Blank* (Table 9.4). Which, if any, leisure activities would you like to take up or develop further?

NOTES

1. Super, D. E. (1981) Approaches to occupational choice and career development. In A. G. Watts, D. E. Super and J. M. Kidd (eds), *Career Development in Britain* p. 9. Cambridge: Hobsons Press. Full reference pp. 7–51.
2. Holland, J. L. (1973) *Making Vocational Choices: A Theory of Careers* p. 85. Englewood Cliffs: Prentice-Hall.
3. Murray, H. A. (1938) *Explorations in Personality*. New York: Oxford.
4. Holland, J. L. (1959) A theory of vocational choice. *Journal of Counseling Psychology*, **6**, 35–45.
5. Holland, J. L. (1966) *The Psychology of Vocational Choice: A Theory of Personality Types and Model Environments*. Waltham, Massachusetts. Blaisdell.
6. Holland, J. L. (1973) *Making Vocational Choices: A Theory of Careers*. Englewood Cliffs, NJ: Prentice-Hall.
7. Holland, J. L. & Gottfredson, G. D. (1976) Using a typology of persons and environments to explain careers: some extensions and clarifications. *The Counseling Psychologist*, **6**, 3, 20–29.
8. Holland, J. L. (1973) *Making Vocational Choices: A Theory of Careers* pp. 2–4. Englewood Cliffs, NJ: Prentice-Hall.
9. *Ibid.* pp. 11–13. Table 9.1 is adapted from material contained in these pages.
10. Holland, J. L. & Gottfredson, G. D. (1976) Using a typology of persons and environments to explain careers: some extensions and clarifications. *The Counseling Psychologist*, **6**, 3, 21.
11. Holland, J. L. (1973) *Making Vocational Choices: A Theory of Careers* p. 5. Englewood Cliffs, NJ: Prentice-Hall.
12. Holland, J. L. (1958) A personality inventory employing occupational titles. *Journal of Applied Psychology*, **42**, 336–342.
13. Guilford, J. P., Christensen, P. R., Bond, N. A. & Sutton, M. A. (1954) A factor analysis study of human interests. *Psychological Monographs*, **68**, (4, whole no. 375).
14. Holland, J. L. (1966) *The Psychology of Vocational Choice: A Theory of Personality Types and Model Environments* pp. 15–41. Waltham, Massachusetts: Blaisdell.
15. Holland, J. L. (1973) *Making Vocational Choices: A Theory of Careers* pp. 11–36. Englewood Cliffs, NJ: Prentice-Hall.
16. Holland, J. L. (1966) *The Psychology of Vocational Choice: A Theory of Personality Types and Model Environments* pp. 52–62; and Holland, J. L. (1973) *Making Vocational Choices: A Theory of Careers* pp. 111–117. Englewood Cliffs, NJ: Prentice-Hall.
17. Holland, J. L. (1965) *Manual for the Vocational Preference Inventory*. Palo Alto: Consulting Psychologists Press.
18. Holland, J. L. (1973) *Making Vocational Choices: A Theory of Careers* pp. 108–109. Englewood Cliffs, NJ: Prentice-Hall.
19. Holland, J. L. (1970) *The Self-directed Search*. Palo Alto: Consulting Psychologists Press.
20. Holland, J. L. (1973) *Making Vocational Choices: A Theory of Careers* pp. 118–131. Englewood Cliffs, NJ: Prentice-Hall.
21. Strong, E. K. (1943) *Vocational Interests of Men and Women*. Stanford: Stanford University Press.
22. Campbell, D. P. & Holland, J. L. (1972) Applying Holland's theory to Strong's data. *Journal of Vocational Behaviour*, **2**, 353–376.
23. Holland, J. L. (1973) *Making Vocational Choices: A Theory of Careers* p. 3. Englewood Cliffs, NJ: Prentice-Hall.
24. *Ibid.* pp. 110–117.
25. *Ibid.* p. 23. Adapted from diagram on this page.
26. *Ibid.* pp. 24–26.
27. Linton, R. (1945) *The Cultural Background of Personality*. New York: Century, Appleton-Century-Crofts.

28. Holland, J. L. (1973) *Making Vocational Choices: A Theory of Careers* p. 27. Englewood Cliffs, NJ: Prentice-Hall.
29. Astin, A. W. & Holland, J. L. (1961) The environmental assessment technique: a way to measure college environments. *Journal of Educational Psychology*, **52**, 308–316.
30. Holland, J. L. (1973) *Making Vocational Choices: A Theory of Careers* p. 34. Englewood Cliffs, NJ: Prentice-Hall.
31. Holland, J. L. & Gottfredson, G. D. (1976) Using a typology of persons and environments to explain careers: some extensions and clarifications. *The Counseling Psychologist*, **6**, 3, 23.
32. Holland, J. L. (1973) *Making Vocational Choices: A Theory of Careers* pp. 37–40. Englewood Cliffs, NJ: Prentice-Hall.
33. *Ibid.* pp. 41–43.
34. Holland, J. L. & Gottfredson, G. D. (1976) Using a typology of persons and environments to explain careers: some extensions and clarifications. *The Counseling Psychologist*, **6**, 3, 24.
35. *Ibid.* pp. 25–26.
36. Holland, J. L. (1973) *Making Vocational Choices: A Theory of Careers* pp. 85–91. Englewood Cliffs, NJ: Prentice-Hall.
37. *Ibid.* pp. 110–117.
38. Thoresen, C. E. & Ewart, C. K. (1976) Behavioural self-control and career development. *The Counseling Psychologist*, **6**, 3, 33. Full reference pp. 29–43.
39. Holland, J. L. & Gottfredson, G. D. (1976) Using a typology of persons and environments to explain careers: some extensions and clarifications. *The Counseling Psychologist*, **6**, 3, 26–27.
40. Crowley, A. D. (1979) Work environment preferences and self-concepts: an investigation of Holland's theory. *British Journal of Guidance and Counselling*, **7**, 57–63.
41. Law, W. (1981) Careers theory: a third dimension? In A. G. Watts, D. E. Super and J. M. Kidd (eds), *Career Development in Britain* p. 300. Cambridge: Hobsons Press. Full reference pp. 300–337.
42. Roberts, K. (1968) Entry into employment: an approach towards a general theory. *Sociological Review*, **16**, 165–184.
43. Roberts, K. (1977) The social conditions, consequences and limitations of careers guidance. *British Journal of Guidance and Counselling*, **5**, 1–9.
44. Roberts, K. (1981) The sociology of work entry and occupational choice. In A. G. Watts, D. E. Super and J. M. Kidd (eds), *Career Development in Britain* pp. 279–299. Cambridge: Hobsons Press.
45. Daws, P. P. (1977) Are careers education programmes in secondary schools a waste of time? – a reply to Roberts. *British Journal of Guidance and Counselling*, **5**, 10–18.
46. Daws, P. P. (1981) The socialisation/opportunity-structure theory of the occupational location of school leavers: a critical appraisal. In A. G. Watts, D. E. Super and J. M. Kidd (eds), *Career Development in Britain* pp. 246–278. Cambridge: Hobsons Press.
47. Blau, P. M., Gustad, J. W., Jessor, R., Parnes, H. S. & Wilcock, R. C. (1956) Occupational choice: a conceptual framework. *Industrial and Labour Relations Review*, **9**, 531–543.
48. Roberts, K. (1977) The social conditions, consequences and imitations of careers guidance. *British Journal of Guidance and Counselling*, **5**, 3.
49. Willis, P. (1978) *Learning to Labour: How Working Class Kids Get Working Class Jobs*. Westmead: Saxon House.
50. Roberts, K. (1977) The social conditions, consequences and limitations of careers guidance. *British Journal of Guidance and Counselling*, **5**, 6–9.
51. Roberts, K. (1981) The sociology of work entry and occupational choice. In A. G. Watts, D. E. Super and J. M. Kidd (eds), *Career Developments in Britain* pp. 23–33. Cambridge: Hobsons Press.
52. Daws, P. P., *Social Determinism of Personal Choice?* Manuscript sent to author, June 1979.

53. Daws, P. P. (1977) Are careers education programmes in secondary schools a waste of time? – a reply to Roberts. *British Journal of Guidance and Counselling*, **5**, 10–18.
54. *Ibid.* pp. 9–26.
55. Halsey, A. H. (1975) Sociology and the education debate. *Oxford Review of Education*, **1**, 9–26. Table 9.3 is adapted from Table 1 on p. 14.
56. Daws, P. P. (1981) The socialisation/opportunity-structure theory of the occupational location of school leavers: a critical appraisal. In A. G. Watts, D. E. Super and J. M. Kidd (eds), *Career Development in Britain*, pp. 255–261. Cambridge: Hobsons Press.
57. Goldthorpe, J. H. & Llewellyn, C. (1977) Class mobility in modern Britain: three theses examined. *Sociology*, **11**, 257–287.
58. Daws, P. P. (1981) The socialisation/opportunity-structure theory of the occupational location of school leavers: a critical appraisal. In A. G. Watts, D. E. Super and J. M. Kidd (eds), *Career Development in Britain*, p. 262. Cambridge: Hobsons Press.
59. Nelson-Jones, R. & Fish, D. G. (1970) Woman students in Canadian medical schools. *British Journal of Medical Education*, **4**, 97–108.
60. Nelson-Jones, R. & Fish, D. G. (1970) Career performances of first-year students at Canadian medical schools, 1966–67 to 1968–69. *Canadian Medical Association Journal*, **103**, 29–33.
61. Tiedeman, D. V. (1961) Decision and vocational development: a paradigm and its implications. *Personnel and Guidance Journal*, **40**, 15–20.
62. Tiedeman, D. V., O'Hara, R. P. & Baruch, R. W. (1963) *Career Development: Choice and Adjustment*. Princeton, NJ: College Entrance Examination Board.
63. Krumboltz, J. D. & Baker, R. D. (1973) Behavioral counseling for vocational decisions. In H. Borow (ed.), *Career Guidance for a New Age* pp. 235–283. Boston: Houghton Mifflin.
64. Thoresen, C. E. & Ewart, C. R. (1976) Behavioral self-control and career development. *The Counseling Psychologist*, **6**, 3, 29–43.
65. Arroyba, T. (1977) Styles of decision making and their use: an empirical study. *British Journal of Guidance and Counselling*, **5**, 150. Full reference pp. 149–158
66. Gelatt, H. B., Varenhorst, B. & Carey, R. (1972) *Deciding*. New York: College Entrance Examination Board.
67. Arroyba, T. (1977) Styles of decision making and their use: an empirical study. *British Journal of Guidance and Counselling*, **5**, 149–158.
68. Williams, R. S. (1977) Psychological approaches to the study of leisure. *Bulletin of the British Psychological Society*, **30**, 8–12.
69. Overs, R. P. (1977) Avocational counselling. *The Counseling Psychologist*, **2**, 85–88.
70. Super, D. E. (1980) A life-span, life-space approach to career development. *Journal of Vocational Behaviour*, **16**, 282–298.
71. Super, D. E. (1953) A theory of vocational development. *American Psychologist*, **8**, 185–190.
72. McDowell, C. F. (1974) Toward a healthy leisure mode: leisure counseling. *Therapeutic Recreation Journal*, **3**, 96–104.
73. McKechnie, G. E. (1974) The psychological structure of leisure: past behaviour. *Journal of Leisure Research*, **1**, 27–45.
74. McKechnie, G. E. (1974) Psychological foundations of leisure counseling: an empirical strategy. *Therapeutic Recreation Journal*, **3**, 4–16.
75. *Ibid.* p. 8.
76. Roberts, K. (1981) The sociology of work entry and occupational choice. In A. G. Watts, D. E. Super and J. M. Kidd (eds), *Career Development in Britain* p. 296. Cambridge: Hobsons Press.

Part Two: Practice

10–Goals and Stages

SUMMARY: *All counsellors make decisions about goals and each counselling theory has its own goals. The values of both counsellors and clients are involved in their acceptance of and adherence to goals. There are a number of different roles in which counselling goals may be implemented. An important consideration is the extent to which clients, counsellors or society determine counselling goals.*

The goals of the theories discussed in Part One of this book are presented. Then a number of dimensions of counselling goals are discussed. These include whether the goals are: (a) medical or psychological; (b) ultimate or mediating, including mediating goals based on counsellor behaviours; (c) from the client's internal viewpoint or from other people's; (d) intrinsic or derived; (e) general or specific; (f) remedial, developmental or preventive; (g) developmental tasks to be attained during different age periods; (h) grouped according to topic areas; (i) individual, institutional or societal; and (j) limited in their attainment by both client and counsellor considerations.

Two possible ways of integrating goals are presented: first, the notion of positive mental health and, second, viewing goals in terms of experiencing, thinking and acting. The latter way lends itself to a view of goals and related counsellor interventions in terms of the stages of the counselling process. A model is proposed in which the early stages of counselling focus on increasing the client's capacity for experiencing, with the later stages being focused more on effective thinking and acting. The interrelated nature of experiencing, thinking and acting is acknowledged and some limitations of a stages view of the counselling process are mentioned. The chapter concludes with a case presentation in which differing client and counsellor goals emerge as counselling proceeds.

In Chapter 1 we took the view that the counsellor is a decision-maker, and that decisions in counselling practice basically fall into three categories: role, responding, and treatment decisions. Figure 1.1 depicted a treatment decision-making model in relation to client needs, a model largely based on humanistic and behavioural theory. In this chapter we discuss a number of issues relevant to counsellor decisions about what are mainly treatment goals. Many, if not all, of these issues are present regardless of theoretical orientation, and thus our discussion encompasses all the theories covered earlier in the book. Furthermore, we look at goals in relation to stages in the process of counselling and suggest that this is one way of reconciling some of the apparent differences between theoretical positions. In short, this is intended as a bridging chapter between the theory and practice parts of the book. The remaining chapters in the practice part of the book are focused more on how to handle specific aspects of the counsellor's role, be it individual counselling, group counselling, or psychological education. Before starting our discussion on goals, perhaps it should be re-emphasized that what distinguishes counselling psychology from fields like psychiatry and clinical psychology is a focus on wellness and self-realizing rather than on sickness, maladjustment and severe disturbance.

Goals involve individuals, singly or collectively, in roles concerned with attainment of the goals. Thus it is necessary both to have some conception of what the nature of effective human functioning is, and to allow that within the area of counselling psychology there will be different roles and methods of achieving the same overall goals. For instance, there are many roles within counselling psychology, including self-help, psychological education, counsellor training, theorizing and conducting research to develop the field. Each of these roles calls for variations in goals, yet they share common overall goals. However, the major emphasis in this chapter is a discussion of the dimensions of the overall goals rather than the specific goals of the various roles. Thus we deal with goals for human development and behaviour more than with methods of attaining these goals.

Decisions about goals also involve values. Patterson observes that the counsellor's own values enter into counselling and psychotherapy in the choice or acceptance of a goal.[1] Furthermore, counsellors may not only be espousing goals and basing their treatment interventions on them, but also modelling behaviour which may or may not be in accord with their goals and stated values. Counsellors who say that their *interventions* are value-free lack a real awareness of the dimensions of their interviewing and its impact on their clients. In a well-known study, Truax analysed excerpts from tape recordings of a single, long-term, successful counselling case with Rogers as the counsellor. Despite Rogers' method of counselling and psychotherapy being termed 'client-centred', Truax produced evidence suggesting that Rogers was responding with varying degrees of empathy, warmth and directiveness to some classes of his client's behaviour.[2] Similarly, counsellors who imply that their *goals* are value-free, like some behaviourists, also fail to acknowledge that they set limits concerning which of their clients' goals they are prepared to work towards. Krumboltz acknowledges the role of values in negotiating goals for behavioural counselling when he observes that client goals need to be 'compatible with, though not necessarily identical to' the values of their counsellors.[3] Thus, when discussing counselling goals and interventions, it is helpful to acknowledge that value dimensions are involved, and that such value assumptions may well merit exploration both in counsellor training and afterwards.

A fundamental issue in relation to decisions about goals is the basis on which a person is determined to be, and hence is labelled, the 'client'. Szasz observes: 'In the animal kingdom, the rule is, eat or be eaten; in the human kingdom, define or be defined'.[4] For instance, in families the 'disturbed' child may be reflecting the disturbed behaviour of one or both parents, each of whom may be more disturbed than the child. Another example may be the need for counselling by some predominantly homosexually oriented people, possibly reflecting the disturbed attitude and behaviour of many members of society towards their sexual orientation. In both the above instances it might be perceived that the more powerful have defined the less powerful as clients, thus avoiding a real examination of their own contribution to the 'disturbance'. Similarly, counselling psychologists have to beware of automatically labelling awkward client behaviour, such as anger at the counsellor, as disturbed when really it may rather be disturbing and threatening to their own sense of competence.

DIMENSIONS OF GOALS

Table 10.1 shows the goals for counselling and for living derived from the counselling psychology theories presented in the first part of this book. There appear to be a plethora of goals in counselling and psychotherapy and a number of books have appeared describing the goals of different theoretical positions.[5, 6] Our approach to the statement of goals includes identifying both some of the different dimensions against which these goals may be viewed and some important integrating themes.

There are a number of different dimensions against which the goals of counselling psychology in Table 10.1 may be viewed. Though the dimensions are often stated here in 'either/or' terms, there tends to be overlap within each dimension and thus the 'either' and 'or' may represent degrees of emphasis rather than mutually exclusive entities.

Medical or Psychological

Goals may be based on a medical or sickness model involving the treatment and, if possible, the cure of mental diseases. Such medical classification schemes focus on mental disorders frequently of an organic nature. For instance, the British psychiatry textbook by Trethowan adopts the following broad classificatory categories: (a) organic disorders: delirious and other acute states; (b) organic disorders: chronic brain syndromes; (c) alcoholism and drug dependence; (d) epilepsy; (e) affective disorders; (f) schizophrenia; (g) paranoid states; (h) abnormal emotional reactions; (i) anxiety states; (j) hysteria; (k) obsessive-compulsive disorders; (l) personality disorders; and (m) disturbances of sexual behaviour.[7] The American Psychiatric Association worked out a classification scheme for mental disorder in conjunction with the World Health Organization. As well as neuroses, its categories include mental retardation, organic brain syndromes and psychophysiologic disorders.[8] The point being made here is that, as stated in Table 10.1, the goals for counselling are in psychological rather than medical terms. This is not to deny that, especially with more severely disturbed clients, there may be overlap between the medical and the psychological. Also, some clients may need exclusively medical or psychiatric

Table 10.1 Goals for counselling and for living from different theoretical positions

Humanistic				Psychoanalytic	Behavioural	Occupational
Person-centred	Reality	Rational-emotive	Transactional analysis	Freudian	Composite*†	Composite*
Realistic perception	Attainment of successful identity	Rationality	Autonomous behaviour	Absence of neurotic symptoms	Absence of deficits in behaviour	Optimum matching of person and work
Openness to experience	Acceptance of reality	Appropriate emotionality	Awareness	Absence of debilitating repressions	Absence of weaknesses in behaviour	Formulation of realistic vocational self-concept
Trust of organismic valuing process	Acceptance of responsibility own behaviour	Maximization of pleasure	Spontaneity	Ego strength	Absence of maladaptive behaviour	Adequate exploration of career preferences
Rationality		Minimization of anxiety	Intimacy	Ability to meet instinctual needs	Absence of debilitating anxiety reactions	Decision-making skills
Responsibility	Capacity to formulate and implement plans	Minimization of hostility	Integrated adult attractiveness and responsiveness objective data-processing personal responsibility	Capacity to love	Capacity to relax	Absence of maladaptive anxiety reactions
Self-regard		Enlightened self-interest		Capacity to work	Assertive behaviour	Capacity to plan
Acceptance of others	Involvement with others	Self-direction	I'm OK—You're OK life position	Adherence to realistic moral standards	Adequate sexual functioning	Vocational satisfaction and stability
Capacity for good personal relations	Engagement in worthwhile activity	Tolerance	Absence of games		Self-control	Effective performance
Creativity	Ethical behaviour	Acceptance of uncertainty			Adequacy as behavioural model	Transcendence of adverse socialization
Ethical living		Flexibility				Optimization of opportunity structures
		Commitment				Healthy leisure behaviour
		Risk-taking				
		Self-acceptance				

* Derived from a number of different writers.
† Acknowledgement is made again that behavioural counsellors state goals for individual clients much more specifically.

attention and so are outside the scope of counselling psychology except for referral to the medical profession. There is a fuller discussion of medical considerations in counselling in Chapter 13.

Ultimate or Mediating

Parloff suggests that the goals of counselling and psychotherapy can be better understood if they are divided into two categories: mediating and ultimate.[9] He proposes that the ultimate goal of all therapy is to reduce discomfort and increase the effectiveness of the client or patient in his biological and social functioning. Furthermore, he considers that the differences between counselling theories in the stated ultimate goal will in all likelihood be small. Mediating goals, however, involve the counselling psychologist's or clinician's assumptions about the steps to be taken in achieving the ultimate goal, and here the goals appear to differ from one theory of counselling to another.

Referring to Table 10.1, it is possible to state that the ultimate goal of the person-centred position is the fully functioning or highly self-actualizing person; of reality therapy, the responsible person; of rational-emotive therapy, the rational person; of transactional analysis, the integrated Adult; and of Freudian psychoanalysis, the person with ego-strength. Furthermore, it could be argued that despite differences in terminology there is a considerable degree of agreement between humanistic, psychoanalytic and even behavioural models about the ultimate goal of counselling or about the psychologically well person in Western culture. Thus the *major* differences between the theoretical positions may revolve around means rather than ends. For instance, should the counsellor be aiming to provide a facilitative atmosphere in which clients can become open to their experience and hence more rational, or a rational atmosphere in which clients can become rational and hence more open to their experience? Here, depending on how counsellors answer this question, which is about mediating rather than ultimate goals, they may engage in the practice of person-centred or rational-emotive counselling. However, other counsellors may agree that, although being able to experience one's emotions and be rational are desirable ends, the way to encourage such adaptive behaviour may be through conditioning, counterconditioning, modelling, and self-control procedures. Such people will probably engage in the practice of behavioural counselling.

Parloff's distinction between ultimate and mediating goals seems insufficiently clear about the nature of mediating goals. Another possibility is to propose that, for example, for the person-centred position the *ultimate* goal is self-actualizing, whereas the items listed in the person-centred column of Table 10.1 are really client *mediating* goals. A second set of mediating goals, focused on counsellor interventions rather than on clients, would be that of providing high levels of empathy, genuineness, and non-possessive warmth. Figure 10.1 depicts this other way of viewing ultimate and mediating goals and provides a basic framework that will vary only in content, according to the theoretical position illustrated. The differences between Figure 10.1 and Parloff's distinction is that mediating goals here clearly refer not only to clients, but also to counsellor behaviours. Another way of stating this is to say that desirable

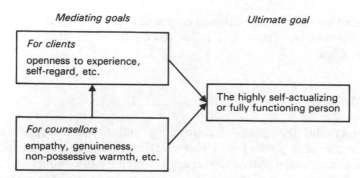

Figure 10.1   Ultimate and mediating goals for person-centred counselling.

counsellor behaviours represent the attainment of mediating goals on the counsellor's part which will in turn help clients to attain mediating goals involving their own behaviour. Mediating goals relating to counsellor behaviours may be more different and more controversial between the counselling approaches 'than client mediating goals of the sort depicted in Table 10.1.

Internal or External

Internal goals are those that clients state as their own, whereas external goals are those stated for the clients by other people, e.g. parents, spouses or counsellors. We shall develop the idea of the internal as contrasted with the external frame of reference or viewpoint in the next chapter. Goals from the internal viewpoint of clients are frequently stated by them as problems, which imply the need for a solution. Examples of *internal* goals are: 'I feel sad and depressed much of the time and wish I could get out of this.' 'I really haven't any idea as to what I should do with my life. In fact, just thinking about it really frightens me.' 'Things are going from bad to worse in my marriage and I wonder what I can do about it.' 'Since I've come to college the work has been piling up, but somehow I just can't get into it.' 'I feel lonely and isolated and seem to have no friends.'

The goals in Table 10.1 tend to be *external* goals derived from theories to which different counsellors adhere. Sometimes the differences between internal and external goals are differences in the language in which they are stated rather than real differences. However, there may be other instances where the differences are such that client and counsellor do not feel that they can work with each other. The emphases and terminology of every counselling approach are likely to prove uncongenial to some clients. Also, some counsellors may feel that they can offer a better or more personally rewarding service to certain kinds of clients with certain categories of problems and therefore they discourage other clients. In continuing counselling cases there tends initially to be an implicit or explicit orientation and negotiation process in which, to some degree at least, client and counsellor come to feel that they share mutual goals.

Intrinsic or Derived

Rogers' view of an actualizing tendency motivating clients towards enhancement and wholeness assumes that the goals of counselling are largely intrinsic to the organism. The goal of the counsellor is to provide the emotional climate and 'core' conditions in which clients can become more attuned to and act on their basic directional tendency towards self-actualization. In fact, Rogers says little about individual differences in the strength of the actualizing tendency and thus differences in people's intrinsic capacity to self-actualize. Humanistic psychologists consider that the counselling interaction should not be geared to a possibly superficial adjustment to culturally subscribed values, but should be representative of a deeper attempt to help the client to engage in a continuing process of autonomous self-realizing. On the other hand, to a behaviourist like Skinner the influence of the environment is pervasive. Although such psychologists acknowledge the influence of biological evolution, they view people and hence counselling goals as largely determined by, or derived from, the environmental contingencies of reinforcement in their societies.

General or Specific

Goals may be stated in broad terms, such as a high level of self-realizing, or in specific terms, such as the steps in a behavioural counselling approach using successive approximation to acquire a particular piece of behaviour systematically, or to countercondition a specific phobic area. The humanistic theorists tend to state their goals in more general terms than the behaviourists, though humanistic theorists, such as Glasser and Ellis, also use techniques involving planning and homework assignments in which specific goals may be set. Needless to say, the issue of general and specific goals is related to theoretical assumptions about human nature and the ways in which people acquire, perpetuate and can change their behaviour. Sometimes in practice counsellors offer their clients a basic helping relationship focused on improving their general sense of worth and ability to cope with life, at the same time focusing on specific areas of behaviour or thinking when they and their clients deem it appropriate.

Remedial, Developmental and Preventive

Often the possible goals for counsellors and for counselling services are stated in terms of being remedial and/or developmental and/or preventive. These are not discrete categories but represent differences in emphasis. One way of viewing remedial goals is that they are aimed at getting people to function at normative levels in their particular group or culture. For instance, individuals who become very anxious in social situations might be seen as being in need of remedial counselling assistance. Another way of viewing remedial goals is that they involve bringing about the absence of negative qualities. Developmental goals, on the other hand, focus on helping people to acquire psychological abilities rather than assuming the need for remedy of psychological disabilities. As such they involve working towards the presence of positive qualities. Indeed, developmental goals might include getting people to function at above normative levels for their culture. Developmental goals, sometimes known as growth goals, encompass deeper and more enriching personal relations, better use of leisure time, and a greater degree of identification with and concern for mankind. Maslow's description of the characteristics of self-actualizing people represents an attempt to state goals in developmental rather than remedial terms.[10] In counselling practice, attainment of remedial goals may accompany, if not be a prerequisite of, attainment of developmental goals. In fact, as remedial goals are attained, developmental goals may emerge.

Preventive goals focus on lessening the need for remedial counselling interventions. This may be by making the remedial interventions unnecessary or by reducing the level of disturbance of a potential client and thus reducing the time and financial investment involved in later counselling. For instance, pre-marital counselling and psychological education may lessen the amount and severity of later marital counselling. Daws observes that, in schools, sound prophylactic measures must not only screen children regularly for signs of distress and maladjustment, but must also provide healthy children with insights and skills so that their vulnerability to breakdown is reduced. This necessitates the personal and social education of all pupils,[11] and here there is a high degree of overlap between preventive and developmental goals.

Goals as Developmental Tasks

Some writers believe that it is hard to consider counselling goals independent of the individual's age and hence developmental status in his culture or sub-culture. Super's and Ginzberg's contributions regarding occupational choice and development are

Table 10.2   *Erikson's eight ages of man and their developmental conflict*[12]

Age	Conflict
Oral sensory	Basic trust versus mistrust
Muscular-anal	Autonomy versus shame, doubt
Locomotor-genital	Initiative versus guilt
Latency	Industry versus inferiority
Puberty and adolescence	Identity versus role confusion
Young adulthood	Intimacy versus isolation
Adulthood	Generativity versus stagnation
Maturity	Ego integrity versus despair

based on such an assumption. Freud also took an age-related view of the psychosexual development of children which has implications for counselling young people, and Erikson's work is based largely on Freudian psychology. Table 10.2 depicts Erikson's eight ages of man showing what he considers to be the critical developmental conflict for each age.

Erikson assumes that, in principle, the human personality develops according to predetermined and interrelated steps which 'all depend on the proper development in the proper sequence of each item'.[13] Psychosocial development proceeds by a series of critical steps or conflicts between forces making for progress and integration and those making for regression and retardation. During each age or stage the conflict, which previously had existed in some form, comes to the forefront, meets its crisis, and finds its solution, which may be for good or for ill.

Another developmental viewpoint, which focuses on behavioural goals, is that of Havighurst.[14] He views living in modern society as a long series of learning tasks which are frequently interrelated and sometimes recurrent. Havighurst defines a developmental task as 'a task which arises at or about a certain period in the life of the individual, successful achievement of which leads to his happiness and to success with later tasks, while failure leads to unhappiness in the individual, disapproval by the society and difficulty with later tasks'.[15] His six major age periods, with illustrative developmental tasks, are: infancy and early childhood (birth–6), forming concepts and developing language; middle childhood (ages 6–12), learning an appropriate masculine or feminine social role; adolescence (ages 12–18), achieving more mature relations with both sexes; early adulthood (ages 18–30), getting started in an occupation; middle age (ages 30–60), assisting teenage children; and later maturity (age 60+), adjusting to decreasing physical strength and health.[16] Havighurst considers that the tasks based mostly on biological maturation, such as learning to walk, show the least cultural variation, whereas those growing out of social demands show most variation. He acknowledges that his 'particular statement is based on American democratic values seen from a middle-class point of view'.[17]

It is probable that, regardless of their orientation, all counsellors assess their clients against some notion of what constitutes an effective way of living for a person of a given age. Furthermore, clients may also be assessing themselves against their capacity to attain goals representing developmental tasks for someone of their age. For instance, in early adulthood, vocational indecision and not having entered into a long-term committed relationship may, rightly or wrongly, give both counsellor and client pause for thought. Goals based on realistic developmental tasks can be useful in providing a guideline for effective functioning. However, one possible drawback is insufficient allowance for individual differences in life-styles. Additionally, both clients and non-clients may use failure to attain developmental tasks as sticks with which to beat themselves and others rather than as carrots for goal-oriented behaviour, thus eroding rather than sustaining motivation for change.

A desirable implication of goals based on developmental tasks is that counselling psychology services cease to become the preserve solely of children and young adults. Adjusting to mid-life, retirement and bereavement are examples of the developmental tasks of middle and old age providing counselling goals. Blocher is a writer who has written about counselling goals in relation to developmental tasks.[18] He views identity formation as seeking answers to questions such as 'Who am I?', 'Where am I going?' and 'What do I value', as a central developmental task for humans 'in every age and under every circumstance'.[19] He also considers that developmental tasks involve different social roles and coping behaviour depending on the life stage in which they fall.

Topic Area

Another dimension against which the goals of counselling are frequently viewed is that of topic area. Partly because of the large number of counsellors working in school and college settings, a common distinction is that between personal, educational and occupational counselling and their related goals. The practice part of this book focuses on counselling goals by topic areas, such as thinking, personal relations, learning, and occupational decision-making. Behavioural writers such as Krumboltz aim to state goals specifically even within topic areas. For instance, goals in the topic area of personal relations might include 'increasing socially assertive responses' and 'learning to discriminate between insults and friendly teasing'.[20] These goals might then be further broken down into sub-goals.

Individual, Institutional or Societal

Many counselling goals are stated in terms of individuals and small groups. However, a number of theorists, such as Rogers in *Freedom to Learn*[21] and *Carl Rogers on Personal Power*,[22] Freud in *Civilization and its Discontents*,[23] and Skinner in *Beyond Freedom and Dignity*,[24] are concerned with large-group and societal goals. Thus the goals for counselling and living depicted in Table 10.1 also tend to be viewed by the theorists as desirable goals for human societies. Carkhuff is a leading writer about the application of counselling skills and knowledge to the development of human resources.[25, 26] At the institutional and societal levels, counselling goals may provide a basis for social and political change.

Limitations on Goals

Counselling goals frequently have to be tailored to meet the realities of clients and their situations. Furthermore, the practice of counselling psychology is still evolving and as time goes by it may be possible to provide more potent counsellor treatment interventions. Thus limitations in goals are caused by client, counsellor and contextual considerations. Regarding client limitations, Havighurst notes that there may be sensitive or critical periods during which specific kinds of learning, such as learning to talk, may occur more quickly and in which certain experiences must occur if the person is to develop adequately.[27] Rutter observes that experiences occurring under the term 'maternal deprivation' are too heterogeneous for the term to have any usefulness and that it should now be abandoned. However, he concludes: 'That "bad" care of children in early life can have "bad" effects, both short-term and long-term, can be accepted as proven'.[28] Many biological and developmental influences may make it difficult to attain high levels of the goals of the different counselling positions. Although certain adverse developmental influences, such as absence of adequate bonding with another person early in life, may possibly be irreversible, other influences may still be reversible, but only with great difficulty. Changing disturbed behaviour involves unlearning as well as learning, and this is a more complex procedure than learning the appropriate behaviour in the first place. Rogers and his colleagues' scale to measure process changes in client-centred therapy is an example of a counselling outcome measure which acknowledges limitations on goals.[29] Here clients may be assessed on seven strands, such as 'manner of experiencing' and 'communication of self'. They start at different positions and then make progress by moving along the strands without necessarily reaching the end points. At higher levels of functioning the various strands converge, whereas they measure more discrete qualities at lower levels of functioning.

Concluding Comment

As the preceding discussion has indicated, counsellor decisions about goals are often more complex than they appear at first. It is important for counsellors to think through their goals in respect of both their overall roles and how they behave with specific clients or groups of clients. Our discussion of goals is intended to help counsellors to formulate goals and possibly to become more aware of some of their underlying or hidden assumptions. Counsellors, like their clients, have to resist tendencies to engage in self-protection. Here the professional and the personal may get intermingled and, for instance, a counsellor may be barred from a full consideration of possible goals for clients by an emotional rather than a rational need to adhere to a particular theory.

INTEGRATION OF GOALS

One approach to the goals of the different theoretical positions is to see whether some integration is possible by identifying common themes across theories. Two ways of doing this are discussed below.

Concepts of Positive Mental Health

Jahoda, in her review of literature on positive mental health, identified six major categories of concepts, to which all ideas on the topic could be assigned with relative ease, even though there might be some overlap. These six categories may be seen in Table 10.3, which also shows illustrative criteria for each category. There are two issues about Jahoda's list: first, the adequacy of the concept of positive mental health and, second, the adequacy of various ways in which it has been defined.

Many counselling psychologists and other social scientists have reservations about the term 'mental health', whether it is defined in positive or negative terms. These reservations include its connotations of a sickness model in which someone from outside provides a cure. Mental health is a value-laden term which causes some people seeking help with psychological concerns to evaluate themselves negatively, since,

Table 10.3 *Jahoda's six major categories of criteria for positive mental health*[30]

Categories	Illustrative criteria
Attitudes towards the self	Appropriate accessibility of the self to consciousness Realism of self-concept Acceptance of self, yet realistic evaluation of strengths and weaknesses Clarity and stability of sense of identity
Style and degree of growth, development, or self-actualization	Degree of motivation for actualizing capacities and talents Level of achievement of higher goals, such as concern with others, work, ideas and interests
Degree of integration, this being a central synthesizing psychological function	An appropriately flexible balance of psychological forces (such as id, ego, super ego) A unifying outlook or philosophy of life Resistance to stress and capacity to tolerate and cope with anxiety
Autonomy or degree of independence from social influences	Regulation of behaviour from within in accordance with internalized standards Optimal degree of independent behaviour
Adequacy of perception of reality	Perception free from need distortion and concern for evidence to support what is seen and anticipated Empathy or social sensitivity to the inner life of other people
Environmental mastery	Ability to love and to have satisfactory sexual relations Adequacy in love, work and play Adequacy in interpersonal relations Adequacy in meeting reasonable situational requirements Capacity for adaptation and adjustment Efficiency in problem-solving

almost by definition, they are labelled as mentally ill. Others may for this reason be deterred from seeking help or working on their problems. Additionally, the term 'mental health' leads to the treatment of psychological concerns being seen as the prerogative of the medical profession, whereas in fact, especially for the concerns of the less disturbed, medical knowledge, as contrasted with psychological knowledge, tends to be inappropriate, if not redundant.

Although they would be unlikely to use either the same categories or the same language, it is probable that Jahoda would gain a considerable measure of support from humanistic, psychoanalytic and behavioural counselling psychologists for the various elements she has identified as defining positive mental health. This reiterates the point made earlier that differences between theoretical positions may have more to do with counselling approaches to achieving goals than with the goals themselves.

Experiencing, Thinking and Acting

Another way of identifying common elements across theories is to view the different goals (see Table 10.1) in terms of experiencing, thinking and acting, even though these elements are interrelated. *Experiencing* may be expressed as the feeling or undergoing by the organism's sensory and visceral equipment of inner and outer facts and events which are potentially available to conscious awareness. The notion fairly common across counselling approaches is that people learn to block, distort, repress or become anxious about certain of their feelings as a result of their interactions with significant others while growing up. The term 'awareness' is often used to describe being aware of one's *own* experiencing and feelings, as contrasted with false experiencing and feelings based on *others'* attitudes and values. Examples of the concept of experiencing in theoretical positions include Rogers' idea of conditions of worth blocking experiencing, Berne's ideas on script injunctions hampering awareness, spontaneity and intimacy, Freud's ideas on repression interfering with the gratification of instinctual needs, and Wolpe's ideas on the need for counter-conditioning to facilitate adequate sexual experiencing. Areas of difference between theorists tend to centre on such issues as the positiveness or negativeness of human nature and the extent to which human nature allows for intentionality or free will. Despite such differences, capacity for experiencing is a significant implicit or explicit goal of all counselling theories.

Experiencing is not considered a sufficient goal for counselling, so the further goal of effective *thinking* is added to guide or help to achieve the attainment of appropriate experiencing. Effective thinking and capacity for experiencing are interrelated, in that feelings may be a basis for effective thinking as well as effective thinking being a vehicle for appropriate feeling. Virtually all the theorists in Table 10.1 cite effective thinking as a counselling goal, whether it is called rationality, as by Ellis and Rogers, acceptance of reality and responsibility, as by Glasser, an effective Adult, as by Berne, a strong ego as by Freud, self-control or self-regulation, as by Skinner and Bandura, or vocational maturity and effective career decision-making, as by Super and Krumboltz. Areas of difference concern the degree to which humans are capable of autonomous thinking, which is the free will issue, and whether or not counsellors should teach various specific skills of effective thinking, such as accurate attribution of responsibility for one's life, rational self-analysis using Ellis's A–B–C framework, helping clients to become aware of ego-defence mechanisms, or self-control and self-reinforcement procedures. A further area of difference is the extent to which theorists focus on ethical and even spiritual considerations.

Experiencing and thinking may together be insufficient goals for counselling if they are not accompanied by effective *acting*. Sometimes, as in Jahoda's concepts of positive mental health (Table 10.4), effective acting is expressed as environmental mastery. Her list of criteria for environmental mastery, relating to capacity for effective action in love, work, play, personal relations and meeting situational requirements, would, as indicated earlier, find little objection among the different theorists. Needless to say, the behaviourist position focuses most directly and specifically on effective acting, with its goal being a response repertoire adequate in terms of breadth, strength and adaptiveness. The theorists differ on the extent to which they emphasize behavioural goals as part of their counselling approach. For instance, among the humanistic theorists, Rogers tends not to, whereas Ellis and Glasser negotiate and set quite specific homework assignments. One of the reasons for this is a difference of opinion about the extent to which action is a necessary prelude to, part of, or consequence of increasing a person's capacity for experiencing.

Concluding Comment

The position we take in this book is that none of the theoretical viewpoints we have presented, as formulated at present, is comprehensive enough to cover the various goals of experiencing, thinking and acting. Allport wrote: 'The trouble with our current theories of learning is not so much that they are wrong, but that they are partial',[31] and the same might be said about the various counselling theories. For example, the person-centred approach has a major focus on capacity for experiencing, the humanistic-rational approaches have a major focus on thinking, and the traditional behaviourists have their major focus on acting. Counsellors must always remember that they are dealing with whole persons who, if they are to function effectively, need to be able to experience, think and act effectively. Thus the practice part of this book is based on an attempt to analyse where counselling clients are facing difficulties and to present an integrated approach which is more comprehensive than, yet derived from, the individual counselling theories reviewed earlier.

There is some evidence that many practising psychologists are also finding individual theories lacking. In a 1974 survey of theoretical orientations among a sample of American clinical psychologists, almost 55 per cent of those surveyed labelled themselves as eclectics.[32] When asked the two theoretical orientations most characteristic of their eclectic views, the three most common combinations were psychoanalytic and learning theory, neo-Freudian and learning theory, and neo-Freudian and Rogerian. The most common reason they adopted eclecticism was that they used 'whatever theory or method seems best for the client'.[33] There was a large decline between surveys reported in 1961 and in 1974 in the proportion of clinical psychologists adhering to psychoanalytic and related orientations. It is notable that analytic orientations featured in each of the three leading eclectic combinations, indicating reservations about the use of psychoanalysis in clinical practice.

STAGES IN COUNSELLING

The concept of stages in counselling may be looked at from the viewpoints of client development and of corresponding counsellor behaviours related to their assessments of 'where the client is at'. Discussing stages in counselling introduces the concepts of client *readiness* and the *timing* of counsellor interventions, both of which are extremely pertinent to the practitioner. Another way of saying this is that decisions on counsellor interventions tend to involve four dimensions: *what* to do, to *whom*, *when*, and *how*.

A number of writers have suggested frameworks for counselling based on a stages model of client development and related counsellor interventions. For instance, Carkhuff observes that the following stages appear to be operative in most effective helping processes:

1. a minimal translation of the helpee's explorations into self-understanding;
2. the development of some direction, however tentative, based upon this minimal understanding;
3. acting upon this directionality;
4. incorporating the feedback from the action;
5. reflecting back upon prior understanding and sharpening earlier discriminations;
6. acting more constructively based upon finer and more sensitive understanding.[34]

Carkhuff proposes a two-phase model of helping, with suggested counsellor interventions, such as empathy, specificity and confrontation, timed to coincide with the level of readiness of the client. The first phase is the downward or inward phase of self-exploration, and the second phase is the upward or outward phase of emergent directionality and action.[35]

Egan's model of helping seems designed to help clients to cope with problems in relatively time-limited counselling. It has a pre-helping phase and three stages, each defined by helper and client goals. In stage one the helper's goal is responding, whereas the client's goal is self-exploration. In stage two the helper's goal is integrative understanding, whereas the client's goal is dynamic self-understanding, which involves seeing the need for action. In stage three the helper's goal is facilitating action, whereas the client's goal is acting.[36] Hamblin also proposes a stage model of the counselling process for the British secondary school. Phase one is concerned with developing pupil powers of comprehension, facilitating self-understanding, and developing goals and insights. Phase two is concerned with the development of constructive coping strategies and with the translation of attitudes and aims into practice in the daily life of the pupil.[37]

Underlying Carkhuff's, Egan's and Hamblin's stages of the counselling process is the assumption that, in general, counsellors and their clients should focus on goals relating to experiencing, thinking and acting, in that order. The practice part of this book also assumes a stages concept of the counselling process and we are in broad agreement with the viewpoint that a nurturing or facilitative stage of counselling, focused on improving the client's capacity for experiencing, should precede a stage focused on thinking and acting. In the next chapter we propose the concept of basic empathy as being the appropriate counsellor behaviour for the experiencing or nurturing stage, whereas other interventions or additive elements may be more relevant to the thinking and acting stages.

There are many qualifications to the stage conception of the counselling process presented here. Perhaps most important, it is a model based on central tendencies and, as such, inadequately covers exceptions to the rule. For instance, counsellors may need to be flexible in dealing with specific concerns, such as phobias, or when faced with client time constraints, such as getting through next week's examination. Furthermore, it is a model which tends, especially in its first stage, to assume that others, such as parents, have contributed strongly to the client's problems through being too restrictive. With clients brought up in a permissive or deviant environment and whose behaviour is too 'loose' and lacking in self-control rather than too 'tight' and inhibited, this is an untenable assumption. Additionally, constraints may be imposed by the extent and directions of different counsellors' knowledge and skills. Furthermore, the goals and needs of individual clients may indicate that only part of the model can or should be implemented. For instance, less disturbed clients may be ready from the start for the stage in counselling emphasizing thinking and acting.

The stages view of the counselling process suggests a possible reconciliation between the goals and methods of humanistic and behavioural counselling positions as formulated at present. Also, it has implications for the development of a more comprehensive theory than those now existing. The person-centred approach may have most to offer during the nurturing stage focused on experiencing; the humanistic-rational approaches may be useful during that part of the action-oriented stage focused on thinking, and the behaviourist approaches may be helpful when the focus turns to acting. However, it must be stressed not only that the above reconciliation is suggested tentatively, but also that frequently there is overlap in counselling practice between emphases on experiencing, thinking and acting.

CASE ILLUSTRATION

When working with clients goals may emerge and alter as counselling preceeds. Below is an example of this:

> John, a single 22-year-old student, entered counselling after a suicide attempt in March of his final year at college. The counsellor's initial goal was to establish a relationship with him in which he would feel safe and free to discuss the concerns which previously were experienced as overwhelming. Therefore John needed to feel understood on his own terms and to perceive that the counsellor was a competent and trustworthy person. Furthermore, having had no adult in the past with whom he could really talk, he needed time in which to experience and explore his thoughts and emotions about his past and current life. A goal which emerged during the initial sessions was that John, despite being far behind in his work and revision, wanted to obtain his degree. Therefore a study skills emphasis was introduced to help to attain this goal. On obtaining his degree, he went overseas for some months. On his return he was still relatively isolated and unsure of himself. Part of his lack of confidence was associated with his anxieties about his hand shaking, to the point where he would draw attention to himself, if he were to drink coffee or eat in public. He felt that getting a job was out of the question while he had this problem. Therefore priority was given to the goal of overcoming his anxieties about eating and drinking in public. Once progress was made on overcoming this problem, he started thinking about employment. However, he had no strong career preferences, so then there emerged the counselling goal of exploring his occupational self-concept and helping him to enter the world of work. An important reason for employment at this stage was to earn money so that he could improve his social life and find a girlfriend. During his occupational exploration he rediscovered his liking for outdoor activity and then obtained a fulfilling job as a park-keeper. Soon afterwards he found a girlfriend.[38]

During the stages of the counselling process, as different goals emerged for John, there were different emphases on experiencing, thinking and acting. Since it is not the purpose of this chapter to discuss treatment approaches, suffice it for now to say that the interventions used by the counsellor were drawn from both humanistic and behavioural approaches. A final point is that the counsellor perceived his role as assisting this client in obtaining the confidence, knowledge and skills for *effective self-help*, the ultimate goal of all counselling psychology.

PRACTICAL QUESTIONS

It may help you to understand this chapter better if, either individually or as part of a skills group, you think about and answer the following questions:

1.   Why are goals important in counselling psychology?

2.   Who do you think should determine goals in counselling? Give reasons for your answer.

3.   Describe the main values which will influence your performance as a counsellor.

4.   To what extent are both client and counsellor goals culturally and socially determined?

5.   Discuss the goals of counselling in relation to the following dimensions:
   (a)   medical or psychological;
   (b)   ultimate or mediating;
   (c)   internal or external;
   (d)   intrinsic or derived;
   (e)   general or specific;
   (f)   remedial, developmental or preventive;
   (g)   goals as developmental tasks;
   (h)   categorization by topic area;
   (i)   individual, institutional or societal goals;
   (j)   limitations on goals.

6.   To what extent do all clients have similar goals? Discuss possible similarities and differences in client goals.

7.   Critically assess the idea of distinguishing counselling goals on the dimensions of experiencing, thinking and acting.

8.   Give your reactions to the view that there are different stages in counselling, with different goals appropriate to each stage.

NOTES

1. Patterson, C. H. (1974) *Relationship Counseling and Psychotherapy* p. 22. New York: Harper and Row.
2. Truax, C. B. (1966) Reinforcement and non-reinforcement in Rogerian psychotherapy. *Journal of Abnormal Psychology*, **71**, 1–9.
3. Krumboltz, J. D. (1966) Behavioral goals for counseling. *Journal of Counseling Psychology*, **13**, 154. Full reference pp. 153–159.
4. Szasz, T. S. (1973) *The Second Sin* p. 20. London: Routledge and Kegan Paul.
5. Mahrer, A. R. (ed.) (1967) *The Goals of Psychotherapy*. New York: Appleton-Century-Crofts.
6. Huber, J. L. & Millman, H. L. (1972) *Goals and Behavior in Psychotherapy and Counseling*. Columbus, Ohio: Charles E. Merrill.
7. Trethowan, W. H. (1979) *Psychiatry* (4th edition). London: Ballière and Tindall.
8. American Psychiatric Association (1968) *Diagnostic and Statistical Manual of Mental Disorders* (2nd edition). Washington: American Psychiatric Association. Presented in modified form in Coleman, J. S. (1972) *Abnormal Psychology and Modern Life* (inside of back cover). Glenview, Illinois: Scott, Foresman.
9. Parloff, M. B. (1967) Goals in psychotherapy: mediating and ultimate. In A. R. Mahrer (ed.), *The Goals of Psychotherapy* pp. 5–19. New York: Appleton-Century-Crofts.
10. Maslow, A. H. (1970) Self-actualizing people: a study of psychological health. In A. H. Maslow, *Motivation and Personality* (2nd ed.) pp. 149–180. New York: Harper and Row.
11. Daws, P. P. (1973) Mental health and education: counselling as prophylaxis. *British Journal of Guidance and Counselling*, **1**, 2–10.
12. Erikson, E. H. (1963) Eight ages of man. In E. H. Erikson, *Childhood and Society* (2nd ed.) p. 273. New York: Norton. Full reference pp. 247–274.
13. *Ibid.* p. 271.
14. Havighurst, R. (1972) *Developmental Tasks and Education* (3rd ed.). New York: David McKay.
15. *Ibid.* p. 2.
16. *Ibid.* Age periods and illustrative tasks form the contents of the book.
17. *Ibid.* p. 34.
18. Blocher, D. (1966) *Developmental Counseling* pp. 45–71. New York: Ronald.
19. *Ibid.* p. 8.
20. Krumboltz, J. D. (1966) Behavioral goals for counseling. *Journal of Counseling Psychology*, **13**, 155.
21. Rogers, C. R. (1969) *Freedom to Learn*. Columbus, Ohio: Charles E. Merrill.
22. Rogers, C. R. (1977) *Carl Rogers on Personal Power: Inner Strength and its Revolutionary Impact*. London: Constable.
23. Freud, S. (1962) *Civilization and its Discontents*. New York: W. W. Norton. Original edition 1930.
24. Skinner, B. F. (1971) *Beyond Freedom and Dignity*. Harmondsworth, Middlesex: Penguin Books.
25. Carkhuff, R. R. (1971) *The Development of Human Resources: Education, Psychology and Social Change*. New York: Holt, Rinehart and Winston.
26. Carkhuff, R. R. (1972) New directions in training for the helping professions: toward a technology for human and community resource development. *The Counseling Psychologist*, **3**, 3, 12–20.
27. Havighurst, R. (1972) *Developmental Tasks and Education* (3rd ed.) pp. 6–7. New York: David McKay.
28. Rutter, M. (1972) *Maternal Deprivation Reassessed* p. 128. Harmondsworth, Middlesex: Penguin Books.
29. Walker, A. M., Rablen, R. A. & Rogers, C. R. (1960) Development of a scale to measure process changes in psychotherapy. *Journal of Clinical Psychology*, **16**, 79–85.

30. Jahoda, M. (1958) *Current Concepts of Positive Mental Health*. New York: Basic Books. Table 10.3 was derived from material in pp. 22–63.
31. Allport, G. W. (1962) Psychological models for guidance. *Harvard Educational Review*, **32**, 380. Full reference pp. 378–381.
32. Garfield, S. L. & Kurtz, R. (1974) A survey of clinical psychologists: characteristics, activities and orientations. *The Clinical Psychologist*, **28**, 7–10.
33. Garfield, S. L. & Kurtz, R. (1977) A study of eclectic views. *Journal of Counseling and Clinical Psychology*, **45**, 78–83.
34. Carkhuff, R. R. (1969) *Helping and Human Relations: Volume 2, Practice and Research* p. 47. New York: Holt, Rinehart and Winston.
35. *Ibid*. pp. 81–102.
36. Egan, G. (1975) *The Skilled Helper: A Model for Systematic Helping and Interpersonal Relating* pp. 28–54. Monterey: Brooks Cole.
37. Hamblin, D. H. (1974) *The Teacher and Counselling* pp. 21–65. Oxford: Blackwell.
38. The counsellor was the author.

11 – *The Fundamental Counselling Relationship*

SUMMARY: *This chapter begins by discussing the intellectual, didactic, experiential and integrated intellectual-didactic-experiential approaches to the practical training of counsellors. An integrated approach is advocated. The idea of a fundamental counselling relationship is examined, focusing on Fiedler's research into the characteristics of an Ideal Therapeutic Relationship, independent of counselling 'school', and on Rogers' necessary and sufficient conditions for therapeutic personality change. A distinction is made between basic empathy, understanding and responding to the client's current reality, and additive empathy, or counsellor interventions which go beyond basic empathy in helping clients to realize their potential. Basic empathy is a necessary ingredient of all successful counselling relationships, though it is sometimes insufficient. Nevertheless, the skills and attitudes of basic empathy constitute the fundamental counselling relationship.*

The remainder of the chapter comprises a series of exercises, with accompanying text, designed to focus on aspects of counsellor provision of basic empathy. The main emphasis of the early exercises is on accurate listening, both to the counsellor's own attitudes and self-evaluations and to the client's personal viewpoint or internal frame of reference. Additionally, some of the early exercises focus on creating an awareness of the importance of empathic non-verbal and para-verbal communications. Next the concept of empathy is described more fully, followed by an exercise on discriminating its presence or absence in counsellor responses. The remaining exercises focus on developing empathic responding through appropriate use of words. These exercises cover reflection of content, reflection of feeling, and reflection of content and feeling together, as well as empathic co-counselling. Suggestions are made for further practising of empathic responding; also, for ways of integrating counselling-skills exercises into an introductory laboratory or pre-practicum seminar, prior to counselling real clients under supervision.

In the previous chapter we reviewed the goals of and explored the idea of stages in counselling. This chapter will focus on the fundamental interviewing relationship, involving helping clients to feel comfortable in the counsellor's presence, helping them to talk, and understanding what they are saying. In short, this chapter will focus on the attitudes and skills involved in a fundamental or facilitative counselling relationship, drawing heavily on the insights of the person-centred approach. Training in such a fundamental relationship is necessary because there is research evidence that many people starting counsellor training, and even some counsellor trainers, are deficient in the ability to listen and respond empathically. Also, some counsellor training may be ineffective, if not detrimental, if trainer counselling skills are poor.[1,2,3]

The person-centred approach to counselling is mainly about the level of emotional development of the counsellor, and hence her attitude of respect and caring for her clients, and not just about techniques. Although practising techniques may be better than nothing, it lacks the potency of the person-to-person contact between a highly self-actualizing and therapeutically genuine counsellor and her clients. In short, a narrow skills emphasis is both insufficient for really good counselling and an incomplete model for counsellor training.

There are a variety of models of or approaches to the practical part of counsellor training, or the counselling practicum, to use the American term. One model is the *intellectual* approach, where the counselling interview is discussed with a possible emphasis on experimental research evidence and on intellectual analysis of clients as 'cases'. In this approach it is possible for aspiring counsellors to receive little or no interview experience with clients.

Another model is the *didactic* or pedagogic approach where 'the emphasis is upon the direct teaching, structuring, or shaping of the thinking and responding of the trainee in accord with the teacher's belief system concerning what dimensions of the therapeutic process are most conducive to constructive change'.[4] Sometimes this may take the form of a skills training approach to the practice of counselling, where the skills objectives are stated as precisely as possible. Then behavioural programmes to attain these objectives are designed, implemented, monitored and evaluated.

A further model is the *experiential* or relationship-based approach. Here the goal is that trainees should develop their own orientations to counselling, based on their own experience. The role of the trainer is twofold: first, to provide a safe and secure emotional climate in which the trainee can experience and explore her concerns about counselling; and second, to provide adequate practical learning experiences, including fairly early contact with clients. The trainer is a facilitator of significant experiential learning and, though intellectual learning may broaden the trainee's comprehension of counselling, it is viewed as a very inadequate basis for engaging in it.[5]

A fourth model is an *integrated* intellectual-didactic-experiential model which, especially for trainees who wish to engage in theory building and research, acknowledges the importance of intellectual learning. At the same time, however, trainees are encouraged to focus on their personal development both through their relationships with their trainers and, if possible, through providing them with suitable opportunities to participate as clients in both individual and group counselling.[6] Also, they are encouraged to develop the attitudes and skills of the effective counsellor through experiential, small-group laboratory training as well as, when ready, being provided with suitable placements entailing the opportunity to counsel real clients and so monitor and develop their interviewing competence. *We support and advocate an integrated approach to counsellor training*, viewing each of the three preceding approaches as a partial and insufficient approach for maximizing training outcomes. Furthermore, we stress the need for counsellor trainers who are also skilled as counsellors and who continue to practise and develop their interviewing competence. Just as an integrated approach is needed for counsellor training, so are counsellor trainers needed who can perform well in each of its elements.

Possibly of all the chapters, this lends itself most easily to a 'how-to-do-it' approach. Consequently, integrated with the text are practical exercises and also suggestions for further practice. Although the chapter may be read on its own, its full impact will be derived only if readers work through the exercises in pairs or as part of a larger group, preferably with a good counsellor trainer who models the required skills and attitudes. The material contained here is part of what might be the content of a counselling skills laboratory or pre-practicum seminar, for which other suggestions are given at the end of the chapter.

THE FUNDAMENTAL COUNSELLING RELATIONSHIP

In 1950 Fiedler published two important articles that raised the issue of whether there is an ideal therapeutic relationship transcending various schools of counselling and psychotherapy.[7,8] His method of investigation was to ask therapists of different orientations to describe the relationship which they considered ideal. In the first article the statements most characteristic of an ideal therapeutic relationship included:

> An empathic relationship
> Therapist and patient relate well
> Therapist sticks closely to the patient's problems
> The patient feels free to say what he likes
> An atmosphere of mutual trust and confidence exists
> Rapport is excellent

Statements rated least characteristic of an ideal therapeutic relationship included:

> A punitive therapist
> Therapist makes the patient feel neglected
> The therapist seems to have no respect for the patient
> An impersonal, cold relationship
> The therapist often puts the patient 'in his place'
> The therapist curries favor with the patient[9]

The second article, a comparison of therapeutic relationships in psychoanalysis and non-directive and Adlerian therapy, indicated that expert therapists of any of the three schools create relationships more closely approximating the ideal therapeutic relationship than relationships created by non-experts. Also, the most important dimension which differentiated experts from non-experts was 'related to the therapist's ability to understand, to communicate with, and to maintain rapport with the patient'.[10]

In 1957 Rogers elaborated Fiedler's theme and presented his six necessary and sufficient conditions for therapeutic personality change.[11] He stated that the following conditions had to exist and continue over a period of time for constructive personality change to occur:

1. Two persons are in psychological contact.
2. The first, whom we shall term the client, is in a state of incongruence, being vulnerable or anxious.
3. The second person, whom we shall term the therapist, is congruent or integrated in the relationship.
4. The therapist experiences unconditional positive regard for the client.
5. The therapist experiences an empathic understanding of the client's internal frame of reference and endeavours to communicate this experience to the client.
6. The communication to the client of the therapist's empathic understanding and unconditional positive regard is to a minimal degree achieved.[12]

The third, fourth and fifth of Rogers' six conditions are: congruence, otherwise known as genuineness or authenticity; unconditional positive regard, sometimes called prizing, warmth, non-possessive warmth or, most commonly, respect; and empathic understanding. Advocates of the client or person-centred position regard these as the core conditions or core dimensions of a counselling relationship,[13] and a considerable amount of research has pointed to their efficacy when used by person-centred counsellors.[14] In a later paper, Rogers reaffirmed his belief that 'in a wide variety of professional work involving relationships with people . . . it is the *quality* of the interpersonal encounter with the client which is the most significant element in determining effectiveness'.[15]

Though there are three core conditions, especially in his later works Rogers seems most heavily to emphasize empathy, a 'very special way of being with another person', as the central condition of his counselling approach.[16] Dictionary definitions of empathy include 'intellectual or emotional identification with another'[17] and 'the power of projecting one's personality into (and so fully comprehending) the object of contemplation'.[18] Other ways of defining empathy include Fiedler's succinct summarization 'to understand, to communicate with and to maintain rapport with the patient', and research scale definitions by Truax and Carkhuff,[19] and by Carkhuff.[20] We take the position that high levels of counsellor empathy entail counsellors' being genuine and respecting their clients. Consequently we use the single term 'basic empathy' for the three core conditions described by Rogers in his 1957 paper. Here Rogers raises two issues in regard to basic empathy, namely, whether it is (a) necessary and (b) sufficient for desirable changes to occur in clients. There seems little doubt that basic empathy is a necessary ingredient of virtually all successful counselling relationships. As well as person-centred counsellors, this has been made explicit or implied by psychoanalytic, Adlerian[21] and, to a lesser extent, rational-emotive[22] and behavioural counsellors,[23] to mention but some. In fact such empathy is the basic interviewing competence common to all schools and approaches.

The assertion that basic empathy is sufficient for all clients, with many different presenting concerns and levels of self-realizing, is much less tenable. Basic empathy is vital, especially for the more disturbed, who may be inhibited and unable to experience their emotions. For the less disturbed, however, and also for those with specific concerns such as certain phobias, basic empathy is likely to be neither sufficient nor, in many instances, sufficiently expeditious. The above statement is not in accord with Rogers' position, but neo-client-centred writers such as Carkhuff, with his early stage of self-exploration and his later stage of emergent directionality or action,[24] and Egan, with his later stages of integrative understanding and facilitating action,[25] acknowledge that further interventions involving additive or advanced empathy may be necessary.

The dictionary definitions of empathy imply identifying and understanding clients as they currrently view themselves. Often such understanding or *basic empathy* is capable of helping clients to higher levels of self-realizing or attainment of their goals. However, a major assumption underlying the exclusive provision of basic empathy by counsellors is that their clients have latent resources which only need the right emotional climate to become manifest. The position we take is that many clients, especially after the nuturing stages of counselling, need more active interventions by counsellors to help them to still higher levels of self-realizing. Such interventions have a more specific rather than a general focus. At later stages in counselling the identification is with clients' potentials rather than with their current realities. To the extent that interventions beyond basic empathy are effective in helping clients to achieve their potentials, they might justifiably be viewed as *additive empathy*. The remainder of this chapter, however, focuses on basic empathy, or on the skills and attitudes of the fundamental counselling relationship, while those relevant to additive empathy are discussed in later chapters. The goal of both basic and additive empathy is to help clients towards a continuing process of more effective self-help.

A MODEL OF THE COUNSELLING INTERVIEW

Table 11.1 is a diagrammatic representation of an individual counselling interview. It can also be expanded to make it appropriate for group counselling. The interview relationship is a continuing process between two people one of whom is termed the counsellor and the other the client. Psychologically, especially for the client, the relationship is likely to continue outside the scheduled interview time, even though the participants will probably not be in physical contact. Counselling contact may be brief, e.g. from one to six interviews, or more extensive, up to 100 interviews or more. Additionally, it may take place on an individual, group, or combination of individual and group interview bases.

Table 11.1 focuses on some of the dimensions common to all counselling interviews. Communication takes place in both the private and the public domain. Within the private domain both the client and the counsellor have their thoughts, feelings and expectations, which they may conceal or, alternatively, reveal to the other, intention-

Table 11.1 *Diagrammatic representation of the counselling interview*

Client: private	Client and counsellor: public	Counsellor: private
Private thoughts, feelings and expectations	Client's verbal communications and self-exploration	Private thoughts, feelings and expectations
Availability to awareness of thoughts and feelings	Counsellor's verbal communications	Availability to awareness of thoughts and feelings
Degree of self-acceptance	Client's intended and unintended bodily communications	Degree of self-acceptance
Anticipation of risk in self-disclosure	Counsellor's intended and unintended bodily communications	Internal dialogue
Internal dialogue	(Accuracy of client's perception of counsellor's verbal and bodily communications)	
	(Accuracy of counsellor's perception of client's verbal and bodily communications)	

ally or unintentionally, in words and/or body language. Most of the counsellor's thoughts and feelings should be accessible to awareness because of her greater degree of self-acceptance, though most, if not all, counsellors have areas of their experiencing about which they remain insufficiently aware. In successful counselling, clients are likely to become increasingly aware of their experiencing. Since a focus of the counselling relationship is on client disclosure, anticipation of risk in self-disclosure is likely to be more prominent in client than in counsellor private thinking. This private thinking for both client and counsellor may be viewed in terms of an internal dialogue. What is revealed in the public domain may be accurately perceived by one or both parties or, for various reasons, it may be inaccurately perceived. Inaccurate perception of the other's disclosures may be a feature of earlier rather than later stages of counselling relationships. Contributing to this phenomenon are the facts that counsellor and client may be reacting to each other partly in terms of previous experiences and that both parties may be anxious as they adjust to a new relationship.

LEARNING BASIC EMPATHY: PART ONE EXERCISES

The remainder of this chapter consists of 12 exercises plus additional material. In part, these exercises resemble those of other writers such as Porter,[26] Carkhuff,[27] Ivey and Authier[28] and Egan.[29] However, all the exercises have been designed specifically for this chapter and some are very different from those found elsewhere. The approach by which counselling skills are taught in small segments is called microcounselling. Such an approach may consist of the trainees' reading a manual defining a specific skill, viewing a demonstration of the skill by an expert, practising the skill, getting feedback, and then engaging in further practice. Although skills are necessary for counsellor trainees, they are not sufficient and, as mentioned earlier, need to be supplemented by supervised contact with many clients and work focused on the trainee's personal and intellectual development.

The exercises that follow are focused on encouraging trainees to explore and listen to themselves, become aware of their non-verbal and para-verbal communication, learn to listen to and understand clients, and finally to be able to communicate this understanding. There is thus a major emphasis on learning to listen properly, with use of words in responding being left until the later exercises. Many clients have not been listened to and understood adequately in the past, and hence they badly need the experience of being listened to and accepted if they are to learn to listen to, understand and value themselves. Rogers cites a beautiful saying of Lâo-Tsze in this regard:

> It is as though he listened
> and such listening as his enfolds us in a silence
> in which at last we begin to hear
> what we are meant to be[30]

Counsellor Trainee Self-exploration

The philosophical and attitudinal orientation of the counsellor is fundamental to the practice of counselling. Exercise 1 is based on theoretical and practical issues in counselling. Complete Exercise 1, check your answers in the 'Responses for Exercises' section at the end of the chapter, and then read on.

Exercise 1. Assessing your counselling attitude

After considering each statement, write down on a piece of paper whether or not you are in basic agreement (A), disagree (D), or cannot decide (?). Do not use (?) unless absolutely necessary and do not spend too much time on any one item. Answer all items.

1.   The counsellor's goal is to make people better adjusted to society.
2.   The counsellor should be in control of the interview at all times.
3.   If counselling is to be successful, the counsellor must depend for the most part on the client's own potential for growth.
4.   A complete case history is unnecessary before the counsellor actually begins counselling with the client.
5.   If the client talks about a number of problems at the same time the counsellor should tell him/her to concentrate on one problem at a time.
6.   One of the counsellor's main functions is to try to convey to the client that he/she accepts the client's feelings and attitudes.
7.   If the client presents a point of view that is obviously prejudiced or distorted, the counsellor should set him/her straight.
8.   Verbalization of insight is not crucial in counselling.
9.   After a therapeutic working relationship has been established the counsellor should begin to interpret the client's unconscious attitudes and feelings.
10.   After a client has stated his/her problem the counsellor should offer one or more possible solutions to serve as a basis for further discussion.
11.   It is rarely helpful for the counsellor to let the client know what he/she would do when faced with the same problem.
12.   The counsellor should give advice when the client requests it.
13.   If the counsellor feels the client persists in wasting interview time, he/she should share his/her feeling with the client.
14.   The counsellor should allow the client to make self-derogatory statements.
15.   The counsellor should never take a client's statements at face value, since the client is not aware of the hidden import behind them.
16.   The counsellor should refrain from adapting the counselling relationship to the expectations of the client.

The above items have been taken from a 70-item *Counsellor Attitude Scale*[31] which purports to measure the central *attitudinal* hypothesis of the person-centred counsellor 'that the individual has a sufficient capacity to deal with all those aspects of his life which can potentially come into conscious awareness'.[32] The central *implementation* hypothesis, based on respect for and reliance on the capacity of the person, is that growth is most likely to take place when the counsellor is able to enter the client's internal frame of reference and respond with empathic understanding. Thus a very high score on the Counsellor Attitude Scale would indicate that the rater considers basic empathy to be both necessary and sufficient for effective counselling. A factor analysis of the Counsellor Attitude Scale suggests that a counsellor whose verbal and non-verbal behaviour correspond to an attitude reflecting basic empathy will: (a) be very reluctant to impose much counsellor direction; (b) unconditionally accept the attitudes and feelings of her clients; (c) allow them the moral responsibility for finding solutions to their problems; (d) de-emphasize diagnosis and interpretation; (e) de-emphasize the collection of information, including case histories, prior to counselling; (f) rely on clients' abilities to solve their own problems; and (g) permit them to express and to feel self-derogation and self-pity.[33]

The point of Exercise 1 is not only to encourage trainee self-exploration and awareness, but also to highlight some of the ways in which would-be counsellors can learn to become safe people so that clients can disclose sensitive information. A number of trainees may themselves require counselling to work on their own lack of self-acceptance and possible need to control and direct others. Although counsellors outside the client-centred orientation may subscribe to many items on the scale, they will differ on others. Neo-client-centred writers like Carkhuff and Egan would probably be inclined to view the scale as more representative of the earlier than the later stages of a counselling relationship.

Though Exercise 2 is focused on those working in pairs or in a skills training group, it may also be done by readers not training with others. The idea here is to encourage people to explore their areas of positive and negative self-evaluation and the degree of risk or fear of losing self-esteem attached to disclosing in these areas. There are various possibilities for counsellor-client interaction in skills training sessions. These include role-playing would-be clients, role-playing the concerns of others, or being oneself. Counsellor training tends to be more real if trainees are prepared to share and explore their own concerns. By rating the degree of risk, trainees can assess their readiness to explore various areas of their lives. Furthermore, it may help them to understand the position of their clients, who may often be making such assessments.

Exercise 2. Self-disclosure and self-exploration areas

Take some paper and make a list of areas of your life which you might wish to explore when it is your turn to be a client in skills training. Express these in self-referent terms (for example, 'I find it hard to acknowledge positive things about myself and seem constantly to be putting myself down') and indicate, using the following rating scale, how risky you anticipate it would be for you to disclose and to explore yourself in each of these areas. Risk involves the degree to which you anticipate you might be esteemed less as a result of your disclosures.

> 5. Impossible, much too risky
> 4. Very risky

3. Moderately risky
2. Slightly risky
1. Not risky at all

Non-verbal and Para-verbal Communication of Basic Empathy

An empathic attitude on the part of the counsellor is communicated to clients partly by non-verbal and para-verbal communication. Also, the counsellor is more likely to understand clients accurately if she is able to respond to non-verbal and para-verbal as well as verbal aspects of their communication. Non-verbal or bodily communication includes gestures, head movements, posture, facial expression, eye contact, proximity and spatial position, touch, clothes, and physical environment, for example the design and decor of the counsellor's office. Para-verbal or vocal-auditory communication includes speech rate, timing, pitch, stress of utterances, and 'framing' signals, which are an expressive commentary on a particular utterance by the speaker.[34]

Silence is an important form of non-verbal communication. One of the main ways in which counsellors can show acceptance is to give clients both permission and psychological space to reveal their thoughts and feelings. Gordon rightly makes the point that non-intervention and saying nothing may be potent ways in which parents can communicate acceptance to their children.[35] The same holds true for counsellors with clients.

Both clients and counsellors attribute characteristics to each other on the basis of non-verbal and para-verbal communication. For instance, if a counsellor persistently looks out of the window, the client may interpret this as lack of interest. Similarly, if a client talks in a very flat voice, the counsellor may attribute this to feelings of depression. Non-verbal and para-verbal communication may be used to support or to replace words. Like words, such communication may be used to conceal, as well as to reveal, thoughts and feelings. Counsellors need to be careful not to misinterpret clients' non-verbal and para-verbal communications. Often it is helpful to check with clients what they are really thinking and feeling.

There is a growing amount of literature on non-verbal communication in counselling and psychotherapy.[36] Mention of the findings of two research studies may highlight its importance for communicating empathy. Haase and Tepper[37] asked counsellors to rate a number of ten-second videotaped interactions between a 'counsellor' and a 'client'. They varied levels of eye contact (eye contact – no eye contact), trunk lean (forward – backward), body orientation (direct – rotated), distance (36 – 72 inches) and verbal empathy (high – medium – low). They found that maintaining eye contact, forward trunk lean, close distance, and medium-rated and high-rated verbal empathy all independently contributed to higher levels of judged empathy. They concluded that, except for low verbal empathy messages, certain non-empathic behaviours could be compensated for by engaging in other empathic behaviours. However, even high levels of verbal empathy could be reduced to unempathic messages when the counsellor uttered the message without eye contact, in a backward trunk lean, rotated away from the client, and from a far distance. Another study, by Shapiro and his colleagues, produced data indicating that judgements of counsellor empathy can reliably be made by both trained and untrained raters from photographs, with facial cues being particularly important.[38] Also, counsellors need to be careful not to misinterpret the effects of their own non-verbal and para-verbal communications on their clients.

Exercises 3 and 4 focus on counsellor non-verbal and para-verbal behaviours pertinent to offering basic empathy. If possible, do Exercise 3 before reading on. If you have access to a video cassette recorder, viewing yourself might help to reinforce some of the points.

Exercise 3. Non-verbal communication

This exercise needs to be done in pairs, possibly also using video feedback.

A.   Seating position:

1.   *Distance.* You sit in a chair and listen to your partner talking: (a) with your heads 18 inches apart; (b) with your heads 6–8 feet apart. Then start moving in until your partner says it feels a comfortable distance for being counselled. You and your partner then reverse roles, followed by discussion.
2.   *Height.* Your partner talks and you listen while you: (a) sit in a noticeably higher chair; (b) sit in a noticeably lower chair; and (c) sit in a chair which is the same height. You and your partner reverse roles, then discuss.
3.   *Angle.* Your partner talks and you listen while: (a) sitting squarely opposite so that your right shoulder is directly across from your partner's left shoulder; (b) sitting at 90 degrees so that the front of your chair faces the right side of your partner's chair. Then move your chair until your partner indicates this to be a comfortable angle for being counselled. You and your partner reverse roles, then discuss.

B.   Body position:

1.   *Posture.* Both seated, your partner talks and you listen while you: (a) have your arms and legs tightly crossed; (b) sprawl loosely in your chair; and (c) try to adopt a relaxed and attentive body posture. You and your partner reverse roles, then discuss.
2.   *Trunk lean.* Both seated, your partner talks and you listen while you: (a) lean right back; (b) lean far forward; and (c) lean slightly forward. You and your partner reverse roles, then discuss.
3.   *Eye contact.* Both seated, your partner talks and you listen while you: (a) avoid your partner's gaze altogether; (b) stare at your partner; and (c) maintain good eye contact, yet look away every now and then. You and your partner reverse roles, then discuss.

C.   Seating and body position:

Your partner talks for a few minutes while you listen in a correct seating position and combining a relaxed posture, slight forward trunk lean and good eye contact. You and your partner reverse roles, then discuss.

While we do not wish to imply more certainty than at present exists, all the parts of Exercise 3 are designed to increase awareness of important considerations in getting started with counselling clients and minimizing the chances of being perceived as unempathic. The word 'proxemics' is used to describe the study of the use of and rules regarding territorial space. For instance, if the counsellor and client sit 18 inches apart this may be regarded as too intimate, whereas if they sit seven feet apart this may be regarded as not only physically but also emotionally distant. Anthony and Carkhuff suggest that the counsellor sit three to four feet away from the client,[39] which is a comfortable distance for personal discussion, allowing privacy yet not signalling great intimacy. This is sometimes called the far personal distance and, unlike the intimate and close personal distances, the other person is not within easy touching distance.[40]

The ideal height for counselling is two people seated at the same level. If the counsellor is higher, the client may feel dominated and talked down to. A more democratic message is conveyed by sitting at the same level. Regarding the angle between counsellor and client, some writers, such as Egan[41] and Anthony and Carkhuff,[42] suggest facing the client squarely. Possibly a better position is for counsellor and client to be at a slight angle to each other. Many clients find direct eye contact difficult, and being at a slight angle rather than facing squarely makes it easier for both counsellor and client to be flexible about eye contact.

Posture, trunk lean and eye contact all convey messages about attentiveness and interest. Ideally all three should combine to help to create a safe environment for the client which conveys the message 'I am with you; please continue'. Behavioural psychologists would view good counsellor body position as helping to reinforce 'self-talk' on the part of the client. Counsellors, however, tend to relax their posture as they get to know their clients. Such matters as slight forward trunk lean become less important, since, after a few interviews, the client usually knows whether or not the counsellor is interested. In getting started, however, it seems advisable to sit up with an open posture, appear moderately but not too relaxed, and lean slightly forward for much of the time. Again, with eye contact, there seems to be a happy medium and the counsellor needs to be sensitive to clients who find this very difficult. The writer has had a number of clients who felt that too much eye contact by the counsellor revealed their inner rottenness, one who could not bear to see himself reflected in shop windows for the same reason, and another who sat facing the door with his hand shielding his eyes and who, session by session, gradually moved round to face the counsellor.

If possible, now work through Exercise 4. If you have access to an audio cassette recorder, listening to yourself is likely to emphasize its message.

Exercise 4. Para-verbal communication

This exercise should be done in pairs, preferably using audio feedback.

1. *Loudness.* You listen while your partner: (a) talks very loudly for a couple of minutes; (b) talks very softly for a couple of minutes; and (c) talks while you direct him/her to a loudness that seems appropriate for being a counsellor. You

and your partner reverse roles, then discuss, possibly also listening to audio feedback.

2. *Speech rate.* You listen while your partner: (a) talks very quickly for a couple of minutes; (b) talks very slowly for a couple of minutes; and (c) talks while you direct him/her to a speech rate that seems appropriate for being a counsellor. You and your partner reverse roles, then discuss, possibly also listening to audio feedback.

3. *Loudness and speech rate.* Your partner talks and you respond with a loudness and speech rate appropriate for being a counsellor. After a few minutes, you and your partner reverse roles, possibly also listening to audio feedback.

As with bodily communication, clients are likely to attribute characteristics to counsellor para-verbal communication. For instance, a very soft voice, besides being scarcely audible, may be perceived as weak, while a very loud voice may be perceived as aggressive and domineering. Counsellor para-verbal communication should help to create a calm and safe, yet emotionally expressive atmosphere which allows the client space for exploration. Many counsellor trainees tend to talk too softly and sometimes this results in an undesirable reciprocal mumbling between them and their clients. Easy audibility and a relaxed pacing of speech, with time for clients to follow their own trains of thought, are desirable. Very rapid counsellor talk may create a tense, pressurized environment, whereas very slow talk may be perceived as boredom, or may be boring. Given the ready availability of cassette recorders, this is an area which lends itself relatively easily to self-monitoring.

Accurate Listening

In the chapter on person-centred theory, the point was made that it adopts the perceptual, subjective or *internal frame of reference*. The ability of counsellors to place themselves in the internal frames of reference of their clients is crucial to empathically understanding them. For instance, statements like 'I feel attractive', 'I am poor at maths' and 'I like my brother' are all statements from the internal frame of reference. Much counselling involves accepting the client and listening to her personal meanings. If the counsellor were to reflect the above statements in the internal frame of reference, they would become, at the simplest level, something like 'you feel you are attractive', 'you consider you are poor at maths' and 'you like your brother'.

Counsellors too have their internal frames of reference, which may impede their accurately listening to clients, since a counsellor's viewpoint and needs may be different from her client's. Hence the counsellor's internal frame of reference may constitute an *external frame of reference*, or view from outside, for the client. Thus, if a counsellor were to respond to the client from an external frame of reference, the earlier statements might become 'Why do you think you are attractive?', 'I don't think you are poor at maths' and 'How can you like a brother like that?'. With the client statement 'I feel attractive', the response 'You feel you are attractive' is an attempt by the counsellor to listen accurately to the client's internal frame of reference, while the response 'Why do you think you are attractive?' is a request for information coming from the external or counsellor's frame of reference. While the former response is client-centred, the latter is counsellor-centred. Paraphrasing Gordon, who called one of his chapters 'How to listen so kids will talk to you: the language of acceptance',[43] one might say for counsellors 'How to listen so that you understand your clients and they will talk to you: responding from the internal or client's frame of reference'.

Now work through Exercise 5 and then check your answers at the end of the chapter.

Exercise 5. Identifying the counsellor's frame of reference

This exercise consists of a number of client statements in various counselling settings. There are three counsellor (Co.) responses to each client (Cl.) statement. On a piece of paper write IN or EX for each of the counsellor responses according to whether you consider the response to be in the internal or external frame of reference.

1. Woman to marriage counsellor.
   Cl. When Bill and I were engaged and first married we used to be able to talk about everything that was important. Now, regrettably, the relationship is much more distant.
   Co. How long have you been married?
   You are disappointed that you and Bill are no longer as close as you were.
   I think it would be a good idea if you asked Bill to come along as well.
2. Student to student counsellor.
   Cl. For some time now I haven't been able to concentrate. My parents badly want me to succeed at college and I'm upset at the thought that I'm letting them down.
   Co. Your concentration difficulties are causing you concern about disappointing your parents.
   You really should be able to study effectively by the time you come to college.
   It's upsetting not being able to concentrate and feeling that you are letting your parents down.
3. Pupil to school counsellor.
   Cl. I'm the only girl and I have three brothers. They tend to tease me a lot and it would be really nice to have a sister so that I wouldn't feel so outnumbered.
   Co. You seem pretty hostile towards your brothers.
   Can't you get your parents to help you out in this situation?
   It would be great to have a sister so that you could have some support.
4. Unemployed man to occupational counsellor.
   Cl. I lost my job two months ago. At first I enjoyed not having to go to work but now I'm getting increasingly frustrated and depressed.
   Co. It's starting to really get you down, not having a job.
   Not going to work was all right for a bit, but now you find the situation getting pretty desperate.
   How hard have you been looking for jobs?

5. Patient to nurse.
    Cl.   I'm really worried about the fact that I have cancer of the breast and have
          come into hospital for surgery. Will it be painful and will it succeed?
    Co.   You'll be all right.
          You've got a number of important concerns in relation to your operation.
          You seem to be feeling pretty sorry for yourself.

Look again at any of the answers you got wrong and try to see why this was the case. If
working in pairs or as part of a training group, discuss reasons for right and wrong
answers.

Exercise 6 is another accurate-listening exercise. Although the focus of this exercise
is on building your listening skills by asking you to listen and not talk, and also to
concentrate on understanding your partner's frame of reference, other elements are
also involved. You are asked to use your body in such a way as to create an empathic
emotional climate which expresses interest in and concern for the other. Furthermore,
you might also use the exercise to listen to your own feelings about being in the
counsellor and client roles. The term 'co-counselling' is used here to indicate working
together by counselling each other sequentially. If possible use video feedback but, if
this is not possible, try to use audio feedback.

Exercise 6. Internal frame of reference co-counselling listening exercise

You act as counsellor to your partner for five minutes by listening and using body
language, such as body posture, nods and facial expressions, but *not* using words.
Then summarize for your partner what he or she was saying and ask your partner to
comment on the accuracy of your feedback. You and your partner reverse roles, then
discuss, possibly using video or audio feedback. This exercise may later be done for
periods of 10, 15 or more minutes each way.

Patterson[44] states that the function of the counsellor, especially at the beginning of
counselling, is to respond to the client and that often interviews in which the client is
responding mainly to the counsellor are interrogations rather than counselling
interviews. Chapter 13 will discuss the initial interview, but for the moment it is
enough to say that if the client is always responding to the counsellor, the client may
find it difficult to talk about and acknowledge important concerns. Therefore the
counsellor may never understand the client's perceptual world or subjective reality
and hence will not have the information base from which to make the client feel
empathically understood. Thus it is critically important that beginning counsellors
learn how to listen. Although the focus in Exercise 6 was on learning to listen to the
words of clients, it is also extremely important to 'listen' to their gestures and nuances,
or non-verbal and para-verbal communications.

Openers and Continuation Responses

This section still focuses on listening, but adds some minimal verbal responding. When clients come for counselling it is important that they are given early the opportunity to describe their area or areas of concern. Table 11.2, while not

Table 11.2 *Openers and continuation responses*

Openers	*Continuation responses*	
Hello, I'm . . . Would you care to:	Um-hmm	And
tell me why you've come to see me	Nods (non-verbal)	So
tell me what is concerning you	I see	Go on
tell me how you see your situation	Then	Really
put me in the picture	Oh	Ah
	Indeed	Yes
	Tell me more	
You've been referred by . . . Now, how do	Would you like to elaborate?	
you see your situation?	That's interesting	
Where would you like to start today?	How do you see things?	

comprehensive, gives some examples of possible counsellor *opening sentences*. All these sentences contain the common emphasis that they are asking the client to help the counsellor to get into her frame of reference. *Structuring* is a term used to describe attempts by counsellors to define and establish expectancies for the counselling relationship. The structuring contained in these opening sentences is: 'I'm interested. I'm prepared to listen. Please let me understand your situation and personal meanings'. The last of the openers, 'Where would you like to start today?', unlike the others, is more appropriate for later interviews in which there is a heavy emphasis on a person-centred approach.

There are, of course, other openers. For instance, with a visibly distressed client, the counsellor may respond directly to the bodily communication and acknowledge the client's unhappiness. Small talk, apart from very brief initial comments, tends to be discouraged, since it may waste valuable interview time, block clients' needs to express their concerns, and provide a structuring for a social rather than for a counselling relationship.

Continuation responses are designed, once clients have started talking, to help them to continue. The message they provide is: 'I am with you. Please go on'. Such responses provide a link between what clients have just said and what they want to go on saying. Although almost all the continuation responses listed in Table 11.2 are verbal, there are many non-verbal continuation messages, perhaps the chief one being the head nod.

Great care needs to be taken with continuation responses to ensure that they help clients to continue in their own frame of reference rather than being obvious or subtle ways of getting the client to focus on the interests of the counsellor. An obvious example of using continuation responses to lead into the counsellor's frame of reference would be a question related to counsellor interest in what the client was saying, rather than a response allowing the client to develop her own theme. A less obvious way would be for the counsellor to nod only when something was of personal interest. It may be helpful here to imagine two parallel railway tracks. Counsellor and client can either continue along their own separate tracks and make little contact, or the counsellor can cross over and help the client to proceed along the client's own track. If, however, the counsellor gets the client crossing into the counsellor's track, this means that the contact is in the external frame of reference. Patterson observes that it is very easy to determine from a tape recording who is responding to whom.[45]

Ivey states that too many counsellors are unaware of the power and importance of what he terms 'mimimal encourages to talk'.[46] Good verbal and non-verbal continuation responses can be a key ingredient in successful counselling. Often awkward pauses and clients' inability to express and experience their feelings are due to counsellor lack of skill at providing appropriate continuation responses. An illustration is television 'chat shows', where you can see examples of both good and poor continuation responses and of the effects they have on those being interviewed.

Exercise 7 is an integrative listening exercise combining non-verbal and para-verbal communication, listening in the internal frame of reference, and using openers and continuation responses. You should consciously try to develop your skills in each of these areas. This will be helped by using video or audio feedback.

Exercise 7. Co-counselling listening and minimal responding exercise

You act as counsellor to your partner for five minutes by using an opener, listening, using body language and continuation responses, but *not* using additional words. Then summarize for your partner what he or she was saying and ask your partner to comment on the accuracy of your feedback. You and your partner reverse roles, then discuss, possibly using video or audio feedback. This exercise may later be done for periods of 10, 15 or more minutes each way.

DESCRIBING EMPATHY FURTHER

Before continuing with exercises involving increased counsellor verbal responding, we expand on our earlier description of empathy. In 1975 Rogers published an updating of his views on the process of being empathic. What he termed his current definition of empathy includes the following:

> . . . entering the private perceptual world of the other and becoming thoroughly at home in it.
> . . . being sensitive, moment to moment, to the changing felt meanings which flow in this other person.
> . . . sensing meanings of which he/she is scarcely aware, but not trying to uncover feelings of which the person is totally unaware since this would be too threatening.
> . . . communicating your sensings of his/her world as you look with fresh and unfrightened eyes at elements of which the individual is fearful.
> . . . frequently checking with him/her as to the accuracy of your sensings, and being guided by the responses you receive.
> . . . pointing to the possible meanings in the flow of his/her experiencing you help the

person to focus on this useful type of referent, to experience the meanings more fully, and to move forward in the experiencing.[47]

Rogers sensitively and elegantly describes the process of being an empathic companion. He strongly affirms Fiedler's earlier finding that the ideal counsellor is first of all empathic.[48]

Tables 11.3 and 11.4 relate to variables associated with the presence or absence of basic empathy in a counselling relationship. These tables elaborate Rogers' description and go some way towards providing an operational definition of the concept. The figures also resemble Fiedler's lists of items most and least characteristic of the Ideal Therapeutic Relationship. Although the tables contain some duplication, neither of them would be sufficient to present the information contained in both. If empathy is described only positively, a number of valuable warnings are excluded. On the other hand, if empathy is defined only by absence of negative qualities, it is hard to capture fully the flavour of a really good empathic relationship. Nevertheless, both tables fall short of conveying the process which, for better comprehension, needs to be experienced.

Emotional Climate

The desired emotional climate for a counselling relationship is often expressed in terms like respect, caring and acceptance for the client, and genuineness and non-possessive warmth on the part of the counsellor. Both Porter[49] and Gordon[50] have stressed the relationship of counsellor self-acceptance to acceptance of the client. Porter defines self-evaluative attitudes as those regarding the worth, competence, capability, guilt, and adequacy or similar evaluations of oneself as a person. He observes that such attitudes may be held consciously or denied to awareness, and that counsellors may compensate for unconsciously held negative self-evaluations by striving for the enhancement of positive self-evaluations.[51]

The outcomes of lack of self-acceptance on the part of the counsellor include possessive warmth and conditional acceptance of the client. Such characteristics militate against a democratic person-to-person relationship and have the effect of reifying the client or turning the counselling relationship into an I–it relationship. The client, instead of being responded to in terms of her potential for self-realizing, is responded to in terms of the counsellor's unresolved needs and conflicts.

Counsellor Behaviours

Basic empathy requires both counsellor and client to work together to promote the client's happiness and fulfilment. Some of the exercises in the earlier part of this chapter focused on improving counsellor listening ability to provide an empathic atmosphere in which the client can feel safe to disclose herself. Now the exercises focus on further improving listening capacity and on learning how to respond. If anything, the exercises emphasize variables associated with presence of empathy.

It has been suggested that counsellors or therapists offering low levels or absence of

Table 11.3 *Some variables associated with the presence of basic empathy in a counselling relationship*

Emotional climate and counsellor attitude	Counsellor behaviours	Client behaviours
Caring and warmth Acceptance of client Self-acceptance by counsellor Safety and confidentiality Respect for client's integrity A person-to-person relationship	*Receiving communications* Sensitivity to client's private world Sensitivity to client's flow of experiencing Sensitivity to client's strengths and defences Sensitivity to own experiencing Listening for verbal content, feelings and nuances Accuracy in understanding client's meanings Appropriate tentativeness in understanding *Sending communications* Effective communication of empathic attitude and understanding Clarity and freshness of expression Easily comprehensible language Appropriate timing of responses Good body language Good para-verbal communication Where appropriate, tentatively checking out understandings Where appropriate, verbally self-disclosing Working *together* with client	Self-disclosure Self-exploration Increased sensitivity to internal flow of experiencing Increased capacity for self-direction Increased trust of counsellor, of self, and of the counselling process

Table 11.4 *Some variables associated with absence of basic empathy in a counselling relationship*

Emotional climate and counsellor attitude	Counsellor behaviours	Client behaviours
Lack of interest Coldness and impersonality Conditional acceptance Threat and lack of confidentiality Overt or subtle lack of respect I–it rather than I–thou relationship	*Receiving communications* Insensitivity to client's private world Insensitivity to client's strengths and defences Listening to own rather than client's needs Understanding client mainly from counsellor's own viewpoint Understanding client in rigid terms Ignoring and misidentifying obvious relevant feelings Ignoring and misidentifying underlying relevant feelings *Sending communications* Ineffective communication of empathic attitude and understanding Technique rather than person orientation Defensiveness and hiding behind a professional facade Inappropriately directing and leading Judging and making evaluative comments Moralizing, preaching and patronizing Intellectualizing and blocking experiencing of feeling Interrogation and clumsy use of questions Diverting and humouring Inability to accept range of client's positive and negative feelings Over-interpretation Talking too much or too little Interrupting Poor body language Poor para-verbal communication Inappropriate lack of tentativeness in responding Egocentricity and inappropriate self-disclosure	Lack of self-disclosure Disclosure to ingratiate self Lessened self-exploration Lessened sensitivity to flow of experiencing Dependency Lack of self-direction Mistrust and dissatisfaction

empathy may make clients worse rather than better.[52] As well as poor listening or poor capacity to receive information accurately, there are numerous pitfalls to be avoided in responding or sending basic empathy communications to clients. These include:

1. Directing and leading: for example, 'You should be doing this' and 'I would like you to talk about that'.
2. Judging and evaluating: 'I think that is wrong' or 'You are over-possessive'.
3. Moralizing, preaching and patronizing: 'Sex is not everything in life'.
4. Intellectualizing and blocking experiencing of feelings: 'Now let's analyse that situation in detail' or 'Let's talk about your feelings'.
5. Labelling and diagnosing: 'You have an inferiority complex' or 'You're behaving in a neurotic way'.
6. Interrogation and clumsy use of questions: questions are often unnecessary and come from and lead back to the counsellor's frame of reference; they should be used sparingly to facilitate rather than hinder client self-exploration.
7. Reassuring, diverting and humouring: 'You will be all right'.
8. Inability to accept the client's range of positive and negative feelings: 'You shouldn't boast' or 'Don't let yourself get so depressed'.
9. Over-interpretation: 'Your reluctance to socialize may indicate some unresolved conflicts, possibly sexual'.
10. Inappropriate self-disclosure: 'My relationship to my mother had these features'.
11. Defensiveness: 'Your lack of progress is due to your resistances'.

Although the above examples may seem parodies of what actually happens in counselling relationships, with unskilled or untrained counsellors this may not be the case. Some of the examples selected were beginning counsellor trainee responses to single client statements.

Client Behaviours

Assuming counsellor empathy to be both present and, to some extent, perceived, the client should show an increasing capacity for self-disclosure, self-exploration and self-awareness.[53] In 1963 Truax developed a nine-point client *Depth of Self-exploration Scale*[54] which was adapted by Carkhuff into a five-point scale.[55] At the lowest level of Carkhuff's scale the client does not disclose personally relevant material, whereas at the highest level 'The helpee actively and spontaneously engages in an inward probing to newly discovered feelings and experiences about himself and his world'. Thus basic empathy may make it easier for clients to talk about and learn to accept themselves.

Absence of basic empathy, on the other hand, tends to make it more difficult for clients to disclose and explore themselves. Truax and Carkhuff[56] analysed the effects of varying levels of empathy and warmth with three patients. They discovered that depth of client self-exploration was significantly poorer when levels of therapist empathy and warmth were low than when they were high. It is also possible that low empathy may increase dependency and lessen client capacity for responsible self-direction.

LEARNING BASIC EMPATHY: PART TWO EXERCISES

A distinction common in the counsellor training literature is that between *discrimination* and *communication*. *Discrimination* involves perceiving what is right or wrong in one's own or in someone else's counselling. *Communication* involves actually being able to do what is right in responding to clients. The difference is that between knowing what is right and being able to put it into practice. Whereas good communication of basic empathy almost by definition entails good discrimination, it is quite possible to be good at discriminating without being able to translate these perceptual skills into good responding skills.

Discriminating Basic Empathy

Exercise 5, on identifying the counsellor's frame of reference, was an exercise in discrimination. Exercise 8, on discriminating empathic responding, is another such exercise. In the light of the above discussion on basic empathy, work through Exercise 8. Before reading on, check your answers with those suggested at the end of the chapter.

Exercise 8. Discriminating empathic responding

Empathic responding involves accurately understanding, from the internal frame of reference, what your client is telling you and then sensitively communicating back your understanding in a language attuned to your client's needs. Take a piece of paper and rate the three counsellor responses to each of the client statements using the following scale:

> 5   Very good empathic response
> 4   Good empathic response
> 3   Moderate empathic response
> 2   Slight empathy in the response
> 1   Response not at all empathic

Write down the reason or reasons for each rating. If you are working with a partner either rate each item independently and then discuss, or rate all items and then discuss.

1. Parishioner to pastoral counsellor.
    Cl.   There are times in my life when religion is very important to me. I don't mean just births, marriages and deaths, but at times I really feel that praying is a meaningful activity. Right now I'm at a bit of a loose end and I can't get as involved in prayer as I would like.
    Co.   (a)   You have obviously done something wrong and this is getting in the way of your relationship with God.

   (b)　We all go through these difficult periods. I feel your need to get closer
          to God but somehow you can't manage it.
   (c)　You would like to get more involved in prayer and you want religion
          to be important again, but just at the moment the feeling and
          involvement just aren't there.

2.　Youth to youth counsellor.
   Cl.　I went with my mates to the football match on Saturday afternoon. I
          expected our team to be thrashed. Well, they weren't. It was a terrific game
          and we spent most of the evening at the pub celebrating. It's one of the
          happiest days I've had for a long time.
   Co.　(a)　I'm delighted that you really enjoyed yourself.
        (b)　Well, I still think your team is going to be relegated at the end of the
              season.
        (c)　How are you going to spend next Saturday?

3.　Disabled woman to rehabilitation counsellor.
   Cl.　You know when I woke up to find that I no longer had my right leg I cried
          and cried and cried. It's still too soon to know whether I will be able to cope
          and at times I get tremendously low. My family have been marvellous
          throughout it all.
   Co.　(a)　You need all the help and encouragement you can get in your
              situation.
        (b)　You appreciate your family, but are there any other ways that they
              could be helping you?
        (c)　It was and still is a bitter blow to have lost your leg and at times you
              get tremendously depressed. You aren't sure you will be able to cope,
              yet your family certainly seem to care.

4.　Businessman to industrial counsellor.
   Cl.　Recently my stomach has been upset and I've found it difficult to keep food
          down. My doctor says it is my liver, but I wonder. The firm want me to go
          to another part of the country and have given me three months to make up
          my mind. I've told them that I don't want to move and that they can have
          the three months to change theirs. Things are pretty tense and uncertain.
   Co.　(a)　Have you got any plans for what you will do if you have to leave the
              job?
        (b)　Your doctor thinks your stomach and digestive difficulties are purely
              medical, but you are in a tense situation and wonder whether your
              health is being affected by this.
        (c)　Underneath it all you seem very angry.

5.　Student to student counsellor.
   Cl.　This is the first time I've been away from home. I enjoyed my final year at
          school and had some good friends at home. I don't quite know what to
          expect here.
   Co.　(a)　Well, we all have to leave home and grow up some time.
        (b)　You enjoyed your previous life and your friends and now wonder how
              you are going to get on here, being away from home.
        (c)　You seem bright and personable and should get by all right.

The three counsellor responses to the first client statement are discussed below to illustrate the kind of reasoning behind the suggested ratings. The first response, 'You have obviously done something wrong . . .', shows no empathy at all and thus received a rating of 1. The reasons for this rating include: (a) it is almost totally within the counsellor's frame of reference; (b) it is judgemental; and (c) there is no evidence that the client has done anything wrong. The second response, 'We all go through these difficult periods', is harder to rate than the previous response, since, depending on the way it was said, the first part of the statement could be sympathetic or patronizing. The rating of 3 indicates that, though some effort has been made to get into the client's frame of reference, nevertheless the response is slightly more counsellor-centred than is desirable. Furthermore, the response insufficiently amplifies the client's concerns. The third counsellor response receives a rating of 5 because it communicates to the client that she has been fully understood.

When doing discrimination and communication exercises it is often useful to think in terms of a three-link chain comprising: (a) the client's first statement; (b) the counsellor's response; and (c) the client's second statement. One way of assessing the adequacy of a counsellor's response is to think about how it might affect the client's second statement. In the above example 'You have obviously done something wrong . . .' might lead to client defensiveness or to a search for a sin, whereas 'you would like to get more involved in prayer . . .' communicates understanding and permission to carry on exploring personal concerns.

Communicating Basic Empathy

There are four exercises in this section on communicating basic empathy: reflection of content, reflection of feeling, reflection of content and feeling, and empathic co-counselling. This section adds to the previous exercises by focusing on the use of words in responding.

Reflection of content involves restating or paraphrasing what the client is saying. Remember, however, that basic empathy is more concerned with emotional climate than with technique; in fact, Rogers was appalled by the caricature 'In nondirective therapy you repeat the last words the client has said'.[57] With this *caveat*, reflection of content is a useful skill which helps the client to know that the counsellor understands the content of her communications, if not the underlying feelings.

Reflection of content is also a way of building up the skill of getting into and responding from the client's frame of reference. In order to make sure the instructions to Exercise 9 are clear, here are some responses to the first client statement. The *repetition* response is: 'You love your children, who mean more to you than anything in the world. If the marriage were to break up you would really miss not having them always with you. Also, you would worry about whether you had done the right thing by them'. A possible *paraphrase* or *restatement* response is: 'You really care for your children and would like to always have them around. If your marriage were to break up this would not be possible. Also, you would be concerned about whether you had hurt them'. Using simple, clear English, work through Exercise 9, including your version of the first statement. Some possible restatement responses are given at the end of the chapter, but it should be understood that there is no single correct restatement response.

Exercise 9. Reflection of content

Part A

For each of the following client statements: (a) repeat the statement using 'you' or 'your' where the client uses 'I', 'me' or 'my'; and (b) again using 'you' or 'your', restate or paraphrase the content of the statement in clear, simple and, where appropriate, colloquial language. If working in pairs, either independently answer the requirements for each statement, then discuss, or answer the items for all statements, then discuss.

1. Husband to marriage counsellor: 'I love my children, who mean more to me than anything in the world. If the marriage were to break up I would really miss not having them always with me. Also, I would worry about whether I had done the right thing by them.'
2. Retired woman to leisure counsellor: 'I really enjoyed my career. I had to try extra hard to make a success of it, since business is basically a man's world. I'm the sort of person with plenty of energy and I hate being idle for long.'
3. Male student to student counsellor: 'I talked with my tutor, Mr Simpson, and he . . . uh . . . he said I should come and talk to you. I want to improve my record, since it's important for me to do graduate work.'
4. Male pupil to school counsellor: 'I don't think I've . . . I've mentioned this to anyone before. I masturbate both first thing in the morning and in the evening too. I don't seem to want to stop doing this, though there are times when I don't feel good about it.'
5. Mother to medical counsellor: 'My son, Bill, is overseas with his new wife. Recently I've been getting quite a lot of back trouble. Part of me says don't write and let them know because it will only worry them and they can't do anything about it anyway. Then another part of me says that they would prefer it if I were open with them.'

Part B

You counsel your partner for five minutes, focusing especially on reflecting the content of his/her statements in your responding. You and your partner reverse roles, then discuss possibly also using audio feedback.

Reflection of feeling is different from reflection of content in that it emphasizes the overt or underlying feelings in what the client is saying. There is often overlap between reflection of feeling and reflection of content; indeed, Exercise 11 combines the two. Nevertheless, reflection of feeling is a skill which merits attention on its own, since it is a powerful way of helping clients to feel understood and to identify and experience their emotions. Experienced counsellors sometimes become very skilled in: (a) creating an emotional atmosphere in which the client can express feelings; (b) understanding the obvious feeling messages that are being conveyed; (c) understanding underlying less obvious feeling messages which, while possibly being hidden in the verbal content, may become revealed in the non-verbal and para-verbal communication; and (d) responding to the client in a way which both demonstrates understanding and also, where appropriate, goes some way towards sharing the emotion.

Because it is a written exercise, Exercise 10 cannot convey the feeling nuances of either the client's messages or your responses. To help you do Exercise 10 correctly, here are some answers regarding the first client statement. The *words* and *phrases* the client uses to describe his feelings are: 'dominates', 'avoid', 'hold back', 'feel so wet'. *Additional words* that might be used to describe the client's feelings include: 'engulfs', 'overwhelms', 'be conspicuous', 'retreat from', 'be inhibited about', 'worthless', 'inadequate', 'useless'. A possible *response* is 'You feel that your fear of blushing is the main thing in your life; also, that you are a terribly inadequate person for avoiding questions and not participating in group discussions'. Again there are many possible words and different responses that might be appropriate for our hypothetical client. In formulating a response try to match, rather than add to or subtract from, the feeling intensity of the client. Work through Exercise 10, including your version of the first statement. Some possible responses are provided at the end of the chapter.

Exercise 10. Reflection of feeling

Part A

For each of the following client statements: (a) identify the words or phrases the client has used to describe how he/she feels; (b) suggest other words or phrases to describe how the client feels; and (c) formulate a response to the client focusing on and reflecting his/her feelings, starting with the words 'You feel . . .'. If working in pairs, either answer the items for each statement independently and then discuss, or answer the items for all statements, then discuss.

1.   Trainee salesman to industrial counsellor: 'My blushing problem dominates my whole life. I try to avoid the trainer's eye so that I won't be asked a question. Also, I hold back from participating in group discussions. I feel so wet for behaving this way.'
     (a)   Client's own words and phrases which might be used to describe client's feelings . . .
     (b)   Additional words and phrases which might be used to describe client's feelings . . .
     (c)   Your response: 'You feel . . .'
2.   Young woman to student counsellor: 'I seem to be more attracted to other women than to men. I get so depressed and low and it's hard for me to get up and face the day sometimes. Today has been a bad day. I suppose coming to see you has forced me to acknowledge that I'm not normal.'
3.   Immigrant to social worker: 'I'm as good as they are. They seem to think they can

push me around; well, they can't. I've got my rights, too. I'm mad at being treated like dirt and I'm not going to put up with it any longer.'

4. Youth to probation officer: 'You know, when I first saw you I thought I was going to hate you. Well, I've been proved wrong. You remind me of my dad, but you've behaved differently. You really do seem concerned that I'm happy and that's great. I like coming here.'

5. Fourteen-year-old girl to school counsellor: 'I want to have friends and be liked. I try very hard to be popular, but the other girls either ignore me or make fun of me. Why do they keep hurting me? What's wrong with me?'

Part B

You counsel your partner for five minutes, focusing especially on his/her feelings in your responding. You and your partner reverse roles, then discuss using audio feedback.

Exercise 11 is on *reflecting content and feeling*. Though the exercise adopts a standard format, this is for didactic purposes and there are other ways of combining reflection of content and feeling. A possible response to the first client statement is: 'You feel discouraged and in a no-win position because you don't like trying hard and coming over as forcing it, nor not trying hard then counselling poorly'. Work through Exercise 11, including your version of the first statement. Again, some possible responses are given at the end of the chapter.

Exercise 11. Reflection of content and feeling

For each of the following client statements formulate a response which reflects both feeling and content using the standard format: 'You feel . . . because . . .'. If working in pairs, either formulate a response for each statement independently and then discuss, or formulate responses for all statements, then discuss.

1. Trainee to counsellor trainer: 'I seem to be in a double bind. The harder I try the more unnatural I get and, if I don't try hard, I don't like the way I counsel. I seem to lose out either way and it's getting very discouraging.'

2. Pupil to school counsellor: 'It's not easy for me. I've never discussed my family with anyone before. My parents might not like my discussing them with you. Also, I might feel disloyal. Anyway, I'm not sure what to do.'

3. Male student to student counsellor: 'I get really nervous at the prospect of going on campus. Somehow I seem afraid of everyone and feel as though I just want to withdraw. When I'm like this even if I did go, everyone would see that there was something wrong with me.'

4. Woman to bereavement counsellor: 'I'm confused. My husband died a couple of years ago and this left me without companionship and a role in life. I would like to sort out my values and find out what is important to me. Then I would be able to do something about it.'

5. Woman to pregnancy counsellor: 'I'm very undecided. Then I get nervous and this

makes it even harder to decide. There are so many things to consider and, even if I were feeling happy and confident, I would find it a difficult decision. But now I'm feeling guilty and depressed it seems impossible.'

Exercise 12 focuses on integrating the different aspects of empathic responding covered in the earlier exercises. The following excerpt from an interview with a male college student indicates a sequence of empathic responding such as required by this exercise.

Cl.   How in fact is a kind way to respond to . . . ah . . . what basically is totally irrational behaviour?

Co.   Is this on the part of your mother?

Cl.   Yeah . . . very often . . . um hmm . . . either I get very annoyed or I'm tempted to ignore her.

Co.   So one way to handle the situation is to get very annoyed and another possibility is to ignore her.

Cl.   But neither of these ways is totally satisfactory because she is a desperately unhappy woman.

Co.   So how can you work towards a way of relating to your mother in which, on the one hand, you don't get angry with her and, on the other hand, you don't ignore her. Is there another way . . .?

Cl.   Yes, how can I work towards a kind of detachment which isn't so detached that I'm treating her as an object but which isn't so involved that I keep getting irritated?

Co.   You want to treat her as a person, yet at the same time . . . contain your feelings.

The above brief excerpt illustrates an attempt by the counsellor both to respond within the client's frame of reference and to help him to explore his concerns about how to handle his mother, whom he perceived as very difficult. Throughout the excerpt the counsellor is trying to convey the message 'I am with you. Please go on'. To emphasize the importance of emotional climate in 'thawing' clients, when he entered counselling the above college student found it much too threatening to talk about his parents.

If possible, now do Exercise 12. This is the kind of exercise that should be done again and again as you build up your interviewing skills and confidence. Video or audio feedback can be a great help in monitoring your performance.

Exercise 12. Integration: empathic co-counselling

You act as counsellor to your partner for 15 minutes by using an opener, listening, using body language and continuation responses and, where appropriate, reflecting content, feeling, and feeling and content together. Your partner should pause every now and then to allow you to practise responding. You and your partner reverse roles, then discuss, possibly also using audio or video feedback. This exercise may be done for longer periods with one person counselling for, say, 30 or 50 minutes. With these longer sessions you may not wish to reverse roles until you have had an adequate break.

Practising Basic Empathy

The old adage that 'practice makes perfect' is highly relevant to learning counselling skills and attitudes. Table 11.5 makes many suggestions for practising empathic responding either on your own or with others. Suggestions for practice, building on the exercises in this chapter, include: (a) making up additional statements and

Table 11.5 *Suggestions for practice of empathic responding*

Discrimination	Communication
Look at film and video-recordings of other interviewers and observe and discuss their body language and para-verbals.	Write out an internal dialogue in which you act as your own counsellor.
Obtain transcripts, tapes or cassettes of interviews by people like Rogers and rate for empathy single responses or three- to four-minute groupings of responses.	Get a transcript of an interview by someone like Rogers, go down the page covering up Rogers' responses, formulating your own, then checking Rogers' responses.
Practice listening to whole interviews and focus on the counsellor, the process and the client.	Do the same as above with a cassette by switching it off after client statements, formulating your responses, then swtiching it on and checking Rogers' responses.
For breadth and comparison, listen to interviews of counsellors working within a number of different frameworks, such as the behavioural or rational-emotive.	Practise your counselling where possible, using audio or video playback as appropriate.
Try to obtain the experience of being counselled by a highly empathic counsellor for at least one session.	Deliberately try to use your empathic responding skills in appropriate situations in your own life.

responses for identifying the counsellor's frame of reference (Exercise 5), discriminating empathic responding (Exercise 8), and reflection of content, feeling, and content and feeling together (Exercises 9, 10 and 11); (b) doing further work on the co-counselling exercises, namely internal frame of reference listening (Exercise 6), listening and minimal responding (Exercise 7) and empathic co-counselling (Exercise 12). Where appropriate, use audio or video cassettes.

The further *discrimination* practice suggestions in Table 11.5 tend to involve access to additional material, though discrimination work can be done on material generated by pairs or by a training group. Counselling interview cassettes by leading psychologists are available in both Britain[58] and America.[59] Often it is possible to obtain the interview transcripts as well. Furthermore, many counselling books contain segments of interviews. Being counselled by a highly empathic counsellor is strongly recommended, not just for therapeutic reasons, but because it provides a rich learning experience in bodily communication, timing, pacing, good emotional climate, and accuracy and appropriateness of responding.

The further *communication* practice exercises in Table 11.5 also include use of transcripts and cassettes, but this time in such a way that interviewer responses are neither seen nor heard until you have formulated your own. In checking your responses against the interviewer responses, remember that often there is no single correct response and that even the best of interviewers sometimes responds inappropriately.

The suggestion of an internal dialogue is to make out a personal transcript along the lines of the excerpt provided to explain Exercise 12. Basic empathy is also a central feature of good personal relations and therefore it is appropriate to develop listening and understanding skills outside, as well as inside, the counselling setting. In one study of college students it was found that experienced counsellors offered students significantly higher levels of empathy than their best available friends.[60] However, counsellors are at risk of not being empathic in situations where their own needs are involved.

CONCLUDING COMMENTS

Using the Exercises

Earlier in this chapter we mentioned that the use of exercises, such as those above, is only part of the content of a counselling skills laboratory or pre-practicum seminar. In a 30-hour (two 1½-hour sessions over ten weeks) introductory graduate seminar on the practice of counselling, the writer tends to spend approximately the first third dealing with exercises (apart from the longer counselling sessions entailed in Exercise 12). We try to get trainees progressing quickly through the exercises for a number of reasons. First, the exercises lend themselves, in the first instance, to being completed as homework. This homework, which may or may not be done in a timetabled practice period, saves valuable class time, which can be used for discussing trainee work. Second, for some of the exercises class time need only be spent to the point where the group understands what is being taught, thus further economizing on time. Third, we like to get trainees progressing quickly to handling longer interview sessions with each other, where there is more time to facilitate client self-exploration and more likelihood that the trainee-clients will share real concerns. Again, many such counselling sessions can be audio or video recorded on a homework basis, either inside or outside a timetabled practice period. Playback and discussion of these longer counselling sessions constitutes the major portion of the middle third and some of the latter third of the 30-hour seminar. Fourth, spending too much time on exercises may mean that other elements, on which we hope to focus in the latter third of the seminar, receive insufficient attention. These elements include the conduct of initial interviews, making treatment decisions, responding to different kinds of interview behaviour (e.g. silence, talkativeness), and dealing with special categories of clients (e.g. the severely disturbed, clients in crisis).

A fifth and major reason for limiting the use of time spent on exercises is that a skills approach to the fundamental counselling relationship has risks. A good trainer tries to facilitate person-to-person contact between trainees and then clients. There is a danger that just teaching counselling skills in a mechanical way may distance trainees from themselves, their healing potential, and their clients. In fact a heavy counselling-skills emphasis might be used by some trainees (and indeed some counsellors) as a defence against real personal contact with clients. Clearly an important part of the counsellor trainer's role is to help trainees to explore and better resolve their own anxieties and blocks to effective interviewing.

After their initial laboratory or pre-practicum experience, counsellor trainees need to have placements which offer them responsibility for a range of clients with different concerns and levels of severity. Adequate supervision will include individual or small-group sessions in which cassette material is listened to and commented on. Larger-group sessions, in which trainees and supervisors share their concerns, skills and experience, may also be helpful.[61] Even after formal training, counsellors need to be conscientious about monitoring and evaluating their capacity to offer basic empathy to their clients and to others.

Necessary and/or Sufficient

In this chapter on the fundamental counselling relationship, the contribution of the client-centred or person-centred school of counselling, particularly of Rogers, has been emphasized. Thus this chapter has provided a moderately thorough introduction to the practice of person-centred counselling, where, as indicated earlier, the fundamental counselling relationship is considered both *necessary* and *sufficient* to help clients to become more self-actualizing. However, we reiterate the point that it is *necessary* for all counsellors and counselling psychologists, whatever their orientation, to be skilled at listening to their clients, understanding them, and communicating back to them that they are accepted and understood. Even though basic empathy may not form so large a part of the content of non-person-centred interviews, nevertheless, as Fiedler's work suggests, it is always present in successful counselling whatever the stated orientation.

RESPONSES FOR EXERCISES

Exercise 1

1. D   2. D   3. A   4. A   5. D   6. A   7. D   8. A   9. D
10. D   11. A   12. D   13. A   14. A   15. D   16. A
The scale is scored by summing correct answers and ignoring incorrect and (?) answers.

Exercise 5

1. EX, IN, EX
2. IN, EX, IN
3. EX, EX, IN
4. IN, IN, EX
5. EX, IN, EX

Exercise 8

1. (a) 1; External frame of reference, judgemental.
   (b) 3; Partial attempt to get into internal frame of reference, possibly patronizing and slightly egocentric.
   (c) 5; Communicates full understanding.
2. (a) 5; Alive, spontaneous, sharing at the same time as understanding.
   (b) 2; Slight attempt to get into the internal frame of reference, but this is more a social than a therapeutic response. As such it might lead to an 'intellectual' discussion rather than an exploration of personal meanings.
   (c) 1; Leads and directs the client's next response.
3. (a) 2; Could be more specific, too external.
   (b) 2; The first four words are good, but the remainder leads and directs the client's next response.
   (c) 5; Communicates full understanding.
4. (a) 2; Seems concerned, but fails to pick up the full impact of what the client is saying and thus blocks his exploring the psychological dimensions of his problem.
   (b) 4; Slightly clumsily worded, but a good attempt at a full understanding. Perhaps 'digestion problems' would be better than 'stomach and digestive difficulties'.
   (c) 1; Given just the verbal content, this is an interpretation from the counsellor's frame of reference.
5. (a) 1; Judgemental and patronizing, a real 'put-down'.
   (b) 4; Good attempt at understanding client's viewpoint.
   (c) 2; False reassurance which fails to fully acknowledge the client's doubts and uncertainties.

The above ratings are the author's and are based on an assessment of the verbal content only.

Exercise 9

Restatement responses. The following are intended only as suggestions. There is no single correct response.

1. 'You really care for your children and would like always to have them around. If

your marriage were to break up this would not be possible. Also, you would be concerned about whether you had hurt them.'

2. 'You very much liked your work. You had to put a lot into making a go of it, since you were a woman in a male setting. You're an active person who badly needs to keep doing things.'

3. 'You discussed your situation with your lecturer, who referred you to me. You want to get better results so that you can achieve your ambition to go on to more advanced work.'

4. 'I seem to be the first person you've talked to about giving yourself orgasms at the beginning and the end of the day. You still want to persist with it, though sometimes you don't like what you do.'

5. 'Your recently married son and daughter-in-law are abroad. You're experiencing a fair amount of back pain and are wondering whether or not to put them in the picture. On the one hand, you don't want to get them needlessly concerned. On the other hand, you feel that they might rather be told the situation.'

Exercise 10

Part A. Again, there are no single correct responses other than for (a).
1. (a)   dominates, avoid, hold back, feel so wet
    (b)   engulfs, overwhelms, be inconspicuous, retreat from, be inhibited about, worthless, inadequate, useless
    (c)   'You feel that your fear of blushing is the main thing in your life; also, that you are a terribly inadequate person for avoiding questions and not participating in group discussions.'

2. (a)   attracted, depressed, low, hard for me, get up and face, bad, forced me to acknowledge, not normal
    (b)   homosexually oriented, down, dislike myself, difficult for me, have confidence to get through the day, poor, made me realize, I'm different
    (c)   'You feel more homosexual than heterosexual. Some days you feel very down and don't even have the confidence to get by. This has been one of those days. Your appointment with me has forced you to realize you're different.'

3. (a)   as good as, push me around, well they can't, my rights too, mad, treated like dirt, not going to put up with it
    (b)   as all right as, bully me, I'm not having it, a person too, angry, being made to feel small, fight back
    (c)   'You feel you're being bullied and belittled and this makes you furious. You're every bit as much a person as they are and you damn well intend standing up for your rights in future.'

4. (a)   hate, proved wrong, reminded me of, behaved differently, concerned, happy, great, like
    (b)   dislike, made a mistake, seemed like, acted otherwise, to care, well-being, fantastic, enjoy
    (c)   'You feel grateful that I genuinely seem to care that you're happy. You felt

when you first saw me that you were going to dislike me intensely. I seemed like your father, but I've acted differently and you enjoy our meetings.'

5. (a) want to have friends, be liked, try very hard, be popular, ignore me, make fun of me, hurting, wrong with me

    (b) needs friends, want to be accepted, make a big effort, be one of the group, take no notice, tease, causing me pain, the problem with me

    (c) 'You feel a terrific need to have friends and be liked but, despite your best efforts, you get ignored or teased by the other girls. This really hurts and you wonder what's wrong with you.'

Exercise 11

Again, there are no single correct responses. The following are suggestions.

1. 'You feel discouraged and in a no-win position because you don't like trying hard and coming over as forcing it, nor not trying hard then counselling poorly.'
2. 'You feel ill at ease and unsure about how to proceed because you've never discussed your parents with anyone before and wonder whether they would approve and also whether you would feel right by them.'
3. 'You feel really upset at the prospect of going on campus because somehow people seem frightening and you just want to withdraw from them. Also, even if you did make the effort, they would notice that you were in difficulty.'
4. 'You feel confused because your husband's dying two years ago left you with a vacuum and you need to sort out your values and find a purpose in life so that you can fill that vacuum.'
5. 'You feel very undecided, which makes you nervous and even less able to decide, because you're depressed and there are so many considerations that the prospect of deciding seems overwhelming. Even if you were on top form, it would still be difficult.'

NOTES

1. Nelson-Jones, R. & Patterson, C. H. (1974) Some effects of counsellor training. *British Journal of Guidance and Counselling*, **2**, 191–199.
2. Pierce, F. M. & Schauble, P. G. (1970) Graduate training of facilitative counselors: the effects of individual supervision. *Journal of Counseling Psychology*, **17**, 210–215.
3. Carkhuff, R. R., Kratochvil, D. & Friel, T. (1968) Effects of professional training: communication and discrimination of facilitative conditions. *Journal of Counseling Psychology*, **15**, 68–74.
4. Traux, C. B. & Carkhuff, R. R. (1967) *Toward Effective Counseling and Psychotherapy: Training and Practice* p. 219. Chicago: Aldine.
5. Rogers, C. R. (1957) Training individuals to engage in the therapeutic process. In C. R. Strother (ed.), *Psychology and Mental Health* pp. 76–92. Washington DC: American Psychological Association.

6. Nelson-Jones, R. (1974) Some thoughts on counsellor training. *British Journal of Guidance and Counselling*, **2**, 182–190.
7. Fiedler, F. E. (1950) The concept of an ideal therapeutic relationship. *Journal of Consulting Psychology*, **14**, 239–245.
8. Fiedler, F. E. (1950) A comparison of therapeutic relationships in psychoanalytic, nondirective and Adlerian therapy. *Journal of Consulting Psychology*, **14**, 436–445.
9. Fiedler, F. E. (1950) The concept of an ideal therapeutic relationship. *Journal of Consulting Psychology*, **14**, 241.
10. Fiedler, F. E. (1950) A comparison of therapeutic relationships in psychoanalytic, nondirective and Adlerian therapy. *Journal of Consulting Psychology*, **14**, 444.
11. Rogers, C. R. (1957) The necessary and sufficient conditions of therapeutic personality change. *Journal of Consulting Psychology*, **21**, 95–104.
12. *Ibid*. p. 96.
13. Patterson, C. H. (1974) *Relationship Counseling and Psychotherapy* pp. 49–50. New York: Harper and Row.
14. Traux, C. B. & Mitchell, K. M. (1971) Research on certain therapist interpersonal skills in relation to process and outcome. In A. E. Bergin and S. L. Garfield (eds), *Handbook of Psychotherapy and Behavior Change* pp. 299–344. New York: Wiley.
15. Rogers, C. R. (1962) The interpersonal relationship: the core of guidance. *Harvard Educational Review*, **32**, 416. Full reference pp. 416–429.
16. Rogers, C. R. (1975) Empathic: an unappreciated way of being. *The Counseling Psychologist*, **5**, 2, 2. Full reference pp. 2–10.
17. *Webster's New World Dictionary of the American Language* (pocket-size ed.). New York: World Publishing Co., 1958, p. 180.
18. *The Concise Oxford Dictionary* (fifth ed.). Oxford: Clarendon Press, 1964, p. 397.
19. Traux, C. B. & Carkhuff, R. R. (1967) *Toward Effective Counseling and Psychotherapy: Training and Practice* p. 58. Chicago: Aldine.
20. Carkhuff, R. R. (1969) *Helping and Human Relations: Volume One, Selection and Training* pp. 174–175. New York: Holt, Rinehart and Winston.
21. Fiedler, F. E. (1950) The concept of an ideal therapeutic relationship. *Journal of Consulting Psychology*, **14**, 243.
22. Ellis, A. (1962) *Reason and Emotion in Psychotherapy* p. 155. New York: Lyle Stuart.
23. Wolpe, J. (1969) *The Practice of Behaviour Therapy* pp. 12–13. Oxford: Pergamon Press.
24. Carkhuff, R. R. (1969) *Helping and Human Relations: Volume Two, Practice and Research* p. 101. New York: Holt, Rinehart and Winston.
25. Egan, G. (1975) *The Skilled Helper: A Model for Systematic Helping and Interpersonal Relating* p. 30. Monterey, California: Brooks/Cole.
26. Porter, E. H. (1950) *An Introduction to Therapeutic Counseling*. Boston: Houghton Mifflin.
27. Carkhuff, R. R. (1969) *Helping and Human Relations: Volume One, Selection and Training*. New York: Holt, Rinehart and Winston.
28. Ivey, A. E. & Authier, J. (1978) *Microcounseling: Innovations in Interviewing, Counseling, Psychotherapy and Psychoeducation* (2nd ed.). Springfield, Illinois: Charles C. Thomas.
29. Egan, G. (1975) *Exercises in Helping Skills*. Monterey, California: Brooks/Cole.
30. Rogers, C. R. (1980) *A Way of Being* p. 41. Boston: Houghton Mifflin.
31. Nelson-Jones, R. & Patterson, C. H. (1975) Measuring client-centred attitudes. *British Journal of Guidance and Counselling*, **3**, 228–236.
32. Rogers, C. R. (1951) *Client-centred Therapy* pp. 19–64. Boston: Houghton Mifflin.
33. Nelson-Jones, R. (1977) A factor analysis of the Counsellor Attitude Scale. *British Journal of Guidance and Counselling*, **5**, 185–188.
34. Argyle, M. (1975) *Bodily Communication* p. 152. London: Methuen.
35. Gordon, T. (1970) *Parent Effectiveness Training* pp. 35–39. New York: Wyden.
36. Gladstein, G. A. (1974) Nonverbal communication and counseling/psychotherapy: a review. *The Counseling Psychologist*, **4**, 3, 34–57.

37. Haase, R. F. & Tepper, D. T. (1979) Nonverbal components of empathic communication. *Journal of Counseling Psychology*, **19**, 417–424.
38. Shapiro, J. G., Foster, C. P. & Powell, T. (1968) Facial and bodily cues of genuineness, empathy and warmth. *Journal of Clinical Psychology*, **24**, 233–236.
39. Anthony, W. A. & Carkhuff, R. R. (1976) *The Art of Health Care: A Handbook of Psychological First Aid Skills* p. 33. Amherst, Massachusetts: Human Resource Development Press.
40. Hall, E. T. (1966) *The Hidden Dimension*. Garden City, New York: Doubleday.
41. Egan, G. (1975) *The Skilled Helper. A Model for Systematic Helping and Interpersonal Relating* p. 65. Monterey, California: Brooks/Cole.
42. Anthony, W. W. & Carkhuff, R. R. (1976) *The Art of Health Care: A Handbook of Psychological First Aid Skills* p. 11. Amherst, Massachusetts: Human Resource Development Press.
43. Gordon, T. (1970) *Parent Effectiveness Training* p. 29. New York: Wyden.
44. Patterson C. H. (1974) *Relationship Counseling and Psychotherapy* p. 104. New York: Harper and Row.
45. *Ibid.* p. 104.
46. Ivey, A. E. & Authier, J. (1978) *Microcounseling. Innovations in Interviewing, Counseling, Psychotherapy and Psychoeducation* (2nd ed.) p. 153. Springfield, Illinois: Charles C. Thomas.
47. Rogers, C. R. (1975) Empathic: unappreciated way of being. *The Counseling Psychologist*, **5**, 2, 4.
48. *Ibid.* p. 5.
49. Porter, E. H. (1950) *An Introduction to Therapeutic Counseling* pp. 45–60. Boston: Houghton Mifflin.
50. Gordon, T. (1970) *Parent Effectiveness Training* pp. 13–28. New York: Wyden.
51. Porter, E. H. (1950) *An Introduction to Therapeutic Counseling* p. 45. Boston: Houghton Mifflin.
52. Traux, C. B. & Wargo, D. G. (1966) Psychotherapeutic encounters that change Behavior: for better or for worse. *American Journal of Psychotherapy*, **20**, 499–520.
53. Patterson, C. H. (1974) *Relationship Counseling and Psychotherapy* pp. 119–145. New York: Harper and Row.
54. Traux, C. B. & Carkhuff, R. R. (1967) *Toward Effective Counseling and Psychotherapy: Training and Practice* pp. 194–208. Chicago: Aldine.
55. Carkhuff, R. R. (1969) *Helping and Human Relations: Volume Two, Practice and Research* pp. 38–39. New York: Holt, Rinehart and Winston.
56. Traux, C. B. & Carkhuff, R. R. (1965) Experimental manipulation of therapeutic conditions. *Journal of Consulting Psychology*, **29**, 119–124.
57. Rogers, C. R. (1975) Empathic: an unappreciated way of being. *The Counseling Psychologist*, **5**, 3
58. Films, tapes and cassettes are available on hire from the British Association for Counselling, 1a Little Church St, Rugby, Warwicks, England.
59. An American source of tapes and cassettes is the American Academy of Psychotherapists, 1040 Woodcock Road, Orlando, Florida, 32803.
60. Martin, J. C., Carkhuff, R. R. & Berenson, B. G. (1966) Process variables in counseling and psychotherapy: a study of counseling and friendship. *Journal of Counseling Psychology*, **13**, 356–359.
61. Nelson-Jones, R. (1979) Some issues in placement work. *The Counsellor*, **2**, (5), 9–15.

12 – Basic Behavioural Counselling Methods

SUMMARY: *Behavioural counselling methods are based mainly on principles of learning, though also on counselling and clinical experience. Behavioural counselling starts with a behavioural assessment to specify treatment goals and methods. The assessment may include data collected both during interviews and from other sources, some of which are described. Progressive relaxation, which consists of tensing and relaxing various muscle groupings, can be a treatment method in itself, or may be part of a more complex method. Other relaxation procedures reviewed include: brief relaxation, differential relaxation, verbal relaxation and mental relaxation. Considerations for counsellors in conducting relaxation training are discussed. Systematic desensitization involves three elements: (a) training in deep muscular relaxation; (b) the construction of hierarchies of anxiety-evoking stimuli; and (c) presentation of hierarchy items to the imagination of a deeply relaxed client. Variations of systematic desensitization involve real-life hierarchies, group desensitization, and different cognitive elements. Participant modelling is a behavioural method which uses observational learning to help the client to perform the feared tasks.*

Behaviour rehearsal involves the counsellor in shaping and rehearsing the client's behaviour for various target situations. Assertive training, or training in the accurate communication of positive and negative feelings without inhibition or aggression, is the main area for behaviour rehearsal. Additionally, cognitive rehearsal, involving mental role-playing and coaching in assertive self-statements, may be useful. Assertive training may be on an individual counselling, group counselling and/or a self-help basis. Reinforcement methods aim to modify behaviour by altering its consequences. Ways of discovering what clients find reinforcing are reviewed. Counselling may be seen as a process of social influence or reinforcement. Clients may be helped to increase the number and scope of reinforcers available to them, an approach which shows promise in the treatment of those who are depressed. Reinforcement programmes and token economies are aimed at changing the behaviour of both individuals and groups, for example in a classroom. Tokens are tangible conditioned reinforcers which may be exchanged for back-up reinforcers such as prizes and food. All reinforcement program-

mes should plan to overcome extinction of the target behaviours after removal of the reinforcers. Time out is a punishment procedure involving removal of clients from situations in which they receive reinforcement. The chapter concludes with practical exercises for learning each basic behavioural counselling method.

This chapter provides an introduction to some of the basic methods of behavioural counselling. The terms 'behavioural counselling' and 'behaviour therapy' are both used to describe a series of counselling interventions which are based mainly on the principles of learning described in Chapters 6 and 7. Wolpe, however, observes that the behaviour therapist need not be confined to methods derived from principles, but may also employ methods that have been empirically shown to be effective.[1]

Definitions of behavioural counselling tend to differ according to whether the psychologist's main emphasis is based on classical conditioning, operant conditioning, or cognitive change or changing clients' thinking. For instance, Wolpe defines behaviour therapy as a conditioning therapy involving 'the use of experimentally established principles of learning for the purpose of changing maladaptive behaviour. Unadaptive habits are weakened and eliminated; adaptive habits are initiated and strengthened'.[2] Wolpe's approach to behaviour therapy is based largely on classical conditioning. A definition of behavioural counselling which is focused more on cognitive change is that of Krumboltz and Thoresen, who write: 'Behavioral counseling is a process of helping people learn how to solve certain interpersonal, emotional and decision problems'.[3] Elsewhere, Krumboltz has observed that there are three types of behavioural goals for counsellors: altering maladaptive behaviour, learning the decision-making process, and preventing problems.[4] This chapter deals predominantly with approaches to altering observable behaviour rather than with cognitive change approaches.

BEHAVIOURAL ASSESSMENT

Behavioural counselling invariably begins with a behavioural assessment, sometimes known as a functional analysis of the client's problem area or areas. One of the main purposes of the assessment is to arrive at an informed specification of treatment objectives in behavioural terms to guide the counsellor's choice of counselling methods. Behavioural assessment thus has two foci: first, specification of the client's problem areas; and second, specification of the most appropriate techniques to be used by the counsellor. An adequate behavioural assessment allows counsellors to identify the stimulus antecedents of the responses they wish to treat, while an inadequate behavioural assessment may lead to the wrong approach being applied to the wrong problem.

When a client makes a statement like 'I seem to be very depressed these days', 'I don't seem to have many friends' or 'I get very tense at work', the behavioural counsellor attempts an analysis based on an *SORC* assessment, where *S* refers to the *stimulus* or *situational antecedents*, *O* to physiological or cognitive mediating *organismic variables*, *R* to the *response variables* and *C* to the consequences or *consequent variables*.[5, 6] The purpose of the *SORC* analysis is to search for the key variables which control the client's behaviour. Sometimes these may be masked: for instance, aggression at work may reflect a poor marital relationship. Behavioural analysis aims for a high degree of specificity. For instance, in analysing a response, information on length, frequency, generality, and strength of the response should be collected. Behavioural assessment may take place both within and outside the counselling interview. Furthermore, there is much scope for client self-assessment as part of or in addition to counsellor assessment.

Within Interview Assessment

Though a behavioural assessment interview tends to have a high degree of focus and of counsellor direction, the kinds of counsellor characteristics described as basic empathy play an important role. This is because they help to build rapport and facilitate client self-disclosure as well as ensuring that the counsellor listens accurately to material. Apart from collecting basic information, such as the client's age, sex and marital and occupational status, two early objectives of the counsellor are to allow the client to convey his problem area or areas in his own words and to provide for him some minimal clarification concerning the goals of the initial behavioural assessment. At this stage some counsellors may also mention that much behaviour is learned and may be unlearned. The interview may continue with the counsellor asking specific questions as part of an *SORC* analysis of presenting concerns. Much of the focus of the assessment will be on current variables which are maintaining the problem behaviours. Behavioural counsellors differ in the extent to which they gather historical material concerning how the presenting concerns were learned, though this may be important in obtaining an accurate picture. Wolpe, for instance, gathers historical material on his clients' presenting concerns, family life, educational and occupational development, and sexual development. Wolpe also explores his clients' current social relationships.[7] Potential pitfalls of a high degree of counsellor direction and questioning are that clients may feel threatened and also may become blocked from discussing areas not being focused on by the counsellor.

Other possible elements of an initial assessment include the counsellor's observations about the verbal and non-verbal behaviour of the client, who, as in the case of socially awkward people, may be demonstrating at least part of his problem during the interview. The counsellor may explore additional problem areas which emerge as the assessment proceeds. The client's personal assets and ways of coping or avoiding coping with problems should be noted. Furthermore, an assessment should be made of the client's motivation for change, any influences in the client's environment which are likely to hinder or help change, and the client's expectancies regarding the possibility of change. The counsellor is also likely to observe the kinds of things which the client finds reinforcing, such as personal attention or praise, since these may be useful for eliciting behaviour change.

Additional Sources of Assessment Data

There are a number of additional sources of assessment data, one or more of which the behavioural counsellor may find useful in generating more accurate hypotheses about treatment goals and objectives. These include the following.

Medical information

A medical examination is essential if there is any suspicion of a physiologically based problem or one with medical implications. For such clients, a behavioural assessment is incomplete until such data have been collected and, even then, the counsellor may have further consultation with a physician.

Previous record of psychological treatment

More information about the client's concerns and the likely outcomes of treatment strategies may be gained from any records of previous psychological or psychiatric treatment which are available. Again, further consultations with the relevant psychologist or psychiatrist may be indicated.

Self-report questionnaires

Clients may be asked to fill in self-report questionnaires. Such measures may focus on overt *behaviour*, or how the client acts, on *emotions*, or how the client feels, and on clients' *perceptions* of their environments. Perhaps the most commonly used type of questionnaire is the sort which asks clients to indicate the kinds of situations which cause them anxiety. One such questionnaire is Wolpe and Lang's *Fear Survey Schedule* in which clients are asked to indicate on a five-point scale, ranging from 'not at all' to 'very much', how disturbed they currently feel in 108 situations, such as 'People in authority', 'Angry people', 'Darkness' and 'Airplanes'.[8] A questionnaire focused on self-report of behaviour is Alberti and Emmons' assertiveness checklist, with such items as 'Do you speak out or protest when someone takes your place in line?'.[9] Another kind of questionnaire, which focuses on activities, events and experiences which clients find rewarding, is the *Pleasant Events Schedule* of MacPhillamy and Lewinsohn.[10,11] Such a questionnaire is useful in identifying actual and potential reinforcers which may be used in conjunction with treatment.

Client self-monitoring

Here clients are asked to collect baseline data by monitoring their current behaviour. One way to go about this is to ask clients to fill in daily diary sheets investigating the *SORC* elements of a specific behaviour being monitored. Table 12.1 illustrates such a

Table 12.1 *Example of an entry in a behavioural monitoring diary*

Behaviour being monitored: fear in public-speaking situations

Stimulus	Organismic mediation	Response	Consequences
3.30 p.m. Was about to give a brief presentation to 15 colleagues concerning a sales project I'm working on. The colleagues were seated round a conference table and I was to stand at one end.	I felt fairly anxious, since I remembered not doing very well on a previous occasion. I was very conscious of wanting to make a good impression.	Tried to hurry my talk through as quickly as possible. Kept little eye contact with my audience. Felt threatened by their questions after the talk.	Felt relieved when talk was over. Disappointed that I had performed only moderately. Feel not very confident about next time.

behavioural monitoring diary, which might be kept for a week or however long it takes to obtain the relevant information. Such diaries imply that the assessment has arrived at the stage where further information is required for specific target behaviours. Sharpe and Lewis provide examples of monitoring sheets across a wide range of behaviours based on a stimulus, response, consequence, 'what I would like to have done' format.[12]

Direct observation in naturalistic settings

Sometimes a behavioural counsellor may go with a client into a real-life setting to observe how the client behaves. An example of this might be going into a pub or a restaurant with clients who may have difficulty drinking or eating in public, then observing and discussing their behaviour and emotions as they happen or shortly afterwards. However, clients may behave differently from usual when being observed in this way.

Indirect observation in naturalistic settings

Another form of observation in naturalistic settings is to collect information from those who interact with clients in their everyday lives, such as teachers or parents in the case of children, or spouses in the case of married people. The counsellor needs to bear in mind the degree to which the reported behaviours may be representative of their clients' behaviours in particular situations and also the extent to which the reports may be contaminated by observer bias. Again, if clients know they are being observed they may behave differently. On the other hand, there are ethical problems in observing and reporting on clients without their knowledge or consent. Some of the problems of the validity of indirect observation in naturalistic settings may be overcome by the use of behaviour monitoring codes involving frequency counts of various categories of behaviour.

Direct observation in simulated settings

Role playing is one form of direct observation in simulated settings. The client might be asked to enact a piece of behaviour as he would normally behave, with the counsellor, and possibly others, playing various roles in the situation. Such enactments might simulate pupils and students having difficulty talking to their parents, or marital partners who are failing to communicate. Another form of observation, which may be direct by the counsellor or indirect by other raters, is to observe behind a one-way mirror the behaviour of clients in a group. Lewinsohn and his colleagues have devised a behavioural rating schedule focused on the actions and reactions of each group member. This leads to a quantitative representation of aspects of social skill such as total amount of behaviour emitted by and directed towards each individual, use of positive and negative reactions, and range of interactions.[13]

Specification of Goals

A *behavioural analysis* needs to be conducted and formulated before goals are specified. Such an analysis entails a description of what the problems are, how they appear to have arisen, and what maintains them. These are in the form of hypotheses to be tested in counselling. The end product of the behavioural analysis is an exact specification of what variables are in need of modification 'be they situational antecedents, organismic variables, components of the problem behavior itself, and/or consequent reinforcers'.[14] This in turn leads to a specification of the behavioural counselling methods which will be used to attain the goals. Usually counsellors establish behaviour modification goals in consultation with their clients and elicit their co-operation for various treatment strategies. Clients tend to have more than one area of concern and, though it may be possible to deal with those simultaneously, sometimes an ordering of priorities is necessary. Here a prime consideration is the extent to which the problem behaviours are interfering with the client's ability to lead a satisfactory life. In most instances, client and counsellor will agree on goals and treatment procedures. Where disagreement exists, further discussion may be all that is necessary to resolve the issue. Referral to another counsellor may be indicated if disagreement persists.

Behavioural assessment and monitoring take place throughout a course of treatment and not just at the beginning. One function of such monitoring is to see whether treatment goals are being achieved. Another function is to see whether counsellors or clients feel that it is advisable to alter or reformulate their goals. Perhaps some new situation, such as the client's getting married or acquiring a more responsible position at work, may precipitate such a reformulation. If goals are altered, treatment methods have to be amended accordingly. It is to some of the principal methods of behavioural treatment that we now turn. However, we again stress that an adequate initial assessment is essential before choosing any of these methods.

RELAXATION PROCEDURES

Relaxation procedures may be used on their own or may form part of more complicated procedures, such as systematic desensitization. The acknowledged pioneer of relaxation training is Edmund Jacobson, the first edition of whose major work, *Progressive Relaxation*, appeared in 1929.[15] Jacobson saw what he termed neuromuscular hypertension 'as a condition marked by reflex phenomena of hyper-excitation and hyperirritation'.[16] He was aware that symptoms of hypertension were very common and not restricted only to the severely disturbed. He hypothesized that his progressive relaxation treatment could bring absolute or relative rest to the neuromuscular system, including the mind. His term 'progressive relaxation' refers to the progressive cultivation of the relaxation response. Perhaps Wolpe is responsible for the present popularity of relaxation methods based on Jacobson's work, since they form a major part of his systematic desensitization technique. Relaxation procedures are now used as a complete or part of a behavioural treatment approach to such problems as tension headaches, insomnia and general feelings of tension.[17,18]

Progressive Muscular Relaxation

There are many variants to Jacobson's original progressive muscular relaxation procedures, including those described by Wolpe,[19] Vitalo,[20], Sharpe and Lewis,[21] Goldfried and Davison,[22] and Bernstein and Borkovec.[23] Although the latters' manual, *Progressive Relaxation Training*, provides a particularly clear introduction to the subject, the following description is drawn from a number of sources, including the author's counselling experience.

The physical setting of the counsellor's office should be conducive to relaxation. This involves absence of disruptive noise, interior decoration that is restful and lighting which may be dimmed. The client may be taught to relax in a recliner chair, or on a mattress or, at the very least, in a comfortable upright chair with a headrest. It is assumed that the behavioural assessment has indicated that relaxation training is a means towards one of the client's behavioural targets, such as a reduction in feelings of tension and irritability, or being able to get to sleep within a stipulated time of going to bed. Since a noticeable investment of time and effort is required of clients for learning relaxation, it is important that they clearly understand the relevance of the procedures to alleviating their problems.

At an early stage the counsellor may explain that much tension is learned and that by training and practice it can be unlearned. The counsellor may from the beginning make an effort to see that clients view relaxation training as learning a coping skill which can be used in daily life rather than just treating them as passive persons.[24] Furthermore, clients should understand that success at learning relaxation, just like success at learning any other skill, requires practice and that relaxation homework will be required. Before starting relaxation, the counsellor should suggest that the client wear loose-fitting, comfortable clothing both during interviews and when doing relaxation homework. Furthermore, that it is helpful to remove items such as glasses and shoes.

Bernstein and Borkovec observe that in teaching muscular relaxation there is a succession of events which must be observed with each muscle group. This tension–relax cycle has five elements: (a) *focus*, by which is meant focusing attention on the muscle group; (b) *tense*, i.e. tensing the muscle group; (c) *hold*, maintaining the tension for five to seven seconds; (d) *release*, releasing the tension in the muscle group; and (e) *relax*, focusing attention on the letting go of tension and further relaxation of the muscle group.[25] Clients need to learn this *focus–tense–hold–release–relax* cycle so that they may apply it in their homework.

Having explained the basic tension–relax cycle, counsellors may then demonstrate it by going through the cycle in relation to their own right hand and forearm and at each stage asking their clients to do the same. Thus, 'I'm focusing all my attention on my right hand and forearm and I'd like you to do the same' progresses to 'I'm clenching my right fist and tensing the muscles in my lower arm . . .', then on to 'I'm holding my right fist clenched and keeping the muscles in my lower arm tensed . . .', followed by 'I'm now releasing as quickly as I can the tension from my right fist and lower arm . . .', ending with 'I'm relaxing my right hand and forearm, letting the tension go further and further and letting these muscles become more and more relaxed . . .'. The final relaxation phase tends to last from 30 to 60 seconds, frequently accompanied by counsellor relaxation 'patter' about letting the tension go and acknowledging and experiencing feelings of deeper and deeper relaxation as they occur. Having been through the tension–relax cycle once, especially in the initial sessions the client may be instructed to go through it again, thus tensing and relaxing each muscle grouping twice.

The counsellor is then likely to take the client through the muscle groups, modelling them as necessary. Table 12.2 shows 16 muscle groups and suggested tensing instructions. The arms tend to come at the beginning, since they are easy to demonstrate. For most clients the face is particularly important because, as Wolpe observes, 'the most marked anxiety-inhibiting effects are usually obtained by relaxations there'.[26]

Once clients have learned how to tense the various muscle groups, they are instructed to keep their eyes closed during relaxation training and practice. After a tension–relax cycle, the counsellor may ask whether the client has been completely relaxed and indicate that, if this has not been the case, they should raise the index finger of the hand nearest to the counsellor. To facilitate genuine relaxation, counsellors should ensure that their clients feel safe to share any feelings of residual tension. Furthermore, counsellors should be observing their clients' body posture and breathing as a check on the extent of relaxation. Complete relaxation is not to be expected immediately. Consequently, counsellors should use their judgement about whether to repeat the tension–relax cycle. Given persistent failure to relax a muscle group, another approach is to alter the muscle group strategy. For instance, in the neck and throat muscle group, shrugging the shoulders by pulling the head down and the shoulders up may be an alternative to pulling the chin down hard towards the chest and resisting having it touch the chest. Clients differ in the muscle groups in which they experience much of their tension and counsellors may have to pay extra attention to such individual differences.

Towards the end of a relaxation session, counsellors may ask clients for a summary of their relaxation, along the lines of 'Well, how was your relaxation today?' and discuss any issues that arise. Termination of a relaxation session may be achieved by counsellors counting from five to one and when they get to one asking their clients to wake up pleasantly relaxed as though from a peaceful sleep. Bernstein and Borkovec advocate relaxation sessions ending with an 'enjoyment period' of a minute or two in which the counsellor suggests that the client focus on the very pleasant state of relaxation prior to the counting procedure for terminating relaxation.[27]

The importance of practising muscular relaxation may be further stressed at the end of the initial relaxation session. Clients are likely to be given the homework assignment of practising muscular relaxation for one or two 15-minute periods a day. Counsellors should ask their clients whether they anticipate any obstacles to such practice, such as finding a quiet place, and help them to devise strategies for ensuring good homework. There is some evidence that clients who monitor their relaxation practice are much more likely to continue doing it.[28] Consequently, it may be helpful

Table 12.2 *Muscle groups and tensing instructions for muscular relaxation training*

Muscle group	Tensing instructions*
Right hand and forearm	Clench your right fist and tense the muscles in your lower arm.
Right biceps	Bend your right arm at the elbow and flex your biceps by tensing the muscles of your upper right arm.
Left hand and forearm	Clench your left fist and tense the muscles in your lower arm.
Left biceps	Bend your left arm at the elbow and flex your biceps by tensing the muscles of your upper left arm.
Forehead	Lift your eyebrows as high as possible.
Eyes, nose and upper cheeks	Squeeze your eyes tightly shut and wrinkle your nose.
Jaw and lower cheeks	Clench your teeth and pull the corners of your mouth firmly back.
Neck and throat	Pull your chin down hard towards your chest yet resist having it touch your chest.
Chest and shoulders	Pull your shoulder blades together and take a deep breath.
Stomach	Tighten the muscles in your stomach as though someone was about to hit you there.
Right thigh	Tense the muscles of the right upper leg by pressing the upper muscle down and the lower muscles up.
Right calf	Stretch your right leg and pull your toes towards your head.
Right foot	Point and curl the toes of your right foot and turn it inwards.
Left thigh	Tense the muscles of the left upper leg by pressing the upper muscle down and the lower muscles up.
Left calf	Stretch your left leg and pull your toes towards your head.
Left foot	Point and curl the toes of your left foot and turn it inwards.

* With left-handed people, tensing instructions for the left side of the body should come before those for the right.

Table 12.3 *Monitoring log for relaxation homework*

Date	Time, place, length	Comments
3 Oct.	6 p.m., living room at home, 15 minutes	Started off feeling tense after day at work. Tensed and relaxed the 16 muscle groups. Distracting thoughts about work interfered with relaxation. Nevertheless, ended feeling considerably better.

for the counsellor to give the client a log for monitoring their relaxation homework. An example of an entry in such a monitoring log is provided in Table 12.3.

Brief Muscular Relaxation Procedures

When the full muscular relaxation procedures have been learned and the client is able to attain deep relaxation, briefer muscular relaxation procedures may be introduced. The idea here is to learn to attain deep relaxation with less time and effort. This skill may be useful both within and outside the counselling interview. Brief muscular relaxation procedures may involve sequential or simultaneous application of the tension–relax cycle to various muscle groups, albeit interrelated.

Bernstein and Borkovec provide examples of sequential brief muscular relaxation procedures.[29] One variation is to tense seven muscle groups: the right arm muscles, the left arm muscles and the facial muscles are each tensed as single groups; the neck and throat muscles are tensed as previously; and the chest, shoulder and stomach muscles, the right leg and foot muscles and the left leg and foot muscles are each tensed as single groups. The four muscle group variation, which, even more than the seven muscle group variation, involves simultaneous as well as sequential relaxation, refers to: arm muscles; face, neck and throat muscles; chest, shoulder and stomach muscles; and leg and foot muscles.

Simultaneous muscular relaxation involves tensing virtually all muscles at once. An introductory counsellor statement might be 'When I give the signal, I would like you to close your eyes tightly, take a deep breath and simultaneously clench your fists and flex your biceps, frown very deeply, pull your shoulder blades together and tense your legs and feet. Now take a deep breath and tense everything . . . hold for five seconds . . . now release and relax as quickly and deeply as you can'. Simultaneous muscular relaxation may provide the counsellor with useful economies in interview time when using systematic desensitization procedures. When ready, brief muscular relaxation procedures should be incorporated into the client's relaxation homework.

Verbal Relaxation Procedures

Verbal relaxation procedures can involve either the counsellor giving instructions to a client or the client engaging in self-instructional procedures. The latter may be particularly useful where the client is in public situations, such as a business meeting, where the tensing of various muscle groupings might appear rather incongruous, to say the least! Thus verbal procedures give clients a useful self-help strategy for stressful situations.

One verbal relaxation format is, without any further tensing, to ask the client to *focus* on the tension in a muscle grouping and then follow a *relax* procedure, with the client's attention being directed to letting go and experiencing relaxation replace tension as it leaves the body. This may be done with all or some muscle groupings. Again, attention to facial muscles may be particularly important for many clients.

Another verbal relaxation procedure involves counting. A simple version is to count from one to ten and instruct clients to notice the tension flowing out of their bodies. A variant of this is to count from one to ten but, for example every two digits, draw the client's attention to noticing the tension leaving particular muscle groupings, such as the arms, legs, trunk of the body, face, and whole body. Again, when ready, clients should be encouraged to practise these verbal relaxation procedures on a homework basis.

Mental Relaxation

Usually in conjunction with other relaxation procedures, clients may be encouraged to engage in mental relaxation. Such relaxation usually involves imagining a peaceful scene, such as 'lying in a meadow on a nice warm summer's day, feeling a gentle breeze, watching the clouds'. Counsellors can discover from their clients which particular scene they find most conducive to relaxation. Mental relaxation might be used after going through a muscular relaxation procedure.

Differential Relaxation

Jacobson defined differential relaxation as 'a minimum of tension in the muscles requisite for an act along with the relaxation of other muscles'.[30] For instance, a golfer who gets inappropriately tense wrecks a shot, which frequently leads to further tension and further mistakes. Differential relaxation necessitates identifying the muscles requisite for an act and then relaxing all other muscles. Jacobson gives an example of a man sitting reading a book whose back, arms, head, legs and trunk are suitably relaxed rather than unnecessarily tense.[31] Differential relaxation may involve muscular or verbal relaxation procedures to (a) get the appropriate tension level in certain muscle groups and (b) eliminate tension in all other muscle groups. Again, it may be a helpful strategy for handling tension in everyday life.

Conditioned Relaxation

Another procedure which may be helpful in handling stress is conditioned relaxation. Here the client is conditioned to associate a cue word such as 'calm' or 'relax' with a deeply relaxed state which may have been attained by progressive muscular relaxation. The client may then use the cue word to contain or reduce anxiety when faced with or during stressful situations.

Relaxed Life-style

As well as the various relaxation procedures described above, counsellors need to be sensitive to whether or not their client's life-style is sufficiently relaxed. Straight-forward precautions like proper holidays, leaving adequate time for meals, not taking on excessive commitments, keeping reasonably fit physically, and having regular recreations may be very important relaxation goals for clients. Such areas should be identified in an adequate behavioural assessment.

Relaxation Training Considerations

Behavioural counsellors and therapists differ in the number of sessions they take for relaxation training. Indeed, clients also differ in the speed with which they attain a capacity to relax. Wolpe teaches progressive muscular relaxation in six 'lessons' and asks his patients to practise at home for two 15-minute sessions per day.[32] Bernstein and Borkovec suggest a ten-session relaxation training timetable, with the first three sessions devoted to training in relaxing all muscle groups, the next four sessions to brief muscular relaxation, and the final three sessions to verbal relaxation procedures.[33] Again, daily homework practice is assigned. Counsellors may vary their relaxation training timetable according to their clients' needs and their own workload. Nevertheless, it is important that subjects have sufficient sessions to learn relaxation adequately.

Frequently, counsellors cassette-record relaxation instructions for their clients to play back during home practice. A risk here is that inadequate attention may get paid to muscle groupings which the client finds difficult to relax. One approach to this problem is to alert clients and ask them, if necessary, temporarily to switch off the cassette recorder and spend extra time relaxing a particular muscle grouping. Goldfried and Davison suggest there comes a time when clients should be weaned from their cassettes.[34] One way to achieve this is to encourage clients to relax for a stipulated period of time without their cassettes, then turn their cassettes on. As the difference in depth of relaxation diminishes between the periods when the cassette is off and when it is on, there is less need for the cassette.

Sometimes clients experience difficulties in getting deeply relaxed. We have already mentioned repeating the tension–relax cycle and altering the tensing strategy as ways of handling certain client difficulties. Also, some psychiatrists use tranquillizing drugs to induce relaxation. One way of dealing with the problem of interfering thoughts is to get clients engaged in mental relaxation. Sometimes clients are afraid of losing control and may be reassured by the counsellor's including in the relaxation instructions a statement to the effect that they will not lose control. Some clients have practice difficulties and we reiterate the desirability of counsellors' monitoring the relaxation homework of their clients and dealing with any issues that arise. One method of checking on the extent of client relaxation both in interviews and at home is to ask them to rate themselves on a quantitative scale ranging from zero, representing maximum relaxation, to 100, representing maximum tension. A further point is that some relaxation difficulties may be more a matter of unrealistic expectations on the part of counsellors or clients rather than actual difficulties.

Borkovec and Sides reviewed 25 controlled studies using progressive muscular relaxation and found that 15 studies reported the superiority of and 10 studies its equivalence to control group outcomes.[35] However, of the seven studies characterized by three or more training sessions, live rather than taped training, and clinical as contrasted with normal subjects, only one failed to prove progressive relaxation superior to control group conditions. The authors concluded 'In the case of progressive relaxation, we suggest that multi-session, live training with subjects for whom there is a relevant physiological response component involved in the target behavior represents a minimum requirement on both clinical and empirical grounds'.[36]

SYSTEMATIC DESENSITIZATION

Systematic desensitization is a behavioural counselling method of which relaxation is an important component. Where a behavioural assessment indicates that the client has certain specific areas of anxiety or phobic areas, rather than just general tension, systematic desensitization may be the preferred method of treatment. However, an adequate behavioural assessment is essential. For instance, anxiety about tests or about occupational decisions may be the consequence of inadequate revision or poor decision-making skills. In such instances the anxiety is likely to be more effectively diminished by skills training than by systematic desensitization. There are numerous different theoretical explanations of the efficacy of systematic desensitization, some of which also have procedural implications.[37]

Wolpe was the originator of systematic desensitization,[38] a treatment he considers to be based on the reciprocal inhibition principle described in Chapter 7. He acknowledges that systematic desensitization may be conducted concurrently with other behavioural interventions.[39] Systematic desensitization involves three elements: (a) training in deep muscular relaxation; (b) the construction of hierarchies of anxiety-evoking stimuli; and (c) asking the client, when relaxed, to imagine items from the anxiety-evoking hierarchies.

Rationale

The behavioural counsellor is likely to start systematic desensitization by presenting a rationale for its use in relation to the client's concerns as identified by the behavioural assessment. This may involve remarks about the reciprocal inhibition principle. Also, the three elements of systematic desensitization are likely to be briefly explained. Additionally, possibly the counsellor will mention the usefulness of learning relaxation as a coping skill for anxiety-evoking situations. Having already discussed relaxation training, we now turn to the construction of hierarchies.

Construction of Hierarchies

Wolpe writes: 'An anxiety hierarchy is a list of stimuli on a theme, ranked according to the amount of anxiety they evoke'.[40] There are a number of considerations in the construction of desensitization hierarchies. First, suitable themes have to be identified around which anxiety-evoking stimuli can be clustered. Needless to say, precedence needs to be given to themes or areas which are proving most debilitating to the client's functioning. Such themes are likely to emerge from the behavioural assessment and may concern any one of a number of stimulus situations, for example public speaking, examinations, eating in public, being with a member of the opposite sex, and sexual intercourse.

Second, the client has to be introduced to the notion of a subjective scale of anxiety or fear. A common way of checking on the anxiety-evoking potential of an item in a hierarchy is to say that zero is a feeling of no anxiety at all, and 100 is the maximum anxiety possible in relation to a particular theme. Thus individual items can be rated according to their positions on this subjective anxiety continuum or scale.

Third, appropriate hierarchy items need to be generated around each theme. Since clients are going to be asked to imagine the items, the situations need to be specifically and graphically described. The counsellor indicates the appropriate way for items to be formulated. Sources of hierarchy items may include data gathered in the behavioural assessment, homework involving self-monitoring, suggestions from counsellor or client, and questionnaire responses.

Fourth, the items generated around a particular theme need to be ordered into a hierarchy (see Table 12.4). This involves rating the items on a subjective anxiety scale

Table 12.4   *Hierarchy for a client with fear of examinations*

1. (Rated 5)	Thinking about exams while revising at my desk three months before the exams.
2. (Rated 10)	Thinking about exams while revising at my desk two months before the exams.
3. (Rated 15)	Thinking about exams while revising at my desk one month before the exams.
4. (Rated 20)	Thinking about exams while revising at my desk one week before the exams.
5. (Rated 25)	Thinking about exams while revising at my desk on the night before the exams.
6. (Rated 30)	Being driven in a car on the way to the examinations.
7. (Rated 35)	Waking up on the morning of an examination.
8. (Rated 40)	Going up to the notice board to have a look at the exam results.
9. (Rated 50)	Waiting outside the exam room.
10. (Rated 60)	Going into the exam room.
11. (Rated 70)	Looking at the exam paper for the first time.
12. (Rated 80)	Sitting down in the exam room.
13. (Rated 90)	Sitting in the exam room thinking of the inescapability of three hours in a hall full of people.
14. (Rated 95)	Experiencing a panic attack during the exam with the feeling of wanting to leave.
15. (Rated 100)	Having to leave the exam room due to panic.

and ordering them accordingly. Some of this work may be done as a homework assignment, but the counsellor will need to check any hierarchy before starting treatment. Also, during treatment, hierarchy items may need to be re-ordered or reworded, or additional items introduced. Some counsellors write, or ask their clients to write, items on index cards to facilitate ordering. In general, gaps of over ten units on the subjective anxiety scale are avoided. Where they occur, counsellor and client may spend additional time formulating an intervening item or items.

Presentation of Hierarchy Items

During desensitization sessions the counsellor asks clients to imagine various scenes when relaxed. A basic assumption is that the client is capable of imagining the scene in such a way that it represents the real-life situation. Goldfried and Davison observe: 'It is therefore essential that one check whether a client can become anxious from an image even before considering this procedure'.[41] They suggest that clients' imaginal capacities should be tested by asking them, when not relaxed, to imagine a situation which, on the basis of their assessment data, causes them anxiety in real life. Sometimes clients can be helped to imagine scenes by being asked to verbalize what they can see in the situation. Also, counsellors may provide a fuller verbal description of scenes.

A desensitization session may start with the counsellor verbally relaxing the client. After the counsellor is assured that the client has attained a state of deep relaxation, he may start presenting scenes along the lines of 'Now I want you to imagine that you are thinking about exams while revising at your desk three months before exams . . .'. The counsellor starts with the least anxiety-evoking scene on a hierarchy and asks the client to raise an index finger if any anxiety is experienced. If no anxiety is experienced, after five to ten seconds the counsellor asks the client to stop imagining the scene and go back to being pleasantly relaxed. After 30 to 50 seconds, the client may be asked to imagine the same scene again. If this causes no anxiety, the counsellor withdraws the scene, possibly spends time further relaxing the client, and moves on to the next item in the hierarchy.

In instances where the client's index finger is raised to indicate anxiety, the scene is immediately withdrawn and the client is encouraged to relax more deeply before one or more further presentations of the scene. If a scene repeatedly causes anxiety, the counsellor may consult the client about the presentation of a less anxiety-evoking hierarchy item.

An important assumption underlying systematic desensitization is that once a low anxiety-evoking item, for example ten units, has ceased to cause anxiety, all the other items in the hierarchy become less anxiety-evoking by ten units. Thus the 100-unit item becomes a 90-unit item, and so on. In general, only weak anxiety-evoking stimuli are presented to clients during desensitization sessions.

Counsellors may work from more than one hierarchy during a desensitization session. Indeed, time spent on desensitization may form only part of a longer interview in which the counsellor is focusing on other problems using other methods. A record is kept of all scene presentations and their outcomes. Wolpe's desensitization sessions last 15–30 minutes and he observes that 'whereas at an early stage 8 or 10 presentations may be the total at a session, at an advanced stage the number may be 30 or even 50'.[42] Goldfried and Davison indicate that it is more useful to cover from two to five items in a given session.[43]

Variations of Systematic Desensitization

There are a number of different ways in which the basic systematic desensitization procedure described above may be varied. These include the following.

In vivo desensitization

Two kinds of considerations may make *in vivo* or real-life rather than imaginal desensitization the method of choice. First, clients may have difficulty in imagining scenes, and second, the stimuli in clients' hierarchies may lend themselves to real-life presentation. Even using imaginal desensitization, it may be helpful, if not essential, to encourage clients to try out in reality the situations to which they have been desensitized in imagination.

Relaxation may be used as part of *in vivo* desensitization. For instance, a client with a fear of public speaking may be relaxed at the start of each session, then over a number of sessions be asked to give a short talk in front of increasingly large numbers of people, who may also ask increasingly demanding questions. The procedure differs from imaginal desensitization mainly in that the hierarchies are constructed out of real-life situations. Otherwise, many of the imaginal desensitization considerations, such as the level of anxiety within which to present items, apply.

Group desensitization

Systematic desensitization may be used as a group as well as an individual procedure. For instance, a counsellor might work with eight test-anxious college students simultaneously rather than with one at a time, thus possibly saving resources. Group approaches tend to involve the construction of standard rather than individual hierarchies and thus assume some proximity of the ordering of members' anxieties to this standard hierarchy.[44] The standard hierarchy may be compiled from items previously collected or may be evolved in consultation with current group members. The counsellor may move the group through the hierarchy, ensuring that further scenes are not presented until all members do not experience anxiety with the present scene.

Cassette-recorded desensitization

Cassettes may be used not only for the relaxation training part of systematic desensitization, but also for imagination training and for presenting actual hierarchy scenes at home.[45,46] Any number from one to five homework items may be placed on cassette, with the assumptions being either that all of the items generate only a small amount of anxiety, or that the client will not move on to later, more anxiety-evoking items until comfortable with earlier items. Clients who find themselves getting very tense may be instructed to switch off the cassette-playback and relax themselves for a few minutes before going on. Like group desensitization, the use of cassettes may save interview time.

Cognitive variations of desensitization

Goldfried has presented a view of systematic desensitization as self-control training in coping with anxiety-evoking situations.[47] This anxiety-management approach focuses on increasing the client's feelings of self-efficacy in relation to these situations. Procedural changes from traditional systematic desensitization include: (a) presenting a rationale which views desensitization as the learning and application of an active coping skill; (b) learning to recognize the proprioceptive feedback associated with tension so that relaxation may be applied as a coping skill; (c) only constructing a single hierarchy composed of situations involving increasing amounts of anxiety rather than focusing on hierarchies constructed around a number of different themes; (d) encouraging clients to continue imagining scenes, even though experiencing anxiety, and learn to relax away the tension; and (e) possible greater encouragement for clients to practise their anxiety-management skill *in vivo*.

Meichenbaum has suggested a further cognitive variation of desensitization.[48,49] First, an attempt is made to make subjects aware of their self-defeating thoughts, self-verbalizations and instructions in relation to their area of difficulty. This insight procedure is derived mainly from Ellis's rational-emotive technique. Next, a coping imagery procedure is added to the presentation of desensitization scenes in which subjects are asked to visualize themselves becoming anxious and tense and then coping with these feelings by means of incompatible relaxation behaviours, slow deep breaths, and self-instructions generated to facilitate task-oriented and inhibit non-task-oriented thoughts.

MODELLING

Observational learning or modelling may be used for helping to inhibit anxiety as well as for learning new responses, such as social skills. Indeed, as when the counsellor uses modelling to teach a client how to relax, modelling may be serving both anxiety-inhibiting and skills-acquisition functions. Modelling forms a part of the techniques of behaviour rehearsal and assertive training, to be discussed later. Here the focus is on participant modelling, a technique which emphasizes anxiety inhibition as well as increasing clients' feelings of self-efficacy.

Participant Modelling

Participant modelling might almost be considered a variant of systematic desensitization. However, the emphasis is on *in vivo* performance of feared tasks, with successful performance being viewed as the primary vehicle of psychological change.[50] Participant modelling involves a number of stages. First, the feared activities are repeatedly *modelled* both to show clients how they can be successfully performed and to show them that the feared consequences do not occur. For instance, the counsellor might repeatedly model handling a feared object such as a cat, dog or snake. Second, *joint performance* with the counsellor may enable people to start engaging in activities which would be too frightening for them to engage in on their own. Hierarchies of sub-tasks of increasing difficulty are used. The counsellor's function is partly that of anxiety inhibitor as well as guide. Third, *response induction aids* or protective conditions may be introduced to reduce the anticipated likelihood of feared conse-quences and thus help clients to perform the desired tasks. For instance, when treating snake phobias, response induction aids might include the model's holding the snake securely by the head and tail, use of protective gloves, and presentation of a smaller snake. Fourth, gradual *withdrawal of performance supports* takes place to ensure that clients can function effectively without assistance. Fifth, a period of *self-directed performance*, in which clients spend time interacting with the feared objects on their own, may follow. During the initial period of self-directed performance the counsellor may stay in the room with the client, but later withdraws, possibly to observe the client behind a one-way mirror. The idea here is that perceived self-competence is best strengthened by independent achievements in which it is clear that clients' successes are due to their ability to master the feared situations on their own.[51] A final comment is that the success of participant modelling, which has been conducted mainly under experimental conditions, should encourage further validation in clinical and counselling settings.

BEHAVIOUR REHEARSAL AND ASSERTIVE TRAINING

Often a behavioural assessment will highlight client deficits in the areas of assertion and other interpersonal skills. Behaviour rehearsal is one counselling method used for such areas of concern. Although behaviour rehearsal involves dramatic enactment or role playing, it differs from Moreno's psychodrama in that clients are encouraged to role-play new appropriate responses rather than existing maladaptive responses.[52] There are a number of stages in behaviour rehearsal, including: (a) assessment and analysis of the areas in which the client is having difficulty; (b) enlisting the client's motivation for the behaviour rehearsal method; (c) working with the client to define what might be appropriate behaviour in given situations; (d) giving the client practice in appropriate responding by means of role playing, with the counsellor role-playing the other person in the interaction; and (e) encouraging the client to try out the rehearsed behaviours in real-life situations and offering appropriate praise and reinforcement when this is accomplished. Behaviour rehearsal involves the counsellor in shaping the client's behaviour in certain situations. Counsellor behaviours while doing this may include modelling, coaching, hierarchy construction and sometimes specific cognitive interventions.

Assertive Training

Assertiveness is probably the main target behaviour for behaviour rehearsal. Wolpe writes: 'Assertive behaviour is defined as the proper expression of any emotion other than anxiety toward another person'.[53] An early trend in assertive training was that of standing up for one's rights or what might be termed *oppositional* behaviour. More recently, assertive training has been extended to include the expression and accurate communication of *affectionate* behaviour where appropriate. Thus assertive behaviour now encompasses the expression of positive as well as of negative feelings.

Alberti and Emmons have distinguished between: (a) non-assertive or *inhibited* behaviour, in which the individual is self-denying; (b) *aggressive* behaviour, in which the individual is self-enhancing at the expense of another; and (c) *assertive* behaviour, in which the individual is self-enhancing in a way likely to enhance both parties in an interaction.[54] Furthermore, they observe that lack of assertiveness or aggressiveness can be *general* traits or *specific* to particular situations.

After a behavioural assessment, possibly including an assertiveness questionnaire, has indicated a need for assertive training in general and/or in specific target areas, the second step may be for the counsellor to enlist the client's motivation for this method. Sometimes the counsellor may need to spend time reviewing the client's religious or philosophical position, which may be perceived as encouraging effacement rather than assertion. For instance, some Christians may need help in understanding that they can be more effective both as people and as Christians if they allow themselves to become whole persons and not deny their needs and feelings, with the likely psychological toll that is entailed.

During the third stage counsellor and client work together to define what may be appropriate behaviours in a situation. Such situations may be asking a boss for a rise or a girl for a date. This stage involves the generation and consideration of alternative responses. Additionally, clients may be encouraged to observe effective models. It is important to realize that assertiveness must take into account the style of individual clients and the fact that appropriate assertive behaviour should be as 'natural' for them as possible. In other words, what may seem an appropriate response for a counsellor may not be an appropriate response for a particular client. Timing is also important, in that clients should not be encouraged to engage in assertiveness tasks for which they are not ready. Consequently, it may be necessary to construct a hierarchy of progressively more difficult assertion tasks.

The fourth stage is that of the behaviour rehearsal of assertiveness. Alberti and Emmons stress that assertive training should not focus only on verbal behaviour, but also on other components such as eye contact, body posture, gestures, facial expression, voice tone, inflection and volume, and fluency and timing of assertion.[55] Counsellors need to rehearse and coach their clients in these non-verbal and para-verbal aspects of assertiveness and should not be content with correct verbal behaviour only. Also, part of behaviour rehearsal might include rehearsing clients in handling the negative and positive consequences of their assertion.

The fifth stage is enactment in real life. The client might be set assertiveness homework assignments of an appropriate degree of difficulty. Furthermore, observing and monitoring assertive behaviour undertaken between sessions is likely to be helpful. Feedback from real-life attempts at assertive behaviour indicates the adequacy of the behaviour and where, if necessary, it might be improved. Furthermore, the attention of clients can be drawn to any positive consequences of their assertive behaviour. If the consequences have been negative, counsellor and client can review the appropriateness of the behaviour.

A number of cognitive interventions may be used as part of assertion training. We have already mentioned the need with some clients to focus on their basic philosophy in regard to assertiveness. Sometimes cognitive rehearsal may be used as part of assertion training. This is a variation of the behaviour rehearsal stage with, instead of an actual role play, the client role-playing appropriate assertive behaviour in imagination at the same time as verbalizing for the counsellor what he is doing in the imagined situation.[56] Cognitive or rational restructuring, involving coaching in assertive self-statements such as 'Remember that saying "no" to a friend probably won't make him dislike me for ever', may also be helpful as an adjunct to a treatment procedure using overt behaviour rehearsal.[57] Such self-talk, which may be used in real life as well as in rehearsal, is designed to help the client neither panic nor engage in self-derogation, but constructively think through what can be done in a situation.[58] A further cognitive element in assertion training may be that of setting homework reading assignments. Two useful introductory books for counsellors, clients and interested lay people are Alberti and Emmons' *Your Perfect Right*[59] and their later *Stand Up, Speak Out, Talk Back!*.[60]

Assertive training may be applied on an individual or group interview or on a self-help basis. An issue in the implementation of group assertive training is whether to have heterogeneous or homogeneous groups, such as women's groups, men's groups, etc.[61] Without wishing to prejudge the issue, homogeneous groups seem increasingly common in non-clinical settings. Cassettes and video-recorders are used by some counsellors for their assertive training. Last, assertiveness may lead to conflict, and we deal with approaches to conflict resolution in Chapter 15.

REINFORCEMENT METHODS

Reinforcement methods aim to modify behaviour by altering its consequences and, as such, reflect operant rather than classical conditioning principles. To recapitulate, both positive and negative reinforcement strengthen the probability of a response. Positive reinforcers involve presenting and negative reinforcers removing something in a situation. Punishment, or the presentation of a negative state of affairs, aims to weaken the probability of a response without necessarily increasing the frequency of other behaviours. Extinction also aims to weaken the probability of a response by withdrawal of customary reinforcers. Readers are referred to the section on Skinner in Chapter 6 for further discussion of reinforcement concepts, such as schedules of reinforcement.

Assessing Reinforcers

Many reinforcers, such as praise, affection and attention, are given out relatively unthinkingly during the course of everyday life. Reinforcement methods, however, involve the systematic application of reinforcement to initiate and strengthen adaptive behaviours and to weaken and eliminate maladaptive behaviours. In order to use reinforcement systematically, it is necessary to discover what is reinforcing for individual clients. Ways in which counsellors can find out what their clients consider reinforcing include asking them, asking others about them, observing what they say and do in the interview setting and getting them to observe and monitor themselves outside the interview setting.

There are some self-report questionnaires for assessing reinforcers. Cautela has devised a *Reinforcement Survey Schedule* to identify possible reinforcing stimuli together with their relative reinforcing values.[62] The focus of the schedule is on identifying those stimuli which can be used to evoke adaptive responses. The schedule is divided into four major sections: (a) reinforcers that can be presented in many conventional settings; (b) reinforcers that can be presented only through facsimile or imagination; (c) situational contexts that 'I would like to be in'; and (d) a frequency count of frequently occurring daily behaviours and thoughts. Both counsellor and client can use the schedule for assessing the nature, range and strength of the client's reinforcers.

Another self-report questionnaire is the MacPhillamy and Lewinsohn *Pleasant Events Schedule*.[63] This instrument consists of 320 events and activities generated after an extensive search of possible 'pleasant events'. Subjects rate each item in the schedule on a five-point scale of pleasantness. A shortened version of the *Pleasant Events Schedule* might be derived from those items shown to be associated with improved mood for a substantial proportion of people. Lewinsohn and Graf list 49 such items and suggest that they fall into three categories: social interactional, effects incompatible with depression, and ego supportive, or activities leading to feelings such as adequacy and competence.[64,65]

When working with children, pictures may be used instead of words to portray reinforcers. An example of this is the 'reinforcement menu' devised by Daley for finding effective reinforcers for eight-year-old to eleven-year-old mentally retarded children.[66] Twenty-two high-probability activities, such as talking, writing and colouring, were drawn in colour by an artist and enclosed in a single book or 'menu' with one activity per page. Children were encouraged to identify the activities in which they wanted to engage.

Counselling as Reinforcement

A reinforcement view of counselling sees the role of the counsellor as that of controlling the interview by dispensing intentional and, sometimes, unintentional reinforcers. Thus the counsellor is conceptualized as an influencer or as a social reinforcement machine who shapes or manipulates client behaviour.[67] Inasmuch as social-influence processes exist anyway in counselling interviews, a behaviourist would argue that counsellors should be trained to maximize their efficiency in the influencing process. Also, they should become aware of ways in which clients may be reinforcing maladaptive interview behaviours by the counsellors themselves.

Counsellors may reinforce their clients with such variables as praise, attention, eye contact, empathy, warmth and genuineness. Truax argues that counsellors offering high levels of empathy, non possessive warmth, and genuineness are more effective than those offering low levels of these conditions because they become more potent positive reinforcers. Counsellors offering low levels of the conditions may be noxious stimuli who serve primarily as negative influences. Reasons why high levels of the 'therapeutic conditions' are important include reinforcement of human relating by the client, reinforcement of self-exploratory behaviour, and reinforcement of positive self-concepts and self-evaluations.[68] Truax also conducted a study to explore whether Rogers was differentially using the core therapeutic conditions to reinforce certain categories of client behaviour. Counsellor-client-counsellor interaction units were selected randomly from the middle one-third of counselling hours from throughout an 85-interview, single, long-term, successful case handled by Rogers. Truax reported that Rogers significantly responded selectively with differential levels of empathy, warmth or directiveness to high and low levels of five out of nine classes of client behaviour. Furthermore, of the classes of client behaviour to which the counsellor selectively responded or reinforced, four out of five showed significant changes during counselling in the predicted direction.[69]

Behavioural counsellors may sometimes reinforce their clients in very overt ways. For instance, during the behaviour rehearsal phase of assertion training, client behaviour will be shaped by reinforcement until it stands a reasonable chance of success when enacted in real life. Also when clients report successful attainment of assertive training homework goals, they are likely to find that behaviour being reinforced by a counsellor comment like 'good'.

Helping Clients to Obtain Reinforcement

A very important aspect of behavioural treatment may be that of helping clients to increase the number and scope of reinforcers available to them. Another way of saying this is that, instead of passively relying on others, clients can be helped to identify and actively seek out people, activities and situations that provide the desired reinforcements. Lewinsohn and Libet assert that a low rate of positive reinforcement is a critical antecedent of depressive behaviours and that improvement is likely to be accompanied by an increase of positive reinforcement.[70] They report the findings of a study in which the 160 items from the *Pleasant Events Schedule* which a subject judged to be most pleasant were made into an activity schedule for that subject, who, for 30 consecutive days, was asked to indicate at the end of each day the activities in which he or she engaged. They found a significant association between mood and pleasant activities over their 30 subjects, though there were large individual differences. They see the clinical utility of activity schedules as including: (a) assessing which activities are potentially reinforcing; (b) illustrating to clients their low rates of emitting behaviours which bring positive reinforcement; (c) goal setting; and (d) monitoring behaviour change.

A more recent study by Turner and his colleagues in which the subjects were moderately depressed college students confirmed the effectiveness of using activity schedules and also instructing the subjects to increase their pleasant activities over their usual level.[71] A further study by Zeiss, Lewinsohn and Munoz indicated that, with depressed outpatients, treatments focusing on interpersonal skills, or cognitions, or activity schedules (with increasing frequency of target activities) all significantly alleviated depression. The authors concluded that all treatments ameliorated depression because they provided training in self-help skills which increased patients' feelings of self-efficacy regarding the obtaining of positive reinforcement as a result of their own skilfulness.[72]

Reinforcement Programmes and Token Economies

Hosford observes that four crucial elements are necessary in any counselling programme implementing operant reinforcement procedures.[73] First, the reinforcements need to be potent enough to motivate the client to continue performing the desired behaviours. Second, reinforcement must be applied systematically. Third, the contingency between the demonstration of the desired behaviour and the application of the reinforcement must be clear. Fourth, counsellors must be able to elicit the behaviours which they plan to reinforce. It is particularly important that, when a behaviour is initiated, the reinforcement contingent upon that behaviour is immediate, otherwise its differential effect may be lost. It should also be remembered that acquisition of desired behaviours may initially involve reinforcement of related behaviours and building up the desired behaviours by successive approximation.

Reinforcement may either be administered directly, by provision of the actual reinforcer, or indirectly, by means of tokens which may later be exchanged for reinforcers. Furthermore, clients may be reinforced vicariously by observing models obtain rewards for desired behaviours. An example of direct reinforcement is Sanborn and Schuster's use of sweets to reinforce desired behaviours in a remedial reading class.[74] For instance, the first boy to sit down was rewarded with a sweet and the contingency for the reward was verbally transmitted. 'This is for taking your seat'. As the class progressed pupils were rewarded for other specific behaviours.

Tokens are tangible conditioned reinforcers which may be exchanged for back-up reinforcers such as prizes, opportunities to engage in special activities, food or other purchases. Token economies or token reinforcement programmes have been used with schoolchildren, delinquents and hospital patients. In their review of token reinforcement programmes in the classroom, O'Leary and Drabman observe that different investigations repeatedly reported significant decreases in disruptive behaviour associated with token programmes and add 'the most obvious dramatic changes in token programs seem to have occurred in programs where non-academic behaviors served as the dependent variable.'[75]

Kadzin and Bootzin suggest that extinction of the desired behaviours generally follows removal of token reinforcement.[76] They state that generalization should be planned rather than depended on as an inadvertent consequence of the token economy. One way of enhancing resistance to extinction is to focus on teaching those behaviours which will continue to be reinforced after training. Another way involves gradually removing or fading the token reinforcement, possibly offering substitute kinds of reinforcement such as praise as the fading takes place. Yet another way of maintaining the behavioural gains is to encourage clients to use self-reinforcement by giving themselves reinforcers contingent upon the performance of desired behaviours.

Reinforcement programmes and token economies may involve the co-operation and training of significant others in the client's environment. For instance, counsellors may need to work with teachers or parents in devising reinforcement procedures for individuals or groups of children. Furthermore, both teachers and parents may need to become aware of how they may inadvertently be reinforcing some of the behaviours they say they are trying to stop. Teaching the skills of effective reinforcement involves both theoretical learning and relevant practice. Furthermore, counsellors may need to support and guide teachers and parents as they apply their new skills in real-life settings.

Punishment

Goldfried and Davison observe that there are three basic punishment procedures, each of which attempts to reduce the frequency of a behaviour: presentation of an aversive event, time out, and response costs.[77] Anger, striking a person, and threats if he performs an undesired behaviour are all aversive events which may reduce the probability of repetition of the behaviour. Time out is a procedure frequently recommended by behavioural counsellors for use with disruptive children. It involves removal of clients from situations in which they might otherwise be receiving reinforcement. For instance, a child's attention-seeking behaviour in a classroom may be being reinforced by teacher attention and peer approval, neither of which is available when the child is made to leave the classroom for a set period of time. Time-out procedures involve a clear instruction, adequate warning that the time-out procedure is contingent upon the undesired behaviour and, if this goes unheeded, application of time out in a systematic and unemotional way. Response costs involve deductions of certain amounts from clients' collections of reinforcers if they perform undesired behaviours. For instance, participants in a token economy may lose some of their tokens.

AVERSIVE AND IMPLOSIVE METHODS

This chapter has focused on basic behavioural counselling methods. Other less common and more controversial approaches exist, for example aversion therapy and implosive therapy. Both these methods tend to be used in clinical rather than counselling settings and so are only briefly mentioned. Aversion therapy, which entails the presentation of an aversive event such as an electric shock contingent upon some undesired behaviour, might be viewed as a punishment technique. Although the issue of homosexual orientation is a more complex one than their study indicates, MacCulloch and Feldman used an aversion-therapy procedure incorporating a special schedule of reinforcement in an attempt to decrease the homosexual and increase the heterosexual orientation of predominantly homosexually oriented patients.[78]

Stampfl, the founder of implosive therapy, views the symptoms of his patients as 'conditioned fear reactions, and/or conditioned anger reactions, acquired from past experiences involving punishment, frustration and pain'.[79] Usually after two information-gathering clinical interviews, the therapist presents scenes to the client's imagination which get progressively closer to what the patient finds most threatening. Some of the scenes are very gruesome. Stampfl's scenes aim to provide as good an approximation as possible to original conditioning events and may be highly anxiety-evoking. However, he hypothesizes that continued repetition of these scenes should lead to a decrease in their anxiety-evoking potential through extinction.[80] Since many of the original conditioning events are associated with the patient's childhood, Stampfl has found the psychodynamic literature, with its emphasis on toilet training, infantile sexuality and aggression, to be useful in indicating sensitive areas of early aversive conditioning. He states that the single strategy of implosive therapy is for patients to confront and stare down their nightmares.[81]

CONCLUDING COMMENT

Behavioural methods are very varied and behavioural counsellors draw upon procedures other than those listed in this particular chapter. For instance, there are a number of common behavioural methods focused on self-reinforcement and self-control. A discussion of such cognitive or thinking-focused methods, which are likely to be an important part of the behavioural counsellor's repertoire, forms part of Chapter 14. Another useful behavioural counselling method is social skills training, which was covered in part in the section on behaviour rehearsal and assertive training in this chapter and is later discussed in Chapter 15.

PRACTICAL EXERCISES

It may help you to develop your skills in the methods described in this chapter if, either individually or as part of a group, you perform the following exercises.

Behavioural Assessment

1.   Conduct a behavioural assessment, preferably on another member of a skills group (if not, perform a self-assessment). Write out a report focusing on the following kinds of information: basic details of client (age, sex, marital status, occupation); interview observations about client; client's view of presenting concerns; SORC analysis of presenting concerns;

relevant historical information; details of other concerns; *SORC* analysis of other concerns; client's motivation, expectancies, likely co-operation; treatment goals expressed in behavioural terms.

2.   Identify an area of your own behaviour that you wish to change. Formulate your objective in behavioural terms. For one week, keep a behaviour monitoring diary collecting material in an *SORC* format.

Relaxation Procedures

3.   Practise relaxing yourself for 15 to 20 minutes a day over a period of at least a week. Keep a monitoring log of your relaxation homework (Table 12.3). During your relaxation homework cover:
(a)   progressive muscular relaxation (Table 12.2);
(b)   brief muscular relaxation;
(c)   verbal relaxation;
(d)   mental relaxation;
(e)   differential relaxation.

4.   Role-play being a counsellor who is getting another person into a state of deep relaxation by means of progressive muscular relaxation.

5.   Assess your life-style to find out whether it is sufficiently relaxed regarding (a) the pace at which you lead your life and (b) having sufficient relaxation outlets.

Systematic Desensitization

6.   Identify themes in your own life which are appropriate for hierarachy construction and then, along the lines of Table 12.4, construct one or more hierarchies around them.

7.   Work with another person in identifying and constructing hierarchies round anxiety-evoking themes in his or her life.

8.   Role-play being a counsellor who is conducting systematic desensitization, including presentation of hierarchy items, with another person as client.

Participant Modelling

9.   Identify areas in your own life where a participant modelling approach might help you to start performing certain behaviours successfully and thus attain a greater feeling of self-efficacy.

10.   If possible, devise and enact a participant modelling session with yourself acting as counsellor and another person as client.

Behaviour Rehearsal and Assertive Training

11.   Assess yourself on the following dimensions:

    (a)   general assertiveness, non-assertiveness, and aggressiveness;
    (b)   assertiveness, non-assertiveness, and aggressiveness in specific situations which are important to you;
    (c)   oppositional and affectionate assertiveness.

12.   Role-play being a counsellor who works with a client to define appropriate assertive behaviours, conducts the necessary behaviour rehearsal, then encourages the client to try out the new behaviours in appropriate real-life situations.

13.   Conduct a cognitive rehearsal, including verbalizing what you are doing, for a situation in which at present you are finding it difficult to be assertive.

Reinforcement Methods

14.   Either make a list of at least 25 items which you personally find reinforcing, or help your partner to compile such a list, or do both.

15.   Design a token reinforcement system which has utility in an applied setting, such as an educational institution or a family. Specify:

    (a)   the behavioural goals of the programme;
    (b)   the population and setting for the programme;
    (c)   the token and back-up reinforcers involved;
    (d)   the precise contingency or contingencies for award of the tokens;
    (e)   features in the programme designed to avoid extinction of the behaviours learned in the programme;
    (f)   steps to be taken in training and supporting any significant others.

16.   Design a time-out procedure which has utility in an applied setting, such as an educational institution or a family. Specify:

    (a)   the behavioural goals of the procedure;
    (b)   the population and setting for the procedure;
    (c)   the actual time-out procedure, including a clear set of instructions, an adequate warning, and details of the systematic application of the procedure;
    (d)   Steps to be taken in training and supporting any significant others involved in the procedure.

NOTES

1. Wolpe, J. (1973) *The Practice of Behavior Therapy* (2nd ed.) p. XI. Oxford: Pergamon Press.
2. *Ibid.* p. XI.
3. Krumboltz, J. D. & Thoresen, C. E. (eds) (1976) *Counseling Methods*. New York: Holt, Rinehart and Winston.
4. Krumboltz, J. D. (1966) Behavioral goals for counseling. *Journal of Counseling Psychology*, **13**, 153–159.
5. Goldfried, M. R. (1976) Behavioral assessment. In I. B. Weiner (ed.), *Clinical Methods in Psychology* pp. 313–315. New York: Wiley. Full reference pp. 281–330.
6. Goldfried, M. R. & Davison, G. C. (1976) *Clinical Behavior Therapy* pp. 18–54. New York: Holt, Rinehart and Winston. These pages cover conceptual issues in and methods of behavioural assessment.
7. Wolpe, J. (1973) *The Practice of Behavior Therapy* pp. 22–52. Oxford: Pergamon Press.
8. Wolpe, J. & Lang, P. J. (1969) *Fear Survey Schedule*. San Diego, California: Educational and Industrial Testing Service. An 87-item version appears as Appendix 3 in Wolpe, J. (1973) *The Practice of Behavior Therapy* pp. 283–286. Oxford: Pergamon Press.
9. Alberti, R. E. & Emmons, M. E. (1975) *Stand Up, Speak Out, Talk Back!* pp. 25–27. New York: Pocket Books.
10. MacPhillamy, D. J. & Lewinsohn, P. M. (1971) *Pleasant Events Schedule*. Mimeograph, University of Oregon.
11. Lewinsohn, P. M. & Graf, M. (1973) Pleasant activities and depression. *Journal of Consulting and Clinical Psychology*, **41**, 261–268.
12. Sharpe, R. & Lewis, D. (1976) *The Success Factor*. London: Souvenir Press.
13. Lewinsohn, P. M., Weinstein, M. S. & Alper, T. (1970) A behavioral approach to the group treatment of depressed persons: a methodological contribution. *Journal of Clinical Psychology*, **26**, 525–532.
14. Goldfried, M. R. (1976) Behavioral assessment. In I. B. Weiner (ed.), *Clinical Methods in Psychology* p. 321. New York: Wiley.
15. Jacobson, E. (1929) *Progressive Relaxation*. Chicago: University of Chicago Press.
16. Jacobson, E. (1938) *Progressive Relaxation* (2nd ed.). Chicago: University of Chicago Press.
17. Tasto, D. L. & Hinkle, J. E. (1973) Muscle relaxation treatment for tension headaches. *Behavior Research and Therapy*, **11**, 347–349.
18. Bernstein, D. A. & Borkovec, T. D. (1973) *Progressive Relaxation Training: A Manual for the Helping Professions* p. 11. Champaign, Illinois: Research Press.
19. Wolpe, J. (1973) *The Practice of Behavior Therapy* pp. 104–108. Oxford: Pergamon Press.
20. Vitalo, R. (1969) Systematic desensitization manual for helper instruction and treatment procedure. Appendix B in R. R. Carkhuff, *Helping and Human Relations: Vol. 1* pp. 272–273. New York: Holt, Rinehart and Winston. Full reference pp. 271–290.
21. Sharpe, R. & Lewis, D. (1976) *The Success Factor* pp. 33–38, 57–58. London: Souvenir Press.
22. Goldfried, M. R. & Davison, G. C. (1976) *Clinical Behavior Therapy* pp. 81–111. New York: Holt, Rinehart and Winston.
23. Bernstein, D. A. & Borkovec, T. D. (1973) *Progressive Relaxation Training: A Manual for the Helping Professions*. Champaign, Illinois: Research Press.
24. Goldfried, M. R. & Trier, C. S. (1974) Effectiveness of relaxation as an active coping skill. *Journal of Abnormal Psychology*, **83**, 348–355.
25. Bernstein, D. A. & Borkovec, T. D. (1973) *Progressive Relaxation Training: A Manual for the Helping Professions* p. 25. Champaign, Illinois: Research Press.
26. Wolpe, J. (1973) *The Practice of Behavior Therapy* p. 104. Oxford: Pergamon Press.
27. Bernstein, D. A. & Borkovec, T. D. (1973) *Progressive Relaxation Training: A Manual for the Helping Professions* p. 29. Champaign, Illinois: Research Press.

28. Tasto, D. L. & Hinkle, J. E. (1973) Muscle relaxation treatment for tension headaches. *Behavior Research and Therapy*, **11**, 347.
29. Bernstein, D. A. & Borkovec, T. D. (1973) *Progressive Relaxation Training: A Manual for the Helping Professions* pp. 33–38. Champaign, Illinois: Research Press.
30. Jacobson, E. (1938) *Progressive Relaxation* (2nd ed.) p. 83. Chicago: University of Chicago Press.
31. *Ibid.* pp. 81–100.
32. Wolpe, J. (1973) *The Practice of Behavior Therapy* pp. 104–108. Oxford: Pergamon Press.
33. Bernstein, D. A. & Borkovec, T. D. (1973) *Progressive Relaxation Training: A Manual for the Helping Professions* p. 37. Champaign, Illinois: Research Press.
34. Goldfried, M. R. & Davison, G. C. (1976) *Clinical Behavior Therapy* pp. 97–98. New York: Holt, Rinehart and Winston.
35. Borkovec, T. D. & Sides, J. K. (1979) Critical procedural variables related to the physiological effects of progressive relaxation: a review. *Behavior Research and Therapy*, **17**, 119–125.
36. *Ibid.* p. 124.
37. Thoresen, C. E. & Coates, T. J. (1978) What does it mean to be a behavior therapist? *The Counseling Psychologist*, **7**, 3, 11. Full reference pp. 3–21.
38. Wolpe, J. (1958) *Psychotherapy by Reciprocal Inhibition* pp. 139–165. Stanford: Stanford University Press.
39. Wolpe, J. (1973) *The Practice of Behavior Therapy* pp. 95–140. Oxford: Pergamon Press.
40. *Ibid.* p. 108.
41. Goldfried, M. R. & Davison, G. C. (1976) *Clinical Behavior Therapy* p. 122. New York: Holt, Rinehart and Winston.
42. Wolpe, J. (1973) *The Practice of Behavior Therapy* p. 125. Oxford: Pergamon Press.
43. Goldfried, M. R. & Davison, G. C. (1976) *Clinical Behavior Therapy* p. 126. New York: Holt, Rinehart and Winston.
44. Emery, J. R. & Krumboltz, J. D. (1967) Standard versus individualized hierarchies in desensitization to reduce test anxiety. *Journal of Counseling Psychology*, **14**, 204–209.
45. Wolpe, J. (1973) *The Practice of Behavior Therapy* pp. 142–144. Oxford: Pergamon Press.
46. Goldfried, M. R. & Davison, G. C. (1976) *Clinical Behavior Therapy* pp. 128–131. New York: Holt, Rinehart and Winston.
47. Goldfried, M. R. (1971) Systematic desensitisation as training in self-control. *Journal of Consulting and Clinical Psychology*, **37**, 228–234.
48. Meichenbaum, D. H. (1972) Cognitive modification of test anxious college students. *Journal of Consulting and Clinical Psychology*, **39**, 370–380.
49. Meichenbaum, D. H., Gilmore, J. B. & Fedoravicius, A. (1971) Group insight versus group desensitisation in treating speech anxiety. *Journal of Consulting and Clinical Psychology*, **36**, 410–421.
50. Bandura, A., Jeffry, R. W. & Wright, C. L. (1974) Efficacy of participant modeling as a function of response induction aids. *Journal of Abnormal Psychology*, **83**, 56–64.
51. Bandura, A., Jeffry, R. W. & Gajdos, E. (1975) Generalizing change through participant modeling with self-directed mastery. *Behaviour Research and Therapy*, **13**, 141–152.
52. Wolpe, J. (1958) *Psychotherapy by Reciprocal Inhibition* p. 118. Stanford: Stanford University Press.
53. Wolpe, J. (1973) *The Practice of Behavior Therapy* p. 81. Oxford: Pergamon Press. Chapter on assertive training.
54. Alberti, R. E. & Emmons, M. L. (1974) *Your Perfect Right* (2nd ed.) pp. 9–24. San Luis Obispo: Impact.
55. Alberti, R. E. & Emmons, M. E. (1975) *Stand Up, Speak Out, Talk Back!* pp. 85–92. New York: Pocket Books.
56. Goldfried, M. R. & Davison, G. C. (1976) *Clinical Behavior Therapy* pp. 146–147. New York: Holt, Rinehart and Winston.
57. Lineham, M. M., Goldfried, M. R. & Goldfried, A. P. (1979) Assertion therapy: skill training or cognitive restructuring. *Behavior Therapy*, **10**, 372–388.

58. Meichenbaum, D. (1975) Self-instructional methods. In F. H. Kanfer and A. P. Goldstein (eds), *Helping People Change* pp. 368–372. New York: Pergamon Press. Full reference pp. 357–391. *Helping People Change* is now available in a 1980 edition.
59. Alberti, R. E. & Emmons, M. L. (1974) *Your Perfect Right* (2nd ed.). San Luis Obispo: Impact.
60. Alberti, R. E. & Emmons, M. E. (1975) *Stand Up, Speak Out, Talk Back!* New York: Pocket Books.
61. Schmidt, J. P. & Patterson, T. E. (1979) Issues in the implementation of assertion training in applied settings. *Journal of Behavior Therapy and Experimental Psychiatry*, **10**, 15–19.
62. Cautela, J. (1967) A Reinforcement Survey Schedule for use in therapy, training and research. *Psychological Reports*, **20**, 1115–1130.
63. MacPhillamy, D. J. & Lewinsohn, P. M. (1971) *Pleasant Events Schedule*. Mimeograph, University of Oregon.
64. Lewinsohn, P. M. & Graf. M. (1973) Pleasant activities and depression. *Journal of Consulting and Clinical Psychology*, **41**, 265.
65. Lewinsohn, P. M. (1970) Activity schedules in treatment of depression. In J. D. Krumboltz and C. E. Thoresen (eds), *Counseling Methods* pp. 74–83. New York: Holt, Rinehart and Winston.
66. Daley, M. F. (1969) The 'reinforcement menu': finding effective reinforcers. In J. D. Krumboltz and C. E. Thoresen (eds), *Behavioral Counseling: Cases and Techniques* pp. 42–45. New York: Holt, Rinehart and Winston.
67. Krasner, L. (1962) The therapist as a social reinforcement machine. In H. H. Strupp and L. Luborsky (eds), *Research in Psychotherapy* (vol. 2) pp. 61–94. Washington: American Psychological Association.
68. Truax, C. B. (1966) Some implications of behavior therapy for psychotherapy. *Journal of Counseling Psychology*, **13**, 160–170.
69. Truax, C. B. (1966) Reinforcement and nonreinforcement in Rogerian psychotherapy. *Journal of Abnormal Psychology*, **71**, 1–9.
70. Lewinsohn, P. M. & Libet, J. (1972) Pleasant events, activity schedules and depression. *Journal of Abnormal Psychology*, **79**, 291–295.
71. Turner, R. W., Ward, M. F. & Turner, J. (1979) Behavioral treatment for depression: an evaluation of therapeutic components. *Journal of Clinical Psychology*, **35**, 166–175.
72. Zeiss, A. M., Lewinsohn, P. M. & Munoz, R. F. (1979) Nonspecific improvement effects in depression using interpersonal skills training, pleasant activity schedules, or cognitive training. *Journal of Consulting and Clinical Psychology*, **47**, 427–439.
73. Hosford, R. E. (1969) Behavioral counseling–a contemporary overview. *The Counseling Psychologist*, **1**, 4, 1–33.
74. Sanborn, B. & Schuster, W. (1969) Establishing reinforcement techniques in the classroom. In J. D. Krumboltz and C. E. Thoresen (eds), *Behavioral Counseling: Cases and Techniques* pp. 131–152. New York: Holt, Rinehart and Winston.
75. O'Leary, K. D. & Drabman, R. (1971) Token reinforcement programs in the classroom: a review. *Psychological Bulletin*, **75**, 385. Full reference pp. 379–398.
76. Kadzin, A. E. & Bootzin, R. E. (1972) The token economy: an evaluative review. *Journal of Applied Behavior Analysis*, **5**, 343–372.
77. Goldfried, M. R. & Davison, G. C. (1976) *Clinical Behavior Therapy* p. 209. New York: Holt, Rinehart and Winston.
78. MacCulloch, M. J. & Feldman, M. P. (1967) Aversion therapy in management of 43 homosexuals. *British Medical Journal*, **2**, 594–597.
79. Stampfl, T. G. (1975) Implosive therapy: staring down your nightmares. *Psychology Today*, February, 68. Full reference pp. 66–73.
80. Stampfl, T. G. & Lewis, D. J. (1968) Implosive therapy – a behavioral therapy? *Behavior Research and Therapy*, **6**, 31–36.
81. Stampfl, T. G. (1975) Implosive therapy: staring down your nightmares. *Psychology Today*, February, 73.

13 – The Initial Interview and Psychiatric Considerations

SUMMARY: *Counsellor objectives for the initial interview are fourfold: establishing a working alliance with the client; forming a working model of the client; formulating working goals; and deciding on working methods. A five-stage plan of the initial counselling interview is presented and discussed. The stages are: introductions; exploration of presenting concerns; reconnaissance or a broader exploration of the client's background and current functioning; contracting or presentation, discussion, and agreement on treatment goals and methods; and termination, involving clarification of administrative details and parting. Some issues pertinent to initial interviews are discussed, namely note-taking, working with silent and talkative clients, and counselling clients in crisis. Counsellor considerations which may negatively affect the success of initial and subsequent interviews include theoretical limitations and rigidity, and counsellor distress and vulnerability, though vulnerability may also be constructive.*

Psychiatric considerations pertinent to counselling are: identification of severe psychiatric illness, awareness of possible psychosomatic symptoms, and knowledge of the major drugs used in psychiatry. Indications of schizophrenia, paranoia, manic depression, and symptoms which may be psychosomatic are reviewed. Some tranquillizing, hypnotic and anti-depressant drugs are discussed, along with their indications for use and possible toxic or side effects.

The chapter ends with a discussion of termination of counselling relationships, whether it is suggested by counsellor, client, or both. Ideally, clients terminate because they are much better able to cope with their decisions and problems of living, but this is not always the case. Termination may be premature, indicating lack of further progress or client dissatisfaction.

In the last three chapters, our aim has been to engage in a discussion of goals for counselling practice (in Chapter 10) and then introduce the reader to basic aspects of the practice of humanistic counselling (in Chapter 11) and to basic behavioural counselling methods (in Chapter 12). In Chapter 10 we expressed broad agreement with the notion that a nurturing or facilitative phase, focused on improving the client's capacity for experiencing, precedes a more action-oriented phase, focused on thinking and acting. However, clients come to counselling at different stages of psychological development and with different problems and concerns. Thus, any counsellor not agreeing with the interrelated ideas of a common or unitary diagnosis for all presenting problems and, hence, a single treatment approach, is forced into the role of a decision-maker. In this chapter we explore considerations relevant to counsellor decisions and behaviour in the initial interview. In particular this chapter focuses on assessment and the making of *treatment decisions*.

THE INITIAL INTERVIEW

Assessment

The initial interview is defined here as covering the initial assessment period in the counselling process and therefore may last for more than one interview. The term 'assessment' is preferred to 'diagnosis', which is a more medical term with connotations of a classification scheme of psychiatric illness amenable to diagnosis, treatment and prognosis. Nevertheless, the concept of assessment in counselling has its critics. The major argument against assessment is that counselling is a relationship process the efficacy of which depends on the quality of the interaction between counsellors and clients. If, however, counsellors engage in assessment, they are stepping outside the frame of reference of their clients and thus endanger the very relationship whose quality is their main counselling tool. The basic client need is to be accepted as a whole person rather than being judged according to parts of that person. The lack of acceptance implicit in assessment is recreating the conditions of lack of respect and empathy which brought the client into counselling in the first place. Furthermore, a climate of assessment may inhibit clients, and thus they may not disclose much of the information vital to making an adequate assessment. Anyway, assessment implies a valid psychological classification system which those who favour a unitary diagnosis of psychological problems assert is unavailable. Patterson writes: '. . . despite the apparent logic of specific treatment for specific conditions, there is evidence for the unitary nature of emotional disturbance and for a single method of treatment'.[1] He continues by saying that the human interpersonal relationship is the effective factor in all counselling.

The major argument for assessment is that clients have different concerns and are at different stages of psychological development and, therefore, assessment is necessary to ensure that they obtain the most effective counselling help. At the very least, assessment is necessary to decide whether clients are suitable for counselling or whether they need to be referred elsewhere. For instance, some very disturbed clients require psychiatric rather than counselling assistance. As the treatment decision-making model of the counselling interview depicted in Figure 1.1 indicates, the position of this book is that assessment is a desirable part of counselling and does not preclude a subsequent emphasis on a nurturant relationship where necessary.

Possibly the 'assessment versus no assessment' debate gets unnecessarily polarized. It is important that assessment takes place within the framework of a facilitative counselling relationship. The abilities to create a safe environment and to get inside the client's frame of reference are major skills of competent assessment. Also, assessment is not carried out just by the counsellor, but in conjunction with the client, and may illuminate rather than obscure client concerns. Additionally, sensitive assessment may improve rather than hinder the quality of the counselling relationship. Furthermore, assessment need not imply rigidity but is best done with flexibility in regard to the varying concerns and communication patterns of different clients. Also, as Tyler observes, 'a large part of diagnostic thinking goes on *between*, rather than during interviews',[2] thus contributing to more of a relationship emphasis during interviews.

Objectives

Initial interviews always take place within environmental contexts, and counsellors need to be alert to the constraints and expectancies generated by such contexts. For instance, counselling a person in a medical setting generates a different set of expectancies from counselling someone in a careers service setting. Thus, though in this chapter we offer a number of suggestions for the initial and subsequent interviews, they may have to be adapted in respect of environmental considerations as well as to individual clients.

The initial interview can be viewed as having four interrelated objectives. The paramount objective is to establish rapport with the client, or a *working alliance*. Counsellors who are unable to establish rapport with their clients are unlikely to keep them. Rapport involves the setting up of a communication or relationship base with the client. Ideally, elements of such a relationship base should be that the client feels respected, liked and understood by the counsellor, who also appears as trustworthy and competent.

The second objective is the formulation of a *working model* of the client. Sullivan, writing about the psychiatric interview, talks of its purpose as 'elucidating *characteristic patterns of living* of the subject person, the patient or client, which patterns he experiences as particularly troublesome or especially valuable, and in the revealing of which he expects to derive *benefit*'.[3] Similarly, Tyler observes that from the first encounter with a client, the counsellor begins to form a 'working image' of the person.[4] This working image will not necessarily be divulged to the client, but is a set of hypotheses concerning client strengths, coping strategies and limitations, around which the counsellor will make both responding and treatment decisions.

The third objective is that of charting a course for subsequent counselling interviews, which involves the formulation of *working goals*. These goals are derived from the tentative model of the client and take into account the client's particular needs and state of readiness. A colloquial rule of thumb for working goals is: 'always start at where the client is'. By this is meant not expecting too much or too little of the client's resources. A further possible guideline is that it is better to err on the side of caution than to generate avoidable threat and anxiety. Again, working goals may not be fully divulged to the client. For instance, it may be hard for clients to appreciate certain goals which they have not yet attained, such as increased capacity for realistic perception or awareness.

The fourth objective is to make some initial decisions regarding *working methods*. The previous two chapters discussed some of the basic working methods of the person-centred and behavioural approaches. Later chapters present further counselling methods. Needless to say, decisions made at the end of an initial interview regarding working methods are of the nature of tentative hypotheses to be monitored and adjusted appropriately according to feedback and client progress.

Some counselling services run an intake interview system by which a duty counsellor makes initial assessments and then refers clients on to other counsellors. A rationale for such a system is that a large counselling service can employ counsellors with strengths in different working methods. Thus the purpose of the intake assessment is to match client goals with counsellor methods.

Stages of the Initial Interview

In this section we tentatively present a five-stage plan of the initial counselling interview. The word 'tentatively' is intended to be taken seriously, since there is a danger of expecting exactitude in a series of interpersonal events which at times may be confused and unpredictable and also, possibly, all the better for it. A certain amount of 'milling around' by both counsellor and client is to be expected in initial interviews.[5] Each person is striving both to avoid, through their own anxieties, and to create a relationship, and also, to develop a working model of the other. Additionally, expectancies of the counselling process may need to be tested and worked through. Furthermore, for many clients genuine self-disclosure and insight are difficult. If they were able to be highly rational about their personal concerns, they would probably not need to be in counselling.

Table 13.1 presents a five-stage plan of the initial counselling interview. Again, we reiterate the need to be sensitive to environmental context, to the differences of individual clients, and to developments which transpire during the interview process. Also, we stress the importance of an emotional climate which is facilitative rather than coldly interrogative. A good distinction is that made by Zaro and her colleagues between task orientation and person orientation.[6] A skilled counsellor is neither too concerned with information at the neglect of the person, nor too concerned with the client's feelings at the expense of collecting relevant information.

Stage one: introductions

The ostensible purpose of the introductions stage can be summarized as meeting, greeting and seating. Counsellors can maximize the success of this stage in a number of ways, some of which are preparatory. For instance, good publicity about the

Table 13.1 *A five-stage plan of the initial counselling interview(s)*

Stage	Illustrative counsellor tasks

Introductions	Meeting, greeting, seating
	If necessary, establishing confidentiality
	  or its limitations
	Starting the development of rapport and
	  trust
	Basic data collection (?)

Presenting concerns	Facilitating client self-disclosure and
	  self-talk
	Exploration of presenting concerns
	  assisting client amplification and specification
	  engaging in clarification

Reconnaissance	Structuring
	Facilitating client self-disclosure and
	  self-talk
	Broader exploration of client's mode of
	  living, background, current stresses,
	  self-concept, coping abilities, motivation,
	  expectancies, etc.
	Assisting exploration
	Engaging in clarification

Contracting	Summarizing Formulating and discussing goals Presenting a treatment method or methods Handling questions Establishing a treatment 'contract'
Termination	Clarifying administrative details Arranging next appointment Parting

counselling service may structure expectancies in a helpful way. The efficiency and warmth of the receptionist may ease client anxieties. Also important is a pleasant, quiet office with a good seating plan.

Coming to counselling may involve clients in talking about and facing up to problems which are sensitive and threatening. From the start counsellors need to create a safe environment. Before meeting their clients for the first time, counsellors should make sure that they know their clients' names and have read any referral material about them. When meeting clients in a waiting area, as well as calling out their names, it may be more friendly to go over to them and show them into the office rather than just stand at the door. They should be politely shown to a seat, possibly given permission to smoke if requested, and helped to feel at ease. At an appropriate moment, there will be a greeting along the lines of 'Hello, I'm . . ., a counsellor (counselling psychologist) here'. The issue of what counsellors and clients call each other can be handled during the initial interview according to the preferences of both parties.

There are a number of other considerations in the introductions stage, some of which may reflect the environmental context of the agency. For instance, the counsellor may feel the need to establish clearly the confidentiality of the interview. Alternatively, if there are limits to confidentiality, it may be advisable to share these.

Also, some agencies require basic data, such as name, age, sex, marital status, address and telephone number, which counsellors may be required to collect at the start. However, counsellors need to be flexible, and first they may decide to respond to their client's distress rather than collect basic data. Furthermore, counsellors observe their clients' verbal, non-verbal and para-verbal communication from the initial moment of waiting-room contact so that they can start to formulate their working models and to respond appropriately.

Stage two: presenting concerns

Even in specialist counselling services, clients may come to counselling with one or more of a variety of concerns. Table 13.2 lists some illustrative presenting concerns by

Table 13.2 *Illustrative presenting concerns by topic area*

Topic area	Presenting concerns
Experiencing and feelings	'I'm feeling depressed and lonely' 'I feel tense and anxious a lot of the time' 'I feel that I just can't cope'
Thinking	'I'm always putting myself down' 'It's hard for me to accept that I have positive qualities' 'I've had a strict religious upbringing and find it hard to enjoy myself'
Relationships	'I don't seem to be able to make close relationships' 'My marriage is breaking up' 'I'm impotent'
Learning	'I keep putting off my work' 'I'm worried about exams' 'I can't contribute in discussion groups'
Occupational	'I don't know what to do with my life' 'I can't decide between engineering and architecture' 'Now I'm retired, I want some leisure interests'

topic area. This table assumes both that there may be overlap between topic areas for a single concern and that the best way to approach presenting concerns is not necessarily to treat them as discrete entities.

The first counsellor task in the presenting concerns stage is to give clients *permission* to divulge the reasons they have come for counselling. Counsellor opening statements include 'Tell me why you've come to see me', 'What brings you here?' and 'Put me in the picture about what is concerning you'. If the client has been referred, this will also be acknowledged. To begin counsellors may just make it easy for clients to talk about their presenting concern or concerns. The second counsellor task is to engage with the client in *mutual exploration* of these concerns with the aim of amplification and clarification. Briefly, this involves focusing on past and current manifestations of the concerns. Remarks to elicit the previous history of the concern include 'When did it start?', 'To what extent has it interfered with your life?', 'How have you attempted to cope with the problem in the past?' and 'Have you seen anyone about it before coming here?'. Remarks focusing on current manifestations of the concern include 'How frequently?', 'How severe?' and 'Under what circumstances?'. Further clarification statements include 'Would you care to elaborate?' and 'Can you give me a specific example?'.

An important area to explore is the personal meanings that the presenting concerns have for the client. For instance, a client who stammers may regard this as overt evidence that she is a worthless person. Another client may be terrified of failing exams, less for academic reasons than for fear of losing the approval of significant others. Put differently, each client's presenting concern is likely to involve: (a) details of the presenting concern; (b) the client's self-evaluations (usually negative) about the presenting concern; and often (c) the client's feelings of loss of self-esteem in regard to others' evaluations of the presenting concern. Another consideration in the exploration of presenting concerns includes the time dimensions involved. For example, does the executive who is afraid of public speaking have to make a formal presentation in two weeks? Such information is relevant to treatment. A final, but important, point is that the presenting concerns are mainly from the client's viewpoint. The counsellor uses the material to help construct her working model, without necessarily committing herself to dealing with the concerns directly as presented.

Stage three: reconnaissance

The term 'reconnaissance' was used by Sullivan to indicate 'obtaining a rough outline of the social and personal history of the patient . . . to get some notion of the person's identity . . .'.[7] We use the term 'reconnaissance' to refer to a continuation of the joint exploration started in the presenting concerns stage. This covers the client's background and life-style and generates further material for the counsellor's working model. In some contexts and for some client presenting concerns, the counsellor may decide to bypass or shorten the reconnaissance stage. For instance, a student client anxious about an imminent exam is probably best helped by focusing on the presenting concern. Clients who come for career counselling are unlikely to want a survey of their personal relations. Furthermore, for other clients, the counsellor may decide that the reconnaissance stage should be handled without much probing until a better relationship is established and the client's level of threat is lowered. For example, some student clients are highly threatened by being asked to talk about their parents.

'Structuring' is a term used to describe the clarification by the counsellor of roles and expectancies in counselling. The counsellor may have structured the initial interview at the beginning by describing its purpose and stages. Often, however, it is more natural for clients to be encouraged to share their presenting concerns and then for structuring to take place at the start of the reconnaissance stage. The counsellor may structure the reconnaissance by saying that often it is helpful to obtain a fuller picture of the client before deciding on how best to proceed.

For the most part, the reconnaissance focuses on the client's current functioning rather than past history. Nevertheless, one area for reconnaissance is the client's *family background*. The purpose of this is to obtain an idea of the emotional climate in which the client grew up, the degree to which the client was encouraged to develop as an independent person, and the ways in which such development may have been impeded. Other family background areas include relationships with siblings and significant others, the effects of deaths and other disruptions of family life, and key parental values such as religion.

The area of *relationships* covers the client's experience of friendship and intimacy, and any current perceived difficulties in relating to others. Issues which may emerge here include fears about intimacy, difficulty in self-disclosure, sexual concerns, and problems in marital and parent–child communication. Specific areas of concern may be explored further, along the lines of the exploration of the presenting concern.

The *occupational* area relates to the client's occupational aspirations and functioning. To what extent does the client feel occupationally fulfilled by being in an interesting job and performing satisfactorily? Also, does the client have any important leisure activities and lead a balanced life?

For those counsellors dealing with pupils and students, an exploration of the *learning* area forms an important part of the reconnaissance. This area consists of the client's educational aspirations and past and current academic functioning. Areas to focus on include satisfaction with course of studies, degree of achievement anxiety, ability to concentrate, motivation difficulties, interpersonal difficulties related to learning, and possession of the requisite learning skills, such as effective work planning and reading. Again, in both the occupational and learning areas, specific concerns may be explored further.

A further reconnaissance area is that of the client's *physiological* functioning. This may have been covered earlier but, if not, inquiries might be made about the client's eating and sleeping and about any physical manifestations of anxiety. We deal with psychosomatic symptoms and with indications of severe disturbance later in this chapter. Suffice it for now to say that the counsellor should be alert for these. Additionally, the counsellor should be aware of whether the client is taking medication and, if so, the name and dosage of the drug and any possible side effects.

If it is not apparent, the counsellor should ask whether there are any particular *current stresses* in the client's life. Also, it may be helpful to ask what the client's living situation is and assess whether her environment is likely to help or hinder counselling progress. Some counsellors may ask their clients to identify and describe their perceived strengths. However, clients often find it difficult to acknowledge positive attributes and find it easier to describe their negative qualities. Another area which may be explored is the client's motivation and expectancies concerning counselling. For instance, if a miracle cure is expected, a more realistic expectation should be indicated to avoid disappointment and the risk of consequent demotivation.

Counsellor skills during the reconnaissance include structuring, facilitating disclosure, engaging in focused exploration, clarifying pertinent areas, and handling transitions from one area to another. Possible transition statements include 'Well, we seem to have explored . . . area; now let's move on to . . . area of your life', 'I would also like to explore the work area of your life' and 'I'm now wondering whether there are any current stresses in your life that you've not already mentioned'. Additional counsellor skills include consultation with other professionals, such as doctors and psychiatrists, concerning medication. Furthermore, counsellors may need skills in using relevant tests and measures to assess material generated in the presenting concerns and reconnaissance stages.

Stage four: contracting

The term 'contracting' is used to describe the process of counsellor and client arriving at a formal, or relatively informal, agreement concerning treatment goals and methods. The first counsellor task is likely to be that of summarizing the major points of the presenting concerns and reconnaissance stages. Possible summarization statements include 'As I see it, your major areas of difficulty appear to be . . . Would you agree with me?' and 'Well, we've explored a number of areas now. Perhaps the time has come to summarize and to have a discussion about where we go from here. As well as a general problem of lack of confidence, you seem to have a number of more specific concerns . . . (mention main concerns.) Additionally, you feel your situation isn't being helped by some additional stresses in your life . . . (mention additional stresses). Do you think I've got the picture clearly?'.

The summarization statement is the bridge between the exploratory work of the initial interview, aimed at arriving at a working model, and the formulation of working goals and methods. It is important that the summarization statement is clear and checked with clients for accuracy and adequate coverage of their major concerns. Counsellors need to tailor for individual clients the nature, level and amount of material in their summaries.

Arising out of the summarization process, and somewhat interrelated, is the formulation and discussion of working goals. An issue here is the degree to which a discussion of goals is meaningful to an individual client. For some clients it may be sufficient to indicate that a goal of focusing on self-confidence and helping the client to experience her own feelings may come first, with more specific goals being taken into consideration as counselling develops. For less disturbed clients, it may be appropriate to formulate specific goals from the beginning.

Summarizing and formulating working goals are part of the process of making decisions about working methods. Counsellor decisions at this stage include:

1. the suitability of the client for counselling rather than referral elsewhere or no treatment;
2. the client's level of psychological development and the degree to which a facilitative basic empathy relationship should be engaged in;
3. what additional interventions are desirable;
4. whether individual and/or group counselling methods are indicated;
5. the order in which the treatment methods should be used;
6. whether medication is indicated;
7. whether consultation with another counselling, medical, or other professional person is indicated.

The presentation to the client of the proposed working methods varies according to the outcomes of the above counsellor decisions. The presentation needs to be clear, free of psychological jargon, and designed to enlist the client's motivation for what is proposed. It has the function of structuring the subsequent interviews, since different working methods involve different roles for both counsellor and client. The counsellor may need to answer questions about the proposed methods and their likely outcomes. These questions should be answered tactfully and truthfully without raising false expectations. Finally, the counsellor will need to check whether the client is prepared to proceed with the proposed methods. If the answer is affirmative, a treatment 'contract' has been entered into by both parties. If the answer is negative, further clarification and negotiation may be necessary. Alternatively, counsellor and client may agree to terminate the proceedings.

Stage five: termination

The counsellor takes responsibility for time-keeping in an interview and indicates that the interview is drawing to a close. If the client has anything pressing she would like to say, she should be invited to do so. Any outstanding administrative details, such as duration and frequency of meetings, can be clarified. In emergencies, the counsellor may allow telephone contact between interviews and mention how to do this. Furthermore, if fees are involved, the amount and method of billing should be explained. Closure of the interview may be achieved by agreeing on the time of the next appointment. If there are any homework assignments relating to their next meeting, the counsellor should ensure that they are clearly understood by the client. As with the initial meeting and greeting, parting from a client is friendly and polite.

SOME INITIAL INTERVIEW ISSUES

There are numerous interview issues, some of which relate only to the initial meetings and others which are also relevant to subsequent meetings. A few such issues are reviewed here.

Note Taking

So long as it neither becomes too intrusive nor has a negative impact on the client, note taking may be helpful for remembering details of the client, discussing the client with colleagues, planning treatment interventions, and for a number of other reasons. Since the initial interview has an information-gathering function, which presumably is agreed with the client, it seems logical for the counsellor to take notes during the interview. Furthermore, when the client has left the office, the counsellor may spend time adding to these notes. The fact that the initial interview has had an assessment focus does not preclude more experiential working methods, for which note taking may be less appropriate, being used during subsequent interviews.

Silent and Talkative Clients

Sometimes there may appear to be long silences in an initial interview. There are a number of considerations in relation to such silences. First, does the silence really exist or is it more a matter of counsellor perception, anxiety and pressure for results? Second, the silence may be performing a useful function in allowing the client to delve deeper into what she is trying to convey. Sometimes it is the talkative clients who erect a wall of 'silence' in terms of genuine communication. Third, the silence may be attributable, in part at least, to counsellor lack of interview skills. Counsellors who are good at empathic responding and creating a safe emotional climate are less likely to have silent clients. Fourth, silence may indicate that the client is not yet ready to trust the counsellor with certain information, though may trust her later. Fifth, there are various counsellor strategies which may help silent clients. For instance, the counsellor can ensure that she gives a good and reinforcing empathic response to any statements made by the client. Also, the counsellor can reflect the client's difficulty in talking and, possibly, ask her to describe what is going through her mind. Additionally, the skilful use of questions may aid some clients. Other clients may need help to discover that it is not necessarily selfish to talk about themselves or disloyal to talk about others in a confidential setting. Still other clients may continue to say very little in interviews, but still feel they are receiving something of value from counselling.

Talkative clients may also be a problem in counselling, in that their talk may mask fears about really being known. Frequently, the talkativeness is just symptomatic of anxiety connected with the initial encounter with a counsellor, and subsides when the client feels safer. Again, counsellors may contribute to their client's talkativeness through: not creating a safe environment; allowing their clients to go on talking and not being prepared to make responses themselves; responding poorly; and not focusing their client's talk where appropriate.

Clients in Crisis

A crisis may be defined as a situation in which the client's coping resources are severely stretched, if not overwhelmed. Clients may come to either initial or subsequent interviews in a crisis. Often crises are precipitated by unusual stresses, such as a death or the break-up of a close relationship. Some crises are immediate, while others simmer and then suddenly overwhelm the client. A nervous breakdown might fall into the latter category. Some clients may become excessively withdrawn when in crisis, whereas others may be in an overt state of heightened emotionality.

As Zaro et al observe, when a client is in crisis it is often also a crisis for the counsellor.[8] Counsellors can prepare for crises by ensuring that they have a good support system which, if necessary, they can mobilize for their clients, for instance ready access to a competent physician. Also, counsellors who have adequately thought through the limits of their responsibility to clients may be better able to remain calm than those who have not. Counsellor skills in a crisis include the following.

Remaining calm

Since an important objective of crisis counselling is to help the client to become less emotional, counsellors need to be in control of their own anxieties and emotions.

Listening

The client may become calmer simply by being able to share her problems and their related emotions. Another word for this process is catharsis. Here, good empathic responding skills may be helpful both in understanding and in helping the client to feel understood.

Assessing client risk

The counsellor needs to be realistic about the severity of the crisis and be sensitive to the client's personal meanings in relation to it. Relevant considerations are the degree of risk to self and to others and the degree of contact with reality.

Assessing client coping capacities

It is important to obtain some idea of whether the client has the strength and resources to cope with the crisis. Also pertinent is whether the client lives alone and the degree to which support is available from friends and relatives.

Assisting exploration and clarification

Crises tend to involve very intense feelings. Possibly the feelings are so intense and unusual for the client that she feels she is losing her ability to control her life. After an initial cathartic period, the counsellor can sometimes help the client to get the problem much more in perspective by assisting exploration and clarification of the factors generating the strong emotions.

Assisting the development of coping strategies

With counsellor support and a diminution of anxiety, the client is likely to be in a stronger position for developing coping strategies. Possibly because of the strong feelings generated by the crisis, clients may either have felt totally overwhelmed, and thus unable to act, or else have developed 'tunnel' vision and become incapable of seeing the range of available alternatives. The counsellor's role is both to help clients to develop strategies for coping with their immediate distress and, if appropriate, to initiate the process of coping with any longer-term problems. As far as possible, clients should be responsible for making their own decisions, both to increase their sense of control over their lives and also because they have to live with the consequences. After alternatives have been explored, plans for coping with the immediate situation should be formulated as specifically as possible.

Mobilizing additional resources

The counsellor may feel it necessary to mobilize additional resources to help the client in crisis. For instance, a physician may be consulted if medication or hospitalization is a possibility. Also, the counsellor may need to contact and explain the situation to at least one relative, friend or significant other if the client needs further support. The client can advise the counsellor on whom to contact if she does not feel up to doing it herself.

Advising on own availability

There are a number of issues here. First, the counsellor may want to make a further appointment with the client, if only to check up on her well-being. Second, there is the issue of between-interview contact and the extent and limits of the counsellor's availability. This can be indicated and, if needed, written down. Third, the counsellor may tell the client whom to contact, for example a physician, if there is an emergency and she is unavailable. Often the fact that the counsellor makes her future availability known is sufficient support for the client until the next interview.

The Chinese use two symbols for the concept of crisis: the symbol for danger is linked with that for opportunity.[9] Many crisis interviews are likely to provide opportunities for both clients and counsellors. Such opportunities include the development of an effective counselling relationship and the obtaining for the client of the skills to prevent or cope with future crises.

COUNSELLOR CONSIDERATIONS

There are a number of counsellor considerations relevant to the initial interview in which personal characteristics and skill deficiencies may intermingle and negatively affect outcomes. Bugental observes that '. . . emotions, conflicts, biases and anxieties of the therapist's own life inevitably have their effects on the client's life . . .'.[10] Many of the adverse effects of the counsellor's own deficiencies may be heightened in an initial interview, with its added anxiety of two strangers meeting for the first time. Without going into an exhaustive discussion, below are two pitfalls related to counsellor personality which may lower effectiveness.

Theoretical Limitations and Rigidity

Many counsellors identify with counselling 'schools' ostensibly to meet the needs of their clients. Another set of reasons may be less creditable: namely, to meet their own needs for security, simplicity, approval of significant others within the school, and avoidance of the hard work involved in keeping up with theoretical and practical advances in the counselling literature. The other extreme to conceptual rigidity is an undisciplined eclecticism, which may also have negative consequences. Counsellors are faced with a difficult task in making sense of the conflicting theoretical and practical approaches and of their own counselling and life experiences. This, however, does not absolve them from continuing to try to develop both as professionals and as people.

Counsellor Distress and Vulnerability

In an ideal world counsellors would be models of the desired outcomes of their theoretical positions. Sometimes it is recommended that counsellors-in-training themselves become counselling clients. The usefulness of this procedure depends in some measure on the counselling effectiveness of the helpers. For counsellors who have completed training, continued self-monitoring is necessary to minimize the effect of their own distresses on clients. All counsellors are wise to identify and develop contact with people from whom they may obtain professional and personal support in time of need or crisis. Also, counsellors may find it necessary to have counselling themselves to overcome areas of difficulty which may lower their counselling effectiveness. Gray writes: 'Vulnerability is an aspect of being which is conducive to the growth of individuals through openness to experience of self and others'.[11] However, the vulnerability of counsellors may be either constructive or destructive. For a list of possible destructive implications of counsellor vulnerability the reader is referred back to Table 11.4, which presents some variables associated with absence of basic empathy in a counselling relationship.

PSYCHIATRIC CONSIDERATIONS

Three kinds of psychiatric considerations pertinent to the conduct of initial interviews are identification of severe psychiatric illness, awareness of possible psychosomatic symptoms, and knowledge of the major drugs used in psychiatry.

Identification of Severe Psychiatric Illness

The three main areas of psychiatric diagnosis are the organic, the psychoneuroses, and the psychoses. Though the role of psychiatrists is debatable where the psychoneuroses are concerned, their special medical knowledge and skills are particularly relevant to the organic and psychotic categories. Here we focus mainly on the psychoses on the grounds of urgency, severity, and likelihood of counsellor contact. Psychosis has been defined as 'severe mental disorder involving loss of touch with reality',[12] and the psychoses include schizophrenia, paranoia and manic depression.

The counsellor needs to be able to identify severe disturbance and to refer severely disturbed clients for psychiatric assistance. Thus it is important that the counsellor not only has the requisite assessment skills, but also has developed professional links with one or more competent psychiatrists. Table 13.3 presents some of the main indicators of schizophrenia, paranoia and manic depression. Willis observes that psychiatric illness is recognized by observing and discerning abnormalities in: (a) behaviour; (b)

Table 13.3   *Some indicators of schizophrenia, paranoia and manic depression*

Disorder	Indicators
Schizophrenia	Extreme emotional withdrawal
	Thought disorders, e.g. inability to focus coherently
	Speech disorders, e.g. loss of consensual use of language
	Delusions (irrational fixed ideas) of self-reference, persecution and grandeur
	Hallucinations (illusions), most commonly auditory, e.g. 'hearing voices'
	Behavioural disturbances, lowered activity, bizarre mannerisms and postures, altered morals
Paranoia	Delusions, without the personality disorganization of schizophrenia
	Thinking characterized by suspiciousness, selective perception to confirm suspicions, blame and hostility (persecutory delusions)
	Possibly also grandiose, religiose and hypochondrial delusions
Manic depression	*Depression*
	Pervasive lowered vitality and fatigue
	Pervasive negative self-image
	Ideas of guilt and unworthiness
	Suicidal ruminations
	Psychomotor retardation–slowing of speech and movement
	Slowing of thought processes
	Sleep disturbance, especially early waking
	Loss of appetite and weight
	Decreased libido
	Mania
	Elation and over-optimism
	Irritability with criticism or restraint
	Grandiose delusions and plans
	Decreased judgement
	Decreased attention span
	Mental acceleration, flight of ideas
	Hyperactivity
	Accelerated speech
	Heightened libido

mood; (c) perception; (d) thought content; (e) intelligence level; (f) memory; (g) concentration; and (h) orientation in space and time.[13] A good guideline for counsellors who consider a client to be psychiatrically disturbed is 'When in doubt, check it out'. Checking it out means either the client or the counsellor having a consultation with a psychiatrist about the client's condition.

Schizophrenia

Schizophrenia is a term used for a group of psychotic disorders characterized by severe disorganization in perception, thought and emotion. Schizophrenia tends to begin mainly in the younger age groups, late teens and early 20s, and really means the *disintegration*, rather than the splitting, of the personality.[14] The onset of schizophrenia may be gradual, a pattern referred to as *process* schizophrenia, the prognosis of which is considered generally unfavourable. More typically, schizophrenia has a sudden onset related to specific precipitating stresses, a pattern called *reactive* schizophrenia. These acute episodes may disappear in weeks, though sometimes they initiate a more chronic pattern.[15] The incidence of schizophrenia is approximately 0.85 per cent of the general population, a figure Willis describes as 'remarkably constant whatever populations are surveyed'.[16]

Schizophrenia may be divided into four main interrelated types: *simple, hebephrenic, catatonic*, and *paranoid*. Additionally, less well defined varieties are described as *undifferentiated* forms. The symptoms presented in Table 13.3 vary according to the type of schizophrenia. For instance, simple schizophrenia is characterized by progressive mental deterioration and a general lowering of all mental activity. Hebephrenia tends to be characterized by hallucinations, incongruent emotional behaviour such as depression interspersed with euphoric laughter, and thought disorder. Catatonic schizophrenia occurs in two main forms: catatonic stupor and wild excitement. Paranoid schizophrenia tends to be found in the older age groups (30 and over) and is characterized by the progressive development of systems of paranoid delusions.

Paranoia

Paranoia is characterized by delusions and impaired contact with reality, without the severe personality disintegration of paranoid schizophrenia. A distinction is sometimes made between *paranoia*, which develops slowly, and *paranoid state*, characterized by transient delusions usually related to a precipitating stress. Paranoid delusions are usually persecutory, but often also contain a grandiose element: 'I am being persecuted because I am so important'.

Manic depression

Manic depressive psychoses are of different types. First, there is the *manic type*, characterized only by manic reactions. Second, there is the *depressive type*, characterized only by depressive reactions. Third, there is the *circular type*, characterized by alterations between mania and depression. Manic depressive reactions tend to be episodic and their duration may be weeks, months or years. Coleman observes that where no formal treatment is received, manic reactions usually run their course in three months and depressive reactions in about nine months.[17] Depressive reactions are considerably more frequent than manic reactions.

Manic reactions are characterized mainly by varying degrees of elation and overactivity. The manic person tends to lose hold on reality, engaging in grandiose enterprises which may spell financial, social and marital ruin, since judgement is lacking. Hypomania is the term used to describe mild to moderate degrees of mania. Mania tends to be an acute illness and, unlike depression, chronic mania does not exist.[18]

The *depressive* type tends to exhibit symptoms which are the opposite of mania, namely varying degrees of pessimism and underactivity. Depressive illness is sometimes called *endogenous* depression to distinguish it from *reactive* depression, or depression which is reactive to one or more precipitating events. Depression may also be caused by clients not having developed adequate attitudes and skills to meet their needs. It thus becomes difficult to talk about endogenous depression as a discrete entity. Nevertheless, there are some indications of predominantly endogenous depression, including: (a) sudden onset, unrelated to a precipitating event; (b) diurnal variation of mood; (c) early morning waking; (d) the delusional quality of thoughts, such as being evil, diseased, guilty, etc.; and (e) marked biological features, such as severe weight loss and insomnia. Suicidal thoughts and attempted and actual suicide are features of endogenous depression, though not exclusively so.

Psychosomatic Disorders

One definition of psychosomatic disorders is that they represent maladaptive physical changes in the body systems, primarily of psychological origin. Trethowan states that more recently this narrow definition 'has been widened to include all conditions in which psychiatric investigation may contribute to the aetiology, prevention and

Table 13.4   *Disorders which may be psychosomatic*[20]

Part of body	Examples
Skin	Eczema, acne, hives
Musculoskeletal	Backaches, muscle cramps, tension headaches
Respiratory	Bronchial asthma, hyperventilation, recurring bronchitis
Cardiovascular	Hypertension, heart attacks, migraine headaches
Blood and lymphatic	Disturbances in the blood and lymphatic systems
Gastrointestinal	Peptic ulcers, chronic gastritis, mucous colitis
Genitourinary	Disturbances in urination and menstruation
Endocrine	Hyperthyroidism, obesity, and some other endocrine disorders
Organs of special sense	Chronic conjunctivitis (pink-eye)
Disorders of other types	Disturbances in the nervous system in which emotional factors play a significant role, e.g. multiple sclerosis

Table 13.5 *Some tranquillizing, hypnotic and anti-depressant drugs in medical and psychiatric use*[23]

Category	Indication for use	Duration	Possible toxic or side effects
Minor tranquillizers e.g. Librium* (Chlordiazepoxide) Valium (Diazepam)	Anxiety states	Short-term (weeks or months) Action is immediate, but tolerance develops rapidly	Drowsiness† Ataxia† (loss of muscle co-ordination) Decreased libido Dependency
Major tranquillizers e.g. Largactil (Chlorpromazine) Also long-acting versions given by intramuscular injection every two to four weeks. e.g. Modecate (Fluphenazine decanoate)	Mania Schizophrenia	Intermediate or long-term (many years)	Parkinsonism† Sunburn† Giddiness† Allergy (e.g. skin rash) Tardive dyskinesia (irreversible involuntary movements) Decreased libido
Hypnotics e.g. Mogadon (Nitrazepam) Barbiturates less used now because of toxic effect and habituation	Insomnia	Short-term (in theory, however, a marked tendency for patients to become regular users and for tolerance to develop)	Few Dependency (mild)
Anti-depressants (a) Tricyclic (non-tranquillizing) e.g. Tofranil (Imipramine)	'Endogenous' depression	Intermediate (months or years) Action is slow, two to four weeks, but tolerance is not a problem	Giddiness† Dry mouth Sweating Blurring of vision Difficulty urinating (especially males) Trembling Constipation
(tranquillizing) e.g. Triptizol (Amitriptyline)		The bulk of the daily dosage may be given at night, aiding sleep and avoiding daytime sedation	As above, plus drowsiness†

| (b) Monoamine oxidase inhibitors e.g. Nardil (Phenelzine) | 'Endogenous' depression (more toxic than Tricyclics and usually used if the former are unsuccessful) | Intermediate (months or years) NB: Patients taking MAOIs must not at the same time take alcohol, barbiturates, other drugs or certain foods (e.g. meat and yeast extracts, cheese, broad beans, yoghurt) | Giddiness Headache Ataxia Tremor Drowsiness |
| *Lithium carbonate* Used to prevent recurrence in cyclic endogenous mood disturbance both of frequency and severity | Mania and depression | Long-term This is a toxic element and close monitoring is required | (a) Mild Tremor Nausea Diarrhoea (b) Severe Vomiting Abdominal pain Confusion Ataxia |

* The names of drugs are proprietary (i.e. the names used by the manufacturer). The names in brackets are non-proprietary names; generally they are the approved names given in the *British Pharmacopoeia*.
† These effects are enhanced by alcohol and are frequently more severe in the elderly, or those with circulatory, liver or kidney disease.
Note: Amphetamines and barbiturates were once widely used, but now there are virtually no grounds for their prescription except under strict supervision in certain exceptional cases.

treatment of a considerable number of physical complaints'.[19] Table 13.4 is a list of disorders which are likely to be, but are not necessarily, psychosomatic. The American Psychiatric Association uses the term 'psychophysiologic' to emphasize that the disorders are caused and maintained primarily by psychological and emotional factors rather than by organic ones, reserving 'psychosomatic' for the general approach to medicine in which physical, psychological and sociocultural factors are taken into consideration.[21]

Counsellors need to be sensitive to psychosomatic signs of distress, since responding to these symptoms can be an important way of empathizing with a client. It is important that counsellors work closely with physicians to ensure that such symptoms are correctly identified and, where necessary, appropriate medication is provided. Also, such collaboration minimizes the possibility of client and counsellor resources being misspent in dealing with organic problems. In America, the five most common types of psychosomatic disorders are: peptic ulcers, migraine and tension headaches, asthma, high blood pressure, and heart attacks.[22] Counsellors can work with clients to ease the emotional stress which usually plays a key causal role in the development of these disorders. A final point is that psychosomatic disorders are distinguished from hysterical or conversion symptoms, which are imitative rather than actual physical disorders.

Psychiatric Medication

It is helpful for counsellors to have a basic knowledge of the main drugs used in psychiatry and psychological medicine. For instance, in an initial interview a client's behaviour may be being affected by medication, a fact which must be taken into account in making a valid assessment. Another reason is that counsellors may be working with clients who are taking medication on a long-term, short-term, or on an *ad hoc* basis. It is useful to know what medication the client is taking, including the dosage and its possible side effects. Table 13.5 presents some tranquillizing, hypnotic, and anti-depressant drugs in medical and psychiatric use. Counsellors can work closely with physicians and psychiatrists to obtain, maintain and, when ready, wean clients off medication. In Britain, when counsellors need to have basic information about a drug, they can either ask a physician or look it up, if available, in MIMS.[24] There is also an Australian version of MIMS.[25]

POSTSCRIPT: TERMINATION OF COUNSELLING

The initial interview lays the basis for subsequent counselling work. However, further monitoring of client progress and counsellor behaviour will undoubtedly be necessary. Such monitoring may lead to decisions regarding continuing along the same treatment approach, changing part or most of the treatment approach, or terminating counselling.

Termination decisions are best made jointly by counsellor and client for positive reasons, namely, that the client is now much better able to cope with her problems and decisions of living. If the counsellor raises the issue of termination, this is likely to be because either the client has reached her counselling goals or further progress seems unlikely. Especially where client and counsellor have had a long-standing relationship, termination should be gradual. The counsellor can prepare her client for termination by tactfully sharing what is in her mind and allowing time for the relationship to achieve satisfactory closure. One possibility is to 'fade' the relationship by seeing the client less frequently. In the final session it may be useful to summarize and review the counselling work and ask the client for her reactions. Also, with certain clients it may be worth mentioning that, if necessary, they can return. With other clients, such a statement may introduce an unnecessarily negative note.

The client may also suggest termination or simply fail to attend subsequent interviews. There are numerous reasons for missed interviews, for example a genuine misunderstanding over the time, an unavoidable crisis, or negative feelings about continuing in counselling. Some follow-up by the counsellor is usually indicated to find out whether the client is all right and, if necessary, to fix another appointment. When the client suggests termination during an interview, there is no problem if the counsellor deems this desirable. When the counsellor considers that the client's suggestion is premature, the reasons for the suggestion merit exploration. If the counsellor still considers that termination is premature, the counsellor can share her reasons, but in such a way that it allows the client the responsibility for coming to her own decision. Client suggestions regarding termination may be threatening to the counsellor's own sense of competence and, hence, over-reactions and inappropriate reactions need to be guarded against.

A final point is that after termination counsellors may follow up the progress of their clients. Though possibly time-consuming, this may be helpful both for clients and for evaluating the effectiveness of the counsellor's work and the impact of the counselling agency. Given shortage of resources, it may be desirable for individual counsellors and counselling agencies to follow up only sample groupings of their clients at periodic intervals.

PRACTICAL EXERCISES AND QUESTIONS

It may help you develop your skills and knowledge of the material in this chapter if, either individually or as part of a group, you perform the following exercises and answer the following questions.

Practical Exercises

1.   With a partner, role-play conducting an initial assessment interview,

including taking appropriate notes. Remember to achieve all four 'working' objectives of the initial interview.

2. With a partner, role-play counsellor strategies for handling:
    (a) silences;
    (b) talkativeness.

3. With a partner, role-play a counsellor interviewing a client in crisis. Afterwards, discuss the issues involved.

4. With a partner, role-play terminating a counselling relationship. Afterwards, discuss the issues involved.

Questions

1. What do you consider to be the main advantages and disadvantages of assessment in counselling?

2. Do you agree that the objects of the initial interview are adequately described by focusing on a working alliance, a working model, working goals and working methods?

3. Do you agree with the five-stage model of the initial counselling interview described in this chapter? Give reasons for your answer.

4. To what extent do you consider it appropriate for counsellors to counsel very severely disturbed clients? Give reasons for your answer.

5. What place do you consider the use of medication has in conjunction with counselling? Cite uses and misuses.

NOTES

1. Patterson, C. H. (1974) *Relationship Counseling and Psychotherapy* p. 173. New York: Harper and Row.
2. Tyler, L. (1961) *The Work of the Counsellor* (2nd ed.) p. 63. New York: Appleton-Century-Crofts.
3. Sullivan, H. S. (1954) *The Psychiatric Interview* p. 4. New York: W. W. Norton.
4. Tyler, L. (1961) *The Work of the Counselor* (2nd ed.) p. 63. New York: Appleton-Century-Crofts.
5. Rogers, C. R. (1970) *Encounter Groups* p. 15. London: The Penguin Press. Rogers uses the concept of milling around to describe the initial stage of the process of the encounter group.

6. Zaro, J. S., Barach, R., Nedelman, D. J. & Dreiblatt, I. S. (1977) *A Guide for Beginning Psychotherapists* p. 41. Cambridge: Cambridge University Press.
7. Sullivan, H. S. (1954) *The Psychiatric Interview* p. 40. New York: W. W. Norton.
8. Zaro, J. S., Barach, R., Nedelman, D. J. & Dreiblatt, I. S. (1977) *A Guide for Beginning Psychotherapists* p. 125. Cambridge: Cambridge University Press.
9. Norfolk, D. (1977) *The Stress Factor* p. 15. Feltham, Middlesex: Hamlyn Paperbacks.
10. Bugental, J. F. T. (1978) *Psychotherapy and Process* p. 34. Reading, Massachusetts: Addison Wesley.
11. Gray, K. (1979) Aspects of counsellor vulnerability. *British Journal of Guidance and Counselling*, **7**, 188. Full reference pp. 188–198.
12. Wingate, P. (1972) *The Penguin Medical Encyclopaedia* p. 346. Harmondsworth, Middlesex: Penguin Books.
13. Willis, J. (1974) *Lecture Notes on Psychiatry* (4th ed.) p. xi. Oxford: Blackwell. The fifth edition of this book was published in 1979.
14. *Ibid.* p. 39.
15. Coleman, J. C. (1976) *Abnormal Psychology and Modern Life* (5th ed.) p. 293. Glenview, Illinois: Scott Foresman.
16. Willis, J. (1974) *Lecture Notes on Psychiatry* (4th ed.) p. 39. Oxford: Blackwell.
17. Coleman, J. C. (1976) *Abnormal Psychology and Modern Life* (5th ed.) p. 341. Glenview, Illinois: Scott Foresman.
18. Willis, J. (1974) *Lecture Notes on Psychiatry* (4th ed.) p. 34. Oxford: Blackwell.
19. Trethowan, W. H. (1979) *Psychiatry* (4th ed.) p. 309. London: Ballière Tindall.
20. Coleman, J. C. (1976) *Abnormal Psychology and Modern Life* (5th ed.). Glenview, Illinois: Scott Foresman. Adapted from material on pp. 268–269.
21. *Ibid.* p. 268.
22. *Ibid.* p. 270.
23. Table 13.5 was compiled from material given to the author by Dr Martin Davies, Consultant psychiatrist at the Midland Nerve Hospital, Birmingham.
24. MIMS, Haymarket Publishing, 38/42 Hampton Rd, Teddington, Middlesex TW11 0JE. Published monthly, MIMS is an index of proprietary preparations available for prescription in general practice.
25. Australian MIMS, 68 Alexandra St, Crow Nest, Sydney, Australia.

14 – Thinking Difficulties

SUMMARY: *Though all counselling might be thought of as involving the ways in which clients think, this chapter discusses a number of specific areas of thinking or cognitive difficulty as well as some relevant counsellor interventions. Clients' areas of thinking difficulty mentioned here are: an inadequate conceptual framework for understanding their own and others' behaviour; internal rules or standards which lead to dysfunctional self-evaluations; using various stratagems to operate on information at variance with their self-conceptions; difficulty accurately attributing the causes of, and realistically assuming responsibility for, what happens in their lives; inaccurately anticipating the risks and gains from various courses of action; possessing an inadequate set of ethical guidelines; restricted thinking, for example 'tunnel vision'; and difficulties in decision-making, problem-solving and self-control.*

There are numerous possible counsellor interventions for helping clients to think more effectively. Sometimes counsellors will need to clear up clients' misinformation about their condition. Acceptance and empathic understanding are also important counsellor tools. Counsellors may explore with their clients in a focused way areas of thinking difficulty. Specificity or concreteness can help to clarify exploration and needed actions. Various confrontations or ways in which counsellors can reflect and bring attention to discrepancies in their clients' feelings, thoughts and actions are discussed. At times counsellors may dispute their clients' reasoning and encourage them to do likewise. Interpretations, which may be shallow or deep, are counsellor explanations of client behaviour and psychological processes. Counsellors may also engage in teaching, providing their clients with information external to themselves or about themselves, and in persuasion. Modelling, role playing and arranging for clients to practise desired behaviours are additional interventions. Furthermore, counsellors may train clients in effective thinking skills, such as those of decision-making and of using self-instructional methods for handling stress. Some issues and hazards of counsellor interventions focusing on client thinking difficulties are discussed, including the possibility of too much counsellor direction and poor timing of interventions, which leads to client resistance.

In Chapter 10 a distinction was made between experiencing, thinking, and acting. This chapter focuses on approaches to clients who would function better if they thought more effectively. There are a number of ways of viewing a focus in counselling on clients' thinking. First, the position may be taken that all the concerns of clients are best described in thinking or cognitive terms, be they called misconceptions of the self,[1] automatic thoughts and distorted internal communications,[2] constricting personal constructs,[3] or dilemmas, traps and snags.[4] Taking such a position, not only the objectives but also the methods of all counselling approaches focus on the way clients think. Furthermore, alterations in clients' thinking are always involved in changes in their experiencing and acting. Second, it is possible to differentiate between counselling approaches in terms of the extent to which counsellors focus directly on attempting to alter their clients' thinking. For instance, this was a basis for our suggested distinction between humanistic-perceptual and humanistic-rational theory. Third, it is possible to identify and describe thinking components of different counselling theories, acknowledging that there may be similarities as well as differences. For example, the concept of faulty self-evaluations is common to many counselling theories. Fourth, counselling focused on thinking entails a number of different counsellor interventions aimed at altering specific areas of clients' faulty thoughts. Fifth, counsellors can aid clients in developing thinking skills, such as problem-solving and decision-making, so that they may engage in self-help independent of a counsellor. This chapter focuses on two main areas: first, on identifying and describing *clients' areas of thinking difficulty*, and second, on *counsellor interventions for altering clients' thinking*, including developing some self-help skills of effective thinking.

Though having some sympathy with the notion that all counselling involves altering thinking, we nevertheless feel that there are differences in the extent to which counsellor interventions focus on cognitive change. For instance, basic empathy may bring about such change, but in a less focused way than the ABCDE analysis of rational-emotive therapy. Considerations of appropriateness and timing are always involved in counsellor decisions to use interventions focused on thinking. Again, the point is made that some clients, possibly the more disturbed ones, need a highly non-threatening basic empathy relationship before their own thoughts are in an appropriate state of readiness to handle more focused interventions. However, even the exploration involved in a basic empathy relationship is likely to involve the ways in which clients think about themselves, about others, and about their situations.

AREAS OF CLIENT THINKING DIFFICULTY

Counsellors and clients meet each other within the framework of their thoughts and styles of thinking. Although this section focuses on some areas of thinking difficulty for clients, counsellors themselves may have similar difficulties both inside and outside their counselling work. We discuss clients' thinking difficulties before discussing counsellor interventions since we hope that having the two foci may make for greater clarity than simultaneously emphasizing both difficulties and interventions. Also, a simple pairing of difficulties and interventions is unrealistic, since difficulties are often interrelated, and since the same interventions may be appropriate for more than one difficulty.

Conceptual Framework

A conceptual framework can be viewed as a set of concepts or a set of working hypotheses about human behaviour which govern the individual's approach to life. A reasonably accurate conceptual framework is necessary if clients are to be able to understand, predict and control events in their lives. Furthermore, a shared conceptual framework may provide a basis for communication with others. Hobbs writes that learning an adequate cognitive system is one of the five major sources of gain in psychotherapy. He observes: 'The individual has got to have a cognitive house to live in to protect himself from the incomprehensibilities of existence as well as to provide some architecture for daily experiencing'.[5] Some clients may enter counselling with a very inadequate set of concepts with which to understand their own and others' behaviour. Theories of counselling almost by definition involve elaboration of conceptual frameworks which either implicitly, as in person-centred counselling, or explicitly, as in rational-emotive therapy and transactional analysis, get communicated to clients. An assumption of possibly all counsellors is that their conceptual framework is superior to that of their clients. Thus, for many clients, deficiencies in regard to their conceptual framework are regarded as important barriers to more effective living. For instance, clients may be in a state of misinformation or lack of information about themselves. Many of the areas discussed below elaborate faulty components of conceptual frameworks or thinking systems.

Self-evaluations and Internal Rules

The notion of positive and negative self-evaluations is common in counselling psychology. For instance, the Freudian superego is composed of rules which generate feelings of pride if adhered to, and feelings of conscience or guilt if broken. In transactional analysis, the term 'Parent' is used to describe tribal and childhood rules and injunctions. Rogers uses the term 'conditions of worth' to describe people's self-evaluations based on others' experiencing and judgements rather than on their own valuing processes. Ellis talks of irrational beliefs which generate faulty positive and negative self-evaluations. Similarly, in Bandura's social learning theory, there is the notion of functional and dysfunctional self-evaluative standards.

There are two interrelated issues involved in thinking difficulties concerning positive and negative self-evaluations: first, the extent to which the self-evaluations are helpful or harmful; and second, if harmful, identification of the internal rules or self-standards which generate such self-evaluations. Almost invariably harmful self-standards involve words like 'must', 'ought', and 'should'. Often they involve overgeneralization from what may have been appropriate in some situations, possibly in the past, to situations where they are now inappropriate. Sometimes they involve unnecessary comparisons with others, concerning such matters as personal characteristics or levels of performance at given tasks.

Both positive and negative self-evaluations and the internal rules on which they are based form part of clients' self-conceptions. Furthermore, harmful self-evaluations may have a cumulative effect, leaving the individual in an overall state of low self-worth or lack of self-esteem. Most counsellors, one way or another, attempt to alter the self-conceptions of their clients so that they are less negative than previously and, also, based more on realistic internal rules. Possibly the most frequent counsellor interventions focused on clients' thinking difficulties concern their faulty self-evaluations and internal rules.

Handling Information at Variance with Self-conceptions

Since clients' self-conceptions form the basis on which they interact with the world, there is a need for them to be reasonably stable. Additionally, clients need to be able to perceive themselves and the world accurately. Often client self-conceptions do not interfere with such accurate perception. On other occasions, however, when incoming information is discrepant with clients' pictures of themselves, client self-conceptions may definitely interfere with accurate perception of reality. Clients use varying stratagems for 'processing' such information, whether it is positive or negative. Such stratagems include processes like Rogers' denial and distortion of information. For instance, to maintain his self-concept of being a worthless person, a male student may operate on positive feedback regarding an essay by saying that the grader did not read it properly. Negative feedback may also be operated on, as in the case of an aggressive person who sees others' coolness towards him as resulting from their character deficiencies rather than from his hostile behaviour towards them. Furthermore, as Laing points out,[6] people not only operate on discrepant information, they also operate on their operations so as not to be aware of them. Undoubtedly, the Freudian defence mechanisms are some of the most important examples of such operations.

Another way of handling information that is at variance with self-conceptions is to operate on other people's experiencing and self conceptions in such a way that they collude in sustaining one's own inaccurate self-conceptions. Laing uses the term 'induction' for this process of transforming another person's experiencing.[7] In his example, a man's wife accepts his projection of his mother onto her and she is induced to act in accordance with the expected role. Another instance is that of the aggressive man cited above who may be trying to make, and possibly succeeding in making, others feel that they have wronged him rather than *vice versa*. Berne's concept of games is a further example of people operating on one another's experiencing to sustain self-defeating positions.

Attributions of Causality and Responsibility

Counsellors are increasingly becoming aware of the significance in counselling of the concept of attribution. The term 'attribution' is used in social psychology to refer to the ways and processes by which people attribute causes and meanings to their own behaviour, to others' behaviour, and to environmental events. Another way of viewing attribution is that it relates to the ways in which people make inferences. Some such inferences are concerned with personal characteristics of self and others and, in some measure, we have already covered this area in our earlier section on self-evaluations and internal rules. Another set of inferences is concerned with the causes of our own and others' behaviour. This area, sometimes known as causal attribution, is the focus of the present discussion.

There are a number of assumptions underlying the notion of causal attribution. First, individuals attempt to identify and assign causes to important instances of their own and others' behaviour; second, their assignment to causes is determined in a systematic manner; and third, the particular cause that they attribute to given events has important consequences for their subsequent feelings and behaviour.[8,9] Strong observes that a key to successful counselling is to help clients to identify causes of their problems in events in which they could behave differently, such as the way they perceive events, their thoughts, beliefs and attitudes about and in the events, and their actions towards others in the events.[10] Clients who understand the causal misattributions involved in their problems are in a position to gain greater control over their behaviour.

Elements of causal attributions on which counsellors may wish to focus include single or multiple, internal or external, facilitative or inhibitory, and accurate or inaccurate attributions. Clients may attribute a single cause or multiple causes to events in their lives. Sometimes attribution of a single cause, such as in the statement 'It's all her fault', is a simplification of an event which has multiple causes, such as the client's behaviour, the other person's behaviour, and external events in both their lives. Attribution of behaviour to external or environmental causes represents the radical behaviourist position. Here the counsellor's job is to find the key environmental considerations which can be modified in such a way as to control their clients' behaviours. Attribution of behaviour to internal causes means that individuals control their behaviour. Frequently, however, behaviour is the result of both internal and external causes and of their interactions. Attributions also affect motivation in that some attributions facilitate appropriate action while others inhibit it. Furthermore, attributions in all of the above categories may be accurate or inaccurate. At different times and in different situations, varying combinations of single or multiple, internal or external, and facilitative or inhibitory attributions may be accurate or appropriate for effective living.

An example of the relevance of causal attribution to counselling is its possible influence on motivation. Weiner *et al* postulate that individuals use four categories of causal attribution both to anticipate and, when completed, to evaluate, the outcome (O) of an achievement-related event.[11] The four causal elements are ability (A), effort (E), task difficulty (T), and luck (L), making for the equation $O = f(A, E, T, L)$. Weiner and Kukla have produced evidence suggesting that individuals who are high and those who are low in achievement motivation differentially attribute the causes of success and failure.[12] High achievement motivation individuals are more likely to attribute success to effort and failure to lack of proper effort. On the other hand, low achievement oriented individuals are less inclined to persist given failure, because they are less likely to ascribe their failure to lack of effort and more likely to attribute it to a deficiency in ability. Consequently, low achievement motivation individuals are less likely to obtain the reward of goal attainment, thus sustaining a negative self-concept and ineffective behaviour.

A critical counselling task is for clients to acquire accurate causal attribution in regard to the extent of their personal responsibility for their internal and external events. Often, as a result of counselling, clients are likely to assume increased responsibility for their role in creating events. For instance, a husband in a marital conflict may start by blaming his wife for all the strife in the home. As counselling progresses, however, he may become aware that some of his own internal rules, self-evaluations and behaviours are harmful. Furthermore, he may also become willing to risk behaving more affectionately, which, in turn, is likely to influence his wife's behaviour positively toward him. The above is an example of a client starting with inappropriate external attribution and moving towards more realistic internal attribution. Sometimes, as in the case of excessive self-blame, clients' internal attributions may also be inaccurate. Glasser's reality therapy, which emphasizes making the client face the basic truth that he is responsible for his behaviour, is a counselling approach in which accurate attribution of responsibility is both central and explicit.

There are a number of further attribution of responsibility dimensions which may be causing clients difficulty. One dimension is the extent to which clients are actors or reactors in their lives. If they are actors, they are more likely to be creating their lives. Another dimension is the extent to which clients are capable of perceiving the choices in their lives. Strong writes: 'In psychotherapy, clients often perceive that they have no choice but to behave as they do (be depressed, be angry with their spouse, and so on)'.[13] Counsellors may help clients to assume more personal responsibility through working with them to develop the capacity to generate alternatives in problem areas in their lives.

Anticipations of Risk, Gain and Competence

One function of people's self-conceptions is to regulate the ways in which they anticipate events. Since self-conceptions have a tendency towards stability, there will also be a tendency towards stable anticipation of events. For instance, individuals who see themselves as good at a task are consistently likely to anticipate doing that task well and *vice versa*. However, self-conceptions may be of varying levels of accuracy and, hence, anticipations tend to be at different levels of realism.

Perhaps Kelly is the psychologist who has most stressed human future orientation, since the fundamental postulate of his psychology of personal constructs is that 'a person's processes are psychologically channelized by the ways in which he anticipates events'.[14] Clients have difficulty in a number of areas of anticipation. A common difficulty is that of inaccurate assessment of risks and gains from various actions. Since counselling clients tend not to be very confident, most often they overemphasize the risks and underemphasize the potential gains. Also, clients often have implicit or explicit negative anticipations which sabotage their efforts for change. Ryle calls these 'snags' or Subtle Negative Aspects of Goals used in the sense 'I want to change, but the snag is . . .'.[15] To the Freudians, giving up the 'secondary gain' of neurosis is an anticipation interfering with motivation for change or a 'resistance'.

Recently much attention has been paid in the psychological literature to concepts such as White's sense of competence,[16,17] Rotter's internal-external locus of control,[18,19] and Bandura's self-efficacy. All of these are essentially future-oriented concepts which relate to peoples' perceptions of their ability to act on their environments in such a way as to have desired effects. Clients frequently have very negative anticipations about their abilities to influence their environments. For instance, Beck observes that depressed patients often have fantasies about failing every task they undertake.[20] Anticipations affect actions and such patients are correspondingly less likely either to test reality or, if they do, to succeed.

Ethical Development

A number of writers on children's moral development have observed a shift with age from respect or submission to external authority towards greater self-government and a morality based on individual principles of conscience.[21,22,23] In the earlier section on self-evaluations and internal rules, we focused on the development of too harsh ethical standards. Another kind of cognitive difficulty is failure to develop adequate ethical standards. Both Mowrer and Glasser stress this aspect of counselling problems. Mowrer emphasizes the need to help the neurotic person get psychologically better by being morally better.[24] Similarly, Glasser's reality therapy emphasizes that to feel worth while clients must maintain a satisfactory standard of behaviour.

Undoubtedly, many clients have either insufficient or confused ethical standards with which to guide their lives. Humanistic psychologists, such as Rogers, would consider that in part this reflects a failure to get in touch with their organismic valuing processes. Additionally, as in reality therapy, counsellors who specifically help their clients to explore values or personal ideas of right or wrong may engender greater ethical development.

For some clients the development of ethical standards cannot be viewed independently of a broader framework or philosophy of life, involving assumptions about life's purposes and reflecting long-range goals and strivings. For instance, May observes that for existential analysts the confronting of death 'makes the individual existence real, absolute and concrete'.[25] Thus counselling involving existential, philosophical and spiritual concerns can be an important area. Such counselling is likely to involve helping clients in their philosophical and spiritual self-exploration and also, where necessary, referring them to specialists in facilitating such self-exploration.

Restricted Thinking

'Tunnel vision' is one of the main forms of restricted thinking. If clients feel threatened they may experience a narrowing of their perceptual field and only be able to focus on certain variables in a situation. This increase in rigidity is likely to be inefficient for, as Combs and Snygg point out, resolution of problems often requires a broad rather than a narrow differentiation of perception, enabling people to take into account all significant information, including being open to the range of available actions prior to acting.[26] Other thinking difficulties related to threat include memory difficulties, concentration difficulties, inability to think coherently, and thought blocking or inability to follow a train of thought. Additionally, there are psychotic delusions and hallucinations.

Another form of restricted thinking is known as dichotomous thinking, or thinking in false either/or dichotomies that restrict the range of choice. Ryle gives the example 'In relationships, I am *either* close to someone and feel smothered, *or* I am cut off and feel lonely'.[27] The opposite of *dichotomous* thinking is sometimes known as *relativistic* thinking, where varying shades of meaning are taken into account.

Yet another form of restricted thinking is the making of arbitrary inferences. Beck observes that it generally does not occur to people to question the validity of their thinking. Nevertheless, in thinking, people continually come to conclusions based on untested inferences. These possibly distorted inferences are treated as fact, since they are not subject to challenge and reality testing.[28] Possible if/then arbitrary influences are '*If* I am to be masculine, *then* I have to be loud and insensitive' or '*If* I blush, *then* people will think I am a weakling'. Another way of looking at the concept of arbitrary inference is that it entails arriving at false conclusions involving untested attributions.

Decision-making and Problem-solving

Almost by definition clients are restricted in their capacity to make effective decisions. This is partly because such factors as faulty self-evaluations, attributions and anticipations lead to a restricted range of perceptions. On many occasions, however, the client lacks basic decision-making skills. Various kinds of decisions occur in many different areas of life. One distinction made by Cronbach and Gleser is that a decision may be terminal or investigatory. An investigatory decision involves calling for additional information until a terminal or final decision is made.[29] Decisions may also be good or bad. Gelatt suggests that a 'good' decision is one in which the person has more 'free choice' through: (a) being more aware of the alternatives; (b) having an increased understanding of the factors involved in the choice, including the perceived desirability of the consequences; and (c) being willing to accept responsibility for the consequences.[30] Another variable in good decision-making, which humanistic psychologists emphasize, is the extent to which the decision reflects the chooser's own valuing process rather than introjected conditions of worth.

Clients need both to make good decisions in specific areas of their lives and to acquire the processes of effective decision-making. Krumboltz and Baker have outlined the following steps in decision-making which the behavioural counsellor wishes to achieve with clients:

(a) Defining the problem and the client's goals.
(b) Agreeing mutually to achieve counselling goals.

(c)   Generating alternative problem solutions.
(d)   Collecting information about the alternatives.
(e)   Examining the consequences of the alternatives.
(f)   Revaluing goals, alternatives and consequences.
(g)   Making the decision or tentatively selecting an alternative contingent upon new developments and new opportunities.
(h)   Generalizing the decision-making process to new problems.[31]

Possibly problem-solving is a term which suggests a more complex process than decision-making, in that it also encompasses feelings and actions as well as cognitive decision-making skills. Elements of problem-solving include the following: (a) general orientation; (b) problem definition and formulation; (c) self-examination; (d) examination of other variables in the problem; (e) generation of alternatives; (f) decision-making; (g) planning how to implement the decision; (h) having or generating sufficient commitment to implement the plan; (i) implementing the plan; and (j) evaluating feedback during and after implementing the plan. These elements are often interrelated.

Goldfried and Davison observe that three key features of a general problem-solving orientation are: (a) the assumption that problems constitute a normal part of life and can often be coped with; (b) the capacity to identify and define situations as problem situations as they arise; and (c) restricting the tendency to respond with one's first impulse.[32] Problem definition involves a clear statement or formulation of the problem to be solved. This is a process which is likely to involve both self-examination, including beliefs, attitudes, and one's *own* contribution in generating and sustaining the problem situation, as well as examination of the external parameters in the situation, such as other people and their beliefs, attitudes and capacity for change. Generation of alternatives may involve 'brainstorming', or trying to generate as many solutions as possible before assessing the feasibility of any one. On the other hand, only a few solutions may be necessary. Decision-making involves assessing alternatives and their consequences and making either a terminal or an investigatory decision. In either case, realistic planning is necessary to carry out the decisions; motivation may need to be explored and strengthened until it becomes commitment; and the plan needs to be carried out and evaluated. Often it is helpful if the plan is broken down into sub-goals which can be approached sequentially. Furthermore, it is often useful to write the plan down and to display it where it may be seen clearly. Realistically assessing feedback involves the capacity for accurately processing information that is at variance with self-conceptions, since without accurate perception of one's own feelings and of external feedback, mistakes are likely to be perpetuated. As in reality therapy, when the plan turns out to be unreasonable, clients and their counsellors can work together to develop a better one.

Self-control

Self-control is defined here as increasing the probability of desired behaviours through manipulating their inner and outer controlling events. Inner events include the individual's self-standards or internal rules, whereas outer events involve external rewards and punishments. Sometimes the term 'self-management' is used instead of 'self-control'. Kanfer observes that such procedures usually combine techniques that involve standard-setting, self-monitoring, self-evaluation and self-reinforcement.[33] Self-monitoring or self-observation essentially involves charting one's behaviour in a target area over a period of, say, a week or so. Self-evaluation involves assessing the discrepancy between what one is doing and what one ought to be doing. Self-reinforcement involves the administration of reinforcers contingent on presence and increase of desired behaviours, such as relaxing and taking more exercise, or on decrease and absence of undesired behaviours, such as smoking and eating bread.[34]

Thoresen and Mahoney indicate that there are two general self-control strategies.[35] First, there is environmental planning or stimulus control, in which an attempt is made to control the target behaviour *prior* to its execution. Both putting food out of sight and out of easy reach and using locations conducive to studying are examples of stimulus control. Second, there is behavioural programming, which involves self-administered consequences *following* the occurrence of a target response. For instance, the golfer who rewards himself with a drink after an hour's practice is engaging in this kind of behavioural self-control. Central to the self-control procedures discussed here is the client's ability to think effectively.

Cognitive therapists such as Meichenbaum consider that self-control difficulties involve not only manipulation of environmental consequences but what clients say to themselves about these consequences.[36] As with Ellis, whose work has been seminal to cognitive therapists, the idea is that clients have continuous internal dialogues which often include faulty self-statements. However, where Ellis focuses on a set of core irrational beliefs, Meichenbaum is more interested in idiosyncratic thought patterns.[37] Clients may have faulty self-statements in a number of areas, such as: (a) inaccurate assessment of the reality of a situation; (b) negative, catastrophizing, anxiety-engendering and task-irrelevant ideation; (c) faulty labelling of the anxiety they are experiencing, which may lead to feelings of lack of control rather than coping; (d) inability to 'psych' themselves up to perform a phobic or stressful task; and (e) absence of or inadequate reinforcing self-statements on completion of a task.[38]

COUNSELLOR INTERVENTIONS FOR THINKING DIFFICULTIES

In this section we focus on some of the interventions which may be used by counsellors, for the most part in interview settings, in helping clients with their thinking difficulties. These interventions are not necessarily discrete entities and it is likely that a number of different kinds of interventions focused on thinking will be used with a single client and, possibly, in a single interview.

Clearing up Misinformation

Clients sometimes come to counselling with overt misinformation or misattributions about their condition. For instance, some clients may consider that they are schizophrenic or on the verge of a nervous breakdown. What may be happening in these instances is that the clients find their symptoms bizarre, frightening and incomprehensible in terms of their current conceptual framework for understanding human behaviour. Furthermore, they may have sought assistance from others, such as doctors and friends, who directly or indirectly may have colluded in their mislabelling of themselves. A competent initial assessment interview should help the counsellor to develop a working model of the client, including whether or not he is schizophrenic or on the verge of a breakdown. At this stage it may be appropriate to try to clear up the client's misattributions, if indeed they exist, by pointing out that his subjective assessment of his situation is not supported by the evidence that he has presented. Additionally, it may be necessary to discuss the symptoms of, say, schizophrenia so that clients can make their own assessment. Wolpe observes that sometimes sophisticated individuals need to be given supporting facts.[39]

What sometimes happens is that clients' fears and anxieties take on the status of facts in their minds. For instance, a fear about homosexual orientation may not constitute the fact of homosexual or even of bisexual behaviour once the evidence is examined. In this instance, an appropriate counsellor intervention may be to acknowledge the fear, but then to provide information that the fear seems unsupported or scarcely supported by the evidence. A brief discussion about the nature of a sexual orientation, including the fact that people differ on a homosexual-heterosexual continuum rather than always being either exclusively homosexual or exclusively heterosexual, may be helpful.

Acceptance and Empathic Understanding

Person-centred advocates consider that the basic empathy relationship is necessary and sufficient for therapeutic personality change and, hence, for changing thinking. The potential of such a relationship for changes in the way clients think should not be underestimated. Given the assumption of an organismic valuing process, it is vital that clients become more centred in their own experiencing. It is arguable that with a high degree of acceptance, safety and freedom (what is sometimes termed 'psychological space') a number of necessary elements of the counselling process have a higher probability of occurring. First, experiences and viewpoints, especially threatening ones, are more likely to come to the client's awareness, be disclosed, and be available for further exploration. Second, the client has a greater prospect of genuine inward searching, exploration and self-experiencing, which is the prerequisite to becoming strongly autonomous. Third, the experience of being accepted and valued as a whole person may accelerate clients' self-acceptance more rapidly than a focus on specific areas of thinking difficulty. A high level of counsellor acceptance and empathic understanding may be very helpful to clients who do not have access to their latent resources for rational thought. The idea here is that thinking difficulties often involve defensive restrictions of thought, which may best be altered by diluting or 'bypassing' them with a basic empathy relationship than by confronting them directly with interventions specifically focused on thinking.

Another way of looking at acceptance and empathic understanding is in terms of facilitating *broad* rather than *focused* exploration. An underlying issue here is the extent of counsellor direction of the content of the interview. In facilitating broad rather than focused exploration the counsellor will be leaving more of the directing of the interview to the client than when engaging in focused exploration. Broad exploration, however, does not mean that the client may not cover a number of the areas, such as exploration of self-evaluations, which may be dealt with more specifically in focused exploration. Furthermore, broad exploration is likely to be influenced by the counsellor's theoretical position and therefore will have some implicit focus. Thus the broad versus focused exploration issue is really one of emphasis rather than an either/or issue. Additionally, both broad and focused exploration may be used at different stages of the counselling process with the same client, with the likelihood of broad exploration taking place more in the early and focused exploration more in the later interviews.

Before indicating some areas of focused exploration, a vignette is provided of the client whose thinking and behaviour were altered by a counselling approach based mainly on acceptance and empathic understanding.

> John was a 25-year-old single law student whose self-conceptions or thoughts about himself on entering and in the early stages of counselling included: (a) I am a worthless person and, in fact, a few years ago I attempted suicide; (b) talking about myself to the counsellor is self-indulgent and wasting the counsellor's time; (c) talking about the difficulties of my home life is disloyal to my parents; (d) having homosexual tendencies and, when feeling low, seeking sex partners in public lavatories makes me even more worthless, especially since I'm Catholic; (e) I can't see why anybody in his right mind would want to give me a legal apprenticeship and, therefore, I don't even bother applying; and (f) counselling, emphasizing talking about myself, is a waste of time. John's non-verbal and para-verbal behaviour indicated a high degree of diffidence and lack of confidence.
>
> John had 40 sessions of individual counselling stretching over two years, at the end of which the above self-conceptions had been altered to the following: (a) I am now a reasonably worthwhile person and no longer get very depressed; (b) the counsellor's listening to me talk was part of his job, for which I am grateful; (c) talking about my parents has helped me both to understand myself better and to relate to them in a more effective way; (d) I am now much more accepting of my homosexual orientation and no longer feel the need to seek sex partners in public lavatories; (e) I am employable and have fixed up a legal apprenticeship; (f) talking about myself in counselling has helped me to accept myself much more and has 'drawn the poison' from me. John's gains were maintained at the time of a sixth-month follow-up interview.[40]

Focused Exploration

Focused exploration involves helping a client to explore one or more specific areas in some depth. Both counsellors and clients may suggest areas for focused exploration and also have views on the speed, extent and duration of such exploration. Focused exploration tends to assume a decision on the part of the counsellor about what areas of the client's functioning are fruitful to develop, though clearly counsellors must be sensitive to their clients' wishes. As Zaro *et al* observe, 'These decisions about the clinical importance of topics are dictated in large part by the goals of therapy and by your choice of treatment approach'.[41]

Focused exploration may arise fairly naturally as part of a counselling interview.

Alternatively, it may be introduced by the client with a statement like 'Well, in this interview I would like to focus on my relationship with my husband', or by the counsellor, with a statement like 'It might be useful if we take a more detailed look at the ways in which you are putting yourself down'.

Focused exploration can be in a number of areas, including: one or more areas of thinking difficulty; client problem areas such as work or family life; assessing and monitoring counselling progress; and looking at the counsellor-client relationship. Here we deal only with exploration of areas of thinking difficulty, though such difficulties are likely to be involved in other kinds of focused exploration. Counsellors who help clients to explore areas of thinking difficulty are likely to have one or both of the following objectives: first, trying to facilitate their clients' *awareness* of the difficulties; and second, going beyond exploration with a number of further interventions designed to help clients to *change* their faulty thoughts and styles of thinking.

As indicated, one of the characteristics of focused exploration is that it involves a degree of counsellor direction and guidance of the exploration, though there are differences in the extent to which such direction is either necessary or takes place. The following are a few suggestions for focused exploration of areas of thinking difficulty.

Conceptual framework

This may involve exploration of the adequacy of the concepts clients have for understanding their own and other's behaviour. One concept, stressed by behaviourists, is that since most behaviour is learned it can also be altered. A fuller understanding of the concepts of stress and anxiety may also help some clients to monitor and regulate their behaviour. When a counsellor focuses on exploration of a client's conceptual framework, the counsellor's own framework tends to be either implicit or explicit in the discussion.

Self-evaluations and internal rules

Foci of exploration here may involve: identification of internal rules or self-standards by which evaluations of personal characteristics are made; exploring the effects on emotions and behaviour of internal rules and their related self-evaluations; assessing the realism of the rules; exploring how the rules have been derived and are maintained; and working with the client on discarding or reformulating internal rules which are blocking effective living.

Information at variance with self-conceptions

This is a sensitive area which often needs to be handled delicately, since clients may need to gain insight into the fact that they actually deny and distort information about themselves and others, as well as into the extent and ways in which they do it. Client willingness to explore such areas depends in part on their level of self-worth, their degree of psychological sophistication, and the quality of their relationship with the counsellor. Also, some areas may be easier to perceive or less threatening than others. Foci of exploration may include the ways in which clients handle positive and negative feedback about themselves, coping styles and defensive mechanisms, and the ways in which clients influence other people to sustain their own self-image.

Attribution of causality and responsibility

Here counsellors may help their clients to explore the extent to which they are prepared to assume personal responsibility not only for how they act but also for how they think and feel. For instance, in a situation where an external change is impossible, internal changes of thoughts and feelings about the situation may be possible. Areas of focused exploration may include: the concept of personal responsibility; areas in which cause is wrongly being attributed by blame and self-blame; the degree to which clients are active in meeting their needs; the relationship between accurate attributions and effective action in problem areas such as a marital difficulty; and generation of alternative ways of perceiving and of alternative courses of action in specific situations.

Anticipations of risk, gain and competence

Here clients may be helped to become more aware of the ways in which they anticipate situations, usually more negatively than desirable. A focus on clarifying and elaborating the gains as well as the risks of changes in lifestyle and actions may be helpful. The accuracy of client assessments of personal competence in specific areas may also be explored, the idea being to achieve more realistic anticipations of competence.

Ethical development

Two areas for exploration here are, first, everyday ethical guidelines for relating to others and, second, the rational, philosophical and spiritual framework on which ethical guidelines may be based.

Restricted thinking

Counsellors may work with clients to increase their awareness of ways in which they restrict their thinking and the effects of this on problem-solving. Such restrictions include tunnel vision, dichotomous thinking, and treating their thoughts as facts rather than as testable hypotheses

Decision-making and problem-solving

A focus on decision-making and problem-solving may involve helping clients to a greater awareness of their current problem-solving styles. Sometimes it may involve analysis of specific situations and areas of difficulty. Often this focus goes beyond exploration into skills training.

Self-control

One area of exploration is the extent to which clients adequately arrange variables in their environments so as to increase the likelihood of their behaving in ways that meet their needs. We have already given examples of environmental planning strategies to reduce eating and to increase studying. Another area to explore is how much encouragement clients give themselves after completing a task, especially one that requires effort and possibly is not rewarding during its execution. For instance, do clients take success for granted and only notice failure, or do they allow themselves appropriate internal and external reinforcement?

Specificity

Counsellors may help their clients to be more specific about their concerns in at least three ways. First, they may respond to their clients' utterances with clarity and conciseness. This may help clients who are somewhat incoherent or struggling to really get in touch with what they are thinking and feeling. Vague and rambling counsellor responses may only serve to confuse the client and also risk creating distance in the counselling relationship. Second, by questions and reflections, counsellors may help clients to understand all the relevant aspects of their areas of concern. Third, as counselling moves from a focus on exploration to facilitating action, counsellors may help their clients to greater specificity concerning necessary actions.

Concreteness is another term for specificity. Carkhuff observes that concreteness enables clients 'to discuss all personally relevant feelings and experiences in specific and concrete terms'.[42] He further observes that counsellors will find that they are most effective when they view and implement the concreteness dimension in stages.[43] In other words, the exploratory phase of counselling, with an emphasis on experiencing and problem clarification, requires a different kind of facilitation involving specificity than later, when the client is formulating, planning and assessing courses of action. A final point is that specificity is helpful to counsellors as well as to clients. It enables them to understand clients' feelings and thoughts more closely, problem areas more fully, and possible courses of action more realistically.

Confrontation

Confrontation means reflecting and/or bringing attention to discrepancy. In varying degrees it involves presenting to clients information that is at variance with their self-conceptions. Confrontation may be used to facilitate both exploration and action. There are a number of possible areas of discrepancy and hence of confrontation, some of which are mentioned below:

1. Discrepancy between *utterances in and behaviour outside counselling*. Example: 'You say that you are not bothered about what your colleagues think of you and yet you get very tense every time you are with them.'
2. Discrepancy between *utterances and behaviour in counselling*. Example: 'You indicate that being rejected really hurt you and yet you smile as you talk about it.'
3. Discrepancy between *utterances in and intentions outside counselling*. Example: 'You've said a number of times that you would like to spend more time with your children and yet you never seem to get around to it.'
4. Discrepancy between *what is being said and what is left unsaid about the counsellor-client relationship*. Example: 'You say your previous counsellor was always very gentle with you and I wonder whether you're not asking me to go easy on you too.'
5. Discrepancy between *self-evaluation and the counsellor's perception of the client's assets*. Example: 'You seem to feel very inadequate about handling this difficulty in your life and yet you have a lot of resources, such as intelligence and persistence, and have coped well with difficult situations in the past.'
6. Discrepancy between *self-evaluation and the counsellor's own feelings about the client*. Example: 'Though you indicate you're boring me, I certainly don't feel that way and enjoy our sessions together.'
7. Discrepancy between *attribution of responsibility and behaviour*. Example: 'You feel that you are taking responsibility for your life and yet you blame your wife and daughter for everything that is wrong in your relationship with them.'
8. Discrepancy between *past and present statements in counselling*. Example: 'Now you say that you have no friends, but earlier you mentioned that you considered Jane and Bill as friends.'

Confrontation aims to expand the range of clients' perceptions by increasing their awareness of discrepancies in regard to feelings, thoughts and actions. In the early stages of counselling it may be advisable to ignore opportunities for confrontation or to confront tentatively. Later in counselling, or earlier with less disturbed clients, confrontations may be more direct and forceful. Carkhuff sees well-timed confrontations as offering clients crises that offer the possibility of moving to higher levels of awareness and functioning.[44] Even though counsellors may not feel it appropriate to share their observations, throughout counselling their understanding and behaviour should be 'keenly and continually attuned to discrepancies in the helpee's behaviour'.[45] Incidentally, there is some evidence that unskilled counsellors confront their clients with their pathology, weaknesses and liabilities much more frequently than do skilled counsellors.[46] However, though unskilled counsellors may use confrontations of weakness destructively, it seems desirable for skilled counsellors at appropriate times to confront their clients with areas in need of further attention.

Disputation

Disputation may be considered a sustained form of confrontation. Some counsellors, such as Ellis, use disputation frequently and forcefully. For instance, when Ellis detects an irrational belief on the part of a client he disputes both the belief and the client's attempts to justify the belief. Rational-emotive counsellors are likely to ask questions such as 'Why must everybody approve of you all the time?' or 'Why must you be perfectly competent all the time?'. The reasons given for the irrational beliefs are then strongly disputed and more rational and less demanding beliefs are suggested. Furthermore, clients are encouraged to engage in self-disputation or challenging their own reasoning.

Interpretation

Interpretations are counsellor explanations of client behaviour and psychological processes. Almost by definition interpretations come from the counsellor's *external* frame of reference and not from the client's *internal* frame of reference. The purpose of interpretation is to heighten awareness by prompting the client to consider an explanation or explanations hitherto not considered. Ideally, interpretations are made on the basis of a good knowledge of individual clients, though even then there is a danger of imposing a theoretical framework on clients irrespective of their particular concerns and needs. Interpretations should lead clients to insight involving a fuller understanding of their behaviour. As such, though coming from the external frame of reference, it could be argued that interpretations take the client further into their own internal frame of reference than if left to their own devices. Raimy makes a distinction between *shallow* interpretations, explanations which clients themselves are almost ready to recognize, and *deeper* interpretations, 'which draw upon information somewhat remote from the patient's immediate preoccupations'.[47] He mentions that, in general, shallow are thought preferable to deeper interpretations.

Perhaps interpretation is a term most commonly associated with psychoanalysis, though it is possible to make interpretations from a number of different theoretical orientations. For instance, the area of transactional analysis known as game analysis might be considered highly interpretive. Depending on the counsellor's theoretical orientation, information for interpretations is obtained from such sources as: clients' behaviour during the interview, including their non-verbal and para-verbal behaviour; clients' reports of their behaviour outside counselling; dreams and slips of the tongue; and clients' relationships with their counsellors.

Interpretations may be made either tentatively or persistently and firmly. Since interpretations often go beyond the intended meaning of the client's utterances, they can be threatening and sometimes downright inaccurate. A great risk in using interpretation is that it may arouse client resistance and thus block rather than facilitate the process of exploration and insight. Consequently, the timing and the wording of interpretations are important. Furthermore, counsellors may have to be prepared to supply supporting evidence for their interpretations. Last, counsellors must guard against projecting their own needs and unresolved areas into their explanations of their clients' behaviours.

Teaching

Teaching here means deliberate instruction of the client by the counsellor into a predetermined conceptual framework or body of knowledge. Such teaching almost invariably involves lecturettes, sometimes accompanied by use of visual aids such as a blackboard or flip-chart. Furthermore, directed reading may be assigned as homework. In humanistic-rational approaches such as rational-emotive therapy, transactional analysis and reality therapy, the counsellor role has a fairly large teaching element. For instance, a prerequisite of work in transactional analysis is that the client be taught its Parent–Adult–Child conceptual framework. Similarly, in rational-emotive therapy it is essential that the client learns the basic A–B–C framework, including the possibility of both rational and irrational beliefs at B. Also, in reality therapy clients are taught that their basic needs are for love and worth and that they must learn to be more responsible in meeting those needs. Furthermore, the role of the counsellor in behavioural counselling is viewed basically as that of a teacher. For instance, elements of the behaviourist conceptual framework, such as the notion of behaviour being sustained by environmental contingencies, may be deliberately and explicitly taught to clients.

Information-giving

Earlier we mentioned clearing up misinformation, which is one form of information-giving. Though there tends to be a presumption in counselling that the counsellor role is to facilitate client information-*getting* rather than to engage in counsellor information-*giving*, nevertheless there are occasions on which counsellors either provide information themselves or make the necessary referrals. Possibly a distinction may be made between teaching and information-giving on the basis of counsellors deciding what is taught and of clients deciding what information they need.

Information-giving may be divided into providing clients with *information external to themselves* and providing them with *information about themselves*. Client needs for *external information* may vary from welfare matters such as legal, housing and financial difficulties, to information in various areas of their personal functioning, such as sexual techniques or occupational opportunities. Such needs may be met by reflection, answering questions, referring the client, running courses such as those in sex and careers education, and providing reading suggestions and access to relevant information libraries. Tests and measures are one way of providing clients with *information about themselves,* though the feedback from these measures must be given to clients in such a way that it facilitates rather than blocks further exploration and self-clarification.

Persuasion

Some counsellors use persuasion as a way of altering their clients' thinking. Bandura lists verbal persuasion as one of the means of altering efficacy expectations. Possibly persuasion is most used in counselling to change client anticipations and thus induce clients to perform a given task. Such persuasion may involve both exhortation, or advocating a course of action, and encouragement, or giving reassurance about success in the course of action. Furthermore, persuasion may involve disputing clients' perceptions of the risks and getting them to see much more clearly the gains of acting. Sometimes, however, counsellors use persuasion to stop clients behaving in certain ways, particularly if likely to damage their long-term interests. Risks of persuasion are that at least some of the client's motivation is provided by the counsellor rather than by themselves. Also, in the events of both success and failure, there may be misattributions of causality and of responsibility.

Modelling

Modelling or observational learning may be used both in acquiring and in strengthening thoughts relevant to adaptive behaviour and also for inhibiting and eliminating thoughts relevant to unwanted behaviour. Modelling may take place in counselling in a number of ways. First, when interviewing, the counsellor may be modelling desirable thinking skills and behaviour which may, for instance, improve the client's capacities for problem-solving and human relating. Second, in behaviour rehearsal, the counsellor may model desirable thoughts and behaviours for clients in specific problem areas of their relationships. Third, in group counselling, other members of the group may model both desirable thoughts and behaviours and also different life-styles. Fourth, the counsellor may sometimes induce behaviour change by getting the client to observe either the counsellor or a third person performing tasks feared by the client, such as handling a dog. Modelled behaviour may both alter the client's anticipations concerning performing the task and provide information on how to go about it. Earlier, in Chapter 7, we mentioned that Bandura considers that modelling plus enactment of the modelled behaviour is a more potent form of learning to overcome fears than is modelling alone.

Role Playing

Role playing is an intervention used both for exploring and for altering the ways in which clients think about themselves. Moreno used psychodrama, dramatic enactment of clients' psychological concerns, to increase their awareness of thoughts, feelings and perceptions.[48] In other words, instead of just talking about their concerns, clients acted them out with the aid of the counsellor and other group members. Thus, in psychodrama, material is generated for exploration and, hence, for changes in self-conceptions, conceptions of others and changes in behaviour.

Behavioural counsellors use role play in their behaviour rehearsal technique. This helps counsellors to explore the ways in which their clients think about their various roles and how they might think and act differently, and also changes clients' anticipations of the likely outcomes of trying out the roles in real life. Additionally, sometimes clients use imagery in their behaviour rehearsal homework by imagining coping with an anxiety-engendering role before actually playing it.

Another form of role play, focused on changing thoughts and influenced by Moreno, is Kelly's fixed-role therapy.[49] Here the client writes a self-characterization and possibly also completes a self-description type of personality inventory. One or more counsellors read and re-read the self-characterization and attempt to write a new personality sketch, the fixed-role sketch, suitable for enactment by the client. This sketch invites the client, under a protective screen of make-believe, to explore behaviours in sharp contrast to the self-characterization and thus test new hypotheses about living. The client is rehearsed in the role and asked to enact it at all times and in all situations. Concurrently the client also has several interview sessions with the counsellor for help in meeting specific situations and for general discussion. Fixed-role enactments are often of two weeks' duration, but may be for as long as three months. The fixed-role procedure may be used in conjunction with other procedures or by itself.

Encouraging Performance

Actual performance of a behaviour or way of living can be a cogent way of altering thinking, though frequently performance is the result of preparatory work involving other thinking-focused interventions. Many counsellors, for example behavioural and rational-emotive, arrange that clients practise desired behaviours by way of homework assignments. Sometimes these assignments are graded in ascending order of difficulty to build up clients' confidence that they can handle more difficult situations. Reality testing is another way of viewing client performance of desired behaviours. Successful performance generates positive evidence which, if ready, clients can integrate into their self-conceptions. Likewise, unsuccessful performance may generate failure anticipations or lack of self-efficacy regarding competence at a given task. Often, during and after reality testing, clients notice that their anticipations about the task, for example giving a talk in public, were much more negative than warranted, thus challenging previously held thoughts.

Skills Training

Many of the interventions discussed so far are likely to have the effect of improving clients' thinking skills outside counselling. Sometimes counsellors deliberately and systematically train their clients in the skills of effective thinking. Some areas of training in effective thinking include decision-making,[50] problem-solving,[51] and self-control.[52,53]

Training in self-instructional methods is an increasingly important counsellor intervention. We have mentioned Meichenbaum's interest in altering faulty client self-statements. He describes a 'stress inoculation' training procedure for treating clients with intense phobic fears.[54] The programme involved three elements: (a) discussion of the nature of emotion and stress reactions; (b) rehearsing coping skills; and (c) testing those skills under actual stress conditions. The counsellor suggested that the course of stress reactions follows four stages: preparing for, confronting or handling, coping with the feeling of being overwhelmed, and reinforcing oneself for having coped with a stressful situation. Clients were encouraged to identify self-statements which they could use during each stage. Sample coping self-statements were: preparing for a stressor, 'Just think about what you can do about it. That's better than getting anxious'; confronting and handling a stressor, 'You can convince yourself to do it. You can reason your fears away'; coping with the feeling of being overwhelmed, 'Don't try to eliminate fear totally, just keep it manageable'; and reinforcing self-statements, 'It's getting better each time you use the procedures'.[55] Clients then rehearsed self-instruction, first aloud, and then silently. Also, they were taught and practised relaxation and breathing exercises. Once the self-instruction techniques and relaxation skills were mastered, clients practised using them in actual stressful situations, such as watching a gruesome film.

Cautela's covert sensitization is another treatment approach involving training the client in thinking self-help skills.[56] Covert sensitization involves imaginal punishment of maladaptive approach behaviours. For instance, as soon as alcoholics have thought of drinking or are about to drink, they are asked to imagine aversive situations in detail, for example nausea and vomiting all over themselves. They are also asked to imagine a feeling of relief as they turn away from the pleasurable object. After several practice trials in the counsellor's office, clients are instructed to continue treatment with regular homework assignments involving further practice. Covert sensitization, like self-instruction, is a control of thinking procedure focusing on manipulating inner rather than outer controlling events.

Use of Audio-visual Aids and Written Homework

Audio-visual aids may fruitfully be used in individual or group work focusing on thinking difficulties. For instance, a blackboard or a flip-chart may be used for teaching concepts, such as those of transactional analysis. Also, individual clients' thoughts are sometimes highlighted for them by having them visually, as well as aurally, presented. For example, using a flip-chart, the counsellor may work with a client in eliciting his significant faulty internal rules and misattributions and then reformulating them. Films, cassettes and tapes may also be used to present material to clients. Furthermore, the effectiveness of some counselling interviews may be heightened by cassette-recording them and then asking the client to play the recording as a homework assignment, thus providing a further, and possibly more relaxed, opportunity for learning from the interview.

Some counsellors use homework sheets as an adjunct to their interviews. For instance, a rational-emotive counsellor may get a client to fill out a rational self-help form: starting with *A*, the activating experiences or events; and analysing *B*, rational and irrational beliefs; *C*, the desirable and undesirable emotional and behavioural consequences; *D*, disputing the beliefs in the form of questions ('Why is it awful to get rejected for a job?'); and *E*, the cognitive, emotional and behavioural effects of disputing irrational beliefs.[57] Other counsellors may also use brief questionnaires in which clients are asked to assess themselves in one or more areas of thinking difficulty or to analyse the relevant thoughts in a situation in which they are experiencing difficulty, such as a worker-boss or marriage relationship. Also, in behavioural counselling, clients may regularly complete forms designed to monitor their thinking and behaviour, including its antecedents and consequences.

ISSUES AND HAZARDS

There are a number of issues, which are also potential hazards, in using interventions focused on clients' thinking. These include the following.

Counsellor Direction

An important issue here is the degree to which counselling should be centred within the client's frame of reference, or whether there should be counsellor direction. Counsellors focusing on their clients' areas of faulty thinking are implementing a degree of counsellor direction. At worst, this direction may involve assuming power over clients and controlling them against their interests. What may be involved is teaching clients not only how to think, but also what to think. Thus clients may be taken even further from valuing their own experiencing and risk additional loss of self-esteem. Furthermore, they may develop an unhealthy dependence on their counsellors.

Use of Questions

Related to the area of counsellor direction is that of use of questions by the counsellor. Questions may often be used beneficially to help the counsellor to assess the client, to aid the client in self-exploration, and to focus the client's attention on various areas of thinking and other difficulties. However, maladroit use of questions can block and sometimes curtail the counselling process. Clients may resent being under interrogation, possibly in sensitive areas. Also, they may feel that counsellors are treating them as objects rather than as people and are more intent on pursuing their own line of questioning than on genuinely understanding their concerns.

Intellectualization

An approach focused on thinking may be criticized for paying insufficient attention to clients' needs for experiencing feelings. What may happen is that a rather controlled counsellor interviews the client in a rather controlled and intellectual way, with the outcome being less satisfactory than if the counsellor had possessed the skills to facilitate experiencing as well as thinking. The problem for some clients is that they are already remote from their experiencing and an approach which is too focused on thinking may sustain this remoteness. Also, sometimes counsellors collude in the defences of their clients, such as intellectualization and rationalization.

Projection

One sense in which projection is used here is that the difficulties focused on are those of the counsellor rather than those of the client. For instance, some counsellors may focus on client anger or sexuality, masking their own unresolved needs. Similarly, they may consistently and persistently perceive certain faulty internal rules, defences or misattributions which relate more to themselves than to their clients.

Counsellors may also project their theoretical frameworks onto their clients. An accusation sometimes levelled at Freudian psychoanalysis is that clients are asked to accept interpretations from a theoretical framework which may have limited relevance to their concerns. The same comment may be made about other counselling approaches, such as rational-emotive therapy, transactional analysis and behavioural counselling; indeed, possibly also about person-centred counselling.

Timing and Resistance

On a number of occasions we have mentioned the importance of timing for counsellor interventions focusing on their clients' thinking. Since these interventions tend to focus on altering habitual processes of thinking or ways of perceiving specific situations, there is always the risk that clients are not ready for the intervention and may, in fact, strongly resist them. Various kinds of confrontations, interpretations and lines of focused exploration may either initially or consistently be rejected by a client. Sometimes the counsellor may return later to an area which has initially been rejected. On other occasions this may not be necessary, since the client's thinking may have altered in the period between interviews. Another possibility is to engage in focused exploration of the client's resistance, but even this needs to be well timed. Yet another consideration is that the client's resistance is justified and that the counsellor's intervention may have been inaccurate and irrelevant. In such instances counsellors may need to explore their own resistances.

Above we have mentioned five potential pitfalls for counsellors making interventions focused on their clients' thinking difficulties. Nevertheless, such interventions can, in varying degrees, be beneficial for many clients. Perhaps the criteria for good interventions focusing on clients' thoughts and styles of thinking are common to all counselling approaches. A good intervention is accurate, relevant, well expressed, well timed and develops rather than diminishes the ability of clients to take effective direction of their own lives.

PRACTICAL EXERCISES AND QUESTIONS

It may help you to develop your skills and knowledge of the material in this chapter if, either individually or as part of a group, you perform the following exercises and answer the following questions.

Practical Exercises

1.　　Work as counsellor with a partner as client and practise your skills of focused exploration in the following areas:

　　(a)　self-evaluations and internal rules;
　　(b)　information at variance with self-conceptions;
　　(c)　attributions of causality and of responsibility.

2.　　Work as counsellor with a partner as client and practise your skills of confrontation, focusing on such areas as:

　　(a)　discrepancy between partner's utterances and behaviour in counselling;

　　(b)　discrepancy between partner's self-evaluation and your perception of your partner's assets;

　　(c)　discrepancy between what is being said and what is left unsaid by your partner concerning your counsellor-client relationship;

　　(d)　discrepancy between your partner's utterances in and behaviour outside counselling.

3.　　Working as counsellor with a partner as client, identify one or more of his or her dysfunctional internal rules, and dispute with him or her the reasoning for the internal rule(s). Then formulate a more appropriate internal rule(s).

4.　　Work as counsellor with a partner as client and make out a brief self-control programme to alter one of his or her unwanted behaviours. The programme should include:

　　(a)　a clearly stated goal;
　　(b)　the ways of monitoring current behaviour to collect baseline data;
　　(c)　the self-reinforcers which might be applied;
　　(d)　an outline of the plan to achieve the goal;
　　(e)　the contingencies for self-reinforcement.

5.   Work as counsellor with a partner as client and write out a series of self-instructional statements for an area which causes him or her stress. List a minimum of two statements in each of the following categories:

  (a)   preparing for the stressful situations;
  (b)   confronting and handling the stressful situation;
  (c)   coping with the feeling of being overwhelmed in the stressful situation;
  (d)   making self-reinforcing statements on completion of the task.

6.   Work as counsellor with a partner as client and practise making some:

  (a)   shallow interpretations;
  (b)   deeper interpretations.

  Then, afterwards, mutually explore your feelings and thoughts concerning making and being the recipient of these interpretations.

7.   Work as counsellor with a partner as client on one of his or her specific problems in need of solving. Cover the following areas:
  (a)   orientation to problem-solving;
  (b)   analysis of the problem;
  (c)   decision-making;
  (d)   action planning.

Questions

1.   Critically discuss the use of counsellor interventions focusing on client areas of thinking difficulty. When are they justified and why?

2.   List at least three significant internal rules or self-standards by which you evaluate yourself:

  (a)   positively;
  (b)   negatively.

3.   What are the main ways in which you handle information at variance with your self-conceptions?

4.   To what extent do you consider that you accurately attribute responsibility for what has happened and is happening in your life? Give specific examples of:
  (a)   accurate attribution of responsibility;
  (b)   inaccurate attribution of responsibility.

5.   Assess the degree to which you are realistic in your anticipations of risk, gain and competence. Cite specific instances as evidence for your answers.

NOTES

1. Raimy, V. (1977) *Misunderstandings of the Self*. London: Jossey-Bass.
2. Beck, A. T. (1976) *Cognitive Therapy and Emotional Disorders*. New York: International Universities Press.
3. Kelly, G. A. (1955) *A Theory of Personality: The Psychology of Personal Constructs*. New York: W. W. Norton.
4. Ryle, A. (1979) The focus in brief intensive psychotherapy. *British Journal of Psychiatry*, **134,** 46–54.
5. Hobbs, N. (1962) Sources of gain in psychotherapy. *American Psychologist*, **17,** 746. Full reference pp. 741–747.
6. Laing, R. D. (1969) *The Politics of the Family* pp. 89–102. London: Tavistock Publications.
7. *Ibid.* p. 119.
8. Jones, E. E., Kanouse, D. E., Kelley, H. H., Nisbett, R. E., Valins, S. & Weiner, B. (eds) (1971) *Attribution: Perceiving the Causes of Behavior* p. XI. Morriston, NJ: General Learning Press.
9. Shaver, K. G. (1975) *An Introduction to Attribution Processes* pp. 4–5. Cambridge, Massachusetts: Winthrop.
10. Strong, S. R. (1978) Social psychological approach to psychotherapy research. In S. L. Garfield and A. E. Bergin (eds), *Handbook of Psychotherapy and Behavior Change: An Empirical Analysis* (2nd ed.) p. 115. New York: Wiley. Full reference pp. 101–135.
11. Weiner, B., Frieze, I., Kukla, A., Reed, L., Rest, S. & Rosenbaum, R. M. (1971) Perceiving the courses of success and failure. In Jones, E. E., Kanouse, D. E., Kelley, H. H., Nisbett, R. E., Valins, S. & Weiner, B. *Attribution: Perceiving the Causes of Behavior* p. 96. Morriston, NJ: General Learning Press.
12. Weiner, B. & Kukla, A. (1970) An attributional analysis of achievement motivation. *Journal of Personality and Social Psychology*, **15,** 1–20.
13. Strong, S. R. (1978) Social psychological approach to psychotherapy research. In S. L. Garfield and A. E. Bergin (eds), *Handbook of Psychotherapy and Behavior Change: An Empirical Analysis* (2nd ed.) p. 123. New York: Wiley.
14. Kelly, G. A. (1955) *A Theory of Personality: The Psychology of Personal Constructs* p. 157. New York: W. W. Norton.
15. Ryle, A. (1979) The focus in brief intensive psychotherapy. *British Journal of Psychiatry*, **134,** 48.
16. White, R. W. (1959) Motivation reconsidered: the concept of competence. *Psychological Review*, **66,** 297–333.
17. White, R. W. (1973) The concept of healthy personality: what do we really mean? *The Counseling Psychologist*, **4,** 2, 3–12.
18. Rotter, J. B. (1966) Generalized expectancies for internal versus external control of reinforcement. *Psychological Monographs*, **80,** No. 1, whole No. 609.
19. Rotter, J. B. (1975) Some problems and misconceptions related to the construct of internal versus external control of reinforcement. *Journal of Counsulting and Clinical Psychology*, **43,** 56–67.
20. Beck, A. T. (1976) *Cognitive Therapy and Emotional Disorders* p. 41. New York: International Universities Press.
21. Piaget, J. (1932) *The Moral Judgment of the Child*. London: Routledge and Kegan Paul.
22. Hoffman, M. L. (1970) Moral development. In P. H. Mussen (ed.), *Carmichael's Manual of Child Psychology. Volume 2* (3rd ed.) pp. 261–349. New York: Wiley.
23. Allport, G. W. (1955) *Becoming*. New Haven: Yale University Press.
24. Mowrer, O. H. (1966) *Abnormal Reactions or Actions?* p. 32. Dubuque, Iowa: W. C. Brown.
25. May, R. (1972) Existential therapy. In J. T. Huber and H. L. Millman (eds), *Goals and Behavior in Psychotherapy and Counseling* p. 240. Columbus, Ohio: Merrill

26. Combs, A. W. & Snygg, D. (1959) *Individual Behavior* (rev. ed.) pp. 170–172. New York: Harper and Row.
27. Ryle, A. (1979) The focus in brief intensive psychotherapy. *British Journal of Psychiatry*, **134,** 47.
28. Beck, A. T. (1976) *Cognitive Therapy and Emotional Disorders* pp. 245–246. New York: International University Press.
29. Cronbach, L. & Gleser, G. C. (1957) *Psychological Tests and Personnel Decisions* pp. 16–27. Urbana: University of Illinois Press.
30. Gelatt, H. B. (1962) Decision-making: a conceptual frame of reference for counseling. *Journal of Counseling Psychology*, **9,** 240–245.
31. Krumboltz, J. D. & Baker, R. D. (1973) Behavioral counseling for vocational decisions. In H. Borow (ed.), *Career Guidance for a New Age* p. 240. Boston: Houghton Mifflin. Full reference pp. 235–283.
32. Goldfried, M. R. & Davison, G. C. (1976) *Clinical Behavior Therapy* p. 188. New York: Holt, Rinehart and Winston.
33. Kanfer, F. H. (1975) Self-management methods. In F. H. Kanfer and A. P. Goldstein (eds), *Helping People Change* p. 312. New York: Pergamon Press. Full reference pp. 309–355.
34. Sharpe, R. & Lewis, D. (1976) *The Success Factor* pp. 55–57. London: Souvenir Press.
35. Thoresen, C. E. & Mahoney, M. J. (1974) *Behavioral Self-control* pp. 1–22. New York: Holt, Rinehart and Winston.
36. Meichenbaum, D. (1975) Self-instructional methods. In F. H. Kanfer and A. P. Goldstein (eds), *Helping People Change* pp. 357–391. New York: Pergamon Press.
37. Mahoney, M. J. & Arnkoff, D. B. (1978) Cognitive and self-control therapies. In S. L. Garfield and A. E. Bergin (eds), *Handbook of Psychotherapy and Behavior Change* (2nd ed.) p. 705. New York: Wiley. Full reference pp. 689–772.
38. Meichenbaum, D. (1975) Self-instructional methods. In F. H. Kanfer and A. P. Goldstein (eds), *Helping People Change* p. 370. New York: Pergamon Press.
39. Wolpe, J. (1973) *The Practice of Behavior Therapy* (2nd ed.) p. 56. Oxford: Pergamon.
40. The counsellor was the author.
41. Zaro, J. S., Barach, R., Nedelman, D. J. & Dreiblatt, I. S. (1977) *A Guide for Beginning Psychotherapists* p. 104. Cambridge: Cambridge University Press.
42. Carkhuff, R. R. (1969) *Helping and Human Relations: Volume 1, Selection and Training* pp. 181–184. New York: Holt, Rinehart and Winston.
43. Carkhuff, R. R. (1969) *Helping and Human Relations: Volume 2, Practice and Research* pp. 87–89. New York: Holt, Rinehart and Winston.
44. *Ibid.* pp. 92–95.
45. Carkhuff, R. R. (1969) *Helping and Human Relations: Volume 1, Selection and Training* pp. 189–191. New York: Holt, Rinehart and Winston.
46. Berenson, B. G., Mitchell, K. M. & Laney, R. C. (1968) Level of therapist functioning, types of confrontation and type of patient. *Journal of Clinical Psychology* **24,** 111–113.
47. Raimy, V. (1977) *Misunderstandings of the Self* p. 49. London: Jossey-Bass.
48. Moreno, J. L. (1959) Psychodrama. In S. Arieti (ed.), *American Handbook of Psychiatry* (*vol. 2*) pp. 1375–1396. New York: Basic Books.
49. Kelly, G. A. (1955) *The Psychology of Personal Constructs: Volume 1* pp. 360–451. New York: Norton.
50. Krumboltz, J. D. & Baker, R. D. (1973) Behavioral counseling for vocational decisions. In H. Borow (ed.), *Career Guidance for New Age* pp. 235–283. Boston: Houghton Mifflin.
51. Goldfried, M. R. & Davison, G. C. (1976) *Clinical Behavior Therapy* pp. 186–207. New York: Holt, Rinehart and Winston.
52. Thoresen, C. E. & Ewart, C. K. (1976) Behavioral self-control and career development. *The Counseling Psychologist*, **6,** 3, 29–43.
53. Thoresen, C. E. & Mahoney, M. J. (1974) *Behavioral Self-control.* New York: Holt, Rinehart and Winston.
54. Meichenbaum, D. (1975) Self-instructional methods. In F. H. Kanfer and A. P. Goldstein

(eds), *Helping People Change* pp. 369–372. New York: Pergamon Press.
55. *Ibid.* p. 371.
56. Cautela, J. R. (1967) Covert sensitization. *Psychological Reports*, **20**, 459–468.
57. Ellis, A. (1976) Rational self-help form. New York: Institute for Rational Living.

15 – Personal, Marital and Sexual Relationship Concerns

SUMMARY: *The chapter begins by discussing the nature of marriage, marital disharmony and breakdown, and some distinctive features of marital as contrasted with other kinds of counselling. Relationships can be complex because of such factors as limitations of awareness by both parties, overt and covert communication, the contexts and rules under which they take place, and distorted thinking. Basically relationships involve sending and receiving verbal, vocal and bodily communications. Receiving information involves effective listening. Counsellors can help their clients to listen better by providing an empathic relationship in which they may learn to be more open to their own experiencing and, hence, more free to listen to others. Client listening may also be improved by appropriate thinking-focused interventions and by skills training. Sending information involves effective self-disclosure. Again, counsellors can help their clients to self-disclose better by helping them to become more in touch with their own experiencing. The way clients think is inextricably related to their self-disclosures. For instance, counsellors may focus on rules about disclosure, positive and negative evaluations of their personal characteristics, attributions of causality and responsibility, and anticipations of risk and gain concerning their disclosures. The notion of appropriate self-disclosure is discussed and 12 self-disclosure skills, such as sending 'I' messages and reciprocity, are reviewed. Conflict resolution is an important application of good listening and self-disclosure. Counsellors may focus on helping their clients to reduce aversive communication, increase helpful communication, increase positive behaviours, and improve their abilities at negotiation and problem-solving.*

Sexual relations also involve effective listening and self-disclosing. The human sexual response cycle is described. Mention is made of issues in sexual relationship counselling such as individual or conjoint counselling, degree of focus, use of co-counsellors, and the duration of counselling. Approaches to sexual relationship concerns range from enhancing unsatisfactory relationships to remedying specific sexual dysfunctions. Sensate focus helps couples to 'think and feel' sensuously. Counsellors may engage in focused exploration of the ways in which their clients think about sex, including whether they consider it sinful or dirty, their body image, and their fears about their own and

their partner's performance. The main female and male sexual dysfunctions are
described, along with specific exercises which may be used in remedying them. Some
data are presented about the incidence of bisexual and homosexual orientation.
Counsellors may work to improve existing homosexual relationships. Also, they may
work with clients with sexual identity concerns in such areas as correcting faulty
self-labelling, increasing heterosexual behaviour, accepting homosexual behaviour, and
facilitating 'coming out', or publicly proclaiming homosexual tendencies. Counselling
approaches for sexual identity concerns are described briefly.

In the previous chapter we reviewed some ways in which counsellors might focus on
their clients' thinking difficulties and expressed sympathy with the notion that all
counselling involves altering thinking. In this chapter we discuss some ways in which
counsellors, beyond offering a fundamental counselling relationship, may approach
their clients' personal, marital and sexual relationship concerns. As with thinking
difficulties, relationship difficulties are pervasive among clients and, hence, improving
clients' effectiveness at relationships is a widespread counselling objective.

MARITAL RELATIONSHIPS

In general this chapter focuses on partner relationships rather than on marital
relationships as such. However, there are some distinctive issues concerning marital as
contrasted with other kinds of partner relationships and we wish to acknowledge some
of these before taking a less specific approach.

The Nature of Marriage

Though there are different views of marriage in Western society, the predominant
one is still that of a life-long psychological, legal and financial commitment on the part
of each partner. Furthermore, most marriages involve children and hence the
commitment becomes broadened to the family as well as to the partners' relationship.
Thus the major distinguishing feature of marital as contrasted with other heterosexual
partner relationships is that of the level of commitment and, as time goes by,
emotional investment in the relationship. Consequently many of the issues and strains
which occur in any partner relationship may occur with greater intensity in marriage.
Such issues include those involving: religious, racial and ethnic differences; power and
decision-making; different expectations from the relationship; the extent to which
gender roles are different; amount and nature of time spent together; quantity and
quality of sex life; friends and social life; budgeting; housing; and miscellaneous
issues, such as tidiness. Other issues more specific to marriage include: number of
children; rearing of children; and treatment of in-laws.[1] Furthermore, there are

several psychological issues, such as the degree of dependency or autonomy of each partner, and the extent to which they are reacting to the current relationship in maladaptive ways derived from their past experiences of intimacy in their initial family. The other side of the picture is that not only may the issues be more intense, but the partners' commitment to working through the issues may be greater than outside marriage, though this is not always so.

Marital Disharmony and Breakdown

In any continuing relationship there are bound to be areas of difference of opinion, if not conflict. Many marriages, however, suffer from more severe forms of disharmony in which the partners either covertly or overtly harm their own, each other's and their children's self-realizing. Table 15.1 shows that, during the 1961–1975 period, while the

Table 15.1 *Marriages and divorces in England and Wales 1961–1975*[2]

| Year | Marriages (000s) | Divorces | |
		Petitions filed (000s)	Absolute decrees (000s)
1961	346.7	31.9	25.4
1966	384.5	46.6	39.1
1971	404.7	110.9	74.4
1975	380.6	140.1	120.5

number of marriages in England and Wales remained relatively stable, the number of divorces increased sharply. The introduction of the more liberal 1969 Divorce Reform Act and the readier availability of legal aid contributed to the increase in divorces. Nevertheless, Table 15.1 indicates that there is much marital disharmony in Britain, especially since the data include neither those separated but not divorced or filing for divorce, nor those who are unhappily still living together, possibly because of family commitments. Furthermore, the impact of divorce is not restricted to marital partners, as evidenced by the 120 522 couples in England and Wales who were granted a decree absolute in 1975 having 202 475 children, of whom 145 096 were under 16 years old.[3]

Dominian considers that marital breakdown can be divided into two phases. During the first five years of marriage, breakdown is more likely to occur through failure to establish the necessary minimum emotional and physical relationship. Later stresses include: partners maturing at different rates; the reliving of unresolved emotional difficulties with parents, with the spouse being related to as the unsatisfactory parent; and the gaps left by children leaving the home.[4] Marriages are continuing processes which take place in changing social contexts and a further reason for disharmony and breakdown may be that, whereas previously 'marital disharmony occurred in a social context strongly supportive of the institution of Christian marriage', nowadays 'society and the law have become less concerned with marriage as an institution than as a source of personal well-being and happiness'.[5] Since marriages are increasingly based on consent not only at the start of but during their lives, this leaves them more vulnerable to withdrawal of that consent by either or both partners.

Marital Counselling

Allied with marriage being a distinctive kind of relationship, there may be some special issues in counselling married people. In counselling involving partners in any relationship, there are issues concerning whether only one or both partners are willing to be clients. Especially in marital work, if one partner is prepared to seek outside assistance, this may be perceived as disloyalty by the other partner. Even where both partners are prepared to seek counselling, there are considerations concerning the use of a single counsellor or of dual-counsellor teams as well as the extent to which partners should be interviewed together or separately.

Marital partners may pressurize the counsellor to collude in their definition of reality instead of being prepared to explore their own contribution to the disharmony and its possible solution. Counsellors may be especially at risk of colluding when they are seeing only one of the partners and hence hearing only one side of the story. Other issues in marital counselling include the long-standing nature of many of the problems, with the corresponding emotional investment of the partners in their defences. Furthermore, marital counsellors need to be skilled at handling greatly heightened emotionality, such as anger and depression. Also, in some instances, the focus of marital counselling may best be extended to family counselling in which the children's perceptions and needs can be directly considered.

ASSUMPTIONS CONCERNING RELATIONSHIPS

Having acknowledged that both marital relationships and marital counselling are somewhat different from other relationships and other relationship counselling, we now focus on areas of common ground. At first glance a focus on relationship difficulties might appear a simple matter of teaching the correct social skills. However, this is often not the case. Thus it is worth exploring some of the reasons why the areas of personal, marital and sexual relationships can be complex. These reasons include the following

Illusion of Individuality and Restricted Awareness

A common illusion is that of a greater degree of autonomy than we actually possess. Thus, when the personal pronoun 'I' is used, we may be motivated more by conditions of worth or injunctions than by our own valuing process or unique individuality. Sullivan observes: 'It is, I believe, a statistically demonstrable fact that the interpersonal relations of any person, even though he feels very full of the conviction of his individuality, are under ordinary circumstances rather strikingly restricted in variety, freedom you might say'.[6]

Another way of viewing the illusion of individuality is that it restricts awareness. For effective personal relationships, people need inner empathy or awareness of their own needs and experiencing so that they may be adequately attuned to and realistically perceive other people's needs and experiencing. A lack of inner empathy coupled with an illusion of more individuality than is actually the case is likely to make for poor communication, especially if the other person or persons in the relationship share similar restrictions.

The Johari window, a modified version of which is depicted in Figure 15.1, helps to

A Known to others Known to ourselves	B Known to others Not known to ourselves
C Not known to others Known to ourselves	D Not known to others Not known to ourselves

Figure 15.1   Modified version of the Johari window.

illustrate some of the problems of awareness occurring in relationships.[7] Area A may be viewed as the open area; area B, the blind; area C, the secret; and area D, the unconscious.[8] In general, the purpose of counselling focused on relationship concerns is to increase area A or, stated differently, to increase honest and open communication.

Overt and Covert Communication

Argyle observes: 'In discussions of communication it is usually supposed that there is an encoder, a message, and a decoder. We need to discover the meaning of particular signals to encoders and decoders'.[9] Satir puts the same point another way when she states that a communication can be said to have at least two levels: (a) a *denotative* level, the literal content; and (b) a *metacommunicative* level, which is a comment on the literal content as well as on the nature of the relationship between the people involved.[10] Metacommunication involves non-verbal and para-verbal communication which may be congruent or incongruent with the accompanying literal or verbal communication. In other words, the covert communication may contradict and be more significant than the overt communication. In any event, it needs to be acurately decoded, a process which is more likely to happen if the receiver is relatively unconstricted by limitations of awareness.

People camouflage their real meanings where they do not feel safe. Sometimes this camouflaging is intentional and realistic, such as when sending a message to a receiver who has limited ability to absorb information at variance with her self-concept. On other occasions the camouflaging may be both unintentional and unrealistic. Here it may be motivated by earlier habits of blocking off full communication, possibly to avoid the prospect of parental disapproval. Sometimes what is thought and felt is suppressed and does not get communicated at all. At other times, both the experiencing and the awareness of the process of blocking off the experiencing are repressed and, again, there is no communication. People may also camouflage their real meanings to maintain their own self-esteem. For instance, they may find it easier to acknowledge anger than anxiety and so use anger to mask anxiety.

Contexts and Rules

Relationships are heavily influenced by their cultural, social and situational contexts. There are explicit and implicit rules which establish the nature and limits of permissible behaviour in various contexts. For example, the same woman may adhere to different rules about the amount and contact of her talking, depending on whether she is attending a committee meeting, having a dinner party with friends, or spending a quiet evening with her husband. Rules, or expectations of appropriate behaviour, may be influenced by other personal and situational variables. Personal variables include culture, social class, marital state, age and gender. An instance concerning gender is that in the past assertive behaviour has tended to be considered more appropriate for males than for females. Situational variables include tasks and goals, such as whether the individual is eating, buying or working.[11] Sexual behaviour is also influenced by contexts and rules. Writing of cultural themes in sexuality, Tiefer observes: 'Every society fashions the development and expression of sexuality in a unique fashion, tailored to fit the social, political and economic conditions of its own existence'.[12] An important issue concerning the rules of relationship behaviour in various contexts is whether they promote or prevent human happiness and fulfilment.

Thinking Aspects of Relationships

In addition to involving feelings and actions, relationships take place between thinking people in social contexts. Figure 15.2 attempts to illustrate some relevant thoughts in a two-person relationship. Many of these areas of thinking were described in the previous chapter, and their relevance to counselling focusing on effective relating will be illustrated here in a subsequent section on self-disclosure. Suffice it for now to indicate that thinking plays a large part before, during and after communicating. In fact, it is a chain-like process in which evaluations of the outcomes of previous communications affect the nature of and anticipations about future communications. A final point is that, on both sides, perception of self and other may be inaccurate. Sullivan used the term 'personification' to illustrate the ways in which people made up or constructed thought images of themselves and others.[13] Putting this another way, my personification of me is in a relationship with my personification of you and *vice versa*. Sullivan acknowledged that, in the psychiatric interview, the '*real* characteristics of the other fellow . . . may be of negligible importance to the interpersonal situation. This we call *parataxic distortion*'.[14] Whether they are called parataxic distortions, transferences or unrealistic perceptions, the purpose of counselling is to minimize distorted cognitions which impede genuine person to person relationships.

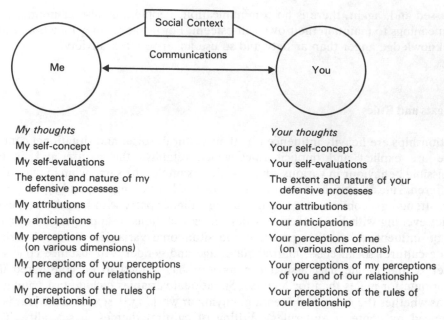

Figure 15.2   Illustration of some relevant areas of thinking in a two-person relationship.

Verbal, Vocal and Bodily Communication

In Chapter 11 we discussed empathy in terms of verbal, non-verbal and para-verbal considerations. Already in this chapter we have mentioned the power of metacommunications and the need to decode verbal messages. Sometimes, also, non-verbal language may be used to replace language and express emotions. Table 15.2 depicts some areas of vocal or para-verbal and of bodily or non-verbal communication. An interesting aspect of vocal and bodily communication is that frequently it falls into area B (known to others, not known to ourselves) on the Johari window. Thus, it would appear that these signals are less easy to bring under conscious control and therefore are more likely to be genuine. Ekman and Friesen have written of non-verbal movements, such as those of arms and legs, as conceivable leakages which may be clues to deception.[15] It is possible, however, for vocal and bodily communication to be deliberately manipulated in such a way as to disguise real motivation, such as the smile which indicates friendliness but may mask the attempt of one individual to take advantage of another. Much of the communication in counselling interviews takes place on the vocal and bodily level. A further dimension of non-verbal communication relates to the furnishing and decoration of the area in which counselling takes place.

Table 15.2 *Some areas and dimensions of vocal and bodily communication*

A. Vocal areas (para-verbals)	
Area	*Illustrative dimensions*
Volume	Loudness, quietness, audibility
Stress	Modulated, unmodulated
Pitch	High, low
Clarity	Good enunciation, mumbling, slurring
Pace	Fast, slow, ease of following
Timing	Late, early
Speech disturbances	Stammering, repetition

B. Bodily areas (non-verbals)	
Area	*Illustrative dimensions*
Proximity	Closeness, distance, ability to touch
Posture lean	Forwards, backwards
Posture orientation	Facing, turned away
Posture focus	Tense, relaxed, rigid, slouched
Clothes	Conforming, rebellious, attractive, dull, showing group identification
Physique	Thinness, fatness, muscularity
Hair	Length, shortness styling
Grooming	Neat, unkempt, clean, dirty
Face	Expressive of emotions, blank
Gaze	Staring, avoidance of eye contact
Gesture	Amount, variety
Smell	Body odour present, deodorized, fragrant, pungent
Touch	Intimacy, aggression, part of a social ritual

Relationships as Sending and Receiving Information

All relationships, whether they are personal, marital, sexual or otherwise, involve a process of sending and receiving information. Senders of information are also receivers and receivers of information are also senders. Sending and receiving information takes place in the experiential, thinking and action modalities. For instance, as senders, we may experience a feeling, put it into words, think whether it is appropriate to say it, then say it, using verbal, vocal and bodily communication. As receivers, we may experience the verbal, vocal and bodily communication of another's message, decode it, think about its consequences, possibly frame a response, and so on. As the interaction progresses, both parties are assessing the information and making decisions such as whether and at what level they wish to stay in the relationship. Thus a continuing or dynamic process of social co-ordination is going on throughout a relationship. In the sections which follow we look at three areas of relationships: (a) *receiving information*, or listening; (b) *sending information*, or self-disclosure; and (c) *conflict resolution*, or handling differences. All of these are areas on which counsellors may wish to focus, be it in individual counselling with one person; or conjoint counselling, one counsellor with the two partners in a relationship; or group counselling, in which the group may be composed of individuals and/or couples.

RECEIVING INFORMATION: LISTENING

An important aspect of any relationship, be it between friends, marital partners, or parents and their children, is the capacity to listen. Relationships often suffer because one or both people feel they are not, or only partially, understood. Recently there has been increased emphasis on 'active listening' as a way to help children to feel accepted by their parents[16] and 'empathic responding' as a basic skill of relationship enhancement between partners.[17] We have already described training counsellors in empathic responding (see Chapter 11), which we called the fundamental counselling relationship. In this section we focus on ways in which counsellors may help their clients to listen better.

Listening and Experiencing

An important aspect of accurate listening is that the receivers be aware of or open to their own experiencing. Since all clients have difficulty in this area and some have great difficulty, counsellors may have to engage in basic empathy relationships with their clients to free them to acknowledge their own thoughts and feelings and hence be less restricted and defensive in receiving information from others. For instance, it may be very difficult for clients who feel misunderstood to acknowledge that their own remoteness from their experiencing may be causing them to misunderstand others. It is also difficult for clients with limited access to their own emotionality to be sensitive to the emotions of others.

The basis for listening to others is to be able to listen accurately to oneself. Putting this another way, though the two are interrelated, a reasonable degree of inner empathy or awareness of one's own thoughts and feelings precedes outer empathy or awareness of another's thoughts and feelings. Limited inner empathy will probably lead to limited outer empathy. Both inner and outer empathy may be further blocked when clients are striving to maintain their self-esteem in a relationship. Thus there can be a number of reasons why clients do not listen to their own experiencing. Some of those reasons relate to the injunctions and conditions of worth derived from their past. However, especially where there is a power struggle between partners, the level of threat to one or both partners may be so high that it provides present reasons which reinforce the blocking effect of past injunctions.

A crucial role of counsellors in helping many clients to listen is to reduce their anxiety level to the point where they can acknowledge much more of their experiencing and hence not engage in processes which Sullivan aptly called 'selective inattention'.[18] Counsellors need to offer an empathic relationship to all clients. However, with less disturbed clients they may use additional interventions, such as focusing on faulty thinking. On the other hand, with severely disturbed clients, a continuing empathic relationship with few embellishments may be indicated to the point where they feel safe enough to have a reasonable capacity to listen to themselves and hence be able to explore their relationships with others.

Listening and Thinking

Thinking is involved in listening in a number of ways. For instance, just as a disturbed listener may decode messages to receive what is not there, the good listener decodes messages to receive their real meaning. As well as a capacity for emotionally experiencing the message, this may entail thinking about its verbal, vocal and bodily aspects. Where appropriate, counsellors may use focused exploration to help to make clients more aware of their thought processes in decoding information from others. For instance, by what signals do clients know that the messages they receive are received correctly? Another focus of exploration is clients' awareness of the context and rules of the relationships in which communications take place.

Client listening skills may also be improved by focused exploration of a number of areas of thinking difficulty mentioned in Chapter 14. For example, a person's internal rules, self-evaluations, evaluations of others, and expectations of a situation may interfere with effective listening. Transference, where a client relates to a personified other in terms of a past relationship, impairs effective listening. Consistent attribution of blame to the other partner for what is wrong in a relationship definitely interferes with good mutual listening. Having 'tunnel' vision about another person causes 'tunnel' listening. Furthermore, counsellors may need to confront their clients with the ways in which their defensive mechanisms and psychological games interfere with their ability to listen to themselves and to others.

Listening and Action

Listening and acting come together when a receiver becomes a sender and responds to another's communication. The response focused on here is that of active listening, or empathic responding. Needless to say, empathic responding involves thought processes, such as the ability to get inside another's frame of reference and to understand her personal meanings and emotional nuances. Also, empathic responding involves sufficient thought to formulate a clear and specific response in language appropriate to the occasion.

As well as the experiential and thinking emphases mentioned earlier, there are a number of counsellor strategies for helping clients to respond more empathically. For instance, good counsellors model empathic responding in such a way that some of their skills are likely to be transmitted to their clients. Some counsellors work with clients either conjointly or in encounter groups and, where appropriate, make interventions which focus on the accuracy with which people are picking up each other's messages and on what is being communicated by their own verbal, vocal and bodily responding. An advantage of groups is that counsellors may observe clients responding in conditions approximating real life, for example under stress. Also, counsellors may teach empathic responding skills fairly systematically, along the lines suggested in Chapter 11. Gordon's parent effectiveness training[19] and Guerney's relationship enhancement approach[20] are two other programmes for teaching listening skills.

SENDING INFORMATION: SELF-DISCLOSURE

The area of self-disclosure is treated in moderate detail in this chapter since, unlike empathic responding, it has previously received little attention in this book. Derlega and Chaikin describe self-disclosure as 'the process by which one person lets himself be known by another person'.[21] Cozby defines self-disclosure as 'any information about himself which Person A communicates verbally to a Person B'.[22] Another way of looking at self-disclosure is in terms of intentional verbal disclosure of self-referent information. However, as indicated earlier, people's self-disclosure can also be through unintentional vocal and bodily communications. Thus the process by which people let themselves be known to others includes unintentional as well as intentional, and non-verbal as well as verbal, disclosures. However, the clearer people are in their verbal and non-verbal self-disclosures, the easier it is for other people to receive their messages accurately and without a difficult decoding process. Furthermore, people disclose themselves by their actions, independent of when they are conversing. Sometimes such actions are consistent or congruent with their verbal self-disclosures, but this is not always the case.

Another facet of self-disclosure involves what people conceal as well as what they reveal. As indicated by the Johari window, they may be revealing more than they think. However, to a greater or lesser degree, everyone engages in a process of information control by which she reveals certain things and conceals others. Goffman considers that the effect of people's information control is to control the conduct of others, especially responses to themselves.[23] He writes of the presentation of self in everyday life, a process of both revealing and concealing information in such a way that people project a definition of a situation and hence influence others' behaviour according to their wishes. An example might be that of parents who control their children's perceptions of them by censoring the aspects of themselves they disclose to their children. Thus, as well as outright lying, partial disclosure or 'economizing on the truth' is a form of concealment.

Appropriate self-disclosure is critical in good human relationships. For instance, a marital partner who says little about herself may be giving her husband little chance to know her subjective self, thoughts, feelings and personal meanings. Furthermore, if she were to talk about herself more she might get to know her husband better, since she would be creating an emotional climate in which it was easier for him to self-disclose. Additionally, our low self-disclosing marital partner may be blocking her own knowledge of herself, since an important way to discover herself is to talk about herself and assess her own and her husband's reactions to her disclosures. Jourard, paraphrasing the 'Know Thyself' advice of the Delphic Oracle, states: 'Make Thyself Known, and then Thou wilt Know Thyself'.[24] Another way of stating this is that appropriate self-disclosure diminishes not only alienation from a partner, but also self-alienation. Furthermore, Jourard argues that real self-disclosure is both a symptom of personality health and a means of ultimately achieving a healthy personality.[25] He considers that openness, including sexual openness and absence of prudery, is a basic ingredient of a good marriage.[26]

Self-disclosure and Experiencing

The concept of self-disclosure begs the question of whether a person is disclosing something which is authentically herself or whether she is disclosing something which is introjected or scripted by others and is not genuinely her own. People who authentically self-disclose are aware of and in touch with their own experiencing. Thus, real self-disclosure first entails inner self-disclosure or the capacity to acknowledge one's own experience prior to the communication of outer or verbal and bodily self-disclosures to others. In a sense, we are back with the notion of inner empathy, the ability to listen to the unfolding of our own experience. Earlier we stated that inner empathy helped us to receive the messages of others without distortion. Here we are saying that inner empathy helps us to send messages to others which are authentic self-disclosures.

The notion of expressiveness is another way of looking at the experiential element of self-disclosure. Here it is insufficient just to acknowledge accurately our own experience, since it needs to be genuinely shared with another. A good expressive message is one which uses appropriate verbal, vocal and bodily communication to convey the inner experiencing in such a way that the receiver is also allowed to listen to our experiencing.

Counsellors can help their clients in a number of ways to listen to and express themselves. We have already stressed the importance of a good basic empathy counselling relationship, involving person-to-person companionship. Here, the counsellor needs to be real, not hiding behind a professional facade. Furthermore, she can increase clients' openness to their experience if her reflections focus accurately and expressively on their feelings.

Beyond basic empathy, deliberate counsellor self-disclosure may help some clients to become both more aware and expressive of their experiencing. Counsellor self-disclosure involves the counsellor in sharing some of her views, attitudes, experiences and feelings, including her reactions to the client. Sometimes counsellors self-disclose in response to clients' requests and, on other occasions, they initiate self-disclosure in response to their own perceptions of their clients' needs and concerns. There are a number of rules of thumb for counsellor self-disclosure. Such disclosures, especially if they are comments about the client, should be owned as personal reactions which also may be saying something about the counsellor. This calls for a degree of humility. Counsellor self-disclosures may be more appropriate in well-established counselling relationships, though this depends on the depth of the disclosure. Counsellor self-disclosures may be most helpful if they are made in ways which model respect and appropriate expressiveness. In other words, such disclosures are best made by skilled counsellors who are functioning reasonably well in their own lives. Last, counsellor self-disclosures should reflect the client's rather than the counsellor's needs and interests, since counselling is for the client. Carkhuff observes that counsellor self-disclosure is often, although not necessarily, related to genuineness, since sometimes counsellor 'disclosures' are more concealing than revealing. He states 'although a helper may be genuine and not self-disclosing or self-disclosing and not genuine, frequently, and particularly at the extremes, the two are related'.[27]

Other ways in which counsellors can facilitate emotional experiencing include psychodrama and behaviour rehearsal. Furthermore, the various techniques of gestalt therapy are designed to increase awareness and experiential self-disclosure. For instance, an important gestalt technique is that of skilful frustration, though this is not recommended for beginning counsellors. Here the therapist tries to find out what the client avoids and her ways of failing to make real contact with others in her environment. Then the therapist works as a catalyst in two ways: providing situations in which the client can experience being stuck in frustration; and then frustrating her avoidances still further until she is willing to mobilize her own resources and engage in authentic rather than phoney communication. Perls writes: 'This is what we are again and again trying to do, to frustrate the person until he is face to face with his blocks, with his inhibitions, with his way of avoiding having eyes, having ears, having muscles, having authority, having security in himself'.[28] Gestalt therapy focuses heavily on the *how* of present behaviour: how what is said is said, with what facial expression, tone of voice, syntax, posture and effect.

Self-disclosure and Thinking

Self-disclosure and thinking are inextricably related, since people tend to think about their self-disclosures before, during and after they are made. Furthermore, as mentioned earlier, relationships take place between personifications, or people who construct thought models of themselves and each other. Thus, for instance in a marital relationship, a wife's disclosure to her husband indicates both her conception of herself and the influence of her conception of him. Although all the areas of thinking difficulty mentioned in the previous chapter have relevance to self-disclosure, only four areas, albeit interrelated, on which counsellors and clients can work together will be discussed here, namely, evaluations and internal rules, attributions of causality and responsibility, anticipations of risk and gain, and defensive processes and styles.

Evaluations and internal rules

Two areas on which counsellors and clients may wish to work are: (a) evaluations and rules concerning disclosure; and (b) positive and negative evaluations of personal characteristics. Counsellors who work with people who feel it is wrong to self-disclose may have to offer an empathic relationship until the client feels safe to make disclosures. On the other hand, with less disturbed clients, counsellors can engage in focused exploration and discussion with their clients on the harmfulness or helpfulness of the rule about not self-disclosing. As with assertion, some people with Christian backgrounds may need to be given permission, backed by reasons, to talk about themselves more openly. For instance, it may be useful for some clients to learn that they can be more helpful to themselves and their friends if they are more revealing. Other self-disclosure rules which may merit attention include those concerning disclosing positive or negative things about oneself and giving positive or negative feedback to others.

People tend to positively and negatively value their personal characteristics. For instance, in a study using a sample of 150 male and female British university students, Nelson-Jones and Strong[29] found that the characteristics most positively valued were being happy, healthy and reasonably honest, having good relationships with parents, and getting on with other people. Those characteristics most negatively valued concerned self-hatred, self-pity, having attempted suicide and having suicidal thoughts. Homosexual tendencies were negatively valued, as was having a fear of the opposite sex. Violence was also negatively valued. Despite some variation in individual responses, the values placed on the personal characteristics were widely subscribed. Furthermore, in general, males and females evaluated personal characteristics much the same on positive and negative dimensions.

The point here is that in any relationship, self-disclosure is affected by the ways in which each person evaluates her own and the other's personal characteristics. Here counsellors may work with clients in increasing awareness of their evaluations and the internal standards or rules on which they are based, exploring the effects that such evaluations and rules are having on the amount and pattern of disclosure in a relationship, and working with one or both partners on discarding or reformulating rules and evaluations of self and the other person which are interfering with effective and open communication.

Attributions of causality and responsibility

One area of attribution relevant to self-disclosure that counsellors may explore with their clients is that of who is responsible for initiating, deepening and, if necessary, terminating a relationship. Some clients may have a tendency to be passive and to wait for things to happen to them when it would be more in their interests to initiate or deepen a relationship. One of the reasons for this may be that either consciously or unconsciously they consider it the responsibility of other people to develop their relationships. Other clients may be assuming too much responsibility in their relationships and might try to make the responsibility for maintaining and deepening disclosure more mutual.

Another area of attribution in a relationship is that of acknowledging responsibility for one's own thoughts and feelings. The following vignette illustrates this point.

> Sue 'you make me feel this way' is a young married teacher who is having difficulties in both her job and her marriage. Despite her erratic behaviour she feels that neither her headmaster nor her husband understands her. Whenever her headmaster discusses her work, Sue gets sullen and inwardly resentful. When her husband makes even the mildest criticism, Sue gets openly aggressive. She blames both her husband and her headmaster for her aggressive feelings and actions.

In a sense, Sue's self-disclosures about the above feelings are governed by her assumption that other people, rather than herself, are responsible for them. Though this may be partially true, she has failed to acknowledge her own contribution in generating her feelings. If, with the help of a counsellor, she were to challenge and change her assumption, she would be increasingly able to take control of her own life, with a corresponding alteration in the nature of her self-disclosures.

Attribution of responsibility for disclosing in ways which make change in a relationship possible is related to the capacity to acknowledge responsibility for much of one's own emotional life. When, for instance, Sue blames her husband for her feelings, she is also indicating that it is his responsibility to change their relationship for the better. Counsellors can help their clients to explore the attributions they make in regard to who is responsible for changing their disclosures once a relationship gets into difficulty. Here a useful question is that of how a person's current pattern of disclosure is helping her, irrespective of how badly she perceives her partner to be behaving.

Anticipations of risk and gain

In general, people anticipate that disclosure of characteristics which they value negatively is more risky than disclosure of characteristics which they value positively. However, this anticipation is not always accurate, since, in building a relationship, disclosure of negative characteristics can have *positive* consequences and disclosure of positive characteristics can have *negative* consequences.[30] A partial explanation of why people may inaccurately anticipate the effects of their negative self-disclosures is that they see them as more risky than if a friend were to make similar self-disclosures to them,[31] especially if they do not first stop to consider what their own reactions to their friend would be.[32]

People in continuing relationships, such as marriage, may anticipate difficulties in changing an established pattern of disclosure, since this may involve disrupting the current equilibrium of a relationship by presenting the other partner with a new or revised version of themselves. Thus anticipations relating to self-disclosure in a relationship pertain to a number of areas, which include anticipations about own feelings, anticipations about the other's reactions, and anticipations about the effect of change in the relationship.

Counsellors may work with a range of clients, from those who negatively anticipate the outcome of nearly all their disclosures to those wondering about the effect of certain disclosures in specific situations. In general, counselling clients are very willing to see *risks* in altering their pattern of self-disclosure. Counsellors may work with clients in exploring the realism of such risks, some of which are listed in Table 15.3. Clients may be less apt to focus on the *gains* of appropriate self-disclosure. Thus, even more important than exploring the risks, it may be helpful if counsellors work with their clients to identify possible gains of greater self-disclosure. There may be an element of 'consciousness raising' involved in this exploration to make clients more aware of the impact they can have on themselves and their relationships.

Defensive processes and styles

Defensive processes and interpersonal styles act as barriers to direct and open communication by distancing and confusing the other person or persons in the relationship. When appropriate, counsellors can focus their clients' attention on the ways in which they may be interfering with genuine self-disclosure. These defensive processes include the following.

Table 15.3 *Anticipations of gain and risk in altering self-disclosure in general or in a specific relationship*

Possible gains	Possible risks
Lessened loneliness and alienation	Rejection
	Not liking self, being ashamed
Greater intimacy	Being misunderstood
More friendships	Lack of confidentiality
Self-definition rather than being defined by default	Feeling tense
	Feeling vulnerable
Standing up for self	Too much intimacy too soon
Easier for others to self-disclose	Too many close relationships
Excitement of discovering others	Too much self-knowledge
	Having to change
Greater self-knowledge	Upsetting equilibrium of relationship
Lessened tension	
Greater self-acceptance	Breaking injunctions about disclosure
Greater control of own life	

Concealment and partial disclosure. Clients may be leading either very secret lives or partially secret lives in which they are engaging in a high degree of information control. Stated another way, these clients are closed and defensive about their lives and, as Mowrer points out, may be violating their basic human 'connectedness' and be out of 'communion' with their fellow humans,[33] including their marital partners.

Distortions of others. As already indicated, people construct thought models or personifications of themselves and each other. Our disclosures to others depend in part on our personifications of them. For instance, the concept of transference implies that, by distorting the other person, people react to a current relationship with old responses and disclosures used in a past relationship. Also, where people's own needs are involved, it is possible for them to have 'tunnel' vision in regard to significant others, possibly focusing exclusively on their negative rather than their positive qualities. Such tunnel vision may involve projection of their own negative qualities onto the other.

Collusion. Partners in a relationship may tacitly agree to acknowledge and disclose only certain aspects of themselves and selected reactions about their partner. With collusion, fantasy and reality get confused. For instance, for the sake of minimizing anxiety, a wife may tacitly agree to maintain her husband's fantasy about himself, but she in turn will probably require that he tacitly agrees to maintain her fantasy about herself. Sometimes people are aware that they are colluding and, in other instances, they are either unaware or find it more convenient to suppress such an awareness. Berne's idea of games assumes that both people are colluding in playing the game. For instance, in the game 'Why Don't You – Yes But', it is essential to have both a person offering suggestions and a person refuting them.

Defensive interpersonal styles. Interpersonal styles are the characteristic ways people have of relating to each other. Defensive interpersonal styles use 'phoney' disclosure and communication as a way of preventing real disclosure and communication.

Sometimes such interpersonal styles can be identified by their predominant feature. Powell gives a catalogue of such defensive styles, which he calls roles. These include the braggart, the clown, the cynic and the loner.[34] For instance, whenever a conversation gets personal and might involve genuine self-disclosure, the clown may start being funny and thus keep the relationship on a superficial level. Berne's games also involve defensive interpersonal styles on the part of both players.

Self-disclosure and Action

Appropriateness

Counsellors need to have some concept of appropriateness when focusing on the ways in which their clients self-disclose. One criterion of appropriateness is whether or not the self-disclosure helps the client to meet her needs. Another way of viewing appropriateness is whether the self-disclosure is suitable or fitting for a particular occasion. Table 15.4 shows some of the areas of appropriateness which apply to

Table 15.4　*Some areas of appropriate self-disclosure*

Area	Description
Amount	The quantity of information which is being disclosed
Topic area	The area of disclosure, e.g. work, feelings, sex
Breadth	The range of areas that are disclosed
Depth	The extent of intimacy of personal disclosure
Timing	When to make a disclosure in a relationship
Target person	The person or persons to whom a disclosure is made
Situational rules	The rules of the context of the disclosure

virtually any self-disclosure a person makes. These self-disclosure areas refer to: how much?; in what area?; in how many areas?; how intimate?; when?; to whom?; and in what context?

Self-disclosure skills

Counsellors may work with clients in individual counselling, marital and family counselling, group counselling, and skills training sessions to develop self-disclosure skills. Twelve self-disclosure skills on which counsellors might focus are discussed below. At this stage, as well as increasing client awareness, we emphasize correct performance of the skill, which may involve practice and homework.

Initiation. Some clients are passive in initiating relationships and self-disclosing. They may often question the other person in such a way that it deflects the conversation from any need to reveal themselves. After a discussion of the problems of initiation, clients may be encouraged to practise initiation by appropriate self-disclosure rather than being silent or hiding behind questions. The idea is to increase self-disclosure and use questions with more discrimination.

Development of relationships. Altman and Haythorn suggest that individuals generally disclose more information on both breadth and depth dimensions as the relationship advances from strangers to casual acquaintances to close friends.[35] Some clients, even partners in long established marriages, may need help in learning how to develop the range and intimacy of their relationships.

Sending 'I' messages. 'I' messages involve acknowledging when we are expressing our own thoughts and feelings. Below is an example of an indirect communication which is then rephrased into an 'I' message:

> Judy (indirect): A lot of people round here, such as Ken and Bill, feel that you are not pulling your weight on this project.
> Judy ('I' message): I feel that you are not pulling your weight on this project and this is creating much extra work for me.

Expressiveness. The ability to express feelings and emotions rather than just to talk about them is very important in real relationships. Clients can be helped to develop flexibility in the expression of their feelings and emotions. Another way of saying this is that in some situations they may need to express emotions spontaneously, whereas in other situations the emotions may need to be acknowledged but controlled.

Positive and negative self-disclosure. Real intimacy involves the capacity to let ourselves be known. Some clients find it difficult to acknowledge and divulge their strengths, while others are perpetually trying to hide their perceived weaknesses. In either case, they may need counsellor assistance in learning to overcome these barriers. Even in relationships between casual acquaintances or workmates, people who are continually boasting or running themselves down can be distancing and tedious.

Reciprocity. Reciprocity, or an attempt to match the intimacy level of another's self-disclosure, is a fairly consistent finding in self-disclosure research studies.[36] Some clients may need to focus on becoming better at matching intimacy levels in their relationships by not responding in too shallow or too intimate a way.

Specificity. Specificity, or concreteness, means communicating clearly and specifically rather than in vague and abstract terms. An illustrative example is given below:

> Jane (vague): Sometimes I don't get on with my boss.
> Jane (specific): Today Mr Jones came in and started pressurizing me about not having finished typing the firm's annual report. I feel really frustrated, since the reason I haven't finished is that he keeps giving me other work to do.

Confrontation. In the previous chapter confrontation was described as reflecting, or otherwise focusing attention on, discrepancy. Just as counsellors need to develop their skills of disclosing discrepancies between their own perceptions and those of their clients, so people in non-counselling relationships need to be able to give similar feedback to one another. Confrontation always entails an element of challenge, but need not be destructively aggressive (see Chapter 14).

Assertion. Confrontation may be thought of as one form of assertion. However, assertion is a broader concept involving the capacity to express, where appropriate, positive and negative thoughts and feelings. Behaviour rehearsal is frequently used in helping people to become more assertive (see Chapter 12).

Immediacy. Earlier we noted that frequently people have in their relationships tacit agreements not to notice or talk about certain areas of the relationship. Immediacy relates to the capacity of people to respond immediately to their experiencing of a relationship and to disclose what otherwise might be left unsaid. Immediacy involves one person in a relationship relating what the other person is saying to what they consider to be going on in their relationship at the immediate moment. Carkhuff gives the example of a client talking about her difficulty in relating to her physician, with the counsellor relating this to the immediate counsellor-client relationship: 'What you're trying to tell me is how difficult it is for you to relate to me–here–now'.[37] Immediacy is a form of sending 'I' messages and also of confrontation. Though valuable, it needs to be used with discrimination.

Handling feedback. An important skill for clients to develop is that of being able to handle the feedback from their self-disclosures. For instance, if people receive negative feedback, their options include: agreeing, if they feel the comments are justified; calmly restating the initial disclosure; reflecting the message of the other person; sending an 'I' message reacting to the feedback; or remaining silent. Not only may clients need to develop overt skills of handling feedback, but they may also need to develop covert skills to deal with their emotions relating to the feedback.

Vocal and bodily disclosure. Much work has been done in Britain on social skills training focusing on vocal and bodily communication.[38,39] Such training approaches may involve assessment of the client, modelling and teaching the skill, rehearsing and practising, and further homework aimed at achieving a transfer of the skill into real life. Audio-visual aids may be used both to model desired skills and to provide clients with feedback about their behaviour.

A final comment about helping clients towards better and more appropriate self-disclosure is that self-disclosure always involves experiential, thinking, and action elements. Consequently, though different clients may need different emphases at different stages of their counselling contact, counselling approaches which do not take all three elements into account run the risk of being less effective than well thought out approaches encompassing these elements together.

CONFLICT RESOLUTION: HANDLING DIFFERENCES

Conflict resolution is an important application of being able to listen well and to self-disclose appropriately. Sooner or later there comes a time in any relationship when differences of interest can either can no longer be ignored or can be ignored only at further cost to the relationship. Such conflicts of interest have potential for both good and ill. Poorly handled, this may lead to additional overt and covert negative behaviour on the part of one or both parties. Such behaviour includes defiance, aggression, getting back, gossiping, forming alliances, and psychological and physical withdrawal. However, if conflicts are handled well this may clear up the immediate problem or problems as well as helping the relationship.

Conflict Resolution and Experiencing

As with listening and self-disclosure, conflict resolution is more likely to succeed if both parties are in touch with their own experiencing and not just creating and engaging in conflicts on the basis of injunctions, conditions of worth and irrational beliefs. If this is not the case, either or both may need individual counselling so that they may understand and experience themselves more fully as individuals. Individual counselling may precede or be concurrent with conjoint counselling focused on enriching their relationship.

The issue of self-worth or how valuable people experience themselves as being is critical in viewing how people create, sustain and handle conflicts. Satir writes of individuals with a low sense of worth: 'Because they feel they have little worth, they expect to be cheated, stepped on, deprecated by others. Expecting the worst, they invite it and usually get it'.[40] Psychological size is another way of viewing people's experiencing of their sense of worth. When not feeling confident, people tend to feel small and sometimes view others as disproportionately large and powerful, hence more threatening. Thus their experiencing of a situation as being one of conflict may have more to do with their low self-esteem than with any external characteristics of the situation. Again, individual counselling may be desirable for such vulnerable people so that they can receive and send messages less defensively.

Conflict Resolution and Thinking

Each of the areas of thinking earlier explored in relation to self-disclosure has relevance to conflict resolution. For example, evaluations and internal rules are pertinent to the expectancies people have of themselves, each other, and their relationship. These expectations may insufficiently allow for the other person's differentness and, hence, people may relate to each other as though they were extensions of themselves rather than autonomous. This may lead to a need to control the other and to see independent behaviour on their part as a threat or rejection.[41] Furthermore, people may have rules about conflict itself. An example of such a rule is 'peace in the home at all costs'. Either in individual or in conjoint counselling, counsellors can help their clients to explore the realism of the rules and evaluations of self, others and the relationship which are relevant to the areas of conflict. Furthermore, counsellors can help their clients to adopt a more constructive attitude towards conflict resolution, viewing conflicts as situations to be coped with as best as possible.

When appropriate, counsellors can also help their clients to explore the realism of their attributions about who has caused the conflict and who is responsible for resolving it. Distressed marriages, for instance, tend to involve much blaming and mutual recrimination. Here the attributions may be not only that the other person has caused the problem, but because of this the other person is solely responsible for righting the situation. Counsellors can also help their clients to explore the realism of their anticipations about the risks and gains of changing their behaviour in conflicts. Often the gains may be obscured behind the risks or fears of losing out in a competitive power struggle. Also, some clients may need to learn compromise, including ridding themselves of the overgeneralization that not getting everything they want means getting nothing.

Counsellors may also work with their clients' defensive processes and styles. For instance, real conflict resolution may not be possible where one or both parties are concealing or only partially disclosing significant thoughts and feelings. Also, genuine conflict resolution involves absence of transference, with its distortion of the other person, and of tunnel vision. Furthermore, instead of passively colluding to ignore conflicts which are festering in and upsetting a relationship, clients may need to become aware of and actively change their behaviour. Counsellors may also help their clients to identify and discard roles which interfere with conflict resolution, such as the martyr, the placator and the distractor.[42] Furthermore, games such as 'If it weren't for you' and 'Why don't you . . . yes but' obstruct the honest listening and disclosing necessary for working through problems and also need to be identified and discarded.

A final point on conflict resolution and thinking is that conflicts, especially if they are long-standing, as in many marriages, may generate an enormous amount of emotion in one or both parties. Putting this another way, the level of defensiveness and hostility may be extremely high. Consequently, before they are able to think more effectively, some clients may need the opportunity to express or release their emotions in a safe environment.

Conflict Resolution and Action

A number of attempts have been made to suggest behaviours which help to solve conflicts. When working with partners, such as distressed marital couples, counsellors may use audio-visual aids to discover how clients are currently handling an area of conflict, illustrate more effective ways, and monitor changes in behaviour. Several areas on which counsellors may focus are now reviewed.

Reducing aversive communication

Hollingsworth observes that, unlike assertion, aggression entails the use of coercive power involving psychological, and sometimes physical, threats and punishment to gain compliance.[43] Aggressive responses can be verbal, such as rejection, ridicule, disparagement and other forms of negative evaluation. Also, aggressive responses can include vocal and bodily components, such as shouting, tut-tutting, turning away, finger shaking, physical violence and other threatening behaviour. Hops observes: 'Some individuals have non-verbal responses that are obvious put-downs but they simply act as if they were unaware that they are behaving like that'.[44] Part of the treatment of marital problems he describes involves identifying aversive and side-tracking behaviours, illustrating the effect they are having on the partner, and reinforcing reductions in the frequency of such behaviours. Video feedback is used as part of this procedure.

Increasing helpful communication

Partners may be taught empathic listening skills.[45,46] Furthermore, where one partner is dominating the dialogue, they can be taught sharing behaviour in which partners are encouraged to alternate the duration of their responding.[47] Many of the self-disclosure skills mentioned earlier, such as sending 'I' messages and specificity, are relevant to clients who need to develop conflict resolution skills.[48] Also, using video feedback, partners can be shown their behaviour in negotiation sessions and encouraged to identify the responses of each other that they find helpful. This may lead to training in making appropriate helpful responses.[49] The idea of both reducing aversive and increasing helpful communication is to create an open as contrasted with a closed communication system. Satir observes that an open system provides for change whereas a closed one provides for little or no change and operates through force, both physical and psychological.[50]

Increasing positive behaviours

Partners can be asked to observe or note on a checklist which of each other's behaviours they find pleasing and displeasing. One such measure is the *Spouse Observation Checklist* of Hops and his colleagues.[51] The counsellor may encourage a discussion on the couple's satisfaction with their relationship and the daily exchange of rewarding and punishing behaviours. Partners can then be encouraged to increase behaviours that are regarded as positive by each other.[52]

Negotiation and contracting

Negotiating conflicts involves setting aside a suitable period of time when both partners are reasonably fresh and can avoid other distractions. The first partner may describe what the other partner is doing and how it makes them feel while the second partner paraphrases, with the roles then being reversed. An attempt is made to avoid aversive communication. Both partners then pinpoint and list specific changes in the behaviour of the other person that would make their life more pleasant. The pinpointing procedure also includes giving feedback on specific behaviours already seen as positive. The partners then negotiate behaviours to be changed. Written contracts are made stating consequences contingent upon the specific behaviours to be changed within them. In this contingency contracting process there may be positive consequences for compliance and negative consequences for non-compliance. Sometimes such contracts are *quid pro quo* arrangements in which one partner agrees to do something in exchange for a behaviour change from the other. However, *independent consequences* arrangements, in which positive consequences are independent of whether the other person changes, may be preferable.[53,54] Hops gives an example of Dick's objective being ten minutes of talk each day about his studies and future. His reward was one bottle of beer per ten minutes and his penalty for non-compliance was to write two letters to friends or relatives. His spouse's objective was to sleep in the nude every night, except during her periods. June's reward was 30 cents a day to be spent in any way she thought fit and her penalty was heavy housework, such as washing windows or cleaning the oven.[55] Contingency contracting has been criticized as a cumbersome procedure often disliked by both counsellors and clients.[56] Furthermore, it may reinforce an overemphasis on always wanting something in exchange rather than gaining pleasure through giving.

Problem-solving

Apart from the above negotiating and contracting methods, there are several approaches to conflict resolution through problem-solving. Gordon's 'no-lose' approach, which he calls Method III, involves both parties in a conflict participating in a joint search for some solution acceptable to both. Gordon's method, claimed not to involve coercive power, involves six separate steps: (a) identifying and defining the conflict; (b) generating possible alternative solutions; (c) evaluating the alternative solutions; (d) deciding on the best acceptable solution; (e) working out ways of implementing the solution; and (f) following up to evaluate how it worked.[57] A similar approach is the Main-Roark consensus method. With the aid of a counsellor, both parties involved: (a) describe the situation as they see it; (b) describe how they feel about the conflict and what personal meaning it has for them; (c) describe a desired situation to reduce the conflict; (d) determine what changes are necessary to achieve that situation; and (e) outline an agenda or plan of action to reach that situation.[58] Further problem-solving approaches are presented by Jacobson[59] and Goldfried and Davison,[60] the latter being described in Chapter 14.

SEXUAL RELATIONSHIP CONCERNS

Sexual difficulties may often contribute to distressed relationships inside and outside marriage. Like conflict resolution, sexual relations are another area in which it is important to be able to listen well and to self-disclose appropriately. Good sexual relations require a capacity to listen to sexual feelings and to disclose this experiencing to a partner. Furthermore, they entail the capacity to listen empathically to a partner's sexual feelings and to act as a good companion in facilitating the experiencing of such feelings. A recent study by Hite of the sexual experiences of American women, albeit methodologically deficient, indicated the following: fairly widespread misunderstanding of the physiology of female sexual responsiveness by both sexes; poor body image for a number of women, including disparagement of their genital area; the inability of many men to listen adequately to and to facilitate their partner's sexual experiencing; and the difficulty many women had in understanding and constructively disclosing their sexual and emotional needs.[61] There seems little reason to believe that the situation is very different in Britain or elsewhere in the English-speaking world.

Although they acknowledge variation within the cycle, Masters and Johnson assert that both the human female's and male's sexual response cycle can be broken down into four separate phases.[62] First, there is the *excitement* phase, in which sexual tension develops from any source of somatogenic or psychogenic stimulation. Second, if effective sexual stimulation is maintained, there is the *plateau* phase in which 'sexual tensions are intensified and subsequently reach the extreme level from which the individual ultimately may move to orgasm'.[63] Third, there is the *orgasmic* phase, which is limited to those few seconds during which the involuntary climax is reached. Here, though the male pattern of ejaculation is fairly standard, there is great variation in both the duration and the intensity of female orgasmic experience. Fourth, there is the *resolution* phase, which is an involuntary period of tension loss which returns the individual through the plateau and excitement phases to an unstimulated state. However, women have the capacity for multiple orgasm, especially if effectively stimulated again at plateau tension level. Residuals of sexual tension usually disappear slowly in both females and males. Masters and Johnson observe that the excitement and resolution phases take up most of the time expended in the complete human sexual response cycle.

Some Issues in Sexual Relationship Counselling

Prior to reviewing some approaches, we discuss some issues which counsellors may need to bear in mind when dealing with clients' sexual relationship concerns.

Individual or conjoint counselling

Leading writers on sex counselling and therapy, such as Masters and Johnson[64] and Kaplan,[65] advocate working with both partners rather than just one. In fact a basic premise of Masters and Johnson's work is that, 'although both husband and wife in a sexually dysfunctional marriage are treated, the marital relationship is considered as the patient'.[66] The Masters and Johnson approach entails individual sessions with each partner as well as conjoint sessions. Reasons for working with both partners include the need to focus on their patterns of communication as well as the desirability of their performing joint homework assignments. Focused group counselling is also a possibility for couples with sexual concerns.

Degree of focus

Here the issue is that of the extent to which sexual concerns can be treated independently of both the broader marital relationship and the state of psychological development of each partner. Kaplan writes: 'It is the integrated use of systematically structured sexual experiences with conjoint therapeutic sessions which is the main innovation and distinctive feature of sex therapy'.[67] She asserts that, though in the course of sex therapy intrapsychic and transactional conflicts are likely to be dealt with to some extent, traditional approaches to sexual disorders, such as psychotherapy and marital therapy, may be more comprehensive than necessary. In many instances, relatively focused sex counselling may be sufficient. However, sometimes marital and/or individual counselling for one or both partners may need to precede or accompany sex counselling.

Use of co-counsellors

Opinions are divided on the use of co-counsellors. Masters and Johnson state: 'Definitive laboratory experience supports the concept that a more successful clinical approach to problems of sexual dysfunction can be made by dual-sex teams of therapists than by an individual male or female therapist'.[68] This is because each counsellor may be more likely both to understand the sexual responsiveness of and to interpret sympathetically the views of the same-sex client. Kaplan, however, asserts that experience suggests that mixed-gender co-counsellor teams are not always essential. She states that a counsellor may effectively conduct sex counselling on a solo basis so long as he or she is 'sensitive, well trained, and experienced, and when he or she is specifically sensitized to the erotic responses and reactions of the opposite gender . . .'.[69] However, mixed-gender co-counsellor teams should be used in specific instances, such as when strong resistances to disclosing and working on sexual concerns are engendered by the sex of an individual counsellor. Some sexual homework assignments, such as some of the 'sexpieces' to make sex more pleasurable described by Brown and Faulder,[70] can be attempted without a counsellor, though this tends to assume a lack of a deep-seated problem.

Duration of counselling

Masters and Johnson advocate a 'two-week phase of rapid education and/or symptom reversal' involving 'the isolation of the marital-unit partners from the demands of their everyday world'.[71] Though this gives the partners the opportunity to develop their personal as well as their sexual relationship in a relaxed atmosphere, it has the disadvantage of being too expensive for many couples. Kaplan, on the other hand, observes that, in the Sex Therapy and Education Program of the Payne Whitney Psychiatric Clinic of Cornell University, couples continue to live at home and are seen once or twice a week. No prior time limit is placed on treatment, which is terminated when seemingly permanent good sexual functioning has been established.[72]

Medical considerations

Sexual functioning can be affected both by physical disease and by the effects of medical drugs. A medical history is part of the assessment procedure advocated by Masters and Johnson for all couples, but other sex counsellors require a medical examination only when they consider it specifically indicated.[73] Our view is that, especially in cases of remediation of sexual dysfunction as contrasted with enhancement of moderately satisfactory sexual relationships, it is better to err on the safe side and to suggest, if not require, a medical examination. Some sex counselling programmes also require couples to have a psychiatric examination before they are accepted for treatment.

Referral

Counsellors who lack the requisite knowledge and skills to engage in focused sex counselling may refer clients to doctors, clinical psychologists, or to other counsellors specializing in sexual difficulties. The British Association for Counselling publishes a directory of agencies offering counselling for psychosexual problems.[74] Furthermore, the National Marriage Guidance Council has a number of counsellors in all regions trained or in training to carry out structured treatments of sexual dysfunctions.[75] In other instances, counsellors may feel it preferable to work with their clients on their sexual relationship concerns, sometimes because appropriate referral sources are unavailable. However, relevant training is strongly recommended.

Counsellor knowledge and attitude

Counsellors possess varying degrees of insight and knowledge about their own and other people's sexuality. Some counsellors may be uncomfortable about discussing sexual material, and such discomfort is transmitted to clients and inhibits them. Other counsellors may have difficulty setting limits, both inside and outside the interview situation, on their sexual attraction to certain clients. Though it is helpful for counsellors to acknowledge their sexual feelings about their clients as a way of understanding both their clients' behaviour and also themselves, 'such feelings should not be "acted out", i.e., motivate self-serving behaviour'.[76] Another area in which counsellors should have some insight relates to the nature and extent of their personal and cultural biases concerning what constitutes appropriate sexual behaviour.

Clients without partners

Clients without sexual partners may seek or need counselling assistance for a number of reasons, such as being out of touch with their own sexuality, lack of knowledge and inhibitions about masturbation, having difficulty initiating sexual relations, and having been sexually dysfunctional in a previous relationship. Unattached people may gain both from exploring their sexuality in a counselling relationship and from increasing their awareness of their own sensuality through relevant homework assignments. Further sex counselling may either await their obtaining a partner who will co-operate in treatment or involve the more controversial involvement of a surrogate partner.

Some Approaches to Sexual Relationship Counselling

Some clients may request counselling assistance to enhance a less than satisfactory sex life. Other clients may be in relationships in which one or both partners act in a sexually dysfunctional way (see Table 15.5). Thus both sexual relationship enhancement and remediation of sexual dysfunction can be foci for counselling. In the following section we discuss counsellor approaches to sexual relationship concerns under the rather arbitrary and somewhat interrelated categories of facilitating appropriate experiencing, thinking and action. Under the action category, specific exercises for the remediation of sexual dysfunctions are reviewed.

Sexual relations and experiencing

As indicated earlier, some clients may require individual counselling to experience themselves more fully as persons and to gain basic self-esteem and a separate identity. Many clients, however, may be functioning moderately well in other areas of their life and need specific assistance in helping them to acknowledge and explore their own and their partner's sexuality.

Masters and Johnson have introduced the technique of *sensate focus* to help couples to 'think and feel' sensuously.[77,78] Sensate focus acknowledges the importance of touch in experiencing and stimulating sensuality. Partners are asked to time their periods of sensate focus when they feel a natural sense of warmth and compatibility and to continue for as long as it is pleasurable. Both partners should be unclothed, with a minimum of emotional and physical fatigue and tension. Avoiding specifically sexual stimulation, including the genitals and the female's breasts, the 'giving' partner is instructed 'to trace, massage, or fondle the "getting" partner with the intention of giving sensate pleasure and discovering the receiving partner's individual levels of sensate focus'.[79] The rules of sensate focus for the receiving partner are that they have to protect the 'pleasuring' partner from causing discomfort or initiation, and that there is no requirement for them verbally or non-verbally to comment on their experiencing, unless such expression is completely spontaneous. The giving partner is committed not only to giving pleasure, but also to acknowledging his or her own sensations in giving pleasure, exploring another's body by touch, and receiving the reactions of another's pleasure. After a reasonable time, partners exchange roles. Sensate focus tends to give couples time, space and permission to be sensual without feeling that they have to perform intercourse. Kaplan observes that, though most couples experience positive reactions to sensate focus, some people experience very little reaction and others negative reactions.[80] These neutral and negative reactions may be indicative of deeper inhibitions about experiencing sensuality.

Sexual relations and thinking

Counsellors may use thinking-focused interventions for clients' sexual relationship concerns. Some interventions may focus on the realism of evaluations and rules concerning sex in such areas as: whether sex is dirty or sinful; the use or misuse of masturbation; some aspect of the body, such as breasts, vulva or penis, being too small or ugly; fears about homosexual orientation; fears about pregnancy and methods of contraception; the extent to which gender differences, such as the 'active' male and the 'passive' female, are desirable or harmful in sexual behaviour; what constitutes realistic levels of sexual performance and pleasure in any given relationship; and the extent to which sex should be used for reproduction, strengthening a primary relationship, or for recreation, possibly involving secondary relationships.

Counsellors may also focus on their clients' attributions about their sex life. For instance, Brown and Faulder's book assumes the importance of partners taking responsibility for their own feelings, thoughts, actions, and mutual pleasure in sexual relations.[81] Another area of counselling focus is that of performance fears, or rather, anticipations and fears about lack of performance. Masters and Johnson observe that 'fear of inadequacy is the greatest known deterrent to effective sexual functioning, simply because it so completely distracts the fearful individual from his or her natural responsivity by blocking reception of sexual stimuli either created by or reflected from the sexual partner'.[82] They place great emphasis on educating the partners of sexually dysfunctional people so that they understand more fully the fear component involved in the dysfunction and can hence be more supportive and less devaluing of both their partner and themselves.

Counsellors may also explore their clients' defensive processes and styles. For instance, their clients may be concealing or partially disclosing some relevant thoughts and feelings concerning their own and their partner's sexual functioning. A simple example is that of a woman who fails to disclose her need for more manual stimulation from her partner. Sometimes people's perception of their partners is distorted and they relate to them in terms of past relationships, possibly of a non-sexual nature. Any transference from past relationships which interferes with here-and-now sexual intimacy may merit exploration. Furthermore, some clients may adopt roles, such as the female martyr or the 'macho' male, which block full intimacy. Also, they may play sexual games, such as seducing and then rejecting. Counsellors may help their clients to become aware of and work towards discarding those roles and games which destroy rather than add spice to sexual relations.

Sexual relations and action

Some couples may feel that their sexual relations are in a rut. One possibility is that their sex life is suffering from excessive repetition and that some variety needs to be introduced. Counsellor recommendation of books like those of Comfort,[83,84] Brown and Faulder,[85] and Hite[86] may be sufficient to widen horizons and increase the range of behaviour, especially if the books are well illustrated. Also, relevant films and video-tapes may be helpful.

Sometimes couples' sexual relations suffer because of conflicts in other areas of their relationship. Some couples agree to try, if possible, to keep such conflicts from affecting their sex life. Also, there is the possibility that sexual relationships will generate their own areas of conflict regarding such issues as how, how frequent, where and when. Counsellors working with couples whose sexual relations are harmed by conflicts arising within or outside their sex life may focus on facilitating communication along the lines suggested in the conflict resolution section of this chapter. This may include helping couples to reduce aversive communication, increase helpful communication, increase positive behaviours towards each other, and use skills of negotiation and of problem-solving to reduce their differences.

Table 15.5 lists the main female and male sexual dysfunctions. Counselling approaches to them are likely to include both sensate focus and an exploration of the relevant thoughts of both partners to identify those inhibiting full sexual expression. Additionally, for each area of sexual dysfunction counsellors may suggest structured exercises, examples of which are provided below. Fuller information on structured exercises may be found in the books by Masters and Johnson, Kaplan, and Brown and Faulder, whose approaches may differ somewhat. Though the structured exercises emphasize techniques, they may also be viewed as part of a broader attempt to establish good communication between partners. In all instances the structured exercises are interspersed with counselling sessions.

General sexual dysfunction. Here the task is to give the woman 'permission' to experience and express herself sexually, thus attaining what Masters and Johnson refer to as a sexual value system involving 'the pleasure in, the honoring of, and the privilege to express need for the sexual experience'.[87] Three kinds of exercises are used in sequence: sensate focus, non-demand genital stimulation and non-demand coitus. Specifically, in non-demand genital stimulation, manual stimulation by the male should be gently conducted in the mons area, particularly along either side of the clitoral shaft. Especially initially, this stimulation should be under the woman's guidance. When ready, non-demand coitus involves the male thrusting in a slow and exploratory manner with the woman focusing on the physical sensations she is experiencing and then progressing towards full intercourse.

Table 15.5 *Female and male sexual dysfunctions*

Dysfunctions	Description
Female	
General sexual dysfunction	Little or no arousal from sexual stimulation, severe sexual inhibition
Orgasmic dysfunction	
primary	Never having experienced orgasm by any method
secondary	Inhibition of orgasm after a period of being able to reach orgasm
Vaginismus	Involuntary tightening or spasm of the muscles surrounding the vaginal entrance which prevents penetration
Male	
Erectile dysfunction	
primary	Never having experienced orgasm inside a woman either through not getting an erection hard enough to enter the vagina or through not being able to maintain erection long enough after entry
secondary	Erectile difficulties after a period of functioning well
Premature ejaculation	Reaching orgasm very quickly after vaginal containment
Retarded ejaculation	Ejaculatory inhibition despite firm erection in the vagina

Orgasmic dysfunction. Kaplan observes that orgasmic difficulties are probably the most common female sexual complaint. She stresses that 'there is only one kind of female orgasm, and it is neither clitoral nor vaginal, but has *both* clitoral and vaginal components'.[88] Her treatment of primary orgasmic dysfunction involves encouraging clients to masturbate to orgasm in private, if necessary also using a vibrator. When ready, couples are instructed to make love in the ordinary way with the female being told not to make any special attempt to achieve orgasm. Other structured exercises are suggested for secondary orgasmic dysfunction.[89]

Vaginismus. The treatment of vaginismus may start by showing the partners that a vaginal spasm is real. The structured exercises involve a successive approximation approach to having objects inside the vagina up to full intercourse. Masters and Johnson instruct the couple to insert vaginal dilators in graduated sizes.[90] Kaplan encourages females to gently insert their own or their partner's finger into their vagina and, when ready, to move the finger back and forth repeatedly. Counsellors may have to help their clients through a transient period of psychological discomfort if they are to overcome this problem.[91]

Erectile dysfunction. Masters and Johnson state that the goals in treating erectile dysfunction are: removing the male's fear of sexual performance; moving him out of his spectator role into being an active participant; and relieving the female's fears for his sexual performance.[92] The man must become convinced that he does not have to *do* anything to have an erection but allow a physiological response to sexual stimuli to occur. As with general sexual dysfunction, three kinds of exercises may be used in sequence: sensate focus; non-demand genital stimulation, this time by the female; and non-demand coitus.

Premature ejaculation. Premature ejaculation is a common male sexual dysfunction. Use of the squeeze technique is the main structured exercise for helping males who prematurely ejaculate to gain ejaculatory control.[93] Here the female stimulates the male's penis until the sensation just prior to ejaculation is experienced by the male. At this stage she squeezes fairly hard at the top of the shaft of his penis, which makes him lose his urge to ejaculate and may also make him lose some of his erection. This procedure gets repeated a number of times. When the male feels he has learned some ejaculatory control, the next step is to insert his penis in the vagina without thrusting, leading in successive steps to full intercourse.

Retarded ejaculation. Masters and Johnson use the term 'ejaculatory incompetence' rather than 'retarded ejaculation'. After sensate focus, the next exercise is a masturbatory one in which the female stimulates and teases the male's penis to orgasm. After the masturbation technique has succeeded and ejaculation can be accomplished easily, the penis, which has been manually stimulated close to ejaculation, is inserted into the vagina. The female is instructed immediately to institute a demanding style of pelvic thrusting. After initial ejaculatory success, the couple work on prolonging the amount of time the penis is in the vagina before ejaculation 'by including a period of voluntary lowered levels of male sexual excitation before coital connection is initiated'.[94]

HOMOSEXUAL RELATIONSHIP AND SEXUAL IDENTITY CONCERNS

Homosexual inclinations and behaviour may be a concern in marriages as well as a concern of many unmarried people. The world is not divided into heterosexuals and homosexuals; rather people may be placed on a continuum according to their sexual preferences and behaviour. Kinsey *et al* used a 0–6 scale to rate individuals' sexual orientation on both psychologic reactions and overt experience: with 0 indicating exclusively heterosexual with no homosexual; 1, predominantly heterosexual, only incidentally homosexual; 2, predominantly heterosexual, but more than incidentally homosexual; 3, equally heterosexual and homosexual; 4, predominantly homosexual, but more than incidentally heterosexual; 5, predominantly homosexual, but incidentally heterosexual; and 6, exclusively homosexual.[95]

Though the Kinsey data are restricted to white North Americans and were collected a long time ago, they nevertheless provide some indication of the prevalence of varying degrees of homosexual orientation. For females, by age 45, 28 per cent had *responded homosexually*, described as 'homosexual experience, arousal, and orgasm', with 13 per cent of the overall sample having had *overt experience to the point of orgasm*.[96] For males, the corresponding figures were 50 per cent for *homosexual response,* and 37 per cent for *overt experience to the point of orgasm*.[97] Regarding being exclusively homosexual, between 1 and 3 per cent of unmarried females and previously married females, but less than three in a thousand of the married females, were in this category.[98] Four per cent of the males were exclusively homosexual throughout their lives.[99] Males tended to continue their homosexual activities over a longer period of years than females. Furthermore, they tended to have more partners, with 71 per cent of the females, but only 51 per cent of the males who had any homosexual contact restricting their homosexual activities to a single partner or two partners.[100] The Kinsey data indicate that approximately 25 per cent of females and 50 per cent of males engage in both heterosexual and homosexual activities, or react to people of both sexes, in the course of their adult lives. Kinsey *et al* consider that, in the absence of the prevailing very considerable social constraints, homosexual activity would occur in the histories of a much larger proportion of the population.[101]

Counselling Homosexual Relationship Concerns

Assuming the Kinsey data have some relevance to Britain, counsellors may have a number of clients who are bisexual or exclusively homosexual in their sexual preferences and behaviour. Some data and case histories of predominantly British people are to be found in Wolff's study on bisexuality.[102] Some clients – perhaps an increasing number – may come to counsellors because they wish to strengthen existing homosexual relationships. Here, much of what has been written in this chapter on listening, self-disclosing and conflict resolution may be relevant to what are emotional as well as sexual relationships. Furthermore, some homosexual partners may wish to enhance their sex life or to overcome a sexual dysfunction. Masters and Johnson have extended their researches to include the treatment of female and male homosexual dysfunctions.[103] Again, much of what has been written earlier in this chapter on sexual relationship concerns is relevant to homosexual as well as heterosexual couples. A final point is that, like heterosexual relationships, homosexual relationships can be tender, caring and enhancing of both partners, or exploitative and destructive.

Counselling Sexual Identity Concerns

Counsellors working with homosexual and bisexual clients need to understand their own feelings, anxieties and possible prejudices in this area. The objectives of counselling people with sexual identity concerns include: clearing up misconceptions in people who have inaccurately labelled themselves as homosexual; increasing heterosexual and decreasing homosexual inclinations and behaviour; helping homosexually and bisexually oriented people towards greater self-acceptance, possibly including an alternative life-style; and supporting homosexually and bisexually oriented people during the process of 'coming out', the public proclamation and demonstration of their homosexual inclinations.

Increasing heterosexual orientation

Some clients, usually those with little exposure to the opposite sex, may label themselves as homosexual with slight or no evidence to support their assessment. Here their problem may have much more to do with fear of homosexuality than with homosexuality itself. A counselling approach which includes a review of the evidence for their sexual self-labelling may be sufficient to clear up misconceptions.

Other clients may present homosexual inclinations at any stage on the Kinsey continuum and request that the counsellor help them to become more heterosexual. Attitudes to homosexual orientation are so strongly influenced by cultural and societal considerations that it is hard to assess how much individuals wish to change for their own reasons and how much they wish to change to please others. Furthermore, there is the question of the extent to which an increase in heterosexual orientation is possible. In general, such changes may be more likely for people who are younger and have low Kinsey ratings (i.e. 1 and 2) than for older people and for those with high Kinsey ratings (i.e. 5 and 6).

Definitive research has yet to be performed on the genetic element in homosexuality. Some psychologists and psychiatrists, such as Freud, consider that humans are basically bisexual, and many consider that there is a large learned, as contrasted with genetic, element in sexual orientation. For instance, writing about males, Wolpe observes that 'in a great many cases the homosexual inclination is attributable to one or more of the following factors: (1) a generalized timidity towards other human beings that is most marked in relation to women . . .; (2) conditioned fear of certain kinds of contacts with females; and (3) sexual arousal conditioned to males'.[104] He argues that clients need to be treated by programmes relevant to their concerns rather than by uniform approaches.

Interventions for clients who present wishing to become more heterosexually oriented range from broad counselling approaches to specific behavioural approaches. For instance, a person-centred counsellor would tend to see the client as a person who needs an empathic relationship in which she can discard conditions of worth and thus become more fully functioning. Thus the counsellor would offer a certain kind of *relationship* for developing the *person* rather than use one or more specific *techniques* for solving a *problem*. The behavioural counsellor, on the other hand, might offer one or more specific techniques to deal with one or more specific aspects of the client's problem: conceivably, assertion training for generalized timidity; desensitization for conditioned fear of certain kinds of heterosexual contact; and possibly even aversion therapy (e.g. use of electric shock) for sexual arousal conditioned to the same sex. Heterosexual approach responses would be positively reinforced and behaviour rehearsal might be used to increase client skills. Also, relevant information on heterosexual lovemaking might be provided through discussion, reading suggestions, or films and videotapes. For those whose homosexuality appears to be associated with living in single-sex environments, change to a mixed-gender environment might be suggested.

Increasing homosexual and bisexual self-acceptance and capacity for relationships

Counsellors may see some clients who are extremely depressed and negative both about their homosexual tendencies and about their whole worth as human beings. Some such people may acknowledge that they are predominantly or exclusively homosexual. Others may be striving hard to prevent themselves from such an awareness. Sometimes counselling to increase heterosexual inclination may have been attempted without success. Still others may have difficulty in acknowledging a homosexual element in a predominantly heterosexual orientation.

There are numerous ways in which homosexually oriented people acquire and perpetuate a negative self-image. As Weeks observes, over the years the homosexually oriented in Britain have been branded as sinful by the Church, criminal by the law (if male), and sick by the medical profession.[105] Frequently the validity of homosexual feelings and behaviour is disparaged by the media, ignored in history and sex education, and discriminated against in employment. Predominantly homosexually oriented boys and girls are rarely, if ever, exposed to role-models of successful homosexual relationships. Furthermore, homosexually oriented people's sense of isolation is increased by the widespread concealment and partial disclosure of homosexual tendencies in our culture, involving what Goffman refers to as information management for a discreditable stigma.[106] Also, there is the problem of heterosexual people overemphasizing the sexual aspect of the homosexual and bisexual life-style and consequently undermining their personhood. Thus, added to any unfortunate experiences which may have taken place in their family life, people with homosexual tendencies often bear a very heavy burden of negative feedback. This may lead not only to lack of self-acceptance but also to what some regard as active self-oppression.

Counsellors need to be aware that coming to counselling may be very threatening for the homosexually oriented, possibly involving for the first time openly acknowledging their orientation to themselves as well as disclosing it to others. Sometimes such people need reassuring telephone contact before risking face-to-face contact.[107] Many of the counsellor attitudes and skills already mentioned in this book are relevant to counselling the homosexually oriented. A high level of acceptance and of empathic understanding is important to people who may find it very hard to accept themselves and fear rejection. Also, such empathy means that clients may explore and experience themselves as whole persons and not just in terms of their sexual functioning. Focused exploration may be used to help clients to examine such areas as: the nature of their homosexual-heterosexual balance; the realism of their rules or standards concerning homosexual behaviour; the harmfulness or helpfulness of their self-evaluations derived from these rules; their anticipations of other people's reactions to their sexual orientation; and the options they have for meeting their relationship and sexual needs. Clients may also have concerns, other than those relating to sexual orientation, on which they may wish to focus.

When ready, clients may wish to explore the advantages and disadvantages of 'coming out', involving openly disclosing their sexual preferences. 'Coming out' is a process which tends to start with self-acceptance of homosexual tendencies and behaviour; then, disclosure of homosexual orientation to other homosexually oriented people and to close friends; followed by being open about their homosexuality to everyone, including other friends, family and colleagues at work. Counsellors may help clients to assess how much they want to disclose, to whom, in what way, and how to handle anticipated feedback. At some stage counsellors may also consider it appropriate to refer clients to gay self-help and contact groups, such as Lesbian Line,[108] Gay Switchboard,[109] Campaign for Homosexual Equality,[110] Gay Legal Advice,[111] and Friend.[112] Also, much self-help and contact information is available in the newspaper *Gay News*.

PRACTICAL EXERCISES AND QUESTIONS

It may help you to develop your skills and knowledge of the material in this chapter if, either individually or as part of a group, you perform the following exercises and answer the following questions.

Practical Exercises

A.   Listening

1.   Practical exercises on basic listening skills are contained in Chapter 11. Some which may be particularly helpful for listening skills training include:

(a)   Exercise 5. Identifying the counsellor's frame of reference.
(b)   Exercise 8. Empathic responding discrimination exercise.
(c)   Exercise 9. Reflection of content.
(d)   Exercise 10. Reflection of feeling.
(e)   Exercise 11. Reflection of content and feeling.

B.   Self-disclosure

2.   Counsel a partner and engage in focused exploration of her or his thinking in the following areas, then reverse roles:

(a)   rules concerning self-disclosure;
(b)   thoughts and feelings about disclosing positive and negative aspects of her/himself;
(c)   attributions of causality and responsibility concerning self-disclosure;
(d)   anticipations of risk and gain concerning self-disclosures;
(e)   defensive processes and styles in regard to: concealment and partial disclosure; distortions of others; collusion; characteristic roles and games.

3.   Working in pairs or in a small group, discuss and role-play possible

counsellor interventions for working with clients in each of the following areas:

(a)   initiation of self-disclosure;
(b)   development of relationships;
(c)   sending 'I' messages;
(d)   expressiveness;
(e)   positive and negative self-disclosure;
(f)   reciprocity;
(g)   specificity;
(h)   confrontation;
(i)   assertion;
(j)   immediacy;
(k)   handling feedback;
(l)   vocal and bodily disclosure.

C.   Conflict resolution

4.   Counsel a partner and engage in focused exploration of the adequacy of her or his characteristic ways of experiencing, thinking about, and handling conflicts in her or his personal relationships.

5.   Working in pairs or in a small group, describe each of the following possible conflict resolution skills, assess your own competence in each skill, and describe and role-play possible counsellor interventions focused on each skill:

(a)   reducing aversive communication;
(b)   increasing helpful communication;
(c)   increasing positive behaviours;
(d)   negotiation and contracting;
(e)   problem-solving.

6.   Counsel a partner by together focusing as best you can on the five steps of the Main-Roark consensus method of problem-solving in an area of conflict in her or his personal relationships; then reverse roles. Though you will be working with only one party in the conflict, the five steps are that both parties:

(a)   describe the situation as they see it;
(b)   describe what they feel about the conflict and what personal meaning it has for them;
(c)   describe a desired situation to reduce the conflict;
(d)   determine what changes are necessary to achieve that situation;
(e)   outline an agenda or plan of action to reach that situation.

D. *Sexual counselling*

7.   Assess your adequacy in counselling clients with concerns regarding their
         sex life. If you consider that you require further training in sex counselling,
         explore the available resources in your area and draw up an action plan to
         obtain additional training. In your action plan be specific regarding: (a)
         your goals; (b) your intended steps towards each goal; and (c) the time
         schedule.

8.   Counsel a partner and together explore how her or his counselling might be
         influenced by her or his:

         (a)   extent of knowledge about female and male sexuality;
         (b)   sexual attitudes and ethics;
         (c)   feelings of discomfort when clients discuss their sexual concerns;
         (d)   feelings of sexual attraction to clients.

         Then reverse roles.

9.   Either in pairs or in a small group, discuss counsellor interventions for
         helping clients with the following concerns:

         (a)   general sexual dysfunction;
         (b)   orgasmic dysfunction;
         (c)   vaginismus;
         (d)   erectile dysfunction;
         (e)   premature ejaculation;
         (f)   retarded ejaculation.

E. *Counselling homosexual and bisexual concerns*

10.   Counsel a partner and together explore:

         (a)   the nature of and how at ease she or he is with her or his own sexual
               orientation;
         (b)   the ways in which her or his gender and her or his sexual orientation
               might influence her or his counselling of homosexually and bisexually
               oriented clients.

11.   Either in pairs or in a small group, discuss approaches for helping clients
         to:

         (a)   increase heterosexual feelings and behaviour;
         (b)   accept homosexual and bisexual feelings and behaviour;
         (c)   come out and publicly proclaim their homosexual tendencies.

Questions

Marital counselling

1.   In what ways, if any, do you consider that marriages are different from other kinds of partner relationships? Please be specific.

2.   In what ways, if any, do you consider that counselling married couples is likely to be different from counselling unmarried partners? Please be specific.

3.   If you are married, in what ways might your own marital experiences influence your counselling? Please be specific about: (a) helpful influences; (b) harmful influences.

NOTES

1. McGinnis, T. C. & Finnegan, D. G. (1976) *Open Family and Marriage: A Guide to Personal Growth* pp. 32–48. St Louis: C. V. Mosby.
2. Working Party on Marriage Guidance (1979) *Marriage Matters* p. 15. London: HMSO.
3. *Ibid.* p. 16.
4. Dominian, J. (1968) *Marital Breakdown* pp. 19–20. Harmondsworth: Penguin Books.
5. Working Party on Marriage Guidance (1979) *Marriage Matters* p. 1. London: HMSO.
6. Sullivan, H. S. (1950) The illusion of personal individuality. *Psychiatry*, **13,** 330. Full reference pp. 317–332.
7. Luft, J. & Ingham, H. (1955) *The Johari Window: A Graphic Model for Interpersonal Relations*. University of California at Los Angeles, Extension Office: Western Training Laboratory in Group Development, August. The word 'Johari' is derived from a combination of the Christian names of Joe Luft and Harry Ingham.
8. Yalom, I. D. (1970) *The Theory and Practice of Group Psychotherapy* p. 350. New York: Basic Books.
9. Argyle, M. (1975) *Bodily Communication* p. 11. London: Methuen.
10. Satir, V. (1967) *Conjoint Family Therapy* pp. 75–90. Palo Alto, California: Science and Behaviour Books.
11. Trower, P., Bryant, B. & Argyle, M. (1978) *Social Skills and Mental Health* pp. 30–33. London: Methuen.
12. Tiefer, L. (1979) *Human Sexuality: Feelings and Functions* p. 18. New York: Harper and Row.
13. Sullivan, H. S. (1953) *The Interpersonal Theory of Psychiatry* p. 167. New York: W. W. Norton.
14. Sullivan, H. S. (1954) *The Initial Interview* p. 26. New York: W. W. Norton.
15. Ekman, P. & Friesen, W. V. (1969) Nonverbal leakage and clues to deception. *Psychiatry*, **32,** 88–105.
16. Gordon, T. (1970) *Parent Effectiveness Training* pp. 29–94. New York: Wyden.
17. Guerney, B. G. (1977) *Relationship Enhancement* pp. 26–29. San Francisco: Jossey-Bass.
18. Sullivan, A. S. (1953) *The Interpersonal Theory of Psychiatry* p. 170. New York: W. W. Norton.
19. Gordon, T. (1970) *Parent Effectiveness Training* pp. 29–94. New York: Wyden.

20. Guerney, B. G. (1977) *Relationship Enhancement* pp. 25–121. San Francisco: Jossey-Bass.
21. Derlega, V. J. & Chaikin, A. L. (1975) *Sharing Intimacy: What We Reveal to Others and Why*. p. 1. Englewood Cliffs, New Jersey: Prentice-Hall.
22. Cozby, P. C. (1973) Self-disclosure: a literature review. *Psychological Bulletin*, **79**, 73. Full reference pp. 73–91.
23. Goffman, E. (1959) *The Presentation of Self in Everyday Life* p. 15. Harmondsworth: Penguin.
24. Jourard, S. M. (1964) *The Transparent Self* p. 11. Princeton, New Jersey: Van Nostrand.
25. *Ibid*. pp. 19–30.
26. *Ibid*. pp. 31–39.
27. Carkhuff, R. R. (1969) *Helping and Human Relations: Volume One, Selection and Training* pp. 186–187. New York: Holt, Rinehart and Winston.
28. Perls, F. S. (1969) *Gestalt Therapy Verbatim* pp. 41–42. New York: Bantam Books.
29. Nelson-Jones, R. & Strong, S. R. (1977) British students' positive and negative evaluations of personal characteristics. *Journal of College Student Personnel*, **18**, 32–37.
30. Nelson-Jones, R. & Strong, S. R. (1976) Positive and negative self-disclosure, timing and personal attraction. *British Journal of Social and Clinical Psychology*, **15**, 323–325.
31. Nelson-Jones, R. & Dryden, W. (1979) Anticipated risk and gain from negative and positive self-disclosure. *British Journal of Social and Clinical Psychology*, **18**, 79–80.
32. Nelson-Jones, R. & Coxhead, P. (1980) Neuroticism, social desirability and anticipations and attributions affecting self-disclosure. *British Journal of Medical Psychology*, **53**, 169–180.
33. Mowrer, O. H., Vattano, A. J. & others (1975) *Integrity Groups: The Loss and Recovery of Community* p. ii. Urbana, Illinois: Integrity Groups.
34. Powell, J. (1969) *Why Am I Afraid to Tell You Who I Am?* pp. 121–167. London: Fontana/Collins.
35. Altman, I. & Haythorn, W. W. (1965) Interpersonal exchange in isolation. *Sociometry*, **28**, 411–426.
36. Cozby, P. C. (1973) Self-disclosure: a literature review. *Psychological Bulletin*, **79**, 81–82.
37. Carkhuff, R. R. (1969) *Helping and Human Relations: Volume One, Selection and Training* pp. 192–195. New York: Holt, Rinehart and Winston.
38. Argyle, M. (1975) *Bodily Communication*. London: Methuen.
39. Trower, P., Bryant, B. & Argyle, M. (1978) *Social Skills and Mental Health*. London: Methuen.
40. Satir, V. (1972) *Peoplemaking* p. 22. Palo Alto, California: Science and Behavior Books.
41. Satir, V. (1967) *Conjoint Family Therapy* pp. 11–19. Palo Alto, California: Science and Behavior Books.
42. Satir, V. (1972) *Peoplemaking* pp. 59–79. Palo Alto, California: Science and Behavior Books.
43. Hollingsworth, J. G. (1977) Differentiating assertion and aggression: some behavioral guidlines. *Behavior Therapy*, **8**, 347–352.
44. Hops, H. (1976) Behavioral treatment of marital problems. In W. E. Craighead, A. E. Kadzin and M. J. Mahoney (eds), *Behavior Modification: Principles, Issues and Applications* p. 441. Boston: Houghton Mifflin. Full reference pp. 431–446.
45. *Ibid*. p. 440.
46. Guerney, B. G. (1977) *Relationship Enhancement* pp. 25–121. San Francisco: Jossey-Bass.
47. Hops, H. (1976) Behavioral treatment of marital problems. In W. E. Craighead, A. E. Kadzin and M. J. Mahoney (eds), *Behavior Modification: Principles, Issues and Applications* p. 440. Boston: Houghton Mifflin.
48. Egan, G. *You and Me: The Skills of Communicating and Relating to Others* (1977) pp. 42–107. Monterey, California: Brooks-Cole.
49. Margolin, G. & Weiss, R. L. (1978) Communication training and assessment: a case of

behavioral and marital enrichment. *Behavior Therapy*, **9**, 508–520.

50. Satir, V. (1972) *Peoplemaking* pp. 113–117. Palo Alto, California: Science and Behavior Books.

51. Hops, H. (1976) Behavioral treatment of marital problems. In W. E. Craighead, A. E. Kadzin and M. J. Mahoney (eds), *Behavior Modification: Principles, Issues and Applications* pp. 436–439. Boston: Houghton Mifflin.

52. Jacobson, N. S. (1979) Increasing positive behavior in severely distressed marital relationships: the effects of problem-solving training. *Behavior Therapy*, **10**, 315–316. Full reference pp. 311–326.

53. Patterson, G. R. (1975) *Families: Applications of Social Learning to Family Life* pp. 87–92. Champaign: Research Press.

54. Hops, H. (1976) Behavioral treatment of marital problems. In W. E. Craighead, A. E. Kadzin and M. J. Mahoney (eds), *Behavior Modification: Principles, Issues and Applications* pp. 443–446. Boston: Houghton Mifflin.

55. *Ibid*. p. 445.

56. Jacobson, N. S. (1979) Increasing positive behavior in severely distressed marital relationships: the effects of problem-solving training. *Behavior Therapy*, **10**, 312.

57. Gordon, T. (1970) *Parent Effectiveness Training* pp. 194–264. New York: Wyden.

58. Main, A. P. & Roark, A. E. (1975) A consensus method to reduce conflict. *Personnel and Guidance Journal*, **53**, 754–759.

59. Jacobson, N. S. & Anderson, E. A. (1980) The effects of behavior rehearsal and feedback on the acquisition of problem-solving skills in distressed and nondistressed couples. *Behavior Research and Therapy*, **18**, 29. Full reference pp. 25–36.

60. Goldfried, M. R. & Davison, G. C. (1976) *Clinical Behavior Therapy* pp. 186–207. New York: Holt, Rinehart and Winston.

61. Hite, S. (1976) *The Hite Report*. New York: Summit Books.

62. Masters, W. H. & Johnson, V. E. (1966) *Human Sexual Response* pp. 3–8. Boston: Little, Brown and Co.

63. *Ibid*. p. 6.

64. Masters, W. H. & Johnson, V. E. (1970) *Human Sexual Inadequacy*. London: J. A. Churchill.

65. Kaplan, H. S. (1974) *The New Sex Therapy: Active Treatment of Sexual Dysfunctions*. Harmondsworth: Penguin.

66. Masters, W. H. & Johnson, V. E. (1970) *Human Sexual Inadequacy* p. 3 London: J. A. Churchill.

67. Kaplan, H. S. (1974) *The New Sex Therapy: Active Treatment of Sexual Dysfunctions* p. 16. Harmondsworth: Penguin.

68. Masters, W. H. & Johnson, V. E. (1970) *Human Sexual Inadequacy* p. 4. London: J. A. Churchill.

69. Kaplan, H. S. (1974) *The New Sex Therapy: Active Treatment of Sexual Dysfunctions* p. 272. Harmondsworth: Penguin.

70. Brown, P. & Faulder, C. (1977) *Treat Yourself to Sex*. Harmondsworth: Penguin.

71. Masters, W. H. & Johnson, V. E. (1970) *Human Sexual Inadequacy* p. 17. London: J. A. Churchill.

72. Kaplan, H. S. (1974) *The New Sex Therapy: Active Treatment of Sexual Dysfunctions* p. 230. Harmondsworth: Penguin.

73. *Ibid*. p. 227.

74. Taylor, F. (ed.) (1978) *Psychosexual Problems: A Directory of Agencies Offering Therapy, Counselling, and Support*. Rugby: British Association for Counselling.

75. National Marriage Guidance Council (1979) *Annual Report 1979* p. 2. Rugby: National Marriage Guidance Council.

76. Kaplan, H. S. (1974) *The New Sex Therapy: Active Treatment of Sexual Dysfunctions* p. 278. Harmondsworth: Penguin.

77. Masters, W. H. & Johnson, V. E. (1970) *Human Sexual Inadequacy* pp. 67–75. London: J. A. Churchill.

78. Belliveau, F. & Richter, L. (1970) *Understanding Human Sexual Inadequacy* pp. 103–105. London: Hodder Paperbacks. This book is the authorized non-technical version of Masters and Johnson's *Human Sexual Inadequacy*.
79. Masters, W. H. & Johnson, V. E. (1970) *Human Sexual Inadequacy* p. 72. London: J. A. Churchill.
80. Kaplan, H. S. (1974) *The New Sex Therapy: Active Treatment of Sexual Dysfunctions* pp. 242–246. Harmondsworth: Penguin.
81. Brown, P. & Faulder, C. (1977) *Treat Yourself to Sex*. Harmondsworth: Penguin.
82. Masters, W. H. & Johnson, V. E. (1970) *Human Sexual Inadequacy* pp. 12–13. London: J. A. Churchill.
83. Comfort, A. (1972) *The Joy of Sex: A Gourmet Guide to Lovemaking*. London: Quartet Books.
84. Comfort, A. (1973) *More Joy of Sex: A Lovemakers' Companion*. London: Quartet Books.
85. Brown, P. & Faulder, C. (1977) *Treat Yourself To Sex*. Harmondsworth: Penguin.
86. Hite, S. (1976) *The Hite Report*. New York: Summit Books.
87. Masters, W. H. & Johnson, V. E. (1970) *Human Sexual Inadequacy* p. 298. London: J. A. Churchill.
88. Kaplan, H. S. (1974) *The New Sex Therapy: Active Treatment of Sexual Dysfunctions* p. 418. Harmondsworth: Penguin.
89. *Ibid.* pp. 415–454.
90. Masters, W. H. & Johnson, V. E. (1970) *Human Sexual Inadequacy* pp. 262–265. London: J. A. Churchill.
91. Kaplan, H. S. (1974) *The New Sex Therapy: Active Treatment of Sexual Dysfunctions* pp. 465–471. Harmondsworth: Penguin.
92. Masters, W. H. & Johnson, V. E. (1970) *Human Sexual Inadequacy* p. 196. London: J. A. Churchill.
93. *Ibid.* pp. 101–115.
94. *Ibid.* p. 132.
95. Kinsey, A. C., Pomeroy, W. B. & Martin, C. E. (1948) *Sexual Behavior in the Human Male* p. 638. Philadelphia: W. B. Saunders.
96. Kinsey, A. C., Pomeroy, W. B., Martin, C. E. & Gebhard, P. H. (1953) *Sexual Behavior in the Human Female* p. 452. Philadelphia: W. B. Saunders.
97. Kinsey, A. C., Pomeroy, W. B. & Martin, C. E. (1948) *Sexual Behavior in the Human Male* p. 650. Philadelphia: W. B. Saunders.
98. Kinsey, A. C., Pomeroy, W. B., Martin, C. E. & Gebhard, P. H. (1953) *Sexual Behavior in the Human Female* p. 474. Philadelphia: W. B. Saunders.
99. Kinsey, A. C., Pomeroy, W. B. & Martin, C. E. (1948) *Sexual Behavior in the Human Male* p. 651. Philadelphia: W. B. Saunders.
100. Kinsey, A. C., Pomeroy, W. B., Martin, C. E. & Gebhard, P. H. (1953) *Sexual Behavior in the Human Female* p. 475. Philadelphia: W. B. Saunders.
101. Kinsey, A. C., Pomeroy, W. B. & Martin, C. E. (1948) *Sexual Behavior in the Human Male* pp. 659–660. Philadelphia: W. B. Saunders.
102. Wolff, C. (1977) *Bisexuality: A Study*. London: Quartet Books.
103. Masters, W. H. & Johnson, V. E. (1979) *Homosexuality in Perspective*. Boston: Little, Brown.
104. Wolpe, J. (1977) Inadequate behavior analysis: the Achilles' heel of outcome research in behavior therapy. *Journal of Behavior Therapy and Experimental Psychiatry*, **8,** 2. Full reference pp. 1–3.
105. Weeks, J. (1977) *Coming Out: Homosexual Politics in Britain, from the Nineteenth Century to the Present* pp. 9–44. London: Quartet Books.
106. Goffman, E. (1963) *Stigma* pp. 57–128. Harmondsworth: Penguin.
107. Wainwright, B. (1980) Gay counselling and switchboards. *Counselling News*, **31,** 4–5.
108. Lesbian Line. Address: BM Box 1514, London WC1V 6XX. Telephone: 01–837–8602.
109. Gay Switchboard. Telephone: 01–837–7324.

110. Campaign for Homosexual Equality. Address: BM, CHE, London WC1V 6XX. Telephone: 01–289–9335.
111. Gay Legal Advice. Telephone: 01–262–2892.
112. Friend. Address: 274 Upper Street, Islington, London N1. Telephone: 01–359–7371. Also local addresses and telephone numbers.

16 – Learning Competence Concerns

SUMMARY: *Learning competence describes the student's or pupil's degree of environmental mastery as a learner. A distinction is made between sense of and actual learning competence. Often counsellors need to increase their clients' sense of competence in order to release their actual competence. Learning competence concerns may be relatively isolated or part of a broader picture of client difficulties, which may be developmental or situational. Too narrow an assessment risks ignoring material relevant to treatment decisions. Sometimes clients need an empathic relationship preceding or in conjunction with more specific interventions. Approaches for different learning competence concerns are reviewed. Students with difficulties using their study time effectively may need to monitor their use of time, develop skills at setting realistic study goals, and feel and take more responsibility for their learning. Approaches for avoiding procrastination include: catharsis and empathic understanding; therapeutic study help, including setting minimum goals to help to build up the student's sense of competence; and thinking-focused interventions. Examination anxiety can be debilitating or facilitating. Approaches for examination anxiety include: training in the skills of revision and taking examinations; systematic desensitization, using either individual or group hierarchies; thinking-focused anxiety-management interventions, including use of appropriate self-instructions; and combinations of the above. Mathematics anxiety has been subdivided into mathematics test anxiety and numerical anxiety. Additional mathematics tutorial or laboratory work may take place along with counselling interventions like desensitization, self-instructional training, and support groups. Some students with problems in being creative and thinking critically may be helped by study skills training. Others may need more extended counselling to find a locus of evaluation within themselves and to explore self-defeating standards. Students often have an inaccurate sense of competence in regard to their reading effectiveness and may need a supportive environment to learn the skills and attitudes of effective reading. Approaches to public speaking anxiety include: skills training, systematic desensitization, thinking-focused anxiety-management training, and a mixture of these. Stuttering may be helped by focusing on breath regulation and systematic slowing of speech. Approaches for* *helping clients to make educational decisions are mentioned. The chapter concludes by discussing the institutional role of the counsellor, including collaboration with academic staff, preventive interventions, structural considerations and collaboration with parents.*

This chapter focuses on clients who would function better if they learned more effectively. Though the primary focus of the chapter is on helping students at the college level, much of the material is relevant to counselling in schools. From the start we mention that counselling students with learning competence concerns involves helping them to function more effectively as people, which will not necessarily entail increases in academic performance. For instance, some students may be performing poorly because they are on the wrong course and, hence, may need a change of course rather than an increase in academic performance. Other students may be *overstrivers* rather than *underachievers*, that is, people whose academic performance is purchased at the cost of an excessive workload and, possibly, lopsided development as people. As a result of counselling, such students may decide to place a lower premium on their studies. Still other students may wish to achieve the same level of academic performance, but with less distress and anxiety.

Accounting for differences in academic performance involves considering numerous variables, such as the quality of the students' prior and present teaching, the institutional climate, variation in students' aptitudes, the effect of home environment, and so on. Nevertheless, an underlying assumption made by many counsellors who wish to focus on learning competence is that it contributes to achievement. To test this assumption it is important that aptitude be controlled for, and three such studies are reported here. Lin and McKeachie, using a modified version of the work methods sub-scale of the Brown-Holtzman Survey of Study Habits and Attitudes, found that student study habits contributed to academic achievement independent of scholastic aptitude, particularly for women.[1,2] Spielberger, using the Taylor Manifest Anxiety Scale, found that though grades were unrelated to anxiety for high-aptitude and low-aptitude students, they varied inversely and significantly with level of anxiety for average-aptitude students.[3,4,5] Finally, Alpert and Haber produced evidence that both their facilitating and their debilitating anxiety scales, especially the facilitating scale, were able to contribute to differences in academic performance other than that accounted for by a measure of aptitude.[6] Thus, both good study skills and an appropriate level of anxiety may contribute to academic achievement.

THE CONCEPT OF LEARNING COMPETENCE

The term 'learning competence' seems preferable to terms like 'study skills, habits and attitudes', 'test anxiety', 'achievement anxiety', and so on, because although the latter describe elements of learning competence they are less comprehensive. Also, the term 'learning competence' allows more recognition to be given to emotional, motivational and interest variables in learning than do terms like 'study skills'. Learning competence describes the student's degree of environmental mastery as a learner. It is important, however, to distinguish between *actual* competence and *sense* of competence. Workers in student mental health and counselling often observe that their clients' estimations of their academic competence appear at variance with their past ability and achievement; indeed, often it is the most able students who feel least adequate. Covington and Beery suggest an explanation for this discrepancy.[7] They assert that it is the individual's self-standards or level of aspiration that determine feelings of success or failure. Thus both a sense of failure and feelings of success are experienced in relation to these subjective standards rather than in relation to actual achievement. Furthermore, students' sense of competence is mediated by their subjective levels of aspiration, and both over-estimations and under-estimations of actual competence may be taking place. Consequently, counsellors who work with learning concerns may almost be more concerned with their client's sense of competence rather than their actual competence, in that altering sense of competence may be the key to releasing actual competence.

A recent study on British first-year university students found that most felt a limited sense of competence as learners, with there being some significant differences between faculties.[8] The same subjects were asked about the amount of help they had received from the staff in their pre-university schools and colleges in developing learning competence and in making decisions about universities, university courses, and their careers. Over all items, 30 per cent felt they had been helped minimally, 40 to 45 per cent slightly to moderately, and nearly 30 per cent moderately to very much.[9] The relative lack of a focus on learning competence in the schools may contribute to pupil underachievement, create stresses in transition from schools to higher education, and also contribute to lack of both actual and sense of competence in students in higher education.

ASSESSMENT

Students may present counsellors with a variety of learning competence concerns, some of which are illustrated in Table 16.1. Sometimes these concerns may be indicative only of study skills deficiencies, but on other occasions they may mask or be part of broader difficulties, which may be developmental or situational. Counsellors need to use their judgement about how complete an assessment they make of the student's functioning outside the immediate learning presenting concerns. With some students and in some counselling settings, for example where the expectancy for the counselling service is to focus only on study problems, the broader assessment approach may seem inappropriate. Nevertheless, at the very least, the counsellor might attempt to get a fairly full picture of the client as a learner, along the lines of some of the categories indicated in Table 16.1. Furthermore, if the information is not forthcoming, counsellors should inquire about the current status of the client on his course and, also, the nature and extent of any work to be made up. Additionally,

Table 16.1 *Illustrative presenting concerns by learning competence areas*

Area	Concern
Planning and organizing work	'My work is getting on top of me' 'I've got behind and don't know where to begin'
Procrastination	'I keep putting off my work' 'I get easily distracted from working'
Examination anxiety	'Just thinking about exams makes me nervous' 'I get this feeling of panic in the exam room'
Mathematics anxiety	'Numbers frighten me' 'I block when it comes to numbers'
Critical thinking and creativity	'I find it easier to copy other people's ideas than to think through to my own criticisms' 'I'm too afraid to take the risks of original work'
Reading, writing and note-taking	'I'm a slow reader' 'I take notes in a disorganized way'
Public speaking anxiety	'I dread the thought of making a presentation in class' 'I feel so stupid when I speak in public'
Educational decision-making	'I can't decide what to study' 'I want to change my subject'

counsellors might ascertain any relevant time parameters, such as essay deadlines and examination dates. This review of the client as a learner covers the past, the present and anticipations about the future. Its purpose is not simply to ascertain facts, but to explore and understand the client's personal meanings in relation to study.

The main reason for a broader initial assessment rather than one of solely learning concerns is that, with a narrow assessment, there is always the risk that treatment approaches may be unsoundly based, since some relevant information concerning treatment decisions may not have been elicited. For example, students may be underachieving because they are feeling depressed at lack of social success and once they become socially more confident their work may improve. Another example is that of clients who have an extremely low sense of their own worth and whose learning difficulties are illustrative of more fundamental developmental problems. Such clients may require a continuing facilitative counselling relationship in conjunction with or prior to more specific approaches focusing on their learning concerns. In other words, without a broad initial assessment the counsellor is less likely to know the degree to which the client's problems are localized to learning and, hence, the extent to which approaches specific to learning concerns should be taken.

APPROACHES FOR DIFFERENT LEARNING COMPETENCE CONCERNS

In the following review of approaches to different learning competence concerns we indicate only some of the possible approaches. Ultimately, however, the counsellor must judge each case on its merits and make treatment decisions accordingly.

Planning, Organizing, and Effective Use of Study Time

Though many students may need help in doing more work, others may need to learn to relax, to take adequate recreation and to stop treating themselves as machines. What is important is that counsellors help individual students towards a pattern of studying and living which is congenial to and productive for them rather than encourage adherence to a rigid normative pattern.

Sometimes students feel overwhelmed with work because they have difficulty in ordering priorities and setting goals. As a start to ordering priorities, such students may find it helpful to complete the kind of *termly* study goals schedule depicted in Table 16.2. This goal-setting schedule may be filled out in two ways, both of which

Table 16.2   *Illustrative termly study goals schedule: Autumn term*

Week	Study goals
Week one 8 Oct.–14 Oct.	
Week two 15 Oct.–21 Oct.	
Week three 22 Oct.–28 Oct.	
Week four 29 Oct.–4 Nov.	
Week five 5 Nov.–11 Nov.	
Week six 12 Nov.–18 Nov.	
Week seven 19 Nov.–25 Nov.	
Week eight 26 Nov.–2 Dec.	
Week nine 3 Dec.–9 Dec.	
Week ten 10 Dec.–16 Dec.	
Vacation 17 Dec.–13 Jan.	

students might be encouraged to do. The first way is from the institution's frame of reference or in terms of institutional demands. Here the student fills out what coursework is required and when, including the names and dates of any mid-term or end-of-term tests and examinations. The second way, from the student's frame of reference, involves a personal ordering of priorities, with decisions on which pieces of work are going to be done when. Personal study goals can be amended as circumstances warrant. Either or both of these termly study goals schedules might be displayed prominently in the student's room. Making such schedules may prevent some students from leaving too much of their work until the last moment and then starting to panic. Also, if students are unclear about what is wanted on an assignment, they might be helped to develop skills at eliciting relevant information from academic staff before, rather than after, completing the assignment. The termly goal-setting schedule may be used by students approaching major examinations for listing revision priorities and objectives.

Some clients may find it helpful to fill out a *weekly* time chart (Table 16.3). Such a time chart may be used either *retrospectively*, for monitoring how time has been spent, or *prospectively*, for deciding on how time will be spent. Counsellors working with clients with learning problems often encourage them first to monitor how they are actually spending their time. Then, on the basis of the information generated by this method, clients are encouraged to explore and make decisions about how they might

Table 16.3 *Weekly time chart*

	Monday	Tuesday	Wednesday	Thursday	Friday	Saturday	Sunday
6 a.m.							
7.00							
8.00							
9.00							
10.00							
11.00							
12.00							
1 p.m.							
2.00							
3.00							
4.00							
5.00							
6.00							
7.00							
8.00							
9.00							
10.00							
11.00							
12.00							
1 a.m.							
2.00							
3.00							
4.00							
5.00							

Note: Coloured pen or pencil may be used to indicate fixed commitments.

plan and organize their time more effectively in future. This may lead to filling out a weekly time chart prospectively. Some clients may prefer, within the framework of a termly plan, to set their objectives day by day. Needless to say, the use of time charts does not suit all students, some of whom may be productive on the basis of inspiration rather than systematic planning. Furthermore, some students may use the filling out of time charts as a device for avoiding work.

Poor study conditions sometimes contribute to ineffective use of time. Counsellors may help students to explore locations which act as a stimulus for them to work, otherwise known as acting as stimulus controls.[10] Usually these places will be quiet, well lit, well ventilated, adequately heated or cooled, and suitably furnished. Students can further contribute to controlling their environmental stimuli by keeping their study location clear of distractions, such as magazines and photographs.

Attempts both to get students to organize their study time better and to find suitable locations for studying aim to get students to be more responsible for their learning. DeCharms has produced some evidence that the more elementary-school students characteristically attribute their behaviour as originating from themselves, the higher they tend to achieve.[11] His personal-causation training – aimed at helping students to determine realistic goals, know their strengths and weaknesses, determine actions, and learn how to monitor those actions – may be a valuable approach to poor planning, poor organization, and ineffective use of study time at secondary and tertiary levels.

Further methods of helping students to use their study time effectively include: audio-taped and video-taped study skills programmes;[12] the teaching of others in the student's own area of learning incompetence, or what Wankowski calls learning through teaching;[13] partly structured groups to help students to understand their own study methods;[14] appropriate choice of room-mate;[15] training teaching assistants and peers to provide tutorial help in study skills;[16,17] and use of reading suggestions, such as Rowntree's *Learn How to Study*,[18] Robinson's *Effective Study*[19] or typed handouts giving study skills advice.[20]

Procrastination

Procrastination involves difficulty in getting down to and/or persisting in work. Paraphrasing the old saying that 'procrastination is the thief of all time', in tertiary education procrastination is the thief of much student and staff time, leading to lowered productivity and underachievement. Sometimes students find it difficult to study because of current stresses such as poor health, inadequate food and sleep, financial and housing worries, uncertain career aspirations, and personal and relationship concerns, such as a bereavement or the break-up of an important relationship. In such instances counsellors and their clients may decide to focus primarily on coping with the non-work stresses interfering with study.

On other occasions the problems of difficulty in getting started and of concentrating once started may be more directly concerned with the student's sense of incompetence and lack of skills as a learner. Occasionally the problems involved in procrastination are very deep-seated and pervasive, thus requiring more extensive counselling

assistance than the interventions suggested below. Frequently students who procrastinate compound their problems with much self-devaluation, which further lowers
their confidence and ability to act effectively.

The counsellor's objective with students who procrastinate is to increase their sense
of competence as learners to the point where they are able to demonstrate actual
competence. Ways in which this may be achieved include the following, which are
often interrelated.

Catharsis and empathic understanding

For some clients just sharing and talking about their problem in an accepting
environment may help them to get it more into perspective, as the vignette below
illustrates.

> Bill was a PhD student in his mid-twenties who came to counselling because he found
> himself getting emotional and weepy at his failure to get started on writing his
> dissertation. He had spent the previous two years performing the research studies for
> his PhD yet now felt unable to write them up. This was worrying because he felt he was
> possibly going to waste two years' effort, with very negative implications for his career.
> Furthermore, he disparaged himself both for losing control of his work which he had
> never done before, and for the emotional state he was getting into. An added issue was
> that he had started questioning whether he really wanted his PhD. After two sessions
> of counselling, in which Bill was able to really talk about his concerns for the first time,
> he came to the conclusion that it was in his interests to obtain his PhD, and he had
> started writing his dissertation. During these counselling sessions he explored his
> approach to life and to meeting others' expectations as well as his approach to work.

Therapeutic study help

Some students who feel they have lost control over their work and hence procrastinate
may be helped by what has been described elsewhere as therapeutic study help.[21]
Briefly, this consists of a number of different elements: (a) a clearly recognized need
on the part of the client for this kind of help; (b) co-operation between counsellor and
client, with the counsellor creating a therapeutic emotional climate and hence
avoiding being perceived as another source of pressure; (c) an analysis of the problem
from the client's frame of reference, including the expression of attitudes and
emotions; (d) joint clarification of the problem area or areas, which may include a
review of ability to set goals and order priorities, of things that make it easier and
things that make it more difficult to study, of use of time during the week, of
characteristic ways of handling study difficulties, of interest in subject, of accuracy of
academic self-image and levels of aspiration, of career objectives, and of ability to use
staff and student resources for assistance; (e) joint specification of minimum study
goals until the next interview, followed by the filling out of a time chart which is
specific in terms of task, time and place for achieving the minimum goals; (f)
information on study techniques where this is requested or indicated by the needs of
the client (though the client should be free to reject the information); (g) possibly
fairly frequent contact at first, with brief 15–30 minute interviews for review purposes

and for setting new and, where appropriate, more ambitious goals; (h) interest and non-possessive encouragement by the counsellor; and (i) referral for additional study skills help, such as a study skills or effective reading course, if this is necessary and available. Therapeutic study help requires sensitive monitoring on the part of the counsellor, since some clients can become very easily discouraged at failure to meet goals. The above approach is slightly less formal than the contract approach described by Goldman,[22] and has been devised in a University Health Service setting for students whose disorganization and ineffective use of time is not just a skills deficit but also involves debilitating anxiety.

Thinking-focused interventions

A common feature of many student clients is their tendency to magnify negative feedback and minimize positive feedback, thus sustaining their low sense of learning competence. In an earlier chapter we mentioned that Weiner[23,24] reported that students who were high in achievement motivation tended to attribute success to high ability and positive effort, and failure to lack of effort. On the other hand, students who were low in achievement motivation perceived that success was weakly influenced by effort and that failure was caused by lack of ability. Thus the high-achievement group were more likely to engage in achievement behaviour, including planning and getting down to work. Though counter-productive attributions are deeply embedded elements in many students' self-concepts, a skilled counsellor, by persistently drawing attention to self-defeating attributions and how they might be reworded, may help clients to replace them with more realism and hence they will come to perceive themselves as having more control over their learning.

Another thinking-focused approach to helping people assume more responsibility for their learning involves modelling and cognitive self-instruction. In Chapter 14 we gave illustrative coping self-statements in the areas of preparing for a stressor, confronting and handling a stressor, coping with the feeling of being overwhelmed, and using a reinforcing self-statement for having coped. Meichenbaum and Goodman[25] trained impulsive children appropriately to talk themselves through difficult situations as a means of developing self-control. This approach might also be effective with certain college students who procrastinate. Counsellors can make up audio-cassettes for their clients with appropriate self-instructional statements which can be played and also practised in conjunction with their work as a homework assignment.

Yet another thinking-focused approach to students who procrastinate is that of rational-emotive therapy. Students who procrastinate are often inhibiting themselves by trying to live up to unrealistic perfectionist standards, frequently to please significant others. Irrational beliefs which may contribute to procrastination include: the need to have sincere love and approval almost all the time from significant people; the need to prove yourself thoroughly competent, adequate and achieving; and the idea that you will find it easier to avoid facing many of life's difficulties and self-responsibilities than to undertake some rewarding form of self-discipline. The rational-emotive counsellor teaches clients to dispute such irrational beliefs and replace them with more functional beliefs (see Chapter 3). Counsellors from other orientations also are likely to help procrastinating clients to focus on and explore their perfectionist demands in relation to their work.

Examination Anxiety

Examination anxiety, sometimes called test anxiety, can be either facilitating and helpful to performance or debilitating and harmful to performance, or a mixture of the two.[26] Sometimes debilitating examination anxiety is viewed as consisting of two major components: a thinking or worry component consisting of thoughts about the consequences of failure, and an emotionality component consisting of unpleasant physiological and emotional reactions. Spielberger observes: '. . . worrying thoughts distract the individual's attention from the task, and intense emotional reactions lead to mistakes and cause repression that blocks memory'.[27]

Debilitating anxiety can be divided into pre-examination anxiety, which may manifest itself during revision, and immediately pre-examination and during-examination crises. Ideally students at risk of examination crises should be identified and helped prior to potentially overwhelming examinations. Since this is not always the case, counsellors may be faced with clients in crisis, such as refusing to go into the examination room, or leaving it in panic. Crises are rarely dealt with in the literature on examination anxiety. Practical approaches to examination crises include tranquillizers (assuming no adverse side effects), coffee, emotional support, the opportunity for catharsis and focused exploration so that students may get matters more in perspective, relaxation, coping self-instructions, and the opportunity to take the examination in a more sheltered environment.

In addition to offering clients a facilitative relationship, there are three main approaches, which may be used singly or in combination, to examination anxiety: study skills training, systematic desensitization, and thinking-focused anxiety-management interventions.

Study skills training

Study skills training may be broadly based or focused more directly on skills relevant to examinations, such as revision or examination room skills. It may be part of a separate group training course, or counsellors may work with individual clients. Revision skills include predicting important areas for revision, making use of relevant feedback on prior work and examinations, ordering priorities, assessment of own strengths and weaknesses in the various examination areas, taking notes which lend themselves to easy recall, appropriate use of staff and other students as resource people, and making a realistic schedule for revision including adequate time for rest and recreation. Examination room skills include: arriving at the examination room in reasonable time and, if possible, in a relaxed frame of mind; reading through the examination paper carefully to identify cues about which questions to answer, key words indicating the kind of answer wanted, and indications about marking; outlining well-structured answers; budgeting time realistically; and reviewing work. One way of increasing examination skills is giving students practice at taking simulated or 'mock' examinations and letting them have feedback on their examination technique. Another way involves showing students a video model of a person verbalizing the decision-making processes of a good examination-taker.

Systematic desensitization

Systematic desensitization, a behavioural counselling method described in Chapter 12, has been used widely for treating examination fears. Emery and Krumboltz have produced some evidence indicating that group desensitization for test anxiety, using a standardized hierarchy, did not differ significantly in effectiveness from the use of individual hierarchies.[28] Sometimes systematic desensitization is used in conjunction with study skills training. For example, Mitchell et al report a successful programme for academic and test anxiety of systematic desensitization followed by re-educative study skills training.[29] Also, Katahan et al treated 14 highly test-anxious college students in a programme that combined group discussion, study skills advice and reading, and systematic desensitization for a total of eight sessions, each approximately one hour in length. Post-test results indicated a significant decrease in test anxiety and a significant increase in grade-point average.[30] Furthermore, on measures of debilitating and of state anxiety, Lent and Russell provide evidence of the superiority of desensitization plus study skills training over study skills training alone.[31]

Thinking-focused anxiety-management interventions

Deffenbacher and Shelton report an approach to treating test anxiety based on Suinn's anxiety management training (AMT).[32] AMT involves: (a) muscular and mental relaxation training; (b) use of imagery to initiate anxiety arousal, for instance focusing on a single highly stressful scene such as taking a final examination; (c) focusing on and building an awareness of the physical cues of anxiety arousal; (d) training in switching from aroused imagery to mental and muscular relaxation; and (e) experience in anxiety arousal followed by self-management of tension through relaxation. Suinn observes that clients can use the AMT sequence of anxiety arousal and anxiety reduction as a preventive measure when anticipating difficult interactions or experiences.[33]

Meichenbaum successfully treated test-anxious college students by using a group desensitization procedure with two modifications. First, the use of slow, deep breathing was emphasized.[34] The counsellor would say: 'By means of using slow, deep breaths and by exhaling slowly one can control any feelings of tenseness and anxiety . . . Breathing right slows the bodily processes, lowers arousal'.[35] Furthermore, the counsellor might encourage clients to think silently to themselves the words 'calm' and 'relax' as they slowly let out their breath. Second, clients were to use an active coping imagery procedure when asked to imagine scenes from the group desensitization hierarchy. This procedure required clients to visualize themselves becoming anxious and tense and then to visualize themselves coping with the anxiety by means of slow, deep breaths and self-instructions to attend to the task. Each client was encouraged to choose from an array of self-instructions those that they personally could employ for coping with anxiety and focusing attention on the test-taking task. The coping statements were similar to the 'stress inoculation' training procedure mentioned in Chapter 14 and tended to be general rather than specific to examinations.

A later study by Hussain and Lawrence focused on treating test-anxious college students either by generalized stress inoculation training or by test-specific stress inoculation training.[36] Both sets of subjects received informal relaxation as well as the same rationale for stress inoculation training. This rationale was that their anxiety in the test situation might be due to the self-defeating statements they were repeating to themselves during the test. Those self-verbalizations were lowering their performance by raising their anxiety level. Therefore, in order to lower this debilitating anxiety, positive statements were to be learned to replace their negative self-verbalizations. Subjects in the generalized stress inoculation condition learned general coping statements such as 'when fear comes, just pause'. Subjects in the test-specific inoculation condition learned coping statements with specific references to test-taking, such as 'I know I'm well prepared for this test, so just relax'. Though stress inoculation training was helpful in lowering test and state (as contrasted with trait) anxiety, even after eight months, there were no significant differences between those individuals receiving test-specific stress inoculation training and those who were trained with more general coping statements.

Mathematics Anxiety

Many pupils and students avoid or feel uneasy about enrolling in mathematics courses, learn mathematics inefficiently, and perform poorly on mathematics tests. Richardson and Suinn, who devised a *Mathematics Anxiety Rating Scale*, defined mathematics anxiety as involving 'feelings of tension and anxiety that interfere with the manipulation of numbers and the solving of mathematical problems in a wide variety of ordinary life and academic situations'.[37] However, a later factor analysis of the *Mathematics Anxiety Rating Scale* suggested that mathematics anxiety was not a unitary construct, but rather there were two main factors labelled as *mathematics test anxiety* and *numerical anxiety* independent of test-taking situations.[38] Student anxieties and difficulties with mathematics may stem from a variety of sources, and counsellors should beware of the loose use of mathematics anxiety as a diagnostic label. Mathematics anxiety is a global term encompassing quantitative aptitude, adequacy of preparation in mathematics, socialization which may have created a negative attitude towards mathematics (especially for females), anxiety about test taking, anxiety about handling new or unresolved situations, and specific problems with specific areas of the complex field of mathematics.

Counsellors with mathematics-anxious clients should remember that any of the above factors may be contributing to their difficulties; also, that skills-building interventions may be necessary instead of or in combination with psychological interventions.

Such skills-building interventions may include mathematics tutorials and mathematics laboratories. Here it is important that the material is presented starting at the current level of the student's skills and that these skills are built up sequentially by means of clear instruction and supervised practice. Teachers of such tutorials and laboratories need to be able to offer empathic relationships as well as be competent in their subject.

Counselling approaches to mathematics-anxious clients include empathic exploration of personal meanings about mathematics and its difficulties, systematic desensitization, and thinking-focused anxiety-management interventions. Genshaft and Hirt report a study which successfully used tutoring and self-instructional training to improve the mathematics performances and attitudes of seventh-grade American female pupils.[39] The self-instructional training focused on self-instructions which might influence task performance. These included: (a) attention-directing ('OK, now what is it I have to do in this problem?'); (b) being less self-deprecating ('I know I can do just as well in maths as in other subjects'); (c) verbal self-reinforcement ('It makes me feel intelligent to solve those problems'); and (d) reducing arousal ('Just remember to relax; there's no need to feel nervous'). In another study women's mathematics anxiety was reduced successfully by means of a combination of a mathematics course and a semi-structured counselling support group.[40] Interventions and techniques in the $1\frac{1}{2}$-hour weekly support group included a mathematics autobiography, cognitive restructuring, weekly goal setting relevant to mathematics, discussion of study skills, assertiveness relevant to asking questions in class, and a brief introduction to desensitization relaxation exercises.

Creativity and Critical Thinking

Creativity and critical thinking are central to high levels of attainment, yet there is a dearth of counselling literature dealing directly with those topics. Possibly this is because clients tend to come to counselling services with overt deficiency problems, such as examination anxiety, rather than with less obvious concerns, such as lack of originality in their work. Thus a criticism of the learning-competence counselling literature is that it focuses mainly on the mechanics of being a student, such as planning work and taking examinations, and relatively ignores the more intellectual skills and attitudes such as critical thinking and creativity. Sometimes, however, good study skills can help creativity. For instance, students with good essay-writing skills may plan their work and pace themselves so that they have sufficient time and energy to write a good integrative and critical discussion section at the end of their essay. Also, students with relatively little debilitating examination anxiety are more likely to be able to use their critical and creative abilities in examinations than are their less fortunate colleagues.

Counselling has a role to play in helping many students and staff to find a locus of evaluation within themselves by which they can be genuinely creative and constructively critical. Some students may need a loosening of their self-concept before they can make a personal contribution to their work. Also, they may need to become less afraid of assessment, and here focused exploration may help them to identify and alter self-defeating standards. Rogers, in *Freedom to Learn*, has focused on ways of creating a freer environment for learning.[41] Some students may need specific training in the skills and attitudes of being more effectively responsible for their learning, including realizing that creativity is likely to involve considerable self-discipline. Furthermore, attention could be paid to the skills of being creative, such as the origination of ideas and risk-taking, and of critical thinking, such as the gathering and analysis of evidence.

Effective Reading, Writing and Note-taking

Probably the majority of both students and staff perform below their optimum effectiveness partly because of reading skill deficiencies. Effective reading is a case where often students' sense of competence is misplaced and interferes with their achieving greater competence. Two assumptions sometimes made by students are: first, that their reading skills are adequate; and second, that even if their reading skills are inadequate there is little they can do about them. Furthermore, by the time they arrive at college, students' reading habits and attitudes are likely to be deeply entrenched, giving rise to resistance to change.

Effective reading necessitates students' reading in the most appropriate way to meet their needs. It covers such dimensions as motivation, purpose, speed, flexibility, comprehension and availability for recall of relevant material. Students and staff often work under the pressure of deadlines and, consequently, they have to read in a very focused way, ruthlessly ignoring extraneous material. Robinson argues for an SQ3R method of reading – survey, formulate questions, read, recite and review – which 'when polished into a smooth and efficient method should result in faster reading, picking out the important points, and fixing them in memory'.[42]

Sometimes client reading difficulties are due to pressures and anxieties in other areas of their life. Also, sometimes there are medical considerations, such as poor eyesight or dyslexia, which require appropriate consultation or referral. Counsellors may explore the extent and nature of their clients' reading difficulties and the personal meanings that such difficulties have for them. Additionally, they may suggest that their clients look at the chapters on reading in selected study skills books.[43,44] They may also refer clients to effective reading courses, which preferably integrate reading skills with the reading required by the students' work. Such a course might be organized along the lines of the Evelyn Wood Reading Dynamics courses, which run for two hours a week over eight weeks, supported by daily practice.[45] Some follow-up session will probably be desirable. The Evelyn Wood method uses the hand to direct the eye at various speeds over the material being read. In Britain, Gibbs and Northedge have attempted a semi-structured group discussion method, consisting of reading tasks and subsequent discussion, for helping students to understand and improve their reading effectiveness.[46] Their intention is to integrate understanding and doing in such a way that it transfers to realistic reading situations.

Writing and note-taking, like effective reading, may best be handled by the counsellor through referral to an appropriate course, preferably involving practice and discussion. Overseas students especially are likely to have problems with their

English, and English language and writing courses may be useful either before or during their courses. British students, too, may profit from brief courses on such topics as how to write an essay or research paper, correct use of English, use of the library, how to take good notes, how to store notes, and so on. For some students, reading the relevant chapters in a study skills textbook will be sufficient.

Public Speaking Difficulties

Public speaking is a skill required of many students both during and after their courses. Nevertheless, for some students considerable anxiety is associated with public speaking, ranging from participation in discussion groups to making more formal presentations. For instance, Jane, a biology graduate student, was on the point of not completing her research degree because she was required by her department to present her research findings in a departmental seminar. Similarly, Bob, an under-graduate in public administration, dreaded the possibility of having to give evidence in court in cases connected with contraventions of public health regulations.

Sometimes students' public speaking difficulties are indicative of broader problems of lack of self-esteem and identity and, as such, may require facilitative counselling instead of, preceding, or concurrent with more specific interventions focused on public speaking. On many occasions counsellor and client may decide to focus mainly on the public speaking difficulty by using specific interventions. The three broad categories of specific interventions are skills training, desensitization, and thinking-focused anxiety-management techniques. Sometimes it is preferable to use more than one of these interventions with the same client.

Skills training

Fremouw and Zittler report the successful use of group skills training for the treatment of speech-anxious undergraduates.[47] The training consisted of modelling, behavioural rehearsal, and videotape feedback on speaking tasks of increasing complexity. They focused on seven elements of public speaking in the following order: rate of speech, volume, inflection, body stance, eye contact, gestures, and speech organization. Subjects were instructed to do homework consisting of practising their skills between sessions. Other skills which might be included in training programmes are answering questions and handling feedback concerning a talk, and appropriate use of audio-visual aids and hand-outs. The fact that most students previously have had limited opportunity to acquire the skills of public speaking makes some form of skills training a useful element in most treatments of speech anxiety. Furthermore, self-disclosure training, though not directly focused on public speaking anxiety, may help to reduce such anxiety by helping students to become less self-conscious about revealing themselves.

Systematic desensitization

Systematic desensitization may be used with imaginal or real-life presentation of scenes. Trussell reports a study which used graduated behaviour rehearsal, increasing the size of the audience and the focus of the speaker, either alone or in combination with systematic desensitization.[48] In the combination group, about half of the time was spent practising progressive muscular relaxation and desensitizing subjects on a single hierarchy consisting of eight items developed from pilot studies with speech-anxious students. The remainder of the group time was spent practising speeches in a normal classroom. Trussell found no significant differences on any dependent measure between the graduated behaviour rehearsal and the graduated behaviour rehearsal combined with systematic desensitization groups.

In an earlier study Paul and Shannon[49] used a 'combined group desensitization' approach consisting of a modified version of individual systematic desensitization plus intensive group discussion aimed at increasing confidence, skills and awareness of effects in interpersonal relations. Two groups of five subjects met for nine weekly one-hour sessions, and were evaluated on the basis of personality and anxiety scales in comparison with subjects individually undergoing insight-oriented psychotherapy, systematic desensitization, and an attention-placebo treatment. Group treatment compared favourably with individual desensitization, and subjects' improvement was maintained over a two-year follow-up period.[50]

Thinking-focused anxiety-management procedures

Meichenbaum and his colleagues used what they then termed a group insight-oriented psychotherapy approach as one of their experimental conditions for treating speech-anxious subjects.[51] This might now be called a stress inoculation approach. The aim was to help subjects both to become aware of the self-verbalizations and self-instructions they emitted in anxiety-producing interpersonal situations and to produce incompatible self-instructions and behaviour. The following points were emphasized: '(a) the specific self-verbalizations group members had emitted in the pre-treatment speech situation; (b) the range and commonality of interpersonal situations in which they made the same or comparable self-verbalizations; and (c) the irrational self-defeating and self-fulfilling aspects of such statements'.[52] Subjects were encouraged to emit incompatible self-verbalizations and self-instructions. Both the insight group and another group using desensitization were effective in significantly reducing subjects' speech anxiety over control-group levels, though there appeared to be differences in which kind of subject responded best to each treatment.

Self-management of thinking may be used in conjunction with relaxation, both being viewed as coping skills. Fremouw and Zittler[53] taught speech-anxious subjects deep muscle relaxation, which they were instructed to practise daily. Also, their subjects were taught to identify anxiety-arousing negative self-statements such as 'I will sound stupid' and replace them with coping statements such as 'I can only improve'. Coping statements were practised in imagination through covert rehearsal of public speaking. Though each of their relaxation skills training and cognitive restructuring-relaxation groups improved significantly, an integration of skills training and cognitive restructuring was suggested as the best way of increasing the generalization of treatment effects.

Stuttering is a very threatening public speaking difficulty for some students. Two things are probable about students who stutter: their stuttering is central to the way they view themselves and is also evaluated highly negatively. As well as giving stutterers an opportunity to explore themselves more generally as people, specific approaches to stuttering might include training in breath control. Here the client is taught, when in trouble, to control his speech by pausing, inhaling, formulating what he is going to say, and speaking at the top of an exhalation.[54] It may also be useful to get clients to practise speaking at a slower and more regular pace. Resick and her colleagues taught subjects to read and speak progressively at 50, 70 and 90 words per minute over a two-week period. Subjects also received anxiety-management training. The results, for both reading and conversation, indicated a significant decrease in stuttering which was maintained at a six-month follow-up.[55] As well as slowing their speech, counsellors may help clients to identify and practise difficult syllables and words. Also, when ready, clients should practise difficult situations, such as speaking on the telephone.

Educational Decision-making

The making of correct educational decisions is highly relevant to motivation and performance. Newsome et al[56] write that subject-choice problems can be reduced to: (a) difficulty in choosing which subjects to study (applicable in institutions which allow for delayed decisions); and (b) disillusionment with the subjects chosen and possibly a desire to change them. Counselling approaches to such students may vary from a single person-centred interview in which the client's resolve is strengthened as he clarifies his position, to a series of interviews in which such matters as values, interests, aptitudes and possible conflicts with parental wishes may be explored. The information aspect of such interviews may include occupational-interest measures, information about courses and professional requirements, and information about the institutional regulations regarding the taking and changing of courses. The area of occupational and educational decision-making is covered in greater detail in Chapters 17 and 18.

THE INSTITUTIONAL ROLE OF THE COUNSELLOR

We now turn to some issues relevant to the institutional role of the counsellor in regard to learning competence concerns.

Collaboration with Academic Staff

Counsellors may be collaborating with academic staff in the treatment of their clients. For instance, a staff member may have referred the client in the first place. On the other hand, the counsellor, with the client's permission, may have contacted an appropriate staff member to help him better to understand the client's behaviour and provide any needed support. Also, counsellors may be asked by their clients to provide letters for their examining boards, so that the board may take extenuating circumstances into account when assessing the client's academic performance.

There are a number of ways in which counsellors can become more integrated with academic staff and *vice versa*. Thorne and DaCosta[57] have developed an Associates Programme for students and staff who want to engage in self-development and explore their own helping abilities. Thorne also writes of running experiential study skills workshops in which counsellors, staff and students share problems, experience and expertise in a non-threatening context.[58] Biggs sees a role for the counsellor as a developmental education consultant in his relations with staff, and suggests ways in which he can help to take part in staff development programmes in such areas as diagnosis of students with learning and emotional problems, the potential for student personality development in the college years, and ways of using lecturing and tutoring to help students to become better learners.[59] Ratigan gives one example of a tutor training programme in a technological university.[60] Also, Bramley notes the need for departmentally based in-service personal tutor training in higher education, consisting of: didactic input, such as human development theory; experiential input, such as listening skills training or even an encounter group; and case discussions.[61]

In recent years 'outreach' has been a fashionable term in the United States to describe counsellor activities taking place outside the central counselling office. There may be some gain in running learning-competence programmes in specific faculties or departments, not least since it may be easier to obtain staff assistance in fostering the integration and practice of skills with course work.

Preventive Interventions

Counsellors may engage in both environment-focused and student-focused preventive work. Daws,[62] writing about school counselling, observes that counsellors are in an excellent position to evaluate the impact of institutions and individual staff on pupils. He suggests that counsellors should find acceptable ways of introducing their values and insights so that mental-health objectives may become incorporated into the institutional philosophy. One way in which counsellors might affect institutional policy is to undertake research monitoring learning-competence problems and their human and financial costs.

Another preventive measure might be for tertiary institutions to provide counselling facilities for potential students who are undecided about which course to take or whether the institution is suited to them. A further preventive intervention would be to run a screening programme in orientation week or early in the first term to identify students who are likely to experience learning difficulties. Such a programme might include a measure of study habits, e.g. the *Brown-Holtzman Survey of Study Habits and Attitudes*, and a measure of anxiety in academic situations, e.g. the *Alpert-Haber Achievement Anxiety Test*. Students should be given the opportunity to discuss their results, with special effort being made to contact those who seem at risk of underachieving. Probably the number of potential underachievers in tertiary education would be smaller if more attention were paid to facilitating learning competence in the schools.

Structural Considerations

Special structures might be considered for helping students with their learning problems and with their debilitating anxieties. Wankowski[63] has proposed an experimental university learning centre where educational counselling and remedial tuition would be made available to students as a matter of normal academic procedure. Another possibility is to name and staff a tertiary counselling service as a 'counselling and study skills service'. Yet another possibility is to have a teaching and learning methods unit with a dual focus on assisting staff with teaching competence and assisting students with learning competence.

Collaboration with Parents

School counsellors are much more likely than student counsellors to be concerned with issues of collaboration with parents. The range of parental behaviour which may contribute to lowered pupil learning competence is very wide. For instance, marital conflict, possibly also involving erratic and negative parental behaviour towards children, is likely to be detrimental. Negative parental attitudes toward education or lack of interest in their children's progress may be affecting performance, as may poor economic and social living conditions. On the other hand, some parents may lower both their children's sense of learning competence and their actual learning competence by being over-involved, excessively controlling, and much too achievement oriented. School counsellors vary in the extent to which they collaborate with parents. Nevertheless, when they engage in such work, they need to use good facilitative skills plus any other specific interventions appropriate to the case in hand.

PRACTICAL EXERCISES AND QUESTIONS

It may help you to develop your skills and knowledge of the material in this chapter if, either individually or as part of a group, you perform the following exercises and answer the following questions.

1.   *Assessment.* Critically discuss some of the issues in regard to assessment when students or pupils present themselves to the counsellor with learning competence concerns.

2.   *Planning, organizing and effective use of study time.*
   (a)   Draw up a work or study-goals schedule for yourself for the next ten or more weeks in terms of: the external demands and deadlines you have to meet; and your subjective ordering of the priorities and goals.
   (b)   Using a time chart, monitor how you spend your time in a 'representative' week. At the end of the week, evaluate your strengths and weaknesses regarding effective use of work/study time.
   (c)   Again using a time chart, set yourself realistic goals for improving your use of work/study time in a forthcoming week.
   (d)   How good do you think you are at pacing yourself to obtain the most out of your work/study, recreational and personal life?

3.   *Procrastination*
   (a)   Over the coming week monitor your procrastination behaviour by keeping a procrastination log. Each time you procrastinate, record the following details: date and time; the situations and other stimulus variables; how you thought and felt; how you behaved; and the consequences of your behaviour for you and for others.
   (b)   Either for yourself or for a client, make up at least one self-instructional statement in each of the following categories: anticipating a study/work situation in which you are likely to procrastinate; handling the arousal of anxiety feelings when facing a study/work situation in which procrastination is usual; making task-oriented statements; and rewarding success at coping with procrastination.

4.   *Examination anxiety.*
   (a)   List as many approaches as you can for handling examination crises. Discuss the advantages and disadvantages of each approach.
   (b)   What are the skills on which you would focus if asked to design a skills training programme for examination-anxious students? What training methods would you use to achieve your goals?
   (c)   Draw up an examination-anxiety systematic desensitization hierarchy either for yourself or for a fellow counsellor trainee or a client.
   (d)   Either for yourself or for a client, make up at least one self-instructional statement in each of the following categories: anticipating an examination; handling the arousal of anxiety during an examination; making task-oriented statements during an examination; and rewarding success in coping with examination anxiety.
   (e)   Discuss the use of relaxation as a coping skill for examination anxiety.

5.   *Mathematics anxiety.*
    (a)   Discuss the concept of mathematics anxiety. To what extent and on which dimensions, if any, might you describe yourself as maths-anxious?
    (b)   Either for yourself or for a client, make up at least one self-instructional statement in each of the following categories: anticipating a 'difficult' mathematics situation; handling the arousal of anxiety in the situation; making task-oriented statements in the situation; and rewarding success in coping with mathematics anxiety in the situation.

6.   *Creativity and critical thinking.*
    (a)   Assess your own ability to be creative and to think critically.
    (b)   List and discuss counsellor interventions for helping clients: to be more creative; and to develop their powers of critical thinking.

7.   *Public speaking difficulties.*
    (a)   Critically discuss the concept of public speaking anxiety.
    (b)   Assess your own feelings, thoughts and behaviour in public speaking and participation in group discussion situations.
    (c)   What are the skills on which you would focus if asked to design a skills training programme for speech-anxious students? What training methods would you use to achieve your goals?
    (d)   Draw up a real-life systematic desensitization or graduated behaviour rehearsal hierarchy for helping a student to overcome speech anxiety.
    (e)   Either for yourself or for a client, make up at least one self-instructional statement in each of the following categories: anticipating a public speaking situation; handling the arousal of anxiety in the situation; making task-oriented statements in the situation; and rewarding success at coping with public speaking anxiety in the situation.
    (f)   With another person, practise speaking using regulated breath control. Start with just a single word for each exhalation, then gradually build up to your usual number of words for each exhalation.
    (g)   By trial and error find out what is involved in speaking at 50 words per minute, then 70 words per minute, and then 90 words per minute. Practise for at least two minutes at each speed.

8.   *Educational decision-making.* Discuss the role of the counsellor in helping clients with their educating decisions.

9.   *The institutional role of the counsellor.*
    (a)   Discuss ways of establishing effective counsellor-academic staff relationships.
    (b)   Design a screening programme for detecting students who are likely to underachieve through learning competence concerns.

(c)   Identify and discuss structural options for counselling students with learning competence concerns.

(d)   In what situations and how might counsellors collaborate with parents to increase pupil learning competence?

NOTES

1.   Lin, E. & McKeachie, W. J. (1970) Aptitude, anxiety, study habits and academic achievement. *Journal of Counseling Psychology*, **17**, 306–309.
2.   Brown, W. E. & Holtzman, W. H. (1964) *Survey of Study Habits and Attitudes Manual*. New York: Psychological Corporation.
3.   Spielberger, C. D. (1962) The effects of manifest anxiety on the academic achievement of college students. *Mental Hygiene*, **46**, 420–426.
4.   Spielberger, C. D. & Katzenmeyer, W. C. (1959) Manifest anxiety, intelligence and college grades. *Journal of Consulting Psychology*, **23**, 278.
5.   Taylor, J. A. (1953) A personality scale of manifest anxiety. *Journal of Abnormal and Social Psychology*, **48**, 285–290.
6.   Alpert, R. & Haber, R. N. (1960) Anxiety in academic achievement situations. *Journal of Abnormal and Social Psychology*, **61**, 204–215.
7.   Covington, M. V. & Beery, R. G. (1976) *Self-worth and School Learning* pp. 17–41. New York: Holt, Rinehart and Winston.
8.   Nelson-Jones, R., Toner, H. L. & Coxhead, P. (1979) An exploration of students' sense of learning competence. *British Educational Research Journal*, **5**, 175–183.
9.   Nelson-Jones, R. & Toner, H. L. (1978) Assistance with learning competence and decision making in schools and further education. *British Journal of Guidance and Counselling*, **6**, 183–190.
10. Beneke, W. M. & Harris, M. B. (1972) Teaching self-control of study behaviour. *Behaviour Research and Therapy*, **10**, 35–41.
11. DeCharms, R. (1972) Personal causation training in the schools. *Journal of Applied Social Psychology*, **2**, 95–113.
12. Jackson, B. & Van Zoost, B. (1974) Self-regulated teaching of others as a means of improving study habits. *Journal of Counseling Psychology*, **21**, 489–493.
13. Wankowski, J. (1979) Educational counselling and learning through teaching. *British Journal of Guidance and Counselling*, **7**, 72–79.
14. Gibbs, G. & Northedge, A. (1979) Helping students to understand their own study methods. *British Journal of Guidance and Counselling*, **7**, 92–100.
15. Shapiro, J. G. & Voog, T. (1969) Effect of the inherently helpful person on student academic achievement. *Journal of Counseling Psychology*, **16**, 505–509.
16. Menger, R. J., Marx, R. & Trumpeter, P. W. (1972) Effectiveness of tutorial assistance for high risk students in advanced college courses. *Journal of Counseling Psychology*, **19**, 229–233.
17. Fremouw, W. J. & Feindler, E. L. (1978) Peer versus professional models for study skills training. *Journal of Counseling Psychology*, **25**, 576–580.
18. Rowntree, D. (1976) *Learn How to Study* (rev. ed.). London: Macdonald.
19. Robinson, F. P. (1970) *Effective Study* (4th ed.). New York: Harper and Row.
20. Richards, C. S. (1975) Behavior modification of studying through study skills advice and self-control procedures. *Journal of Counseling Psychology*, **22**, 431–436.
21. Nelson-Jones, R. & Toner, H. L. (1978) Counselling approaches to increasing students' learning competence. *British Journal of Guidance and Counselling*, **6**, 19–34.
22. Goldman, G. (1976) Students with learning problems – some practical approaches.

Proceedings of the Seventh Conference on Student Counselling. University of London Institute of Education (mimeo).

23. Weiner, B. & Kukla, A. (1970) An attributional analysis of achievement motivation. *Journal of Personality and Social Psychology*, **15**, 1–20.
24. Weiner, B. (1972) Attribution theory, achievement motivation and the educational process. *Review of Educational Research*, **42**, 203–215.
25. Meichenbaum, D. H. & Goodman, J. (1971) Training impulsive children to talk to themselves: a means of developing self-control. *Journal of Abnormal Psychology*, **77**, 115–126.
26. Alpert, R. & Haber, R. N. (1960) Anxiety in academic achievement situations. *Journal of Abnormal and Social Psychology*, **61**, 204–215.
27. Spielberger, C. (1979) *Understanding Stress and Anxiety* p. 87. New York: Harper and Row.
28. Emery, J. R. & Krumboltz, J. D. (1967) Standard versus individualized hierarchies in desensitization to reduce test anxiety. *Journal of Counseling Psychology*, **14**, 204–209.
29. Mitchell, K. R., Hall, R. F. & Piatowska, O. E. (1975) A group program for the treatment of failing college students. *Behavior Therapy*, **6**, 324–336.
30. Katahan, M., Stenger, S. & Cherry, N. (1966) Group counseling and behavior therapy with test-anxious college students. *Journal of Consulting Psychology*, **30**, 544–549.
31. Lent, R. W. & Russell, R. K. (1978) Treatment of test anxiety by cue-controlled desensitization and study-skills training. *Journal of Counseling Psychology*, **25**, 217–224.
32. Deffenbacher, J. L. & Shelton, J. L. (1978) Comparison of anxiety management training and desensitization in reducing test and other anxieties. *Journal of Counseling Psychology*, **25**, 277–282.
33. Suinn, R. M. (1976) Anxiety management training to control general anxiety. In J. D. Krumboltz and C. E. Thoresen (eds), *Counseling Methods* pp. 320–326. New York: Holt, Rinehart and Winston.
34. Meichenbaum, D. H. (1972) Cognitive modification of test anxious college students. *Journal of Consulting and Clinical Psychology*, **39**, 370–380.
35. Meichenbaum, D. H. (1972) Therapist manual used in study of 'College modification of test anxious college students'.
36. Hussain, R. A. & Lawrence, P. S. (1978) The reduction of test, state, and trait anxiety by test-specific and generalized stress inoculation training. *Cognitive Therapy and Research*, **2**, 25–37.
37. Richardson, F. C. & Suinn, R. M. (1972) The Mathematics Anxiety Rating Scale: psychometric data. *Journal of Counseling Psychology*, **19**, 551. Full reference pp. 551–554.
38. Rounds, J. B. Jr & Hendel, D. D. (1980) Measurement and dimensionality at mathematics anxiety. *Journal of Counseling Psychology*, **27**, 138–149.
39. Genshaft, J. L. & Hirt, M. L. (1980) The effectiveness of self-instructional training to enhance maths achievement in women. *Cognitive Therapy and Research*, **4**, 91–97.
40. Hendel, D. D. & Davis, S. O. (1978) Effectiveness of an intervention strategy for reducing mathematics anxiety. *Journal of Counseling Psychology*, **25**, 429–434.
41. Rogers, C. R. (1969) *Freedom to Learn*. Columbus, Ohio: Merrill.
42. Robinson, F. P. (1970) *Effective Study* (4th ed.) pp. 32–33. New York: Harper and Row.
43. *Ibid*. pp. 15–52, 151–178.
44. Rowntree, D. (1976) *Learn How to Study* (rev. ed.) pp. 39–64, 79–104. London: Macdonald.
45. Wood, E. (1968) *Evelyn Wood Reading Dynamics*. London: EWRD.
46. Gibbs, G. & Northedge, A. (1979) Helping students to understand their own study methods. *British Journal of Guidance and Counselling*, **7**, 96–100.
47. Fremouw, W. J. & Zittler, R. E. (1978) A comparison of skills training and cognitive restructuring-relaxation for the treatment of speech anxiety. *Behavior Therapy*, **9**, 248–259.
48. Trussell, R. P. (1978) Use of graduated behavior rehearsal, feedback, and systematic desensitization for speech anxiety. *Journal of Counseling Psychology*, **25**, 14–20.

49. Paul, G. L. & Shannon, D. T. (1966) Treatment of anxiety through systematic desensitization in therapy groups. *Journal of Abnormal Psychology*, **71,** 124–135.
50. Paul, G. L. (1968) Two-year follow-up of systematic desensitization in therapy groups. *Journal of Abnormal Psychology*, **73,** 119–130.
51. Meichenbaum, D. H., Gilmore, J. B. & Fedoravicius, A. (1971) Group insight versus group desensitization in treating speech anxiety. *Journal of Consulting and Clinical Psychology*, **36,** 410–421.
52. *Ibid.* p. 413.
53. Fremouw, W. J. & Zittler, R. E. (1978) A comparison of skills training and cognitive restructuring-relaxation for the treatment of speech anxiety. *Behavior Therapy*, **9,** 248–259.
54. Azrin, N. H. & Nunn, R. G. (1974) A rapid method of eliminating stuttering by a regulated breathing approach. *Behaviour Research and Therapy*, **12,** 279–286.
55. Resick, P. A., Wendiggensen, P., Ames, S. & Moger, V. (1978) Systematic slowed speech: a new treatment for stuttering. *Behaviour Research and Therapy*, **16,** 161–167.
56. Newsome, A., Thorne, B. J. & Wyld, K. L. (1973) *Student Counselling in Practice* pp. 96–97. London: University of London Press.
57. Thorne, B. & DaCosta, M. (1976) A counselling service as a growth centre. *British Journal of Guidance and Counselling*, **4,** 212–217.
58. Thorne, B. (1979) The study-skills workshop. *British Journal of Guidance and Counselling*, **7,** 101–106.
59. Biggs, D. A. (1976) The student counsellor as a team member. *British Journal of Guidance and Counselling*, **4,** 28–37.
60. Ratigan, B. (1977) Counsellor training for tutors in higher education. *British Journal of Guidance and Counselling*, **5,** 98–101.
61. Bramley, W. (1977) *Personal Tutoring in Higher Education* pp. 114–127. Guildford: Society for Research into Higher Education.
62. Daws, P. P. (1973) Mental health and education: counselling as prophylaxis. *British Journal of Guidance and Counselling*, **1,** 95–113.
63. Wankowski, J. A. (1977) Learning how to learn at University: the case for an experimental centre. *British Journal of Guidance and Counselling*, **5,** 41–48.

17 – Occupational Concerns: Testing and Information

SUMMARY: *Psychological tests are one way of gathering information about people. Their uses include selection and counselling, where they are helpful in educational and occupational decision-making, in clearing up misconceptions, evaluation, diagnosis and screening, and prediction. Tests may be used in occupational counselling to gather information in the following areas: interests and values; aptitude; mental ability; achievement; personality; and, treated separately here, leisure interests. Each area is discussed and mention is made of specific British and American tests. Information is provided on who can use tests in Britain and where they may be obtained. Some considerations of test selection include saturation versus precision testing and the role of the client. Assessing a test involves a careful review of its manual, including its description and rationale, who can take it, administration details, reliability, validity, normative data, item analysis and scale development, and interpretation. There is a discussion of ways in which counsellors can contribute to ensuring standardization before, during and after testing. Some problems of testing include response sets, test anxiety, coaching and practice, counsellor personality, invasion of privacy, and perpetuating the status quo.*

Occupational information is any information pertinent to decisions about careers, jobs and occupations. Occupational information may help clients to explore, understand, elaborate and implement their occupational self-concepts. Classification systems for occupational information include: the British COIC/CRAC Careers Library Classification Index, some details of which are provided; the American Dictionary of Occupational Titles; and the Canadian Classification and Dictionary of Occupations. Sources of occupational information in Britain include: the Careers and Occupational Information Centre (COIC); the Careers Research and Advisory Centre (CRAC); the Central Services Unit for University and Polytechnic Careers Services (CSU); industry training boards; professional institutes; the Department of Education and Science; the Manpower Services Commission's Jobcentres, Professional and Executive Recruitment, and Training Services Division; the Department of Employment; Local Education Authority Careers Services; and special reference sources. The information provided by each of the above sources is described briefly and American, Canadian and Australian occupational information sources are mentioned. The chapter concludes with a short description of audio-visual and computerized information services.

The next two chapters focus on practical approaches to occupational concerns. Although the major focus is on occupational choice and career development in the world of work, some mention is made of leisure. It is sometimes said that occupational counselling is distinguished from other forms of counselling mainly by its use of psychological testing and occupational information. On the one hand, psychological testing provides information about an individual or group of people. On the other hand, occupational information provides data about the world of work. Both sources of information may be necessary for effective decisions about people's occupational choice and development.

OCCUPATIONAL TESTING

Our discussion of occupational testing in this chapter aims to introduce the reader to some of the main tests and issues involved in the area. In the next chapter we deal with integrating tests into the counselling interview. Although a knowledge of statistics and test construction is important, such areas are not covered here, since to deal with them properly would require more space than appropriate in this book. Readers who want to learn more about statistics and test construction are advised that basic references include: Anastasi's *Psychological Testing*;[1] Cronbach's *Essentials of Psychological Testing*;[2] Goldman's *Using Tests in Counseling*;[3] Guilford's *Fundamental Statistics in Psychology and Education*;[4] and *Educational Measurement*, edited by Thorndike.[5]

What is a Psychological Test?

There are many different ways of gathering information about people. These include interviews, which may be either relatively unstructured or highly structured, possibly using an interview schedule in which virtually every question has been decided in advance. Other sources of information include personal and educational records, references, essays and autobiographies. Furthermore, individuals who wish to gather information about themselves may use such methods as introspection, asking others' opinions, and social comparison or comparing themselves with others.

A psychological test is another, yet different, form of information gathering. Anastasi writes: 'A psychological test is essentially an objective and standardized measure of a sample of behaviour'.[6] The idea of taking a relatively small, but carefully elected, sample of behaviour is that it would be far too difficult and time consuming to make observations of the whole of a person's behaviour. 'Standardization' means that the test will be administered in a standard way and scored so that an individual's score can be compared with the scores of the group of similar people. 'Objective' means that the test has been constructed to measure and score the behaviour under consideration in as objective a way as possible, thus minimizing the chances of using invalid samples of behaviour and of subjectivity in marking. However, the use of virtually every test involves problems of interpretation.

Uses of Psychological Tests

Testing is used in occupational psychology in two broad areas: *selection*, focusing mainly on the needs of the organization, and *counselling*, focusing mainly on the needs of the individual. Selection decisions within an organization include: (a) selection, whether or not to employ or admit someone; (b) placement, where to place them for the greatest mutual benefit of person and organization; and (c) advancement, whether to promote or upgrade them.[7]

The use of tests in occupational counselling centres around helping clients to make vocational and educational decisions. More specifically, their uses in occupational counselling include the following, all of which relate to the clarification and refinement of the client's self-conceptions as part of the decision-making process.

Clearing up misconceptions

Many counselling clients underestimate their real intelligence and abilities. Indeed, sometimes their potential is masked by underachievement due to the problems which cause them to see a counsellor. Sometimes the appropriate use of a test, such as an intelligence test, may provide a more accurate indication of their real ability than their actual performance to date.

Evaluation

Tests may be used to help both clients and counsellors to evaluate the client's interests, values, aptitudes, abilities and behaviour. Sometimes such evaluations are *ipsative*, that is, they entail within-the-individual comparison. For instance, Joan may be more interested in social welfare than in persuasive occupations, irrespective of anybody else. Sometimes such evaluations are *normative*, where the comparisons are made between individuals. Such normative evaluations involve comparison with the scores of a normative group, for instance with a group comprising people with certain characteristics similar to Joan's, e.g. age and gender.

Diagnosis and screening

Tests may have a diagnostic function for both clients and counsellors. They may identify areas of ability and aptitude that are below acceptable levels. Also, they may identify personal concerns, such as anxiety, which are above acceptable levels. Furthermore, they may indirectly provide clues to the level of a client's psychological well-being. For instance, a client with scarcely any or no clearly defined interests may be having identity problems. A further use of tests is to screen groups of people for diagnostic purposes as a basis for offering assistance to those identified as being in some way at risk.

Prediction

Cronbach observes that all decisions involve prediction.[8] Although tests report something about a sample of an individual's behaviour at a particular moment, often this information is used to predict future performance against the same or a different criterion. For instance, though an occupational aptitude test may not measure the specific tasks that will be required on a particular job, nevertheless it may have a statistical value in predicting success at that job over and above other predictors. Assuming availability, it is helpful for counsellors to have knowledge about the predictive values of the tests they use and, where appropriate, to present this information in such a way that clients can take it into consideration in their decision-making. Sometimes clients will make their own predictive inferences from the results of tests, for instance either agreeing with or ignoring certain findings from an interest measure.

What Kinds of Tests are Available?

Tests may be used in occupational counselling to gather information in the following areas: interests and values; aptitude; mental ability; achievement; personality; and, treated separately here, leisure interests. Each of these areas, though they are interrelated, is now discussed in turn.

Interests and values

Values are the ends which people seek, whereas interests are the means and activities by which people achieve and express their values. For instance, a person with religious values is likely to express these in religious interests and activities. Super and Crites write that there have been four major interpretations of the term 'interest':[9] first, *expressed* interest on verbal statements about liking or disliking an activity, task or occupation; second, *manifest* interest, or interest inferred from participation in activities; third, *tested* interest, or interest as measured by objective tests which indicate how much relevant knowledge and information an individual has in a given area; and fourth, *inventoried* interest, which is assessed by subjective self-estimates of lists of activities and occupations by measures constructed to yield a pattern of interests. These interest patterns are based on interest types which tend to be derived from a statistical technique called factor analysis, and hence are sometimes called interest factors. Table 17.1 shows interest types or factors of selected American occupational interest inventories. Here it may be seen that the *Strong-Campbell Interest Inventory* has adopted Holland's personality types to describe occupational themes.

Table 17.1 *Types of interests of selected American occupational 'interest' inventories*

Strong-Campbell's occupational themes	Holland's personality types	Kuder's interest areas
Realistic	Realistic	Outdoor
Investigative	Investigative	Mechanical
Conventional	Conventional	Scientific
Enterprising	Enterprising	Computational
Social	Social	Clerical
Artistic	Artistic	Persuasive
		Social Service
		Artistic
		Literary
		Musical

During the past decade or so there has been pressure on the constructors of interest inventories to provide combined rather than separate forms for females and males. For instance, the former *APU Guide* and the *Strong Vocational Interest Blank* have now been revised into combined forms known as the *JiiG-CAL Occupational Interests Guide* and the *Strong-Campbell Interest Inventory* respectively. These changes reflect the facts both that much of a person's interests are learned and that previously separate forms for females and males may have perpetuated stereotypes in regard to appropriate interests, activities and occupations for each sex.

Later we describe the assessment of test manuals and the administration and scoring of tests. British interest inventories include the *JiiG-CAL Occupational Interests Guide*[10] and the *Rothwell-Miller Interest Blank*.[11] At time of writing the *Crowley Occupational Interests Blank*[12] had a unisex version; new male, female and unisex forms of the *Rothwell-Miller Interest Blank* were nearing completion; and the *Connolly Occupational Interests Questionnaire*[13] had been withdrawn. American inventories include: the *Strong-Campbell Interest Inventory*, which has a British edition;[14] the *Kuder Preference Record Form C*;[15] the *Ohio Vocational Interest Survey*;[16] and *Holland's Self Directed Search*, which includes activity and competency scales.[17] Especially where unisex versions of an interest inventory seem to be unavailable, it may be worth checking with the publisher or author of the inventory on recent developments. Values inventories include: *Super's Work Values Inventory*;[18] the *Allport, Vernon and Lindzey Study of Values*;[19] and the *Rokeach Value Survey*.[20]

Aptitude

Super and Crites make a distinction between 'the popular concept of *aptitude for a vocation* and the scientific concept of *aptitude important in vocations* . . .'.[21] They observe that psychologists, who think in terms of individual differences and traits, use the word in the latter narrow scientific term. Nevertheless, aptitude still remains a difficult concept to define and measure. It has connotations of innate rather than learned potential, but these overlap. It may be defined as a capacity to learn and, hence, perform some activity or type of activity. However, there may be difficulty in specifying and measuring both a single aptitude and the varying combinations of aptitudes which are necessary for any given occupation.

Aptitude tests come in the form of either batteries, which are a combination of separate tests, or specific tests for special areas of aptitude, such as music or art. Table 17.2 indicates the aptitudes measured in selected British and American aptitude batteries. British aptitude batteries include: the *Department of Employment Vocational Assessment Test,* abbreviated to DEVAT;[22] the *Morrisby Differential Test Battery*;[23] and the recently produced *British Ability Scales*.[24] American aptitude batteries include: the *Differential Aptitude Tests*;[25] and the *General Aptitude Test Battery*.[26]

Mental ability

Mental ability or intelligence tests may form part of larger aptitude batteries or be special tests on their own. Intelligence is sometimes defined as the capacity for reasoning or for problem-solving. Verbal reasoning tends to be the most generally important type of reasoning, but two other kinds of reasoning are numerical reasoning, using numerical symbols, and abstract reasoning, using geometric symbols. More practical aspects of intelligence include spatial visualization, which is the ability to visualize and judge the relationship of objects to each other, and manual dexterities, referring to motor aptitudes. Intelligence testing is a controversial area because of the nature-nurture issue. Super and Crites write '. . . that whereas both nature and nurture play a part in the development of intelligence, mental ability as indicated by the intelligence quotient is relatively constant from the time a child enters elementary school until late adulthood'.[27] Perhaps a better way of expressing this is that intelligence quotients are relatively constant during this period, but there is considerable controversy over the extent to which intelligence tests measure mental ability.[28]

British mental ability tests include: the *AH2/AH3 Group Tests of General Ability*;[29] the *AH4 Group Test of General Intelligence*;[30] the *AH5 Group Test of High-Grade Intelligence*;[31] the *AH6 Group Tests of High-Level Intelligence*;[32] *Raven's Standard Progressive Matrices*;[33] and *Raven's Advanced Progressive Matrices*.[34] American mental ability tests include: the *Wechsler Intelligence Scale for Children* or WISC;[35] the *Wechsler Adult Intelligence Scale* or WAIS;[36] the *Stanford-Binet Intelligence Scale*;[37] the *Watson-Glaser Critical Thinking Appraisal*;[38] and *Cattell's Culture Fair Intelligence Test*.[39]

Table 17.2 Aptitudes measured in selected British and American aptitude batteries

British		American	
Department of Employment Vocational Assessment Test (DEVAT)	Morrisby Differential Test Battery (DTB)	Differential Aptitude Tests (DAT)	General Aptitude Test Battery (GATB)
Arithmetic	Compound series test	Verbal reasoning	General
Shapes	General ability test–verbal	Numerical ability	Verbal
Same word	General ability test–numerical	Abstract reasoning	Numerical
Reasoning (verbal and/or numerical)	General ability test–perceptual	Clerical speed and accuracy	Spatial
Mechanical	Shapes	Mechanical reasoning	Form perception
Mathematics	Mechanical ability test	Space relations	Clerical conception
Clerical	Speed test–clerical aptitude	Language usage	Motor co-ordination
Reasoning (visual)	Speed test–word fluency	1: spelling	Finger dexterity
	Speed test–fluency of ideas	2: grammar	Manual dexterity
	Speed test–flexibility of thinking		
	Speed test–manual speed		
	Speed test–manual skill		

Achievement

People differ not only in interests, aptitudes and intelligence, but also in achievement or attainment. Frequently educational and occupational achievement is assessed by looking at a person's past performance or 'track record'. Another way of measuring achievement is by the construction of tests which sample behaviour from the content area or areas being measured. For instance, achievement tests may be constructed to measure the effects of a specific course of instruction or training. Alternatively, they may be used to assess an individual's level of readiness to undergo specific kinds of training or to be selected for a particular occupation. Achievement tests can come in the form of either general batteries, which measure achievement across a number of areas, or standardized tests in separate subjects, such as reading, mathematics and English.

Another way in which achievement tests may be divided is into tests of knowledge and tests of skill. Though the distinction is somewhat artificial, tests of academic work might be viewed as tests of knowledge while tests of practical skills, such as typing or shorthand, are tests of skill. Sometimes achievement tests involve measuring both knowledge and skills. Anastasi cites the example of tests in modern foreign languages which use tape recordings to test proficiency in reading, writing, listening and speaking.[40] Counsellors, if they ever need to use achievement tests, are referred to the recent catalogues of reputable test publishers and to Buros' *Mental Measurements Yearbook*[41] as sources for making an appropriate test selection.

Personality

Each personality theory tends to have its own constructs and hence there are numerous possibilities for measuring personality, which is in itself a vague construct. Anastasi observes that 'in conventional psychometric terminology "personality tests" are instruments for the measurement of emotional, motivational, interpersonal, and attitudinal characteristics, as distinguished from abilities'.[42] Personality tests which may be relevant to occupational counselling include: measures of interest, attitudes, opinions and values; measures of personality traits such as introversion and extroversion; measures of anxiety and psychopathology; and behavioural measures indicating how people behave across or in particular environments. Anastasi's distinction between personality and abilities becomes very blurred when personality is defined in behavioural terms, for example by specific social skills.

Many counsellors, while remaining sensitive to the psychological and social parameters of occupational life, have reservations about the use of personality measures other than interest inventories. This is especially the case where the constructs and items of the measure do not have a direct link with the occupational decision under review. Furthermore, some careers counsellors may have an inadequate background in the constructs measured by certain personality tests and, in such instances, would be well advised not to use them. However, there are times when personality measures may have an incremental predictive value against some criterion such as occupational success or satisfaction. Where such data exist, taking a personality measure may provide useful information for the counselling process

We have already listed some British and American interest inventories. A British measure of personality traits is the *Eysenck Personality Inventory* or EPI[43] and an American measure is the *Minnesota Multiphasic Personality Inventory* or MMPI,[44] which is used in clinical settings as a measure of psychopathology. The EPI scales are Extroversion/Introversion and Stability/Neuroticism. In its regular administration, the MMPI provides scores on ten 'clinical scales': Hypochondriasis, Depression, Hysteria, Psychopathic deviate, Masculinity-femininity, Paranoia, Psychasthenia, Schizophrenia, Hypomania and Social Introversion. Holland's work on personality types, described in Chapter 9, is a more specific application of the notion of personality traits to occupational counselling and the world of work. Furthermore, writers like Astin and Holland, with their *Environmental Assessment Technique*,[45] and Pace and Stern, with their *College Characteristics Index*,[46] have attempted to measure environmental personality traits, thus broadening the concept of personality testing from individuals to environments.

Leisure

Leisure has been listed as a separate area of testing more because of its future potential as an important area of test development than because of the current availability of many valid measures. At time of writing there appears to be no British leisure interests inventory. American leisure inventories include *McKechnie's Leisure Activities Blank*, in which subjects rate their past participation (manifest interest) and future participation intentions for each of a number of activities,[47] and Overs and his colleagues' *Avocational Title Card Sort* and *Avocational Picture Card Sort*.[48]

Issues in Test Selection

There are numerous issues involved in selecting tests, ranging from basic practical considerations, such as who can use tests and how to obtain them, to considerations about the effect of testing on the counselling relationship and process.

Who can use tests?

Probably the major test publisher in Britain is the National Foundation for Educational Research (NFER). In accordance with the requirements of the British Psychological Society and international practice, all test materials supplied by the Test Department of the NFER Publishing Company are subject to a test user qualification system, illustrated in Table 17.3. Other test publishers may not be so fastidious about the qualifications of test users. However, there is an ethical obligation for counsellors to be trained and competent in the use of any test they select.

Table 17.3 *NFER test user qualification system*

Categories of tests	User qualifications
Level A (Attainment tests)	Responsible people who have had some experience at testing.
Level P (Group tests of ability)	Successful attendance at a course of training in test administration and interpretation approved by BPS or equivalent supervised experience.
Level T	Available to teachers and lecturers.
Level Q (Personality questionnaires)	Those with a thorough knowledge of the principles underlying testing and a fairly wide practical experience in addition to specific training in the type of test ordered.
Level R (Individual tests of mental ability)	Associate Membership of BPS or equivalent training and experience.
Level K (Special clinical instruments)	Normally a clinical psychologist or psychiatrist specifically trained in the instruments ordered.
Level L (Projective techniques)	Associate Membership of BPS or equivalent training and experience, normally with a background of clinical training.

Availability of tests

Selecting tests involves knowledge of the available tests in print plus the ability to obtain them. Test publishers are usually very willing to send their catalogues on request. Below are the names and addresses of some of British and American test publishers.

Britain

Careers Research and Advisory Centre (CRAC),
Publications Department, Hobsons Press, Bateman Street, Cambridge CB2 1LZ (0223–69811)

Educational and Industrial Tests Services,
83 High Street, Hemel Hempstead, Hertfordshire, HP1 3AH (0442–56773)

Hodder and Stoughton Educational,
PO Box 702, Dunton Green, Sevenoaks, Kent TN13 2YD (0732–50111)

National Foundation for Educational Research (NFER),
Test Division, NFER Publishing Company Ltd, Darville House, 2 Oxford Road East, Windsor, Berks SL4 1DF (075–35–69345)

Science Research Associates Ltd (SRA),
Reading Road, Henley-on-Thames, Oxon RG9 1EW (04912–5959)

America

Consulting Psychologists Press, Inc.,
577 College Avenue, Palo Alto, Calif. 94306, USA

The Psychological Corporation,
304 East 45th Street, New York, NY 10017, USA.

Another source of possible tests in print and their publishers is Buros' *Mental Measurements Yearbook*, the eighth edition of which was published in 1978.[49] Further sources of information on test availability are recent editions of psychological testing textbooks, such as those by Anastasi[50] and Cronbach.[51]

Whether and how to test

Super and Bohn observe that psychological tests are indicated in occupational psychology when the questions have been thought through and when specific answers can be helpful.[52] Tyler writes that a test is useful for counselling purposes if, first, there is a considerable amount of evidence about just what characteristic it is measuring and, second, 'if the counsellor can state in clear unambiguous terms what the significance of an individual's score is in relation to various life decisions'.[53] Another way of stating this is that tests should not be used unless the information generated will be helpful in clarifying the client's self-conceptions as part of their occupational decision-making process. Earlier we listed four uses of psychological tests: clearing up misconceptions, evaluation, diagnosis and screening, and prediction. Thus, for each of these uses, there is a basic decision of whether to test or not to test.

Other test selection decisions involve saturation versus precision testing and the role of the client. *Saturation* testing involves the use of a comprehensive battery of tests, whereas *precision* testing involves the use of only that test or tests appropriate to the needs and state of readiness of the individual client. An example of saturation testing would be group administration of a comprehensive battery of aptitude and interest tests to the whole of a school fifth form. An example of precision testing might be the tailor-made administration of a mechanical aptitude test for someone making a career decision about an occupation for which that test has known predictive validity. Often a reason for saturation testing is that of administrative practicality, where there is insufficient counselling time to discover individual testing needs. Saturation testing implies little participation by the client in the test selection process. Also, sometimes the client, especially in groups, may have little chance to say 'no' to the testing itself, quite apart from saying 'yes' or 'no' to individual measures. Factors involved in whether and how clients participate in the test selection process include: their age, the purposes and institutional context of the testing, how forceful clients are in making their wishes known, and the theoretical orientation of the counsellor.

Assessing a Test

Another issue in test selection is that of assessing the relevance and quality of a particular test. This usually involves the counsellor being able to assess the manual for any test under consideration. Sometimes the counsellor may gain additional insights by reading the reviews of instruments mentioned in Buros' *Mental Measurements*

Yearbook or in psychological testing textbooks. Additionally, if they are considering the instrument seriously, counsellors are well advised to look at the items on, if not actually complete, the questionnaire itself.

Two important reference sources for counsellors wishing to assess tests are the British Psychological Society Professional Affairs Board's 'Technical recommendations for psychological tests'[54] and the American Psychological Association's *Standards for Educational and Psychological Tests*.[55] The following are some important considerations in assessing a test manual; readers who wish more detail are referred to the BPS and APA publications.

Description of and rationale for the test

Review the nature of the test constructor's purposes in devising the instrument. Also look for the date when the test and its manual were first published and for the dates of any subsequent revisions.

Who can take the test?

The population for which the test is intended should be examined carefully.

Administration details

Administration details include: availability of the test; difficulty of administration from the counsellor's viewpoint; whether any special training or professional qualifications are needed by the tester; the time the test takes to complete; whether it is for group or for individual administration; the format or formats in which the test is available; whether there are practice items; whether the administration instructions are clear and unambiguous, including indicating any allowable variations in administration and their likely consequences; and whether the test is machine and/or hand scored and the ease with which scoring can be performed.

Reliability

Reliability refers to the consistency, stability and dependability of a test. There are different ways of assessing reliability, including: the same test taken at two different times, or *test-retest* reliability; two different forms of the same test, or *alternate-form* reliability; and measuring internal consistency by assessing scores on comparable halves of a test from a single administration, or *split-half* reliability. Usually reliability is expressed in terms of correlation coefficients indicating the extent to which two measures are related, with test-retest coefficients and internal consistency coefficients being most common. High reliability is not in itself a measure of high validity

Validity

Validity, a central concept in testing, means how well a test measures what it sets out to do. In fact, different tests can have different purposes and a single test can have multiple purposes, so validity is not a unitary concept, but rather there are different kinds of validity. The three main kinds of validity are predictive, content and construct. *Predictive* or criterion-oriented validity refers to the soundness with which predictions can be made on the basis of a test score against some future criterion, such as successful performance of a task. *Content* validity refers to how well the test samples the content and behaviour it is seeking to test. It is highly relevant to attainment tests. *Construct* validity 'involves setting up a number of hypotheses about the test variable as a construct or concept and then examining the evidence relative to these hypotheses'.[56] When assessing the validity of a test, counsellors need to be clear about their own purposes, since the kinds of validity that are important relate to these counsellor purposes and the decisions their clients wish to make.

Item analysis and scale development

Test items can be analysed qualitatively, in terms of their content and form, and quantitatively, in terms of their statistical properties, such as item difficulty and item validity. Some manuals provide details on how the items for a test were selected and analysed. Furthermore, many tests add the scores on groups of selected individual items to form scales. Again, a manual can provide details on the rationale, statistical and otherwise, for the selection of items to form a test's scales.

Normative data

Psychological tests are generally interpreted by reference to *norms* which illustrate the performance on the test of the population or populations for which the test was intended. Normative data enable the test score of an individual to be related to the distribution of scores of a suitably large and relevant reference group. Earlier we mentioned that some test scores may involve ipsative or within-person rather than normative or between-persons comparisons.

Interpretation

The test constructor's intentions for interpreting the scores should be clearly indicated. Information should be provided on common errors and on any other special factors which can affect interpretation.

Administration of Tests

Psychological tests are standardized tests, which means that they are designed to be administered and scored in a standard way or else they lose their real statistical meaning. The counsellor can contribute to ensuring standardization before, during and after any test session.[57] Before the session a suitably quiet, spacious, heated or cooled, lighted and furnished room has to be located. The counsellor should organize the test situation so that the spacing of desks, availability of testing materials, and briefing of any helpers have all been adequately attended to beforehand. Notices should be available to be placed on doors announcing 'testing in progress'. Also, any necessary permissions to conduct the testing should have been obtained.

During testing the instructions in the test manual should be followed precisely, with the counsellor or tester speaking in a slow, clear and suitably loud voice. If it is a group administration, periodic visual checks should be made to ensure that the clients or testees have understood the instructions and are completing the test properly. If any circumstances arise which might invalidate the test findings for an individual or group, these should be noted in writing. When collecting test materials, it can be important to check that adequate personal details have been given. After testing the counsellor might check through the materials to ensure that they are suitable for scoring. Needless to say, the safe storage and transit of completed test materials is vital.

Some Problems in Testing

There are a number of problems in testing which all, directly or indirectly, raise issues about the validity of test findings. Again, readers who wish more detailed information are referred to the specialized textbooks in psychological testing mentioned earlier.

Response sets

The concept of response sets implies that some people answer tests in fixed ways, thus distorting their true scores. Faking or conscious misrepresentation is sometimes included in this category. Some tests, such as the EPI and the MMPI, have lie-scales to detect faking. Less conscious response sets are those concerning social desirability, or wishing to be seen in an approved light, and acquiescence, or the tendency to agree and answer 'yes' to questions. Testee confidence in the complete confidentiality of test findings may sometimes lessen tendencies to social desirability and acquiescence.

Test anxiety

Test taking may be threatening to many testees and thus may give rise to test anxiety, which debilitates rather than facilitates performance. For instance, some testees may worry about the prospect of moderate or low intelligence-test scores in a way which increases the probability of obtaining them. Counsellors who are good at establishing rapport with testees may help to lessen test anxiety.

Coaching and practice

A distinction may be made between coaching, i.e. giving people supervised instruction and experience in taking a test, and practice, or just giving them the experience. Good item selection can minimize the possibility of coaching and practice bringing much invalidity into test results. Not suprisingly, coaching may have rather more pronounced effects than just practice or repetition.[58]

Counsellor personality

Emotional factors may influence the ways in which counsellors use tests. For instance, some counsellors may hide behind tests to give themselves a spurious feeling of expertise and power. Other counsellors, however, may reject tests out of hand as being too numerical, cold or authoritarian without properly considering how tests might help the client's decision-making process. Emotional factors may influence test administration as well as selection. For example, a warm and interested tester is likely to be better than a cold and distant one at stimulating client motivation and co-operation.

Invasion of privacy

Some resistance to psychological testing may stem from feelings that it constitutes an invasion of individual privacy. Personality tests particularly give rise to such reservations. Anastasi observes that protection of privacy involves two key concepts: relevance and informed consent.[59] Relevance means that the information the individual is asked to reveal must be relevant to the stated purposes of testing. Informed consent refers to agreement by the individual, after being adequately briefed about the nature and purpose of the test, to participate in a testing session. Another invasion of privacy is when an agreement to keep test findings confidential is broken.

Perpetuating the status quo

Sometimes tests are criticized for being measures which lead to faulty labelling of people as well as to faulty self-labelling in such a way as to maintain less desirable aspects of our society. Recently, occupational-interest measures have come under attack as perpetuating gender stereotypes. The result of this has been a move towards unisex interest inventories. Also, there is a risk of the faulty labelling of recent immigrants to Britain, such as those from Asia and the West Indies, unless their special circumstances are taken into account when they participate in testing here. In other countries similar problems are likely to arise in testing members of cultural minorities.

OCCUPATIONAL INFORMATION

Hoppock defines occupational information as 'any and all kinds of information regarding any position, job, or occupation, provided only that the information is potentially useful to a person choosing an occupation'.[60] Such information can encompass numerous areas, such as: the functions or nature of the work; the work environment; education, training and qualifications; hours, pay and prospects; method of entry; location, housing and transportation; and trade union affiliation. There are other less tangible, yet still important, aspects of occupational information relating to where the satisfactions are in differing kinds of occupations and to the social and psychological characteristics of specific work environments.

Uses of Occupational Information

Occupational information provides another means by which clients can clarify and implement their occupational self-concepts. Furthermore, such information may contain details about occupational availability, thus indicating whether a choice of occupation is realistic as well as desired. Counselling clients have often had limited access to occupational information in the past and, furthermore, this information may have been circumscribed by social class considerations and distorted by occupational stereotypes. Additionally, clients may have lacked the skills to seek out information and to assess it adequately.

Tyler implies that there are three main uses of occupational information in counselling.[61] First there is the *exploratory* use, by which clients are helped to search for promising alternative courses of action. Second, there is the *understanding* use of information, which is an outgrowth of the exploratory phase and involves getting a fuller understanding of the occupational life-style of particular occupations. This phase may include work observation or work experience as well as assimilation of written information. Third, there is the *elaboration* use of information, when the client needs information for effective implementation of an occupational choice.

Both occupational information and testing have uses for society as well as for the individual. In this regard they may help to obtain the most efficient use of the society's labour force as well as lessen the distress caused by unemployment or unsatisfactory employment, with its social consequences. Needless to say, for occupational information to be fully useful, it should be accurate, well prepared, presented at the level of the potential consumer, and easily available to take advantage of the right timing of its use for different clients' needs and states of readiness.

Classification of Occupational Information

Counsellors may need to build up an occupational information library or filing system. There are many ways in which occupations can be classified, such as: by level, e.g. manager, foreman, skilled worker, unskilled worker; by field, e.g. manufacturing, finance, insurance; by industry, e.g. chemical engineering, textile, steel, motor car; by activity, e.g. typing, book-keeping, selling; by measured interest pattern, e.g. social welfare or persuasive; by predominant environmental personality type, e.g. artistic, realistic, and so on.

There are a number of occupational classification systems in use in Britain. One of the most prominent is the Careers and Occupational Information Centre/Careers Research and Advisory Centre (COIC/CRAC) *Careers Library Classification Index*.[62] The Index is based on groups of careers and consists of an Alphabetical Index listing some 500 careers, each with a classification symbol, and a Classified Index listing the main groups of careers (see Table 17.4). The Classified Index career groupings are

Table 17.4   *Career groupings in the COIC/CRAC careers library classification index*

Basic reference services	Finance
Armed services	Marketing
Administration	Business services
Art and design	Science
Teaching and cultural activities	Engineering
Entertainment and recreation	Manufacturing (excluding engineering)
Catering and personal services	Building and civil engineering and land services
Health and medical services	
Social work	Agriculture, horticulture, forestry and fisheries
Law	Transport and material handling
Security and protective services	Opportunities overseas

subdivided into a number of more specific topics. For instance, Finance is subdivided into General Information, Accountancy, Banking, Building Society Work, Insurance and Actuarial Work, Stock Exchange Work, and Others not specified. Other British classification systems include the Department of Employment's *Classification of Occupations and Directory of Occupational Titles*, or CODOT,[63] used by its Jobcentres and listing and defining some 3500 occupations, and its *Professional and Executive Recruitment Directory of Occupational Titles*, or PERDOT, [64] used by its PER offices.

The major American classification system is the *Dictionary of Occupational Titles*.[65] Here thousands of job titles are listed and briefly described. Each title is assigned a code number and the groupings of related occupational titles are reflected in numerical proximity to each other. In Canada there is the *Canadian Classification and Dictionary of Occupations*.[66] At the time of writing the *Australian Standard Classification of Occupations* was being jointly produced by the Department of Employment and Youth Affairs and the Australian Bureau of Statistics. Originally based on the Canadian classification system, it was undergoing substantial local modification. Perhaps the main American classification system by industry is the *Standard Industrial Classification Manual*.[67] An international classification system by industry is the International Labour Office's *International Standard Classification of Occupations*.[68]

Sources of Occupational Information

Even though counsellors may not be able to answer specific questions about occupations themselves, often they can help people by having appropriate information at hand or at least by knowing how people can get hold of it. Much of this information is presented formally in publications of one sort or another. However, often it will be in a client's interests before accepting employment to use informal sources of information, such as word of mouth and site visits, to obtain a fuller picture of a job.

In Britain, apart from advertisements, etc., there are many sources of occupational information, mainly published, including the following.

Careers and Occupational Information Centre (COIC)

COIC is part of the Government's Manpower Services Commission. COIC's classroom materials for use with and by groups include filmstrip/tape and overhead transparency presentations about career/job choices. COIC also produces several types of material for private study. These materials tend to be in leaflet and booklet form and to provide information on specific careers. COIC's services to assist the careers adviser include up-to-date manuals giving labour market information and details of career entry and training, and *Newscheck*, a monthly newsletter providing news about occupations and industries and reporting developments in education and training. The address of COIC is: Careers and Occupational Information Centre (COIC), Pennine Centre, 20–22 Hawley Street, Sheffield S1 3GA (0742–739022). Further information may be obtained from its most recent booklet on publications and services.

Careers Research and Advisory Centre (CRAC)

CRAC's publications include a series of over 40 separate *Degree Course Guides* giving detailed comparisons of first degree courses in UK universities, polytechnics and colleges. CRAC's other regularly updated guides include the *Directory of Further Education*, covering further education courses in British polytechnics and colleges, *Graduate Employment and Training*, covering graduate employment and 2000 employer organizations which recruit graduates, and *Graduate Studies*, covering postgraduate study in Britain. Additionally, CRAC publishes many other books, films and games.

Central Services Unit (CSU)

The CSU is funded by every university and polytechnic in Britain to support their careers advisory services. CSU publications include the fortnightly *Current Vacancies*, containing details of vacancies for graduates and those about to graduate, and the monthly *Forward Vacancies*. Additionally, CSU publishes a *Register of Graduate*

Employment and Training (ROGET), which is a compendium of graduate employers. Furthermore, in conjunction with AGCAS (Association of Graduate Careers Advisory Services), CSU publishes a national series of information leaflets on various occupations. CSU's address is: Central Services Unit for University and Polytechnic Careers Services, Crawford House, Precinct Centre, Oxford Road, Manchester M13 9EP (061–273–6464).

Industry training boards

There are numerous industry training boards, such as the Agricultural Training Board, the Engineering Industry Training Board, and the Iron and Steel Industry Training Board. These industry training boards publish careers information relevant to their particular industry. A factsheet containing the addresses of industry training boards may be obtained from: The Occupational Information Officer, Birmingham Careers Service, 65 Cornwall Street, Birmingham B3 2EE (021–235–2652).

Professional institutes

Information about professions can be obtained from the relevant professional institutes and associations, such as the Chartered Insurance Institute and the Institute of Chartered Accountants in England and Wales. Addresses for professional institutes may be found in Priestly's *British Qualifications*.[69]

Department of Education and Science (DES)

The DES puts out a series of booklets, updated annually, on the educational courses and qualifications that lead to jobs. Titles in the series include *Getting a Grant, After O Levels, On from A levels, Becoming an Engineer* and *Science at Work*. The DES also publishes *Higher Education – Finding Your Way*, which is a brief guide for school and college students. Copies of DES publications may be obtained from Department of Education and Science, Room 2/11, Elizabeth House, York Road, London SE1 7PH, or in Wales from Room 303, Welsh Office, Oxford House, Hills Street, Cardiff CF1 2XG.

Jobcentres, Professional and Executive Recruitment and Training Services Division

As well as COIC, the Manpower Services Commission provides occupational information through its Jobcentres and PER offices. Additionally, PER publishes *Executive Post*, which is a weekly list of professional and executive vacancies notified to it. The Manpower Services Commission also has a Training Services Division, which publishes information on its Training Opportunities Scheme (TOPS), for training in or updating a job skill, and its Youth Opportunities Programme (YOP), which includes training workshops and opportunities for work experience on an employer's premises or in community service. Government programmes are liable to change, so counsellors should check for the most recent information.

Department of Employment

The Department of Employment publishes a monthly *Employment Gazette* giving information and statistics about employment and employment trends. Its statistics cover such areas as working population, employment, unemployment, unfilled vacancies, hours worked, earnings and wage rates, retail prices and industrial stoppages. Subscriptions and sales of *Employment Gazette* are handled by Her Majesty's Stationery Office, 49 High Holborn, London WC1V 6HB and by other HMSO shops.

Local Education Authority Careers Services

LEA careers services may produce some information themselves. For instance, Birmingham Careers Service prints a series of careers factsheets. Also, it makes available a tape-slide presentation and handouts on how to set up a school careers library.

Additional reference sources

Further reference sources include Priestly's *British Qualifications*,[70] a regularly updated guide to educational, clinical, academic and professional qualifications. Additional British educational and training reference sources are the *Handbook of Polytechnic Courses in England and Wales*,[71] the *Directory of First Degree Courses*,[72] the *Handbook of Degree and Advanced Courses in Institutes/Colleges of Higher Education, Colleges of Education, Polytechnics, University Departments of Education*,[73] *How to Apply for Admission to a University*,[74] *A Compendium of University Entrance Requirements for First Degree Courses in the UK*,[75] and the *Schedule of Postgraduate Courses in United Kingdom Universities*.[76] Publications focusing on Scotland include the *Compendium of Information*,[77] the *Memorandum on Entry Requirements for Admission to Courses of Teacher Training in Scotland*,[78] and the *Handbook of Scottish Central Institutions*.[79] Reference sources concerning overseas education and training opportunities include the American Council on Education's *American Universities and Colleges*,[80] the Association of Commonwealth Universities' *Commonwealth Universities Yearbook*,[81] and the Council of Europe's *European Directory for the Student*.[82] A further useful British guide, this time to careers publications themselves, is *The Directory of Careers Publications*.[83]

In America a major source of occupational information is the *Occupational Outlook Handbook*, published biennially by the US Department of Labor Bureau of Labor Statistics.[84] The handbook provides a wide range of information on occupations, income, training and employment conditions. An abridged version of the handbook is the *Occupational Outlook for College Graduates*.[85] Further and more frequent information from the Bureau of Labor Statistics is provided by the *Occupational Outlook Quarterly*. An American directory of employers is the *College Placement Annual*,[86] while in Canada there are the *Directory: Employers of New University Graduates*,[87] and the *Directory: Employers of New Community College Graduates*.[88]

In Australia much information is collated by the Occupational Information Section of the Department of Employment and Youth Affairs, GPO Box 2817 AA, Melbourne, Victoria 3001. The Department of Employment and Youth Affairs has a national publication called *Job Guide for Australia*[89] as well as an annual *Careers Guide* for individual states. Furthermore, the Department has Careers References Centres in the capital cities of each state and in some other large towns. Open during normal shopping hours and with an informal atmosphere, people are encouraged to use each Centre's resources themselves. These resources include both written information and as video and audio tapes of personal comments by job incumbents.

There is a body called the Graduate Careers Council of Australia (University Grounds, Parkville, Victoria 3052), which publishes pamphlets on careers for graduates in various fields, e.g. accountancy, and general handbooks to help graduates who are looking for employment, e.g. handling an employment interview. Some Australian colleges and universities have an office to help prospective students to decide (a) whether or not to study and (b) which courses would suit their needs, e.g. the University of Melbourne's Office for Prospective Students. Also, most Australian universities and colleges of advanced education have careers and appointments boards.

Audio-visual aids and computerized information services

Every now and then in the above discussion of occupational information mention has been made of films and tape/slide presentations. Some careers counsellors prefer tape-slide presentations to films since they are easier to update. COIC publishes a *Catalogue of Careers Films and Other Audio Visual Aids* listing material suitable for careers counselling purposes. Each entry includes information about the content of the item and reflects an advisory panel's view of its effectiveness and limitations. Other sources of films are the industry training boards and the Central Film Library, whose address is Government Building, Bromyard Avenue, Acton, London W3 7JB (01–743–5555).

Another audio-visual development is the provision of careers information by *Prestel*, the computerized information service introduced by the Post Office. Prestel enables the user to draw information from a central computer via a telephone line, for display on a modified domestic TV receiver. For instance, PER uses Prestel to provide executive job displays, graduate appointment displays, and advice on changing jobs. As mentioned in the following chapter, computers can also be used to match coded information on clients with information on occupations.

PRACTICAL EXERCISES AND QUESTIONS

It may help you to develop your skills and knowledge of the material in this chapter if, either individually or in pairs, you perform the following exercises and answer the following questions.

Practical Exercises

1.   With a partner, assess a test manual and test materials for at least one of the tests mentioned in the chapter in each of the following areas:

(a)   interests and values;
(b)   aptitude;
(c)   mental ability;
(d)   personality.

2.   With a partner, administer, score and report, verbally or in writing, each other's results for at least one of the tests mentioned in the chapter in each of the following areas:

(a)   interest and values;
(b)   aptitude;
(c)   mental ability;
(d)   personality.

3.   With a partner, work together to decide what occupational information is necessary and how to obtain it for any educational or career decision(s) that each of you may have.

Questions

1.   Critically discuss:
(a)   what a psychological test is;
(b)   the uses and misuses of testing in counselling;
(c)   whether and why you might or might not use tests in any counselling work you do now or in the future.

2.   In selecting tests:
(a)   what are the advantages and disadvantages of saturation versus precision testing?
(b)   to what extent and in what ways should clients be involved in the test selection process?

3.   What do you understand by occupational information? Critically discuss the uses and misuses of occupational information in counselling.

4.   If you were setting up a careers library, what classification system would you use and why?

5.   If you were setting up a careers library, what sorts of occupational information would you want in it and why?

6.   Critically discuss the use of audio-visual aids, including Prestel, in occupational counselling and education.

NOTES

1. Anastasi, A. (1976) *Psychological Testing* (4th ed.). New York: Macmillan.
2. Cronbach, L. J. (1970) *Essentials of Pscyhological Testing* (3rd ed.). New York: Harper and Row.
3. Goldman, L. (1971) *Using Tests in Counselling* (2nd ed.). Pacific Palisades, California: Goodyear Publishing Co.
4. Guilford, J. P. (1965) *Fundamental Statistics in Psychology and Education* (4th ed.). New York: McGraw Hill.
5. Thorndike, R. L. (ed.) (1971) *Educational Measurement* (2nd ed.). Washington DC: American Council on Education.
6. Anastasi, A. (1976) *Psychological Testing* p. 23. New York: Macmillan.
7. Super, D. E. & Bohn, M. J. (1971) *Occupational Psychology* pp. 46–47. London: Tavistock Publications.
8. Cronbach, L. J. (1970) *Essentials of Psychological Testing* (3rd ed.) p. 22. New York: Harper and Row.
9. Super, D. E. & Crites, J. O. (1962) *Appraising Vocational Fitness* (Rev. ed.) pp. 377–380. New York: Harper and Row.
10. Closs, S. J. (1980) *Computer Assisted Career Guidance: Manual for the JiiG-CAL System.* Sevenoaks: Hodder and Stoughton.
11. Miller, K. M. (1968) *Manual for the Rothwell-Miller Interest Blank.* Windsor: NFER Publishing Co.
12. Crowley, A. D. (1976) *Crowley Occupational Interest Blank Manual.* Cambridge: CRAC.
13. Fox, J. (1974) *Interests and Occupations: An Introduction to the Design and Use of the Connolly Occupational Interests Questionnaire.* Cambridge: CRAC/Hobsons Press.
14. Strong, E. K. & Campbell, D. P. (1977) *Manual for the Strong-Campbell Interest Inventory.* Stanford, California: Stanford University Press. Distributors of the Strong-Campbell include The Psychological Corporation (address in text).
15. Kuder, G. F. (1960) *Administrator's Manual Kuder Preference Record: Vocational Form C.* Chicago: Science Research Associates Inc.
16. Ayres, G., D'Costa, A. G., Winefordner, D. W., Odgers, J. G. & Kolns, P. B. Jr (1969–70) *Manual for the Ohio Vocational Interest Survey.* New York: Harcourt, Brace, Jovanovich.
17. Holland, J. L. (1979) *Professional Manual for the Self Directed Search.* Palo Alto, California: Consulting Psychologists Press.
18. Super, D. E. (1968–70) *Manual for the Work Values Inventory.* Boston: Houghton Mifflin.
19. Allport, G. W., Vernon, P. E. & Lindzey, G. (1960) *Study of Values: A Scale for Measuring Dominant Interests in Personality* (3rd ed.). Boston: Houghton Mifflin.

20. Rokeach, M. (1973) *The Nature of Human Values.* Riverside, New Jersey: Free Press – Macmillan.
21. Super, D. E. & Crites, J. O. (1962) *Appraising Vocational Fitness* (Rev. ed.) p. 70. New York: Harper and Row.
22. Employment Service Agency. *The DEVAT Manual.* London: Department of Employment.
23. Morrisby, J. R. (1970) *Administrative Manual for the Differential Test Battery.* Hemel Hempstead: Educational and Industrial Tests Services.
24. Elliott, C. D., Murray, D. J. & Pearson, L. S. (1977) *The British Ability Scales.* Windsor: NFER Publishing Co.
25. Bennett, G. K., Seashore, H. G. & Wesman, A. G. (1966) *Manual for the Differential Aptitude Tests Forms L and M* (4th ed.). New York: The Psychological Corporation.
26. United States Department of Labor: Manpower Administration (1970) *Manual for the USES General Aptitude Test Battery.* Washington DC: US Employment Service.
27. Super, D. E. & Crites, J. O. (1962) *Appraising Vocational Fitness* (Rev. ed.) p. 84. New York: Harper and Row.
28. Eysenck, H. J. & Kamin, L. (1981) *Intelligence: The Battle for the Mind.* London: Macmillan.
29. Heim, A. W., Watts, K. P. & Simmonds, V. (1974) *Manual AH2/AH3.* Windsor: NFER Publishing Co.
30. Heim, A. W. (1970) *AH 4 Group Test of General Intelligence Manual* (Rev. ed.). Windsor: NFER Publishing Co.
31. Heim, A. W. (1968) *AH 5 Group Test of High-Grade Intelligence* (Rev. ed.). Windsor: NFER Publishing Co.
32. Heim, A. W., Watts, K. P. & Simmonds, V. (1970) *Manual for the AH6 Group Tests of High-Level Intelligence.* Windsor: NFER Publishing Co.
33. Raven, J. C. (1960) *Guide to the Standard Progressive Matrices.* London: H. K. Lewis.
34. Raven, J. C. (1965) *Advanced Progressive Matrices: Plan and Use of the Scale with a Report of Experimental Work.* London: H. K. Lewis.
35. Wechsler, D. (1974) *Manual: Wechsler Intelligence Scale for Children – Revised.* New York: The Psychological Corporation.
36. Wechsler, D. (1955) *Manual for the Wechsler Adult Intelligence Scale.* New York: The Psychological Corporation.
37. Terman, L. M. & Merrill, M. A. (1960) *Stanford-Binet Intelligence Scale: Manual for the Third Revision, Form L – M.* Boston: Houghton Mifflin.
38. Watson, G. & Glaser, E. M. (1964) *Manual: Watson-Glaser Critical Thinking Appraisal.* New York: Harcourt, Brace and World.
39. Cattell, R. B. & Cattell, A. K. S. (1959) *Handbook for the Culture Fair Intelligence Test.* Champaign, Illinois: Institute for Personality and Ability Testing.
40. Anastasi, A. (1976) *Psychological Testing* (4th ed.) p. 411. New York: Macmillan.
41. Buros, O. K. (ed.) (1978) *The Eighth Mental Measurements Yearbook – vols 1 and 2.* Highland Park, New Jersey: Gryphon Press.
42. Anastasi, A. (1976) *Psychological Testing* (4th ed.) p. 493. New York: Macmillan.
43. Eysenck, H. J. & Eysenck, S. G. B. (1964) *Manual For the Eysenck Personality Inventory.* Sevenoaks: Hodder and Stoughton.
44. Hathaway, S. R. & McKinley, J. C. (1967) *Minnesota Multiphasic Personality Inventory Manual* (revised 1967). New York: The Psychological Corporation.
45. Astin, A. W. & Holland, J. L. (1961) The environmental assessment technique: a way to measure college environments. *Journal of Educational Psychology*, **52**, 308–316.
46. Pace, C. R. & Stern, G. G. (1958) An approach to the measurement of psychological characteristics of college environments. *Journal of Educational Psychology*, **49**, 269–277.
47. McKechnie, G. E. (1974) Psychological foundations of leisure counseling: an empirical strategy. *Therapeutic Recreation Journal*, **3**, 4–16.
48. Overs, R. P. (1975) Avocational counseling: gateway to meaningful activity. *Counseling and Values*, **1**, 36–41.

49. Buros, O. K. (ed.) (1978) *The Eighth Mental Measurements Yearbook – vols 1 and 2.* Highland Park, New Jersey: Gryphon Press.
50. Anastasi, A. (1976) *Psychological Testing* (4th ed). New York: Macmillan.
51. Cronbach, L. J. (1970) *Essentials of Psychological Testing* (3rd ed.). New York: Harper and Row.
52. Super, D. E. & Bohn, M. J. (1971) *Occupational Psychology* p. 34. London: Tavistock Publications.
53. Tyler, L. E. (1961) *The Work of the Counsellor* (2nd ed.) p. 107. New York: Appleton-Century-Crofts.
54. Professional Affairs Board (1980) Technical recommendations for psychological tests. *Bulletin of the British Psychological Society*, **33**, 161–164.
55. American Psychological Association (1974) *Standards for Educational and Psychological Tests*. Washington DC: American Psychological Association.
56. Professional Affairs Board (1980) Technical recommendations for psychological tests. *Bulletin of the British Psychological Society*, **33**, 163.
57. Holdsworth, R. (1978) *Using Tests in Vocational Guidance* pp. 1–23. Stourbridge: Institute of Careers Officers.
58. Anastasi, A. (1976) *Psychological Testing* (4th ed.) pp. 41–44. New York: Macmillan.
59. *Ibid.* pp. 49–52.
60. Hoppock, R. (1976) *Occupational Information* (4th ed.) p. 6. New York: McGraw-Hill.
61. Tyler, L. E. (1961) *The Work of the Counsellor* (2nd ed.) pp. 155–158. New York: Appleton-Century-Crofts.
62. Careers and Occupational Information Centre/Careers Research and Advisory Centre (1976) *Careers Library Classification Index* (Rev. ed.). Sheffield: COIC.
63. Department of Employment (1972) *Classification of Occupations and Directory of Occupational Titles*. London: HMSO.
64. Manpower Services Commission (1972) *Professional and Executive Recruitment Directory of Occupational Titles*. London: HMSO.
65. *Dictionary of Occupational Titles*. Washington DC: US Government Printing Office. See latest edition.
66. *Canadian Classification and Dictionary of Occupations*. Ottawa: Information Canada, Publishing Division. See latest edition.
67. *Standard Industrial Classification Manual*. Washington DC: US Government Printing Office. See latest edition.
68. *International Standard Classification of Occupations*. Geneva: International Labor Office. See latest edition.
69. Priestly, B. (ed.) *British Qualifications*. London: Kogan Page. See latest edition.
70. *Ibid*.
71. Committee of Directors of Polytechnics. *Handbook of Polytechnic Courses in England and Wales*. Bradford: Lund Humphries. See latest edition.
72. Council for National Academic Awards. *Directory of First Degree Courses*. London: CNAA. See latest edition.
73. *Handbook of Degree and Advanced Courses in Institutes/Colleges of Higher Education, Colleges of Education, Polytechnics, University Departments of Education*. Bradford: Lund Humphries. See latest edition.
74. University Central Council on Admissions (UCCA). *How to Apply for Admission to a University*. Cheltenham: UCCA. See latest edition.
75. Committee of Vice-Chancellors and Principals. *A Compendium of University Entrance Requirements for First Degree Courses in the UK*. London: Association of Commonwealth Universities. See latest edition.
76. *Schedule of Postgraduate Courses in United Kingdom Universities*. London: Association of Commonwealth Universities. See latest edition.
77. Scottish Universities Council on Entrance. *Compendium of Information*. St Andrews: SUCE. See latest edition.
78. Scottish Education Department. *Memorandum on Entry Requirements for Admission to*

      Courses of Teacher Training in Scotland. Available from HMSO offices. See latest edition.
79. *Handbook of Scottish Central Institutions.* Paisley: Paisley College of Technology. See latest edition.
80. American Council on Education. *American Universities and Colleges.* Washington DC: American Council on Education. See latest edition.
81. Association of Commonwealth Universities. *Commonwealth Universities Yearbook.* London: Association of Commonwealth Universities. See latest edition.
82. *European Directory for the Student.* Strasbourg: Council of Europe. See latest edition.
83. Hope, G. (ed.). *The Directory of Careers Publications.* Chorley Wood, Herts: Graduate Press Ltd. See latest edition.
84. US Department of Labor Bureau of Labor Statistics. *Occupational Outlook Handbook.* Washington, DC: US Government Printing Office. See latest edition.
85. US Department of Labor Bureau of Labor Statistics. *Occupational Outlook for College Graduates.* Washington, DC: US Government Printing Office. See latest edition.
86. *College Placement Annual.* Bethlehem, Pennsylvania: College Placement Council. See latest edition.
87. *Directory: Employers of New University Graduates.* Ottawa: Department of Manpower and Immigration. See latest edition.
88. *Directory: Employers of New Community College Graduates.* Ottawa: Department of Manpower and Immigration. See latest edition.
89. *Job Guide for Australia.* Melbourne: Department of Employment and Youth Affairs. See latest edition.

18 – Occupational Concerns: Counselling and Careers Education

SUMMARY: *Career development is a concept which encompasses both careers counselling and education. Assumptions underlying career development are discussed. Developmental careers counselling acknowledges the importance of emotional factors in facilitating or blocking effective occupational decision-making. Elements of developmental careers counselling include an empathic counselling relationship, the use of tests to facilitate self-exploration, the use of information to explore the world of work, and assistance in planning the implementation of an occupational self-concept. Behavioural careers counselling is based on a teacher-learner relationship. Behavioural methods include verbal reinforcement of information-seeking behaviour, modelling and teaching decision-making skills, simulated work experience, behaviour rehearsal of interview skills and behavioural self-control. Differentialist careers counselling is based on a matching of individual differences with differences in careers and jobs. Williamson's trait-factor, Rodger's seven-point plan and Holland's 'modern differentialist' approaches are presented. Developmental, behavioural, and differentialist approaches to leisure counselling are reviewed.*

Careers education involves educating people to make career decisions wisely. Objectives include opportunity awareness, self-awareness, decision learning and transition learning. Careers education may save interview time. In secondary schools it is best viewed as a team effort involving careers staff, careers officers, teachers, and people from the world of work. The clientele for careers education includes teachers, parents and employers as well as pupils. Careers education may be integrated into the teaching of regular curricular offerings or there may be special courses focusing on one or more careers education objectives. Methods of helping pupils to attain each objective are described. In the future the term 'career' may be defined more broadly to include other roles, such as leisure or coping with unemployment.

Computers extend both client and counsellor access to career-relevant data. Computer-based systems range from information storage and retrieval systems, through job-person matching systems, to interactive exploration, choice and career development systems. Some problems of computer-based careers counselling and education are mentioned, including cost and confidentiality. Nevertheless, in the future computers will have an important role to play.

In this chapter we elaborate our earlier discussion in Chapters 8 and 9 of occupational choice and development theories. We describe the implications for occupational *counselling* practice of developmental, behavioural and differentialist theories. Additionally, attention is paid to the practice of leisure counselling. The chapter also focuses on the broader concept of *careers education*, of which counselling forms a part. Watts observes that the term 'careers education' only started to come into general use around 1970–71.[1] A major distinction in careers education may be made between being *trained for a career* by acquisition of specifically vocational skills, such as building, technical drawing, typing, gardening and motor maintenance, and being *educated to make career decisions wisely* by curricular, extra-curricular and counselling interventions. Although both training for a career and being educated to make career decisions wisely have been emphases in American careers education, British careers education has mainly emphasized making career decisions wisely.[2] After reviewing approaches to careers education, we briefly mention the role of computers in occupational counselling.

CAREER DEVELOPMENT

In its early years occupational counselling was heavily dominated by a cognitive, logical and rational 'talent-matching' (matching of person to job) approach. Over the past 20 or so years there has been a shift in emphasis from a talent-matching to a career-development position. Watts writes concerning this shift:

> Previously the primary tasks of guidance specialists had been to *diagnose* the individual's attributes and to *prescribe* appropriate occupations. Now their tasks were increasingly seen as being to *facilitate* the individual's decision-making processes and to *develop* his or her own decision making skills and competencies.[3]

Furthermore, there has been an increasing tendency to drop the term 'guidance', with its diagnostic-prescriptive connotations, and to replace it with the more developmental term 'counselling'.

The concept of career development provides a rationale both for counselling and for careers education interventions for the problems of occupational choice and development. There are a number of assumptions associated with career development. First, it is assumed that people's occupational lives comprise a series of career decisions relating to such issues as work entry, initial training, in-service training, job enhancement, mid-career mobility, slowing down and retirement, not to mention the possibility of underemployment and redundancy. More colloquially, this may be expressed as 'occupational life is one darned decision after another'. Second, it is assumed that the attainment and implementation of a reasonably satisfying occupational identity is a very important developmental task. Furthermore, continued access to satisfying work can make a sizeable contribution to emotional stability and psychological well-being.

Third, it is assumed that nowadays there are a number of reasons why young people find it difficult to grow up occupationally. Borow writes that 'occupational illiteracy' is a common phenomenon among American youth[4] and probably the same is true of Britain. In Chapter 9 we mentioned structural factors restricting knowledge about the world of work. Other factors which contribute to occupational illiteracy include: the increased complexity of the occupational world; the increased training required for and hence remoteness of some occupations; the lessened opportunities for children to work alongside their parents and learn a trade; the tendency of parents and significant others to teach their children stereotypes about occupations rather than provide them with realistic information; restrictive perceptions of various occupations according to gender; and the tendency of people to distort occupational information to suit their personal needs. Thus career development interventions are perceived as necessary antidotes to the prevailing occupational illiteracy.

A fourth assumption underlying career development is that initial career choices may for varying reasons be voluntarily reversible or compulsorily reversed. For instance, a business executive or a housewife may voluntarily seek more self-enhancing career opportunities in mid-life. On the other hand, redundancy due to an economic recession or technological change may force people to re-evaluate and possibly modify or reverse their initial career decisions. Fifth, there is perhaps a greater emphasis than before on people taking responsibility for their personal decision-making, including the development of and satisfaction they derive from their careers. The notion of career development implies helping people to become effective in such decision-making.

The concept of career development provides common ground in considering approaches for occupational concerns. First, it is implicit in all the counselling approaches described here, whether they are labelled developmental, behavioural or differentialist. Second, the objective of career development is shared both by counselling and by careers education approaches. Though in the sections that follow many different approaches and techniques are discussed, their common objective is to help people more effectively to develop their careers over their life-span.

COUNSELLING APPROACHES

Developmental Careers Counselling

Since the Second World War, psychotherapeutic considerations involving the client's emotions and attitudes have become a more prominent part of occupational counselling. The term 'developmental careers counselling' is used to designate an approach to occupational interviewing heavily influenced by Rogers' client-centred or person-centred therapy as well as by Super's ideas on vocational development. It acknowledges that occupational choice and development decisions tend to be processes involving the whole *person*, including feelings, thoughts and actions, rather than being narrowly circumscribed *problems*. Though our present discussion of developmental careers counselling will focus on decisions relating to the world of work, in 1980 Super provided a broader definition of career as being 'the combination and sequence of roles played by a person during a lifetime',[5] indicating that these roles include leisurite, citizen, worker, spouse and homemaker. Such a definition implies a wider emphasis in developmental careers counselling than that discussed here.

Theoretical concepts

We provide summaries of person-centred and vocational development theories in Chapters 2 and 9 respectively. Here we select some concepts which are particularly important in understanding the developmental approach to careers counselling.

Occupational self-concept. A person's self-concept comprises the many different self-conceptions by which the individual describes and distinguishes himself. Occupational self-conceptions are those parts of the self-concept relating to work and leisure activities. In our review of Super's work we mentioned that he considered that: (a) vocational development involves the continuous development and implementation of a self-concept; and (b) self-concept development takes place in stages relating to approximate ages – growth (age 0–14), exploration (15–24), establishment (25–44), maintenance (45–64), and decline (age 64 onwards).

Organismic valuing process. Person-centred theory posits that the 'organism has one basic tendency and striving – to actualize, maintain and enhance the experiencing organism'.[6] A person's organismic valuing process relates to the continuous weighing of experience and the placing of values on that experience in terms of its ability to satisfy the actualizing tendency. Occupational self-actualizing may be seen as one expression of the individual's self-actualizing tendency. Rogers writes of the infant's trust in his own valuing processes as evidence both that these processes exist and that they may subserve the needs of the organism.[7] Thus all people are seen to have the innate capacity for adequate valuing of experience within themselves, including experiences pertinent to occupational choice and development.

Conditions of worth and occupational self-concept. Rogers believes that most of us accumulate introjected value patterns or conditions of worth and live accordingly.[8] Such value patterns are introjected to the extent that they reflect the assessments of others rather than those of our own valuing process. Some sample conditions of worth relevant to occupational choice are: 'I am not the sort of person who can handle my life without being dependent on other people'; 'Making money is the highest good'; 'High-status occupations are always better than low-status occupations'; and 'Women do not go into engineering and therefore, since I am female, it is not a career possibility for me'. It is probable that most clients in occupational counselling are in varying degrees blocked from accurately perceiving and hence accurately processing information about themselves and the world of work. They are denying and distorting information so as to sustain occupational self-conceptions based on conditions of worth. This leads to faulty career decision-making and to the implementation of plans of action based on incomplete and distorted information.

Occupational self-concept allowing realistic perception. Assuming sufficient and accurate occupational information, people are likely to be successful in their occupational decision-making and self-enhancement to the degree that they are open to the experiencing going on within themselves. Rogers considers that mature people have a locus of evaluation firmly within themselves, yet their valuing is fluid, flexible, and based on the experiencing of the immediate moment. Also, such people are likely to endeavour to sense and clarify their personal meanings in all their complexity. Rogers gives the following example of a student who is moving from values based on conditions of worth to those based on his organismic valuing process:

> The student failing chemistry realizes, as he gets close to his own experiencing – 'I don't value being a doctor, even though my parents do; I don't like chemistry; I don't like taking steps toward being a doctor; and I am not a failure for having these feelings'.[9]

As clients become more fully functioning, their career decision-making is likely to possess a high degree of rationality, with the criterion of their decisions being the degree to which they are self-actualizing and self-enhancing.

Practical considerations

The increasing realization of the fact that most people are unable to adjust to life without distortions of reality has been the impetus behind the trend towards taking psychotherapeutic and emotional considerations into account in careers work. The possibility that both client and counsellor may be misperceiving, sometimes simultaneously, themselves, each other, the world of work and the content of the interview has necessitated a re-examination of the practice of careers work. As previously mentioned, this has involved a shift away from externally directed *guidance* towards a *counselling* approach with an emphasis on facilitating self-direction.

Clients come into counselling at varying states of readiness for making and implementing occupational decisions. For instance, a counsellor working with a moderately to severely disturbed client may decide, in co-operation with the client and given adequate time, to help him to reduce his conditions of worth before focusing on specific career decisions. Put more simply, the client needs to understand himself better before committing himself to a career decision. On the other hand, with less disturbed clients facing the normal problems of occupational choice, the emotional factors present can be worked with concurrently, and as part of a more focused approach to occupational decision-making. It is this latter type of developmental career counselling which we describe here.

The goal of developmental careers counselling is to facilitate the client's self-actualizing by means of a relationship in which the client feels safe and free to explore, clarify and, if necessary, receive help in implementing an occupational self-concept undistorted by emotional factors. Such an approach might include the following elements.

A fundamental counselling relationship. This is the kind of relationship described in Chapter 11 in which the counsellor strives to create an emotional climate of acceptance and understanding. Within this empathic relationship, the client's occupational self-exploration is facilitated and he is allowed 'to express his self-concept in terms of his needs, his conflicts and anxieties, and his hopes, desires, and expectations as they relate to aptitudes, abilities, interests, and concepts of work and occupations'.[10] The counsellor endeavours to make the atmosphere sufficiently trusting for the client to start acknowledging and clarifying ideas and feelings within himself which may be at variance with his current occupational self-conceptions. To a large extent the counselling process is involved with the way the client experiences and perceives himself and his world, and his personal meanings, attitudes and emotions. To the extent that external reality considerations are involved, it is the client's perception of these that is of primary importance.

Use of tests to facilitate occupational self-exploration. Developmental careers counselling differs from the usual person-centred counselling mainly in the use of tests and occupational information. The use of tests in such careers counselling is primarily to help the client to understand and evaluate himself rather than to provide information for external evaluation by the counsellor. Two important issues are the *selection* and the *reporting* of tests. Tests may be introduced into the counselling process either when requested by the client or when the counsellor infers from the client's behaviour that he is ready for the information they might provide. This corresponds closely to Super's idea of precision testing, tailor-made for the client, as contrasted with saturation testing, giving a complete battery of tests at one time, possibly prior to any occupational counselling interviews.[11] The client participates in the test selection process, with the counsellor indicating which tests are available and the kinds of information they generate, including their validity.

When the tests have been taken and scored the counsellor 'communicates' the results to the client as objectively and non-judgementally as possible and responds to the client's attitudes and emotions concerning the information in a psychotherapeutic way.[12] The information provided by tests may be at variance with the client's self-concept and certain clients may have difficulty in assimilating it and using it to plan future behaviour.[13,14] Despite the objective validity of a test's psychometric characteristics, clients may invalidate its results by distorting them to accord with their psychological needs. Thus the counsellor must create a safe environment for the presentation and discussion of test results, since there is always the risk of tests impeding rather than facilitating self-exploration.

Use of occupational information to explore the world of work. Although occupational information may not possess the negative comparison connotations of low test scores, nevertheless it may not be the kind of information that the client wishes to hear. Additionally, it may be presented in written or verbal form in ways inappropriate to the level of, or unlikely to hold the interest of, clients. As with tests, occupational information may be introduced by the counsellor when the client either overtly or covertly seems ready for it. This may be information about sources of careers information and ways of making a decision as well as information about particular careers. Where it is inappropriate to encourage the client to seek out information for himself, the reporting of occupational information should be done in a way that indicates that the counsellor has no vested interest in what the client chooses. Once again, there should be an emotional climate conducive to the client's feeling safe to express and work through his thoughts and feelings about the information.

Planning the implementation of an occupational self-concept. Action planning is likely to follow the crystallization of a career decision. Though the responsibility for the planning is that of the client, information about the planning process itself, as well as specific information about occupations, may be introduced by the counsellor in accord with the client's needs. Whether clients accept or reject this information is their responsibility. Client feelings and emotions should be allowed expression and should be handled therapeutically as part of the client's continuing process of self-exploration.

Some clients may still be in contact with careers counsellors when they engage in the reality testing of implementing their action plans. For school and college students this may involve taking their first job, which can be a challenging and stressful transition period. Any first job is likely to involve an exploratory trial period which may or may not consolidate a career decision, thus providing information which the client may assimilate into future career decision-making. Just as emotional factors may be present in the career-choosing process, so they are very much present in the work situation. During the reality testing period the counsellor's role should be empathically supportive.

Focused exploration to assist occupational decision-making. Some developmental careers counsellors may engage in focused exploration of client thinking difficulties impeding effective occupational decision-making. This exploration may cover areas such as: internal rules or self-standards which lead to dysfunctional self-evaluations relevant to occupations; the extent to which clients can accurately attribute cause to and realistically assume responsibility for what happens in their occupational lives; the accuracy with which clients assess the gains and risks of various courses of action; the ways in which clients distort information, including test information, at variance with their self-conceptions; and the client's competence at making and implementing decisions. Some of these interventions are part of and some possibly may go beyond a strictly person-centred approach. In such focused exploration counsellors may use the skill of confrontation to provide clients with information and feedback discrepant with their current self-conceptions.

Behavioural Careers Counselling

Behavioural careers counselling involves the application of behavioural methods to the problems of occupational choice and development. There is a growing research literature, which is the main source for the following review, on the application of behavioural principles and methods to occupational concerns. The behavioural interventions tend to be relevant to careers education as well as to counselling, and this is hardly surprising, since the counsellor-client relationship in behavioural counselling, unlike that in developmental career counselling, tends to be that of teacher-learner.

A careers counsellor working within the behavioural framework will conduct an initial assessment of his client so that he may make informed decisions concerning: (a) which specific behaviours need to be initiated, strengthened or eliminated; and (b) which are the most appropriate treatment methods to be used. With clients with the usual range of occupational choice problems this is likely to be a more focused assessment than that used for clients presenting with 'personal concerns'. Needless to say, any final decisions concerning counselling goals and treatment methods are taken in consultation with the client, who must desire the goals. The behavioural careers counsellor views his client's interests and career preferences as the outcome of previous instrumental and associative learning experiences. Thus, just as interests and career preferences have been learned, so, given appropriate environmental stimuli, can they be modified. Behavioural careers counselling tends to lay heavy emphasis on clients' acquiring the skills of being effective career decision-makers rather than just on solving particular career problems.

The following are illustrations of how behavioural principles and methods may be used for clients with occupational choice and development concerns.

Systematic desensitization

Systematic desensitization may be used to facilitate careers counselling either directly or indirectly. A direct application might be to use systematic desensitization as a treatment approach for a client who is anxious before and during job interviews. A less direct application might be to use systematic desensitization as a way of reducing a client's anxiety about public speaking, thus allowing jobs involving public speaking to become career options. It should be remembered that clients often make career choices on the basis of their anxieties as well as their strengths and that, consequently, anxiety reduction techniques may play a valuable role in careers counselling. Woody observes that systematic desensitization has been successful in treating numerous on-the-job situations that provoked fear or anxiety in the employee and thus impaired his productivity.[15] Unresolved fears and anxieties can affect career decision-making within the possibilities offered by a present job as well as when considering a future job. Also, as part of or independent of systematic desensitization, verbal and mental relaxation exercises may be a helpful way of coping with work stress.

Verbal reinforcement

Behavioural careers counsellors may use verbal reinforcers to strengthen desired client behaviours. A well known example is the study by Krumboltz and Thoresen[16] in which American eleventh-grade pupils interested in receiving special counselling about their future educational and vocational plans were randomly assigned to individual and group counselling settings involving two control and two experimental conditions. The latter were: (a) counselling using reinforcement of verbal information-seeking behaviour; and (b) presentation of a tape-recorded model of a boy making an educational/vocational decision followed by counselling using reinforcement of verbal information-seeking behaviour. In the experimental conditions each subject received two interviews in which the counsellor reinforced any response judged to be information-seeking by verbal reinforcers which were assumed from past experience to be positive, such as 'Yes, that would be a good thing to know', 'Excellent idea', and 'Mm-hmm'. Non-verbal cues, such as smiling, forward body posture and head nodding, were also used. Additionally, in the first interview, the counsellor periodically used questions designed to increase verbal information-seeking responses, such as 'How would you handle this question of what college to attend?' and 'There are several ways of getting information about a particular job. Where would you begin?'. The counsellor closed the first interview by asking each subject to summarize the specific steps which they might take to seek information about their future plans, then verbally reinforced each summary statement and added any specific steps not mentioned by the subject. Furthermore, the counsellor asked subjects to begin acting on some of the specific steps before the second interview, held approximately one week later.

At the second interview the counsellor asked the clients both whether they remembered the things they might do in getting information about their future plans and whether they had done anything or thought about some ways in which they could get information. Again the counsellor reinforced any verbal information-seeking behaviour from the subject and terminated the interview in a manner similar to the previous one.

The criterion behaviour for this study was the frequency and variety of subjects' information-seeking behaviours occurring outside counselling during a three-week period after the first interview. Such extra-counselling information-seeking behaviour included: writing off for occupational information; reading information; talking to relevant people; visiting or making plans to visit the colleges or places of employment under consideration; and seeing the relevant high-school counsellor to gain information pertinent to future plans. Without wishing to go into detail, both the model reinforcement and the reinforcement counselling conditions produced significantly more information-seeking behaviour than that found in either of the control groups.

Modelling

Live, taped and filmed models may be used in careers counselling to demonstrate desired behaviours. The desired behaviours may include information-seeking behaviour, decision-making skills and effective interview behaviour. For instance, a client who is about to see a counsellor for an occupational decision-making interview may previously watch a film or listen to a tape of a person modelling effective decision-making behaviours in a counselling interview. As well as characteristics of the observer or client, characteristics of the model may be important in determining the effectiveness of such observational learning. For instance, in one study Thoresen and his colleagues found that models differing either on academic or on athletic success levels were associated with significant differences in frequency of information-seeking by subjects, but no such significant differences were associated with models differing on social success.[17] Though there must be at least some degree of perceived similarity between observer and model, there may also be important differences which make different models more effective influencers. The Thoresen *et al* study is an attempt at exploring this area.

Simulated work experience

Krumboltz and his colleagues have tried to overcome the problem of clients making occupational decisions on the basis of inadequate information by simulating work experience. They have designed problem-solving materials to give people exposure to the kinds of problems faced by workers in different occupations. These materials include an accountant's kit[18] and two kinds of electrician's kits, one requiring more active participation than the other.[19] They have also exposed subjects to films about problem-solving in banking jobs, with some subjects being asked to participate more actively than others.[20] Their experiments suggest that occupational problem-solving materials which are life-like and involve active participation may increase career exploration. However, careful consideration must be given to the timing of the introduction of such materials into the career decision-making process. Simulated work experience, which reflects the behaviourist concern with specificity, is also a method by which counsellors can *reinforce* the obtaining of accurate and realistic occupational information by their clients.

Teaching decision-making skills

Verbal reinforcement, modelling and simulated work experience may all be ingredients in the teaching of decision-making skills to clients. Within the available time limits for occupational problem-solving, behavioural careers counsellors attempt to help their clients to learn wise decision-making. We mentioned in Chapter 14 that Krumboltz and Baker outlined the steps which the behavioural counsellor accomplishes with his clients as: (a) defining the problem; (b) mutual agreement on goals; (c) generating alternatives; (d) collecting information about alternatives; (e) examining the consequences of alternatives; (f) revaluing goals; (g) making the decision; and (h) generalizing the decision-making process to new problems.[21] The teaching of decision-making skills may form part of individual or group occupational counselling. Alternatively, teaching decision-making skills may form part of a larger-scale careers education programme.

Behaviour rehearsal

Behaviour rehearsal involves identifying situations in which clients are having difficulty, defining what might be appropriate behaviours, role-playing the appropriate behaviours, and encouraging clients to try out the rehearsed behaviours in real life. In careers counselling, behaviour rehearsal may be used for helping clients to handle job interviews or to engage in occupational information-seeking behaviour. For instance, in one study three formerly hospitalized but vocationally employable psychiatric patients received job-interview training through a behaviour rehearsal procedure focusing on two or more skill components, such as providing positive information about their education and/or work experience, asking the interviewer questions, appropriate gesturing, and expressing enthusiasm about the job.[22] Other categories of people who may find such interview training helpful include unemployed young people and redundant executives. Assertive training also has a role in careers counselling. For instance, some clients may need to be trained to be more assertive in seeking desirable jobs, since they may be inhibited about acknowledging their abilities and afraid of applying and thus risking rejection. Also, there are numerous on-the-job situations, for example relating to subordinates, colleagues and bosses, for which assertive training may be useful.

Behavioural self-control

Thoresen and Ewart have proposed a behavioural self-control approach to career development.[23] They define behavioural self-control as 'learnable cognitive processes that a person uses to develop controlling actions which, in turn, function to alter factors influencing behaviour'.[24] The idea is to help clients to become better architects of their occupational lives on a continuing basis. Four broad areas in which presence or absence of suitable self-control procedures can affect career decision-making are: *commitment*, developing and sustaining motivation; *awareness*, observing one's behaviour; *restructuring environments*, planning situations and environments; and *evaluating consequences and standards for self-evaluations*, assessing and changing current reinforcements and self-standards.

Commitment behaviours include specification of goals and the making of self-contracts to achieve the goals. An example of an *awareness* behaviour is keeping a diary over a two-week period monitoring careers-relevant thoughts, feelings and external actions. *Restructuring environments* might include joining a weekly career development group (restructuring external environment) or using relaxation skills just before asking people for occupational information (restructuring internal environment). *Evaluating consequences and self-standards* includes an assessment of how current consequences, such as being differentially encouraged when talking about various careers, are maintaining present career-related behaviour. Also, career exploration may need to be sustained by short-term as well as longer-term rewards. For instance, a client might treat himself to a coffee each time he engages in specified career exploration behaviours. Thoresen and Ewart suggest that generally in a behavioural self-control approach to career choice the focus is at first on commitment and self-awareness, while later the emphasis shifts to the specific techniques of achieving goals, such as environmental structuring and self-reward methods.

Concluding comments

Behavioural careers counselling methods may be used in varying combinations depending on the mutually agreed goals of client and counsellor. Behavioural careers counsellors are likely to monitor carefully the effectiveness of their interventions and to make changes if necessary. To some extent, behavioural methods such as reinforcement have always been used in careers counselling, but their systematic application to the problems of occupational choice and development is relatively recent. Probably, at the time of writing, the behavioural approach to careers counselling is less accepted in Britain than in America.

Differentialist Careers Counselling

Historically the differentialist or talent-matching approach made its appearance in vocational *guidance*, as contrasted with the later careers *counselling*, before the developmental and behavioural approaches. The differentialist approach is based on a matching of individual differences in people with differences in careers and jobs. In this section we review Williamson's trait-factor, Rodger's seven-point plan and Holland's 'modern differentialist' approaches to the problems of occupational choice and development.

Williamson's trait-factor approach

For a considerable period E. G. Williamson was a leading figure in the American counselling movement. His career at the University of Minnesota spanned the years 1926–1969, after which he was retained as a consultant. He was Assistant Professor and Director of the first Testing and Counselling Bureau in the University from 1931 to 1938, co-ordinator of Student Personnel Services from 1938 to 1941, and Dean of Students from 1941 to 1969. His books include *How to Counsel Students: A Manual of Techniques for Clinical Counsellors*,[25] *Student Personnel Services in Colleges and Universities*,[26] and *Vocational Counselling: Some Historical, Philosophical and Theoretical Perspectives*.[27]

Trait-factor careers counselling rests on a number of assumptions, including the following. First, it is assumed that each individual is an organized and unique pattern of capabilities and potentialities which, for most people, are stable after late adolescence. Second, these individual capabilities and capacities are identifiable by objective 'tests'. Third, different capacities are significantly involved in and correlated with different work tasks. Also, psychological interests are correlated with different work tasks and are differentially characteristic of identifiable criterion groups of workers of known competence. Fourth, success in work tasks and academic achievement is best predicted by a battery of unique trait tests which have low correlations with each other, but cumulatively correlate highly with the criterion under consideration.[28] More recently, Williamson has acknowledged that 'training-on-the-job' may be regarded as an aptitude test in the case of culturally deprived individuals with deficient formal education.[29]

Williamson writes: 'The task of the trait-factor type of counselling is to aid the individual in successive approximations of self-understanding and self-management by means of helping him to assess his assets and liabilities in relation to the requirements of progressively changing life goals and his vocational career'.[30] In an early paper entitled 'The clinical method of guidance',[31] Williamson stated that his method consisted of six steps. These same six steps also provide a framework for his approach to careers counselling. They are as follows:

1. *Analysis.* Williamson considers that counsellors are in a better position to help their clients if they know something about them. Consequently the counsellor, by both subjective and objective methods, collects data from many sources about the client's attitudes, interests, family background, knowledge, educational progress and aptitudes, etc.
2. *Synthesis.* The counsellor collates and summarizes the data using case-study methods and test profiles to highlight the client's uniqueness and individuality.
3. *Diagnosis.* Here the counsellor describes the outstanding characteristics and problems of the client, including diagnosing the causes of the problems. Williamson writes: 'in most guidance programs each counsellor is expected to collect data from many sources concerning a particular student, to synthesize these data, and to arrive at a composite diagnosis'.[32] A skill in diagnosis is to 'tease out' the relevant data so that a valid interpretation of the client's assets and liabilities may be arrived at.
4. *Prognosis.* Prognosis involves predicting the probable consequences of clients' educational and career decisions and any other problems they may have, thereby indicating the advisability of alternative actions and adjustments. Regression or prediction equations, usually but not necessarily based on test scores, are one of the more exact ways of handling some kinds of data for making prognoses. For instance, test scores, high-school grades and family background information may be combined in a regression equation designed to predict college grades.
5. *Counselling or treatment.* Though the trait-factor counsellor is essentially a teacher, effective counselling and effective teaching both depend on a good counsellor-client *personal* relationship. Together, counsellor and client consider and decide what behaviour is to be changed and what the appropriate content for the counselling instruction should be. For instance, the behaviour to be changed may centre around an educational or vocational decision, or a clarification and choice of values or even of life-styles. Williamson observes that no effective counsellor uses only one approach to counselling, since clients are not 'fragmented into any of the classical categories which characterize the chapters of this or any book on counselling'.[33]
6. *Follow-up.* Follow-up consists of repeating the above steps as new problems arise and further assisting clients to carry out desirable programmes of action.

Williamson's trait-factor approach to occupational counselling is not as coldly rational and logical as his assumptions might lead the reader to believe. Though the approach emphasizes the use of test scores and, where possible, appropriate prediction equations, Williamson recognizes that the client's life experience and subjective meanings must also be taken into account. Furthermore, the approach acknowledges that disturbed clients may need special counselling focusing on their emotional concerns and that all clients need a personal relationship with the counsellor. Additionally, Williamson sees occupational counselling in career-development terms and seeks to help clients towards greater proficiency in the lifelong task of self-counselling. However, the role of the counsellor in Williamson's trait-factor approach is likely to be rather more, if not much more, didactic than that of the developmental careers counselling approach described earlier in this chapter. Also, a possible weakness of Williamson's approach is its tendency to rely on the use of tests and prediction equations which may be neither feasible nor available for many working counsellors.

Rodger's seven-point plan

Alec Rodger was Professor of Occupational Psychology at Birkbeck College of the University of London. He devised a system for gathering material to form a working image of a person's occupational assets and liabilities which could be used in personnel selection or vocational guidance.[34] This system, known as the seven-point plan, assumes a matching model of vocational guidance. The term 'guidance', with its implications of counsellor direction, is that used by Rodger himself. The plan as presented is more in terms of the counsellor assessing the client than facilitating the client's self-assessment.

Rodger indicates that the seven points are in no particular order of importance and need not be covered in a set order; nor need 'the questions under the seven headings . . . be put directly to the applicant by his assessor'.[35] The seven headings and the questions that go with them are as follows:

1. *Physical make up.* Has he any defects of health or physique that may be of occupational importance? How agreeable are his appearance, his bearing and his speech?
2. *Attainments.* What type of education has he had? How well has he done educationally? What occupational training and experience has he had already? How well has he done occupationally?
3. *General intelligence.* How much general intelligence can he display? How much general intelligence does he ordinarily display?
4. *Special aptitudes.* Has he any marked mechanical aptitude, manual dexterity, facility in the use of words or figures, talent for drawing or music?
5. *Interests.* To what extent are his interests intellectual? Practical-constructional? Physically-active? Social? Artistic?
6. *Disposition.* How acceptable does he make himself to other people? Does he influence others? Is he steady and dependable? Is he self reliant?

7. *Circumstances.* What are his domestic circumstances? What do the other mem-
    bers of the family do for a living? Are there any special openings available for
    him?

A concluding comment is that Rodger's seven-point plan, which also allows for the
use of tests to collect relevant information, seems to have its origins in selection and
employment interviewing by an external assessor. As presented, it says little about the
process of careers counselling but, by implication, the role of the counsellor is that of
an expert in matching people to types of work, if not to actual jobs. The plan, which is
rather authoritarian, may pay insufficient attention to the client's personal meanings
and anxieties about himself and the world of work. In all, especially with its lack of
emphasis on client self-assessment, the seven-point plan has limitations as a model for
careers counselling. Furthermore, its underlying model of human functioning and
change remains unarticulated.

Holland's 'modern differentialist' approach

Holland and Gottfredson consider that Holland's personality and environmental
model typology (see Chapter 9) suggests a new vocational assistance orientation,
which they tentatively call the 'Exploratory View'.[36] Most people can resolve their
own vocational problems if they have suitable opportunities for obtaining information
and are encouraged in their exploration. They write: 'In short, this view accepts the
person's definition of the problem and helps him/her deal with it by providing
resources and information, but above all this approach emphasizes exploration of self
and the world . . .'.[37] Proposed ways of helping people with their exploration include
the following.

A placement and work experience service. The idea of the work experience service is to
help people to explore a particular kind of work or explore many kinds of work.[38]
Needless to say, the classification of work experience would be based on Holland's
typology.

A translation service. Many people lack sufficient information about themselves or
confidence to translate personal characteristics into occupational opportunities. The
translation service would provide a variety of translation devices so that people could
get exploratory self-directed help without appointments. The service would include
easily available occupational information. Holland observes that career literature,
employer announcements, and listings of vacant positions can all be organized and
filed in a system that uses his classification.[39] Another feature of the translation
service would be self-administered and self-scored inventories, such as the *Self-
directed Search* (SDS). The SDS includes two booklets: a self-assessment booklet and
an occupational classification booklet.[40] A person filling out the self-assessment
booklet indicates: his occupational daydreams; his preferences for six kinds of
activities (realistic, investigative, artistic, social, enterprising, conventional); his
competencies in six areas (realistic, etc.); his preferences for six kinds of occupations;
and his estimation of his ability in six areas. He then scores the booklet to obtain a

three-letter occupational code (e.g. RIE, or realistic, investigative, enterprising). All permutations of the three-letter code are used to locate suitable occupations in the occupational classification booklet, *The Occupations Finder*. Holland considers that the SDS encourages self-direction and initiative in resolving vocational decisions, helps people who do not have access to professional counsellors, and multiplies the number of people a counsellor can serve.

A counselling service. Counsellors would see people who were self-referred or other-referred because of their inability to use the other and main services. The counsellors' job would be to return their clients to the self-directed services as soon as possible. Holland suggests that maladaptive vocational development may be brought about in five major ways: (a) insufficient experience to acquire a well-defined personality type; (b) insufficient experience to learn about the major environmental models; (c) ambiguous or conflicting experience about one's personality type; (d) ambiguous or conflicting information about the major environmental models; and (e) lack of confidence to translate personal characteristics into occupational opportunities.[41] Using this diagnostic scheme, counsellors can work with clients to develop appropriate treatment plans to help them to resolve their vocational decisions. Treatment may involve one or more of: occupational information, work experience, self-directed self-exploration, competence training, and counselling. For instance, a client with an inconsistent and undifferentiated personality profile may require personal counselling prior to vocational counselling. Later he may also require work experience to get a more accurate picture of himself and the major areas of work.

Vocational education. School pupils should be given an opportunity to experience the six curricula and the six kinds of non-school experiences. Holland considers that unless schools, parents and other agencies provide a full range of experience, they lessen students' ability to understand themselves and their future possibilities.[42]

Concluding comments

Though the terms 'developmental', 'behavioural' and 'differentialist' have been used to describe different approaches to career counselling, there are many similarities as well as differences. All the approaches are trying to help clients to obtain greater fulfilment by an adequate matching of their capacities and interests with the world of work. Thus in a sense all occupational choice counselling is based on a matching model. All approaches acknowledge the importance of self-direction and career development. Furthermore, when the developmental careers counselling approach is extended to include careers education focusing on decision-making skills, the differences between it and the behavioural approach become smaller.

Some of the important differences, however, include the following. Developmental careers counsellors may view their role more as facilitators than teachers and are likely to be more concerned than their behavioural or differentialist counterparts with helping clients to become attuned to their underlying valuing process. Put another way, developmental careers counsellors may be more sensitive to the fact that career choosing can be a highly irrational process, distorted by conditions of worth, fears and anxieties. Consequently, these need to be attended to as part of the counselling process. Behavioural careers counsellors are more technician-teachers who are strong in helping clients with the mechanics of career information-seeking, job interviewing and career decision-making. When behavioural counsellors move into the area of self-control, they may be helping clients to explore areas similar to those focused on by developmental careers counsellors. Trait-factor differentialist counsellors may collect and have available useful predictive information for considering the consequences of educational and vocational decisions. Furthermore, modern differentialist careers counsellors use a typology which allows clients to describe and understand occupational environments as well as themselves.

Leisure Counselling Approaches

Leisure or avocational counselling is a developing field in America, if not in Britain. In general, careers counselling provides models for leisure counselling, though some adaptations are in order. For instance, in the area of *testing* there are a number of measures focusing specifically on leisure. These include McKechnie's *Leisure Activities Blank*[43] and Overs and his colleagues' *Avocational Title Card Sort* and *Avocational Picture Card Sort*.[44] Furthermore, behavioural counselling measures, such as MacPhillamy and Lewinsohn's *Pleasant Events Schedule*[45] and Cautela's *Reinforcement Survey Schedule*,[46] are very relevant to leisure counselling and highlight the interplay between avocational activities and psychological well-being.

There is also a need for well presented and easily available leisure *information*. For instance, Overs has developed an *Avocational Activities Inventory* (AAI), which is a systematic way of identifying, classifying and coding avocational activities.[47] The major classifications used in the AAI are: O, Games; 1, Sports; 2, Nature activities; 3, Collection activities; 4, Craft activities; 5, Art and music activities (performing); 6, Educational and cultural activities; 7, Volunteer activities; 8, Organizations; and 9, Social relationships. Additionally, there are sub-categories, such as under 2, Nature activities: 28, Animal raising and breeding, then 287, Raising/breeding of dogs. Paragraph definitions are written for each item. Overs also keeps an Avocational Activities File comprising data on local avocational opportunities which have been collected, classified and filed. Though relatively little has been written about the practice of leisure counselling, like careers counselling it can be viewed within the developmental, behavioural and differentialist frameworks.

Developmental leisure counselling

Developmental leisure counselling is concerned with the clarification and implementation of the client's leisure self-concept. However, leisure self-concepts can contain conditions of worth which block accurate processing of leisure information. The Protestant Work Ethic may be one such condition of worth. McDowell writes of unhealthy leisure modes containing statements like 'I should', 'I ought', 'I'd like to, but', 'I don't have the time', and 'If it weren't for, I'd'.[48] Furthermore, he observes that many of the patients with whom he works wait for things to happen in their leisure time rather than initiating action themselves. Developmental leisure counselling starts with the counsellor providing the client with an empathic relationship in which he feels safe and free to explore his leisure self-concept, including attitudes, values, interests, aptitudes and personal meanings. The counsellor provides testing and leisure information either when the client requests it or when he feels the client is ready for it. The counsellor deals in a therapeutic way with the thoughts and feelings generated by tests and leisure information. Furthermore, once leisure goals are defined, the counsellor may work with the client to design action plans for implementing them, especially since the challenges involved in change may seem difficult. Overs observes that many 'older and disabled people have extensive fears and anxieties about their ability to enter an activity, even though it might be one that had previously been of interest to them'.[49] The developmental careers counsellor also may need to support clients as they try out one or more of the activities they have chosen. Developmental leisure counselling, like behavioural and differentialist approaches, may be performed on an individual or a group basis.

Behavioural leisure counselling

As yet behavioural leisure counselling does not appear to have been developed in any really systematic way. Nevertheless, behavioural principles and methods may be helpful in such counselling. We have already mentioned the use of pleasant events and reinforcement schedules in identifying potentially reinforcing activities. All the behavioural careers counselling methods are relevant to leisure counselling. For instance systematic desensitization may be used to reduce anxieties about participation in one or more leisure activities; verbal reinforcement to encourage leisure information-seeking behaviour; modelling to demonstrate leisure decision-making or participation in a leisure activity; teaching decision-making to ensure that leisure decisions are made wisely; behaviour rehearsal to prepare for handling potentially anxiety-evoking situations in relation to leisure, such as being interviewed for entry to a club; and behavioural self-control to control outer and inner environments and reinforcers relevant to leisure participation, e.g. joining a leisure activities discussion group and altering maladaptive self-standards.

Differentialist leisure counselling

Differentialist leisure counselling involves the matching of characteristics of leisure activities with characteristics of people. In a sense Holland's typology is relevant to leisure counselling and he hypothesizes that 'Personality pattern determines a person's choice of nonvocational activities and recreations'.[50] Extrapolating from his ideas on careers work, planned opportunities for leisure experience, a leisure translation service and leisure counselling are all conceivable. Another differentialist position is that of McKechnie, who considers that leisure counselling will make real progress only to the extent that it 'employs empirically based multivariate techniques of appraisal that are demonstrated to predict validly and reliably the initial response and long-term adjustment of the individual client to a particular leisure or recreation situation',[51] He favours the use of tests, such as his own *Leisure Activities Blank*, to help clients to identify their interests and predict their successful participation in activities. Another approach is the matching of leisure interests with activities by computer. Hartlage reports a program, the Computer Research Avocational Guidance Program, which helps to match interests, measured by a self-report inventory, with rewarding leisure activities. Of his 219 respondents, 94 per cent indicated that they intended to take up at least one of the three avocations selected for them by the computer.[52]

Concluding comment

Leisure counselling is an area which is likely to develop as people seek or are forced by unemployment to seek greater fulfilment in their non-work lives. As well as special groups, such as the elderly and the disabled, leisure counselling has much to offer young people, who may gain a lifetime's fulfilment from good leisure decision-making. Unfortunately, little or no work appears to have been conducted in Britain involving systematic research into the practice of leisure counselling, a situation which it is hoped will be rectified in the coming years.

A final point is that enforced leisure is not leisure in the sense of recreation after a hard day's or week's work. There is scope for unemployment counselling at all age levels, from school leavers up to and including the retired. This requires an extension of the notion of career development to embrace directions of personal involvement in meaningful activity, such as work for voluntary agencies, that move outside the official labour market but may still include gainful occupation. With such a legitimate extension of the notion of a career to embrace other modes of self-fulfilment and 'occupation' as well as paid employment, careers counselling acquires the comprehensiveness and relevance that it should always have had. Nevertheless, there is still room for counselling with an emphasis on leisure as presently understood. What must be avoided, however, is a simplistic compartmentalization of traditional notions of work and leisure, so that individuals may find at any stage of their lives the mixtures of occupational activity that best suit them.

CAREERS EDUCATION

Careers education is an umbrella term to cover a variety of interventions aimed at helping children, mainly at secondary-school level, to become more occupationally literate. By the early 1970s it was not a prominent feature in most English and Welsh secondary schools, with a large-scale Department of Education and Science survey concluding: 'The concept of careers education as that element in the school programme more especially concerned with preparation for living and working in the adult world is not at present generally accepted or put into practice except by a minority of schools'.[53] Since then, it is likely that the concept of careers education has gained some ground.

Objectives

Early in this chapter we commented that British careers education has mainly tended to emphasize making career decisions wisely. Daws views careers education as part of personal education and considers that school leavers should possess the following 'marks of maturity' as a result of a careers education programme:

1. Knowing the opportunities that await them.
2. Having some idea of what they wish to strive for, based on a thorough and realistic self-appraisal.
3. Having the personal and social competencies to satisfy employers and their supervisory staff, and to get on with workmates.
4. Having the personal resources to profit from occupational failure (and higher educational failure) should they meet it, and not to react neurotically.[54]

Many of Daws' 'marks of maturity' were repeated in slightly different form in the summary of themes in British careers education contained in the Schools Council's report *Careers Education in the 1970s*.[55] Here the principal themes were: self-awareness and self-exploration; understanding the working world, the role of the working adult, and the differences between the various occupations and work environments; acquiring decison-making skill and the confidence to be self-determining; and an awareness of social involvement and responsibility.

More recently Watts has stated the objectives of careers education programmes as: (a) opportunity awareness; (b) self-awareness; (c) decision learning; and (d) transition learning.[56] *Opportunity awareness* involves helping pupils or students to gain a realistic understanding of the world of work, including the likely opportunities open to them, requisite entry and training qualifications, and the demands and satisfactions of work. *Self-awareness* involves helping pupils to become more aware of their interests, values and needs. An argument can be made for self-awareness being, as well as a concurrent, an earlier objective than opportunity awareness, since it provides a basis for reacting to the world of work. *Decision learning* relates to teaching pupils the variety of ways in which decisions can be made and giving them the skills to integrate self-awareness and opportunity awareness into making decisions wisely. *Transition learning* means helping pupils towards a realistic appreciation of the environments they are likely to enter and, where possible, giving them the skills to cope with the likely adjustments to be made. Additional objectives of careers education programmes may be helping young people to handle a period of unemployment and, possibly, leisure education.

So far we have dealt with objectives of careers education for pupils and students, but counsellors also may have their own objectives for engaging in careers education. Hoppock suggests some such reasons.[57] For instance, careers education may save counsellor time in answering individual queries, since these may be dealt with on a group basis. Furthermore, it gives clients a background of relevant information which may improve counselling. Also, if counsellors conduct careers education themselves, it gives them an opportunity to meet clients in different settings, provides an opportunity to meet less disturbed or non-problem clients, and helps to keep them up to date on occupational information.

Timing

The recognition of the concept of vocational or career development suggests that pupils and students might have suitable careers education opportunities from primary school onwards. As children grow older, there may be a shift from 'career awareness' to 'career exploration' followed by 'career preparation',[58] but this is just a rough guide. Reasons for starting some form of careers education in primary schools include early prevention of a gap developing between education and work and the fact that primary-school educational and recreational decisions are relevant to later occupational choice. As with primary and secondary schools, careers education is also possible in higher education[59] and for special groups of people, such as unemployed professional executives. In general, careers education interventions are best timed when groups of pupils or students have specific educational and career decisions to make, for example during their last year at secondary school or before choosing A-level subjects. In the review that follows the focus is on secondary education, though many of the comments are relevant to careers education in other settings.

Personnel

Although at least one person, such as a careers counsellor, teacher or tutor, needs to have major responsibility for initiating and co-ordinating a careers education programme, it is best viewed as a team effort involving the skills and contributions of many other groups of people inside and outside the school. Inside the school, teachers may integrate career-relevant material into the curriculum. Also, heads of year and pastoral tutors may become more occupationally literate and, hence, useful to people seeking careers information and counselling. Personnel from outside the school include careers officers who, with their extensive knowledge of local industry and opportunities, can be helpful both in advising on the contents of a careers education programme and in assisting individual pupils. Then there are numerous people from the world of work who can either give talks and seminars in the school or provide varying kinds of careers education experiences in their actual work settings. Another important group is parents, who represent a variety of employments and may be prepared to give talks or offer opportunities for work experience. Furthermore, parents can be encouraged to support their children in their career exploration and decision-making. Last, there is the careers counsellor, teacher or tutor, who, as well as being occupationally literate and having good administrative and teaching skills, also needs to have good counselling skills.

Clientele

Although pupils are the main clientele for secondary-school careers education programmes, there are at least three other possible groups of clientele. First, there is the staff in the school, many of whom might be prepared to become more occupationally literate both to enrich their teaching and to help with their pastoral work. Second, there are the parents, who can be helped to understand more fully their children's educational and occupational choices. Third, careers education can be a two-way process: not only education learning more about the world of work, but employers learning more about schools, including the nature of present-day education and what are realistic expectations to have about school leavers.

Methods

Careers education in the schools is sometimes thought of as part of the broader area of personal and social education. However, the review of methods that follows will focus mainly on interventions specific to careers. The selection of methods is likely to be influenced by the theoretical orientation of the careers counsellor, teacher or tutor. For instance, a person-centred counsellor might heavily emphasize group work, possibly exploring personal meanings about values, work and life-style; the behaviourist might focus on reinforcing information-seeking behaviour and teaching decision-making skills; and the modern differentialist might make Holland's *Self-directed Search* materials available. Similarly, curriculum interventions are likely to be influenced by the educational philosophies of teachers. Thus, depending on the orientation of the careers counsellors and/or the other staff members involved, the same item in the following review may affect pupils differently.

Integration with existing curriculum

Careers education may be integrated into the teaching of regular curricular offerings. For instance, economics students might be introduced to the worlds of banking, insurance and accountancy to gain a more realistic understanding of the kinds of work and decisions that these fields involve. Also, the pupils' reactions to, and learnings and personal meanings from, the site visits could later be discussed in the classroom. Additionally, it is possible to teach some of the content of courses like business studies using the case-study method, which simulates decisions and problems drawn from real life. Social studies, the arts and science subjects might similarly be approached in a way which includes developing career opportunity awareness.

Careers education courses

Careers education courses are either voluntary or prescribed special courses designed to meet one or more of the careers education objectives (e.g. self-awareness, opportunity awareness, decision learning and transition learning). They may be as short as a classroom period a week for half a term or, alternatively, they could be a series of courses tailored to the different educational and occupational decision-making needs of pupils as they progress through secondary education. Some possible approaches to careers education courses are as follows:

Self-awareness. Approaches to self-awareness include group counselling and discussion, possibly with focused exploration of such topics as attitudes, values, interests, needs, motivation and desired life-style. Testing of interests and aptitudes may also help some pupils so long as they are given adequate opportunity to understand and discuss their results. Similarly, less structured self-exploration exercises, which help pupils to clarify and define themselves, may also be helpful.[60]

Opportunity awareness. Approaches to opportunity awareness include: outside speakers; occupational visits; films, television programmes and cassettes showing people at their work, along the lines of 'a day in the life of . . .'; talks and seminars in which occupational information is presented by careers officers and others; use of interest measures keyed to suggest and describe suitable occupations, such as the *JiiG-CAL System for Computer Assisted Career Guidance*[61] and Holland's *Self-directed Search*, which includes his Occupations Finder; projects such as how to go about finding a job in the locality of the school or the making up of a display board regarding a particular occupation; use of a careers library which includes the kinds of occupational information discussed in the previous chapter; exercises such as SPEED-COP (1. Surroundings, 2. Prospects, 3. Entry and training, 4. Effects, 5. Description, 6. Conditions, 7. Organization, 8. People), designed to help people to classify, discover and analyse occupational information;[62] and simulated work experiences, such as management games or working through banking and accounting problems. Opportunity awareness may be further fostered by longer-term work experience schemes, including suitable vacation employment.

Decision learning. Decision learning involves the learning and practising of decision-making skills. Furthermore, good decisions are made to be implemented and, therefore, decision learning should include a focus on action planning. We have already outlined the steps in effective decision-making in Chapter 14 and again in the behavioural section of this chapter. Pupils are more likely to be involved in decision learning if they integrate it with practice in making and implementing current educational and occupational decisions of their own. This means that the timing of decision learning is very important. Good career decisions involve a high degree of self-awareness and opportunity awareness. Since such decisions involve emotions, feelings and conditions of worth, some pupils will also need individual counselling to increase their self-understanding. Furthermore, a behavioural counsellor might include some self-control skills as part of decision learning.

Transition learning. Transition learning may focus on such issues as entering a new environment, handling work stress, learning to identify and create sources of job satisfaction, integrating work and leisure life, information about hierarchical patterns at work, the role of professional associations and trade unions, and other concerns which pupils may have during their final year at school. Many of the methods discussed under opportunity awareness are relevant, perhaps with adaptation, to transition learning. For instance, outside speakers might include recent school leavers discussing their first jobs.

Concluding comments

Realistic careers education programmes, including availability of skilled counselling, are likely to help many pupils to clarify their occupational self-concepts in ways which lead to more fulfilled occupational lives. Furthermore, they are likely to lessen decision-making mistakes which may entail the necessity of starting again in terms of training and experience for a new career. Especially in British secondary education, it seems likely that careers education programmes will become a growing feature, though this growth may come more slowly than some might like. There is room both for the further development of good curriculum materials and for sound research into the processes and outcomes of British careers education. Another future development may be a wider definition of the term 'careers' to include education for other roles, such as leisure and a period of unemployment.

COMPUTERS IN OCCUPATIONAL COUNSELLING

With the development of computer technology, it is not surprising that some occupational psychologists have turned their attention to how computers can support their work. Watts lists five capacities of the computer relevant to careers guidance: (a) *storing* vast quantities of information; (b) *retrieving* information quickly and accurately; (c) *matching* the information retrieved to client characteristics; (d) *updating* information quickly and easily and making it immediately available to all users; and (e) *printing out* information and providing copies for the client.[63] Super is also impressed by the computer's capacity as a dynamic conversational mode[64] and, on a more mundane level, Heginbotham has found it useful for scoring large quantities of aptitude tests in a city careers service.[65]

Computers are a way of extending both client and counsellor access to data. Inquiries may be made *indirectly*, as with a batch processing system in which the inquirer fills out questionnaires that are turned over to the computer centre, or *directly* by the client asking the computer a question and the computer responding either by print-out or by flashing messages on a screen.[66] Super has identified five computer-based systems for educational and vocational guidance:

1. *Information storage and retrieval systems*, for instance a job bank which enables users to find out what opportunities are available in a particular area.
2. *Simple matching systems*. Such systems may match characteristics of person and job or person and college and tend to rely on batch processing.
3. *Interactive matching systems*. These are similar to the above, but the client is given greater freedom in deciding which person characteristics he wishes to match and when.
4. *Interactive exploration and choice systems*. These systems query, analyse and summarize. For instance, the computer asks users what information they would like to know about an occupation they have chosen to explore and allows them to make direct inquiries, interact, and accumulate information step by step according to their needs.
5. *Career development systems*. These systems, themselves still in the process of development, attempt to teach the constructs of life stages and developmental tasks, help users to assess their own level of vocational maturity, and provide guided and evaluated exploratory opportunities.[67]

There are a number of computer-based guidance systems being developed in Britain and these appear to be person-occupation and person-college matching systems.[68] There are, however, problems relating to the use of computers in careers counselling and education. These include cost, protection of individual privacy, adequacy of the occupational data used in the systems, and the narrowness or breadth of the criteria on which users are matched to occupations. Furthermore, there is the problem of counsellor resistance to what they may perceive as impersonal technology.

Assuming that some of the problems mentioned above are adequately dealt with, computers are potentially of great value to counsellors. Not only do they provide a means of storing and presenting a range of information which is far more comprehensive than a counsellor could manage, but they also allow users to engage in self-directed career exploration in a manner which many are likely to find highly motivating. One way in which careers counsellors can view the development of computerized systems is in terms of extending their effectiveness. By providing them with a means of handling much of their occupational information work, computers may eventually free careers counsellors to focus more of their individual and group person-to-person contact where it is most needed. While wishing to be realistic about the limitations of computers and the dangers of computer faddism, they do offer an exciting prospect for the future of careers counselling and education.

PRACTICAL EXERCISES AND QUESTIONS

It may help you to develop your skills and knowledge of the material in this chapter if, either individually or in pairs, you perform the following exercises and answer the following questions.

Practical Exercises

1.   Offer your partner an empathic relationship as he or she explores his or her occupational self-concept. After a suitable period of time reverse roles, then discuss.

2.   Conduct a careers counselling interview with your partner as client in which, both verbally and non-verbally, you reinforce his or her occupational information-seeking behaviour. After a suitable period of time reverse roles, then discuss.

3.   Conduct a behavioural assessment of your partner's occupational choice and development behaviours, including:

   (a)   specifying treatment goals in behavioural terms;
   (b)   indicating treatment methods for each goal.

4.   Administer and score Holland's *Self-directed Search*. Then locate some possible occupations by using *The Occupations Finder*.

5.   Offer your partner an empathic relationship as he or she explores his or her leisure self-concept. After a suitable period of time reverse roles, then discuss.

6.   If you were responsible for designing a careers education programme in a secondary or high school:

   (a)   what objectives would you have?
   (b)   what specific steps would you be taking to attain each of your objectives?
   (c)   what do you consider would be some of the difficulties in implementing your programme?
   (d)   how would you evaluate the effectiveness of your planned programme?

Questions

1.   Critically discuss the concept of career development.

2.   Discuss the respective roles of counsellor and client in:

   (a)   the selection of tests;
   (b)   the presentation of occupational information.

3.   Discuss the relevance to career counselling of Williamson's six 'clinical' steps:
        (a)   analysis;
        (b)   synthesis;
        (c)   diagnosis;
        (d)   prognosis;
        (f)   follow-up.

4.   Critically discuss the feasibility of Holland and Gottfredson's 'exploratory view' of counselling, with its emphasis on client self-direction.

5.   What do you consider to be the similarities and differences between careers education and careers counselling?

6.   Critically discuss the role of computers in careers counselling and education.

NOTES

1.   Watts, A. G. (1973) A structure for careers education. In R. Jackson (ed.), *Careers Guidance: Practice and Problems* pp. 3–17. London: Arnold.
2.   Watts, A. G. & Herr, E. L. (1976) Career(s) education in Britain and the USA: contrasts and common problems. *British Journal of Guidance and Counselling*, **4**, 129–142.
3.   Watts, A. G. (1981) Introduction. In A. G. Watts, D. E. Super and J. M. Kidd (eds), *Career Development in Britain* p. 2. Cambridge: Hobson's Press. Full reference pp. 1–6.
4.   Borow, H. (1970) Career development: a future for counseling. In W. H. Van Hoose and J. J. Pietrofesa (eds), *Counseling and Guidance in the Twentieth Century* pp. 33–46. Boston: Houghton Mifflin.
5.   Super, D. E. (1980) A life-span, life-space approach to career development. *Journal of Vocational Behaviour*, **16**, 282. Full reference pp. 282–298.
6.   Rogers, C. R. (1961) *Client-centered therapy* p. 487. Boston: Houghton Mifflin.
7.   Rogers, C. R. (1964) Toward a modern approach to values: the valuing process in the mature person. *Journal of Abnormal and Social Psychology*, **68**, 160–167.
8.   *Ibid*. pp. 162–163.
9.   *Ibid*. p. 163.
10. Patterson, C. H. (1964) Counseling: self-clarification and the helping relationship. In H. Borow (ed.), *Man in a World at Work* p. 446. Boston: Houghton Mifflin. Full reference pp. 434–459.
11. Super, D. E. (1950) Testing and using test results in counselling. *Occupations*, **29**, 95–97.
12. Crites, J. O. (1974) Career counseling: a review of major approaches. *The Counseling Psychologist*, **4**, 3, 3–23.
13. Bixler, R. H. & Bixler, V. H. (1946) Test interpretation in vocational counseling. *Educational and Psychological Measurement*, **6**, 145–156.
14. Seeman, J. (1948) Psychotechnology and psychotherapy in vocational counseling. *The Personal Counselor*, **3**, 57–61.
15. Woody, R. H. (1979) Vocational counseling with behavioural techniques. In S. G. Weinrach (ed.), *Career Counseling: Theoretical and Practical Perspectives* pp. 180–187. New York: McGraw-Hill.
16. Krumboltz, J. D. & Thoresen, C. E. (1964) The effect of behavioural counseling in

group and individual settings on information-seeking behaviour. *Journal of Counseling Psychology*, **11**, 324–333.

17. Thoresen, C. E., Hosford, R. E. & Krumboltz, J. D. (1970) Determining effective models for counseling clients of varying competences. *Journal of Counseling Psychology*, **17**, 369–375.

18. Krumboltz, J. D. & Sheppard, L. E. (1969) Vocational problem-solving experiences. In J. D. Krumboltz and C. E. Thoresen (eds), *Behavioral Counseling: Cases and Techniques* pp. 293–306. New York: Holt, Rinehart and Winston.

19. Hamilton, J. A. & Krumboltz, J. D. (1969) Simulated work experience: how realistic should it be? *Personnel and Guidance Journal*, **48**, 39–44.

20. Jones, G. B. & Krumboltz, J. D. (1970) Simulating vocational exploration through film-mediated problems. *Journal of Counseling Psychology*, **17**, 107–114.

21. Krumboltz, J. D. & Baker, R. D (1973) Behavioral counseling for vocational decisions. In H. Borow (ed.), *Career Guidance for a New Age* pp. 235–283. Boston: Houghton Mifflin.

22. Furman, W., Geller, M., Simon, S. J. & Kelly, J. A. (1979) The use of a behavior rehearsal procedure for teaching job-interviewing skills to psychiatric patients. *Behavior Therapy*, **10**, 157–167.

23. Thoresen, C. E. & Ewart, C. R. (1976) Behavioral self-control and career development. *The Counseling Psychologist*, **6**, 3, 29–43.

24. *Ibid.* p. 37.

25. Williamson, E. G. (1939) *How to Counsel Students: A Manual of Techniques for Clinical Counselors.* New York: McGraw-Hill.

26. Williamson, E. G. (1961) *Student Personnel Services in Colleges and Universities.* New York: McGraw-Hill.

27. Williamson, E. G. (1965) *Vocational Counseling: Some Historical, Philosophical and Theoretical Perspectives.* New York: McGraw-Hill.

28. Williamson, E. G. (1965) Vocational counseling: trait-factor theory. In B. Stefflre (ed.), *Theories of Counseling* pp. 193–195. New York: McGraw-Hill. Full reference pp. 193–214.

29. Williamson, E. G. (1972) Trait-Factor theory and individual differences. In B. Stefflre and W. H. Grant (eds), *Theories of Counseling* (2nd ed.) pp. 136–176. New York: McGraw-Hill.

30. Williamson, E. G. (1965) Vocational counseling: trait-factor theory. In B. Stefflre (ed.), *Theories of Counseling* p. 198. New York: McGraw-Hill.

31. Williamson, E. G. (1939) The clinical method of guidance. *Review of Educational Research*, **9**, 214–217.

32. *Ibid.* p. 215.

33. Williamson, E. G. (1972) Trait-Factor theory and individual differences. In B. Stefflre and W. H. Grant (eds), *Theories of Counseling* (2nd ed.) p. 172. New York: McGraw-Hill.

34. Rodger, A. (1952) *The Seven Point Plan.* London: National Institute of Industrial Psychology. Reproduced in Hopson, B. & Hayes, J. (eds) (1968). *The Theory and Practice of Vocational Guidance* pp. 359–373. Oxford: Pergamon Press.

35. *Ibid.* p. 362.

36. Holland, J. L. & Gottfredson, G. D. (1976) Using a typology of persons and environments to explain careers: some extensions and clarifications. *The Counseling Psychologist*, **6**, 3, 20–29.

37. *Ibid.* p. 26.

38. Holland, J. L. (1974) Vocational guidance for everyone. *Educational Researcher*, **4**, 24–26.

39. Holland, J. L. (1973) *Making Vocational Choices: A Theory of Careers* pp. 85–96. Englewood Cliffs NJ: Prentice-Hall.

40. Holland, J. L. (1979) *Professional Manual for the Self-directed Search.* Palo Alto: Consulting Psychologists Press.

41. Holland, J. L. (1973) *Making Vocational Choices: A Theory of Careers* pp. 88–91. Englewood Cliffs, NJ: Prentice-Hall.

42. *Ibid*, p. 92.
43. McKechnie, G. E. (1974) Psychological foundations of leisure counseling: an empirical strategy. *Therapeutic Recreation Journal*, **3**, 4–16.
44. Overs, R. P. (1975) Avocational counseling: gateway to meaningful activity. *Counseling and Values*, **1**, 36–41.
45. MacPhillamy, D. J. & Lewinsohn, P. M. (1971) *Pleasant Events Schedule*. Mimeograph, University of Oregon.
46. Cautela, J. (1967) A Reinforcement Survey Schedule for use in therapy, training and research. *Psychological Reports*, **20**, 1115–1130.
47. Overs, R. P. (1970) A model for avocational counseling. *Journal of Health, Physical Education and Recreation*, **41**, 36–38.
48. McDowell, C. F. (1974) Toward a healthy leisure mode: leisure counseling. *Therapeutic Recreation Journal*, **3**, 96–104.
49. Overs, R. P. (1970) A model for avocational counseling. *Journal of Health, Physical Education and Recreation*, **41**, 36.
50. Holland, J. L. (1973) *Making Vocational Choices: A Theory of Careers* p. 26. Englewood Cliffs, NJ: Prentice-Hall.
51. McKechnie, G. E. (1974) Psychological foundations of leisure counseling: an empirical strategy. *Therapeutic Recreation Journal*, **3**, 13.
52. Hartlage, L. C. (1969) The scientific management of leisure time. *Journal of Clinical Psychology*, **25**, 226–228.
53. Department of Education and Science (1973) *Careers Education in Secondary Schools* p. 61. London: HMSO.
54. Daws, P. P. (1971) Careers education in the secondary school curriculum. *Careers Quarterly*, **23**, 33–34. Full reference pp. 33–37.
55. Schools Council Working Party on the Transition from School to Work (1972) *Careers Education in the 1970s* p. 36. London: Evans/Methuen.
56. Watts, A. G. (1977) Careers education in higher education: principles and practice. *British Journal of Guidance and Counselling*, **5**, 167–184.
57. Hoppock, R. (1976) *Occupational Information* (4th ed.) pp. 141–143. New York: McGraw-Hill.
58. Ibid. p. 176.
59. Watts, A. G. (1977) Careers education in higher education: principles and practice. *British Journal of Guidance and Counselling*, **5**, 167–184.
60. Hayes, J. & Hopson, B. (1972) *Careers Guidance: The Role of the School in Vocational Development* pp. 171–181. London: Heinemann.
61. Closs, S. J. (1980) *Computer Assisted Career Guidance: Manual for the JiiG-CAL System*. Sevenoaks: Hodder and Stoughton.
62. Hopson, B. & Hough, P. (1973) *Exercises in Personal and Career Development* pp. 93–119. Cambridge: Careers Research and Advisory Centre.
63. Watts, A. G. (1978) Using Computers in careers guidance in schools. *Journal of Occupational Psychology*, **51**, 34–35. Full reference pp. 29–40.
64. Super, D. E. (1973) Computers in support of vocational development and counseling. In H. Borow (ed.), *Career Guidance for a New Age* p. 313. Boston: Houghton Mifflin. Full reference pp. 285–315.
65. Heginbotham, H. (1978) Computer applications in the careers service of a large city. *Journal of Occupational Psychology*, **51**, 85–93.
66. Super, D. E. (1973) Computers in support of vocational development and counseling. In H. Borow (ed.), *Career Guidance for a New Age* pp. 292–294. Boston: Houghton Mifflin.
67. Super, D. E. (1978) From information retrieval through matching to counselling and to career development: some lessons from the USA. *Journal of Occupational Psychology*, **51**, 19–22. Full reference pp. 19–28.
68. Watts, A. G. (1978) Using computers in careers guidance in schools. *Journal of Occupational Psychology*, **51**, 34–35.

19 – Group Counselling

SUMMARY: *Group counselling consists of the practice of the relationships and activities of counselling in groups. A brief history of the development of group counselling is provided. Group counselling may be used after, concurrently with, or instead of individual counselling. Sources of therapeutic gain in group counselling include: the opportunity for self-exploration and feedback provided in the group; improved motivation for some clients; the experience of being a member of a group; the contributions of other members; the opportunity to practise personal relations; and the value of the participant-observer role of the counsellor.*

Preparatory considerations in establishing counselling groups are reviewed. Counsellor decisions will need to be made about: whether to have one or two counsellors for a group; whether the group is to be closed or open; group size; group composition and selection; whether to conduct intake interviews and engage in other forms of pre-group preparation; the nature of any contracts and guidelines; physical setting; and duration and frequency of meetings.

There are many considerations relating to the counsellor's role in the group process, including leadership style, structuring, handling termination, and coping with personal vulnerability. Furthermore, counsellors can expand some of their individual counselling skills to become proficient at working with groups, including such skills as listening and empathic understanding, focusing on members' manner of relating, focusing on members' thinking difficulties, and handling resistance and aggression. Counsellors also need to make decisions about whether or not to use audio-visual aids or exercises and games in conjunction with their groups. The notion of developmental stages in the life of groups is discussed and some common themes are identified, for example a shift from social distance to intimacy and from avoidance of problem areas to actively working on problems.

Some approaches to counselling which either exclusively or heavily emphasize group work are reviewed briefly, namely, psychodrama, gestalt therapy, integrity groups, and conjoint family therapy. Last, a cautionary word is added about some of the problems of group work, including ethical issues surrounding the counsellor, and difficulties which clients and their significant others may face outside the group.

In the next two chapters on group counselling and psychological education we examine counselling psychology approaches other than the individual interview. In fact, there is much overlap between the rest of the book and these two chapters. All the theoretical positions discussed earlier have group as well as individual counselling applications. Furthermore, group methods are used in occupational counselling and the term 'careers education', almost by definition, implies a group approach. Additionally, many of the interventions discussed in the practice part of the book, such as the fundamental counselling relationship and cognitive interventions, are applicable to group counselling.

Despite the overlap, a chapter on group counselling has been included for the following reasons. First, there are many considerations in group counselling which either do not arise in individual counselling at all or which arise in a different form. Among such issues are practical details about selection and composition of groups, group facilitator or leader behaviours, and the processes or stages of development of groups. Second, we wish to mention some approaches to counselling which are primarily group approaches, namely, psychodrama, gestalt therapy, integrity groups, and conjoint family therapy.

HISTORICAL BACKGROUND

The founder of group psychotherapy is often acknowledged to be Joseph H. Pratt, a Boston doctor who used weekly group meetings as one way of treating far advanced tuberculosis patients. During the inter-war years a number of psychiatrists tried group methods. Prominent among these were Alfred Adler, who was using group techniques in his child guidance clinics in Vienna and who heavily emphasized the need for patients to develop 'social interest', and J. L. Moreno, the founder of psychodrama and sociodrama, who was the first to use the term 'group therapy'.[1] Gazda observes that during this same period the American vocational guidance movement was instrumental in the introduction of such group activities as homeroom guidance and classes in occupational information.[2]

The Second World War accelerated the introduction of group therapy, since there were insufficient mental health workers to allow for individual treatment of military psychiatric casualties. In 1947 the first T (for human relationship skills training) group was held in Bethel, Maine, and afterwards the T group movement, with its educational and laboratory training emphasis, continued growing. Also, Rogers reports that in 1946 and 1947 he was experimenting at the University of Chicago Counseling Center with an intensive group experience for trainee personal counsellors for the Veterans Administration.[3] Yalom observes that during the 1950s the main thrust of the group therapy field was towards the application of group therapy in different clinical settings and for different types of clinical problems, with a number of theoretical approaches, such as Freudian, Sullivanian and Rogerian, having their group applications explored.[4] Possibly the main development in group work during the 1960s and 1970s has been the burgeoning growth of encounter groups, which set out to provide intensive group experiences for less disturbed 'normals' in non-medical settings rather than for moderately to severely disturbed patients in medical settings.

DEFINING GROUP COUNSELLING

In Chapter 1 we indicated that counselling might be viewed as: (a) a special kind of helping *relationship* characterized by the 'core conditions'; (b) a set of practical *activities* based on theoretical principles; and (c) an *area* of services provision focused on less disturbed clients in non-medical settings. A definition of group counselling is that it consists of the practice of the relationships and activities of counselling in groups or, more simply, the counselling of people in groups.

A distinctive feature of group counselling, mentioned either implicitly or explicitly by writers on group work, is that group interaction and relationships are used to help members to attain personal objectives. For instance, an important part of Mahler's definition of group counselling is that it is 'The process of using group interaction to facilitate deeper self-understanding and self-acceptance'.[5] Similarly, Ohlson writes that 'Group counseling is a special relationship in which clients feel safe to discuss what really worries and upsets them, to define desired new behaviours, to practice essential interpersonal skills, and to implement new behaviors'.[6] Yalom also stresses the importance of interpersonal relationships and sees psychotherapy groups as evolving into social microcosms in which curative interpersonal learning may take place.[7]

In practice, counselling groups are defined by their theoretical orientation, e.g. TA or RET, by their focus on a problem area, e.g. examination anxiety or social skills, by their clientele, e.g. singles groups or couples groups, by their length, e.g. marathon groups, and by broad categories, such as T groups or encounter groups. Rogers writes of the encounter group: 'This tends to emphasize personal growth and the development and improvement of interpersonal communication and relationships through an experiential process'.[8] Rogers' emphasis here on personal growth highlights an important feature of many counselling groups, namely, that they are often based on notions of development, growth and optimization of psychological potential rather than on remediation of severe pathology. The terms 'personal growth' and 'personal development' are sometimes used in the titles of such counselling groups.

RATIONALE FOR GROUP COUNSELLING

Group counselling may be used after, concurrently with, or instead of individual counselling. An assumption of counsellors who make treatment decisions favouring group methods is that they offer sources of counselling gain over and above the individual interview. Yalom refers to such sources of gain as 'curative factors' and sees such factors as falling into 11 primary categories: (a) installation of hope; (b) universality; (c) imparting of information; (d) altruism; (e) the corrective recapitulation of the primary family group; (f) development of socializing techniques; (g) imitative behaviour; (h) interpersonal learning; (i) group cohesiveness; (j) catharsis; and (k) existential factors.[9] While not adopting all of Yalom's categories, we now suggest some reasons why group counselling may be the treatment of choice for certain clients.

Opportunity for Self-exploration and Feedback

Given the importance of good personal relationships in effective living, groups can provide their members with many valuable direct and vicarious learning experiences which may not take place in individual interviews yet which may facilitate self-exploration, self-understanding and self-acceptance. For instance, groups may provide an opportunity for members to test their perceptions and possibly to overcome their perceptual distortions in regard to: how they perceive themselves; how others perceive them or the kinds of impressions they make on others; how they anticipate that others in the group will react to their self-disclosures and how they actually do react; and how they themselves react to all kinds of interpersonal situations which may arise in the group and which may be causing difficulty outside, such as situations involving warmth, closeness and hostility.

Improved Motivation

The motivation of some clients both for attending counselling sessions and for making changes in their behaviour is likely to be significantly improved by participation in group counselling. Though groups can be very threatening for an unready client, for others they can be challenging and can meet deep-seated needs for close personal relationships. Furthermore, the encouragement, ideas and support provided by other group members can help members to take the risks of trying new behaviours both inside and outside the group. Additionally, some clients may be motivated to change their behaviour if they perceive the success of other group members in attaining goals.

Experience of Group Membership

The actual experience of group membership itself may be a source of gain. For instance, the group may provide an opportunity for isolated or shy people to relate to others and thus lessen their isolation. Furthermore, the disclosures of others may make members feel that they are not alone in having problems, in coming from unhappy backgrounds, and in having negative thoughts and feelings about themselves. This may lower members' sense of isolation and help them to rate themselves less negatively. Groups tend to differ on the amount of attraction that they have for their members. Yalom argues that the group therapy analogue of the 'relationship' in individual therapy is a broader concept called 'group cohesiveness', encompassing the patient's relationship to the group therapist, to the other group members, and to the group as a whole.[10] Cohesive groups are characterized by a sense of belongingness and mutual support and acceptance.

Contribution of Other Members

As well as the capacity to create a cohesive community in which individual members may gain a sense of belonging, there are other ways in which group members can contribute to each other. For instance, the social microcosm aspect of groups gives individuals the opportunity to widen their perceptions in a number of ways, such as: a close-up view of a number of different personalities and life-styles; the ways in which members can work towards or avoid change; and the chance to get more in touch with some aspect of their own experiencing through the disclosures and sharing of experiencing by others. Furthermore, though at times group members may be overtly helpful and healing, at other times they may provide challenging confrontations and feedback which may also be beneficial to an individual member. Additionally, interacting with other group members can have a valuable here-and-now quality in which there can be spontaneity and the opportunity to explore feelings, defences and interpersonal styles at or near to the time they *actually happen*. This tends to be more difficult in individual counselling, not least because the client relates only to the counsellor.

Practice at Personal Relationships

Group counselling provides members with sheltered but nonetheless valuable practice at initiating, sustaining and, at least when the group ends, terminating a range of personal relationships. Group members have much opportunity for self-disclosure, and sometimes for catharsis, since many of their thoughts and feelings may have been bottled up and festering for a long time. Furthermore, groups may give individual members the confidence and skills to approach others. For instance, previously isolated college-age males and females may become much more at ease with heterosexual relationships as a result of a mixed-group experience. Also, groups may provide individual members with opportunities to be helping and healing to others, to become less threatened and overwhelmed by the emoting of others, and to develop some skills of conflict resolution by working out differences with particular members. One way of viewing counselling groups is as behavioural laboratories where people learn to take risks, define themselves more accurately and move in new directions without some of the deleterious cost and reward contingencies which may have prevailed and which may still be prevailing outside the group.

Participant-observer Role of Counsellor

Another potential source of gain of group counselling as contrasted with individual counselling stems from the counsellors being able to observe clients as they develop or avoid personal relationships in the group. Depending on the counsellor's orientation, she may confront clients with their strengths and favoured coping and defensive interpersonal styles in a way that would be difficult in individual counselling, since much of the data would not be so immediate and available. Furthermore, where appropriate, the counsellor may work together with other group members to help an individual to explore the impact that her behaviour is having on others and its rewards and costs in terms of attaining personal objectives.

CONSIDERATIONS IN GROUP COUNSELLING

Preparatory Considerations

There are many preparatory considerations in establishing counselling groups, some of which are reviewed below. Whatever the theoretical orientation of the group, it is unlikely that decisions relating to these considerations can be avoided.

Number of counsellors

Sometimes counselling groups are led or facilitated by two counsellors rather than one. Though often this may not be feasible in terms of resources, there are reasons why some counsellors consider it desirable. For instance, especially for beginning group counsellors, it may be helpful to have the support of a more experienced counsellor. Furthermore, it is difficult for one counsellor to be sensitive to the range of feelings and interactions within a group and a second counsellor may help to remedy this deficiency. Also, a second counsellor may provide additional valuable insights into the functioning of the group and of particular individuals. Another argument for two counsellors is that they may be of opposite sexes or have different personalities, thus increasing the likelihood that each group member will be able to relate well to at least one of the counsellors. Sometimes the two group counsellors play different roles: for example, one may play a facilitative role whereas the other may be more task-oriented, or more confronting, or more of an interpreter-sum-marizer.

There are, however, some potential pitfalls of having two counsellors; for example, they may not get on well with each other or they may be unable to agree how best to facilitate or lead the group. Furthermore, two counsellors may provide an increased likelihood of blocking the growth of intermember cohesiveness by too frequent and possibly conflicting interventions.

Closed or open groups

When planning a group the counsellor will have to decide whether it is to be *closed* or *open*. The *closed* group is likely to meet for a fixed time-span, say an academic year, and, once established, admits no new members. Counsellors who lead closed groups may start with a few extra members to allow for some drop-out without necessitating taking on new members. An argument advanced for closed groups is that there is a distinct unfolding or series of stages in group work which may be impeded by the introduction of new members. *Open* groups meet for either fixed or unspecified lengths of time. They are open in that new members may be introduced either when previous members leave or when the counsellor feels she has a client who could benefit from the group experience, presumably without badly disrupting the other members. In open groups the counsellor can always discuss with existing members the timing of the introduction of new members. Often the practicalities of running counselling groups dictate that they should be open, since some members change jobs, leave the district, or otherwise find themselves unable or unwilling to attend.

Group size

Yalom observes: 'My own experience and a consensus of the clinical literature suggests that the ideal size of an interactional therapy group is approximately seven, with an acceptable range of five to ten members'.[11] Groups of fewer than five may not provide a sufficiently varied range of personalities, coping and defensive styles, and interactional opportunities. Groups of more than ten may make it difficult to develop intensive interactional experiences. Furthermore, large groups limit the amount of group attention that can be devoted to each member and, hence, may increase the likelihood of certain members willingly or unwillingly avoiding participation. Further reasons for limiting the size of groups are the capacity of the counsellor to be sensitive to the personal needs and interactions of large numbers of people, and the emotional strain that handling groups of ten or more may place on counsellors.

Some counsellors are able to do useful work in groups of more than ten. This may be partly a function of counsellor skill and experience and partly related to duration of meetings. For instance, weekend or marathon intensive encounter groups often have 14 to 20 members. However, when group numbers get above ten, many counsellors may feel under pressure to adopt an educational or training, rather than an interactional, format.

Group composition and selection

Some groups have their potential clientele identified in their titles, such as singles groups, pre-retirement groups, and social skills training groups. In such instances the counsellor has signalled from the start that she wishes to work with a certain category of member. In other instances the counsellor may seek to provide an intensive group experience and, without predetermined restrictions, be left with the problem of trying to put together a group which will last and from which its members will gain benefit.

There are few, if any, hard and fast rules in group composition. Clearly the group must have at least a certain minimal level of attraction for its members or else it will soon run into problems of non-attendance. There are a number of variables which the counsellor forming a group may wish to consider, including age of members, their gender, the number of highly defensive and rigid people in the group, the number of people with some helping skills, the proportion of people who are reasonably talkative rather than shy and silent, intelligence and education, socioeconomic status and cultural background, the range of presenting problems, and the range of personalities.

An issue in group formation is sometimes stated in terms of whether *homogeneous* are preferable to *heterogeneous* groups and *vice versa*. A degree of homogeneity (e.g. age, intelligence, socioeconomic status) may appear to be necessary to ensure that the group has a basic level of inter-member attractiveness and, hence, potential for cohesiveness. However, the matter is not that simple. A group composed entirely of silent and inhibited people is scarcely likely to prove a success. Furthermore, mixed-gender groups have much to recommend them, since people have to relate to both sexes outside the group. Additionally, some members may find learning to relate to people of different personalities and backgrounds a rewarding experience. Perhaps words like 'homogeneous' and 'heterogeneous' are too broad and imprecise adequately to describe desired features of group composition. One consideration which is very important in forming effective groups is that they contain at least two or three people who, despite their problems, have some facility at making human contact. Such people may both act as catalysts for the group and be helpful in a healing capacity.

So far our discussion of group composition has focused on the issue of which members to include. However, group composition also requires some decisions focused more on *exclusion* than *inclusion*. Certain clients may prefer to stay in individual counselling and exclude themselves from groups, since they feel unready for the greater stresses they anticipate in a group setting. On other occasions the client may be willing, but the counsellor may have reservations about that client's readiness. Specific categories of people who might be excluded from a group include: uncommitted people who seem likely to terminate counselling early; extremely hostile and aggressive people; people who are chronic monopolizers in social situations; and people who are in close contact outside either with each other or with the counsellor. Counsellors differ on the degree of contact they consider permissible outside groups, some considering that close contact outside may lead to unproductive sub-grouping inside.

Intake interviewing and preparation

There are many different ways in which groups are formed. A counsellor who is seeing many clients on an individual-interview basis may also run one or more groups for those of her clients whom she considers may benefit. Alternatively, counsellors may circularize their colleagues to obtain members for a group they are about to start. Sometimes counsellors may let their intentions to start a group be known by hand-outs or by an advertisement in, perhaps, a campus newspaper. On other occasions, where a counsellor is known to have an interest in groups, clients who want an intensive group experience may present themselves for group membership.

Some groups may be composed on a 'first come, first served' basis up to the desired group size, but it seems preferable for counsellors who are considering running intensive interactional groups to hold individual intake interviews with those being considered for membership. There are a number of advantages of such intake interviews. First, they allow the counsellor to make more realistic selection decisions on the basis of her criteria of inclusion and exclusion for the particular group in question. Second, intake interviews help prospective clients to clarify their expectancies about the proposed group, including whether they feel at ease with the counsellor. Thus, client decisions on participation are likely to be more realistically based, thereby reducing tendencies to terminate early. Third, and a very important precaution against early termination, individual group members may feel that they have had the opportunity to start developing a relationship with the counsellor. This sense of relationship with the counsellor, or of having a 'friend at court', may provide members with a degree of security as they face the anxieties and stresses of new and possibly more intense personal relationships than they are accustomed to.

Fourth, intake interviews can provide some initial structuring for the group process. Some of this structuring may focus on providing a rationale for membership in a group, though related to the needs of the individual being interviewed. A few of the points mentioned in the rationale for group counselling earlier in this chapter might be stressed. For people who have had past relationship difficulties and are having troubled current relationships, interactional groups can be presented as having a logical connection with remedying their problems. Another area of structuring may be that of indicating desired group member behaviours, such as honesty, openness, and a willingness to take risks in revealing intimate aspects of oneself as well as in trying out new behaviours.

In some kinds of groups, intake interviews are conducted by existing group members. The *ad hoc* intake committees of Mowrer's integrity groups provide an example of this. The intake committees usually consist of four people, two men and two women. The intake session is held at the home of one of the committee members and is based on the assumption that helping 'the new person to *change, starts at once* . . .'.[12] Consequently attempts are made to get the prospective member to 'get honest' and these attempts may include modelling by one or more of the intake committee members in which they tell their stories and describe the difficulties they have encountered. If accepted, new members are placed in groups with at least one or two people who have been on their intake committee.[13]

Some group counsellors seek further to prepare members beyond the intake interview. Ways of doing this include getting them to read a hand-out on desirable group behaviours or some other material concerning the theoretical orientation of the proposed group, such as the basic principles of TA or RET. Another form of preparation involves exposing prospective members to an audio or videotape of a productive group session. Yet another form is that of pre-group training in membership skills, such as self-disclosure and using 'I' messages to give feedback to other members. Here the skills may first be described and modelled on videotape.

Guidelines and contracts

All groups operate on the basis of 'contracts' of varying degrees of formality and explicitness between the group counsellor and group members. At the more formal end of the spectrum, Brammer and Shostrom get new group members to sign a mimeographed sheet, adapted from Bach,[14] on which procedural principles are stated in six areas: size of group; admission of group members; extra-office meetings; sharing of mutual experience; ethical confidence (confidentiality); and the group's goal.[15] Integrity groups have an explicit but slightly less formal 'contract' which governs the structure and activities of the group and to which members must adhere. These are stated in terms of: (a) Ground Rules; and (b) Suggestions and Guidelines. A sample Ground Rule is 'An IG member may be summarily expelled for physical violence (directed at another person or persons or at material objects) or threat thereof'. Sample Suggestions and Guidelines are 'Don't interrupt!', 'Don't blame' and 'Don't mind read or expect others to read yours!'.[16] A positive approach to group contracts is that of Egan, who asks members to engage in and gives guidelines concerning 'core interactions' or personal relations skills.[17] Other groups may operate on a more informal basis, with relatively little structuring from the counsellor and with procedural issues being talked through in the group as they arise.

Minimum attendance and extra-group socializing are two areas which Yalom attempts to clarify when preparing patients for group psychotherapy. He asks prospective members to make a minimum commitment of at least 12 meetings before even attempting to evaluate the ultimate usefulness of the group. Regarding extra-group socializing, he tries tactfully to convey that 'the therapy group teaches one how to develop intimate, long-term relationships, but it does not provide these relationships'.[18] He considers that if, however, members meet outside they should discuss the salient aspects of their meeting inside the group. Though counsellor attitudes to minimum attendance and extra-group socializing vary, these are always likely to be important considerations in formal or informal group 'contracts'.

Physical setting

The group should be in a physical setting which is conducive to interaction. Privacy and quiet are important. Furthermore, a pleasantly decorated room, preferably carpeted, is desirable. This room should comfortably provide space for the numbers in the group, but should not be too large. Sometimes groups lasting for a few days seek a natural setting, such as a woodland, and hold sessions out of doors.

In terms of seating arrangements, a circle is preferable to a rectangle, since members, including the group counsellor, need to be able to see each other. Where there are two counsellors it is preferable that they sit away from each other so as not to focus the leadership in one area. There are three main possibilities for seating. First, the group sits around a table. Possible advantages of this are that vulnerable members feel somewhat protected by the table and that members can write if they want to. However, sitting around a table may create rather than lessen social distance. Second, the group sits in reasonably comfortable chairs in a circle, with nothing blocking their view of each other. Here members can observe each other's non-verbal behaviours more easily. Furthermore, it is a more natural setting than the table arrangement for moving round during the group if, for instance, one member wishes to comfort another. Third, there may be no chairs but a number of cushions on which members may sit, either against a wall or not. Mintz uses the floor-and-cushions format for her marathon groups.[19] Such a format seems desirable for groups in which members perform exercises and play games involving physical movement. Psychodrama groups, in which various parts of the room may become the 'stage', sometimes use the floor-and-cushion format.

Frequency and duration of meetings

Most commonly, counselling groups meet once weekly. However, some therapists, such as Yalom, prefer a twice-weekly schedule considering it conducive to greater intensity and continuity.[20] Some groups meet up to five times weekly, though this may be easier in a hospital setting than where people have work commitments. A further possibility is to meet twice weekly at the start of the group or if there is some urgent business to be dealt with, but otherwise to meet once weekly. Other counselling groups may be scheduled on a bi-weekly or monthly basis, possibly with longer sessions than when the meetings are more frequent. One reason for fewer and longer sessions is that it may make attendance easier for certain members who have domestic commitments or live some distance away. Still other counselling groups, usually lasting at least a full day or a weekend, may be scheduled on a 'one-off' basis.

Duration and frequency of meetings tend to be inversely related: i.e. shorter and more or longer and fewer. Regarding weekly group sessions, anything less than an hour is generally regarded as too short to allow for both warm-up and a number of themes to be dealt with. Consequently, 90-minute or two-hour sessions are considered preferable. Some groups, such as integrity groups, hold sessions of three hours or more. Both counsellor and group members' fatigue may be one of the problems of longer groups. Shorter groups, for example an hour, may have some advantages for school children in terms of their attention span and also may fit more readily into a classroom period.

When groups meet less frequently than once weekly, additional time may be necessary to deal with the various themes members may bring to the group, as well as with the material generated by it. Consequently, for a fortnightly group, a session of three hours might be appropriate. Some counselling groups, known as marathon groups, last for two days or so. This may entail, perhaps, six three-hour sessions spread over a couple of days, with breaks for meals and sleep outside the group room. Alternatively, members may be required to eat and sleep in the group counselling room.

The number of meetings tends to vary with the purposes of the group. Marathon groups tend to be on a 'one-off' basis, though members may choose to enrol in another marathon group of the same or a different theoretical orientation. Groups focused on managing specific problems, such as examination anxiety, may have a fixed number of meetings, perhaps six to eight. Weekly interactional groups may last for up to a year or more. Indeed, Mowrer and his colleagues consider group participation to be a lifetime process, so individuals remain in community both to work on current problems and to avoid 'backsliding' into previous bad habits.[21] However, some counsellors consider that having a group with a clearly stipulated number of sessions provides an incentive for members to work harder.

The Counsellor in the Group Process

Until now we have focused mainly on considerations prior to the initial group meeting. Now we focus on some issues related to the role of the counsellor during the life of the group.

Leadership style

Group counsellors vary tremendously in how they view and enact their roles. This variability is related to such factors as their theoretical orientations, their personal needs, their skills and experience and a number of other factors such as the context in which they work and the different memberships of particular groups. Counsellor directiveness is one dimension of group leadership style, with a high level of directiveness indicating a teacher-learner or trainer-trainee relationship between counsellor and group members. Behavioural counselling groups, with their clearly defined goals and methods, tend to operate on such an assumption. In a group-centred leadership style the counsellor attempts to share the responsibility for the direction and development of the group with its members. This is more the leadership style of person-centred counselling groups where the counsellor is frequently called a 'facilitator'. It is erroneous, however, to suggest that the person-centred facilitator is totally 'non-directive'; she is influencing the process of the group by using skills based on a person-centred model of human behaviour. For instance, though the counsellor has a lower profile than in highly directive groups, nevertheless her presence is felt as she creates a climate in which members can explore and experience themselves more fully. At an extreme end of the directiveness dimension is the leaderless group, which may be leaderless for occasional sessions or for regularly scheduled sessions, such as every other week. Alternatively, the group may spend its whole life on a leaderless basis, with the peer group of members providing what leadership exists.

Another dimension on which leadership style varies is the extent to which the counsellor becomes a participant-member of the group. Some group counsellors prefer to play an expert role in their groups, revealing little of their own personal life and problems. Often these counsellors consider that, particularly in groups with highly vulnerable clients, such self-disclosure and working on their own problems would interfere with meeting their clients' needs. On the other hand, a number of group counsellors consider that they function most effectively as leader-members or facilitator-members of their groups. Here they try to model the attitudes and skills of effective personal relationships. However, even those counsellors who self-disclose less than their more participating counterparts may still be offering some good relationship skills, such as empathic understanding.

Structuring

Some structuring or setting of expectancies goes on in intake interviews and in any other pre-group preparation that may have taken place. Nevertheless, at the initial meeting it may be helpful for the counsellor to engage in structuring, even at the risk of repetition. There is no uniform method of structuring, since the goals and leader and membership roles of groups vary greatly. Rogers observes that he tends to engage in minimal structuring, with such comments as: 'I suspect we will know each other a great deal better at the end of these group sessions than we do now'; 'Here we are. We can make of this group experience exactly what we wish'; and 'I'm a little uneasy, but I feel somewhat reassured when I look around at you and realise that we're all in the same boat. Where do we start?'.[22] In fact, there is quite a lot of structuring of facilitator and member roles implicit in Rogers' comments. The initial structuring in non-person-centred groups may be much more specific in regard to such matters as the goals of the group, its working style, its rules and guidelines, and the theoretical language to be used. As well as the introductory statement, counsellor structuring takes place throughout the initial session or sessions by means of differential responding to various group members' utterances and by the use of body language. Counsellors who are skilled at structuring may enhance client motivation for the work of the group, whereas poor structuring may lead to resistances over and above those already brought into the group by its members.

Listening and empathic understanding

It is important in group counselling for members to feel that there is an emotional climate conducive to sharing personal disclosures. The group counsellor listens carefully to everything that each individual says and she frequently allows other members to respond and interact rather than always responding herself. The group counsellor shows her empathic understanding partly through her attitude and physical presence and partly by the level of understanding she shows when she does choose to respond. As in individual counselling, empathic understanding may take the form of responding to individual members' single statements or, where appropriate, clarifying and summarizing a series of statements from the same member. However, empathic understanding in group work may also involve responding to interactions between two or more members. At its simplest level this may be just reflecting the thoughts and feelings of each person involved. Furthermore, empathic understanding in group work may involve reflecting the mood of the whole group at any given time or clarifying and summarizing themes, such as fear of self-disclosure of difficulty in handling feelings of hurt, which may be at or just below the surface of the group conversation in a session. Another area in which counsellors can use empathic understanding in groups is in being sensitive to the needs of members who are not overtly participating and, where appropriate, facilitating their participation. As the group develops, members should become more skilled at empathically understanding and responding to each other.

Focusing on members' manner of relating

Earlier we mentioned that a possible advantage of group as contrasted with individual counselling is the opportunity for the counsellor to be a participant-observer of members' manners of relating. The counsellor can help individual members as they explore their feelings and reactions to incidents in the group. Furthermore, the counsellor may summarize and reflect the feedback other members are giving an individual about the way she relates. Sometimes the counsellor may actually encourage members to give feedback about the effect an individual member has on them. On other occasions the counsellor herself may be confronting a member with feedback. An example Rogers gives is: 'I don't like the way you chatter on. Seems to me you give each message three or four times. I wish you would stop when you've completed your message'.[23] Rogers tries to make such confrontations in terms of 'I' messages, in which he is willing to claim his thoughts and feelings as his own. At times the counsellor may confront the whole group rather than just individual members.

Counselling groups differ in the extent to which they explicitly engage in personal relations training. On the one hand the group counsellor may, in a relatively unstructured way, be making comments about such matters as: the advisability of calculated risk-taking in personal relationships; the desirability of talking specifically rather than in vague generalities; and being able to acknowledge ambivalence in oneself and one's relationships. On the other hand, as represented by Egan's contract-based encounter groups, group members may be trained in specific ways of relating. Egan describes and then asks members to experiment with and engage in the following core interactions: (a) self-disclosure; (b) the manner of expressing feeling; (c) listening; (d) support; (e) confronting others; and (f) responding to confrontation.[24] In marital counselling groups the counsellor may consider it appropriate to focus on the attitudes and skills of conflict resolution. The use of game analysis in Transactional Analysis, in which the counsellor attempts to make members aware of the moves and ulterior motives in disruptive series of transactions, is a further example of a focus on members' manner of relating, though here the focus is also on members' styles of thinking.[25]

Focusing on members' thinking difficulties

Often counsellor interventions in group counselling focus on members' thinking difficulties. Since these thinking difficulties tend to underlie many of the difficulties members are having in their relationships, it is hard to separate a focus on manner of relating from a focus on thinking difficulties. For instance, a group counsellor may observe that a member rarely initiates contact, but responds only when spoken to. Possible explanations for this behaviour, which might be explored in the group, are concerned with the way the member is attributing cause for what happens in her life and the way she is anticipating the risks of and gains from her actions. The group member may be failing to take initiatives because she does not see herself as having a causal influence on what happens in her life. Also, she may be accentuating this passive stance by a tendency to overemphasize the risks and minimize the gains of initiating contact with others. In the above instance, not only might the counsellor explore the thinking difficulties underlying the group member's behaviour, but the other group members might provide feedback about the effect of the individual member's behaviour on them and, possibly, provide support for future risk-taking. We already have listed in Chapter 14 many other counsellor approaches to thinking difficulties. These difficulties often become more apparent in group than in individual counselling, since members are required to interact with each other. In other words, their defence mechanisms, destructive roles and games are being enacted in the presence of the counsellor and other group members. This provides a rich source of material with which counsellor and members can work.

Handling resistance and aggression

Resistance and aggression are two kinds of client behaviours with which group counsellors often have to deal. Resistances are member behaviours (or lack of them!) which interfere with the work of the group and with the individual member or members gaining benefit from the group. For instance, an individual member may exhibit resistance to any participation at all or to a deeper form of participation. Group counsellor strategies for handling such resistance include: not mentioning it and hence giving the member psychological space to handle it in her own way; empathic reflection; exploration focused on thinking; relying on the modelling effect of other group members' disclosures; rewarding any group participation behaviours, however small; appropriate confrontations, for instance for evasiveness and lack of specificity; and, where necessary, exploring the issue of confidentiality.

Groups may themselves collectively exhibit resistance. For instance, they may develop a set of norms which allow members not to be fully committed to discussing their problems openly. Also, they may arrive at plateaus or times when they appear unwilling to do further work, possibly to avoid facing difficult material. The counsellor needs to decide whether such resistance is a transient phenomenon to be ignored or whether it is better to focus on and explore the resistance. However, as Ohlson observes, 'the best method for coping with resistance is to do everything possible to prevent it . . .',[26] Prevention may take place in such areas as group composition, intake interviewing, structuring, and showing sensitivity to the needs and feelings of the group. Nevertheless, members inevitably will bring individual resistances into the group and probably will exhibit collective resistance during its life.

Group counsellors, rather more than individual counsellors, have to handle the issues raised by client aggression. Writers on group work, such as Rogers[27] and Egan,[28] observe that negative feelings, such as hostility and anger towards other members and the leader, are some of the first *current* feelings to be expressed in encounter groups. When hostility is expressed between group members the counsellor may decide not to intervene. However, there are a number of possible interventions which may be helpful in the area of aggression. First, the counsellor may need to facilitate some members, if not actually give permission to them, to express their hostility. Second, hostility generally is most constructively expressed by encouraging members to use 'I' messages rather than engaging in blaming and passive-aggressive self-pity. Third, the counsellor can help group members to explore the thoughts, requests and feelings which may be masked by the show of anger. For instance, anger may mask hurt (and *vice versa*) caused by someone making unrealistic demands on themselves and/or others. Fourth, members may be helped to explore their reactions to and cope better with other people's anger. Fifth, the counsellor may decide that one or more members in the group needs support or protection and intervene either with direct protection or with a response which indirectly protects, for example by encouraging another member's exploration of rather than just expression of their anger. Some of the above interventions are relevant when the group counsellor has to handle hostility directed at herself. We have indicated earlier that, if it is possible to identify them in advance, certain chronically hostile people might be excluded from a counselling group.

Use of exercises and games

Some counsellors use exercises and games in their group work, while others, such as Rogers, consider that they are artificial unless they occur with real spontaneity.[29] Exercises and games are used in group work for a number of reasons: as warm-up devices either to speed up initial contact in a group or to help it through a plateau; as ways of illustrating points related to the theoretical orientation of the group; and, with non-verbal exercises, as ways of encouraging people to explore their bodily movements and responses and helping them learn to be more physically and emotionally expressive.

An example of a warm-up exercise is for group members to pair off and get to know each other in such a way that one of the pair may introduce and describe the other to the group. An example of a theoretically related exercise is the gestalt exercise of feeling the actual: 'Try for a few minutes to make up sentences stating what you are at this moment aware of. Begin each sentence with the words "now" or "at this moment" or "here and now"'.[30] Pushing is an example of a non-verbal exercise: 'The two participants stand facing each other and clasp both hands, palm to palm, intertwining fingers. When they agree they begin pushing each other, attempting to make the other give ground'.[31] Those who want ideas for further exercises and games are referred to the writings of Perls and his colleagues,[32] Schutz,[33] Mintz,[34] and Hopson and Hough.[35]

Use of audio-visual aids

Many counsellors use no audio-visual aids in conjunction with their group work. Some, however, use felt-tip pens and flip-charts or chalk and blackboard to illustrate points they are trying to make. More recently, counsellors have been experimenting with using the videotape recorder, somewhat along the lines of the old adage that a picture is worth a thousand words. Video feedback may help group members to explore their own self-image and also to obtain some fairly irrefutable evidence about how they relate to others. Furthermore, some counsellors may also use the video-recorder to model desired interpersonal skills. Counsellors using videotape recording vary from those who consider it central to those who consider it an occasional adjunct to their groups. Sometimes the playback sessions are immediate and on other occasions they may be the next group session after the recording. Reservations about using videotape include fears about loss of spontaneity in the group through being recorded, the possibility of having unreliable and distracting equipment both in the recording and in the playback sessions, the need to have a horseshoe seating pattern if only one camera is used, and fears about loss of privacy and confidentiality. Yalom observes that, if anyone, the person who appears to experience the most discomfort is the therapist, only some of whom adjust to using video-recording.[36]

Handling termination

Counsellors may have to handle three kinds of termination: (a) members in open or closed groups who terminate early; (b) members in open groups who terminate when their goals have been achieved; and (c) the termination of all members at the end of a closed group. We have already spoken of approaches to group member preparation in order to reduce the likelihood of premature termination. It possible, the group counsellor needs to be able to identify members whom she feels will leave early. Furthermore, she needs to be sensitive to the degree of resilience of those who are coming under attack in a group and who may handle stress by avoidance. Understanding her group members' feelings, reservations and vulnerabilities is important, since not all those who terminate early announce their intentions before leaving. Potential early terminators can be supported by the counsellor's showing empathic understanding of their needs during sessions, by her protecting them from more aggression than they can handle, and by her being available for individual interviews when necessary. One or more individual interviews are also a way of handling those who announce their intention to terminate, yet whom she does not consider ready. Another way is to discuss the matter in the group, but Yalom points out that this method is rarely successful in dissuading people.[37] However, Yalom is wrong to label premature terminators as unsuccessful patients, since, in some instances, it is the counsellor who is lacking and hence the client is justified in leaving.

In open groups one of the termination issues is to ascertain when a member's goals have been achieved. Ideally, the member considering termination makes an accurate assessment of this in consultation with the counsellor and other group members. In practice, the counsellor may have to guard against tendencies both in herself and in the other group members not to allow a member to leave. In general, it is better for termination decisions to be discussed and made over a series of sessions rather than abruptly and possibly without thought.

Handling the termination of a whole group towards, at and after the end of its life involves the counsellor in at least two important tasks: (a) helping the group to work through its thoughts and feelings regarding the impending termination, including feelings of loss and loneliness; and (b) working with individual group members, who are at varying states of readiness, to handle the practical problems of transition caused by the ending of the group. It is hoped that a number of the group members will be at the point where they can now cope on their own with reasonable success. Others may require or request further short-term support in individual counselling or may wish to join another group.

Counsellor vulnerability

In a number of ways the group counsellor may be more vulnerable to inner and outer pressures than the counsellor engaging only in individual interviews. For instance, there are added stresses in counselling between five and ten people rather than one at a time. These include: the need to understand many more interactions; being the recipient of group and not just single-member emotions; and having to relate to a wider range of personalities and defensive and coping styles. In short, some counsellors feel very threatened in groups. Others, unfortunately, may use groups to handle personal needs for power, status, affection and sex. Ways of increasing counsellor sensitivity and of reducing undesirable aspects of vulnerability include: adequate supervised training in group as well as in individual counselling; working with a more experienced counsellor when learning to be a group counsellor; and, even when experienced, considering working with another counsellor in groups and being prepared to seek out peer and possibly supervisor support.

Stages in Group Counselling

With so many different approaches to group counselling, we must beware of generalizations about various stages in the development of groups. Consequently the following discussion pertains mainly to experiential interactive groups which rely heavily on the contributions of members as well as on the skills of the counsellor. Yalom identifies three stages in the early life of a group.[38] First, there is the initial stage in which members size up one another and the group, attend to social relationships, and search for structure and the rationale of the group. During the second stage the group becomes preoccupied with issues of dominance, control and power, and there is much jockeying for position. Inter-member criticism becomes more frequent and the 'emergence of hostility toward the therapist is an inevitable occurrence in the life sequence of the group'.[39] The third stage involves the development of cohesiveness, in which there is an increase of trust, openness and authentic self-disclosure. Yalom observes that, once a group has survived its first few months and achieves a degree of stability, the long working-through stage begins. During this stage members reveal and work on their problems of living and their relationships with each other.

Other writers echo Yalom's views on the shift from social distance to intimacy, sometimes by way of hostility, during the life of a group. For instance, this shift can be seen in the titles of the 15 elements by which Rogers attempts to chart 'in roughly sequential order' the process of encounter groups: (a) milling around; (b) resistance to personal expression or exploration; (c) description of past feelings; (d) expression of negative feelings; (e) expression and exploration of personally meaningful material;

(f) the expression of immediate interpersonal feelings in the group; (g) the development of healing capacity in the group; (h) self-acceptance and the beginning of change; (i) the cracking of facades; (j) the individual receives feedback; (k) confrontation; (l) the helping relationship outside group sessions; (m) the basic encounter; (n) the expression of positive feelings and closeness; and (o) behaviour changes in the group.[40] Mintz, writing about marathon groups, also observes the shift from social distance to intimacy.[41] She describes the first phase as that in which social masks are worn. During this phase group members' attempts to help each other lack empathy. In the second phase, that of preliminary expression of authentic feelings, participants experiment with revealing their genuine feelings about themselves and one another in any number of ways. Sometimes the first breakthrough of real feeling is anger, using the leader as scapegoat. During this second phase there is a growing concern among members for one another, and participants may start using physical contact in expressing their feelings. The third phase is that of deeper self-exploration and mutual acceptance in which the group itself may truly become the counsellor and the activity of the leader is often minimal.

Another theme implicit, if not explicit, in each of the writers mentioned above is that members shift from positions of defensiveness and avoidance of problems to actively working on their problems, often with the help and collaboration of the rest of the group. In fact Mahler, another writer on stages in group counselling, calls his third stage the working stage. His first, second and fourth stages are the involvement stage, the transition stage and the ending stage.[42] All groups have to deal with problems raised by ending and thus, inevitably, groups conclude with a termination or ending stage, some of the issues of which we have already discussed.

GROUP APPROACHES TO COUNSELLING

We have already mentioned that all the theoretical orientations discussed earlier in this book have group as well as individual counselling applications. Here we briefly present some additional counselling approaches exclusively or heavily emphasizing group work: psychodrama, gestalt therapy, integrity therapy, and conjoint family therapy.

Psychodrama

Moreno, the founder of psychodrama, defined it as 'the science which explores the "truth" by dramatic methods. It deals with inter-personal relations and private worlds'.[43] His underlying hypothesis was that in order to provide people with a new opportunity for reintegration 'therapeutic cultures in miniature' are required in lieu of, or as an extension of, natural habitats.[44] Psychodrama may be viewed as an action approach to group counselling focused on releasing members' potential for constructive spontaneity and creativity.

In psychodrama, some portion of the group setting is designated as a stage, though ideally there is a specially adapted space containing a stage. There are four main participants in psychodramas: the subject or protagonist; the counsellor or director; the other players or auxiliary egos; and the group or audience. The dramas or enactments may be scenes from the protagonist's past, present or even future life. The auxiliary egos function as actors portraying roles, such as a parent or spouse, required by the enactment. The audience is an audience to the enactment, but also may make comments or share their own experiences. The director is a producer of the enactments, but is also a counsellor in helping the protagonist and other group members to handle therapeutically the material generated by the enactments. In a single psychodrama session of, say, three hours' duration, there may be a number of psychodramas consisting of three phases: (a) warming up the protagonist and setting the scene; (b) enacting; and (c) working with the material generated by the enacting.

Psychodrama uses a number of techniques, a few of which we now mention.[45] In the role-reversal technique the protagonist exchanges roles and acts as the other person involved in an interpersonal situation. In the mirror technique the protagonist remains seated in the audience while an auxiliary ego copies her behaviour patterns and shows her 'as if in a mirror' how other people experience her. In the double technique, used to penetrate areas of conflict, an auxiliary ego is placed beside the subject, interacting with the subject 'as herself' and assisting her in the assessment of her problems.

Gestalt Therapy

Though gestalt therapy may be performed on an individual basis, it is frequently conducted on a group basis. Gestalt therapy was created mainly by Fritz Perls, who died in 1970 at the age of 76. The aim of gestalt therapy is to help clients to make strong gestalts, or good contact with their environments. Another way of stating this is that clients are helped to move from environmental support to self-support through their increased ability to use the world actively for their own development instead of manipulating the environment by playing neurotic roles. The methods of gestalt therapy foster 'deliberate awareness of one's various functions, until the sense is spontaneously revived that "it is I who am thinking, perceiving, feeling and doing this".' At this point the patient can take over on her own.[46] Gestalt counsellors help group members to focus on the 'how' and the 'now', or on how rather than why they are feeling the way they are at the present moment. We have already mentioned the work of Perls and his colleagues as a source of ideas for exercises and games.[47,48]

Gestalt counsellors, however, often work with one person at a time in a group setting, though frequently this work turns into a shared group experience. The techniques of gestalt therapy include psychodrama, skilful frustration, helping clients to identify their projections, and getting resentments expressed and understood. The gestalt counsellor may use psychodrama by getting the group member to move forward and back from one seat to another as she engages in a dialogue between parts of herself, between other persons, or between dream objects. In skilful frustration, the counsellor identifies areas in which the member handles threatening situations by avoidance and frustrates her avoidance still further until she is willing to mobilize her *own* resources to cope with the situations, thus realizing that the impasses existed more in fantasy and in her catastrophic expectations than in reality. A part of skilful frustration is helping members to identify their projection on to the counsellor of the characteristics they feel are missing in themselves. Perls writes: 'We are continually projecting threatening fantasies onto the world and these fantasies prevent us from taking the reasonable risks which are part and parcel of growing and living'.[49] The gestalt counsellor works with group members' resentments. Resentment is seen as the weak or incomplete gestalt *par excellence* and the expression of resentment is viewed as one of the most important ways of helping a person to make her life a little easier. Gestalt counsellors consider that behind every resentment there is a demand and they encourage members to express such demands.

Integrity Groups

Mowrer, the founder of integrity groups, considers that the fundamental task of psychotherapy is to help patients or clients to 'establish problem-solving habits which will enable emotions to operate as they are normally intended to'.[50] Also, he considers that the group approach 'encourages the development of rectitude, responsibility, and realism so much more rapidly than do the conventional forms of individual treatment'.[51] His view of human problems is that people are often undersocialized, not living up to their contracts and promises, and engaging in devious and secretive life-styles which keep them out of real community with their fellow humans. Integrity groups, based on a mutual help or peer group model, aim to get members more in tune with others and having better feelings about themselves. They operate on three cardinal principles: (a) honesty, self-disclosure of contracts and promises broken and of temptations; (b) responsibility, correction of contract violations or revision or dissolution of contracts; and (c) involvement (concern, love), giving help to others in becoming more honest, responsible and involved.

Integrity groups consist of eight to ten people, all of whom may be members of a larger integrity group community. Group sessions normally last for three hours and members may request additional special sessions if they feel they need extra time to work on a problem. We have already mentioned integrity group intake committees at which a high level of self-disclosure is both modelled and expected. The same openness is expected during meetings, and members may be challenged for deviations from the three cardinal principles. In keeping with the mutual peer help emphasis, the chairmanship of sessions rotates weekly, usually on an alphabetical basis. Within an integrity group community, group membership may be re-assigned every few months. Integrity groups are not time-limited and become for many a 'distinctive sub-culture and way of life'.[52] The manual for integrity groups is entitled *Integrity Groups: The Loss and Recovery of Community*.[53]

Conjoint Family Therapy

There are many approaches to family therapy, of which the conjoint family therapy approach of Satir will be used here as an illustration.[54,55] Satir views a dysfunctional marital relationship as the main contributor to symptoms in a child and, therefore, the relationship between the marital partners is the counsellor's first concern. Illness derives from inadequate methods of communication, or inadequate giving and getting of information, which is associated with feelings of low self-esteem. The role of the family therapist includes: being a resource person who remains outside the family power struggle as an 'official observer'; being a model of communication; being a teacher of communication, for instance helping clients to be aware of messages that are incongruent, confused or covert, and showing them how to check out invalid assumptions that are used as fact; and being an analyser of the nature and extent of dysfunction in a family by, for instance, focusing on how family members handle the presence of differentness, or on how congruently they are playing their roles, and on the early life models that influenced each of them.

The family therapist structures the initial interviews by taking a family life chronology covering pre-marital and marital life, including parenting. Satir usually sees the marital pair first for at least two sessions and then the children are introduced and, depending on their age, may remain for most of the subsequent sessions. Children's views of their parents and the family situation are also collected as part of the family life chronology. The bulk of the conjoint family therapist's time is spent untangling the dysfunctional relationships which exist in unhappy families by helping members to perceive themselves and each other clearly and teaching them how to communicate in an open system which, unlike a closed system, permits honest self-expression and allows disagreement. Satir is flexible in terms of: session length, from half an hour to weekend long sessions; place, her office or the family's home; how many people in the family are worked with in a session; and having one or more co-therapists, where she feels it appropriate. She is also flexible in her use of techniques and tools, such as audio-taped and video-taped feedback, dancing, body movement exercises, role playing, and communication games.[56]

POSTSCRIPT

On the whole, this chapter has given a favourable account of group work. In conclusion, a brief cautionary word is added about some of the problems of group counselling. We have already mentioned problems like poor attendance, aggression directed towards a member which is beyond her coping capacity, individual and group resistance, fears of confidentiality, and counsellor vulnerability. Another problem in groups is that the norms established may be harmful rather than helpful to individual members. For instance, members may feel pressurized to conform both inside and outside the group. One such pressure within the group may be towards pseudo-authenticity rather than a more gradual working towards genuine disclosure and relationships.

There are a range of ethical issues in group work. These include: truthful rather than exaggerated advertising; accurate representation of the qualifications of the counsellor; adequately informing clients of the nature of the group; protecting clients from psychological and physical harm during the group; and adequate availability of additional counselling or medical help both during and after the group.[57] A further set of issues relates to the feelings of significant others in group members' lives who are outside the group, such as a spouse or an intimate friend. For instance, they may feel left out and worried that they are becoming out of step in their relationships with the group member. Also, the group members themselves may experience problems of re-entry to outside group life where their new perceptions and behaviours may be neither welcome nor accepted. Indeed, some people may develop an undesirable dependency on groups and move from one to another without establishing maintaining satisfactory personal relations outside.

PRACTICAL EXERCISES AND QUESTIONS

It may help you to develop your skills and knowledge of the material in this chapter if, either individually or in pairs or as part of a group, you perform the following exercises and answer the following questions.

Practical Exercises

1.   Identify the possible options in your locality for joining a counselling group as a member. If possible, join the group which seems most likely to help you meet your needs for either good first-hand knowledge of group counselling and/or your personal development.

2.   With a partner, discuss what might be important topics to cover in an intake interview for a counselling group. Then role-play an intake interview, with you acting as the counsellor and your partner as the prospective group member.

3.   With a partner, discuss and practise structuring at the start of a group. What sort of questions do you think group members might ask you after your structuring? Formulate and practise responses to such questions.

4.   Write out what you consider to be a desirable contract for a group that you might lead. Would you wish such a contract to be informal or formal, possibly to the extent of being written and signed?

5.   Groups may present some special problems. If possible, become part of a

group of four to ten members, in which you discuss and practise handling the following problems:

(a) inter-member aggression;
(b) aggression against the leader;
(c) an individual member who resists participating;
(d) a group which resists working on its problems;
(e) two members who are having an affair outside the group;
(f) introducing a new member.

6.   When ready, explore whether there are any possibilities in your locality for you to co-lead a group with a more experienced counsellor. Take any such suitable opportunity that is available.

Questions

1.   In what sort of counselling groups, if any, have you been a member? For each group, assess whether or not you derived any benefit and why.

2.   In future, what sort of counselling groups, if any, might you consider joining for your own benefit? Give reasons for each choice.

3.   Discuss the advantages and disadvantages of group versus individual counselling. For what kinds of clients would you consider group counselling a preferred method of approach?

4.   Discuss criteria for group composition. What procedures would you adopt to select members on the basis of your criteria?

5.   Discuss issues pertaining to (a) client self-disclosure and (b) counsellor self-disclosure in group counselling.

6.   In running counselling groups, what leadership style would you adopt and why?

7.   Do you consider that the idea of stages of development in the lives of groups is useful and why? If you consider the notion of stages useful, identify and briefly describe the stages *you* feel are important.

8.   What criteria would you use to measure the progress of:

(a) individual group members?
(b) a group as a whole?

9.   'Group counsellors tend to lead groups more to meet their own than their clients' needs.' Discuss.

10.   What topics would you include in an ethical code for group counsellors and why?

11.   What sorts of training and experience are desirable before a counsellor leads a group alone?

12.   Discuss your initial reactions to the brief descriptions of the counselling groups listed below. Also, for each approach, how would you go about getting more information and gaining some practical experience?

    (a)   psychodrama;
    (b)   gestalt therapy groups;
    (c)   integrity groups;
    (d)   conjoint family therapy.

NOTES

1.   Yalom, I. D. (1975) *The Theory and Practice of Group Psychotherapy* (2nd ed.) pp. 479–481. New York: Basic Books.
2.   Gazda, G. M. (1969) *Theories and Methods of Group Counselling in the Schools* pp. 13–14. Springfield, Illinois: Charles C. Thomas.
3.   Rogers, C. R. (1970) *Encounter Groups* pp. 2–4. Harmondsworth, Middlesex: The Penguin Press.
4.   Yalom, I. D. (1975) *The Theory and Practice of Group Psychotherapy* pp. 479–481. New York: Basic Books.
5.   Mahler, C. A. (1969) *Group Counselling in the Schools* p. 11. Boston: Houghton Mifflin.
6.   Ohlson, M. M. (1977) *Group Counselling* (2nd ed.) p. 30. New York: Holt, Rinehart and Winston.
7.   Yalom, I. D. (1975) *The Theory and Practice of Group Psychotherapy* pp. 3–44. New York: Basic Books.
8.   Rogers, C. R. (1970) *Encounter Groups* pp. 4–5. Harmondsworth, Middlesex: The Penguin Press.
9.   Yalom, I. D. (1975) *The Theory and Practice of Group Psychotherapy* pp. 3–104. New York: Basic Books.
10.   *Ibid.* pp. 45–104.
11.   *Ibid.* p. 284.
12.   Mowrer, O. H. (1972) Integrity groups: principles and procedures. *The Counseling Psychologist*, **3**, 2, 17. Full reference pp. 7–33.
13.   *Ibid.* pp. 16–22.
14.   Bach, G. R. (1954) *Intensive Group Psychotherapy* pp. 29–30. New York: Ronald.
15.   Brammer, L. M. & Shostrom, E. L. (1968) *Therapeutic Psychology* (2nd ed.) pp. 338–339. New Jersey: Prentice-Hall.
16.   Mowrer, O. H. (1972) Integrity groups: principles and procedures. *The Counseling Psychologist*, **3**, 2, 26–27. Full reference pp. 7–33.
17.   Egan, G. (1970) *Encounter: Group Processes for Interpersonal Growth* pp. 25–67. Belmont, California: Brooks/Cole.

18. Yalom, I. D. (1975) *The Theory and Practice of Group Psychotherapy* p. 293. New York: Basic Books.
19. Mintz, E. E. (1971) *Marathon Groups* p. 14. New York: Appleton-Century-Crofts.
20. Yalom, I. D. (1975) *The Theory and Practice of Group Psychotherapy* p. 278. New York: Basic Books.
21. Mowrer, O. H., Vattano, A. J. & others (1975) *Integrity Groups: The Loss and Recovery of Community*. Urbana, Illinois: Integrity Groups.
22. Rogers, C. R. (1970) *Encounter Groups* pp. 46–47. Harmondsworth, Middlesex: The Penguin Press.
23. *Ibid*. pp. 54–55.
24. Egan, G. (1970) *Encounter: Group Processes for Interpersonal Growth* pp. 55–59. Belmont, California: Brooks/Cole.
25. Berne, E. (1964) *Games People Play*. New York: Grove Press.
26. Ohlson, M. M. (1977) *Group Counseling* (2nd ed.) pp. 124–125. New York: Holt, Rinehart and Winston.
27. Rogers, C. R. (1970) *Encounter Groups* pp. 18–19. Harmondsworth, Middlesex: The Penguin Press.
28. Egan, G. (1970) *Encounter: Group Processes for Interpersonal Growth* p. 186. Belmont, California: Brooks/Cole.
29. Rogers, C. R. (1970) *Encounter Groups* pp. 56–57. Harmondsworth, Middlesex: The Penguin Press.
30. Perls, F., Hefferline, R. F. & Goodman, P. (1951) *Gestalt Therapy* pp. 30–41. London: Souvenir Press.
31. Schutz, W. C. (1967) *Joy* p. 143. Harmondsworth, Middlesex: Penguin.
32. Perls, F., Hefferline, R. F. & Goodman, P. (1951) *Gestalt Therapy* pp. 30–224. London: Souvenir Press.
33. Schutz, W. C. (1967) *Joy*. Harmondsworth, Middlesex: Penguin.
34. Mintz, E. E. (1971) *Marathon Groups* pp. 47–85. New York: Appleton-Century-Crofts.
35. Hopson, B. & Hough, P. (1973) *Exercises in Personal and Career Development*. Cambridge: Careers Research and Advisory Centre.
36. Yalom, I. D. (1975) *The Theory and Practice of Group Psychotherapy* pp. 437–440. New York: Basic Books.
37. *Ibid*. pp. 365–374.
38. *Ibid*. pp. 301–364.
39. *Ibid*. p. 307.
40. Rogers, C. R. (1970) *Encounter Groups* pp. 14–37. Harmondsworth, Middlesex: The Penguin Press.
41. Mintz, E. E. (1971) *Marathon Groups* pp. 113–134. New York: Appleton-Century-Crofts.
42. Mahler, C. A. (1969) *Group Counselling in the Schools* pp. 64–167. Boston: Houghton Mifflin.
43. Moreno, J. L. (1953) *Who Shall Survive?* p. 81. New York: Beacon House.
44. Moreno, J. L. (1959) Psychodrama. In S. Arieti (ed.), *American Handbook of Psychiatry* (Vol. 2) p. 1395. New York: Basic Books. Full reference pp. 1375–1396.
45. *Ibid*. pp. 1390–1391.
46. Perls, F., Hefferline, R. F. & Goodman, P. (1951) *Gestalt Therapy* p. 235. London: Souvenir Press.
47. *Ibid*. pp. 30–224.
48. Levitsky, A. & Perls, F. (1970) The rules and games of gestalt therapy. In J. Fagan and I. L. Shepherd (eds), *Gestalt Therapy Now*. Palo Alto, California: Science and Behavior Books.
49. Perls, F. S. (1969) *Gestalt Therapy Verbatim* p. 42. New York: Bantam Books.
50. Mowrer, O. H. (1966) *Abnormal Reactions or Actions?* p. 30. Dubuque, Iowa: Wm C. Brown.
51. Mowrer, O. H. (1965) Foreword to Glasser, W. (1965) *Reality Therapy* p. xvii New York: Harper and Row. Full reference pp. xi-xxii.

52. Mowrer, O. H. (1972) Integrity groups: principles and procedures. *The Counseling Psychologist*, **3**, 2, 26. Full reference for 'Basic principles, ground rules, and guidelines for integrity groups' pp. 26–27.
53. Mowrer, O. H., Vattano, A. J. & others (1975) *Integrity Groups: The Loss and Recovery of Community*. Urbana, Illinois: Integrity Groups.
54. Satir, V. (1972) *Peoplemaking*. Palo Alto, California: Science and Behavior Books.
55. Satir, V. (1967) *Conjoint Family Therapy* (Rev. ed.). Palo Alto, California: Science and Behavior Books.
56. *Ibid.* pp. 91–188.
57. Patterson, C. H. (1972) Ethical standards for groups. *The Counseling Psychologist*, **3**, 2, 93–101.

20 – Psychological Education

SUMMARY: *The growth of psychological education programmes is relatively new and has been stimulated by a desire to meet widespread developmental and preventive, rather than just remedial, needs. Definitions of psychological education encompass: training people in life skills; an academic/experiential approach to teaching psychology; humanistic education; training paraprofessionals in counselling skills; a range of outreach activities, including consultancy; and public education in psychological matters. Several examples of psychological education are described. In the schools, deliberate psychological education is a practicum and seminar way of teaching psychology to attain both academic and personality development goals. Some British approaches to personal and social education are reviewed, as well as American approaches to humanistic education. Psychological education in colleges and universities can focus on making the curriculum relevant to student personality development and also on extracurricular activities such as training in life skills, paraprofessional training, and offering consultancy services to individuals and groups.*

In recent years there has been a growth in psychological education programmes relevant to women, including: women's study courses both inside and outside psychology departments; consciousness-raising groups; and making counsellor trainers more sensitive to gender-related issues. There is an overlap between the psychological education methods of the women's and homosexual/bisexual movements, including an emphasis on public education. Four approaches to psychological education for effective parenting are described: Gordon's parent effectiveness training; Carkhuff's systematic group training; Adlerian parent-child educating centres; and expectant parent and fathering classes. There are many other types of clientele for psychological education, including the health professions, the police and prison officers.

Counsellors engaging in psychological education need additional skills to those of individual and group counselling. These skills are in such areas as making role decisions, designing and implementing training programmes, consultancy, and programme evaluation. Psychological education programmes have risks and potential weaknesses, including: lack of an adequate theoretical base; ineffectiveness through teaching mechanistic skills in a superficial way; brainwashing, leading to conformity; and lack of competent and psychologically well developed trainers. The extent to which parents should be involved is relevant to psychological education in the schools. Psychological education will be an important, though by no means exclusive, part of the future work of counsellors.

Psychological education, sometimes called personal and social education, is an important and relatively new direction in counselling psychology. It involves an expansion of the role of counsellors beyond their traditional individual and group counselling activities. Though psychological education requires counsellors to have additional knowledge and skills, it nevertheless draws heavily on the kinds of counselling theory and practice described earlier in this book.

Paraphrasing the French statesman Talleyrand's aphorism that 'War is much too serious a thing to be left to military men', an underlying assumption of the psychological education movement is that 'Psychology is much too serious a thing to be left to psychologists'. In his influential 1969 presidential address to the American Psychological Association, George Miller talked of the need for psychologists to give psychology away in such a way that scientific results could be practised and used by nonpsychologists.[1] Developing Miller's theme, there are a number of reasons for the emerging interest among counsellors in psychological education. First, as Miller himself observes: 'There simply are not enough psychologists, even including non-professionals, to meet every need for psychological services. The people at large will have to be their own psychologists, and make their own applications of the principles that we establish'.[2]

A second reason is that many counsellors feel that too much of their effort in the past has been devoted to remedial work for the few, consequently with insufficient time devoted to developmental work for the many. In 1976 Ivey wrote that a report of the Professional Affairs Committee of APA's Division of Counseling Psychology stated that the educational/developmental role of the counselling psychologist must now be considered primary, followed by the preventive and then by the remedial or rehabilitative roles.[3] Some counsellors may recognize the need for more educational/developmental work without necessarily considering it their primary function.

Third, psychological education often has a *preventive* or prophylactic as well as a developmental focus. Daws, writing of the need for preventive work in British schools, observes that recognizing and working with especially vulnerable children, though an important preventive function, is only a starting point. He argues that the strongest expression of the preventive principle is work devoted to the personal and social education of *all* pupils in such a way that it anticipates their developmental needs.[4] Also, psychological education and consultancy efforts can focus on preventing the ill effects of poor institutional environments.

Fourth, pressures on counsellors to become more accountable for their expenditure of resources have forced many to question traditional individual and group counselling approaches. Some counsellors argue that their cost effectiveness is much greater if they engage in active outreach activities, such as psychological education and consultancy, rather than passively waiting in their offices for clients needing remedial counselling. Drum and Figler write: 'Literally, *outreach* means to reach out both physically and psychologically to seek additional ways to be impactive on the total population'.[5]

DEFINING PSYCHOLOGICAL EDUCATION

Psychological education is far from a unitary phenomenon. It is a catch-all term which tends to mean different things to different people depending on such variables as their theoretical orientation and current job. Six broad uses of the term 'psychological education' are identified below.

Training People in Life Skills

Advocates of this form of psychological education aim to help people to acquire important life skills by means of structured programmes conducted on a group basis. These skills include: listening, such as empathic understanding; sending information, such as the various form of appropriate self-disclosure; conflict resolution; problem-solving and planning; decision-making; anxiety management; coping with sexuality; and the effective making of important life transitions, such as getting married, becoming a parent, handling a bereavement, and redundancy or retirement. The term 'personal and social education' has a similar meaning to this use of the term 'psychological education'.

An Academic/Experiential Approach to Teaching Psychology

A distinction is sometimes made between academic and experiential approaches to teaching and learning. Whereas the former emphasizes intellectual skills, the latter emphasizes learning by doing. A psychological education approach to teaching psychology at the secondary school or undergraduate level would incorporate experiential teaching of life skills and/or the skills of applied psychological practice as well as intellectual teaching of academic skills. In fact, Sprinthall argues that including an experiential emphasis may enhance academic results.[6]

Humanistic Education

Humanistic education focuses on the whole pupil or student and sees the objective of both counselling and education as the production of self-actualizing people. The role of teachers is that of facilitating learning. As well as having subject matter knowledge, they need to possess an empathic attitude and be able to offer their pupils or students the person-centred 'core' interpersonal conditions.

Training Paraprofessionals in Counselling Skills

Counsellors can extend their effectiveness by training paraprofessionals and lay people in counselling skills. There are numerous instances in which paraprofessionals have been so trained. For instance, Anthony and Carkhuff have trained health care personnel in human relations skills,[7] and Thorne and Da Costa have extended their Associates Programme at the University of East Anglia to include the training of selected Associates in the skills of personal counselling.[8] A variant of paraprofessional training is that sometimes peers are trained to counsel each other, whether they are students in educational settings, women in the women's movement, or members of racial minorities. All agencies involved in training and using voluntary counsellors might be viewed as engaging in psychological education as defined in this section.

A Range of Outreach Activities

Sometimes psychological education is not only a form of outreach activity, but an overall term for the range of outreach activities. Such activities include life skills training and the training of paraprofessionals in counselling skills in settings, such as living and working environments, outside the counsellor's office. Additional outreach activities may include consultancy to an institution or community, or to groups within it, and also providing individuals with psychological self-help information through a 'phone-in' service.

Educating the Public in Psychological Matters

Halmos observed that the counselling literature, ever since the time of Sigmund Freud, has had a far-reaching influence both on the cultural and moral leadership in society and on its rank and file.[9] Sometimes this influence has been indirect. On other occasions, for example in relation to the women's movement and to a greater understanding of the homosexual and bisexual experience, counsellors have joined in direct attempts at public education, including, where necessary, lobbying to alter discriminatory legislation.

In conclusion, though there is no single definition of psychological education, there are some recurrent themes which go some way to distinguishing it. Such themes include: providing psychological services for all; no assumption of severe disturbance among the receivers of psychological assistance; a strong developmental and preventive rather than just a remedial emphasis; providing services outside as well as inside traditional counselling settings; training in skills as a preferred mode of treatment; the extension of the provision of psychological services to include the use of paraprofessionals and peer self-help; and the use of both small-group and large-group methods of training.

SOME EXAMPLES OF PSYCHOLOGICAL EDUCATION

Psychological education programmes vary in several ways. For instance, programmes may use a behavioural skills acquisition model, or may be based on humanistic assumptions, or may be a mixture of the two. The focus may be on one or more of a number of life skills or on bringing about broader changes, such as in community racial attitudes. The targets or clientele may be school children, young adults, parents, women, coloured people, the homosexual, bisexual and heterosexual, an institution or community, or the public at large. The personnel conducting the psychological education may be psychologists, counsellors, teachers, or peers who either have been or are in the same situation as the learners. Its various settings include education, industry, medicine, the social services, marriage guidance councils and other community settings. We now turn to some examples of psychological education, but the categories under which the programmes are discussed are not discrete. For instance, we discuss separately programmes in the schools and programmes targeted at women, yet the schools are one of the settings for women's programmes.

Psychological Education in the Schools

In Chapter 18 we looked at careers education in the schools. Here we review some other areas of psychological education in British and American schools.

Deliberate psychological education

One of the best known attempts at psychological education has been Mosher and Sprinthall and their colleagues' programme to promote 'deliberate psychological education' in the American high school.[10,11,12] Their objective was to make personal development a central focus of education. Having experimented with various models, they settled for a practicum and seminar format similar to that employed in professional graduate schools. This format was applied to a number of different units offered for academic credit as one-semester courses in psychology. The course in counselling was essentially a practicum and seminar in peer counselling. The *practicum* part of the course involved role-playing counselling, listening under supervision to tape-recordings of their attempts at counselling, and discussion of various aspects of the helping relationship. Later in the semester, seniors on the course counselled under supervision some underclassmen in the school. The *seminar* focused on issues of supervision of individual counselling, general issues, and discussions of tapes and films by other counsellors, such as the Rogers, Perls and Ellis film series, 'Gloria'.

Over the course, the high-school students made significant gains in counselling skills as measured by Carkhuff's Empathy, Genuineness and Immediacy scales. In fact, their mean post-test scores on all three scales were above the 'minimally facilitative' level 3 rating. The Kohlberg Moral Judgement Scales and the Loevinger Sentence

Completion Form were used to measure students' moral and ego development respectively. A significant pre-post test gain was reported for the Loevinger test, and a near significant gain for the Kohlberg test.[13]

Mosher and Sprinthall observed after two years' experience in the field that school personnel, such as counsellors and English and social studies teachers, could become effective as supervisors after one semester's participation in a section of the counselling laboratory.[14] Regarding the pupils, they stated: 'Essentially we found that teenagers work and learn optimally in a context where the expectation and the objective of the curriculum is to consider them capable, with supervision of "adult" responsibility in genuine tasks'.[15]

Two other courses in Mosher and Sprinthall's programme were those in educational psychology and in child development. Each course followed the practicum and seminar format, with the practicum being teaching in elementary school for the educational psychology class and nursery-school work for the child development class. In a later paper, Sprinthall observes that experiential learning by itself is as arid an approach to learning as is the more traditional content focus. However, he strongly criticizes an exclusive focus on teaching psychology as a narrow academic discipline in secondary schools, an approach irrelevant to the pupils' needs and interests as well as being less than optimally productive in stimulating their intellectual and psychological growth.[16]

Some British psychological education programmes

The need for personal and social education in British schools has been strongly urged by writers such as Daws[17] and Hopson and Hough.[18] However, with the possible exception of careers education, the literature describing British psychological education programmes is not extensive. Table 20.1 shows Hopson and Hough's statement of personal growth goals in the areas of sensing, feeling, thinking and doing.[19] These are the kinds of life skills from which those designing personal and social education programmes for schools might choose their goals. Hopson and Hough have also designed a series of class exercises in personal development, broken down into the areas of sensing, feeling, thinking and doing.[20]

The Schools Council Social Education Project was an attempt at social education in the British secondary school.[21] The objectives of the project were to encourage an awareness of the social environment and the ability on the part of individuals and groups to effect changes in it. The programme started by training pupils, particularly by means of role playing and sociodrama, in the skills of observation and communication. Then, in small-group projects, pupils developed profiles of the groups which had an immediate impact on them, such as their class, family, school, peer group and local community. Film, videotape, photography, creative writing, graphs, drawing, diagrams and tape recordings were all used in presenting these profiles. Two recurrent themes which were explored as part of the project were man-woman relationships and crises of personal responsibility. The final stage of the programme focused on participation in the community and its affairs by means of identifying problems, conducting a community survey, and formulating suggestions for action. One

Table 20.1   *Hopson and Hough's personal growth goals**

Areas	Objectives
Sensing	Awareness of *physical* senses in self and others Control of *bodily systems* Awareness of relationship between physical and emotional expression
Feeling	Awareness of *emotions* in self and others Effective *expression* of feelings Learning to *accept all feelings* as valid How to handle negative feelings in self and others
Thinking	Develop *creativity* Develop and *crystallize* values Awareness of *interests and needs* Examining the *rationality of needs* Developing *commitments* Awareness of *strengths and weaknesses* *Moral* development Developing *behavioural goals*
Doing	How to *make effective decisions* Operating efficiently in *groups* *Helping others* to solve problems How to *receive help* from others How to *initiate relationships* How to *maintain relationships* How to *use conflict constructively* How to be *assertive* effectively How to *create and manage personal change* How to *communicate interpersonally*, verbally and non-verbally How to approach *personal problem-solving*

* Acknowledgement is made to the editors of the *British Journal of Guidance and Counselling* for permission to copy the above table. From Hopson, B. & Hough, P. (1976). The need for personal and social education in secondary schools and further education. *British Journal of Guidance and Counselling*, **4**, 18. The original figure was entitled 'A model of personal growth'.

conclusion drawn from the project 'was that social education work offers an opportunity for children to develop talents and skills of which they and their teachers were unaware'.[22]

Hamblin sees what he terms 'social education' as 'a carefully planned attempt to develop general social skills, whilst group counselling is intended to resolve the specific problems of individuals'.[23] Social education should be a co-ordinated and sequential programme of activities running throughout the school years. The year head and his form tutors should be responsible for devising the activities, which should focus on situations of immediate concern to the pupils. Hamblin favours an approach which presents situations from the everyday lives of pupils, such as 'learning to give a favourable impression of myself' and 'when I feel I am being picked on', as problem situations which need solving. Principles underlying behaviour are extracted by the teacher from the pupils as they reveal the solutions they have reached. The teacher also helps pupils to discover other situations, inside and outside school, where the principles can be applied. Role play, decision-making exercises and simulations and games are all part of social education, which, as well as social skills, may focus on how to work in a group and, if there is time, on community issues.[24,25]

Humanistic education

Humanistic education is mentioned in the section on psychological education in the schools, though it is applicable to other levels and types of education. In the prologue to his book *Freedom to Learn*, Rogers states that he believes learning can be viewed along a continuum of meaning with, at one end, memorization of nonsense syllables and, at the other end, significant, meaningful experiential learning.[26] Humanistic or person-centred education aims to help pupils to self-actualize through fostering both their intellectual and their personal development. It is an attitude and approach to areas such as working in the classroom, affective education, school administration and teacher training.

The key to classroom learning is the teacher-pupil relationship, which should be characterized by empathy, respect and genuineness on the part of the teacher. Thus, teachers need to be more than subject-matter experts; they must offer good human relationships to pupils.[27] Rogers states that a precondition for person-centred learning is a teacher 'sufficiently secure within himself and in his relationship to others that he experiences an essential trust in the capacity for others to think for themselves and to learn for themselves'.[28] If this precondition exists, the following are likely to happen: (a) the facilitative person shares with others the responsibility for the learning process; (b) the facilitator provides learning resources; (c) the student develops his own programme of learning, alone or in co-operation with others; (d) a facilitative learning climate is provided; (e) the focus is primarily on fostering the continuing process of learning; (f) the discipline necessary to reach the student's goals is a self-discipline; (g) the evaluation of the extent and significance of the student's learning is made primarily by the learner himself; and (h) the learning is deeper, more rapid and more pervasive than learning acquired in the traditional classroom.[29] Rogers gives some examples of person-centred learning both in *Personal Power*[30] and in *Freedom to Learn*.[31]

Humanistic educators would claim that their approach to the 'academic' curriculum contains elements of affective education in which the pupil's personhood was being facilitated by identification and then self-directed development of his intellectual potential. However, humanistic educators are also concerned with valuing, identifying and developing pupils' human relations potential. One approach is to teach aspects of the present curriculum, such as English and social studies, in such a way that pupils are able to explore their own feelings and emotions in relation to the material. Another possible approach is that of deliberate psychological education. A further approach, advocated by Patterson, is participation by all pupils in small encounter groups, facilitated on person-centred lines, throughout their school careers.[32]

Humanistic education requires the preparation of humanistic teachers. Such teachers should be grounded in a systematic theoretical approach to human behaviour, such as that suggested by Rogers and by Combs and Snygg.[33] Adequate supervised experience in teaching within a humanistic framework is necessary. Trainee teachers should also be given the opportunity both to participate in a basic encounter group and to learn to facilitate such groups. Additionally, Patterson suggests that they should participate in a continuous integrative seminar in which they are encouraged to respond to and evaluate their total experience in teacher education.[34]

School administrators may also be targets for psychological education regarding their administrative styles and understanding of the purposes of humanistic education. Rogers favours an 'influence and impact' rather than a 'power and control' approach to administration. Characteristics of person-centred 'influence and impact' administration include giving autonomy to people and groups, expressing own ideas and feelings as one aspect of the group data, offering feedback and receiving it, encouraging and relying on self-evaluation, and finding rewards in the development and achievements of others.[35] Rogers has presented a plan for self-directed change in an educational system, consisting of intensive group experiences for administrators, for teachers, for parents, for class units, and for a mixed or 'vertical' group.[36] The anticipated outcome for administrators is that they will move more in the direction of person-centred administration, become less defensive and self-protective, listen better, and make fuller use of the resource potential of their staff.

Psychological Education in Colleges and Universities

Psychological education in colleges and universities takes place both inside and outside the curriculum. The objectives of college education may be viewed on an intellectualistic-holistic continuum. At the intellectualistic end the goal of an institution is purely intellectual development, while at the holistic end the goals are to develop a whole person in his personal and social as well as his intellectual functioning. Psychological education is a reflection of a holistic approach to college education.

The curriculum

The curriculum itself may be used as a vehicle for student personality development. For instance, Crookston has argued for the establishment of a human development curriculum in which teaching is organized around the needs of the student and not the subject. Education for human development focuses on the concerns of the student age-range, such as identity and the search for meaning in life. One of the goals of such education is *affective rationality* or 'the capability to recognise and understand feelings and to translate them into rational action'.[37] The role of the developmental teacher is to arrange both intellectual and experiential learning experiences that make students better able to cope with such concerns. Teaching skills include both counselling skills and supervising projects using the scientific method to inquire into developmental tasks. A human development unit, with the status of a special academic subdivision such as a school or college, is suggested as an appropriate structure.

As in secondary schools, another curricular approach is that of teaching counselling skills. Ivey observes that, in America, 'Undergraduate programs in helping skills are a booming aspect of many college degree offerings'.[38] Indeed, it could be argued that such skills are necessary for virtually all branches of applied psychology, including research into applied problems, and that learning them is an important part of any balanced undergraduate psychology curriculum. Furthermore, the teaching of counselling skills is relevant to several professional and paraprofessional courses, such as social work and nursing.

Counsellors are increasingly attempting to *co-operate* with other sectors in their institution, both in the formal and the informal curriculum. For instance, at the University of East Anglia (UEA) medical, counselling and physical education specialists combine to offer an interdisciplinary course in health education. The objectives of the course are to get participants to learn how to take more responsibility for their own health. Its contents encompass relaxation, body awareness, physical exercise, and personal relationships. Spiritual awareness groups are another *co-operative* outreach venture at UEA. Here counsellors and chaplains jointly offer an opportunity for those of any belief or none who wish to explore the spiritual dimensions of their own and others' experience without having any religious or philosophical views imposed upon them. Also at UEA, counsellors, careers advisers and faculty members combine to offer programmes for final-year undergraduates focused on values, career objectives and the transition to employment. Such programmes may focus on the needs of students in a particular faculty.[39] Further UEA psychological education projects include: study skills workshops; a programme of workshops for first-year Overseas Students; and a weekly cross-cultural group for students who wish to develop communication skills across cultural frontiers.

Training in life skills

Especially in America, counselling services are offering members of college and university communities developmental programmes involving training in various life skills, particularly those relevant to personal relations. Such skills were further outlined in the previous section on defining psychological education and in Table 20.1. The main training method is the structured group experience consisting of a mixture of didactic instruction, role play and discussion. Though many of these programmes may be offered on the counselling service premises, others may be held in the students' working or living environments. Though often the target populations for such programmes are students in general, some training programmes may focus on the needs of specific subgroups, such as women, the homosexual and bisexual, and coloured students. Sometimes these training groups are not restricted to students, but include other members of the campus community, such as non-academic staff and faculty spouses.

A British example of a life skills programme is the University of East Anglia Student Counselling Service's Associates programme. The programme aims to help members of the university community to develop their 'own awareness and relationship skills and as a result become more helpful, more sympathetically useful to others and to the community in general'.[40] The programme enrols ten people at any one time and consists of five two-hour evening sessions and one 24-hour residential weekend encounter group. The encounter group is held between the first and second evening sessions. The evening sessions include self-exploration and awareness exercises, working through unfinished business after the encounter group, counsellor-client role plays, elementary peer counselling, and theoretical input introducing the concepts of self-actualization, self-concept development, and the core conditions of a facilitative relationship. Many who complete the programme engage in follow-up activities, either as clients in peer counselling or, after further training, as auxiliary counsellors. Furthermore, the Associates play a useful role in generating an understanding of counselling on the campus and in advertising the Student Counselling Service.

Training paraprofessionals

In some institutions there has been a move towards training staff counsellors and student peer counsellors as paraprofessionals who, backed by professional staff, will perform much of the counselling in those institutions. Such training tends to focus on offering a fundamental counselling relationship along the lines described in Chapter 11. However, if training 'normals' in life skills becomes a more important objective of college counselling services, then there is likely to be a corresponding growth in training paraprofessionals, who themselves become trainers of 'normals' in such life skills. Other groups who might benefit from paraprofessional training in counselling skills include: members of a college's student support team, such as chaplains, welfare workers and health service personnel; academic staff who wish to become better tutors; and student union officers.

Some paraprofessionals may also become trainers of other paraprofessionals. This is in line with Carkhuff's model of human and community resource development in which (a) persons indigenous to the target community are selected and trained as helpers and (b) some such helpers are further selected and trained to be trainers of helpers.[41] An example of paraprofessionals in a training function is the use of selected University of East Anglia Student Counselling Service Associates to train other Associates and to help conduct preparatory training workshops for the student self-help organization, 'Nightline'.[42] In future, with the current dearth of counselling skills among British academic psychologists, if counselling skills are ever going to be taught widely in psychology departments some academic staff will need to be trained to teach these skills.

Consultancy

There are many ways in which counsellors may perform a consultancy function in higher education. For instance, they can help in the design of education for human development and of deliberate psychological education curricula. Furthermore, they can offer assistance in such areas as the design of systems of assessment, the psychological implications of any new buildings being planned, helping academic staff to handle their own stress problems, and supporting academic staff who are working with 'problem' students. Furthermore, counsellors can make known their availability to serve as consultants to various groups within an instituition, for example academic departments, student government or residence hall groups. Some counselling services may conduct institutional research on such matters as monitoring and identifying causes of student underachievement and attrition and on sources of stress for students and staff. Feeding back the findings of such research to appropriate people is another way in which counsellors can act as consultants.

An example of consultancy, albeit overlapping with training in life skills, is the workshop run in recent years by the Leicester Polytechnic counselling service staff for and at the request of the incoming Student Union Executive. This workshop lasts for one or two days in mid-September and has two parts. The first part focuses on basic listening and helping skills, and uses exercises and role play. The second part focuses on communication and team building, and here approaches have included asking the group to plan and then make a three-minute 'video film' advertising what the Student Union is and does. The workshops have been attended by the Executive and also by the permanent staff of the Student Union. There has been consistent feedback that the group members have got to know each other at a crucial stage of the year as well as getting to know the student counsellors.[43]

Use of audio-visual aids

Psychological education may involve many forms of audio-visual aids. For instance, the telephone can be used to play on demand pre-recorded information in any one of a number of areas of student concern. Furthermore, some colleges have arrangements for person-to-person telephone counselling which may protect the anonymity of clients as well as ridding them of the need to go for an interview. Increasingly, clients may be able to interact with computers to gather information, advice and skills relevant to their concerns. Films and video and audio cassettes and tapes may also be used to expand the impact of a counselling service and to teach life skills. Last, some people may find it helpful to have easy access to books and hand-outs relevant to their concerns.

Psychological Education for Women

In recent years there has been an increased questioning, sometimes vehement, of the status of women in Western society. The women's movement aims to increase the opportunities and abilities for women to become more highly self-realizing. Fried writes that the primary aims of women's new self-concept 'are toward a sense of equality, though not identity with the male; a conviction of capability; acknowledgement and open pursuit of sexual desires; social activeness; and a first-rate human, economic and social position'.[44] The questioning of women's status and role has been accompanied by an examination of men's status and role. In many instances this has entailed viewing men as being too powerful and oppressive, but another strand has been to see men as well as women as being victims of constricting gender identities which make it difficult for either sex to give full expression to their human potentialities. Though a great simplification, there is more than a little truth in the Reverend William Sloane Coffin's comment: 'The woman who most needs liberating in this country is the woman in every man, and the man who most needs liberating is the man in every woman'.[15] Thus, though in this section we focus on psychological education for women, our view is that there also exists a corresponding need for psychological education for men. Furthermore, both men and women need to become more empathic to each other's gender difficulties.

Deliberate psychological education

Erickson describes a course entitled 'Psychological Growth for Women' carried out and evaluated with a group of 23 self-registered sophomore girls in the social studies department of an American high school.[46,47] The course, which lasted for a term, adopted Mosher and Sprinthall's practicum-seminar format. The initial practicum sessions involved teaching communication and interviewing skills until the pupils could reach level 3, representing accurate content and feeling responses on an empathy scale. Then followed role-play interviews and actual interviews with classmates. The pupils also learned the skills of asking questions which illuminated women's thought processes and values. They then conducted a series of field interviews with girls and women across the generational span to discover their major motivations and values both in general and in their vocational, educational, intellectual and marital roles.

The seminar sessions were used in a number of ways: examining, restructuring and integrating the field interviewing experiences; reflecting on current articles about sexual stereotypes, language and inequality, and the equal rights amendment; and taking a historical as well as a developmental perspective by examining the role of women in plays and short stories, such as Sophocles' Antigone and Nora in Ibsen's *A Doll's House*. Throughout the seminars the pupils began to explore, in small-group discussions, the implications of their literary reading and interview experience for their own emerging choices and personal development. The course was conducted by a team consisting of Erickson, a female English teacher, and a female school counsellor. Significant pre-post course and one-year follow-up gains were reported both on the Kohlberg Moral Maturity Test and on selected Loevinger ego development scales, indicating that it is possible to promote positive psychological growth for women in a secondary-school class.

Women's studies courses

Possibly more academically oriented than the deliberate psychological education programme described above, women's studies courses seek to make women more aware of their history and culturally assigned roles. Fitzgerald comments how, as long ago as 1973, it was estimated that in America more than 1000 courses were offered by more than 300 colleges and universities, and even a few high schools.[48] Such courses are found most frequently in English literature, sociology, history, psychology, and law departments. Illustrative English literature courses are women in literature and women as writers. Examples of courses in other areas are: sociology, women's roles in society; history, women heroines in history; psychology, the female personality; and law, women and the law. Counsellors may both help to stimulate the offering of such courses and advise on teaching methods and possibly content. Women's studies courses seem less developed in Britain than in America. However, the 'New Opportunities for Women' (NOW) courses run by the University of Newcastle's Department of Adult Education might be considered a British example. The courses take place one day a week from 9.45 a.m. to 3 p.m. for the first two terms of the academic year. Although 40 of the 60 sessions are devoted to academic subjects, seemingly without a feminist emphasis, the remaining 20 sessions are devoted to 'opportunities'. As part of this element, individual and group counselling sessions are held both to help to clarify the women students' interests and abilities and to explore and provide support in such areas as the conflict of domestic and career commitments and uncertainties about their transition to the world of work.[49]

Consciousness raising groups

Though consciousness raising (CR) groups for women have different levels of structure, they tend to share basic assumptions. Elias states two of the assumptions: that 'sexism is a corrosive emotional poison that retards the growth of people' and that it is not necessary 'that each sex must emit certain distinctive behaviours in order to be healthy, just because of gender'.[50] Brodsky states another important assumption: 'that the environment, rather than intrapsychic dynamics, plays a major role in the difficulties of individuals'.[51]

Some CR groups are an opportunity for an intellectual rather than an experiential learning about sexism. For instance, the groups may focus on a different topic each week, such as ageing, dependence/independence, rape, and mothers and daughters. In other groups, women are confronted with the need to act as individuals and are encouraged to explore their uniqueness independent of their present family or job roles. More experienced group members model alternative life-styles. As well as encouraging self-exploration, such groups often engage in assertive training, since two of the major problems confronting women are dependency and low self-esteem. Such assertive training has to take into account the fact that it may be aiding women to behave in ways which society does not condone and that, hence, there may be little outside reinforcement for bolstering motivation.[52] Jakubowski-Spector gives examples of facilitating women's assertive behaviour in such areas as altering the nature of their partner's love-making and refusing a request to babysit.[53]

CR groups may encourage women both to take the risks involved in more active pursuit of their male equals and to be open to new forms of emotional friendship with each other.[54] Furthermore, CR groups may develop beyond individual solutions to encompass group action to alter the environment. Such action may consist of organized protests, political lobbying and educational programmes. There is no precise dividing line between CR groups and group counselling or therapy for women. However, if anything, CR groups have more of an educational/training/political emphasis, whereas counselling groups are more likely to be arenas where women have the space to work through their individual problems.

Counsellor training

In 1978 APA's Division of Counseling Psychology approved a statement of 13 principles concerning the counselling and therapy of women.[55] These principles cover academic background and training as well as practical and ethical guidelines. These guidelines reflect concerns about sexism in regard to counsellor knowledge, values, expectations and practice. To combat inadequate training, Johnson suggests a knowledge base for counsellors of women, including: the history and sociology of sex-role stereotyping; the psychophysiology of women and men; theories of sex-role development; life-span development; career development; and counselling and psychotherapy. The counselling and psychotherapy element might consider: the effects of counsellor-client gender on interaction; power relationships; alternatives to traditional counselling, such as consciousness raising and women's study courses; and particular problems of women, such as depression, low self-esteem, rape and battering.[56] Harway, in her model for sex-fair counselling and counsellor training, advocates that at least 40 per cent of the faculty should be women, that there should be more research on women and on women's career development, the development and use of sex-fair materials and books, and prohibition of the use of male pronouns when referring to both sexes.[57] Perhaps enough has been said to indicate that counsellor training is an important area for psychological education regarding the effects of both female and male gender.

Psychological Education Regarding Homosexual and Bisexual Orientation

The preceding section on psychological education for women overlaps with this section on homosexual and bisexual orientation in a number of ways. For instance, homosexual and bisexual women are part of the women's movement. Furthermore, the issue of gender conditioning is central to both the women's and the gay movements. Both groups consider that sexism, which they perceive as the gender and role supremacy of the heterosexual male, has given them an inferior status which is reinforced by 'self-oppression, the internalization of guilt, of self-hatred, or the values of the oppressors'.[58] Additionally, both groups feel the need to work towards an identity of their own, including an affirmation of their sexuality. With so much common ground, it is to be expected that the women's and gay movements adopt similar psychological education techniques, such as consciousness-raising groups of varying degrees of structure. Furthermore, both movements have a peer support and self-help emphasis, though trusted professional help may also be welcome. Additionally, each movement has turned its attention to changing the attitude of the wider public to their situations.

Public education

Though this section focuses on public education regarding homosexual and bisexual orientation, much of it is equally relevant to public education regarding the status and the role of women. The provision of an accurate body of knowledge regarding homosexual and bisexual orientation is one of the ways in which counsellors can contribute to public education. Though much research has already been conducted, it has by no means exhausted the topic, especially since it has been concerned more with male than with female homosexuality.

There are various target populations for education about homosexual and bisexual orientation. Counsellors themselves need to be knowledgeable about the area. Relatively recently, the American Psychiatric Association removed homosexuality from its classification of personality disorders, thus reflecting a change in professional opinion. Nevertheless, it is probable that many counsellors lack adequate information, and many also possess varying degrees of prejudice against homosexual and bisexual people. Davison and Wilson's data, based on a survey conducted in the early 1970s on the attitudes of British and American behaviour therapists towards homosexuality, lend some support to the above assertions.[59] Thus it is important for counselling trainees to have adequate exposure to academic, practical and personal issues in regard to working with homosexual and bisexual people.

Another important target population is the wider public, including their legislators. In Britain public opinion is altering, albeit slowly, towards greater acceptance of homosexual and bisexual orientation. In 1954 the Home Office established a Committee on Homosexual Offences and Prostitution, the term 'homosexual offences' referring exclusively to males, since there has never been a legislation in Britain about homosexual behaviour between women. Wolfenden, its chairman, writes of the then climate of opinion: 'In those days the topics with which we were to be concerned were not mentioned in polite society'.[60] In 1957 the Committee proposed that homosexual behaviour in private between consenting adults should no longer be a criminal offence. In 1967 this proposal became law in England and Wales for males aged 21 and above, with exceptions regarding the armed forces and the merchant navy. Weeks views the legislation as still being harshly restrictive and observes that homosexuality was not, as such, legalized.[61]

Undoubtedly counsellors and mental health professionals played some role in bringing about legislative change. During the mid–1960s, Anthony Grey, later to be a founder Executive Committee member of the British Association for Counselling, was Secretary of the Homosexual Law Reform Society. Nowadays some counsellors participate in the work of the Campaign for Homosexual Equality (CHE), the organization currently carrying on public education to end discrimination against homosexual and bisexual people. Such counsellors tend to feel strongly that, though the homosexuality oriented may have their personal problems, there is also the wider social problem of numerous 'straight' people suffering from ignorance and prejudice against homosexuality, hence the need for public education which may in time lead to further legislative changes.

In America homosexual groups have tried to bring about changes in legislation through their political power as voters. In San Francisco 'homosexuals have become by general agreement the largest "liberal" voting bloc in the city courted by candidates of both parties'.[62] San Francisco, along with a number of other American cities including Washington and Detroit, has introduced laws barring discrimination against homosexual people in employment and, as a result, they are welcome to join the city's police force. Other cities and states have not moved so far. However, as the Kinsey data indicate, there are really large numbers of homosexually and bisexually oriented people. In Britain, as in America, more and more of these people are likely to 'come out' and, both inside and outside politics, make their needs for acceptance known, if not legally enforced. Counsellors, who should be knowledgeable about homosexual and bisexual orientation, can work to bring about a state of affairs in which both 'gays' and 'straights' are more accepting both of themselves and each other. As well as counselling, their contribution can include provision of accurate information, helping with education, and support for responsible legislative change attempts.

Psychological Education for Effective Parenting

As indicated earlier in this chapter, a major focus of psychological education is that of training people in life skills. Parents are one category of people whose life skills affect not only themselves but their offspring. Clearly the quality of the relationship between parents creates an emotional atmosphere which may or may not be conducive to their children's development. The kinds of between-partner sending, receiving, and conflict resolution skills that were discussed in Chapter 15 are highly relevant to ensuring a happy family atmosphere. Furthermore, some advocates of psychological education consider that these are the kinds of skills which should be taught in personal and social education programmes in the schools, not only to enhance personal relations between pupils but also as a preparation for parenthood. In this section, however, we do not focus on school pupils, but on four programmes designed for people who either are or are just about to become parents.

Gordon's parent effectiveness training

In 1962 Thomas Gordon started developing his Parent Effectiveness Training or PET.[63] Initially it was a training programme for parents whose children had already developed problems. However, since then, it has attracted parents and would-be parents who want to enhance their relationships with their children, or at least learn how to avoid trouble.

PET focuses on three main skills: active listening, sending 'I' messages, and the 'no-lose' method of resolving conflicts. Gordon has been heavily influenced by Rogers and hence his focus on active listening is really an attempt to explain and teach the concepts of acceptance and empathy with simplicity and clarity. Parents are not only taught active listening skills but, when ready, are encouraged to try them out with their children at home and then share such experiences in class.

Sometimes, however, it is the parent rather than the child who has the problem. Here parents are taught to acknowledge or 'own' their problems in relation to their children. A simple example is that of a tired parent who, not owning his problem, sends a 'You' message to a child, in the form of 'You are a pest', rather than an 'I' message, such as 'I am very tired'. The 'You' message makes the child feel he is bad, whereas the 'I' message is more likely to communicate accurately the parent's tiredness. Again, parents are encouraged to practise their 'I' message skill at home and to report back to class.

In Chapter 15 we mentioned Gordon's 'no-lose' approach to conflict resolution which he claims does not involve coercive power. To recapitulate, the 'no-lose' approach to parent-child conflict resolution involves six steps: (a) identifying and defining the conflict; (b) generating possible alternative solutions; (c) evaluating the alternative solutions; (d) deciding on the best acceptable solution; (e) working out ways of implementing the solution; and (f) following up to evaluate how it worked. Gordon has extended the range of his training programmes to include Teacher Effectiveness Training, Counselor Effectiveness Training and Leader Effectiveness Training. He considers that 'most of these professional people are remarkably similar to parents in their attitudes towards kids and in their methods of dealing with them'.[64]

Carkhuff's systematic group training

Carkhuff observes that effective treatment is a function of an effective helping relationship plus an effective helping programme. Together they are more effective than either is on its own. The systematic and direct training of clients is often the 'preferred mode of treatment'.[65] Systematic training is goal directed, emphasizes group practice, and leaves group members with tangible and usable skills.

Carkhuff reports an only partially successful attempt at systematic group training for the parents of emotionally disturbed children.[66] The group, consisting of five couples, met twice weekly over a two-month period. The training programme included: assessing parents on their level of interpersonal functioning with each other and with their child; the trainer modelling empathic understanding in a helping role-play and being rated for empathy by group members, followed by discussion; parents being cast in helping interactions about adult concerns with parents from other families, plus ratings and discussion; each parent role playing his or her troubled child in working with a parent from a different family unit, plus ratings etc.; each parent role-playing his or her troubled child in working with the other parent from the same family unit, plus ratings etc.; both parents from a family unit working with their troubled child, while the other parents and children viewed from behind one-way vision screens; and, finally, extended interactions between parents with each serving alternatively as helper and helpee. Not surprisingly, given the emphasis of the programme, relationships between parents improved significantly, but not those between parents and children. Future projects were to incorporate more direct parent-child experiences.[67]

Adlerian parent-child education centres

In the 1920s Alfred Adler, the Austrian psychiatrist, used to interview children, their parents, siblings and teachers before groups of professional people and other parents. During the 1920s and 1930s about 30 parent-child education centres were established in Vienna. Since the 1930s, stimulated by an associate of Adler, Rudolf Dreikurs, many such centres have been established in the United States. Adler's individual psychology stresses such concepts as the striving from inferiority to superiority and the need to develop social interest.[68] Dreikurs has elaborated Adlerian psychology in relation to rearing children, many of his ideas being presented in *Children the Challenge*.[69]

An example of Adlerian parent-child education is offered by the Community Parent-Teacher Education Center (CP-TEC) in Eugene, Oregon, in north-west America. The Center offers courses, counselling and discussion groups for parents, teachers, students and professionals interested in improving relationships between adults and pre-school and elementary-school children.[70] It exists under the joint sponsorship of the University of Oregon College of Education and the Eugene Public Schools. The Center runs both parent study groups and teacher study groups, in each of which members discuss Adlerian and Dreikursian principles about managing themselves while working with children. Attending a parent study group is a condition for a parent receiving counselling.

The Center also offers 'open' counselling sessions which are normally held on Saturday mornings to make it possible for parents, teachers and others who are interested to attend and, hence, profit from the concerns of a few. First, the parents are counselled for about 45 minutes to gain an understanding of their attitudes towards and methods of training their child or children. Then the parents are asked to leave and their children are brought in to be interviewed. Lowe and Morse observe: 'There is a strong interaction between the children and the audience . . . Most impressive is the realization by the adults of how much more easily the children understand the nature of their troubles and problems than do their parents'.[71] The children then return to the playroom and the parents are called back to be given systematic explanations of the dynamics of the children's behaviour as well as specific recommendations. This is done in a supportive way, since, like discouraged children, discouraged parents need encouragement too. The parents are urged to become members of the audience in subsequent weeks until they have a follow-up interview session. The follow-up session has the same format as the initial interview: counselling parents, interviewing children, and summarization and recommendations. Lowe and Morse estimate that in 1977 there were almost 200 Adlerian parent-child centres in the United States associated with universities, churches, institutes and county agencies.

Psychological education for fathering

The growing questioning of traditional gender roles has provided an impetus for fathers to become more involved in the rearing of their children. Traditionally the role of the father in Western society has been relatively task-oriented, especially with sons, compared to the more nurturing role of the mother. This has resulted in many fathers not expressing many 'parental feelings of love, tenderness and joy in their interactions with their children', to the impoverishment of both themselves and their offspring.[72] Resnick and her colleagues describe expectant parent classes and fathering classes, both of which are part of a larger humanistic parent-child psychological education and development programme spanning the prenatal period to entry into elementary school.[73]

In the expectant parent classes, the couple, rather than the father only, participate on a weekly basis in groups of six couples. Course content includes: information about labour and delivery; decision-making skills; communication skills including, where appropriate, assertive training; a tour of the maternity suite; sharing of experience by new parents; and an opportunity to attend a session of the existing parent-infant classes. Sometimes the expectant parent class is broken up into same-sex groups since 'men seem to have an easier time dealing with issues surrounding roles, expectations and competency (or lack of it) when not in the presence of women'.[74]

An interesting aspect of the fathering classes is that fathers attend with their infants in classes grouped according to their child's age (under 6 months, 6–12 months, 12–24 months, or pre-school age). The optimal class size is regarded as eight fathers plus their infants. Classes are held for two hours each on a monthly or bi-weekly basis, on a week night or Saturday morning. The first part of the class is devoted to imparting knowledge and skills regarding infant development. Fathers are taught how to communicate with their infants and to facilitate their sensory-motor, cognitive and affective development. The second part of the class is a group discussion and sharing period focused on the impact of fatherhood. Issues discussed include: relationships with wives, for example finding time to be alone; feelings about sexual rejection; handling both work and fathering pressures; and fatigue, anxiety and jealousy. Sometimes the groups have a problem-solving focus. The aim of the group leaders is to help the men to develop confidence and competence in their role as fathers. Resnick and her colleagues conclude that, given a serious invitation, men react enthusiastically to the opportunity to become involved fathers.[75]

Psychological Education for Other Clienteles

Apart from the above examples, there are numerous other clienteles for psychological education programmes. Ivey and Authier state that, among the health professions, counselling relationship skills have been taught to psychiatric nurses, medical students, physician assistants, speech therapists, and physicians training for family practice.[76] Elsewhere, Ivey notes the demands for human relations training for police, prison guards and inmates, state and county officials, business people, teachers and administrators.[77] Furthermore, Carkhuff and Banks have used training in counselling skills to facilitate communication between white teachers and black parents, a project with obvious implications for facilitating understanding between people of different races.[78] In short, in every area of life that involves human relationships there are potential clienteles for appropriate psychological education programmes.

COUNSELLOR SKILLS IN PSYCHOLOGICAL EDUCATION

Counsellors engaging in psychological education need additional knowledge and skills to those required by counsellors who confine themselves to individual and group counselling. Furthermore, they need a different attitude towards their work to perform both functions. We now review some further skills needed by the counsellor who is also a psychological educator.

Role Decision-making

In Chapter 1 we referred to the counsellor as a decision-maker who makes *treatment*, *responding*, and *role* decisions. *Role decisions* refer to the ways in which counsellors, or a counselling service, decide to allocate their time and resources. Figure 20.1 shows

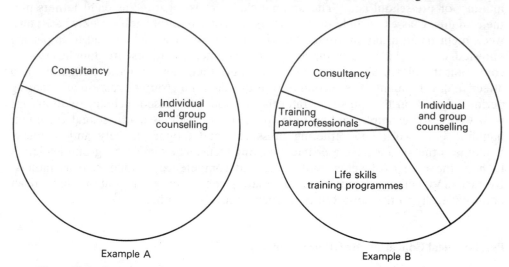

Figure 20.1   Examples of how a counsellor or a counselling service might distribute its time.

two simplified examples of how counsellors or a counselling service might distribute their time. Time spent on administration, which may be as much as a quarter of total counsellor time,[79] is excluded here. Example A is a traditional view of a counselling service where the emphasis is on remedial work with a relatively small percentage of a given community. Example B is based more on a psychological education philosophy, with an attempt being made to reach a much larger proportion of the community. Here training programmes are offered to help 'normals' to develop adequate life skills and to develop the counselling skills of paraprofessionals, with correspondingly less time being spent on individual and group remedial counselling.

Counsellors who engage in psychological education need the skills of making good role decisions. To help with such decisions, Morrill and his colleagues have devised a three-dimensional model of counselling functions.[80] They define counselling interventions as all counsellor functions designed to produce changes in clients, groups or institutions. Three dimensions of counsellor interventions are their target, their purpose and their method. The *target* of an intervention may be: (a) an individual; (b) the individual's primary groups; (c) the individual's associational groups; and (d) the institution or community. The *purpose* of an intervention may be remediation, prevention or development. The *method* of an intervention may be through direct professional involvement with the target population, through consultation and training, or through media approaches. Morrill and his colleagues view their model as a framework for counsellor role decisions which need to be made after a systematic assessment of institutional and individual needs.

Morrill et al's model is similar to Nelson-Jones's three-dimensional counselling functions matrix, in which counsellors are presented with a worksheet with 'actions' (e.g. counselling, research, training) listed on one axis and 'areas' (e.g. academic, occupational, marital) listed on the other axis.[81] The third dimension is that of clientele. For instance, in British higher education, clientele categories might include, among others: departmental heads (D); lecturers (L); postgraduate students (P) and undergraduates (S). The worksheet is completed by making decisions about the categories of clientele, if any, for the various actions by areas boxes and then filling in the designated letter or letters. The counselling functions matrix is a role decision-making tool that counsellors can use according to their local circumstances.

Being an Effective Trainer

Counsellors who make the role decision to spend some time as psychological educators need to develop the skills of being an effective trainer of clients and, possibly, of paraprofessionals. Essentially these skills fall into three areas: designing, implementing and evaluating training programmes. Design of programmes entails setting realistic objectives and then systematically outlining the experiential and intellectual steps necessary to reach those objectives. In this chapter we have reviewed a number of different designs for training programmes. Further ideas might be gained from such books as: Carkhuff's *Helping and Human Relations*, for rating scales of counsellor skills;[82] Ivey and Authier's *Microcounselling*, for ideas on microtraining involving breaking skills down into their component parts;[83] Egan's *You and Me*, for a structured exercise approach to communication skills training;[84] and Pfeiffer and Jones's series of paperbacks *Structured Experiences for Human Relations Training*, which contain numerous ideas for courses and workshops.[85]

In future counsellor training courses are likely to devote more attention to training in psychological education. Already many counsellor trainees undergo fairly systematic training in the skills of empathy, though in many instances they are not taught directly to be trainers of empathy. A broad training to become psychological educators involves being trained to offer a range of skills programmes such as those for self-disclosure and for effective thinking as well as for empathic listening. The skills of implementing training programmes include: effective use of structured exercises; getting a good balance between exploration, thinking and action; use of appropriate hand-outs and reading suggestions; and use of audio-visual aids such as films or a video recorder. We discuss programme evaluation, the third area of being an effective trainer, in a subsequent section.

Consultancy Skills

There are a number of consultancy skills which counsellors need to learn. For instance, it is important to accurately listen to and monitor the institution or community of which they are a part. Another skill is that of working with individuals or groups within a community to facilitate their defining where they perceive their own or the community's functioning might be improved. Further skills are relating to and working through others to develop remedial, preventive and developmental programmes of various sorts. Also, it is important for consultants to have good verbal and written communication skills to increase the likelihood of their ideas being listened to and accepted. However, the counsellor who acts as a consultant must realize that he is part of a team, and, hence, must be sensitive to other people's resistances and to the limits of his effective influence.

Programme Evaluation Skills

Advocates of psychological education tend to be critical of the impact of traditional counselling programmes. To be consistent, then, they need to be rigorous in assessing the impact and effectiveness of the various elements of their own programmes. Programme evaluation skills are relevant to role decisions for both new and existing counselling services. Both kinds of services need to assess institutional or community needs for counselling and psychological education programmes. Once the programmes are established, counsellors need to monitor and obtain feedback on their effectiveness. Furthermore, one of the ways in which counsellors can be helpful in a consultancy capacity is to assist in evaluative research of programmes being conducted by other people and groups. The need for counsellors to possess programme evaluation skills is highlighted by Morrill et al's comment: 'There is evidence that many programs are not effective in achieving their goals, yet counsellors are often guilty of offering programs year after year with no evidence concerning program impact'.[86]

In Chapter 1, as well as viewing counsellors as decision-makers, we observed that they might also be conceptualized as being engaged in a continuing process of making and testing hypotheses. Essentially, counsellors need to view themselves as applied scientists willing to adjust their practice in the light of valid feedback. Such feedback can come either from evaluative studies of their own performance and programmes or from research evaluating other people's programmes. For instance, a training programme in self-disclosure skills might be adopted because of its successful outcomes elsewhere, yet may still need to be evaluated in terms of its local application. In other words, programme evaluation skills for counsellors fall into two interrelated categories: those of *consuming* programme evaluations conducted by others and those of *conducting* evaluations on their own programmes. As well as a scientific attitude and a willingness to be open to evidence, even if it is negative, counsellors need to possess basic research skills. Such research skills include project design, data collection and processing, use of statistics, impartial assessment of evidence, and the ability to write cogent research reports. Such skills are best taught with actual examples of evaluating psychological education programmes. Counsellors are likely to need similar skills for evaluating the outcomes of individual and group counselling.

SOME CRITICAL COMMENTS

Systematic approaches to psychological education are relatively recent. Though developmental objectives and the wish to reach a larger clientele than counsellors reach at present are highly desirable, psychological education still has risks and potential weaknesses and it is to some of these that we now turn.

One of the pitfalls of some psychological education programmes is that of having an inadequate theoretical base. Such programmes need to be soundly based on both a theory of human development and a related theory of instruction. Possible reservations about the theoretical base of current approaches to psychological education include the following. First, psychology is somewhat lacking in theories of optimum psychological as contrasted with abnormal functioning. Such a lack is more likely to constrict programmes targeted on less disturbed than on more disturbed people. Second, though some writers such as Mosher and Sprinthall have attempted to relate their approach to the work of Kohlberg and Loevinger, often there is little attempt to relate the content of psychological education programmes to theory. Furthermore, sometimes there is no real attempt to communicate a theory of human development to clients as part of their psychological education. Third, the teaching methods of psychological education often appear to be based on trial-and-error pragmatism rather than on well thought through theory.

Training in life skills programmes is open to the twin charges of superficiality and ineffectiveness. Arbuckle writes: 'The history of trying to "teach" a person to be a more effective human being is about as dismal as the history of traditional psychoanalysis to "cure" a person of a "sickness"'.[87] He adds that he has known many ineffective people who possessed many of the mechanistic skills of being an effective person. Life skills training programmes may be less open to charges of superficiality if they are based on good theory, take into account their clients' stages of psychological development, and focus on self-exploration and understanding as well as on effective thinking and acting. Furthermore, if psychological educators continue to develop and evaluate their training programmes, then they themselves will provide the necessary research evidence to counter charges of ineffectiveness.

Psychological education programmes also face dangers of superficiality in moving away from a counselling model, with its emphasis on uncovering and bringing out people's existing potential, to a teaching model, with an emphasis on education and training to remedy what is lacking in people's skills and knowledge. Such dangers may be represented by words like brainwashing, manipulation and conformity. There are risks that, instead of encouraging individual personal responsibility, psychological educators may teach a superficial attitude to personal relations and human existence. Areas of psychological education like the women's and the gay movements, which have a combination of a peer-group influence and a deep feeling of injustice, may be especially at risk in terms of demanding conformity of thought and behaviour. Furthermore, there is always the sinister possibility in any society that the state may reach such a position of power that it uses 'psychological education' for its own ends.

An important issue in psychological education is the competence of the trainers, many of whom may not have acquired the requisite knowledge and skills while training to be counsellors. The issue of having adequate competence also applies, perhaps even more so, where paraprofessionals are conducting psychological education programmes. Furthermore, both counselling professionals and paraprofessionals vary in the extent to which they themselves possess the life skills which they purport to teach. Ineffective ways of thinking and relating are so prevalent that it may be the rare psychological educator who is himself functioning at a genuinely high level.

Each area of psychological education is likely to have its own issues and problems. For instance, with psychological education in the schools, there are many issues regarding parental involvement. These concern parents' roles in decisions about enrolment in psychological education, their satisfaction with its content, and whether or not they consider that psychological education programmes are being offered at the expense of basic academic competencies. Another issue is that administrators may be tempted to offer psychological education programmes only to the less academically able, yet the more academically able students are likely to have just as much need for personal development. A further issue concerns the ability of staff to function effectively both as subject-matter teachers and as psychological educators.

In conclusion, psychological education is a promising development within counselling psychology. Consequently, if they have not done so already, counsellors and counselling services should be re-examining their roles to explore whether they could be serving their constituencies better by engaging in psychological education as well as in individual and group counselling interventions. Furthermore, counsellor trainers might profitably spend some time training their students to be psychological educators. Though the area is still developing and has many potential pitfalls, psychological education is likely to constitute an important, though by no means exclusive, part of the future work of counsellors.

PRACTICAL EXERCISES AND QUESTIONS

It may help you to develop your skills and knowledge of the material in this chapter if, either individually, in pairs or in small groups, you perform the following exercises and answer the following questions.

Practical Exercises

1.   As director of a counselling service you are asked by your central administration to be accountable for your existence. In particular, you are asked to present data concerning the impact your service is making on the total institution or community. Make out a case that your service is catering to the needs of many people in the institution or community rather than only providing a counselling service for the moderately to severely disturbed few.

2.   As head of a counselling service you decide that it is desirable to change the institutional or community climate in which you and your clients find yourselves. In regard to a setting of your choice, design an action plan for achieving such change. Be specific about:

(a)   your goals;
(b)   how you would go about achieving each goal.

3.   Choose a life skill for which you think structured psychological education might be appropriate. Design a training programme including:

(a)   a clear and realistic statement of goals;
(b)   a session-by-session outline for achieving your goals;
(c)   ways of evaluating the outcomes of your programme.

4.   What attitudes, knowledge and skills do you consider necessary to be an effective psychological educator? Do you consider that you possess the necessary attitudes, knowledge and skills? If not, design an action plan to enable you to remedy your deficiencies.

5.   Working with a partner as counsellor, explore the extent to which:

(a)   your current behaviour has been shaped by past gender programming;
(b)   your gender programming is likely to affect your own counselling;
(c)   your gender is likely to affect your clients' perceptions of you as a counsellor.

Then reverse roles with your partner.

Questions

1.   Critically discuss the advantages and disadvantages of teaching psychology by means of deliberate psychological education.

2.   If you were a counsellor in an institution or community of your choice:

(a)   what would be the process by which you would make role decisions?
(b)   how much time would you allocate for each element of your job?

3.   If you were a counsellor and/or head of a counselling service, how would you go about evaluating:

(a)   your own effectiveness?
(b)   the effectiveness of your service?

4.   To what extent do you think that there is a need for a men's movement? If so, what methods should it adopt and why?

5.   Discuss the extent to which:

    (a)   individual and group counselling are political activities;
    (b)   psychological education is a political activity;
    (c)   counsellors should become involved in attempting to introduce or to change legislation relevant to the quality of their clients' lives.

NOTES

1. Miller, G. A. (1969) Psychology as a means of promoting human welfare. *American Psychologist*, **24**, 1063–1075.
2. *Ibid*. pp. 1070–1071.
3. Ivey, A. E. (1976) Counseling psychology, the psychoeducator model and the future. *The Counseling Psychologist*, **6**, 3, 72. Full reference pp. 72–75.
4. Daws, P. P. (1973) Mental health and education: counselling as prophylaxis. *British Journal of Guidance and Counselling*, **1**, 2–10.
5. Drum, D. & Figler, H. (1977) Outreach in counseling. In C. Hatcher, B. S. Brooks and associates, *Innovations in Counseling Psychology* p. 17. San Francisco: Jossey-Bass. Full reference pp. 11–36.
6. Sprinthall, N. (1980) Psychology for secondary schools: the saber-tooth curriculum revisited? *American Psychologist*, **35**, 336–347.
7. Anthony, W. A. & Carkhuff, R. R. (1976) *The Art of Health Care: A Handbook of Psychological First Aid Skills*. Amherst, Massachusetts: Human Resource Development Press.
8. Thorne, B. & Da Costa, M. (1976) A counselling service as a growth centre. *British Journal of Guidance and Counselling*, **4**, 212–217.
9. Halmos, P. (1965) *The Faith of the Counsellors* p. 176. London: Constable.
10. Mosher, R. L. & Sprinthall, N. A. (1970) Psychological education in secondary schools: a program to promote individual and human development. *American Psychologist*, **25**, 911–924.
11. Mosher, R. L., Sprinthall, N. A. with associates (1971) Psychological education: a means to promote personal development during adolescence. *The Counseling Psychologist*, **2**, 4, 3–82.
12. Sprinthall, N. A. (1973) A curriculum for secondary schools: counselors as teachers for psychological growth. *The School Counselor*, **20**, 361–369.
13. Mosher, R. L., Sprinthall, N. A. with associates (1971) Psychological education: a means to promote personal development during adolescence. *The Counseling Psychologist*, **2**, 4, 27–33.
14. *Ibid*. pp. 36–37.
15. *Ibid*. p. 38.
16. Sprinthall, N. (1980) Psychology for secondary schools: the saber-tooth curriculum revisited? *American Psychologist*, **35**, 336–347.
17. Daws, P. P. (1973) Mental health and education: counselling as prophylaxis. *British Journal of Guidance and Counselling*, **1**, 2–10.
18. Hopson, B. & Hough, P. (1976) The need for personal and social education in secondary schools and further education. *British Journal of Guidance and Counselling*, **4**, 16–27.
19. *Ibid*. p. 18.
20. Hopson, B. & Hough, P. (1973) *Exercises in Personal and Career Development* pp. 27–91. Cambridge: CRAC.
21. Rennie, J., Lunzer, E. A. & Williams, W. T. (1974) *Social Education: An Experiment in*

Four Secondary Schools (Schools Council Working Paper 51). London: Evans/Methuen Educational.

22. *Ibid*. p. 122.
23. Hamblin, D. H. (1974) *The Teacher and Counselling* p. 318. Oxford: Blackwell.
24. *Ibid*. pp. 316–322.
25. Hamblin, D. H. (1978) *The Teacher and Pastoral Care* pp. 152–160. Oxford: Blackwell.
26. Rogers, C. R. (1969) *Freedom to Learn* pp. 3–5. Columbus, Ohio: Charles E. Merrill.
27. Patterson, C. H. (1973) *Humanistic Education* pp. 97–139. Englewood Cliffs, NJ: Prentice-Hall.
28. Rogers, C. R. (1977) *Personal Power: Inner Strength and its Revolutionary Impact* p. 72. London: Constable.
29. *Ibid*. pp. 72–74.
30. *Ibid*. pp. 74–89.
31. Rogers, C. R. (1969) *Freedom to Learn* pp. 57–145. Columbus, Ohio: Charles E. Merrill.
32. Patterson, C. H. (1973) *Humanistic Education* pp. 191–209. Englewood Cliffs, NJ: Prentice-Hall.
33. Combs, A. W. & Snygg, D. (1959) *Individual Behavior: A Perceptual Approach to Behavior* (Revised ed.). New York: Harper and Row.
34. Patterson, C. H. (1973) *Humanistic Education* pp. 210–225. Englewood Cliffs, NJ: Prentice-Hall.
35. Rogers, C. R. (1977) *Personal Power: Inner Strength and its Revolutionary Impact* pp. 90–104. London: Constable.
36. Rogers, C. R. (1969) *Freedom to Learn* pp. 303–322. Columbus, Ohio: Charles E. Merrill.
37. Crookston, B. B. (1973) Education for human development. In C. F. Warnath and associates, *New Directions for College Counsellors* p. 59. San Francisco: Jossey-Bass. Full reference pp. 47–65.
38. Ivey, A. E. (1976) The counselor as teacher. *Personnel and Guidance Journal*, **54**, 443. Full reference pp. 431–434.
39. Correspondence from B. J. Thorne dated 20 March 1981.
40. Thorne, B. & Da Costa, M. (1976) A counselling service as a growth centre. *British Journal of Guidance and Counselling*, **4**, 212.
41. Carkhuff, R. R. (1972) New directions in training for the helping professions: towards a technology for human and community resource development. *The Counseling Psychologist*, **3**, 3, 12–30.
42. Thorne, B. & Da Costa, M. (1976) A counselling service as a growth centre. *British Journal of Guidance and Counselling*, **4**, 215.
43. Correspondence from Jean Clark, Senior Student Counsellor, Leicester Polytechnic, dated 23 April 1981.
44. Fried, E. (1974) Does woman's new self-concept call for new approaches in group psychotherapy? *International Journal of Group Psychotherapy*, **24**, 265. Full reference pp. 265–272.
45. Quoted in Elias, M. (1975) Sisterhood therapy. *Human Behaviour*, April, 61. Full reference pp. 56–61.
46. Erickson, V. L. (1975) Deliberate psychological education for women: from Iphigenia to Antigone. *Counsellor Education and Supervision*, **14**, 297–309.
47. Sprinthall, N. A. & Erickson, V. L. (1974) Learning psychology by doing psychology: guidance through the curriculum. *Personnel and Guidance Journal*, **52**, 396–405.
48. Fitzgerald, L. E. (1973) Women's changing expectations . . . new insights, new demands. *The Counseling Psychologist*, **4**, 1, 90–95.
49. Aird, E. (1980) The place of counselling in 'New Opportunities for Women' courses. *British Journal of Guidance and Counselling*, **1**, 92–98.
50. Elias, M. (1975) Sisterhood therapy. *Human Behaviour*, April, 58.
51. Brodsky, A. M. (1973) The consciousness-raising group as a model for therapy with women. *Psychotherapy: Theory, Research and Practice*, **10**, 1, 25. Full reference pp. 24–29.

52. *Ibid*. pp. 24–29.
53. Jakubowski-Spector, P. (1973) Facilitating the growth of women through assertive training. *The Counseling Psychologist*, **4**, 1, 75–86.
54. Fried, E. (1974) Does woman's new self-concept call for new approaches in group psychotherapy? *International Journal of Group Psychotherapy*, **24**, 265–272.
55. Division 17 Ad Hoc Committee on Women (1979) Principles concerning the counselling and therapy of women. *The Counseling Psychologist*, **8**, 1, 21.
56. Johnson, M. (1979) A knowledge base for counsellors of women. *The Counseling Psychologist*, **8**, 1, 14–16.
57. Harway, M. (1979) Training counselors. *The Counseling Psychologist*, **8**, 1, 8–9.
58. Weeks, J. (1977) *Coming Out: Homosexual Politics in Britain, from the Nineteenth Century to the Present* p. 190. London: Quartet Books.
59. Davison, G. C. & Wilson, G. T. (1973) Attitudes of behaviour therapists toward homosexuality. *Behavior Therapy*, **4**, 686–696.
60. Wolfenden, J. (1976) *Turning Points: The Memoirs of Lord Wolfenden* p. 132. London: Bodley Head.
61. Weeks, J. (1977) *Coming Out: Homosexual Politics in Britain, from the Nineteenth Century to the Present* p. 176. London: Quartet Books.
62. Foley, C. (1975) San Francisco politicians woo the gay vote. *The Observer*, 5 October, 7.
63. Gordon, T. (1970) *Parent Effectiveness Training*. New York: Wyden.
64. *Ibid*. p. 298.
65. Carkhuff, R. R. (1971) Training as a preferred mode of treatment. *Journal of Counseling Psychology*, **18**, 123–131.
66. Carkhuff, R. R. (1969) Group training as a preferred mode of treatment. In R. R. Carkhuff, *Helping and Human Relations: Volume 2, Practice and Research* pp. 129–185. New York: Holt, Rinehart and Winston.
67. *Ibid*. p. 181.
68. Ansbacher, H. L. & Ansbacher, R. R. (1956) *The Individual Psychology of Alfred Adler*. New York: Harper Colophon.
69. Dreikurs, R. & Soltz, V. (1964) *Children the Challenge*. New York: Harper Colophon.
70. Lowe, R. N. & Morse, C. (1977) Parent-child education centers. In C. H. Hatcher, B. S. Brooks, et al., *Innovations in Counseling Psychology* pp. 146–170. San Francisco: Jossey-Bass.
71. *Ibid*. p. 165.
72. Resnick, J. L., Resnick, M. B., Packer, A. B. & Wilson, J. (1978) Fathering classes: a psycho/educational model. *The Counseling Psychologist*, **7**, 4, 59. Full reference pp. 56–60.
73. *Ibid*. pp. 56–60.
74. *Ibid*. p. 58.
75. *Ibid*. p. 59.
76. Ivey, A. E. & Authier, J. (1978) *Microcounseling: Innovations in Interviewing, Counseling, Psychotherapy and Psychoeducation* (2nd ed.) pp. 247–249. Springfield, Illinois: Charles C. Thomas.
77. Ivey, A. E. (1976) The counselor as teacher. *Personnel and Guidance Journal*, **54**, 433.
78. Carkhuff, R. R. & Banks, G. (1970) Training as a preferred mode of facilitating relations between races and generations. *Journal of Counseling Psychology*, **17**, 413–418.
79. Troy, W. G. & Magoon, T. M. (1979) Activity analysis in a university counseling center: daily time recording or time estimates? *Journal of Counseling Psychology*, **26**, 58–63.
80. Morrill, W. H., Oetting, E. R. & Hurst, J. C. (1974) Dimensions of counselor functioning. *Personnel and Guidance Journal*, **52**, 354–359.
81. Nelson-Jones, R. (1974) The counselling functions matrix. *The Counsellor*, **19**, 4–7.
82. Carkhuff, R. R. (1969) *Helping and Human Relations: Volume One, Selection and Training*. New York: Holt, Rinehart and Winston.
83. Ivey, A. E. & Authier, J. (1978) *Microcounseling: Innovations in Interviewing, Counseling, Psychotherapy and Psychoeducation* (2nd ed.) Springfield, Illinois: Charles C. Thomas.

84. Egan, G. (1977) *You and Me: The Skills of Communicating and Relating to Others.* Belmont, California: Brooks/Cole.
85. Pfeiffer, J. & Jones, J. (1969–77) *Structured Experiences for Human Relations Training.* Iowa City: University Associates Press. Vol. 1, 1969; Vol. 2, 1970; Vol. 3, 1971; Vol. 4, 1973; Vol. 5, 1975; and Vol. 6, 1977.
86. Morrill, W. H., Oetting, E. R. & Hurst, J. C. (1974) Dimensions of counselor functioning. *Personnel and Guidance Journal*, **52,** 359.
87. Arbuckle, D. S. (1976) Comment on A. E. Ivey's paper 'The counselor as teacher'. *Personnel and Guidance Journal*, **54,** 434.

Appendix A – *Provision of Counselling Psychology Services in Britain*

SUMMARY: *The scope of counselling psychology services in Britain is reviewed. Some counselling is performed by clinical, educational and occupational psychologists as part of their professional roles. Also, a number of psychologists have been developing counsellor training courses and writing about counselling. In the past two decades there has been a rapid growth of counselling services, offered mainly by non-psychologist counsellors. Some areas in which services are provided are described briefly: counselling in educational settings; marital counselling; family counselling; careers guidance and counselling; pastoral counselling; youth counselling; medically related counselling, including counselling by doctors and nurses as well as pregnancy/abortion and disablement counselling; bereavement counselling; counselling the suicidal and despairing; minority group counselling; counselling women; the growth movement; and counselling by social workers. Some comments are made assessing the overall provision of counselling services in Britain.*

Counselling psychology services are provided in Britain both by psychologists and by non-psychologist counsellors.

COUNSELLING INVOLVEMENT OF PSYCHOLOGISTS

The term 'psychologist' denotes membership of the British Psychological Society (BPS), whose basic membership requirement is an undergraduate degree in psychology or its equivalent, At the time of writing BPS has no division focused on counselling psychology. It does, however, have three divisions whose work entails the relationships and activities of counselling, namely the Divisions of Clinical Psychology, Educational and Child Psychology, and Occupational Psychology. Some members of the recently formed Division of Criminological and Legal Psychology may also engage in counselling.

504

Clinical Psychologists

·At the end of 1979 there were 885 members of BPS's Division of Clinical Psychology.[1] The vast majority of British clinical psychologists work for the National Health Service, some are academics, some move into areas such as student counselling, while only a handful are in private practice. Counselling is an almost ubiquitous activity among practising clinical psychologists, especially with behavioural approaches now becoming more cognitive. Furthermore, there is a trend in clinical psychology to viewing patients in relation to their social settings, including counselling their relatives. Also, counselling is involved in the move of clinical psychologists towards primary health care in which patients are worked with within general practice. It is hard to assess the amount of support provided by clinical psychologists for the voluntary sector, though psychologists did not feature prominently in a recent Home Office report on marriage guidance.[2] In future, clinical psychologists may have increasing freedom to provide health services in the community outside hospital settings. Though clinical psychologists engage in counselling, they would not claim expertise in certain areas of counselling, such as careers counselling.

Educational Psychologists

At the end of 1979 BPS's Division of Educational and Child Psychology and Scottish Division of Educational and Child Psychology had 496 and 90 members respectively.[3] The majority of British educational psychologists are employed by Local Education Authorities. Educational psychologists are increasingly moving into the child's natural settings and very little of their work is now being performed in Child Guidance Clinics; the main focus is now the school. Other settings in which educational psychologists work include the Social Services and Paediatric Assessment Centres. Also, more work is being carried out in the home. Possibly, at some time, all educational psychologists are using counselling skills in their work, either with children or with their parents. A recent survey of educational psychologists indicated that principals spend a large proportion of their time on administration and planning and field workers correspondingly more time on treatment assessment. Educational psychologists reported that the demands for assessment had increased and that this was curtailing their involvement in treatment (probably including counselling). The same survey indicated that principals and field workers spent 17.8 per cent and 24.3 per cent of their time respectively on direct and indirect treatment, whereas they spent 26.7 per cent and 40.7 per cent of their time respectively on assessment.[4] The survey tended not to use the word 'counselling'.

Occupational Psychologist

At the end of 1979 BPS's Division of Occupational Psychology had 214 members. Also, there were 538 members of BPS's interest-based Occupational Psychology Section.[5] In 1980 Sylvia Downs, the Division's Chairman, wrote:

> Our members are concerned with counselling in a broad range of activities including
> vocational guidance, careers guidance, redundancy counselling, assessment centres, as
> well as identifying training needs in counselling, and designing courses to answer these.
>   Indeed in an ad hoc sample, we are all involved in counselling, whilst our training
> appears far from uniform.[6]

Divisional members probably also use counselling skills in their consultancy work with organizations. With their focus on work, occupations and careers, they are not necessarily competent to counsel in other areas, such as personal anxieties. Many members of the Division may have little formal training in counselling and so have acquired their knowledge and skills through individual initiative. Occupational psychologists in Britain, as well as counselling, work in the areas of industrial and organizational psychology, personnel psychology, including selection, and ergonomics or the study of work methods.

Psychologists Outside BPS's Divisions

Undoubtedly many psychologists, independent of the professional roles represented by the Divisions, are involved in counselling and are influencing its development in Britain. Though few, if any, school counsellors are psychologists, there are a number of psychologists engaged in student counselling in further and higher education. Few of the National Marriage Guidance Council counsellors are psychologists. Psychologists, some of whom are ineligible for membership of the Division of Occupational Psychology, are engaged in careers guidance and counselling, working in tertiary education careers services and in industry or private consultancy. Psychologists are also interested in and involved in pastoral care and counselling within a religious framework, though their numbers are hard to estimate. The same comment might be made about the areas of youth counselling, medically related counselling, minority group counselling, counselling women and the growth or encounter group movement.

Psychologists have been fairly prominent in the area of counsellor training, for instance in staffing educational counselling courses. At present, however, there are no counselling psychology training courses. Little research appears to have been conducted by psychologists into counselling with non-patient populations. However, psychologists have contributed to what counselling research literature exists, have written non-research articles for counselling journals, and have also written some books in the area. Furthermore, three of the four editors of the *British Journal of Guidance and Counselling* are psychologists.

INVOLVEMENT OF NON-PSYCHOLOGIST COUNSELLORS

Counselling in Britain has its origins in mental health, pastoral care, social work and careers guidance. In the past 20 years there has been a rapid growth in the provision of counselling services, many of which are staffed predominantly by non-psychologists. This growth has come about with the increasing acceptance that from time to time most people have problems that they may or may not have the necessary personal resources to cope with on their own. Some initial indication of the extensiveness of counselling activity may be gained from the fact that, in 1980, three years after its establishment, the British Association for Counselling (BAC) had over 1800 ordinary members and 160 organizational members. Furthermore, BAC's 1978 publication *A Directory of Voluntary Counselling and Allied Services*[7] listed over 500 local and national agencies offering counselling services. Additionally, many counselling services are provided by 'non-voluntary' services, such as the Careers Service and educational institutions.

A further way of gaining an idea of the extensiveness of the growth in counselling services is to look at some of the presenting concerns with which they deal. Table A.1 depicts some presenting concerns, along with illustrative agencies providing related counselling services. This list, which is not exhaustive, covers concerns relevant to

Table A.1 *Some presenting concerns and illustrative agencies providing related counselling services**

Presenting concerns	Illustrative agencies providing services
Alcoholism	Al-Anon Family Group, Alcoholics Anonymous
Autism and parenting autistic children	National Society for Autistic Children
Bereavement	Compassionate Friends, Cruse
Career choice	Careers Service, Association of Graduate Careers Advisory Services
Career development and redundancy	Counsellors in work settings, Saville and Holdsworth Ltd
Crisis support	Andover Crisis Support Centre
Delinquency	Probation and parole officers
Family planning	Brook Advisory Centres, Family Planning Association
Family problems	Family Service Units, Family Welfare Association
Identity and transition to adulthood	Counsellors in educational institutions
Learning difficulties	Counsellors in educational institutions
Marriage difficulties and education for marriage	Catholic Marriage Advisory Service, National Marriage Guidance Council
Mental handicap and parenting mentally handicapped children	National Society for Mentally Handicapped Children
Mental illness of relatives	National Schizophrenia Fellowship
One-parent families	Gingerbread
Physical disablement	Multiple Sclerosis Society, Spastics Society
Pregnancy advice	British Pregnancy Advisory Service
Psychosexual difficulties	Sexual Dysfunction Clinic (London Marriage Guidance Council), Forum Personal Adviser Clinic
Sexual minorities	Albany Trust, Friend
Spiritual concerns	Clinical Theology Association, Westminster Pastoral Foundation
Suicide and suicide prevention	Niteline, Samaritans
Youth concerns	YMCA, YWCA, Youth Advisory Services

* The examples are illustrative rather than inclusive.

effective functioning at all stages of the human life-cycle. Some of the concerns, such as realistic career choice and handling bereavement, are common to most, if not all, people at some stage of their lives. Other concerns pertain to the numerous minority groups which form part of our society.

Counselling in Educational Settings

Daws traces the origins of educational counselling in mental health and in vocational guidance.[8] There has also been a strong pastoral tradition in British education which has both helped and hindered the development of school counselling. The first training courses for school counsellors were begun at the Universities of Reading and Keele in 1965. Since then there has been a large growth in the number of counselling courses for teachers. Some of the products of these courses return to the schools as part-time or full-time counsellors, others return to teaching, which they may perform with more of a counselling emphasis than before their counselling training, and still others move into senior roles, such as deputy head or senior mistress, where they may have responsibility for overseeing and co-ordinating pastoral care and counselling developments in their schools. Also, there appears to be a growing concern in British schools for the personal and social development of pupils, and this may be an emerging area of increased counsellor activity. Until the recent establishment of the Counselling in Educational Settings Division in BAC, the main association for school counsellors was the National Association of Counsellors in Education (NACE), with a membership of approximately 400.

There has also been a growth of counselling services in British tertiary education. In 1963 the first counselling service at a British university evolved from the careers and appointments service at Keele. Also, the student health service at the University of London under Malleson gave an early lead to meeting emotional problems among students. Student counselling services have proliferated to the point where they are common in universities, polytechnics, colleges of education and of higher education, and colleges of further education. Sometimes they are separate counselling services, or they may form part of a central welfare service, a counselling and careers service, or a student health service. At present, student counsellors come from a variety of backgrounds, including training courses in student counselling, social work and clinical psychology. Also, a number of chaplains perceive their roles as including counselling. The Association for Student Counselling, now a Division of BAC, was formed in 1970, and in 1980 had approximately 300 members.

Marital Counselling

One of the largest groupings of counsellors in Britain is those who work on a voluntary basis for the National Marriage Guidance Council (NMGC). In 1938 the Marriage Guidance Council was established by a group of people, led by the Reverend Dr Herbert Gray, who were concerned about the rising divorce rate and the breakdown of married and family life. In 1943 the first MGC centre opened in London. Also in

1943 the Home Office made the first grant-in-aid from public funds to the NMGC, the Catholic Marriage Advisory Council and what is now the Tavistock Institute of Marital Studies[9] and, since then, the NMGC has continued to receive government support. By 1956 there were 80 recognized local Marriage Guidance Councils in England, Wales and Northern Ireland and 794 counsellors had been selected and either fully or partly trained. In 1979 there were 145 Marriage Guidance Councils offering a counselling service in over 500 centres. The total number of counsellors was 1614, the total number of cases worked with was 35 400, and the total number of interviews was 165 000. Additionally, NMGC counsellors engaged in extensive education for marriage and family life, mostly on a discussion-group basis, in schools, colleges, youth clubs and other settings.[10] Marital counselling is also conducted by the Catholic Marriage Advisory Council (CMAC). In 1978–79, CMAC had 524 counsellors working in 63 centres. These counsellors worked with 3156 cases and conducted a total of 10 416 interviews. Additionally, nearly 4000 people attended CMAC marriage preparation courses.[11]

Family Counselling

Organizations which provide counselling for family problems include the Family Service Units and the Family Welfare Association. Family Service Units cater for families in severe personal, social and financial difficulties. Their services include counselling for parents, groupwork of many kinds for adults and children, community activities, compensatory education, and providing holidays for children. The Family Welfare Association has centres in London providing professional counselling for marriage and family problems.[12]

Careers Guidance and Counselling

Over the years there has been an expansion not only in the number of careers officers, formerly called youth employment officers, but also in the provision of training facilities for them. Today there are approximately 3000 careers officers in the Careers Service and the 1978-79 intake figure for course centres offering the Diploma in Career Guidance has reached 405 places.[13]

Alongside statutory development, there has been an increasing recognition and expansion of careers work in British schools, colleges and universities. Though the distinction is somewhat artificial, some of this work focuses on careers *counselling*, or helping individuals and small groups to make career decisions, and some of it on *careers education*, or teaching larger groups about the world of work and, possibly, training them in skills such as decision-making and handling job interviews. Careers work in educational settings may be conducted by people employed by the institution, such as counsellors and teachers in secondary education or careers advisory and appointments officers in tertiary education. Further help may be provided by visits from Careers Service Officers to educational institutions.

Not all careers counselling provision is focused on the school-age and young adult population. Some counselling goes on in work settings and possibly this is a growth area in the future provision of counselling services. Some of the early initiatives for counselling at work came from Shell, ICI and British Steel. Also, in 1979, BAC inaugurated a Counselling at Work Division. Either inside or outside careers settings, post-school careers counselling may focus on transitions between jobs or careers, enrichment of existing jobs, problems of redundancy, and pre-retirement and retirement issues. Sometimes these counselling services are provided by private careers and occupational consultants.

Pastoral Counselling

Counselling developments have also taken place in both Anglican and the Roman Catholic Churches, where many of the clergy are redefining their role to include a more professional approach to counselling personal and spiritual concerns. Additionally, there are agencies which offer counselling and pastoral care within a religious framework, such as the Clinical Theology Association in Nottingham and the Westminster Pastoral Foundation in London. The Roman Catholic Dympna Centre in London also provides counselling within a religious framework.

Youth Counselling

The National Association of Young People's Counselling and Advisory Services (NAYPCAS) aims to promote and encourage the growth of young people's counselling and advisory services by means of support, training and publicity. Youth counselling is provided by national agencies, such as the YMCA and the YWCA, and by local agencies, such as the Young People's Counselling Centre in Exeter, the Young People's Information and Advisory Service in Watford and the Open Door in Birmingham.

Medically Related Counselling

Some physicians attempt counselling as part of their work, though this, of necessity, is limited by demands on their time. Additionally, just as some clinical psychologists have started working in conjunction with general practices, so have some counsellors, though their number is probably still small. Some other areas of medically related counselling provision include the counselling work of nurses, pregnancy and abortion counselling and disablement counselling.

Nurse counsellors

Possibly there is a growing trend in nursing education to see the nurse-patient relationship in counselling terms. Sometimes this may be just a matter of ensuring that nurses carry out what may be brief interactions with patients in a psychologically helpful way. On other occasions nurses may have to spend more time with individual patients in what might be considered a counselling capacity.

Pregnancy/abortion counselling

Pregnancy and abortion counselling tends to be brief and focused around the decision of whether to continue or terminate a pregnancy. A national agency working in this area is the British Pregnancy Advisory Service (BPAS), a non-profit-making charitable trust whose branches offer information, counselling and practical help to anyone with problems connected with pregnancy, contraception, sexuality, fertility or sterilization. BPAS also runs an educational service for schools, colleges and youth clubs. Another national agency is the Brook Advisory Centres, whose local branches offer young people advice, treatment and supplies for contraception, pregnancy diagnosis, pregnancy counselling, and counselling on emotional and sexual problems.

Disablement counselling

Disablement counselling focuses on two groups of clientele: the disabled and those who are parents of or are otherwise responsible for the disabled. Illustrative agencies include the Spastics Society, which maintains a range of counselling and supportive services, both individual and group, for the cerebral palsied (spastics) and their families. Another agency is SPOD (the Committee on Sexual Problems of the Disabled). SPOD does not offer continuing advice and counselling itself, but refers clients for counselling and advisory assistance in their own localities. The work of physiotherapists and occupational therapists may also contain a large counselling element.

Bereavement Counselling

Bereavement counselling is conducted by people in many roles, including doctors, clergy and counsellors. CRUSE (the national organization for widows and their children) offers a counselling service to widows and their children throughout the United Kingdom, irrespective of the widow's age, length of bereavement, and social or financial position. Another agency offering help to the bereaved is Compassionate Friends, an international organization of bereaved parents offering friendship and understanding to other bereaved parents.

Counselling the Suicidal and Despairing

The purpose of the Samaritans is to help the suicidal and despairing through discussion by telephone, letter and face-to-face contact. Also, clients may be befriended in crisis to help them to find their own solutions to their problems. The service is free, based on 24-hours availability, and is confidential. The local branches are staffed by selected and trained volunteers. In 1975 there were 200 000 new Samaritan clients in Great Britain and Eire.[14]

Minority Group Counselling

Many counselling services cater for the needs of minority groups, and only a few such services can be mentioned here. A number of agencies are concerned with problems raised by homosexual and bisexual orientation. For instance, Friend, the counselling and advice service of the Campaign for Homosexual Equality, offers counselling and befriending to men and women in their localities. Also, the Albany Trust in London has considerable experience in helping members of sexual minorities. The Trust offers only a limited amount of counselling and, wherever possible, acts as a referral agency. Often the telephone is used to counsel homosexual and bisexual people, some of whom are reluctant to reveal their identity. For instance, Friend offers a telephone service, as does Gay Switchboard in London, which is based on telephone contact only. Counselling services for sexual minorities tend to have a peer self-help emphasis, due to suspicion about both the attitude and the amount of relevant scientific knowledge of many mental health professionals. Other agencies offering counselling to minority groups, often on a peer self-help basis, include: Gingerbread, the association of one-parent families; Alcoholics Anonymous; and Gamblers Anonymous.

Counselling Women

The growth of the women's movement is causing many women to question their identity and attempt to develop more of their potential. Sometimes this takes place in an agency with a broader counselling objective, e.g. NMGC, but on other occasions such counselling takes place within an agency which has a specifically feminist perspective. One such feminist agency is the Women's Therapy Centre in London, whose services include individual counselling, long-term and short-term counselling groups, couple counselling, and half-day theme centred workshops on topics such as assertion, sexuality and compulsive eating.

The Growth Movement

A number of individuals and agencies offer what might be termed 'growth' experiences. Frequently these involve encounter groups of one kind or another. One such agency is Quaesitor, a London-based education centre founded in 1969 to introduce, experience and develop new ideas in creative groupwork applicable to psychotherapy. There are also many other opportunities in Britain to participate in group experiences based on different models, such as transactional analysis, gestalt, psychodrama, and co-counselling.

Counselling by Social Workers

Though social workers are employed mainly by local social services committees, they are also employed by the probation and after-care service and by voluntary organizations. The counselling-related methods used by social workers include casework, groupwork and community work. Their main clienteles are those people perceived as least able to help themselves, such as the young, the old, the sick and the handicapped. Undoubtedly counselling is an important skill of the effective social worker.

CONCLUDING COMMENTS

Both quantitative and qualitative considerations are relevant in assessing counselling services in Britain. Quantitatively, probably the largest groupings of counsellors are those in educational settings, marriage guidance work, and the Careers Service. Nevertheless, even in each of these areas the provision of services is patchy. Many educational institutions have either an inadequate counselling service or no counselling service at all. The Home Office Working Party on Marriage Guidance reported that the NMGC was underfinanced and that the service suffered accordingly.[15] Also, both the NMGC and the CMAC are agencies using part-time voluntary counsellors, which raises the question of whether standards would be raised if counsellors were full-time and paid. Careers officers tend to have time for only brief contacts with individual clients. This state of affairs adversely affects their capacity for effective careers counselling.

The picture that emerges is that, though there has been a growth in the provision of counselling services in the past two decades or so, this growth has not kept pace with potential demand, even in those areas in which most provision has been made. Additionally, there are qualitative issues regarding the provision of services, including the degree to which counselling interventions are based on research evidence, the extent to which counselling services are evaluated adequately, and the quality of basic and continuing training for the various services. Furthermore, alongside their non-psychologist colleagues, British psychologists could be playing a more active role in the provision of counselling services for less disturbed populations. Also, psychologists have an important contribution to make in researching into counselling processes and outcomes, and evaluating counsellor training programmes and the provision of counselling services.

NOTES

1. British Psychological Society (1980) *Annual Report 1979–80* p. 18. Leicester: British Psychological Society.

2. Working Party on Marriage Guidance (1979) *Marriage Matters*. London: HMSO.
3. British Psychological Society (1980) *Annual Report 1979–80* p. 18. Leicester: British Psychological Society.
4. Wedell, K. & Lambourne, R. (1979) *An Enquiry into Psychological Services in England and Wales*. Birmingham University: Department of Educational Psychology (mimeo).
5. British Psychological Society (1980) *Annual Report 1979–80* p. 18. Leicester: British Psychological Society.
6. Correspondence from S. Downs, Chairman of the British Psychological Society's Division of Occupational Psychology, dated 4 July 1980.
7. Humphreys, J. (ed.) (1978) *A Directory of Voluntary Counselling and Allied Services*. Rugby: British Association for Counselling.
8. Daws, P. P. (1976) *Early Days: A Personal Review of the Beginnings of Counselling in English Education during the Decade 1964–74* pp. 13–28. Cambridge: Hobsons Press.
9. National Marriage Guidance Council (1967) *A Short History of the Movement*. Rugby: National Marriage Guidance Council.
10. National Marriage Guidance Council (1981) *The National Marriage Guidance Council Annual Report 1980*. Rugby: National Marriage Guidance Council.
11. Catholic Marriage Advisory Council (1979) *Annual Reports and Accounts 1978–79*. London: Catholic Marriage Advisory Council.
12. Humphreys, J. (ed.) (1978) *A Directory of Voluntary Counselling and Allied Services*. Rugby: British Association for Counselling.
13. Correspondence from General Secretary, Institute of Careers Officers, dated 21 September 1978.
14. Humphreys, J. (ed.) (1978) *A Directory of Voluntary Counselling and Allied Services* p. 110. Rugby: British Association for Counselling.
15. Working Party on Marriage Guidance (1979) *Marriage Matters* p. 33. London: HMSO.

Appendix B–*Development of Professional Associations in Britain, America, Australia and Canada*

SUMMARY: *An insight into the growth of counselling psychology may be gained from a review of the development of professional associations. Accordingly, data on both counselling psychology and counselling professional associations are presented for Britain, America, Australia and Canada. America and Australia have Divisions focused on counselling psychology as part of their national psychological associations, while a Section of Counselling Psychology is under consideration within the British Psychological Society. Britain, America and Canada have national counselling associations.*

Some idea of the spread of counselling psychology may be gained from briefly reviewing the development of professional associations. In this section we examine counselling psychology and counselling professional associations in Britain, America, Australia and Canada, though it is likely that there have also been important developments in other English-speaking countries.

BRITAIN

Counselling Psychology

The British Psychological Society (BPS) was formed in 1901 and received a Royal Charter in 1965. The BPS has a number of Sections, based on interest groupings, and Divisions, based on professional competence groupings. In 1979 BPS's Professional Affairs Board set up a Working Party on Counselling 'To consider the practice of counselling, its reference to the professional interests of the Society, and to make

515

recommendations upon any actions that the Society might take . . . '.[1] In November 1980 the Working Party submitted its report, the major recommendation of which was that the Society should establish a Section of Counselling Psychology.[2] Thus, rather belatedly, BPS appears to be getting involved in counselling psychology, though many of its members have been involved as individuals for some time.

Counselling

In the early 1970s the Standing Conference for the Advancement of Counselling was established and this led to the formation, in 1977, of the British Association for Counselling (BAC). BAC's objects are twofold:

(a) To promote and provide education and training for counsellors working in either professional or voluntary settings, whether full or part time, with a view to raising the standards of counselling for the benefit of the community and in particular of those who are the recipients of counselling.

(b) To advance the education of the public in the part that counselling can play generally, and in particular to meet the needs of those members of society whose development, and participation in society, is impaired by mental, physical or social handicap or disability.[3]

Ordinary membership of BAC signifies either being engaged in or having received suitable minimum training in counselling. Other categories of individual membership include Student Members and Qualified Members, an accredited counsellor category. Additionally, BAC has an Organizational Member category for national and local organizations concerned with training or practice in the furtherance of BAC's objects and acceptable to its Executive Committee. As mentioned earlier, in July 1980 BAC had over 1800 individual members and 160 Organizational Members. BAC publishes a bi-monthly journal called *Counselling* (formerly *Counselling News*). In 1978 a policy and priorities questionnaire was sent out to all BAC members with the February issue of *Couselling News*. The three highest priorities for the approximately 25 per cent of the membership who completed the questionnaire were: development of standards for the ethics and practice of counselling, training events, and development of local branches planning their own programmes. Research into counselling was ranked last among the 14 possible priorities.[4] Thus BAC's members may perceive its role more in terms of facilitating training, practice and in-service support than pursuing the advancement of counselling through scientific investigation.

BAC's structure includes national Divisions representing specialized interests, and local branches, which cut across specialized interests. In 1980 BAC had seven Divisions: counselling in Education, Counselling in Medical Settings, Counselling at Work, Personal/Sexual/Marital/Family Counselling, Pastoral Care and Counselling, Student Counselling and Youth Counselling. Table B.1 shows membership details of these Divisions. Further Divisions may be formed as needed in such areas as disablement counselling, bereavement counselling and counselling the elderly.

Table B.1 *Membership of BAC Divisions, July 1980**

Division	Membership
Counselling in Education†	115
Counselling in Medical Settings	126
Counselling at Work	120
Pastoral Care and Counselling	308
Personal/Sexual/Marital/Family Counselling	299
Student Counselling	288
Youth Counselling	99

* Source: BAC's Membership Secretary.
† In July 1980 the main grouping of counsellors in education was NACE (National Association of Counsellors in Education), which then was not part of BAC, though negotiations for entry were continuing.

AMERICA

Counselling Psychology

In America, counselling and psychology have come together to form a recognized field of psychology called counselling psychology. In 1947 the American Psychological Association (APA) was divisionalized, with Division 17 being the Division of Counseling and Guidance. In 1952 Division 17 officially changed its name to the Division of Counseling Psychology. Division 17, which aims to bring together psychologists specializing in counselling psychology, has objectives in four areas: education and training, scientific investigation, practice, and dissemination of information.[5] The Division formulates appropriate requirements for the scientific and professional education and training of specialists in counselling psychology, encourages both surveys of research and original research, promotes high standards of competence and ethics among practitioners, and organizes meetings and conferences and promotes public understanding of counselling psychology.

Membership of the Division is open to Fellows, Members and Associates of APA provided they satisfy additional conditions in counselling psychology. For instance, a doctoral degree conferred by a graduate school of recognized standing is the minimum standard for election to member status in APA, with the additional stipulation for Division 17 being that applicants shall currently be engaged in teaching, researching into or practising counselling psychology. Only Fellows and Members of Division 17 may vote and hold office. The Division sponsors two journals: the *Journal of Counseling Psychology*, emphasizing research, and *The Counseling Psychologist*, emphasizing the continuing education and training of practitioners. In America official accreditation of counselling psychologists tends to take place on the state rather than the national level and, as such, is not a major function of Division 17.

In 1980 APA had a total of 50 933 members, approximately three fifths of whom were members of one or more of its 40 Divisions.[6] Table B.2 indicates the 1980 membership of some APA Divisions relating to counselling. In quantity of members, the Division of Counseling Psychology was APA's sixth largest Division.

Table B.2   *Membership in 1980 of some APA Divisions related to counselling**

Division number and name	Total	Men	Women	Percentage men	Percentage women
12 Clinical psychology	4520	3602	918	79.7	20.3
16 School psychology	2477	1449	1028	58.5	41.5
17 Counseling psychology	2581	2058	523	79.7	20.3
22 Rehabilitation psychology	872	680	192	78.0	22.0
27 Community psychology	1500	1145	355	76.3	23.7
29 Psychotherapy	4116	3053	1063	74.2	25.8

* Source: 1980 *Membership Register.*

Counselling

As in Britain, much counselling in America is practised outside recognized psychology. The organization analogous to BAC is the American Personnel and Guidance Association (APGA), which is a scientific and educational organization serving members and the public through programmes that advance guidance and counselling in all settings.[7] In 1979 APGA represented more than 40 000 members and had 13 national Divisions and 53 state Branches. APGA's scope may be seen from the titles of its 13 Divisions: American College Personnel Association; Association for Counselor Education and Supervision; National Vocational Guidance Association; Association for Humanistic Education and Development; American School Counselor Association; American Rehabilitation Counseling Association; Association for Measurement and Evaluation in Guidance; National Employers Counselors Association; Association for Non-White Concerns in Personnel and Guidance; National Catholic Guidance Conference; Association for Specialists in Group Work; Public Offender Counselor Association; and American Mental Health Counselor Association. In 1952 *The Personnel and Guidance Journal* was started as APGA's principal publication.

AUSTRALIA

Counselling Psychology

In 1977 a Division of Counselling Psychologists was formed within the Australian Psychological Society (APS). By 1979 the membership of the Division of Counselling Psychologists was 185, as contrasted with: Division of Clinical Psychologists, 253 members; Division of Educational Psychologists, 176; and Division of Occupational Psychologists, 199.[8] Thus the growth in the Division of Counselling Psychologists' membership has been rapid. The purposes of the Division are fourfold: (a) establishing educational standards; (b) safeguarding standards of practice; (c) facilitating and promoting both the personal and the professional development of counsellors and, also, the development of counselling psychology; and (d) co-operating with other societies and organizations with similar interests.

The Division of Counselling Psychologists is becoming a professional competence rather than an interest-based grouping. During a ten-year transitional period APS members may be eligible for membership of the Division basically if they have had two years of experience in counselling under conditions recognized by the Committee of the Division as suitable. After the ten-year period the terms of entry to the Division become exclusively as follows:

(i)   A member of the Division of Counselling Psychologists shall be an Honorary Fellow, Fellow or Member of the Australian Psychological Society;

(ii)   (a)   have successfully completed an approved postgraduate degree or diploma in counselling psychology at a University OR equivalent graduate course at another institution which has been approved by the Committee of the Division for the purpose of this clause;

or   (b)   hold a recognized postgraduate qualification in psychology, or other disciplines substantially related to counselling;

and

(iii)   have completed two years in practice, research, teaching, writing or administration in the field of counselling under the supervision of a person acceptable to the Committee of the Division;

or

(iv)   have other such qualifications as are deemed equivalent by the Committee of the Division.[9]

Additionally, the Division of Counselling Psychologists has a category of non-voting affiliate membership for APS fellows, members, associate members, affiliates or student subscribers who, though not holding the requisite qualifications, signify their wish to become associated with the Division.

The Division runs symposia, publishes a newsletter, makes representations concerning conditions of employment of counselling psychologists and gets involved in working parties. Though there is no separate counselling psychology journal in Australia, academic papers on counselling psychology may appear in the *Australian Journal of Psychology* and applied papers in the *Australian Psychologist*.

Counselling

There is no national counselling association in Australia along the lines of BAC or the APGA.

CANADA

Counselling Psychology

Though the terms 'counselling psychology' and 'counselling psychologist' are well established in Canada, there is no division of counselling psychology within the

Canadian Psychological Association (CPA). The nearest equivalent is a Division of Applied Psychology which, in 1980, was in the process of being renamed the Division of Professional and Applied Psychology. Dr Hogan, Executive Officer of the CPA, observes:

> A person holding a PhD in psychology whether that be in clinical psychology, counselling psychology, experimental psychology, etc. may become a member of the Canadian Psychological Association. I expect that if a person has a PhD in counselling psychology most jurisdictions in Canada (provinces) would certify that person as a practicing psychologist. Most certainly that person would be able to be a member of the various provincial Associations as well as the Canadian Psychological Association.
>
> It is difficult to ascertain how many of our members are counselling psychologists. Most certainly close to half of our members would engage in counselling and/or psychotherapy by some appropriate description.[10]

Counselling

The Canadian Guidance and Counselling Association (CGCA) was founded in 1965 and, by 1980, had approximately 1000 members representing every province in Canada.[11] Criteria of eligibility for Ordinary Membership of CGCA include possessing a graduate degree in guidance and counselling from a college or university recognized by the Association of Universities and Colleges of Canada or, for those holding a university degree, one year of experience in guidance and counselling. CGCA aims to promote counselling and also contacts among its members by a major biennial conference which brings Canadians together from coast to coast. CGCA also publishes the journal *Canadian Counsellor* and the newsletter *Cognica*. Both CGCA and CPA are bilingual associations.

CONCLUDING COMMENTS

Counselling psychology seems to be an accepted professional speciality area in America, Australia and Canada, with America and Australia each having a Division of its national psychological association devoted to it. These Divisions focus on standards of training, practice and continuing education, scientific development of the field, and dissemination of information and public education. Counselling psychology is in the process of becoming established as a speciality area in British psychology with the establishment of a Section of Counselling Psychology currently under consideration by the BPS. National counselling associations have been established in Britain, America and Canada, but not Australia. Though Britain appears to lag behind America in regard to the development of professional associations in counselling psychology and counselling, recent events, such as BAC's establishment and BPS's Working Party on Counselling, indicate that this situation is being altered.

NOTES

1. BPS Professional Affairs Board (1979) *Terms of Reference for Working Party on Counselling*. Leicester: British Psychological Society (mimeo).
2. Nelson-Jones, R., Davis, J., Hamblin, D., Hemming, J., Holdsworth, R. & Hopson, B. (1980) *Counselling: The Report of a Working Party*. Leicester: The British Psychological Society.
3. British Association for Counselling (1979). *Constitution*. Rugby: British Association for Counselling (mimeo).
4. Nelson-Jones, R. & Coxhead, P. (1978) Whither BAC – a survey of members' views on policy and priorities. *Counselling News*, **31**, 2–5.
5. Division of Counseling Psychology (1961). *Revised (1961) By-laws of the Division of Counseling Psychology of the American Psychological Association*. Washington: American Psychological Association (mimeo).
6. American Psychological Association(1980). *Membership Register*. Washington: American Psychological Association.
7. American Personnel and Guidance Association (1979). *APGA Counsels America*. Washington: American Personnel and Guidance Association.
8. Australian Psychological Society (1979) Reports from Divisions. *Bulletin of the Australian Psychological Society*, **1**, 22–26.
9. Division of Counselling Psychologists (1977). *Rules of the Division of Counselling Psychologists*. Melbourne: Australian Psychological Society (mimeo).
10. Correspondence from Dr T. V. Hogan, Executive Officer of the Canadian Psychological Association, dated 12 February 1980.
11. CGCA/SCOC (1980). *Canadian Guidance and Counselling Association/Société Canadienne D'Orientation et de Consultation*. Ottawa: CGCA/SCOC (leaflet).

Name Index

Subject Index